Preface

"*N*urture your mind with great thoughts; to believe in the heroic makes heroes." These words, attributed to British Prime Minister Benjamin Disraeli, provide a kind of rationale for the study of history. Of course, this sort of rhetoric may fit better with the credulous Victorian age than it does with the present. We approach historical study today with a kind of detached irony, eager to debunk heroism, "deconstruct" the past, and rescue the marginalized who attracted little notice during their lives.[1] And to a great extent this more analytical approach to history is valuable. It is essential to question received versions of the past. It has long been understood that our interpretation of events can be coloured by our own biases—our faith, our nationality, our gender, our social class, the very age in which we live. Additionally, we have come to recognize that the very selection of which events are studied is in itself a subjective decision. The term *historiography*, meaning "the writing of history," is a useful one; it reminds us to be conscious of the mediation that has necessarily taken place between the past and the present, and reminds us that only certain facts have been selected for inclusion. History is no longer only "past politics," as it was once described, but instead encompasses all aspects of life in the past—political, economic, social, and ideological.

But history is also about change; historians, after all, tend to follow the action. Any national history will include enormous gaps where historians have leapt across substantial geographic and chronological divides to focus on the next significant upheaval. Change may be constant but the rate of change is not. Social arrangements—for example, marriage or child-rearing customs—may stay comparatively static for generations. French historian Emmanuel LeRoy Ladurie famously described social history as "history that stands still."[2] This is, of course, an exaggeration, but there is no doubt some correlation between the decline of lively narrative history—the kind of stories of great deeds that inspired Disraeli and his generation—and the wish to write a more inclusive history. The real challenge of today's historical writing is to capture the best of both worlds.

Narrating a Nation adopts a narrative approach. Events are followed chronologically, focusing on a story developing over time. This is in contrast to the more usual method of today, in which chapters are divided according to theme, region, or perhaps some combination of both—for example, "Industrialization in the Maritimes." The chronological approach is meant to help events make sense to students, to ground their knowledge of

---

[1] The concept of "deconstructionism"—a notion central to postmodernist literary criticism—involves a close analysis of written texts to discover the implicit assumptions about power relations that underlie them. This concept necessarily implies a skepticism about "meta-narratives"—unified stories that ignore the complexity of human experience and alternative methods of arriving at truth.

[2] Emmanuel LeRoy Ladurie, "History That Stands Still," in Emmanuel LeRoy Ladurie, *The Mind and Method of the Historian* trans. Siân Reynolds and Ben Reynolds. (Chicago: University of Chicago Press, 1984), 1–27.

past societies, in all their social, economic, and ideological complexity, in a clear political context, with the necessary sense of linkage and causality that is at the bedrock of historical understanding. The goal is to help students focus on the events that are significant historical benchmarks or turning points.

Each volume is divided into 12 chapters to correspond to the number of weeks in a typical university academic term. Each chapter revolves around a broad theme. Identifiable trends and significant historic events mark the turning points and provide the structure. Timeline marginal icons serve as a reminder of key dates and developments, a pedagogical tool to reinforce understanding of key moments of change. The chronological approach is meant to help events make sense to students, to ground their knowledge of past societies, in all their social, economic, and ideological complexity, in a clear political context, with the necessary sense of linkage and causality that is at the bedrock of historical understanding. We have avoided the use of devices like text boxes and frequent subheadings that break the narrative flow and give the material an incoherent and undigested quality. Similarly, by avoiding thematic chapters—for example chapters devoted exclusively to Aboriginal peoples or regions of Canada—we can make the narrative more coherent. When such material is woven in to the main story, the reader is better able to piece together information to gain an overall sense of the times. Discussion questions at the end of each chapter are meant to reinforce the reader's understanding of the material and provide an opportunity for reflection.

In some respects, the narrative approach we have adopted recalls a tradition in historical writing. So, too, does the use of a broadly political framework to mark chronological periods. However, we fully recognize that earlier political and narrative textbooks possess major shortcomings, principally deriving from their exclusive focus on the elite—indeed, almost inevitably the male elite. Naturally enough, there must be considerable attention paid to those whose prominence enabled them to shape events. But it is absolutely essential that voice and agency be given to those whose story has been brought to life by social and cultural historians. While politics plays a central role in both volumes of *Narrating a Nation*, we include what older texts traditionally did not, namely the exciting new scholarship in social and cultural history that has so transformed Canadian historiography. We have aimed, therefore, to capture the best of both worlds—the narrative tradition of the past wedded to a more all-inclusive history that our students will recognize as their own.

Where possible, the text and especially the companion readers address issues of historiography—how have historians interpreted an event? How have interpretations changed over time? Such references to more in-depth studies will also signpost works the reader might wish to pursue in order to do further research on an issue. The suggestions for further reading at the end of each chapter are offered in a similar spirit. While they are by no means exhaustive, they suggest a selection of works—primary documents, recent articles, and time-tested standard interpretations—that a student might consult.

The aim of this second volume, *Narrating a Nation: Canadian History Post-Confederation*, is simple: to provide a clear, chronological, and engaging narrative treatment of the history of post-confederation Canada for university students. The idea may be simple, but its execution is a far different matter given the complexity of the country and the dizzying array of books and articles covering, it seems, virtually every imaginable facet of modern Canadian history.

Canadians want a clear and compelling account of their country's past. They want to understand its triumphs and setbacks, visionaries and villains, and giants of industry and champions of social welfare. Stories of exceptional individuals are not only inspiring—biographies can also provide a window through which we can understand the past, a way to appreciate "human-sized" history. It is instructive, for example, to reflect on how truly flawed some of our great Canadians have been and on the fact that they did not wait until they were perfect before making their mark on history. John A. Macdonald, who dominated Canada's nineteenth-century political life, was in the grip of alcoholism and utterly unable to carry out his duties at key moments: On one occasion his government went down to defeat in the legislature while the leader was absent on one of his legendary benders. Donald Smith, later Lord Strathcona, had a hand in myriad key events in Canadian history: He negotiated with insurgents at Red River, drove the last spike in the Canadian Pacific Railway, and became at last Canada's first high commissioner in London. Yet Smith endured public gossip and condemnation for his alliance with another man's wife. A milder liability was his deep dread of public speaking. Called upon to address an audience in London in 1865, the then-chief factor for the Hudson's Bay Company at Labrador fled the room in panic. Emily Murphy, celebrated as the first female magistrate in the British Empire and one of the "Famous Five" who in 1929 won legal recognition of Canadian women as "persons," was also an advocate of eugenics, the sterilization of those deemed to be "mentally defective." Our longest-serving prime minister, William Lyon Mackenzie King, kept an intimate journal that recorded his reliance on supernatural guidance. Using spiritual mediums, he sought advice from the long-deceased Wilfrid Laurier, his late mother, and even his dead dog, Pat. Such very human frailties did not preclude important achievements.

Of course, history in an academic context is more than an exercise in promoting pride in citizenship. It is more than a glorifying meta-narrative imposing false order on a diverse and complicated past. There are dark aspects of our history: Some have been marginalized and persecuted, often on the basis of religion, race, or gender. Canada remains a work in progress with much still to be done. We need only witness urban homelessness, Native reserves that often resemble shantytowns in developing nations, regional inequities and alienation, and the ongoing threat of Quebec separation. Yet these deep-seated problems in need of urgent redress do not undercut the fact that Canada's story is fundamentally a success story, a point that is too often overlooked. Canada is one of the world's most prosperous countries, where the rule of law protects people and property, and where citizens have access to rich array of social programs. It is a beacon to the world, with growing evidence of diversity, opportunity, and social inclusion. Canada's 2001 census revealed the extent of this diversity, with 18.4 percent of Canadians born outside the country and in some urban centres, much higher concentrations of newcomers. Toronto's population, for example, includes 44 percent who are foreign-born. In Richmond, British Columbia, the population of so-called visible minorities stands at 59 percent as of 2001. Many have clearly opted for the Canadian way of life, and old patterns of intolerance are breaking down. Indeed, our resident head of state, Canada's governor-general, Michaëlle Jean, a Haitian-born woman of colour, represents this new face of Canada to the world.

The text seeks to place Canadian events in a larger global context, something that is essential to a sound historical understanding. Confederation itself, for example, owes much to concerns about defence amid the American Civil War. It would be impossible to understand Canada's growing autonomy in the early twentieth century as a former British colony without understanding the scale of Canadian sacrifice during the First World War and the shifting philosophy towards the Empire throughout the Commonwealth. Even such a seemingly "internal" phenomenon as the radical separatist Front de libération du Québec (FLQ) can be properly explored only with reference to the wider movement towards decolonization around the globe, often under Marxist inspiration, in Cuba and in France's former colonies in Africa and Indochina. While it is natural to study history according to national divisions, ideas often migrate across boundaries.

Comprehensive Learning and Teaching Package

We have developed a variety of high-quality supplements for both teaching and learning to accompany this text.

Online Learning Centre   *(www.mcgrawhill.ca/olc/blake)*

Separated into both Instructor and Student areas, each section holds a variety of material for instructors to develop and use in their course and for students to use and review. Instructors will find an Instructor's Manual, chapter-specific PowerPoint lecture slides, and a Test Bank of multiple-choice, true/false, and essay-type questions for each chapter. The student area offers interactive quizzes and study questions to assist students in preparing for tests and exams.

Superior Service

Service takes on a whole new meaning with McGraw-Hill Ryerson and *Narrating a Nation: Canadian History Post-Confederation.* More than just bringing you the textbook, we have consistently raised the bar in terms of innovation and educational research. These investments in learning and the educational community have helped us to understand the needs of students and educators across the country, and allowed us to foster the growth of truly innovative, integrated learning.

Integrated Learning

Your Integrated Learning Sales Specialist is a McGraw-Hill Ryerson representative who has the experience, product knowledge, training, and support to help you assess and integrate any of our products, technology and services into your course for optimum teaching and learning performance.

Whether it's using our test bank software, helping your students improve their grades, or putting your entire course online, your *i*Learning Sales Specialist is there to help you do it. Contact your *i*Learning Sales Specialist today to learn how to maximize all of McGraw-Hill Ryerson's resources!

*i*Learning Services Program

McGraw-Hill Ryerson offers a unique *i*Services package designed for Canadian faculty. Our mission is to equip providers of higher education with superior tools and resources required for excellence in teaching. For additional information, visit www.mcgrawhill.ca/highereducation/iservices.

McGraw-Hill Ryerson National Teaching and Learning Conference Series

The educational environment has changed tremendously in recent years, and McGraw-Hill Ryerson continues to be committed to helping you acquire the skills you need to succeed in this new milieu. Our innovative Teaching, Technology & Learning Conference Series brings faculty together from across Canada with 3M Teaching Excellence award winners to share teaching and learning best practices in a collaborative and stimulating environment. Pre-conference workshops on general topics, such as teaching large classes and technology integration, are also offered. We will also work with you at your own institution to customize workshops that best suit the needs of your faculty.

CourseSmart

CourseSmart brings together thousands of textbooks across hundreds of courses in an e-textbook format providing unique benefits to students and faculty. By purchasing an e-textbook, students can save up to 50 percent off the cost of a print textbook, reduce their impact on the environment, and gain access to powerful Web tools for learning, including full-text search, notes and highlighting, and e-mail tools for sharing notes between class-mates. For faculty, CourseSmart provides instant access to review and compare textbooks and course materials in their discipline area without the time, cost, and environmental impact of mailing print copies. For further details, contact your *i*Learning Sales Specialist or go to www.coursesmart.com.

Create Online

McGraw-Hill's Create Online gives you access to the most abundant resource at your fingertips—literally. With a few mouse clicks, you can create customized learning tools simply and affordably. McGraw-Hill Ryerson has included many of our market-leading textbooks within Create Online for e-book and print customization as well as many licensed readings and cases. For more information, go to www.mcgrawhillcreate.ca.

WebCT and Blackboard

In addition, content cartridges are available for the course management systems WebCT and Blackboard. These platforms provide instructors with user-friendly, flexible teaching tools. Please contact your local McGraw-Hill Ryerson *i*Learning Sales Specialist for details.

Acknowledgments

The two volumes of *Narrating a Nation* have been a collaborative effort from concept to completion, and we owe tremendous gratitude to one another. In accordance with each author's area of expertise, in Volume 1, Norman Knowles wrote the chapters on First Nations and First Contacts, Furs and Faith: New France, 1632–1663, France in America: 1663–1750, The Inevitable Conquest? 1749–1763, Evolution and Revolution: 1763–1791, and A Contest of Identities: British North America: 1770–1815; and Barbara Messamore wrote the chapters on Development and Diversity: 1815–1836, Rebellion in the Canadas: 1826–1838, The Fate of British North America: 1838–1846, Hinge of the Imperial Relationship: 1846–1849, Colonial Societies in Transition: 1849–1864, and Three Weddings and a Divorce: 1858–1867. Similarly, in Volume 2, Raymond Blake wrote the chapters on Negotiation, Compromise, and Statehood: 1864–1873, Consolidating Confederation and Managing Diversity: 1874–1896, Uncertainty and Conflict: 1957–1967, Seeking the Just Society: 1968–1984, Seeking a New Consensus: 1984–1993, and Canada's New Century; and Jeffrey Keshen wrote the chapters on Canada's Century: 1896–1914, War and Upheaval: 1914–1919, The Turbulent Twenties, The Great Depression, War and Upheaval, II: 1939–1945, and Consensus and the Cold War: 1945–1957. Great admiration is also extended to all those scholars and teachers of Canadian history who have written books and articles about Canada. We have depended on their scholarship, and much of their hard work is reflected in this book. So, too, is the wisdom and insight of our colleagues across the country who kindly offered criticism and helpful advice on various drafts, and whose suggestions markedly improved the text. For their careful assessment of the manuscripts, we are grateful to

Jean Manore, Bishop's University

Gillian Poulter, Acadia University

Claire Campbell, Dalhousie University

Thor Frohn-Nielsen, Kwantlen Polytechnic University

Todd Webb, Laurentian University

John Zucchi, McGill University

Ken Cruikshank, McMaster University

John Sandlos, Memorial University

Robert Sweeny, Memorial University

Kathleen Lord, Mount Alison University

Steven Maynard, Queen's University

E.J. Errington, Royal Military College of Canada

Ross Fair, Ryerson University

John Reid, St. Mary's University

Gayle Thrift, St. Mary's University College

James Muir, University of Alberta

Sean Kheraj, University of British Columbia

Alan Gordon, University of Guelph

Greg Marquis, University of New Brunswick, Saint John

Karine Bellerose, University of Ottawa

Esyllt Jones, University of Ottawa

Robert Talbot, University of Ottawa

Selena Crosson, University of Saskatchewan

Jan Noel, University of Toronto

Penny Bryden, University of Victoria

Georgia Sitara, University of Victoria

Roy Hall, University of Western Ontario

Michelle A. Hamilton, University of Western Ontario

Robert Wardhaugh, University of Western Ontario

Carolyn Podruchy, York University

Franc Sturino, York University

As well, the authors have accumulated a debt of gratitude to many individuals. Professor Ged Martin (emeritus, University of Edinburgh) provided valuable advice, as did Scott Sheffield (University of the Fraser Valley), Hamish Telford (University of the Fraser Valley), and Kathryn Magee Labelle (Ohio State University). Research assistants Ron Hughes and Everett Messamore did exceptional work. The editors and staff at McGraw-Hill Ryerson have been a pillar of strength and have shepherded this book from just an idea to a finished product. We wish to thank Lisa Rahn, our acquisition editor at McGraw-Hill Ryerson, for her support, patience, and sage advice, and Jennifer DiDomenico for the initial guidance in development. Katherine Goodes, senior developmental editor, became involved at a crucial stage to offer expert advice and leadership as well as the badly needed—but diplomatically delivered—push to get the volumes done, and, along with her assistant Linda Toms, she did a remarkable job in guiding the text through to the completion of the development stage. Megan Jones, permissions editor, did an excellent job in helping to locate and clear the copyright for the reproduction of photographs, paintings, posters, and maps. The authors also wish to express their appreciation for the work done by the copy editor, Valerie Adams; the proofreader, Dawn Hunter; the supervising editor, Jessica Barnoski; and the production coordinator, Lena Keating.

Finally, the authors would like to express heartfelt thanks to their families for their support throughout this project that, like most in academe, took somewhat longer to complete than first anticipated. Raymond Blake thanks Wanda, Robert, and Ben, as always, who have listened to the woes about particular sections and offered their advice. More important, they were all there as a family at the end of each day that I was writing this book to show me what really is important in my life. Jeff Keshen extends heartfelt thanks to his wife, Deborah, and to his children, Jacob and Madelaine. Norman Knowles wishes to thank his wife, Margaret Anne, and daughters, Emily and Sarah, who provided constant support and encouragement during the production of this work, which coincided with cancer treatments. Barbara Messamore is grateful to the memory of her late husband, Steve, whose good-humoured encouragement meant so much in the completion of this project, as it did in so many other things in life. The loving support of their children, Keith, Neil, Everett, and Joy, has been a continued blessing.

This book is for our students, who shared our love of Canadian history and asked hard questions that helped us to look at events with fresh eyes.

About the Authors

Raymond B. Blake

Raymond B. Blake completed this book while Craig Dobbin Chair of Canadian Studies at University College Dublin in Dublin, Ireland. Also professor of history at Regina, he has taught Canadian Studies at Mount Allison University and was for several years the director of the Saskatchewan Institute of Public Policy. His research interests include nationalism and identity, social policy, and twentieth-century Canadian politics. He is the author and editor of a dozen books, including *Beyond National Dreams: Essays on Canadian Nationalism, Citizenship, and Identity* (with Andrew Nurse), *Social Fabric or Patchwork Quilt? The Development of Social Welfare in Canada* (with Jeffrey Keshen), *From Rights to Needs: A History of Family Allowances in Canada, 1929–92*, and *Canadians at Last: Canada Integrates Newfoundland as a Province*.

Jeffrey Keshen

Jeffrey Keshen, a professor of history at the University of Ottawa, specializes in post-Confederation Canadian political, social, and military history. Jeff has written or edited a dozen books on modern Canadian history, including *Saints, Sinners, and Soldiers: Canada's Second World War* (translated as *Saints, Salauds et Soldats: Le Canada et la Deuxième Guerre mondiale*) and *Propaganda and Censorship during Canada's Great War*.

Norman Knowles

Norman Knowles is a professor of history at St. Mary's University College and holds an adjunct appointment in the Department of History at the University of Calgary. He has written or edited half a dozen books and more than a dozen articles or book chapters on nineteenth- and early-twentieth-century Canadian social, cultural, and religious history. His works include *Seeds Scattered and Sown: Studies in the History of Canadian Anglicanism* and *Inventing the Loyalists: The Ontario Loyalist Tradition and the Creation of Usable Pasts*. He currently serves on the editorial board of the *Journal of the Canadian Church Historical Society*.

Barbara Messamore

Barbara Messamore teaches Canadian history at University of the Fraser Valley in Abbotsford, British Columbia. She completed her Ph.D. at the University of Edinburgh in 2003 and is the author of *Canada's Governors General, 1847–1878: Biography and Constitutional Evolution*. She has published a number of articles on related topics, edited *Canadian Migration Patterns from Britain and North America*, and is co-founder and editor-in-chief of the *Journal of Historical Biography*.

1

*N*egotiation, Compromise, *and* Statehood: *1864–1873*

*O*n July 1, 1867—Canada's first Dominion Day—Adolphus Gaetz, a businessman and Registrar of the Court of Probate for Lunenburg County, was awakened early. It was a holiday and a time of great celebration in Lunenburg, the Nova Scotia seaport town. The Volunteer Artillery Company had gathered on Gallows Hill shortly before sunrise to announce the birth of the Dominion of Canada with several rounds from their cannons. Amid the blast, church bells rang out. At 10 o'clock, Gaetz joined others in a crowded service at the Episcopal Church; in the afternoon, he watched as the children from the grand Lunenburg Academy sang "God Save the Queen" and gave three hearty cheers for the new dominion. As the sun sank over the Western Shore, the artillery company offered another salute of 21 guns to end the day's festivities. Gaetz gathered again with the townspeople to wish "Peace, Happeness [*sic*] & Prosperity to the Dominion of Canada." If Gaetz had been able to visit Yarmouth, further down the South Shore, or had been able to drop in to Pictou or New Glasgow, he would have witnessed a different picture. For some in Pictou there was only sadness. The *Pictou County Advocate* saw no reason to celebrate. It described Confederation as the illegitimate birth of an "infant monster," and lamented the premature death of Nova Scotia. In Halifax, the provincial capital, the mood was mixed. One newspaper,

the *Morning Chronicle*, described the celebrations as a "Fizzle," proclaiming victory in the sombre mood that saw buildings in the city draped in black crepe and flags flying upside down or at half-mast. The *Halifax Evening Express*, on the other hand, shared Gaetz's excitement over the new constitutional arrangement and celebrated Nova Scotia as both a new province and an integral part of the new dominion. "The day of small things has passed away," it rejoiced, and "henceforth we will have our name inscribed among the nations of the Western World." Such were the different reactions to Canada's birth in one of its founding provinces.[1]

After reading this chapter you will be able to:

1. Describe the factors and influences leading to Confederation in 1867.
2. Appreciate that Confederation was a process of negotiation and compromise.
3. Consider Confederation an exercise in nation-building.
4. Understand the concept of federalism and how it made union possible.
5. Evaluate the role of individuals in the creation of Canada.
6. Reflect on Canada as a political nationality.
7. Assess the impact of Canada's economic expansion after 1867.
8. Analyze the attempts to create a sense of nationalism in Canada.

Introduction

The period from 1864 to 1874 was a momentous decade in Canadian history. It saw the emergence of Canada as a nation when three British North American colonies came together as a federation in 1867 under the British Crown. This particular period was marked by conflict, disunity, and political instability, and the historical process that created the country was often cynical, messy, and complicated. Yet, the colonial leaders negotiated a constitutional arrangement to satisfy their particular interests, create national institutions, and forge a new nation. The new state was then able to extend the reach of the country from sea to sea, even if its citizens would remain British subjects for more than two generations.

This chapter begins with the events leading to the creation of Canada. It examines the factors that encouraged and often pushed the colonies towards union. There is no single cause or event that led to Confederation, however. It simply emerged out of a combination of factors and circumstances: the process of industrialization and urbanization that developed in British North America in the 1850s and early 1860s; the termination of the reciprocity agreement in 1866 that had allowed the free exchange of natural products between the British colonies and the United States after 1854; the fear of American reprisal for the British support of the South during the American Civil War (1861–1865), the extensive northern militarization that accompanied the conflict, and a general wariness of American expansionism; the growing concern of British financiers and bankers about their investments; the movement of Britain towards free trade; a politically dysfunctional constitution in the Province of Canada and the burgeoning gap between French-speaking Canada East and English-speaking Canada West; and a growing sense of nationalism and ambition among the elites in the colonies.

The negotiations over Confederation were complicated by the cultural, economic, and regional divisions evident in the colonies. This chapter also explains why some groups favoured union and others opposed it; why the deal sold in most, but not all, colonies; and how the process of negotiation and compromise not only created a new country but also became one of the most effective ways of dealing with many of the tensions inherent in the new nation.

Historians and political scientists have frequently downplayed the significance of Confederation. It has been dismissed as a practical and pragmatic business deal, conducted in a largely undemocratic manner, by elite men who were divisive and often misguided. The critics of the Confederation process cannot be dismissed, especially when viewed from our own time. The politicians behind Confederation, often called the "Fathers of Confederation," were not great democrats; in fact, they were worried about the democratic excesses that, they believed, had contributed to the American Civil War. The electoral system in the mid-nineteenth century allowed only males over the age of 21 who met strict property qualifications to vote; it excluded women, who were disenfranchised by their gender before Confederation, although they had had some limited exercise of the franchise earlier in Canada's colonial history. Others were excluded because of their race. Aboriginal peoples were also ignored, and large minorities, such as the Acadians and Catholics, were underrepresented. Moreover, many of the historians who have examined the early years of Confederation have focused on what divided the provinces.

While it has been easy to emphasize the divisions and discord in Canada and be dismissive of the politics of compromise and negotiation that emerged in the years leading to Confederation and in the first few years of union, it is necessary to recognize that there was enough unity to create a nation and hold it together, even if, in the words of one prominent historian, the architects of Canada took each other "not by the hand but rather by the throat."[2] Admittedly, Confederation can be seen as a practical solution to a series of immediate problems, but creating a country means dealing with practical and pragmatic issues, such as building a national transportation network, establishing a judicial system, designing a commercial policy, and implementing a common system of weights and measures.

The period was also an exercise in nation-building. Some academics have argued that it is inaccurate to dismiss the colonial politicians who negotiated Canada as mere pragmatists. As one recent book insists, many of them were "remarkably well read, and referred easily to philosophical ideas and constitutions from Britain, the United States, and continental Europe."[3] They also had a vision. George Brown, one of the leading confederates, believed that "some among us will live to see the day when … a great and powerful people may have grown up in these lands—when the boundless forests all around us shall have given way to smiling fields and thriving towns—and when one united government, under the British flag, shall extend from shore to shore."

Leonard Tilley, the Premier of New Brunswick, saw little hope for the smaller colonies; it would take statesmen, he told a group at a public dinner in August 1864, "to bind together the Atlantic and Pacific by a continuous chain of settlements and line of communications for that is the destiny of this country." Brown also lauded the architects of the new nation for their "earnest large-minded willingness to subordinate all party interests to the attainment of a larger project."[4]

Canada would be no primordial, traditional nation; it would be a modern one where "nations [are] formed by the agglomeration of communities with kindred interests and sympathies." That was the view of George-Étienne Cartier, another leading figure in the Confederation movement, who noted that in the new nation "we were of different races, not for the purpose of warring against each other, but in order to compete and emulate for the general welfare." Brown shared that vision: "We are endeavouring to adjust harmoniously greater difficulties [linguistic, religious, ethnic, and regional] that have plunged other countries into all the horrors of civil war," he reminded the legislative assembly, noting particularly the descent of the United States into civil war to settle their differences.[5] In the grandiose political rhetoric of the day, the proponents of union had great hopes for the northern half of North America, even if John A. Macdonald saw "the founding of a great nation under the fostering care of Great Britain, and our Sovereign Lady, Queen Victoria." Canada would be the first daughter of the British Empire and loyal to the Crown.

Canada began as a negotiated nation, and it remains one to this day. As the vignette that opens this chapter shows, there were several competing emotions among the new Canadians in 1867, and many did not share the sense of a national spirit. Creating the nation might have been the easier task; governing a country like Canada that spanned the North American continent proved difficult in the early years of Confederation. Much of it was sparsely populated and without rudimentary communication and transportation links. What is remarkable about this period, then, was the ability of Canadians to negotiate a new country, extend it both east and west to include all of the British colonies in North America (with the exception of Newfoundland) within five years of union, and to consolidate the disparate parts into a single political entity. Despite the multitude of divisions and intense conflicts that constantly pulled at its fabric—English–French hostilities, a provincial rights struggle, and Aboriginal resistance to imperial expansion—the country stayed together. Some of the patterns and trends in the early years of Confederation have since become hallmarks of Canada. In many ways, the process of making Confederation and governing the nation in the early years of the union helped to give the nation many of its defining and enduring characteristics. Compromise and negotiation were two, and they became essential elements in the Canadian political culture. By 1874, Canada had emerged as a new transcontinental country and, despite the internal tensions that marked its formative years, it would survive to be celebrated in the early twenty-first century as one of the world's oldest and most successful federations.

John A. Macdonald was Canada's first prime minister and one of the leading players in the Confederation era.

Source: Joseph Purcell, *John A. Macdonald, Prime Minister and Father of Confederation*, 2008. Private Collection of Wanda Blake and Raymond Blake.

British North America in the Era of Nation-Building

Canada emerged as a nation in the middle of the nineteenth century amid the mindset that larger political entities were economically and militarily advantageous. Examples of new nations abound. Most Canadians are familiar with the reinvention of the United States in the American Civil War, which came to an end in 1865; that horrific war stemmed, in part, from the desire of President Abraham Lincoln and his supporters to fulfill the ideals of the Founding Fathers in the 1770s against the intolerable regional interests of the Antebellum, or pre-Civil War period. At the same time, in the late 1850s, there were numerous patriotic nationalist uprisings all over Italy, culminating in the Italian unification in 1866. Also in 1866, Peru repulsed Spanish forces and effectively became an independent nation. Using both political machinations and war, Otto von Bismarck succeeded in unifying Germany by 1871, though the new state placed little value on liberal reforms.

Not all examples of nation-building were born of rebellion and revolution, however. With the passage of the *New Zealand Constitution Act 1852*, it ceased being a Crown colony, won the right of self-governance, and achieved independence in domestic affairs.

The United Kingdom itself has had a long history of reform through non-violent means and, in 1867, with the Second Reform Bill, it moved much closer to becoming a genuine democratic nation, when the franchise was extended to many in the urban working class.

These nation-building movements were also driven by an emerging middle class from the commercial and industrial sectors that was increasingly replacing agrarian interests as the dominant group. They believed that larger nation-states were necessary to capitalize on the technological advances of the era, which was symbolized by the increasing use of the steam engine and the transformative changes occurring in the production of textiles and in metallurgy. The Industrial Revolution was changing the way economies operated, and it placed new demands on the state. Even with rapid expansion in the transportation sector, particularly with a spate of railroad construction, a functioning national market would be more difficult if local governments and interests remained in control. The middle class believed larger states, with a new kind of authority to provide new fiscal and legal structures, were necessary to facilitate the development of efficient economies. Nation-states were created by the middle class as a means to further political and economic goals.

Those new nations were not homogenous, though. Most of the nineteenth-century attempts at nation-building were political enterprises rather than cultural or ethnic ones. They were increasingly defined as political communities that could embrace different cultures and ethnicities. The nation-building impetus was intended to organize nation-states that could administer their territories and allow people to live together despite their differences. Germany, for instance, sought to represent rather than to resolve the tensions within German society; in France and Spain, the state recognized the existence of regional cultures. This approach to nation-building does not mean that peoples within a nation did not share a common interest, as they certainly did. Recently, Benedict Anderson, a prominent historian, has argued that those nineteenth century nations were the beginnings of "imagined communities." In his view, the new nations could rise above the differences created by religion, region, and ethnicity and bring together within a state people who would never meet each other but who would forge a national identity.[6]

What Anderson describes applies to Canada. The primary goal of Canada's nation-building experience was to unite several cultural and ethnographical pluralistic communities that had been a hallmark of Canada's colonial past into a single political community under a stable and prosperous national government. There was in Canada no popular uprising against a tyrannical oppressor; rather, the Canadian process was essentially a liberal one, as it represented the making of a self-determining community against the sectionalism and regionalism of the past. The Canadian experience has often been the story of reconciliation and negotiation.[7]

Change and Anxiety in British North America

There is no obvious starting point for the story of Canadian Confederation. Some of the Loyalists who moved north to the British colonies in the wake of the American Revolutionary Wars (1775–1783) contemplated a union of the British North American colonies. Two of them, William Smith and Jonathan Sewell, published *A Plan for the Federal Union of British Provinces in North America* in 1807, but their idea soon fizzled. Lord Durham, who the British government had sent to the colonies as governor-general to investigate the circumstances leading to the rebellions in Upper and Lower Canada in the late 1830s, also considered the prospects of union for the British North American colonies, but the idea gathered little support. In the immediate aftermath of Durham's 1839 report, only Upper and Lower Canada had been united. Thomas D'Arcy McGee, an Irish-Catholic journalist in Montreal, had declared in 1850, "I see in the not remote distance one great nationality" stretching across the northern half of North America. A year later, Joseph Howe introduced a motion in the Nova Scotia Legislature to approach Britain and the other Canadian provinces "on the subject of a union of the North American provinces, or of the Maritime provinces."

One might consider the proposal in 1858 from Alexander Galt, the minister of finance in the Province of Canada, for a federal union of Canada East (later, Quebec), Canada West (later, Ontario), and the Maritime provinces as indication of the continuing impulse for Confederation. Galt, John Ross, the president of the Executive Council, and George-Étienne Cartier, one of the leading French-Canadian politicians in Canada East, took their proposal to London, but without support from the other colonies, their plan for a federal union of the provinces of British North America received a cool reception. When Cartier met Queen Victoria, he reminded her, however, that an inhabitant of Canada East was an Englishman who spoke French.

The federal principle meant the power and authority of the country would be divided between a federal (national) and a provincial government—a system like that of Canada today, and one that many of the leaders of the period considered as essential for a union among several colonies that were different in so many ways. The colonies were too divided by geography, language, and distance, too different in their histories and outlook, and too worried about losing control over a variety of local matters, such as education, to join in a legislative union with a single, powerful central government. The smaller colonies on the Atlantic Ocean were worried about protecting their interests against the larger inland Province of Canada; Canada East was particularly worried about surrendering control to a largely English-speaking majority. None of the proposals for union found widespread support at the time, but the musings from colonial leaders about a new nation demonstrate that they were thinking about their constitutional future. All colonies in British North America—the Province of Canada, Newfoundland, Nova Scotia, Prince Edward Island, New Brunswick, British Columbia, and even the Red River settlement—were united in their loyalty to the British Crown. In the 1860s a series of factors pushed them towards union.

Confederation was, in part, a reasoned and negotiated response to the changing economic realities of British North America from the late 1840s through to the 1860s. The first major shock for the colonies came with the end of preferential treatment for their products in the British markets in the 1840s. The British and French colonies had been founded in North America to supply the home country with raw materials. In 1846, when the British government cancelled the Corn Laws, which gave colonial wheat and flour a preferential place in the British market (and three years later the British government repealed the Navigation Acts to allow non-British vessels to participate for the first time in the carrying of goods within the British Empire), the colonists felt abandoned, and the search for a new economic order began.

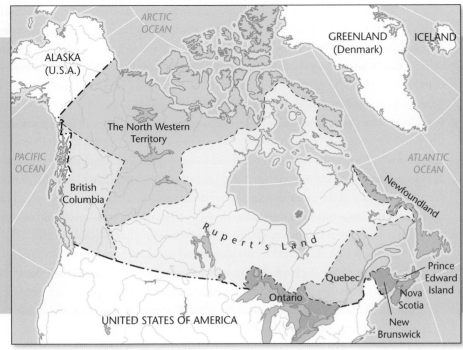

Map 1.1
Provinces and British Territory, 1867

Source: Natural Resources Canada.

After a brief moment of anger towards Britain, the British North Americans realized that they had to secure alternative markets for their exports. Beginning in 1850, they embarked on a plan for intercolonial reciprocity, but with a large and growing population to the south, they looked foremost to the United States. Free trade in natural resources, or reciprocity as it was then called, would restore some of the certainty about markets that had been lost with the end of mercantilism.

Each of the colonies moved towards reciprocity independently, but it was the Province of Canada (the old colonies of Upper and Lower Canada) rather than the Atlantic Colonies that pushed hardest. Reciprocity with the United States was finally realized in 1854, when Maritime and Canadian natural products were granted tariff-free access to the American markets in exchange for allowing American fishers access to the inshore waters in the Atlantic colonies and free navigation on the Great Lakes. The impact of the Reciprocity Agreement was enormous for the export trade of British North America: exports to the United States of items included in the treaty had increased from 40.9 percent in 1854 to 69.2 percent when the treaty was terminated. The American Civil War also contributed to the increase in cross-border trade, but the ending of reciprocity in 1864 created the second economic shock for British North America. Losing what they considered another secure market, colonial leaders saw a union of the British colonies as a way of integrating their colonial economies into a single east–west market.

By the 1860s, the colonies had also begun a process of industrialization and urbanization, had developed banking systems, had launched themselves into the railway era, and some had grand schemes of annexing the interior of the continent and building a railway to link all British territory in North America. The Province of Canada had most aggressively encouraged its manufacturing sector. In Quebec, for instance, the value of manufacturing increased from $600 000 in 1851, to more than $15 million a decade later, and $104.5 million by 1881. Galt, who was a leader in the Montreal business community as well as the minister of finance, increased, in 1859, the general tariff rate from 8.54 percent to 12.11 percent on most imports, and from 15 to 20 percent on finished goods. The government had to raise revenues to cover the costs associated with building railways, but the revised tariff schedule also provided a measure of protection for Canada's nascent industries. It was the first time that the government extended a significant level of protection to the manufacturing sector, an essential element of any nation-state. Colonial leaders were ready to embark on a process of nation-building, and the emerging economic order was one factor driving changes to the existing political structures and institutions. In British North America—as elsewhere—the rise of industrialization had necessitated a new regulatory regime.

Although the British North American colonies had started to move away from a pioneer economy based largely on the staples of wheat, lumber, and fish, by the middle decades of the nineteenth century as they started a process of industrialization, staple production remained important. In Quebec, nearly 78 percent of the population lived in rural areas and continued to depend on farming, driven by the demand from the United States, especially during the reciprocity period and the American Civil War. In 1867, agricultural production contributed more than $90 million to the economy of the Province of Canada. Wood also remained an important export for British North America. Sawn lumber, which produced boards and planks, was in demand in the growing urban American markets. This transition in the forestry sector away from squared timber (unprocessed logs) allowed for the use of smaller trees and led to the expansion of sawmills, which were usually established at the mouth of major rivers. The lumber was carried to markets either by ship or on the expanding railways lines.

The shipping and shipbuilding industry continued to prosper in the 1850s and 1860s, when it was a major driver in the economy of the Maritime provinces. In 1864, 596 vessels were built throughout the Maritimes—the most ever, and the region enjoyed what has been called the "Golden Age of Sail." The Maritime colonies played a prominent role in international shipping.

The fishery was another of the important staples, particularly in Newfoundland, where the industry was still largely controlled by British mercantile firms operating throughout the colony. The "truck system," used in farming and lumbering as well as in fishing, usually kept those engaged in the staple production in the grips of the local merchants. This complex system operated on the basis of credit and not cash. At the beginning of the season, the local merchant would outfit the fishers with the materials required to engage in the fishery and provided supplies the family required to survive. These items were supplied on credit, and at the end of the season the fisher would deliver his salt cod to the merchant who would decide the value of the season's catch. If there was a small profit, the fisher would earn a credit with the merchant and purchase further supplies for the winter. If the debt could not be cleared, the merchant might advance further credit, but the fisher's indebtedness increased. There were risks to the merchant, but in the Newfoundland fishery the merchants usually fared better than the fishers and their families.

Railways and Confederation

Despite the importance of the staple economy, railways were all the rage at mid-century, and all the colonies were engaged in ambitious programs of railway construction. Railways, however, were especially expensive in British North America, where great distances and a rugged environment were the norm. Only about 3.5 million people lived in the British colonies, and it soon became apparent that governments had to be involved in the construction of railways. While governments did not usually favour direct public ownership, they certainly went out of their way to attract private investment. Much of the investment came from Britain.

The railway boom lasted for much of the 1850s when nearly 3000 kilometres of track were laid in the Canadas. The Maritimes dreamed of capturing the trade from the interior of North America bound for Europe and embarked on their own railway projects. By 1867, more than 600 kilometres of track had been put down in the region. Both the Province of Canada and the Maritime colonies had amassed a considerable debt in promoting railways and were finding it difficult to manage their debt load, let alone continue to build new lines. Undoubtedly, governments required a larger financial base to meet their current obligations and to fulfill their hopes for intercolonial and transcontinental expansion.

British bankers were also interested in what was happening in the colonies. They had invested heavily and were worried about instability in British North America, which had a much higher per capita debt than the United States. In the 1850s, British investors had sunk about $100 million into the two Canadas. By the early 1860s, the Grand Trunk Railway (one of the major railway firms) missed interest payments on its bonds and faced bankruptcy. Barings Bank of London was one of the key investors in the Grand Trunk; the bank hired Edward Watkin, a major railway executive in Britain, to investigate the problem. After a visit to Canada, he reported that the only solution to the Grand Trunk's problems was to construct a line from Halifax to Quebec and eventually a transcontinental line across North America.

Watkins and other businessmen with considerable investment in British North America came to the conclusion that political unification of the colonies was the best alternative if they hoped to recoup their investments. In 1862, they created the British North American Association (BNAA) to promote colonial union and worked assiduously to promote the idea, particularly within Britain's Colonial Office. Andrew Smith, a young historian who has studied the connection between British investors and Confederation, claims that "without the support of a small but influential group of investors, Confederation would not have occurred in 1867, if at all." Smith's work follows in the tradition of Ged Martin and others who have attempted to situate Confederation in the contexts of British and comparative imperial history.[8]

Negotiating a Nation

As the economy of British North America was being transformed, the colonies continued to think about the prospects of colonial consolidation or union. The year 1864 would prove to be a momentous one for all of the colonies. In that year, the Maritime colonies of Nova Scotia, Prince Edward Island, and New Brunswick agreed to hold a conference in

*Great Coalition created
in the Canadas, 1864.*

Charlottetown to discuss the idea of a Maritime union. They believed that union could only strengthen their colonies politically, economically, and militarily. They shared with other British North Americans "an enthusiasm for railways, for expanded and more centralized school systems, for improved social services and for governments with enhanced access to credit."[9] They believed that a railway link with central Canada would provide them access to a much larger market, and it should not be forgotten that at the time of Confederation, Nova Scotia was the centre of Canada's mining industry—an advantage in the new industrial age.

Those in the Province of Canada came together in a coalition determined to find a way out of the dysfunctional political system that had effectively rendered their constitution unworkable. From 1862 to 1864, the legislature failed to pass any significant legislation: both attempts to pass a Militia Bill failed even in the face of heightened concerns about American aggression. Moreover, *Canadien* members of the legislature were becoming increasingly worried about the growing demands in Canada West for representation by population, an argument based on the belief that seats should be allocated according to population rather than divided evenly between the two provinces. Within three years, there had been two elections that failed to produce a workable majority, and over that same period four governments had been sworn in and then defeated.

In late spring 1864, the government of John A. Macdonald and Étienne-Paschal Taché was defeated on another vote of confidence. Macdonald asked the legislature for an adjournment so he could consult with the governor-general. Although Lord Monck agreed to dissolve the legislature and call new elections, Macdonald and George Brown met and discussed the constitutional situation. Brown had chaired a legislative committee that had been investigating proposals for a federal system of either the two provinces in Canada or a federation of all British North America. They agreed that a federal union was the only way forward; the Great Coalition was born when Brown, one of the co-founders of the present-day *The Globe and Mail*, joined with his political adversaries, John A. Macdonald and George-Étienne Cartier. They were determined to end the legislative union of the Canadas in favour of a federal union of all British North American colonies. The only political group not included in the coalition was Antoine-Aimé Dorion's radical Rouge Parti, but he had suggested in the legislature in 1861 that he might accept representation by population if the parties agreed to a federation of the two provinces with a limited central government.

Although she was not present at any of the negotiations between Macdonald, Cartier, and Brown, Anne Nelson Brown nonetheless played an important role. George Brown had fought the Conservatives over every major political issue for a decade. Defeated in the 1861 election and suffering from ill health and financial problems, Brown went on an extended holiday to Britain. While there, he met Anne Nelson, the sister of his childhood friends, fell madly in love, and married three months later. Anne was an intelligent and well-educated woman, and even though she missed her Scottish home terribly, she had an enormous impact on her husband and Canadian history. Brown's biographer, J.M.S. Careless, described her as "the mother of Confederation." To Oliver Mowat, Brown's political ally and later premier of Ontario, it was only because of Anne that "the softer side of [Brown's] nature has been developed." After his marriage, Brown re-entered politics with a much calmer disposition than before. Where he had once seen "French domination" of the Province of Canada, he now came to see the need for "constitutional reform."[10]

The goal of separating the English-speaking Protestants of Canada West from the French-speaking Catholics of Canada East remained, and Brown believed federation would provide his province with greater autonomy. Canada East also recognized the constitutional difficulties and realized that its long-term interests would be best served if it were rid of those in Canada West who seemed to harbour opposition to Roman Catholic separate schools and other cultural issues that the *Canadiens*, or French-speaking people, believed so important. Cartier knew that the English-speaking Protestants would soon engulf the French-speaking Catholics, and Quebec's best hope would be to retain control of important areas, such as education and its own legal system.

George-Étienne Cartier (1814–1873). Leader of the Conservatives in Canada East, Cartier joined forces with John A. Macdonald to bring about Canadian Confederation.

Source: McCord Museum I-7956.

The economic imperative was also important. Nearly a decade earlier, Brown's *The Globe* had declared that Canada West was "looking for new worlds to conquer." Macdonald had also started to link the expansion westward to the development of a new nation out of the Province of Canada. They looked to the Maritime market, but the great prize for the Canadian economic interests was extending their control over the lands that lay to the West. Canada West, or Ontario, did not have the financial resources or sufficient credit to acquire Rupert's Land and the North-Western Territory—the vast territory that today extends from Northern Quebec and Ontario to the Arctic Circle south to the U.S. border and west to British Columbia—from the Hudson's Bay Company; that could only come with a larger union of all the British colonies.

When the Canadians learned of the impending conference to discuss Maritime union, they asked to present their thoughts on the prospects of a larger union of all of British North America. In late August 1864, the Canadian politicians boarded the government-owned steamer *Queen Victoria* and set sail for Charlottetown to sell the Maritimers on a confederation of all British North American colonies. Confederation would become the institutional instrument for the Province of Canada to solve its immediate constitutional crisis and to attain its larger economic objectives.

The Great Coalition had come together to search for immediate solutions to the constitutional problems that plagued the Canadas, but the Maritimers were under no such pressure. Still, historian P.B. Waite suggests, that by 1864 "whether for good or ill, there was a national spirit stirring in the Maritime Provinces."[11] When the Canadians arrived on September 1, 1864, the delegates found ample opportunity to get to know each other in the various dinners and galas that were provided both by the Maritimers and the Canadians.

Once they got down to discussing business, the Maritime delegates set aside their discussion on Maritime union to first hear from the Canadians. Over a few days, Cartier, Brown, Galt, and Macdonald made their case, and when the Canadians finished their presentations, the Maritimers considered their options. There was widespread support for consolidating the colonies into a large union throughout the Maritimes. That goal, after all, had led to the Charlottetown Conference. As Phillip Buckner has shown, the Maritimes, too, "equated consolidation with material progress and modernization" and saw the benefits of "larger and more powerful institutional units of government."[12] The Maritime colonies were undoubtedly interested in the prospects of a railway to the Canadas, a project that had excited them since the early 1850s and that they saw as necessary for the further industrialization of the region. Brown reported to his wife Anne the decision that the Maritime politicians made: "They were unanimous in regarding Federation of all the Provinces to be highly desirable—*if the terms of union could be made satisfactory.*"[13]

The Canadians and Maritimers had found enough common purpose to meet in Quebec City in October to hammer out the basis of a constitution for a new nation during what has become known as the Quebec Conference. This time, Newfoundland would be invited. Before the Canadians returned home, however, they toured the region and received a warm welcome. In Halifax, Nova Scotia Premier Charles Tupper proposed a toast to the "Colonial Union." Macdonald responded, emphasizing the importance an intercolonial railway would have on improving the common defence of British North America. As the new nation extended westward, the resources of the West would be moved to market through the Maritime ports. Moreover, Macdonald said, the new nation "would be a great British monarchy, in connection with the British empire, and under the British Queen."[14] The Halifax *Morning Chronicle* commented that there is now a positive desire for union.

At Quebec, the delegates met from October 10 to 27. They were determined to achieve a new union; the representatives from the Canadas spoke with a single voice, but the Atlantic delegates had come as representatives of the four colonies, not as a unified bloc.

The delegates at the Quebec Conference in 1864. Compare this photograph with the Fathers of Confederation that was painted much later and appears on page 3.

Source: Library and Archives Canada/C-016588.

As there was no equality in the size and power of the Maritime colonies and those of the Canadas, the Maritimes negotiated from the terms presented by the Canadians. In the end, they agreed upon 72 resolutions that would provide the basis of the Canadian constitution that was known as the *British North America Act* until it was renamed in 1982 as the *Constitution Act, 1867*.

They agreed that Canada would be a federation that divided powers and jurisdiction between two orders of government: federal and provincial. The federal government was given clear responsibilities for defence, developing a national transportation system, and creating a nationally integrated economy through its control of currency, weights and measures. It was also given jurisdiction over international trade and commerce, and transportation and communications. Section 121 of the *British North America Act* provided for a common market, claiming that "all articles of the growth, produce or manufacture of any one of the Provinces … shall be admitted free into each of the other Provinces."

Much of the discussion about the power of the federal government has centred on the preamble of section 91 of the *British North America Act* that outlines Ottawa's responsibilities. It includes a clause that empowers the federal government to make laws for the "Peace, Order and Good Government of Canada." Frequently referred to as the POGG clause, it was first used when the British Parliament passed the New Zealand constitution in 1852 and was last used in the *West Indies Act* in 1962. This clause has been important for two reasons: First, it clearly establishes for the federal government the sense of a national jurisdiction to meet national needs and govern for the good of the nation; and second, it provides the federal government with general and wide-ranging powers, while leaving provincial jurisdiction to deal with local matters and interests.

At Quebec, the ministers from Canada East and the Maritimes had insisted the provinces have autonomy over education, religious and civil institutions, property rights and social welfare, though the latter at the time of Confederation meant public workhouses, reformatories, prisons, hospitals, asylums, and charities. This meant that the authority to protect and promote the interests of the French in Quebec passed to the province, along with control over municipal affairs, ownership of public lands, and mines and minerals. The provinces could levy direct taxation, but had no equivalent to the POGG clause.

In a classic federal system, the power to legislate is limited to that allocated in the constitution, and because the two orders of government are each assigned exclusive powers, it was understood that neither level of government could encroach upon the powers or jurisdiction of the other. But this was not the form of government that was agreed to at the Quebec Conference. There were plenty of areas where the framers agreed that the federal government could encroach on provincial jurisdiction. Ottawa was given the power of disallowance and reservation of any bill from the provincial legislatures, both of which have been seen as providing a supervisory role for the federal governments over the provinces, which unmistakably indicated Ottawa was the dominant power.

The federal government was also given the responsibility to protect the educational rights of religious minorities that existed by legislation at the time of Confederation. If a provincial majority decided to impose any tyrannical measures against a provincial minority, section 93 of the *British North America Act* provided the federal government the authority to protect minority education rights. The Fathers of Confederation were concerned about the place of minorities in Canada in 1867, and the treatment of minorities would remain a major theme in Canada's history. Although Canada has had less than a stellar record for its treatment of its minority groups, the politicians who created Canada in the 1860s recognized the importance of religious minority rights. Yet, the rights of Aboriginal people attracted little attention at Confederation because in Eastern Canada they were thought to be quickly disappearing or adopting a European lifestyle. The Constitution also did not contain an amending formula explaining how it might be changed, and this was because everyone assumed that changes would be done in concert with the British government.

For much of the twentieth century, there emerged a consensus among historians that John A. Macdonald, who had taken the lead role in the making of Canada, wanted a strong central government with only local responsibilities given to the provinces. There seems little doubt that Macdonald would have preferred a legislative union, which he described as "the best, the cheapest, the most vigorous, and the strongest system of government."[15] But Macdonald accepted the compromised proposal for a federal system because he was convinced that in a country like Canada with such divisions, a federal union was the only practical alternative. He believed that at the Quebec Conference the federal government had secured control of the levers of power necessary to build the nation. Included in those was the authority to regulate trade and commerce and supervisory powers over the provinces, such as the power to veto provincial legislation.

The negotiations over the Senate at the Quebec Conference were difficult, taking nearly a week to resolve, and almost led to a collapse of the meetings. In Charlottetown, the delegates had agreed that each section (Canada East, Canada West, and the Maritimes) would have 24 senators, even though the Maritime provinces collectively had a smaller population than the other two regions. The Senate was designed to represent the regional nature of the new country rather than to resolve the regional tensions, but it recognized the equality of the various sections. The Senate would be an appointed body because if it were elected it might have greater claim to challenge the House of Commons. An elected Senate would have legitimacy. In the view of the Fathers of Confederation, it existed as a check on the democratic excesses of the elected lower house, but it could not be a threat to responsible government as exercised through the power of the House of Commons. Christopher Moore reminds us that in taking this approach to the Senate, the delegates were adhering to John Stuart Mill's 1861 *Representative Government*, the great constitutional text of the period.

What the *British North America Act* and the federal system that was created really meant was settled after 1867. The principle of coordinate sovereignty between the provinces and the federal government was established by a series of rulings from the Judicial Committee of the Privy Council in London, England, which acted as Canada's final court of appeal until 1949. If Macdonald believed that the dominion government would emerge as the superior one (similar to how the imperial Parliament in London had been superior to the colonial legislatures in British North America), he underestimated the desire of the provincial governments to protect their interests. By the 1880s, a strong provincial rights movement had formed that challenged any notion Macdonald had of a strong central government.

Because it is so central to the meaning of the federal arrangement negotiated at the Quebec Conference, it is important to note that many of those involved in the process were committed to provincial autonomy and held important views on federalism. First, they understood that the federal principle meant that the dominion government had no authority to interfere in matters placed under provincial legislatures, just as the provinces had no authority to infringe upon federal powers. Federalism meant that each level of government was sovereign in its own areas of jurisdiction. Second, federalism meant a division of power and not that one level of government was supreme over another. Third, the provincialists argued that Confederation was a contract among the provinces, and Canada was created because the colonies had agreed to be federally united into one dominion. Over time, the provincialists would win acceptance of their views, and before Macdonald died in 1891 many of what he considered supervisory powers (such as disallowance of provincial laws) had been largely discredited.[16]

More recently, however, historians have raised questions about the centralizing features of the Constitution and the notion that Macdonald wanted a strong central government. Paul Romney contends that Canadian historians have forgotten the context in which the *British North America Act* was crafted and those powers given to the federal government did not necessarily mean that Ottawa ruled supreme over the provinces. In the view of Leonard Tilley of New Brunswick, the federal government acquired the powers of the Imperial Government in London rather than the power of the colonies; by 1867, Romney points out, London had lost much of its authority to control Canadian affairs, and it had not disallowed a Canadian law in more than 25 years. The colonies had all acquired responsible government with autonomy over their own affairs by the middle of the nineteenth century, and none of them were about to relinquish those powers to a new central government, especially when it came to local matters. Romney goes to great lengths to suggest that the federal power of disallowance and reservation and Ottawa's right to appoint the lieutenant-governors "were not instruments of federal dominance but symbols of the new national unity."[17] In other words, these articles of the Constitution that historians have long seen as giving superior power to the federal government to control the provinces were to be used only in extreme cases. Still, if John A. Macdonald had been such an ardent supporter of the division of powers and federalism, it raises two questions: Why did he exercise the power of disallowance so readily in the immediate aftermath of Confederation, and why did he come into conflict with the province of Ontario on so many occasions over the question of provincial rights?

Debating Confederation

For Canadians today it might seem most peculiar that there was little consultation with the public about the constitutional deal negotiated at the Quebec Conference. In contemporary Canada it would be practically impossible to have such a development without some form of direct democracy, such as a referendum. Many historians believe the lack of any such public approval of the proposed constitution in 1867 is evidence that Confederation was an elitist exercise. Considering less than 20 percent of all adults had the right to vote because of restrictive property and gender-based qualifications, there is little wonder that contemporaries see the whole process of Confederation as an undemocratic exercise. Yet, in mid-nineteenth-century British North America, there was firm acceptance of representative democracy in the tradition of Edmund Burke, a philosophy that maintains that an elected representative was given the authority by the electorate to make decisions for the people who had elected him.

In the past decade, this matter has been an important debate, led on the one hand by Ian McKay, professor of history at Queen's University in Kingston, and by Janet Ajzenstat, professor emeritus of political science at McMaster University, and Paul Romney on the other. MacKay and others have argued that the "people" were excluded from the Confederation process. In an influential essay published in the *Canadian Historical Review* in 2000, McKay argues that "the Fathers [of Confederation] were convinced that they did not need to attain the approval of the mere human beings for the political order they were designing for individuals."[18] Ajzenstat and Romney disagree. They claim that the debates in the colonial legislatures were not over whether to consult the people but how they should be consulted.[19] Furthermore, they claim the debates in the colonial legislatures show that the Fathers of Confederation made every effort to attain the approval of the populations that would be governed by the new constitution.

Elsewhere, Ajzenstat reminds us, none of the colonies were "to be yanked into Confederation by the British Government or by an ambitious local elite." All of the legislative assemblies of the various British colonies, even the constituent assembly of Red River, debated the issue because the local assemblies represented the people. Moreover, the British North Americans realized that they were making a country even if it was a country within an empire. The colonies' delegates had negotiated a constitution for their new country and they had done so in secret behind closed doors, but Macdonald and others declared that it was a democratic exercise: "We in this house," he said in the debate on Confederation, "are representatives of the people, not mere delegates, and to pass such a law [as to have a referendum on the Quebec proposal] would be robbing ourselves of the character of representatives." He argued further that the elected members "represent the people of Canada and we are here to pass laws for the peace, welfare and good government of the country."[20] They agreed on the supremacy of Parliament on the British model. There was no election or referendum on Confederation in the Province of Canada. In Canada West, the major political figures all supported the Quebec proposals, and there was widespread support for the proposed federation. The whole notion of Confederation was hotly debated in Canada East (Quebec), where the Protestant English-speaking minority held considerable economic and social power.

Confederation offered the opportunity to restore the economic might of the business community in Montreal; however, the *Canadiens-Français* were the majority. For them, the union of all the British North American colonies pivoted on the issue of provincial autonomy. As the *Gazette de Sorel* commented on January 14, 1865, "We must never forget that French Canadians need more reassurance than the other provinces for their civil and religious immunities."[21] The Rouges, the party of reform in the colony led by A.A. Dorion, saw Confederation as a direct threat to the powers of Quebec if Ottawa emerged as the dominant power in the new nation. They were equally worried about the discussion in the English-speaking colonies about the creation of a new nationality, which the French equated with centralization of the English-speaking powers and assimilation. Dorion's motion in the legislature calling on members to repudiate all notions of a new nationality was defeated when it was supported by only 25 *Canadien* members.

The Parti Bleu represented the conservative element in Quebec politics and it saw a different nation emerging with union. Led by George-Étienne Cartier and supported by the Catholic Church, it argued that Confederation would undo the 1840 *Act of Union* and liberate Canada East from Canada West, giving it autonomy over the issues that were important to the province in a new Canada. All issues dealing with the French-Canadian nationality would fall within the domain of the provincial government in Quebec City. Many in Quebec realized that there had to be some form of association with the English-speaking provinces for reasons of economic development and defence against the United States. Still, as Cartier said when he returned from London where he had helped write the Constitution, "That is why I was careful to make sure that the federal government would receive only that amount of power which was strictly necessary to serve the general interests of the Confederation."[22]

La Minerve quoted with approval Cartier's views on Confederation. He said: "As a distinct and separate nationality, we form a state within a state. We enjoy the full exercise of our rights and the formal recognition of our national independence."[23] He declared that "the idea of unity of races was utopian—it was impossible. Distinctions of this kind would always appear ... in our own federation." He further noted that "we should have Catholics and Protestants, French, English, Irish and Scotch, and each by his efforts and his success would increase the prosperity and glory of the new confederacy."[24] Confederation for him created a "political nationality" as a Canadian nation existed, but its citizens did not share common origins or a common race. For Cartier, the strength of Canada came from its diversity—that must sound remarkably prescient to anyone living in Canada today.

When the vote on the proposed union was taken in the legislature at 4:30 A.M. on Saturday, March 11, 1865, it carried easily at 99 to 33. Nineteen French Canadians voted against the motion—six fewer than had supported Dorion's motion opposing the concept of a new nationality for the new nation. There was greater opposition to union in the Atlantic region. When the Maritime and Newfoundland delegates returned home from the Quebec Conference, they discovered considerable opposition to the Quebec Resolutions. The ensuing debate in the colonies was not about the desirability of union but whether the Quebec Resolutions met their needs. In fact, many in the region demanded another conference to renegotiate the terms of union. There were considerable fears that the Quebec arrangements would produce a powerful and distant central government, which would leave the Maritimes with little influence. As the *Woodstock Times* in New Brunswick opined, "Union is one thing and the Quebec scheme is quite another."[25]

This was particularly true of Newfoundland and Prince Edward Island. While there had been considerable enthusiasm in Newfoundland when its delegates returned from the Quebec Conference, the mood quickly turned negative. First, the strong Newfoundland Catholic community, with its deep attachment to Ireland, feared any alliance that was led by a British majority, as Confederation surely was. Second, merchants in Newfoundland saw little benefit to a union that they believed would lead to higher tariff rates and favour the economic development of the continent. Similarly, Prince Edward Island saw little in the Quebec Resolutions that recognized its special circumstances. At Quebec, its delegates were not able to convince the assembly to award them an additional seat in the parliament or to provide a special grant of £200 000 to purchase much of the land in the colony held by absentee landowners. Unlike Newfoundland, however, Prince Edward Island joined the union in 1873, when Canada offered the Island colony most of what it had demanded in 1864, suggesting that the particular resolutions agreed upon in Quebec were the primary obstacle to their joining, rather than any inherent opposition to the principle of Confederation. Canada agreed to help Prince Edward Island with its long-standing grievances with absentee landowners and assume the Island's debt, which had increased dramatically because of its railway building projects. After the Confederate forces were soundly trounced in the 1869 Newfoundland election, the issue crept back into the political debate there on several occasions, but Britain's oldest colony chose to stay out of Confederation until 1949.

1866: New Brunswick rejects Confederation Deal.

In New Brunswick, Leonard Tilley called an election to allow a debate on Confederation, but only when many of his Cabinet ministers refused to support the Quebec Resolutions. His chief opponent, Albert Smith, won the 1865 election that saw only 11 of the members supporting the Quebec Resolutions returned to office. Still, Smith and many of his supporters were not opposed to the principle of union. Charles Tupper faced similar opposition in Nova Scotia, but he chose to delay the debate on the Quebec Resolutions in the face of mounting opposition. Joseph Howe, an earlier proponent of union, led the fight against Tupper because he feared the separation of Nova Scotia from Great Britain. He disagreed with Tupper's refusal to consult the people in an election. Howe saw himself foremost as a British subject and saw little gain for Nova Scotia in a Canadian federation. When he already had London as his capital, he asked, why should he trade it for a new capital in the backwoods of Canada: "Take a [Nova Scotian] to Ottawa, above the tidewater, freeze him up for five months, where he cannot view the Atlantic, smell salt water, or see the sail of a ship, and the man will pine and die."[26]

Howe took a petition opposing the union signed by 18 000 Nova Scotians to the Earl of Carnarvon, the Colonial Secretary, but it had little impact in London where there was general support for union of the British North American colonies. Even though he was dismissed in London, Howe would continue his struggle against Confederation after 1867. After what had happened in New Brunswick, Tupper had the Nova Scotia legislature vote on the Quebec Resolutions, and with a majority in the legislative assembly, Nova Scotia agreed to the union. However, in the federal election that followed Confederation on July 1, 1867, Tupper was the only supporter of Confederation to win his federal seat, and the anti-confederates won the provincial legislature.

In New Brunswick, Smith's coalition of critics (of the Quebec proposal) and reformers started to unravel over patronage, religious disputes, financial support for the railways, and internal confusion. The situation for the government was exacerbated by two factors: First, Smith and his cabinet failed to present any alternative to Confederation; and second, the British Colonial Office dispatched Arthur Gordon to New Brunswick as the lieutenant-governor, with strict orders to promote Confederation. The antics of a group of Irish nationalists known as the Fenian Brotherhood, who harassed the British colonies from their base in the United States, helped to create a panic in New Brunswick. In the face of the Fenian scare and the collapse of Smith's coalition, new elections were held in New Brunswick. The campaign—as most campaigns in British North America were at the time—was swayed by patronage, money, and liquor. Tilley was re-elected to bring New Brunswick into Confederation.

The Fenian Influence

The Fenians proved convenient for those favouring Confederation because they provided seemingly sound footing to argue that union of the colonies was essential for the defence of British North America. The Fenian Brotherhood had been created in 1858 for the purpose of liberating Ireland by holding Britain's North American colonies hostages. Thousands of Irish Americans had joined the U.S. Army during the Civil War and when it ended, many in British North America feared that the Fenians would try to occupy Canada to force Britain out of Ireland. In April 1866, the insecurity of British North America was heightened when several thousand Irishmen arrived in Portland, Maine, and made their way to Eastport, just kilometres from the New Brunswick border. The goal was to occupy Campobello Island in New Brunswick, but when the British dispatched two warships from Halifax and sent 5000 British and New Brunswick militiamen to the area, the Fenians burned a customs warehouse on the island and fled. However, that was not the end of Fenian threat. More than 1500 landed at Fort Erie in Canada West and engaged the militia in Welland County. Nine were killed in the skirmishes before the Fenians fled across the border, where U.S. officials persuaded them to give up the struggle with offers of free passage to their homes.

The Fenians were little more than a nuisance and clearly no real threat to British North America. Yet, the 1860s were a decade when there was considerable fear of the United States among British North Americans. The British Colonies had not been invaded since the War of 1812, when British soldiers, the local militias, and their Aboriginal allies joined forces to repeal the Americans, but the feeling persisted that the colonists had to be vigilant; otherwise the Americans could cross the border at any moment to bring all of North America under their control.

Insecurity heightened during the American Civil War when Britain favoured the losing side. There was enough boisterous rhetoric coming from the Americans to worry those in British North America. William Seward, the U.S. Secretary of State, was a strong proponent of annexation, and Charles Sumner, the chair of the Senate Committee on Foreign Relations, even talked of letting the American South secede from the Union and taking Canada instead. Newspaper articles of the time added to the anxiety; the *New York Times* commented regularly on the inevitability of the United States annexing Canada. Two incidents in particular raised the level of fear in the colonies. First, the U.S. warship *San Jacinto* stopped the *Trent*, a Royal Mail steamship in international waters, and seized two Confederate officers on their way to London to purchase supplies for the Southern armies. Britain considered the incident an act of piracy and provocation, and lodged a formal protest with the Union Government. Even though the pair was released, Britain dispatched 11 000 troops to British North America. By the time they arrived in Canada, the St. Lawrence River had frozen and they had to march overland to Canada, fuelling further demands for an intercolonial railway to ensure the defence of British North America.

The second incident occurred on October 19, 1864, when a small group of Confederate soldiers robbed three banks in St. Albans, Vermont. They fled across the border and sought refugee in Montreal, but not before they had taken $200 000, killed one American, and wounded several others. The bank robbers were arrested but later released on a technicality after a Montreal judge ruled that the men were officially soldiers on a mission. Because of its neutrality in the conflict, Britain could not extradite the soldiers to the United States. When the robbers were released and the money returned to them (by some accounts), the American government interpreted the court's bumbling as British support for the Confederates. The U.S. government demanded that all Canadians entering the United States carry a passport, and many American newspapers renewed their call for annexation.

As tensions built between the British and the Americans, many believed that the colonies were in peril. Some colonial leaders insisted that Confederation would strengthen the resolve of the colonies to remain under the British flag, and the British Colonial Office wanted the colonies to shoulder more of the cost of their own defence. None was more adamant about passing greater responsibility for defence and the costs associated with it to the Canadians than Edward Cardwell, who had been the Colonial Secretary in London since 1864. There was little prospect of that occurring as long as each colony remained separate, but Britain would certainly insist that as a nation Canada should assume greater responsibility for its own defence, and Britain did what it could to encourage Confederation.

Although Canada's Constitution had been adopted in outline form at Quebec City in 1864, it took several years to complete the process and put it into legal language. The *British North America Act*, passed the British legislature and Queen Victoria gave the Bill royal assent on March 29, 1867. It was a conservative document, and Canada remained very much tied to the British Empire, largely because it needed the Empire for markets, capital, and protection from the United States. The preamble of the Constitution, which incidentally did not include the word *Canada* in the title, acknowledged that Canada would have "a constitution similar in Principle to that of the United Kingdom." The Imperial Parliament in London, England, knew it was best not to interfere with the plans of the politicians in the colonies when the principle of responsible government had been long established. As Thomas D'Arcy McGee noted in the debate on Confederation, it was a "scheme not suggested by others, or imposed upon us, but the work of ourselves, the creation of our intellect and of our free, unbiased, and untrammelled will."[27]

The first section of the *British North America Act* declared that the "present and future prosperity of British North America will be promoted by a Federal Union under the Crown of Great Britain." Even if Canada was to be a British nation, that did not mean that those who created Canada could not also be Canadian. As Macdonald had said in 1860, "Since I was five years old, I have been in Canada. All my hopes and dreams and my remembrances are Canadian; not only are my principles and prejudices Canadian, but what, as a Scotchman, I feel as much as anyone else, my interests are Canadian."[28]

Canada in 1867

The new dominion government took office on July 1, 1867. Sir John A. Macdonald, recently knighted for his role in making Confederation, became Canada's first prime minister. Macdonald's government looked to the old Province of Canada for much of the foundation of governing, establishing a trend that has held since that time: Ontario and Quebec largely took control. With Confederation, some might argue, Ontario and Quebec, once united as a single province, won not only control of their own provinces but also control of national politics and economics. For instance, when the civil service was established, it was recruited primarily from Ontario and Quebec. Similarly, the tariff rate for the new nation was adopted from the Province of Canada. The new nation required a regulatory regime for the nation to function and a transcontinental economy to develop. Shortly after Confederation, a national financial and banking system was established that favoured a centralized system with a series of branches across the country rather than the creation of new banks. The federal government adopted new currency and coinage legislation, and provided for patent law, uniform weights and measures, and a number of other mundane, but necessary, rules and regulations for the new nation to function. The federal government had responsibility for defence and economical development, including western land ownership, immigration, canals, dry-docks, fisheries, post offices, and wharves.

At Confederation, the extent of unequal development among the various provinces and regions of Canada was pronounced. Although some believe economic disparity was a result of Confederation, regional economic disparity was a feature of Canada when it was created. Ontario was the richest economy, based largely on its strong agricultural sector; it had per capita commodity incomes 20 percent above the national average. The other provinces fell below the national average. Quebec's per capita commodity income was 86 percent of the national average, and New Brunswick and Nova Scotia lagged with 83 percent and 75 percent, respectively. The Census Reports from 1851 to 1871 also show that Ontario was already emerging as the most populous and dominant province in Canada. In 1851, it accounted for 39.1 percent of the people in British North America, slightly ahead of Quebec with 36.5 percent; a decade later, Ontario would claim 43.2 percent of the population, while Quebec's share had declined to 34 percent, and by 1871 Ontario had 43.9 percent while Quebec had dropped further to 32.3 percent. The Maritime provinces' shares had dropped from 22 percent in 1851 to 20.8 percent in 1871.

By 1867, several large cities had emerged. Montreal was the largest with 100 000 people, followed by Quebec City with 60 000. Toronto was the largest urban centre in Ontario with a population of 50 000. In the Maritime provinces, Halifax and Saint John each had populations around 30 000, yet more than 80 percent of Canada's population of 3.5 million lived in rural areas and were engaged in staple production in agriculture, forestry, mining, and fishing. Agriculture was, by far, the dominant sector, as Table 1.1 illustrates; it accounted for 54 percent of commodity incomes across Canada, though manufacturing had become the second most important commodity-producing sector, accounting for 33 percent of commodity income across the nation. New Brunswick and Quebec, two economies that depended heavily on the forestry sector, were the most dependent on manufacturing. The service sector, including construction, transportation, government services, and retail, accounted for one-third of the nation's gross national product in 1870.

John A. Macdonald becomes first prime minister of Canada.

Table 1.1
Sectorial Distribution of Income, Canada, 1870

Region	Farm	Factory	Forestry	Mines	Fish
Canada	54%	33%	10%	2%	1%
Nova Scotia	46	27	7	12	7
New Brunswick	47	39	11	1	3
Quebec	49	37	12	1	1
Ontario	59	32	9	1	0

Source: Kris Inwood and James R. Irwin, "Canadian Regional Income Differences at Confederation," in Kris Inwood, ed., *Farm, Factory and Fortune: New Studies in the Economic History of the Maritime Provinces* (Fredericton: Acadiensis Press, 1993), table 2, page 102.

With slightly more than half of all Canadians engaged in the agricultural sector, Canada was a rural nation in 1867, but the rural areas were far from homogenous. Clear distinctions existed between those who owned a piece of land and those who did not. The dominant group in any rural village or town was the professional class, those lawyers and notaries, doctors, priests, and local merchants. The merchants continued to be substantial creditors, and farmers, loggers, and fishers were usually indebted to the local merchant. Most towns also had several skilled craftspeople as well as unskilled labourers engaged in production for a local economy. In the transition to industrialization, skilled workers, those with a trade learned over a long period of time, were at the top of the working class. They have been called the aristocracy of labour by some historians. Their wages were well above average, and they were the leaders of the nascent labour movement, mainly to protect their privileged position in society.

Life for women whose families were engaged in staple production was not easy. They played an important role in the farm economy alongside their husbands, but men were unlikely to engage in domestic work. In addition to sharing in the farm work, women were responsible for the domestic chores such as washing the clothes, hauling the water, cooking and cleaning, making the clothes that the family needed, caring for the children, and tending the vegetable gardens. For families engaged in fishing, women were often the ones who cured the salted fish and repaired damaged fishing gear. Though they were active participants in managing and providing for the needs of daily life, women had few legal claims to family property, and the family farm, for instance, was often sold by the husband without any consultation with his wife. If a wife outlived her husband, the farm often passed to the eldest son upon the father's

Work: "My poor husband, you complain of your ten hours of work. I've been working fourteen hours, and my day is not yet over."

Source: C572_A.02.532.1 © McCord Museum.

death. Even if a wife inherited the farm, a husband often placed restrictions on her in his will that she could only keep the farm on the condition of "proper behaviour"; this usually meant she could not remarry.

In the Confederation era, Canada's economic expansion changed. The staple economy expanded into the north and the west. Industrial development was fuelled by the resources of Quebec, Ontario, and British Columbia; imported capital primarily from Great Britain; and cheap labour supplied by immigrants, women, and recent arrivals to the cities from the countryside. The rapid industrial expansion saw the concentration of factories in large urban cities that changed the nature of Canada.

As industrialization started to take hold in the larger towns and cities, neighbourhoods became separated by class and ethnicity. Workers had to live near their places of work, and nearly all workers were tenants living in overcrowded and unhealthy conditions. The rich lived much better, and as the working classes crowded the city centre, new upper-class neighbourhoods emerged where new luxurious houses were built on spacious green lots. Social inequality also became more pronounced and more visible in Canada's cities. Between 1877 and 1896, for instance, the average rate of death for the French-speaking working-class ward of Sainte-Marie in Montreal was 36.7 per thousand, but it was 18.7 per thousand in the English-speaking upper-class ward of Saint-Antoine.[29]

The introduction of industrial production significantly altered both the gender and the age of the labour force. Women played an important role in the economic transformation occurring in Canada as they moved increasingly into wage labour after 1850. The life of a mother and wife had never been easy in the harsh realities of farming before the age of mechanization, and little changed for her with the arrival of the industrial age. For families engaged in the industrial economy, a clear division emerged between paid and unpaid work. The concept of a "family wage" emerged where it was assumed that it was the husband's responsibility to provide for his family, but wage rates were such that this was rarely the case. Because a male wage was rarely sufficient to provide for a working-class family, women and children often supplemented the family income by working in the formal wage economy.

Women also performed many tasks in the informal economy, such as taking in boarders, making clothes, and keeping a garden plot. Many women turned to the factories for work; by 1871, 42 percent of the industrial workforce in Montreal and 34 percent in Toronto consisted of women and children. About a quarter of all children between 11 and 14 worked in factories. Women were often involved in the practice of "putting out," where employers hired women to work at home on a piecework basis; this was especially true of work in the garment industries. Some also entered such professions as teaching and nursing, but the most important paid employment for women was domestic service, and it was one sector of the economy in which Aboriginal women were encouraged to participate.

Women were anxious, though, to escape the drudgery and exploitation of domestic service. The *Globe* reported in 1868 that "our working women dread household service, and hundreds would rather famish than apply at a servants' agency."[30] Life as a domestic servant meant not only long hours of drudgery and hard labour but also the risk of sexual exploitation. Because many domestic servants were young girls, they became pregnant by their employers. The case of Reverend Corbett, an Anglican priest who drugged and raped his servant Maria Thomas and then attempted to perform an abortion, was not unusual. Corbett was sent to jail for six months for his crimes.[31]

Life was not easy in Canada at the time of Confederation, especially for the working class. Workers found themselves in harsh and unsafe working conditions and lived in areas where pollution and filth were commonplace. Crime, prostitution, excessive drinking, and labour unrest marked life in the cities. Most public celebrations, such as Queen Victoria's birthday, were occasions for violence. In 1867, for instance, the popular celebration was marked by gang wars in the Irish neighbourhoods of Montreal, when young men attacked French-Canadian street vendors. Crimes associated with heavy drinking were common. In 1870, of the 11 135 arrests in Montreal that year, 5358 (4313 men, 1045 women) were linked to public drunkenness.[32]

We can also get a glimpse into life in post-Confederation Canada by considering which members of society were allowed to vote. In 1867, voting was a privilege rather than the right and obligation it is today. It was 1885 before the federal government passed a law that gave Parliament control of the right to vote. Until that happened, the voting laws were under provincial control and voters had to meet three basic conditions—male, at least 21 years of age, and a British subject by birth or naturalization—and whatever rules fell under the jurisdiction of the electoral laws of each province. In the first generation of Confederation, most workers earned only modest incomes and the vast majority did not own the homes in which they lived. Because of the property-based qualifications, many Canadians could not vote. Others were excluded for various reasons, including those in the employ of the government; persons receiving social assistance or any help form charitable organizations; Aboriginal peoples living on reserves; and in British Columbia, any person of Chinese origins.

Before Confederation, all of the British North American colonies had used statute law to disenfranchise women, and with provincial laws governing the voting rights, the exclusion of women was entrenched in the new Canadian constitution. In the 1870s, a women's suffrage movement emerged in all of the provinces; the mandate of the movement was to seek social, economic, and political equality with men. New Brunswick was the only province (in 1867) to adopt the secret ballot; other provinces voted in the open, a process that was vulnerable to considerable abuse and intimidation. Moreover, the federal election in 1867 stretched over six weeks and in 1872 took nearly three months. After the 1874 election, the government introduced the secret ballot and mandated that all eligible electors vote on the same day. The legislation also required all candidates to disclose their election expenses.

Consolidation East and Expansion West

John A. Macdonald was well prepared to lead the new nation. He had learned much about holding fractious elements together in the Province of Canada (where he governed for more than a decade), and while he might not have been interested in political philosophy, he was well suited to governing the new country that was divided along regional, ethnic, and partisan lines. He once told a gathering of skilled workers in Toronto that he was a successful cabinetmaker. Indeed he was, and he was determined to create a solid framework for the new country. He began by convincing many of those who had held leadership roles at Charlottetown and Quebec to join him in a coalition that became known as the Liberal-Conservative Party. George Brown split with Macdonald in 1866 and attempted to build a national party to rival Macdonald, but he had scant political success; Brown failed to win a seat in the first Canadian Parliament.

One of the defining features of Canada since 1867 has been the persistence of regional cleavages and strong provincial governments determined to achieve a better deal for their province. One of the first manifestations of this phenomenon emerged in Nova Scotia when the Confederate forces were soundly beaten in the first election after Confederation.

Nova Scotia begins campaign to leave Confederation.

Those Nova Scotians went to Ottawa in 1867 to repeal the Confederation deal; the Bloc Québécois was not the first group of MPs elected on a mandate to withdraw a province from Confederation. The "Repealers"—as the Nova Scotians were called—were worried about the province's identity in Confederation, its economy in the face of impending central Canadian economic expansion, and what they considered the poor deal for Nova Scotia negotiated at Quebec.

Joseph Howe was the nominal leader of the group. He had objected to Confederation because he believed Nova Scotia was better off as a British colony than a Canadian province. He had made his case for the anti-confederate cause in *Confederation Considered in Relation to the Interests of the Empire*, where he described Confederation as an attempt to destroy the British Empire. In his pamphlet, he attacked various interest groups who were plotting to railroad the colonies into union. One of his villains was the Hudson's Bay Company, which he described as standing in the way of "the advancing civilizations of Europe and America," and he accused it of reducing the First Nations to a "state of subjection akin to slavery."[33]

Resolutions for repeal of Confederation were passed in the Nova Scotia legislature, but the Colonial Office in London, England, dismissed such overtures. The imperial authorities favoured a united British North America and had no interest in the protests from Nova Scotia. When his appeal to the British Parliament failed, Howe's

Joseph Howe was a leading Nova Scotia reformer and anti-Confederate before he joined Macdonald's cabinet.

Source: Joseph Purcell, *Joseph Howe*. Private Collection of Wanda Blake and Raymond Blake. Photo Robert Blake.

options were limited because the Nova Scotians had no greater success in Ottawa. When they introduced a resolution demanding that the Canadian Constitution not apply to their province, the motion was immediately dismissed. They found that the other MPs in Ottawa were expansionists—meaning they saw themselves as working together to build a nation in the northern half of North America, and they refused to recognize—let alone debate—the merits of those from Nova Scotia who wanted out of Confederation.

The choices for the Nova Scotians had narrowed considerably. They had to choose between independence, which meant the possibility of annexation to the United States, or working within Confederation for better terms. Macdonald realized that he had to deal with those who opposed the union and turned his attention to Howe, who surrendered to Macdonald's persistence and joined the Cabinet. After all, Macdonald reminded him that Nova Scotia would remain a part of the empire, as Canada was a "British" nation, and in Confederation Nova Scotia would not lose any of its connection to the Crown. With Howe's acceptance of Confederation, the anti-confederates were effectively silenced. Using the federal spending power, Macdonald offered slightly better terms to improve the annual federal subsidy for the province. Through his brand of brokerage politics—the reconciling of the various regional, political, economic, and cultural interests—and his penchant for coalition building, Macdonald and his government had to prove to Canadians that his Confederation leap of faith could actually work.

In the 1872 election, Macdonald's party won 13 of the 21 federal seats in Nova Scotia, and even though many in the province continued to harbour resentment towards Ottawa, the province had cast aside its hope to leave the union. By then, the first section of track for the Intercolonial Railway, built to fulfill the conditions of Confederation, was completed in Nova Scotia. On July 1, 1875, the rail line linking Nova Scotia to Quebec, at a cost of more than $34 million, was complete.

Negotiations and Force: Canada and the Red River Colony

In addition to addressing the anti-Confederate sentiments in Nova Scotia, Macdonald and his government were quick to extend Canada's dominion over the rest of British North America all the way to the Pacific Ocean. An important step in that process was the acquisition of the vast territory to the west and north known as Rupert's Land, which had been granted to the Hudson's Bay Company in the seventeenth century.

For many, the destiny of Canada was linked to the occupation and development of the North West. Ontario was fuelling the expansionist sentiment, driven by the lack of new arable land in that province. A West filled with farmers would also be an important market for eastern manufactured goods coming from Quebec and Ontario, as well as a source of raw materials for their factories. Thomas D'Arcy McGee, among Canada's most fervent nationalists, captured the expansionist sentiment in 1868 when he said that "the future of the Dominion depends on our early occupation of the rich prairie land."[34] At the same time, Canada was increasingly worried about the Americans, who were developing their own western lands and looked with interest to the British prairies. Minnesota had become a state in 1858, and farmers were pouring into the Red River Valley in Minnesota and the Dakotas. The Americans exerted considerable influence in the region through the St. Paul and Pacific Railroad, running along the border, and it captured virtually all of the trade with the Red River settlement and Fort Garry.

1869: Canada acquires Rupert's Land.

In its eagerness to annex the western lands, Canada acted without any consultation or negotiations with the approximately 100 000 Aboriginals and Métis living in the region. George-Étienne Cartier and his colleague William McDougall travelled to London in October 1868 to negotiate with the British government and the Hudson's Bay Company (HBC) for Rupert's Land and the North-Western Territory. Canada acquired the vast territory for £300 000 in March 1869, but the HBC maintained its right to trade throughout the territory. It also received title to considerable tracts of land in the territory, but with the deal Canada acquired more than a quarter of North America. Neither the HBC nor the British government demonstrated any greater interest than had Canada in communicating with the inhabitants of the North West about the impending transfer of their land to Canada.

The Canadian government failed to realize that it was not acquiring an empty land. However, they learned quickly that the right of self-determination was also important to the Métis. Because of its association with the HBC and the fur trade, the Red River settlement consisted mainly of Métis, the descendents of fur traders (Scots and French-Canadians) and their Aboriginal wives. By 1869, over 80 percent of the 12 000 persons at Red River were Métis, and more than 50 percent were French-speaking and Roman Catholic. They had divided the land along the Red River in long narrow lots along the river, a necessity for travel and food. The Métis had their own government, the Council of Assiniboia, established in 1835, as well as their own system of local courts. They had created their own economic and cultural society at Red River and a strong sense of identity, and they were prepared to defend it against intrusions from the Canadians who were intent on extending their influence to the western lands. Moreover, a feeling of discontent and anxiety existed in Red River as the colony had struggled in 1867 and 1868 with a severe grasshopper plague that devastated much of the harvest, causing widespread hunger and hardship. The situation was further aggravated by the disappearance of buffalo from the eastern plains in the wake of American military operations against its Aboriginal population, advancing settlers, and indiscriminate slaughter of the herds.

The Canadian government planned to take control of Red River in December 1869, but the colony had not received any official information about the transfer or about how the new owners of the land would govern the territory. What little information the citizens had been able to gather came from the local newspaper, *The Nor'Wester*, which was controlled by the Canadians in the colony. The settlers must have thought the annexation of the North West was led by English, Protestant, and Orange Ontario rather than the Dominion of Canada. Canada had even appointed McDougall as the first lieutenant-governor to lead the colonial administration until the colony was ready to become a province. He was to arrive in Red River in late November.

1869: Red River Resistance begins.

Led by 25-year-old Louis Riel, a bright, young Métis recently returned to Red River from Montreal where he had attended college to train as a priest, the Red River settlers took great exception to the Canadians who arrived with their surveyor's chains, English language and cultural mores, Protestant religion, and superior attitudes to make this region a hinterland for the more populous provinces in the East. Riel had returned, sensitive to a special mission to defend his people from the threat of impending change. He believed his people represented a new nation in their own right and felt fully justified in stopping the transfer of the land to Canada. Riel even talked about the colony's nation-building aspirations. On October 18, 1869, Riel led the formation of the National Committee of the Métis to decide how to protect their interests and their land; a few weeks later a provisional government of both Francophones and Anglophones was established. Riel and his people did not object to becoming a part of Canada, but they wanted negotiations with the Canadian government for some guarantee of their land, their language, and their religion. The first acts of their self-created government were to drive from the colony Canadian surveyors who were changing the land division from long, narrow strips to square township lots, and to prevent McDougall's entry into the territory.

Councillors of the Provisional Government of the Métis Nation. Note that Riel is clearly the dominant person in the photograph. (Front row): Robert O'Lone, Paul Proulx. (Centre row): Pierre Poitras, John Bruce, Louis Riel, John O'Donoghue, François Dauphinais. (Rear row): Bonnet Tromage, Pierre de Lorme, Thomas Bunn, Xavier Page, Baptiste Beauchemin, Baptiste Tournond, Joseph Spence.

chapter 1

Source: Library and Archives Canada, Copy negative PA-012854.

The Canadians in Red River were mostly young and well-educated from middle-class Ontario families. They were known as the "Canadian party" and included such individuals as Dr. John Schultz, a medical doctor and merchant, who had arrived from Canada West in 1859. They dismissed any notion of Métis nationalism when they paid any attention at all to them. They saw in the North West the creation of a new Ontario, and they wanted annexation to Canada. In January 1867, they had initiated a petition asking to be united with Canada. However, as historian Doug Owram has pointed out, such petitions had dubious beginnings; nevertheless, they played an important role in shaping Canada's image of the Red River colony.[35] The Canadian party did little to cultivate any support among the indigenous population and saw the manoeuvrings of Riel and the provisional government as acts of lawlessness, not the acts of a self-determining people.

The Canadians in Red River opposed Riel's provisional government, and they used Schultz's general store as their headquarters. The Métis raided the store and took the Canadians prisoners. Riel released those who promised to leave the territory or abide by Métis laws. Schultz refused and remained imprisoned with a few others, only later to escape and lead his supporters in an attack on the provisional government at Fort Garry. The Métis suppressed the uprising and captured several of the insurgents, including Thomas Scott, a 28-year-old Irishman, a member of the Orange Order, and a vehement anti-Catholic. Scott had arrived in Red River in 1869 and worked as a labourer on the road from Red River to Lake Superior. He drifted towards Schultz and the Canadian party and was part of the group, along with Schultz and Charles Mair, a poet and columnist in Red River for *The Globe*, that attempted to overthrow the provisional government. Their leader, Major Charles Arkoll Boulton, was sentenced to death for treason by the provisional government, but Riel intervened to save his life. Scott, on the other hand, was not so fortunate. He tormented his guards with insults and contempt. They attempted to silence him with a beating, but when that failed he was charged with insubordination and treason and sentenced to death by a court martial, the usual punishment for treason in the nineteenth century. On March 4, 1870, he was placed in front of a firing squad and shot. Riel reluctantly agreed to Scott's execution so as to placate his men who were upset over the death of one of their own in a previous altercation, and as he said later, "We must make Canada respect us."[36]

1870: Thomas Scott is executed by Riel.

Macdonald realized that the people of Red River had every right to be angry. He said to Cartier on November 27, 1870: "They are handed over like a flock of sheep to us; and they are told that they lose their lands … Under these circumstances it is not to be wondered at that they should be dissatisfied, and should show their discontent."[37] Macdonald soon realized, too, that the events unfolding in Red River would have repercussions throughout Canada as they threatened to accentuate the racial and religious divisions within the new nation. Both Ontario and Quebec watched closely his handling of the affairs in Red River, and Macdonald had to chose a course of action that he hoped would minimize the tension between Ontario and Quebec and resolve the conflict with Riel and the Red River colonists. He could negotiate with Riel and his supporters or he could resort to a show of force. He chose both.

Macdonald sent Donald A. Smith of the Hudson's Bay Company as a special commissioner to help defuse the growing tensions in the colony. Through this approach, Macdonald continued the process of negotiation and accommodation that had marked the earlier confederation process. Smith's negotiations with Riel in January and February 1870 prepared the way for a delegation from Red River to negotiate the colony's entry into Confederation. This entry was achieved in May 1870 with the *Manitoba Act*, which satisfied most of the demands of Riel and the Métis. The *Manitoba Act* promised settlers in Red River secure tenure of the river lots already occupied and a reserve of 566 580 hectares to be allotted to the next generation of Métis. The remaining land in Manitoba and Rupert's Land was deemed Dominion Land to be used for national purposes and, therefore, beyond the jurisdiction of the Manitoba legislature. The *Manitoba Act* also provided for denominational schools and the use of French as a language of record as well as debate in the provincial assembly. French-Canadian leaders, especially in Quebec, were extremely pleased with the *Manitoba Act*, as it fulfilled the promise of the French–English duality of Canada. The Act caused some resentment and disappointment in Ontario, however, which had seen the North West as its hinterland and as a fertile land for the sons and daughters of Ontario farmers.

Manitoba enters Confederation, 1870.

Manitoba's entry into Confederation did not resolve the crisis created by the execution of Thomas Scott, which had accentuated the racial and religious divisions within the new nation. Much of Ontario saw Riel and the Métis as little more than puppets of the Roman Catholic clergy, for whom many in Protestant and English-speaking Ontario harboured great distrust. Ontario did not want negotiations with Riel as it considered the rebellion as a direct threat to the hegemony of Canada and, indeed, the British Empire. Their only solution was to dispatch a military force. When Schultz and Mair escaped from Red River and returned to Toronto, they were met by a crowd of 5000 and hailed at a meeting in St. Lawrence Hall as Canadian and British patriots defending country and Empire against the Métis rebels. Even the mayor of Toronto attended and demanded that the rebellion be suppressed with military force.

Thomas Scott's death added fuel to the nationalist fire raging in Ontario. When news of Scott's death reached Ontario, there was a public outcry for retribution, particularly from the Orange Order, one of the most powerful organizations in English-speaking Canada. There were considerable differences, though, among the Orange population throughout Canada; some of them, such as many of those in Toronto, were fiercely anti-Catholic. In Quebec, however, the relations between French-Canadian Catholics and the Orange Order were much better and, in many ways, they had found some semblance of political accommodation with each other. A resolution from Toronto Orangemen that passed on April 13, 1870, and that later appeared in *The Globe* showed that was not the case in Ontario: "Whereas Brother Thomas Scott, a member of our Order was cruelly murdered by the enemies of our Queen, country and religion, therefore be it resolved that … we, the members of L.O.L. No. 404 call upon the Government to avenge his death, pledging ourselves to assist in rescuing Red River Territory from those who have turned it over to Popery, and bring to justice the murderers of our countrymen."[38] French Canada saw the reaction in Ontario as a threat not only against the Métis but also against anyone who might defend the Catholic faith and French culture in Canada. The events of Red River caused a deep emotional divide in Canada.

Macdonald understood the divisions between Quebec and Ontario perfectly, and he realized that his promise in March 1870 of an amnesty to those engaged in the Red River Resistance was sure to divide the country. In Ontario, Riel was denounced; in Quebec, he was a hero. Macdonald wrote to Adams G. Archibald, the new lieutenant-governor for Manitoba, of his dilemma in offering an amnesty for Riel:

> The French Canadians have identified themselves in sentiment a good deal with their compatriots; and the Protestants, on the other hand, would view with intense dislike any amnesty which would shelter or protect those connected with the murder of Scott. Were it not for that unhappy event all parties would, I think, acquiesce in the propriety of letting by-gones be by-gones, and an amnesty for the political offences would not be seriously objected to.[39]

To appease Ontario, Macdonald dispatched troops to Manitoba in July 1870 on the pretext of preventing further trouble. At the same time, Macdonald encouraged Riel to flee to the United States, and there were rumours that Macdonald offered him money to remain there. Riel was elected twice to the House of Commons, but he was prevented from attending. Mackenzie Bowell, the Ontario Orange leader and later prime minister, introduced a motion in 1873 to expel him from Parliament. In 1875, Riel was offered an amnesty on condition of five years' banishment from Canada, which he took. At the time, though, it seemed that the Métis had achieved their objective. Canada had been dissuaded from annexing their land without consultation with them, and they had won entry into Canada as a province; they had won legislative guarantees that their land, religion, and language would be secure within the new Canadian regime. Within a few years, though, the Métis would call upon Riel to defend their interest again.

After the Canadian government acquired the North West, it recognized that Aboriginal peoples had a right to the land. It continued the process initiated by the British in the eighteenth century of dealing with Aboriginal title and rights and negotiated 11 "numbered treaties" that covered much of present-day Ontario, Manitoba, Saskatchewan, Alberta, and some of the Canadian North. At Confederation, the *British North America Act*, gave the federal government jurisdiction over "Indians and Land reserved for Indians." Beginning in 1871, the Canadian government negotiated a series of numbered treaties (which will be considered fully in the next chapter) with Canada's indigenous peoples that provided for the cession of land by the First Nations to allow expansion of settlement into Western Canada. In addition to the promise of reserve land and annual cash payments, Canada promised hunting and fishing rights, gratuities, the provision of agricultural implements and livestock, schools, and a variety of other benefits to protect the First Nations peoples from hunger and disease. There is ample evidence that in many cases on the plains this did not happen, and the reserve system led to widespread hunger, starvation, and disease that the government had promised to prevent.

By most accounts, Canada never regarded the treaties as being signed between sovereign nations, but as real estate transactions that extinguished Aboriginal title and rights. Aboriginal peoples generally believed that they were sharing, and not surrendering, their land and that these deals were done between autonomous communities. Furthermore, they believed that the elaborate ceremonies accompanying the negotiations were an indication of the highest order of diplomacy and law-making within their communities. Today, the treaties are constitutionally recognized as binding agreements between Aboriginal peoples and the Crown, and their interpretation has fallen to the courts. Over the decade of the 1870s, most of the Aboriginal lands between Manitoba and the Rocky Mountains were transferred from the First Nations to the Government of Canada at almost no immediate cost to the Dominion, but vast areas of certain parts of Canada have never been formally negotiated by the two parties.

Two other developments were of significance in Western Canada. First, the government created the North-West Mounted Police—now the Royal Canadian Mounted Police—in 1873 as an agent of the Canadian government to maintain peace in the West. Their dress was the scarlet tunic to take advantage of the respect that Aboriginal groups had for the British Army. Second, and with no more than a few thousand European settlers in the West, the government passed the *Dominion Lands Act* in 1872 to facilitate white Anglo-European settlement of the West. The Act provided to each head of family, or male 21 years of age, 64 hectares free if he paid a $10 registration fee, resided on the land for three years, cultivated 12 hectares, and built a permanent dwelling. If these conditions were met on the first quarter-section, it was his, and for a small fee he could add a second quarter-section. The government believed that even free land would pay for itself by bringing in immigrants who would need consumer goods, which, in turn, would generate manufacturing and trade in the new Dominion. Despite the offer of free land after 1872, few people ventured into the Canadian West until the 1890s when the American West was settled.

Reaching the Pacific Ocean

The Canadian government was anxious to extend its control across the continent to make Canada a nation from sea to sea, which meant bringing British Columbia into the fold. The European population of the colony had grown rapidly following the gold rush after 1857, even if they were outnumbered by Aboriginal peoples. There was also a great concern that the Americans would extend their influence in the colony. After all, on March 30, 1867, one day after the passage of the Canadian Constitution in the British Parliament, the United States purchased Alaska from Russia. British Columbia was being squeezed on both sides by the Americans, and there was considerable talk—and fear—of annexation. Moreover, the Americans completed their first transcontinental railway in 1869, and were planning a second that would run near the Canadian border. In August 1869, William Seward visited Victoria and left with the impression that British Columbians were eager to join the United States.

British Columbia (1871) and Prince Edward Island (1873) join Confederation.

With its Pacific fleet based at Esquimalt, Britain did not want to lose British Columbia, and it worked after 1867 to have it join Canada. It had facilitated the sale of the Hudson's Bay Company land in the North-Western Territory to Canada to extend Canada's border westward and keep the northern half of North America British. Anthony Musgrave was sent to British Columbia as governor with instructions to promote union. Macdonald agreed with the British government. After all, British Columbia was a natural extension of Canada and necessary for the development of the transcontinental nation. When Macdonald fell ill in early 1871, Cartier again played a key role in the Canadian advance west. "Before very long," he told Parliament, "the English traveler who lands at Halifax will be able within five or six days to cover half a continent inhabited by British subjects"; this was a much shorter trip than the 24 days it took the delegation from British Columbia to get to Ottawa to negotiate union. When the Canadian government promised a rail link within a decade, assumed the colony's debt, and provided the usual subsidies, British Columbia joined. In 1871 when the legislation passed the House of Commons, Cartier shouted "All aboard for the West!"[40]

While the boundaries of Manitoba had been limited to the settled portions of the territory, this was not the case with British Columbia. Although Aboriginal title to the

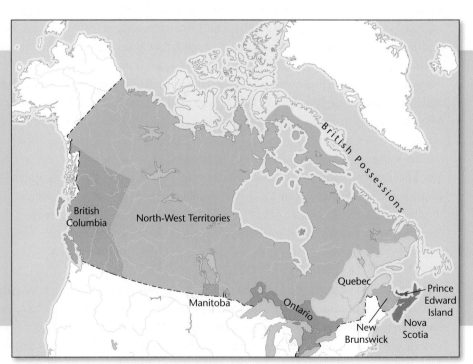

Map 1.2
Canada, 1873

Source: Reproduced with the permission of Natural Resources Canada 2009. Courtesy of the Atlas of Canada.

lands in the colony had not been extinguished by treaty as they had been in much of Eastern Canada, British Columbia entered Confederation with the same boundaries it has today. Resolving Aboriginal title would prove to be a difficult and protracted issue in the province, however. George Brown had not been far off when he said on July 1, 1867, that it was only a matter of time before Confederation would include all of the British colonies in North America. Only Newfoundland would remain outside of the union until 1949. Other parts fell quickly to Canada. In 1880, Britain transferred to it the Arctic Archipelago and in 1905 two new provinces—Alberta and Saskatchewan—would be carved out of the North-West Territories. With the inclusion of all of continental North America, the Canadian nation had rapidly taken shape. Just as the delegates to the constitutional conferences in Charlottetown and Quebec in 1864 had hoped in their lofty dreams, the continent-wide union was complete.

Identity, Culture, and Nation-Building

Even as the national leaders built a regulatory regime and pursued territorial expansion in the new Canada, there were a group of Canadians who were not pleased with the sense of national purpose that was emerging in Canada. Jonathan Vance suggests in his history of Canadian culture that Confederation signalled the beginning of cultural nationalism that was marked by a distinctive boosterism that Canada had to be different from either the old world or the one that lay to the south. One of the earliest proponents of this movement was Thomas D'Arcy McGee. In 1857 McGee wrote: "Every country, every nationality, every people, must create and foster a National Literature, if it is their wish to preserve a distinct individuality from other nations." In his volume of poetry published in 1858, *Canadian Ballads and Occasional Verses*, he expressed his hope "That we shall one day be a great northern nation, and develope [*sic*] within ourselves that best fruit of nationality, a new and lasting literature, is the firm belief, at least of those to whom this volume is mainly addressed ... of all forms of patriotism, a wise public-spirited patriotism in literature, is not the least admirable."[41] Only a few writers heeded McGee's call to action: Alexander Muir wrote "The Maple Leaf Forever" in 1867, which is included below, and others penned patriotic songs, including J.D. Edgar's "This Canada" and Louis Fréchette's "O mon pays, terre adorée."

One of the most expensive publications of the period (at a cost of $14 000) was the *Confederation Debates*. It might not have made fascinating reading nor did it meet McGee's idea of a national literature, but 4000 copies were sold in French and 7500 in English.

There were also some notable achievements in the visual arts. Although he started to paint in the decade before Confederation, Cornelius Krieghoff sold hundreds of paintings that depicted the life of working people, particularly in Quebec. He also painted Aboriginal peoples engaged in the fur trade, as well as lumbermen and merchants, all done on large canvases and in great detail. There is no evidence that he was a member of the Society of Canadian Artists (SCA), which was established in 1867. Any hopes for a national arts community were dashed in the recession in the early 1870s, when the SCA collapsed. Even though many of the cultural activities at the time of Confederation withered quickly, the generation born in the Confederation era would create a more lasting cultural industry.

THE MAPLE LEAF FOREVER

In days of yore the hero Wolfe,
Britain's glory did maintain,
And planted firm Britannia's flag
On Canada's fair domain,
Here may it wave, our boast, our pride,
And, joined in love together,
The Thistle, Shamrock, Rose entwine,
The Maple Leaf forever!

Chorus:

The Maple Leaf, our emblem dear,
The Maple Leaf forever!
God save our Queen, and heaven bless
The Maple Leaf forever!

On many hard-fought battle-fields,
Our brave fathers side by side,
For freedom, homes and loved one dear,
Firmly stood, and nobly died:
And those dear rights which they maintained,
We swear to yield them never!
We'll rally round the Union Jack,
The Maple Leaf forever!

In autumn time, our emblem dear
Dons its tints of crimson hue;
Our blood would dye a deeper red,
Shed, dear Canada for you!
Ere sacred rights our father won,
To foeman we deliver,
We'll fighting die—our battle-cry,
"The Maple Leaf forever!"

God bless our loved Canadian homes,
Our Dominion's vast domain;
May plenty ever be our lot.
And peace hold an endless reign;
Our Union, bound by ties of love,
That discord cannot sever,
And flourish green, o'er Freedom's home,
The Maple Leaf forever!

On Merry England's far-famed land,
May kind heaven sweetly smile;
God bless old Scotland evermore,
And Ireland's emerald isle!
Then swell the song, both loud and long,
Till rocks and forest quiver;
God save our Queen, and heaven bless,
The Maple Leaf forever.

Source: *Raise the Flag and Other Patriotic Canadian Songs and Poems.* Toronto, Rose Publishing Company, 1891.

Alexander Muir submitted this poem in a patriotic poetry contest sponsored by the Caledonian Society of Montreal. It won second prize and became an important anthem for English Canadians until the 1950s. It has been revised several times.

McGee was a part of a small group of nationalists who came together in Ottawa in 1868 with the goal of putting Canada first; they wanted a great outpouring of national sentiment and the development of a national culture. They have been called the Canada First group and believed that territorial expansion, the establishment of currency and tariffs, and other instruments necessary to consolidate the confederation process—while important—were not enough to make a nation. It fell to McGee's friends—poets and intellectuals such as Charles Mair, William Foster, George Denison, and Robert Haliburton—to carry on his dream because McGee was assassinated in Ottawa on April 7, 1868, after he gave a passionate speech arguing for greater national unity. They wanted to continue McGee's hope of fostering a Canadian consciousness in the new nation.

Thomas D'Arcy McGee assassinated in Ottawa, 1868.

One of the first publications of the Canada First group came from William A. Foster, who wrote a pamphlet *Canada First; or, Our New Nationality*. There can be little doubt that today we would call many of their ideas exclusionary and offensive. Canada First had helped to fuel the anger against the Métis and French-speaking Catholics during the Red River resistance, and they favoured British immigration to Canada. They wanted an Anglo-Saxon and Protestant nation and saw a unity between French and British groups in Canada, as both emerged from the "Aryan tribes" of northern Europe and had grown to nationhood in the ice and cold of North America. From them, we can trace the origins of "The True North Strong and Free," but their ideas did not become a unifying dynamic of nation-building in Canada. What is important is that they represented a group committed to fostering a national consciousness immediately after Confederation. Many other Canadians chose to celebrate their nation through their participation on the first day of July each year to mark the anniversary of the birth of the nation. In 1868, for instance, Governor-General Lord Monck issued a Royal Proclamation, calling upon all Canadians to celebrate the first anniversary of the Dominion of Canada. As the poster illustrates, Canadians across the country celebrated Dominion Day even before it was proclaimed a national holiday in 1879.

Creating a new nationality was not limited to cultural matters and celebrations. Historian Suzanne Zeller reminds us that science also played an important role in creating Canada and idealizing Canadian progress: Science "not only enhanced the possibilities of Canada's material progress but also provided a fertile ground for a 'new nationality' to take root as a northern variation of the British nation." It was science and technological innovation that would allow Canadians to dominate their natural environment, prosper, and make the idea of the transcontinental nation possible. Science and

Dominion Day poster, Richmond Hill, Ontario, 1872 showing popular ways of celebrating in the late nineteenth century: athletics, parades, and fireworks.

Source: Copyright © 1999. Canadian Heritage Gallery.

scientists demonstrated, for instance, that agriculture could flourish in areas of the North-Western Territory long considered barren wasteland, and they could discover valuable mineral deposits in the inhospitable Laurentian Shield. Moreover, it was science that allowed Canadians to "devour space" through such technological advances as the railway and the telegraph.[42] Railways had been important since the 1850s, but with Confederation they took on added significance. In a country with a comparatively small population dispersed across a large and often hostile land mass, railways became one of the few means of tying the people together and uniting the various regions.

Canada, Britain, and Foreign Policy

Nationhood did not mean independence for Canada. The *British North America Act* was silent on the conduct of international relations except to note that Canada remained a part of the British Empire and was obliged to uphold any treaties Britain had with other countries. This was no accident, as the Fathers of Confederation realized the advantages, military and economic, of remaining within the Empire. Canada was a British colony and would remain so until the 1930s (although some have argued that it was even much later than that). Because of that, foreign policy was left to the British. However, the federal government realized that it would need representation abroad, especially in London, to promote its interests. Normally, that was left to the governor-general, but, in 1869, Macdonald appointed Sir John Rose, a former finance minister and at the time a London banker, to informally promote Canada. Rose often lobbied British officials on Canada's behalf and promoted emigration to Canada, and he was, in many ways, Macdonald's eyes and ears in London.

Canada's primary concern in international affairs was with its neighbour, the United States, and here it had two objectives: One, not to anger the Americans, and two, renegotiate a reciprocity agreement with them, even as Canada moved towards protectionism—one of the major contradictions in post-Confederation fiscal and economic policy. The British withdrawal of their forces from Canada (with the exception of the naval base at Halifax) in 1871 was an important step in achieving the first objective. Both objectives became linked to a fisheries dispute in 1869.

Access to the fishery resources had been a point of contention between the British colonists and American fishers for more than a generation. American fishers wanted access to the waters of British North America. In 1869, Canada asserted its authority over American vessels trespassing on Canadian fishing grounds when it dispatched cruisers to patrol the inshore waters; in 1870, 16 vessels were charged for illegal fishing. President Ulysses S. Grant was not amused. In his annual address to Congress in 1870, he said (in a veiled threat to the British and Canadians) that "The time is not probably far distant when, in the natural course of events, the European political connection with this continent will cease." Then, he warned ominously, "The course pursued by the Canadian authorities towards the fishermen of the United States during the past season has not been marked by a friendly feeling.... Vessels have been seized without notice or warning, in violation of the custom previously prevailing." Grant wanted a resolution to the vexing problem, and it became one of the important issues facing British and Canadian negotiators who met in Washington in 1871 to resolve a number of pressing issues in Anglo–American relations, some of them dating back to the American Civil War

Macdonald, the newly minted Canadian prime minister, acted as one of the British commissioners. In some respects, the presence of a Canadian at the treaty talks represented a step forward in Canadian autonomy; previous diplomatic agreements were negotiated solely by Britain on Canada's behalf. Yet Macdonald would also be forced to bear the political cost in Canada for failing to win some important diplomatic objectives. New England fishers were flouting Canadian laws, and Macdonald believed that Canada could offer access to the fisheries in an attempt to force the U.S. government to consider some form of reciprocal trade with Canada. As the Canadians saw it, "The fisheries are our trump card," and they wanted to trade them to gain access to the American market; that was the goal when the negotiations began in Washington. The Maritimes disagreed vehemently with this position and used it to show how their interests were not protected in Confederation. However, the Americans were not interested in reciprocal trading arrangements, only access to the waters around Canada and Newfoundland.

Treaty of Washington gives American access to Canadian fisheries.

The Treaty of Washington, signed on May 8, 1871, granted American fishers the right to fish in the territorial waters off Quebec, Nova Scotia, New Brunswick, and Prince Edward Island, while British subjects were granted the same rights in American waters north of the 39th parallel. Fish and fish oil produced in Canada, Prince Edward Island, and the United States were to be admitted without duty on a reciprocal basis. Other contentious issues were sent to arbitration. Yet, because it was gaining the most from these arrangements, the U.S. government provided financial compensation for their access to Canada's fisheries with an amount to be determined by an international board of three commissioners. Macdonald realized that the arrangement was not beneficial for the fishing industry in the Maritimes, but he agreed to it because the British government had promised to guarantee a loan for the construction of railways and canals in the new dominion if the treaty were adopted. With such a promise, Macdonald had Parliament ratify the Treaty of Washington—itself an act of symbolic importance—knowing full well that he had surrendered Maritime fisheries for the perceived good of Canada. As historian R.C. Brown has correctly noted, by 1871 the fishery question was always related to reciprocity and whenever Canada negotiated with the United States, the policy was always the same: Canada's exclusive and undoubted rights in the inshore fisheries could be bargained for something, but this time Canada would have scant success in Washington. Macdonald also discovered that the treaty had not just offended the Maritimes but had also disappointed much of Ontario and Quebec because he had failed to gain free access for agricultural products as he had for Maritime fish. In the aftermath, Macdonald would abandon hopes for reciprocity with the Americans and become a vocal champion of high protective tariffs.

Conclusion

Canada did not emerge from revolution nor was it even a process driven by democratic impulses. Confederation was considered by its proponents as a way to preserve the British connection; it was an exercise in continuity rather than rupture, and it was all completed under the watchful eye of Queen Victoria. That does not mean that Confederation was not debated in the colonies of British North America or completed against the wishes of the citizens of the British North American colonies. Canada emerged out of negotiations among the political leaders of the various colonies in the 1860s. In that sense, Canada was a negotiated nation that took account of some of the various regional, economic, ethnic, and cultural dimensions of the people and colonies that were party to the negotiations in the period from 1864 to 1874.

Even after the nation was created and expanded its boundaries beyond the original four colonies of Nova Scotia, New Brunswick, Quebec, and Ontario to reach across the continent, negotiations and compromise remained the approach to nation-building. Manitoba negotiated French and Catholic rights and its unique land-holding system; Prince Edward Island negotiated a deal with Canada to solve the problem with its absentee landowners; and British Columbia negotiated a transcontinental railway. The government was less generous, though, in its negotiations and accommodations of Aboriginal peoples. Out of the conflict, disunity, and political instability of the period from the early 1860s to 1874, the country was able to remain united in spite of the multitude of divisions that constantly pulled at its fabric, including English–French conflict, a provincial rights struggle, and Aboriginal resistance to imperial expansion. The proponents of Confederation had been able to move beyond their local patriotism and see a nation being created out of the smaller colonies. It was an arrangement designed to recognize the differences in the new nation, but also to make the new nation work. It had survived the first years of union but difficult times lay ahead.

Questions to Consider

1. What is a federal union? Why would the British North American colonies demand such a union?

2. What evidence is there that the colonial leaders in British North America saw themselves as ready to participate in a larger national enterprise in the 1860s?

3. What was more important to Confederation in 1867: internal pressures or external pressures?

4. What sort of national sentiment emerged in 1867? Was it shared by everyone?

5. Was Louis Riel a nationalist?

6. What is the evidence for Confederation as a great moment of nation-making or national purpose?

Critical Thinking Questions

1. What does it mean that Canada began as a negotiated nation?

2. Would Canada have been better to join the United States, as some have suggested?

3. Why weren't Aboriginal peoples given a voice in the Confederation process? Was Canada weaker because of the exclusion of Aboriginal leaders?

Suggested Readings

General

Ajzenstat, Janet, et al., eds. *Canada's Founding Debates*. Toronto: University of Toronto Press, 2003.

Charlottetown Conference of 1864 [online]. http://epe.lac-bac.gc.ca/100/200/301/ic/can_digital_collections/charlottetown/index.html.

Cook, Ramsay, ed. *Confederation*. Toronto: University of Toronto Press, 1967.

Creighton, Donald. *The Road to Confederation: The Emergence of Canada, 1863–1867*. Toronto: Macmillan, 1964.

Gwyn, Richard. *John A. The Man Who Made Us*. Toronto: Random House Canada, 2007.

Harris, R. Cole, and John Warkentin. *Canada before Confederation: A Study in Historical Geography*. Ottawa: Carleton University Press, 1991.

Martin, Ged. "Archival Evidence and John A. Macdonald Biography." *Journal of Historical Biography* 1 (Spring 2007): 42–79.

Martin, Ged, ed. *The Causes of Canadian Confederation*. Fredericton: Acadiensis Press, 1990.

Moore, Christopher. *1867. How the Fathers Made a Deal*. Toronto: McClelland & Stewart, 1997.

Romney, Paul. *Getting It Wrong: How Canadians Forgot Their Past and Imperilled Confederation*. Toronto: University of Toronto Press, 1999.

Russell, Peter. *Constitutional Odyssey. Can Canada Become a Sovereign People?* 3rd edition. Toronto: University of Toronto Press, 2004.

Smith, Andrew. *British Businessmen and Canadian Confederation: Constitution-Making in an Era of Anglo-Globalization*. Montreal and Kingston: McGill-Queen's University Press, 2008.

Vipond, Robert C. *Liberty & Community: Canadian Federalism and the Failure of the Constitution*. Albany: State University of New York, 1991.

Waite, P.B., ed. *The Confederation Debates in the Province of Canada, 1865*. With a New Introduction by Ged Martin. Montreal and Kingston: McGill-Queen's University Press, 2006.

White, W.L., et al. *Canadian Confederation: A Decision-Making Analysis*. Toronto: Macmillan of Canada, 1979.

Atlantic Canada and Confederation

Beck, J. Murray. *Joseph Howe*, 2 Vols. Montreal and Kingston: McGill-Queen's University Press, 1984.

Buckner, Philip A., and John G. Reid, eds. *The Atlantic Region to Confederation: A History*. Toronto: University of Toronto Press, 1994.

Buckner, Philip A., P.B. Waite, and William M. Baker. "The Maritimes and Confederation: A Reassessment," *Canadian Historical Review* 71, 1 (March 1990): 1–45.

Durant, Vincent. *War Horse of Cumberland: The Life and Times of Sir Charles Tupper*. Hantsport, NS: Lancelot Press, 1985.

Hiller, James. "Confederation Defeated: The Newfoundland Election of 1869." In James Hiller and Peter Neary, eds., *Newfoundland in the Nineteenth and Twentieth Centuries: Essays in Interpretation*. Toronto: University of Toronto Press, 1980, 67–94.

Hiller, James K. *The Confederation Issue in Newfoundland, 1864–1869: Selected Documents*. St. John's: Memorial University of Newfoundland, 1974.

MacNutt, W. S. *New Brunswick: A History, 1784–1867*. Toronto: Macmillan of Canada, 1984.

Pryke, Kenneth J. *Nova Scotia and Confederation, 1864–1874*. Toronto: University of Toronto Press, 1979.

Robertson, Ian Ross. "Prince Edward Politics in the 1860s." *Acadiensis* 15, 1 (Autumn 1985): 35–58.

The Canadas and Confederation

Careless, J.M.S. *Brown of the Globe*, 2 Vols. Toronto: Dundurn, 1989.

Cook, Ramsay. *Canada and the French-Canadian Question*. Toronto: Copp Clark Pitman, 1986.

Creighton, Donald. *John A. Macdonald: The Young Politician and the Old Chieftain*, 2 Vols. Toronto: University of Toronto Press, 1998.

Hodgins, Bruce W. *John Sandfield Macdonald, 1812–1872*. Toronto: University of Toronto Press, 1971.

Silver, A.I. *The French-Canadian Idea of Confederation, 1864–1900*. Toronto: University of Toronto Press, 1997.

Swainson, Donald. *Ontario and Confederation*. Ottawa: Centennial Commission, 1967.

The West and Confederation

Barman, Jean. *West Beyond the West: A History of British Columbia.* 3rd edition. Toronto: University of Toronto Press, 2007.

Ens, Gerhard J. *Homeland to Hinterland: The Changing Worlds of the Red River Métis in the Nineteenth Century.* Toronto: University of Toronto Press, 1996.

Friesen, Gerald. *The Canadian Prairies. A History.* Toronto: University of Toronto Press, 1984.

Morton, W. L. *The West and Confederation, 1857–1871.* Ottawa: Canadian Historical Association, 1968.

Owram, Doug. *Promise of Eden: The Canadian Expansionist Movement and the Idea of the West, 1856–1900.* Toronto: University of Toronto Press, 1990.

Nation-Building, 1867–1873

Bliss, Michael. *Northern Enterprise: Five Centuries of Canadian Business.* Toronto: McClelland & Stewart, 1987.

Dickinson, Olive. *Canada's First Nations.* Toronto: McClelland & Stewart, 1992.

Norrie, Kenneth, and Douglas Owram. *A History of the Canadian Economy.* Toronto: Nelson Publishing, 2002.

Stacey, C.P. *Canada and the Age of Conflict. A History of Canadian External Relations.* Volume 1. Toronto: Macmillan, 1977.

Stewart, Gordon T. *The Origins of Canadian Politics: A Comparative Approach.* Vancouver: University of British Columbia Press, 1986.

Social, Cultural, and Intellectual Canada

Gwyn, Sandra. *The Private Capital. Ambition and Love in the Age of Macdonald and Laurier.* Toronto: McClelland & Stewart, 1984.

Light, Beth, and Alison Prentice, eds. *Pioneer and Gentlewomen of British North America, 1713–1867.* Toronto: New Hogtown Press, 1980.

Office of the Chief Electoral Office of Canada. *A History of the Vote in Canada.* Ottawa: Elections Canada, 2007.

Palmer, Byran. *Working-Class Experience: Rethinking the History of Canadian Labour, 1880–1991.* Toronto: McClelland & Stewart, 1993.

Prentice, Alison, et al. *Canadian Women: A History.* Toronto: Harcourt Brace, 1996.

Vance, Jonathan F. *A History of Canadian Culture.* Toronto: Oxford University Press, 2009.

Zeller, Suzanne. *Inventing Canada: Early Victorian Science and the Idea of a Transcontinental Nation.* Toronto: University of Toronto Press, 1987.

Notes

1. This vignette was based on some of the accounts that appeared in several Nova Scotia newspapers in early July 1867. See http://www.collectionscanada.gc.ca/confederation/023001-2600-e.html#NovaScotia.

2. Ged Martin, *Britain and the Origins of the Canadian Confederation, 1837–67* (Vancouver: University of British Columbia Press, 1995), 5.

3. Janet Ajzenstat, Paul Romney, Ian Gentles, and William D. Gardiner, eds., *Canada's Founding Debates* (Toronto: University of Toronto Press, 2003), 1–2.

4. *The Globe*, 1 July 1867, http://heritage.theglobeandmail.com.libproxy.uregina.ca:2048/PageView.asp. A complete run of *The Globe and Mail* newspaper is available online.

5. Peter B. Waite, *The Confederation Debates in the Province of Canada 1865*, 2nd ed. (Toronto: University of Toronto Press, 2006), 27–29, 36, 48, 54.

6. Benedict Anderson, *Imagined Communities: Reflections on the Origins and Spread of Nationalism* (London: Verso, 1991).

7. On this point, see John D. Whyte, "Federalism Dreams," *Queen's Law Journal* 34, 1 (Fall 2008): 1–28.

8. Andrew Smith, *British Businessmen and Canadian Confederation. Constitution-Making in an Era of Anglo-Globalization* (Montreal and Kingston: McGill-Queen's University Press, 2008), 1–10.

9. Phillip Buckner, "CHR Dialogue: The Maritimes and Confederation: A Reassessment," *Canadian Historical Review* 71, 1 (March 1990): 1–45.

10. Richard Gwyn, *John A. The Man Who Made Us* (Toronto: Random House Canada, 2007), 287–288.

11. P.B. Waite, *The Life and Times of Confederation, 1864–1867. Politics, Newspapers and the Union of British North America* (Toronto: University of Toronto Press, 1962), 72.

12. Buckner, "CHR Dialogue: The Maritime and Confederation: A Reassessment."

13. Quoted in Gwyn, *John A.*, 305. Italics in original.

14. Quoted in Gwyn, *John A.*, 308.

15. Quoted in Robert C. Vipond, *Liberty & Community. Canadian Federalism and the Failure of the Constitution* (Albany: State University of New York, 1991), 4.

16. On this point, see Vipond, *Liberty & Community*, 6.

17. Paul Romney, *Getting It Wrong: How Canadians Forgot Their Past and Imperilled Confederation* (Toronto: University of Toronto Press, 1999), 98.

18. Ian McKay, "The Liberal Order Framework," *Canadian Historical Review* 81, 4 (December 2000); and Peter Russell, *Constitutional Odyssey: Can Canadians Become a Sovereign People?* (Toronto: University of Toronto Press, 2004).

19. Ajzenstat et al., *Canada's Founding Debates*, chapters 11 and 12; and *Débats sur la fondation du Canada*, Édition français préparée par Stéphane Kelly et Guy Laforest, Les Presses de l'Université Laval (2003).

20. Quoted in Gwyn, *John A.*, 351.

21. Quoted in A.I. Silver, *The French-Canadian Idea of Confederation, 1864–1900*, 2nd ed. (Toronto: University of Toronto Press, 1997), 34.

22. Quoted in Silver, *The French-Canadian Idea of Confederation, 1864–1900*, 48.

23. Quoted in Silver, *The French-Canadian Idea of Confederation, 1864–1900*, 41.

24. Quoted in Christopher Moore, *1867: How the Fathers Made a Deal* (Toronto: McClelland & Stewart, 1997), 233.

25. Quoted in Buckner, "CHR Dialogue: The Maritimes and Confederation," 32.

26. Quoted in J. Murray Beck, *Joseph Howe*. Volume II. *The Briton Become Canadian, 1848–1873* (Montreal and Kingston: McGill-Queen's University Press, 1983), 201.

27. Quoted in Moore, *1867. How the Fathers Made a Deal*, 236.

28. Quoted in Gwyn, *John A.*, 298.

29 Paul-André Linteau, René Durocher, and Jean-Claude Robert, *Quebec. A History, 1867–1929* (Toronto: James Lorimer & Company, Publishers, 1983), 161.

30 Alison Prentice, et al., *Canadian Women. A History* (Toronto: Harcourt Brace, 1996), 128.

31 Prentice et al., *Canadian Women*, 128–129.

32 John Dickinson and Brian Young, *A Short History of Quebec* (Montreal: McGill-Queen's University Press, 2008), 148.

33 Quoted in Smith, *British Businessmen and Confederation*, 113.

34 Quoted in Doug Owram, *Promise of Eden. The Canadian Expansionist Movement and the Idea of the West, 1856–1900* (Toronto: University of Toronto Press, 1980), 77.

35 Owram, *Promise of Eden*, 81–82.

36 Thomas Flanagan, *Louis "David" Riel. Prophet of the New World* (Toronto: University of Toronto Press, 1979), 29–30.

37 Quoted in "John A. Macdonald," *Dictionary of Canadian Biography Online*, http://www.biographi.ca/009004-119.01-e.php?BioId=40370.

38 "Thomas Scott," *Dictionary of Canadian Biography Online*, http://www.biographi.ca/009004-119.01-e.php?BioId=38817.

39 Sir John A. Macdonald to Adams G. Archibald, in R.C. Brown and M.E. Prang, *Confederation to 1949*. Canadian Historical Documents Series. Volume III (Scarborough: Prentice-Hall of Canada, 1966), 14.

40 "George-Étienne Cartier," *Dictionary of Canadian Biography Online*, http://www.biographi.ca/009004-119.01-e.php?BioId=39006.

41 Quoted in Jonathan F. Vance, *A History of Canadian Culture* (Toronto: Oxford University Press, 2009), 144–145.

42 Suzanne Zeller, *Inventing Canada. Early Victorian Science and the Idea of a Transcontinental Nation* (Toronto: University of Toronto Press, 1987), 1–9.

2

Consolidating Confederation *and* Managing Diversity: *1874–1896*

Lord Stanley became a hockey dad; Lady Constance Stanley, a hockey mom. They arrived in Canada from England on June 11, 1888, and moved into Rideau Hall with four of their eight children. Lady Stanley was not terribly impressed with the official residence of the governor-general of Canada, but the grounds were large and the family found the people of Ottawa welcoming. The Stanleys were also committed to seeing as much of Canada as they could. They attended the Montreal Winter Carnival, which had included an invitational hockey tournament since 1883. There, the Stanleys watched their first game of ice hockey, and they were immediately hooked. They had already enjoyed the skating rink at Rideau Hall that one of Stanley's predecessors, Lord Dufferin, had built in the 1870s, and all of the children had learned to skate. Their son Arthur, then 19, was particularly enthusiastic and so was 12-year-old Isobel. Even Lord Stanley attempted a game or two, once on a Sunday, prompting an Ottawa newspaper to accuse him of blasphemy on the Lord's Day.

Arthur and his brothers organized a game for government workers on Parliament Hill and later formed the Rideau Rebels to travel throughout Southern Ontario to challenge other teams. Arthur also helped organize the Ontario Hockey Association in 1890. Isobel invited other young ladies to play on the Rideau Hall rink. It was perhaps the first game of women's hockey in the nation's capital. Lord Stanley and his wife watched many of the games at Rideau Hall and encouraged their children

in the winter sport. In 1892, he wrote to the Ottawa Amateur Athletic Association that "I have for some time been thinking that it would be a good thing if there were a challenge cup which should be held from year to year by the champion hockey team in the Dominion (of Canada)." For 10 guineas (approximately $50) he had one of the finest silversmiths in London craft the Dominion Challenge Trophy as the symbol of hockey supremacy in Canada. The Trophy was first awarded in 1893 when the Montreal Amateur Athletic Association (AAA) hockey club defeated Ottawa to become Dominion champions. Lord Stanley never saw a championship game, but his trophy, known as the Stanley Cup, became one of the most coveted awards in professional sport. Stanley was inducted into the Hockey Hall of Fame in 1945.

> **After reading this chapter you will be able to:**
>
> **1.** Evaluate Mackenzie's tenure as prime minister.
> **2.** Consider the attempts to define Canada in this period.
> **3.** Describe the National Policy.
> **4.** Identify the features of Canada's immigration policies.
> **5.** Explain relations between Aboriginal peoples and the state.
> **6.** Assess the state of Canadian culture during this period.
> **7.** Discuss the nature of ethnic conflict in Canada.

Introduction

As his first term as prime minister of Canada was coming to an end in 1878, Alexander Mackenzie embarked on a campaign tour of Ontario. In one of his speeches published later that summer, Mackenzie acknowledged the difficulty inherent in governing Canada: "We have a country vast in extent, vast in its territorial magnitude, vast in respect to its sectional views, and in its diversity of creed and race," he said. "It is a task which any statesman may feel great difficulty in accomplishing, to harmonize all those interests, and bring a genuine feeling of union to bear upon the prosperity of the country which he has to govern. Under the most favourable circumstances," Mackenzie remarked, "any one would feel necessitated to ask occasionally not merely the indulgence but the forbearance of friend and foe alike in a country like this."[1] Mackenzie failed to bring harmony to the new country, and he failed to satisfy either friend or foe. He did keep the young nation together, however, and in doing so, he was no different from any of the other political leaders that have occupied the prime minister's office since 1867. They have all managed to keep the country from breaking apart, but as Mackenzie found out, doing so has never been an easy task.

This chapter focuses on the period between the coming to power of the Liberal party in 1873, following the resignation of John A. Macdonald and the Conservatives, and 1896, when Wilfrid Laurier won his first mandate. It highlights the challenges, strains, and sometimes tragedies associated with Canada's growth and maturation in this period and examines the impact on relations between First Nations and Métis people and the Canadian government, and between French-speaking and English-speaking Canadians. It also considers the difficulties that Canada faced in developing a coherent national economic strategy and sustaining an effective federal–provincial relationship, and Canada's role within the British Empire. This is a chapter about managing political, ethnic, and class divisions in Canada, as citizens, institutions, and governments dealt with the tensions inherent in the country. Many of the themes that emerged during this period continue to define the national experience.

The Pacific Scandal and a New Government

Canada's first prime minister, John A. Macdonald, won a small victory in the second general election after Confederation in 1873, but some very damaging allegations were soon made. The Liberal party discovered after the election that Macdonald and other Conservatives had accepted large political contributions from Sir Hugh Allan, who had been awarded a lucrative contract to build Canada's first transcontinental railway prior to Macdonald calling the election. Macdonald attempted to dismiss the Liberal charges of corruption; he rallied his party to defeat a motion that called for an investigation into the matter, promising instead to appoint his own commission. With the evidence mounting against him and other party stalwarts, such as George-Étienne Cartier and Hector Langevin, Conservative members of Parliament were worried. Liberal newspapers published a series of telegrams revealing that Allan had given the Conservatives more than $350 000 during the campaign. Macdonald, who has been the subject of much political folklore, reportedly once told a colleague that what he really needed around him were people who would support him when he was wrong, but when one of his telegrams to Allan saying "I must have another ten thousand; will be the last time of calling; do not fail me; answer today" was published, it was too much for even his staunchest supporters. Many of them deserted the prime minister, when it became clear that even Macdonald had gone too far this time.

It appeared that Macdonald's Conservative party, which had been organized at the time of Confederation as a coalition of the various regional, ethnic, and linguistic groups that had forged the new nation between 1864 and 1867, was finished and his government would not survive. Macdonald quickly appointed his friends and allies to plum positions throughout the government. Some of those sitting on his side of the House rushed across the floor to sit with the Liberals, showing that party allegiance counted for very little, even in Macdonald's day.

Those early politicians who were engaged in partisan politics in the developing party system in Canada practised what political scientists, such as David E. Smith, have called the *clientelist* system. This approach to party politics, which lasted from Confederation in 1867 to the end of the First World War, saw party leaders, as patrons, provide favours, such as employment, infrastructure, and other benefits, to their supporters in exchange for votes. It can be argued that this practice continues in our own time, but in the period before widespread literacy and mass media, which allowed politicians to try to appeal to the imagination of voters, political parties and their leaders depended on delivering material benefits to their supporters. In the Macdonald era, patronage and the distribution of material benefits to local supporters played an important foundational role in the development of the Canadian party system. Macdonald's originality in his approach to party politics stemmed from the fact that he understood that in winning and keeping power in Canada he had to satisfy local demands. It was not uncommon for him to turn his chair towards a rookie MP struggling through his maiden speech in Parliament and cheer him on with a loud and enthusiastic "Hear! Hear!" while other parliamentarians prayed for the misery to end.[2] This approach would facilitate his return to power later, but for the moment the charges of bribery had sealed his fate.

John A. Macdonald resigns amid charges of corruption.

Macdonald resigned on November 5, 1873, without facing a vote of confidence in the House of Commons. He left office in disgrace and found refuge in the bottle. Governor-General Lord Dufferin asked Alexander Mackenzie, the leader of the Reformer-Liberal party, to become prime minister two days later. Mackenzie subsequently revoked many of Macdonald's last-minute political appointments, but he reluctantly let stay Leonard Tilley, who had sought refuge as the lieutenant-governor of New Brunswick. Canada was still some distance from a politically neutral civil service, but the new prime minister, who favoured such an innovation, refused to purge the civil service of all known Conservatives,

Alexander Mackenzie becomes Canada's prime minister.

even though he believed that "All the offices [in Ottawa] are crammed with hostile people so that we can trust no one."[3]

Mackenzie, like Macdonald, was born in Scotland. He followed his sweetheart, Helen Neil, to Canada in 1842, when he was 20 years old. They were married in 1845 and settled in Sarnia, Ontario. He was working-class, having apprenticed as a stonemason at the age of 13, but became a general building contractor and eventually a businessmen and newspaper editor before being elected to the House of Commons in 1867. The federal opposition party had persuaded Mackenzie to become its leader in March 1873, days before the Pacific Scandal broke. The Liberal party that he inherited after the departure of George Brown was, like the Conservatives, a coalition of various interests. In many ways, though, they had been united in their opposition against Macdonald and his followers. Many within the party had been associated with reform politics of pre-Confederation Canada and were steeped in a liberal-democratic tradition. They were largely rural and agrarian and adhered to the principles of nineteenth-century liberalism that believed in minimalist government, free trade, low taxes and fiscal restraint, democratic reform and egalitarianism, and provincial autonomy. Mackenzie would remain committed to his democratic ideal during his term as prime minister: Three times he was offered a knighthood, and three times he refused it.

When Mackenzie sought his own mandate in January 1874, he chose morality as the major campaign theme—an issue that has served several opposition leaders well since Confederation. During the 20-day campaign, the shortest in Canadian history, he promised "to elevate the standard of public morality ... and ... conduct public affairs upon principles of which honest men can approve." Note that women could not vote at the time. His message had considerable appeal: The Liberals captured 53.8 percent of the popular vote and won 138 of the 206 seats in the House of Commons. The Conservatives were routed, but Macdonald managed to hold his Kingston seat by fewer than 40 votes.

During his five years as prime minister, Mackenzie demonstrated a commitment to frugality, reform, and consolidation. He frowned on the Conservative policy of rapid expansion across the continent, and vowed to give Canadians a government that was efficient, honest, and economical. Mackenzie started with electoral reform to improve the democratic system. In the first session of the new Parliament, he introduced legislation to hold general elections on the same day in all constituencies, prohibit the distribution of alcohol by candidates, close pubs on polling day, and control campaign expenditures by requiring all candidates to submit election expenses within two months of the vote. Moreover, the *Election Act* provided for the secret ballot to replace the open voting system, which had been subject to all sorts of abuse and intimidation. It also extended the franchise beyond property owners, but did not give women the right to vote; that would take another four decades, but support for the cause was starting to build. In 1871, American suffragist leader Susan B. Anthony gave a series of lectures in Victoria on women's rights, and a year later a motion was introduced, albeit unsuccessfully, in the provincial legislative of British Columbia for women's suffrage. The Toronto Women's Literary Club, created in 1876, was concerned primarily with women's right to vote, not literature,

Alexander Mackenzie (1822–1892), from Sarnia, Ontario, was prime minister of Canada, 1873–1878.

Source: William James Topley/Library and Archives Canada/PA-026522.

although Dr. Emily Stowe believed that it was necessary to hide the club's real objectives. Only in 1883 would the club change its name to the Canadian Woman Suffrage Association.

The government introduced new insolvency laws for personal bankruptcy so that individuals would not be imprisoned for indebtedness. It also attempted to control the use of alcohol, as the campaign against drinking mounted with the formation of the Women's Christian Temperance Union in 1874. The *Canada Temperance Act*, introduced four years later in 1878, also demonstrated Mackenzie's respect for local authorities, as it left the decision on the sale of alcohol to local governments and municipalities across Canada. Although Mackenzie considered the consumption of alcohol as both wasteful and immoral, he realized, too, that any attempt to ban it would be unpopular with certain groups, notably in Quebec. His legislation diffused the issue somewhat by offloading to local governments the issue of banning alcohol, which was potentially politically unpopular. He had hoped that his legislation would satisfy his core Anglo-Protestant supporters who had demanded action. In the end, few were satisfied. The legislation prompted the liquor interests to support the Conservatives and campaign actively for Mackenzie's defeat in the 1878 election.

Mackenzie was also interested in nation-building and institutional reform. In 1875, the government announced it would create the Supreme Court of Canada as the final judicial body of appeal rather than the Judicial Committee of the Privy Council (JCPC) in London, England. Macdonald had hoped to create a Supreme Court as part of the Confederation process and had twice introduced legislation in Parliament, paving the way for its establishment. For Mackenzie, the Court was a symbol of Canadian nationalism and one that he hoped would instil pride in Canadians. He quickly learned that his initiative did not sit well with Lord Dufferin, the British-appointed governor-general. Dufferin asked London to disallow the legislation. In his view, every British subject—and, at the time, that meant all Canadians—enjoyed the right of appeal to the Crown through the JCPC.

After Confederation in 1867, the authorities in London were reluctant to use its constitutional power to disallow Canadian legislation and whenever a controversy arose, as it did with Mackenzie's announcement of a Supreme Court, it sought a compromise rather than having to resort to the heavy-handed measure of disallowance of Canadian legislation, even though such action was perfectly constitutional. Mackenzie went ahead and created the Supreme Court, but rather than force the issue of Canadian independence in judicial affairs with the governor-general, he continued to permit appeals to the British JCPC. Criminal appeals to London were abolished in 1888.

The government passed the *Post Office Act* in 1875 to regulate the postal system in Canada and coordinate with the American postal services the movement of mail in North America. It also provided for the delivery of door-to-door mail in most Canadian cities. The *Penitentiary Act* was an attempt in 1875 to reform Canada's penitentiaries by imposing greater fiscal control and providing a more rigorous system of inspections. The *Public Accounts Audit Act of 1878* was the first attempt to bring a measure of fiscal management to the federal government and created the office of the auditor general. Mackenzie's Liberal reformism also reached into the Department of Militia and Defence, which he reorganized. He also established the Royal Military College of Canada to train officers for Canada's fledgling army to make the military less susceptible to partisan politics.

Letter carrier making free home deliveries in Montreal, 1874.

Source: Library and Archives Canada/POS-002974.

The Liberals swept into office at the beginning of a severe economic depression that would last for most of the 1870s, however. The economic downturn was precipitated by a crisis in the international markets and an economic collapse in the United States following the American Civil War. Canadian exports began a steady decline in 1873 that continued each year until 1879, as did the value of imports. Because the government earned nearly 70 percent of its revenue from taxes on imported goods, Mackenzie's government had less money to spend. Because the Liberals came to office with a belief in a minimalist role for government, they might have managed the situation reasonably well had they not inherited the expansionist and costly commitments of the previous Conservative government.

One of the most expensive was Macdonald's promise to British Columbia of a transcontinental railway within ten years of its joining Confederation. The Liberals had vehemently opposed Macdonald's deal with the Canadian Pacific Railway in 1872 to build the railway to the Pacific Coast, but any change in the government's commitment risked alienating British Columbia. Once in power, Mackenzie attempted to renegotiate the agreement, but British Columbia Premier George Anthony Walkem had already complained that Macdonald had needlessly delayed construction of the railway, and he rejected Mackenzie's attempt to renegotiate the railway deal. To Mackenzie's dismay, Walkem appealed to the British authorities in London, and Lord Carnarvon, the colonial secretary, became personally involved in what Mackenzie considered an internal Canadian matter. Still, he reluctantly accepted Lord Carnarvon's recommendation to extend the completion date for the CPR to 1890 and build the Esquimalt–Nanaimo line in British Columbia as compensation for the delay.

When the House of Commons passed the legislation for the new line, the Conservative-dominated Senate defeated the Bill. Lord Carnarvon refused to allow Mackenzie to increase the number of senators to get the legislation passed, further angering the prime minister. The matter dragged on for several more years and strained relations between the prime minister and the governor-general, who believed he had the moral and constitutional authority to resolve the matter. One historian has noted that Dufferin "felt a passing urge to hit his prime minister" before the matter was settled in 1876, when Mackenzie promised to start construction of the railway to British Columbia within two years.[4] During Mackenzie's term in office, total Canadian railway mileage increased from 6970 kilometres in 1874 to 11 040 kilometres in 1879, largely because of the completion of the Intercolonial Railway linking Central Canada with the Maritimes.

How Much Independence for Canada?

The Liberal government was annoyed with the governor-general and wanted to clarify his role in Canada. The *British North America Act*, had been largely silent on the role of the governor-general, who was appointed by the British cabinet, not Queen Victoria. As such, the governor-general was essentially a colonial administrator and imperial watchdog, answerable to the Colonial Office. Lord Dufferin, the governor-general, interfered in what Mackenzie considered purely domestic affairs, such as the construction of the railway to British Columbia, the establishment of the Supreme Court, and reduction of the sentence of Ambroise Lépine for his part in the execution of Thomas Scott to two years' imprisonment. Edward Blake, the minister of justice, wanted the instructions for the vice-regal clarified to limit his power. During the turmoil over the delay in building the railway to British Columbia, Mackenzie wrote Dufferin that "Canada was not a Crown Colony (or a Colony at all in the normal acceptation of the term)" and that the dominion "would not be dealt with as small communities."[5] It was hard to exert much control over Dufferin, but the Liberals hoped to rein in his successor. There they had more success. Blake convinced the Colonial Office that the role of the governor-general was not to be an activist one and that Canada would not tolerate London's interference in its domestic affairs. The instruction issued to the Marquess of Lorne when he replaced Dufferin made it clear that the governor-general could not interfere in any way with the operation of responsible government in the country, and he had no authority to pardon any convicted person without the advice of the Privy Council in Canada.[6]

Role of governor-general defined.

Blake was intensely nationalistic, and he outlined his vision for Canada in a speech to a gathering of 2000 in Aurora, Ontario, in 1874. Blake had been a contender for the Liberal leadership when Mackenzie was invited to be prime minister in 1873 and some have maintained that he was terribly disappointed that he was passed over for the top job. Still, Blake saw the necessity of promoting national patriotism in addition to building Canada's infrastructure, extending its territorial boundaries, and providing effective governance. In his Aurora speech he acknowledged the difficult task of governing Canada when the seven provinces were frequently divided by isolation, local interests, and petty jealousies. Can there be real union, he asked, by the government "giving sop now to one, now to another"? The future of Canada, he told the large crowd, "depends upon the cultivation of a national spirit." He also stressed the importance of Canada's independence and its constitutional autonomy within the British Empire. "We are four millions of Britons who are not free," he told the gathering.[7] He then made the case for the reorganization of the Empire upon the basis of an imperial federation, presumably one in which Canada would enhance its sovereignty and independence. Blake was associated with the Canada First movement, a small group of young English Canadians who believed it was important to foster a patriotic spirit among Canadians. He had criticized the Treaty of Washington in 1871 because he believed Britain had sacrificed Canada's interests for favour with the United States. Five days after Blake's Aurora speech, Canada Firsters established the National Club in Toronto and launched a periodical, *The Nation*, as the organization's mouthpiece. *The Nation* promoted a national tariff, or tax on imported goods, to protect Canadian industry, an idea that was subsequently picked up by Macdonald and later also embraced by the Liberals.

Mackenzie hoped for a new reciprocity agreement with the United States, just as Macdonald had when he was prime minister; he came to the prime minister's office believing Macdonald had not done enough to cultivate good relations with the Americans. Even before he met with Parliament after the 1874 election, he dispatched newly appointed Senator George Brown to Washington to push for a new free trade agreement. The Treaty of Washington had given American and Canadian fishers access to each other's inshore fisheries, but the deal certainly favoured the Americans. To compensate Canada for the unfair arrangement, the treaty provided for a commission to determine what compensation the American government should pay to Canada. However, no commission had been appointed at the time of Brown's visit. He hoped that the Americans might consider a free trade agreement rather than sending dollars north to Canada. Brown successfully negotiated a treaty that secured free trade not only in natural products as the 1854 reciprocity deal had but also in a wide range of manufactured goods. To Mackenzie's and Brown's surprise, there was considerable opposition to the deal, especially among Canada's growing manufacturing sector. The Manufacturers Association of Nova Scotia petitioned the government for a higher tariff to protect their finished products from cheaper imports; it did not want reciprocity. Mackenzie's government was saved a quarrel with Canada's growing and increasingly protectionist manufacturing sector when the U.S. government decided not to push the draft treaty through a protectionist Senate. Even though the government increased the tariff several times during its mandate, it was declining government revenues more than anything else that tested Liberal free trade principles. The government needed additional revenue to cover government expenditures. The Conservatives were the first to embrace protectionism for the manufacturing sector, however.

The National Policy

John A. Macdonald and the Conservatives were demoralized after their 1874 defeat. Macdonald contemplated resigning as leader and only slowly recovered his interest in politics. That the Liberals struggled from the beginning helped. By 1876, they were in trouble and over the next two years they lost virtually every by-election held. Quebec was not adequately represented in the cabinet after Antoine-Aimé Dorion resigned in May 1874 to become chief justice of the Quebec Court of Queen's Bench. The continued economic crisis, which saw minor food riots in Montreal, internal party dissension, delays in railway construction, and temperance legislation, all hurt the governing Liberals.

The imminent demise of the government seemed to revive Macdonald and rekindle his interest in politics and national affairs. The Conservatives directed considerable resources into local party organizations and the United Empire Club, a political organization committed to reviving the Conservatives. Macdonald also saw an opportunity for his Conservatives in a tariff policy that would benefit manufacturers, labourers, and farmers alike—the beginnings of a National Policy that would also include settlement of the West and a transcontinental railway across Canada (sometimes referred to as RIT—railways, immigration, and tariffs). Following a wave of rising protectionism across the globe, Macdonald proposed a tariff in the House of Commons in 1876, and in each of the next two summers he promoted his National Policy on the political picnic circuit. Before the September 1878 election, Macdonald told those gathered at a picnic in Southwestern Ontario that "there has risen in this country a Canadian Party, which declares we have Canada for the Canadians (applause).... You cannot get anything by kissing the feet of the people of the United States."[8] Anti-Americanism, the view that too close a relationship with the United States would undermine Canada's ability to act independently, plays well in Canada, and voters were impressed with Macdonald and his new message. They were willing to forgive him for his earlier indiscretions though he stood for election in three different ridings (Kingston, Ontario; Marquette, Manitoba; and Victoria, British Columbia), which was permitted under the electoral laws until 1919, to be sure he would win a seat in the House of Commons. He lost his Kingston seat, but he was clearly more

Macdonald regains power campaigning for the National Policy with 142 seats in Parliament. Macdonald has a second chance at leading the government.

popular in the West, winning seats in both British Columbia and Manitoba. The Liberals were reduced to 64 seats in the 1878 general election.

The election marked a fundamental shift in Canada and in Canadian politics. If Canada could not secure free trade with the United States, it could create its own east–west industrial economy, which, after all, was one of the objectives of Confederation in 1867. The free trade ideology of the Liberal party had little appeal among voters, despite the claims of such Liberal stalwarts as Sir Richard Cartwright, Mackenzie's finance minister, that the tariff was essentially a tax on 95 percent of the people to benefit the top 5 percent. It is important to note that this 5 percent had the ear of Macdonald, particularly the manufacturers, who figured prominently in the 1878 campaign and lobbied hard for a national tariff. Protectionism and high tariffs made good politics, and in his first budget following the election, Sir Leonard Tilley, who had vacated the vice-regal office in Fredericton to become minister of finance in Macdonald's government, raised the tariff on a variety of imports from agricultural implements to iron. He also raised the tariff on a variety of agricultural products. The Conservatives wanted farmers to believe that protection was in their interest as well, yet it was the manufacturers who benefited most from the new policy when the average tariff rate was set at 25 percent on most imported items. As Ben Forster has noted, when manufacturers produced finished products for the Canadian marketplace they could often set the tariff rate, but when one manufacturer's output was another's input, compromise was necessary. What was not in doubt, however, was that for the Conservatives, tariff protection was considered permanent. Permanency, Macdonald argued, was the principle upon which the National Policy was based.

The tariff annoyed the British, but Governor-General Lord Lorne told Macdonald that London would not disallow the tariff legislation as economic policy was for Canada alone to decide. The National Policy was another small step towards Canadian sovereignty, and Tilley found a biblical reference to explain the motives behind the government's protectionist policy: "The time has arrived when we are to decide whether we will be simply hewers of wood and drawers of water … or will rise to the position, which, I believe Providence has destined us to occupy."[9]

The Conservatives adopted a policy of economic nationalism based on protectionism (tariffs), railways and transportation networks, and settlement and immigration that remained in place for more than half a century. The goals were simple: Create an integrated east–west economy by fostering the growth of the manufacturing sector and the settlement of the West and tie it together with a transcontinental railway system. Within a short period of time, the industrial strategy appeared to be working. The Maritime provinces, which had joined Confederation, in part, for access to the larger Canadian market, appeared to be well on their way to economic success. Throughout the 1880s and early 1890s, the region's staple production in agriculture, fishing, and timber enjoyed only modest growth, but the rate of industrial expansion surpassed that of Quebec and Ontario. The rise of the manufacturing sector, particularly in cotton cloth, refined sugars, rope and twine, and iron and steel, accounted for nearly half of the region's value of production in 1890 and brought enormous prosperity; however, the success would be fleeting. Most of the secondary manufacturing was done by small, community-based, and family-oriented enterprises that depended on loans from the chartered banks. These enterprises would struggle against the larger and better organized firms located in Quebec and Ontario when overproduction of many products led to a period of industrial mergers and consolidation early in the twentieth century.

The growing metropolitan centres of Montreal and Toronto quickly added to their economic might. Within a decade of the introduction of the tariff, Ontario increased the value-added of its manufacturing sector by nearly 65 percent. As business historian Michael Bliss has argued, the new tariff structure did not keep foreign capital out of Canada; that was never the objective of Macdonald and his government. Their policies were designed to force American corporations to establish their manufactories in Canada. Although the concern of foreign ownership and control over Canada's economy lay well into the future, John A. Macdonald's National Policy helped shape the Canadian economy in ways never imagined. Macdonald and many of those who supported his policies were concerned only with economic development and providing jobs for Canadians. The National Policy did that, but it also attracted American manufacturers and capital to Canada.

Linking Canada by Rail

Large-scale interprovincial trade was not possible without the completion of a railway network across the country. A transcontinental line was the second plank in Macdonald's National Policy. The Liberals had refused to embrace Macdonald's ambitious railway-building scheme while in power, but upon his return to office, Macdonald had not lost any of his enthusiasm for railways, even if it was tempered slightly by his years out of office. He approached railway expenditures and railway promoters with a little more caution, even as government revenues increased with a hike in tariff rates. Still, Macdonald believed that the railway had to be constructed in advance of settlement—the third pillar of his policy—to stake Canada's claim to the substantial territory in the West and to build an east–west economy. In 1880, Macdonald appointed a royal commission to consider the government's role in building the railway to the Pacific. When the commission reported in 1882, it advised that such schemes should be left to the private sector. Macdonald agreed, although he realized that private companies would have to be amply rewarded for their risk in building a railway through the parts of Canada that in the early 1880s had relatively few European settlers.

The government signed a contract with the Canadian Pacific Railway on October 21, 1882, to complete a railway link from Montreal to British Columbia. The syndicate was headed by George Stephen, the president of the Bank of Montreal, and his cousin, Donald Smith, the chief commissioner of the Hudson's Bay Company. They were already wealthy individuals who had amassed fortunes through various ventures, including successful railway projects in the United States, particularly with a line from St. Paul to Winnipeg. For the new sections of the transcontinental railway to be built, the government paid the CPR $25 million and gave it 10 million hectares of arable land along the proposed route through the North-West Territories, which had been reorganized into several administrative districts, as shown in Map 2.1 (on p. 57). The sections of railway that the government had already built—estimated to be approximately 1300 kilometres and valued at $31.5 million—were turned over to the company. The CPR agreed to operate the railway once completed; the government gave it land for its stations. The company's property and capital stock were free from taxation

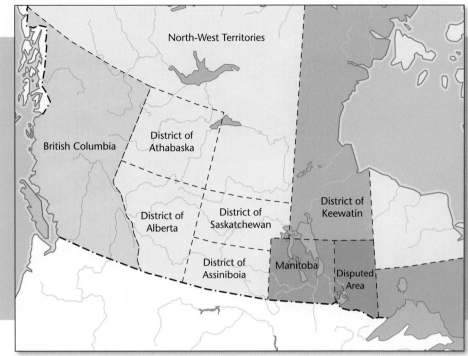

Map 2.1
Western Canada in 1882

The provisional district of Assiniboia, Saskatchewan, Athabaska, and Alberta were created in the North-West Territories in 1882.

Source: Natural Resources Canada, The Atlas of Canada.

in perpetuity, and its landholdings were granted tax-free status for 20 years, an attempt by the government to encourage the railway to participate in attracting settlers to the prairies. They were also given a quasi-monopoly, as the government promised not to allow any other lines south of the CPR in the West.

There was considerable opposition to the CPR contract. The Liberals were certainly critical and wondered if it might be cheaper for the government to build the railway itself. Even the Conservative caucus had to be persuaded that the contract was reasonable. The Toronto business community complained that its interests were sacrificed to those of Montreal, and the West criticized the government for ignoring its interest. The Edmonton *Bulletin* wrote that the contract had been negotiated and signed by people who knew nothing about the West and believed that "the sun rises in Halifax, shines all day straight over Montreal and Ottawa, and sets in Toronto."[10] Manitoba objected because the same capitalists that controlled the all-Canadian route also owned the route south of the Great Lakes.

Opposition grew louder in 1883 when the federal government was forced to loan Stephen and his group an additional $30 million. Charles Tupper, the minister of finance, was able to secure the support of his own MPs only by granting subsidies for railway lines in Quebec and Manitoba. Parliament was in an even greater uproar when Stephen returned for another handout in 1884. The CPR might well have gone bankrupt except for Macdonald—he threatened to resign if the Conservatives failed to support the motion for additional aid for the company—and the beginnings of a second uprising in the West since Confederation. The line to Vancouver was completed in 1885.

A ballast train, headed westward, in 1886, stands on the bridge spanning the Fraser River near Cisco, British Columbia. The bridge, 161 metres long and 43 metres above low water level is adjacent to the Cisco tunnel, a 181-metre bore, the east portal of which is seen in front of the locomotive.

Source: Canadian Pacific Archives, A.11416.

Immigrants: Difficulties, Desirables, and "Undesirables"

The railway was essential to the settlement of the West and to fulfilling the third pillar of Macdonald's National Policy. Settling the West became an important aspect of nation-building, and the government had hoped that its version of the American homestead legislation—the *Dominion Lands Act* introduced in 1872—would attract massive immigration simply by giving away free land. It did not in the period before 1899: Only 1.5 million immigrants chose Canada, while more than 8 million flocked to the United States and nearly 3 million to Australia during the same period. Moreover, more than 2 million people left Canada, primarily from Quebec and the Maritime provinces, mostly for the United States because of better economic prospects there.

Canada's lacklustre performance in attracting settlers did not fail for lack of effort. Shortly after Confederation, the federal Department of Agriculture, which was responsible for attracting settlers, began a massive advertising campaign to sell potential immigrants and Canadians alike on the virtues of the West. The government opened immigration agencies in some Canadian cities, in Britain, and throughout Europe. It also encouraged particular groups, such as Icelanders, Mennonites from Russia, and others, to establish homogeneous communities on the prairies, but the federal efforts resulted in only modest gains, until the 1890s, when the completion of the railway provided easier access for getting to the Western frontier as well as a means for farmers to get their produce to market. By then, such factors as the return of economic prosperity, rising grain prices, innovations in prairie farming, including new agricultural machinery and hardier strains of wheat, and the closing of the American frontier meant that Canada became attractive to thousands of immigrants from the British Isles, Europe, and even the United States.

Immigration to the West did not mean just homesteading. Many came to work in the coal mines that were opening up around Lethbridge and Banff in the 1880s and the new factories opening up across the country. One group that found Canada a particularly unwelcoming place were Chinese migrant workers who were initially recruited to build the Canadian Pacific Railway. Eager to flee the crushing poverty in their homeland, more than 15 000 Chinese labourers were lured to Canada by politicians and businessmen seeking a source of cheap labour for work on laying the CPR tracks through the mountains. Paid less than half of what white workers earned, the Chinese labourers often performed the most dangerous work, including the handling of explosives needed to blast through the mountains. While the estimates vary of the number that died in laying the CPR line, most agree that at least 10 percent succumbed to smallpox or cholera or died in work-related accidents.

The Chinese labourers were considered a cheap form of labour; they were never desirable as immigrants. Many Canadians—politicians and workers, alike—complained that Chinese immigration presented a problem for Canada, especially as the railway was nearing completion. Labour groups protested that they depressed wage rates and took the jobs from white Canadians; others were simply racists and asserted that because the Chinese could not be assimilated, they would alter the character of Canada. The federal government appointed a royal commission to investigate the alleged problem of Chinese immigration. It agreed that immigration from China had to be curtailed and recommended the imposition of a head tax on each new Chinese immigrant. In 1885, after considering the report, Macdonald told the House of Commons that the Chinese worker "has no common interest with us, and while he gives us labour he is paid for, and is valuable, the same as a threshing machine or any other agricultural implement which we may borrow from the United States on hire and return it to the owner on the south side of the line … he has no British instincts or British feelings or aspirations, and therefore ought not to have a vote." Given such a view, it is not surprising that Macdonald accepted the recommendation of the royal commission and imposed a head tax of $50, which would be revised upward on several occasion and remain in place until 1923, when Chinese immigration was banned. In 2006, Prime Minister Stephen Harper offered on behalf of the Government of Canada an apology and compensation for the head tax.

Head Tax imposed on Chinese immigrants.

Life in the Workplace

Chinese workers were not the only ones who endured difficult working conditions in the 1880 and 1890s. These were years of turmoil as factories emerged throughout the country under the auspices of the Macdonald's National Policy. The situation of labour became a matter of considerable concern for the public as strikes became common and unions emerged to protect the interests of some workers. Many looked to the federal government to protect workers in the new industrial era. The Royal Commission on the Relations of Capital and Labour was the federal government's response. This royal commission has been the subject of considerable study among Canadian historians. When Ottawa investigated the plight of workers, it showed that the federal government was concerned not only with industrial and economic development but also with the conditions of Canada's working people, even though governments would be slow to respond to the challenges that labouring men and women experienced in Canada.

The life of workers was harsh in the late nineteenth century. Most were at the mercy of their employers, and such benefits as job security and continued wages in the event of injury and serious illness simply did not exist. Female workers who toiled in the cotton mills and appeared before the royal commission when it visited Halifax in 1888 described a life marked by low wages (between three and four dollars a week, about one-half of that of a man in a comparable job), long hours standing in suffocating heat and dust performing repetitive tasks, strict discipline with fines for lateness and shoddy work, and an unpredictable work schedule. In Ontario knitting mills in 1881, many women and children worked for nearly 60 hours for $1.65 a week. This was not unusual for factory work, which was heavily dependent on women and children to provide the labour.

Early labour unions were for the elite of the workforce: skilled craftsmen. Unions were not particularly interested in organizing women, children, or the unskilled labourers, but after Confederation, as the lines between labour and capital became more pronounced, this began to change. That was one of the major developments of the 1870s and 1880s, and it was reflected in the concerted efforts of labour for the Nine Hour Movement in the 1870s, which campaigned to reduce the working day from 12 hours to nine. Although the movement failed, it led to the creation of the Canadian Labour Union in 1873, which also collapsed a few years later. One of the major initiatives among workers was an import from the United States, the Holy and Noble Order of the Knights of Labor, that organized more than 20 000 workers across Canada into an industrial union. The Knights wanted to organize all workers regardless of skill level, gender, or race (though they excluded Chinese workers), but the Knights had largely disappeared—with the exception of a few chapters in Quebec—by the turn of the twentieth century. In Nova Scotia, the Protective Workman's Association organized most of the workers in the province's coal industries. Organized labour spread across Canada, but in 1890 many of the 240 established unions were located in Ontario and Quebec. The Trades and Labour Congress of Canada was established in Ontario in 1883 but it would be 1900 before it extended its reach across Canada.

Culture and Sport as Nation-Building

While Macdonald pursued economic policies as a basis for national development, others, including several of Canada's governors-general, saw the importance of culture in constructing the new nation. Lord Dufferin, for instance, complained when he was appointed governor-general in 1872 that his income was so insufficient that he would be able to do "very little either for Art or Literature."[11] Still, Dufferin and his wife promoted theatre and drama in Rideau Hall and across Canada, and awarded the Dufferin Medal in 1873 and 1874 to recognize academic and athletic accomplishments among Canadians.

Governor-General Lorne was 33 when he arrived in Canada with his wife, Princess Louise (Queen Victoria's daughter and a skillful painter and sculptor), to replace Dufferin. Working with painter Lucius Richard O'Brien, Lorne convinced artists from provincial associations in Quebec and Ontario in March 1880 to create the Royal Canadian Academy of Arts (RCAA). He wanted the group to become a national association of artists and hold exhibitions in the major cities across the country. Lorne contributed $500 of his own money and convinced Macdonald to help find a venue for the Academy's first exhibition. His efforts laid the foundation for the National Gallery of Canada, which was formally established two years later.

After he opened the RCAA's first exhibition, Lorne wrote to his father saying, "I think myself lucky to have been able to get it on foot, off my own bat the first year, as it will be a lasting thing, and grow with the nation's development."[12] The National Gallery depended initially on donated works until it purchased its first work, *With Dolly at the Sabot-makers*, a painting by contemporary Canadian artist William Brymner, in 1884. But the government had other interests, and the National Gallery struggled for years.

The National Gallery of Canada is created, 1882.

Lorne was also interested in academics. In 1881, he proposed the establishment of a national literary and scientific organization that would combine the scientific interests of the British Royal Society and the literary orientation of the French Academy. He hoped a literary and scientific body would do for scholarship in Canada what the Royal Canadian Academy had done for art. While French-speaking Canadians were excited, English-speaking Canadians were dismissive. When he visited Western Canada later that year and discovered that the Smithsonian Institute had collected a large number of First Nations relics and had taken them to Washington, Lorne was even more convinced that Canada had to organize an academy to prevent such pilfering of the nation's cultural artifacts. In 1882, he created the Royal Society of Canada that would recognize original works in four categories: French-Canadian literature and history; English-Canadian literature and history; mathematical, physical, and chemical science; and geological and biological sciences. The federal government provided $5000 annually so that the Royal Society could publish papers reflecting the intellectual activity of Canadians and facilitate the exchange of new and innovative ideas. Lorne commented that Canadians should be proud of their great enterprises, such as the Canadian Pacific Railway, but he also insisted that the "adornment and elevation of thought" was equally important.[13]

Poets certainly thought so, and a group known as the Confederation Poets represented one of the major literary achievements of the period. At its core were six poets, led by Charles G.D. Roberts, Duncan Campbell Scott, and Bliss Carmen, though Pauline Johnson and Isabella Valancy Crawford were also linked to the group. Johnson, Scott, and some of the others were invited several times to Rideau Hall by Lord and Lady Aberdeen. One of the best-known poems came from Roberts, who called upon Canadians to fulfill their potential through independence. His "An Ode for the Canadian Confederacy" became one of many patriot anthems for English-speaking Canadians and was included in textbooks used in many schools across Canada.

Organized sport was another aspect of culture that grew in the last half of the nineteenth century as part of the broader emergence of an urban industrialized society. In pre-industrial Canada, recreation and leisure had been governed largely by the seasons and as part of the festivities celebrating religious occasions. However, as the life of urban Canadians was increasingly controlled by regular hours in the factory and attendance at school, sport emerged as an important part of leisure and culture. Many in the middle and upper classes maintained that games and sport were of questionable value if they led to the promotion of vices, such as drinking, gambling, and illicit sex. If sport could be properly organized, regulated, and controlled, however, it might be a means to inculcate among the lower and working classes habits of discipline, hygiene, and self-improvement.

Many of the early organized sporting activities were associated with religious groups and churches that had adopted the British notions of amateurism in sports to inculcate desirable social and Christian qualities, such as teamwork, perseverance, honesty, and discipline, in a clear attempt to disseminate among workers middle-class ideals on the ethos of productivity and moral respectability. Women could participate in such activities as rowing, archery, and figure skating, though there were clear boundaries based on sex and race: Aboriginal peoples and blacks, for instance, were excluded from participation with whites. By the late nineteenth century, sport was driven increasingly by economic rather than moral interests. Technological advances, such as electricity, improved transportation, mass circulation of newspapers, and the telegraph, fuelled the growth of professionalization, suggesting that sport would not remain in the hands of amateurs. These changes can be seen in Canada in the evolution of hockey.

The Rise of Hockey and National Parks

There are no doubts about hockey's Canadian origins, but where it began in Canada has been the subject of considerable dispute. Windsor, Nova Scotia, is now the acknowledged birthplace of hockey and, like Canada itself, the winter sport moved rapidly from east to west. It was carried by soldiers and students from Nova Scotia to Quebec and Ontario. When James A. Creighton, a Nova Scotian studying law at McGill College, organized an exhibition game on March 3, 1875, at the Victoria Skating Rink in Montreal, he ordered the first one-piece sticks from Mi'Kmaq carvers—who also claimed their own version of the modern game—and skates from the Dartmouth Starr Manufacturing Company, which manufactured 16 different kinds of skates. The sport was given a boast in Canada when it was included in the Montreal Winter Carnival in 1883.

During their first winter in Canada, Governor-General Lord Stanley and his family travelled to Montreal to attend the winter carnival. After the family's return, Arthur, son of Lord Stanley, organized a Rideau Hall team that included government workers, members of Parliament, and senators. Creighton, who had moved to Ottawa as law clerk in the Canadian Senate, was a member of Stanley's team. Called the Rideau Rebels hockey club, they occasionally travelled in the governor-general's private railway car and helped to promote the sport across southern Ontario. Lord Stanley and his wife, who were avid sports fans, watched many of the games at Rideau Hall and invested in the Ottawa rink where their sons played with the Rebels.

By the late 1880s, there were efforts to regularize competition with the creation in 1886 of the Amateur Hockey Association of Canada (AHAC). The AHAC retained the single-game challenge system and every match was a championship match; the club winning the last match of the season became the champion of the league. Lord Stanley decided in 1892 to offer to the Ottawa Amateur Athletic Association the Dominion Challenge Trophy for the champion hockey team in Canada. He established two trustees for the Stanley Cup whose job it was to prevent it from being hijacked by any one team. The trophy was not presented until March 1893 when the Montreal Amateur Athletic Association (MAAA) hockey club defeated Ottawa to become Dominion champions. In that year, the *Dominion Illustrated News* declared hockey the most popular Canadian sport.

The first Stanley Cup competition set the parameters for hockey in Canada. Nearly 5000 paying spectators attended. Newspapers reported that people donned the colours of their favourite club. Hockey was well on its way to becoming commercialized. The growing urban

Stanley Cup first awarded, 1893.

population of wage earners created new markets for sports as they did for other products and services. At the same time, advertising was becoming common and newspapers, magazines, and trade publications realized that coverage of sporting events generated considerable advertising revenue. Equally important was the growing connection between sport and community and national pride. When teams began to represent their communities, winning was all that mattered. Out of these impulses emerged a market for the best athletes and for competitive and winning teams; such developments ushered in the era of professional sports. This connection had been evident earlier when four rowers from Saint John, New Brunswick, surprised their competition at the World Amateur Rowing Championship in Paris in 1867 to great acclaim across Canada. The team, known as the Paris Crew, attracted large audiences wherever they rowed. They, like Edward "Ned" Hanlan, a six-time world champion in sculling in the 1880s, became a source of a growing national pride. So did Louis Rubenstein, the world champion in figure skating in 1890. By the end of the nineteenth century, there were numerous hockey clubs and regular leagues playing. The Stanley Cup also became the symbol of hockey supremacy in Canada, and the Stanley Cup championship, a major commercial success. When that happened, hockey ceased being an amateur sport and became a business.

Canada's national parks were like hockey in many ways—both came to symbolize national greatness, but both became the preserve of business and venues for economic development. The natural hot springs at Banff became Canada's first national park in 1885. While Banff and several other national parks preserved the natural beauty of Canada, they also became instruments of economic development for the federal government, which gave exclusive control of the mountain parks to the Canadian Pacific Railway. These parks became the preserve of the CPR for its hotel patrons, and the Canadian government was complicit with the railway company in keeping working-class Canadians and First Nations peoples out of the parks. The designation of some of Canada's most spectacular natural scenic areas would not prohibit logging and coal-mining in those areas until the 1930s, however. The democratic ideal of public access to Canada's national parks was a phenomenon that began only in the middle of the twentieth century.

Treaty-Making and Preparing the West for European Settlers

In 1869, when Canada acquired the territory granted to the Hudson's Bay Company in 1670, its goals were simple: to prepare the land for settlement to fulfill the vision of the Fathers of Confederation as a nation that stretched the breadth of North America. Macdonald moved quickly to keep the territory out of the grasp of the Americans, but his haste to annex the Red River settlement, and prepare the territory for the arrival of farmers from Ontario, had sparked an armed confrontation with the Métis and European settlers living there. The situation had been diffused when Louis Riel led the colony into Confederation as the province of Manitoba in 1870. However, in little more than a decade, Macdonald had another crisis on his hands, one for which he and his government cannot escape a fair measure of blame, and one that would cost Riel his life.

Riel has been one of the most interesting and controversial figures in Canadian history, cast as both a villain and a hero. The Métis praised him for defending their rights, and to all

Aboriginal peoples he symbolized their struggle with the European colonizers. The current campaign for a pardon for Riel remains a poignant issue, especially for the Métis peoples. At times, Riel has been seen in Western Canada as the region's first defender against the rapacious forces operating in Central Canada; to Quebec, he was a staunch defender of a bilingual and Catholic society in Western Canada, struggling against the homogenizing Protestant and English-speaking steamroller of Ontario. To many in Ontario, he was a traitor and a murderer.

Like the Red River resistance of 1869–1870, the Northwest uprising in 1885 was the result of accumulated grievances and frustrations, dating from the government's treaty-making process with Western Aboriginal peoples that began in the early 1870s. After Confederation, Canada continued the British colonial practice of negotiating treaties with First Nations whose lands they wanted for settlement. In the words of the policymakers of the 1870s, the ultimate goal of the treaty process was to protect and "civilize" Canada's Aboriginal peoples. To the Canadian government, this meant bringing Christianity to Aboriginal peoples, settling them on agricultural lands to become farmers, and having them adopt European culture. This was without a doubt a process of subjugation, but for the government of the time it was the best means of integrating and assimilating Aboriginal peoples and providing them with a better life. These policy objectives were largely responsible for creating a sense of colonial domination among Aboriginal peoples in Canada that has animated much of the First Nations and Métis activism that marked the final third of the twentieth century.

One of the first steps in the settling of the West was to negotiate a series of treaties with the First Nations in the Northwest Territories. J.R. Miller has pointed out that the Americans were spending about $20 million annually on their "Indian Wars." Since the federal government's budget was only $19 million at the time, it was economically prudent that Canada find some accommodation with the Aboriginal peoples before large number of settlers arrived. Joseph Howe, the secretary of state responsible for Indian Affairs, told his officials that they should "endeavour to secure the cession of the lands [from the Aboriginal peoples] upon terms as favourable as possible to the Government." It should be remembered, too, that some First Nations made it clear to government officials that they wanted treaties, as treaty-making was a way to assert their sovereignty over the land. Other Aboriginal leaders believed they needed some sort of accommodation with the government. Most pressing for them, of course, was the rapid depletion of the resources that they had relied on for centuries. The huge bison herds were rapidly approaching extinction on the North American plains, declining from as many as 30 million in the mid-seventeenth century to a few hundred by the end of the nineteenth, making it one of the worst ecological and environmental disasters of all times. Overexploitation of the bison by American and Canadian hunters might have been the major cause of the bison's decline, but drought and environmental change, as well as advances in Aboriginal hunting technology, also contributed to the bison's demise.[14]

The destruction of the bison herds was a catastrophe of enormous proportions and it changed the way of life of many of the Aboriginal peoples. Starvation and hunger became common. Missionaries pressed the Aboriginals to negotiate with the government, and Aboriginal leaders themselves knew only too well the fate of their peoples in the United

States. Throughout the whole treaty-making process, Aboriginal leaders maintained that the survival and well-being of their people would be assured if they established a good relationship with the government and worked with it to facilitate a transition from a traditional to a "modern" way of life. Many saw agriculture as an acceptable alternative for the future.

Seven treaties dealing primarily with lands required for settlement, generally referred to as the Numbered Treaties, were signed in the 1870s. Treaty One was finalized on August 3, 1871, and it covered much of southern Manitoba; six others were completed between the Canadian government and the various First Nations by 1877.[15] The federal government wanted to prepare the way for European settlement and economic development. The First Nations made a number of demands on the state in the negotiations as a means of protecting their interests. They believed that the negotiations themselves implied recognition of their title to the territory they occupied, even though the federal government wished to extinguish Aboriginal title.

Each treaty usually set aside a reserve large enough in area to provide 64 hectares for each family of five. The federal government agreed to provide and maintain a school on each reserve. Each Aboriginal man, woman, and child was given a gratuity of five dollars and an annuity of five dollars. The treaty also prohibited the introduction and sale of alcohol on the reserves. In return, the First Nations agreed to "cede, release, surrender and yield up to Her Majesty the Queen and successors forever all the lands" included in each treaty and maintain peaceful relations with Her Majesty's white subjects.

The negotiations leading to Treaty Six that covers the area of present-day central Saskatchewan and Alberta is particularly instructive. In 1871, during a major outbreak of smallpox and with the First Nations facing starvation from a dwindling food supply as the bison herds declined, chiefs of the Plains Cree, Woodland Cree, and Assiniboines approached the government to negotiate a treaty. The Aboriginal leaders were growing increasingly worried about their survival; however, the Canadian government had decided to make treaties only when the territory was required for settlement and as settlers had not reached that far west, the government chose to wait. The treaty was finally signed in 1876 at Fort Carlton and included terms similar to those of the other Numbered Treaties across Western Canada during this period. However, this area had had a recent and horrible experience with the smallpox plague against which traditional medicine was largely powerless. As a consequence, the Cree negotiated the promise of assistance from the government in case of a pestilence or a famine. The treaty included a clause that the Indian Agent keep a medicine chest to protect the health of First Nations. With this clause, healthcare became a treaty right. Later, in two separate rulings, including *Regina v. Johnston* in 1966, Canadian courts held that "the Indians are entitled to receive all medical services including medicine, drugs, medical supplies, and hospital care free of charge."[16]

Another important principle included in Treaty Six was peace. As Blair Stonechild, a professor of Indigenous Studies at the First Nations University of Canada, has argued, by the 1870s a strong peace movement had developed among the Aboriginal leaders, largely because they understood the threat to their societies from disease and inter-tribal conflicts. In one such conflict between the Cree and the Blackfoot on the Oldman River in 1870, several hundred warriors were killed. The Aboriginal nations, which had never been at

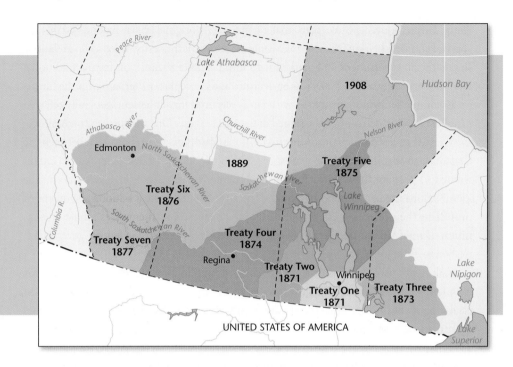

Map 2.2
Maps Showing Treaties
One to Seven

war with European settlers in the Northwest, made peace among themselves and with the settlers, one of the principles of Treaty Six: "They will maintain peace and good order between each other, and also between themselves and others of Her Majesty's subjects."[17]

Not surprisingly, given two different cultures and two different world views of the Aboriginal peoples and the Canadian negotiators, there has been considerable dispute about what the treaties mean for Canada today. There is the general question of interpretation: Are the treaties to be interpreted literally or should the whole culture and history of treaty-making be considered? For the Canadian government, the treaties meant that the Aboriginal peoples in Western Canada had surrendered title to the land in exchange for reserves and annual payments. However, Aboriginal leadership saw the negotiations differently. First, the Aboriginal leaders realized that they could not surrender the land as they did not own it. To them, the treaties were pacts of friendship whereby they received gifts in exchange for permitting settlers to occupy certain sections of land; the treaties did not mean the surrender of huge territories to the government. In fact, the treaties included provisions for the continued use by Aboriginal peoples of the land for the purposes of hunting and fishing. Second, the chiefs did not see themselves as subservient to the Canadian government. J.R. Miller has pointed out that when the Aboriginal peoples talked about the Queen Mother and they being "her Indian children," such language had a different purpose than what the Canadian negotiators thought. To the First Nations' chiefs, such phrases signified freedom—freedom that came from being a child—rather than being a dependant. Of course, the two sides spoke different languages and the interpreters were not always conversant in both. The Numbered Treaties remain a point of contention in Canada today.

Harmonious Aboriginal–state relations in Canada were not improved in the long term when the federal government passed the *Indian Act, 1876*. This was an attempt to bring all the laws and regulations governing Canada's Aboriginal peoples under a single statute. The Act virtually turned Aboriginal peoples into wards of the state, as government policy became steadily more interventionist in the life of Aboriginal peoples and more controlling. The Act set out conditions for the sale of reserve lands, and mandated elections for band councils in spite of traditional practices of Aboriginal governance. It effectively decided who could and could not be considered an Indian under the law. Any woman who married an Aboriginal male would be considered an Indian, but any Aboriginal woman who married a non-Aboriginal male ceased being one and lost all privileges under the Act. Aboriginal peoples of mixed ancestry, such as the Métis, had to choose to either take an Indian identity and become part of a treaty or take scrip (land certificates) and remain outside the treaty arrangements and away from reserve lands. Métis scrip could be used only to acquire lands from the Dominion Lands Office, but many of those land vouchers or certificates were purchased by land agents and financial institutions at considerable discount and then flipped at huge profits to immigrant homesteaders. The scrip process left many Métis landless and without a community base. The *Indian Act* provided for the establishment of residential schools for Aboriginal children between the ages of 5 and 16; attendance became compulsory in 1895, with terrible consequences for Aboriginal societies. The Act was undoubtedly intended to speed the process of assimilation; it was regularly amended as the federal government searched for the most effective policies with which to accomplish its objectives.

As the federal government prepared the prairies for the arrival of European settlers, there was a migration of Métis from Manitoba to present-day Saskatchewan. Historians have disagreed over whether the Canadian government forced the Métis further west to pursue their trade in pemmican and buffalo robes, or whether they moved for economic benefits. D.N. Sprague, formerly a professor of history at the University of Manitoba, has argued that the Métis were deliberately dispossessed of the land promised them in the *Manitoba Act* in 1870; they were the victims of a deliberate conspiracy by the Canadian government to deprive them of their lands. It was the federal government, Sprague insists, that forced the Métis out of Manitoba and further west to Saskatchewan.[18] Scholars Gerhard Ens and Thomas Flangnan disagree.[19] They argue that the federal government met its obligations to the Métis, who then sold much of their lands for considerable profit. Ens has argued that the Métis specialized in the buffalo-robe trade and they followed the animals further west. In his view, the Métis were adapting to the changing economic realities of the period. Both sides in the debate have been criticized because they have worked as researchers for either the federal government or the Manitoba Métis Federation. Those scholars have impeccable credentials and few would question their objectivity, but as Professor J.R Miller, one of Canada's leading historians and a former president of the Canadian Historical Association, recently noted, "historians are going to have to think about if, and on what terms, they are going to participate in remunerative judicial jousting so as to maintain not only their integrity, but also that of their discipline."[20]

Riel and the Northwest Uprising

By the early 1880s, the bison were rapidly disappearing from the prairies, and the Métis who had settled in the Qu'Appelle Valley of Saskatchewan were struggling, as were many

1876: The Indian Act *is proclaimed.*

of the First Nations on their reserve lands. Much of the land they had acquired as a result of the Numbered Treaties was marginal farmland at best. Many of the Indian Agents appointed by Ottawa were unsympathetic to the plight of Aboriginal peoples, and their leaders soon complained that Ottawa was not fulfilling its treaty obligations. European settlers were also disappointed with Ottawa.

Compounding the problem was a series of severe winters, particularly in 1884 and 1885; the whole region was seething with discontent. First Nations, Métis, and settlers who had arrived from throughout Canada all had their legitimate grievances. W.H. Jackson, the secretary of the North-West Settlers' Union, outlined their grievances in several petitions to Ottawa throughout the early 1880s, complaining that the federal government was ignoring them. An important issue for the Settlers' Union was the lack of representation in the House of Commons, which did not happen until 1887. It also demanded provincial status and self-government, which, the settlers maintained, would be the only way to deal with the lack of schools, roads, and other infrastructure in the territories. They complained, too, that land speculators and officials connected with the federal Conservative party wielded too much power in the region and benefited immensely from their connections, usually at the expense of the settlers.

By 1884, Jackson agreed with the Métis that they turn to Louis Riel, who had lived for more than a decade in Montana and had become an American citizen in 1883, to help push for the redress of their grievances against Ottawa. Riel eagerly returned to Canada and played a pivotal role in creating the Northwest Rebellion. The historians who first wrote about the events of 1884–85 saw the rebellions as a clash between two cultures, one sophisticated and advanced, and the other primitive and backward. That interpretation has been dismissed, and historians now agree that there is no simple explanation for the rebellion. The Métis had their grievances with Ottawa, particularly over land title, and the federal government never seemed to take their concerns seriously. Shortly after returning to Canada, Riel came to believe that he had a divine mission to prepare for the second coming of Christ. The white farmers, who shared many of the Métis concerns, realized Riel was unstable, as did the Catholic priests who warned Ottawa and their bishop that Riel was heretical when he adopted "David" as his name and talked of establishing the papacy in Manitoba. Shortly after the federal government announced the appointment of a commission to examine Métis grievances, Riel proclaimed a provisional government on March 19, 1885, as he had in Red River in 1869, and demanded the surrender of Fort Carlton and a North-West Mounted Police detachment stationed there. A week later, the Métis defeated the North-West Mounted Police in a skirmish near Duck Lake, where 12 of the force died and six Métis warriors, including Isidore, the brother of the Métis military commander Gabriel Dumont. The Canadian government believed it faced an armed insurrection and dispatched a large military force to the Northwest. They were confirmed in their belief when word reached Ottawa of the Frog Lake massacre. Macdonald feared he was facing an Indian–Métis alliance after years of neglecting their grievances.

There was no alliance between the Cree Nation and the Métis. The First Nations were disappointed with the federal government over the implementation of the treaties. The list of grievances grew as the Aboriginal population on the prairies declined from approximately 33 000 in 1880 to slightly more than 20 000 in 1885, an annual death rate of 10 percent.

Second uprising of Aboriginal peoples and Métis in the West.

Aboriginal leaders were disappointed with the settling of the reserves and complained to Ottawa about inadequate rations, the lack of agricultural implements, the lack of schools and medical provisions, and how their grievances were being ignored. Yet, they preferred diplomacy and had planned a Grand Council for 1885 that would send a delegation to Ottawa to deal directly with the government. They were confident that their strategy of concerted political action, rather than war, would yield results. When Riel attempted to form a territory-wide insurrection with First Nations, Aboriginal leaders refused; instead, they notified government authorities of their loyalty to the Crown and demanded a role in their own well-being.[21]

However, Mistahimaskwa (commonly known as Big Bear), a Plains Cree chief, had considerable difficulty keeping the younger men in his camp under control. They were impatient with negotiations and believed violence would produce a better outcome. When they learned of the Métis triumph at Duck Lake, Ayimâsis, Big Bear's son, and a number of younger Cree warriors, grew impatient with their situation and attacked the Hudson's Bay Company store and the Indian agent at Frog Lake to protest against the Canadian government's withholding of provisions. The attack was the beginning of what some historians have called the Cree uprising. Nine people were killed at Frog Lake, including Thomas Quinn, the Indian agent, and 70 were imprisoned in Big Bear's camp. The Canadian militia forces engaged the Cree on other occasions throughout the early months of 1885, but recently historians have insisted that the incidents must be kept separate from the Métis uprising, even though the two have been combined in Canadian history. At Fish Creek, Métis military leader Gabriel Dumont won a major victory over Major-General Frederick Middleton, but at Cut Knife Hill, it was Cree forces, led by war Chief Fine Day, that defeated Lieutenant-Colonel William Otter and the 500-strong Canadian militia. This was the final Cree triumph against the government militia. The Métis's last stand came at Batoche in a battle that began on May 9, 1885, and lasted for three days until the Métis ran out of ammunition. Batoche marked the end of the Métis resistance and, some have argued, the end of their independence as a nation. Riel surrendered a few days later. Middleton despatched a letter (shown at right) to Big Bear, warning of the consequences of continued resistance.

Both Big Bear and Poundmaker surrendered in July. Piapot, also known as Payipwat, was the Chief of the Cree in the Qu'Appelle Valley and he stayed out of the rebellion, as did the Blackfoot Confederacy. Poundmaker and Big Bear, however, were prosecuted and each received three-year sentences in a federal penitentiary for their role in the uprising. Fifty others were convicted on various offences, and eight were executed. It is Louis Riel, however, who has attracted much of the attention in the aftermath of the failed rebellion.

On July 20, 1885, Riel was tried for treason in a Regina courtroom and subsequently found guilty before a magistrate and a jury of six English-speaking Protestants. Many have

Letter from General Middleton demanding that Big Bear surrender and release his prisoners.

Source: Library and Archives Canada, MG29-E23.

Métis prisoners outside the Regina Court House after the North West Rebellion, 1885.

Source: Archives of Ontario/Acc. 6876 S-8035.

Louis Riel found guilty of treason.

argued since that his trial was a miscarriage of justice, including Emmett Hall, a former justice of the Supreme Court of Canada, who supported various groups demanding that the Canadian government grant Riel a pardon. Much of the debate about Riel has focused on his mental health: Was he insane? Riel had twice been institutionalized in the 1870s and his lawyers wanted to mount a defence based on insanity, but Riel would have none of it—such a plea would nullify both his religious mission and Métis grievances. He was also an American citizen. The jury seemed to understand that Riel was mentally ill and, although they found him guilty, they recommended that Judge Hugh Richardson show mercy in his sentencing. The law was clear, however: Treason was punishable by death. The verdict was appealed to the Court of Queen's Bench of Manitoba (which had jurisdiction over the Territories), and then to the Judicial Committee of the Privy Council. Both appeals were dismissed. Only the federal government could save Riel from the gallows.

Prime Minister Macdonald knew better than anyone the cleavages that existed within Canada and the dilemma that Riel's fate created for the new nation and its government. Ontario had been outraged that Riel had not been sufficiently punished after a Métis court martial found Thomas Scott guilty on the charge of insubordination and treason on March 3, 1870, and executed him by firing squad the following day. In 1872, the Ontario legislature offered a $5000 reward for the arrest of Scott's "murderers." With Riel finally in custody, English-speaking Protestants throughout Ontario demanded that Macdonald let him hang. On the other hand, Quebec demanded clemency for the Catholic and French-speaking Riel. French-speaking cabinet ministers convinced Macdonald that an independent medical team should be permitted to examine Riel's state of mind. Two of the three doctors found Riel sane. Macdonald decided to let the law take its course: Riel was hanged for treason in Regina on November 16, 1885. Macdonald's decision caused outrage in Quebec and jubilation in Ontario. In time, Riel became an important symbol for Métis and Aboriginal peoples. He was not only a martyred leader but also a visionary who fought for the rights of Canada's First Nations and Métis peoples. In the meantime, Riel brought meaningful change to provincial and national politics throughout Canada. A new political party emerged in Quebec to confront Ottawa, and even though Macdonald and the Conservatives would win the 1887 and 1891 federal elections, the seeds of a major political realignment had been sown in national politics.

Reconciling Diversities: Schooling and Education

It was understood in 1867 that Confederation would not obliterate the differences that existed in the new nation. It was hoped, though, that within the federation, regional and provincial differences, and differences of ethnicity and religion, might be reconciled. George-Étienne Cartier, one of the Fathers of Confederation, had said in the Confederation debates in 1865 that he hoped Confederation would create "a political nationality with which neither the national origin nor the religion of any individual would interfere."

The furor over Riel was only one of a series of incidents in the generation after Confederation that tested the strength of the new political nationality created in 1867. Schooling and education created another. They had often generated conflict in the society of British North America, and when Confederation was negotiated in 1867, exclusive responsibility for education was left with the provinces. Still, the *British North America Act* protected denominational education and warned the provinces not to interfere with any of the denominational rights existing at the time of Confederation. If any minority felt aggrieved by any subsequent legislative changes in the provinces, they could appeal to the Government of Canada for protection through the federal Parliament's remedial power. Education and schooling proved to be nearly as divisive as the hanging of Louis Riel, as Catholic education came under attack in several of the provinces between 1874 and 1896.

In the nineteenth century it became widely accepted that education was an important agent of social and cultural change. Both the state and the church agreed on the need for a formal system of education. While there was general consensus on how education should be funded, there was little agreement on who should control education. Ontario had been one of the pioneers in education with its *Common Schools Act* of 1846 and 1850, and this legislation subsequently became a model for many of the other provinces. The place of religious authorities in the educational system created considerable debate and animosity among Canadians, however. Many argued that education was a public responsibility, necessary for the good of the nation, while others, particularly Catholics, maintained that education could not be separated from religion. Some Protestants, on the other hand, took a more utilitarian view of education, but they, too, saw the educational system as the best way to create in their new nation young people schooled in the English language, British customs and traditions, and even Protestantism itself. These two visions would collide because schooling was key to assimilation and inculcating values in young Canadians. Parents were interested in schooling their children, too, and most children between the ages of seven and twelve attended school for several months each year, even before compulsory education was introduced later in the nineteenth century.

Most of the post-Confederation controversies over education involved Francophone minorities outside of Quebec. Quebec, itself, had established separate Catholic and Protestant systems of education, and this system satisfied both religious groups. New Brunswick opted for a single, tax-supported non-sectarian public school system when it introduced the *Common Schools Act of 1871*. Many Catholics in the province were outraged; they had had their own schools for generations, though by practice and tradition rather than by any legislative authority. They appealed to the federal government, claiming that the *British North America Act* protected religious schools in the province. Macdonald did not want to get involved and asked the province to reconsider its legislation. The Supreme Court of New Brunswick ruled in 1873 that the legislation was constitutional because the provinces had exclusive jurisdiction to make laws for education in the province.

The matter did not end there because religion was very important in late-nineteenth-century Canada. The Catholic bishops in New Brunswick pursued the matter on two fronts: They pressured local Catholic MPs to continue the struggle in Ottawa, and they looked to the Catholic hierarchy in Quebec to intervene with Macdonald and with the New Brunswick government. It was even a minor issue in Quebec during the federal election of 1872. However, New Brunswick Catholics had little success, largely because many of Macdonald's Quebec ministers were worried about setting a precedent for the federal government. They realized that Ontario had often expressed its fears of Catholic domination of the educational system, and they did not want to arouse the militant Protestants there by appearing to bow to the Catholic bishops in New Brunswick. Still, the government paid the costs for the bishops to appeal to the Judicial Committee of the Privy Council in London, which prompted New Brunswick to complain of federal and imperial interference in a local matter, even though the Judicial Committee of the Privy Council ruled in favour of the provincial government. Premier George E. King, who had shepherded the legislation through the New Brunswick assembly as provincial secretary, called an election on the issue in 1874, insisting that a public system offered an equal and efficient education for all children. He won, although he lost every seat in the predominately Catholic and French-speaking districts in the Acadian north.

The final acts of Catholic defiance came from the bishops and priests who refused to pay their taxes to support public education and told Catholic parents to keep their children home and to refuse to pay their local taxes as a form of popular protest. Tax collectors seized property, including Bishop John Sweeney's carriages and horses and Father McDevitt's cows; as well, several parish priests were jailed. The militia was despatched to Caraquet to quell the growing protest, and in the clash with protesters two people were killed: Louis Mailloux, a 19-year-old Acadian, and John Gifford, a constable. Nine Acadians were charged with murder. Soon after, a compromise was reached: In the more populated school districts, all Catholic children could attend the same school, thus providing by default for Catholic schools; members of the clergy were allowed to teach in the schools, but they would have to successfully complete the same examinations as all other teachers; bishops would not be permitted to select textbooks for use in the Catholic schools, but in those texts translated into French any anti-Catholic references would be removed; and religious instruction would be permitted in Catholic schools after the end of the regular teaching day.

The ethnic and linguistic cleavages were played out in other provinces, too, and all of them had implications for the national community. In Quebec, it was Riel and the Jesuit Estates Bill that generated considerable controversy and emotion. Although most of Quebec condemned the violent resistance in the Northwest in 1885, they could not ignore the fact that Riel was also French-speaking and Catholic. His hanging outraged Quebec, which saw his execution as an assault on French Canada. Honoré Mercier, a leading member of the Quebec Liberal party, called for a coalition or *parti national* to protect and strengthen the position of Quebec within Confederation. His Parti National came to power in the wake of the Riel crisis. One of his first initiatives was the *Jesuits' Estates Act*, which attempted to deal with the property or estates that once belonged to Jesuit priests. The British government stripped the society of its Canadian holdings in 1791, some years after Pope had banned the society in 1773. When the society was re-established in Quebec in 1842, it demanded the return of its property. Catholic bishops disagreed and wanted the monies given in compensation for the estates divided among the Catholic schools in the province. The Quebec government decided upon $400 000 in compensation to various Catholic bodies (and $60 000 to the Protestants) following a long arbitration process overseen by the Pope. Many Protestants—both inside and outside Quebec—disagreed with Pope Leo XIII's involvement in the matter, and Ontario, in particular, saw it as further evidence of clerical control of Quebec and the subjugation of the state to the church. A motion introduced in the House of Commons calling for the disallowance of the *Jesuits' Estates Act* was defeated 188 to 13. However, the decisive defeat did not end the matter for radical Protestants as they mounted an aggressive campaign to promote a Canada that was decidedly Protestant and British. At the forefront of that campaign was the Equal Rights Association (ERA), created in Toronto in June 1889, which demanded the separation of church and state and advocated equal rights for all Canadians, but it was, in effect, an anti-French-Canadian and anti-Catholic organization. D'Alton McCarthy, a close colleague of John A. Macdonald, became one of its primary spokespersons, though the prime minister went to great measures to distance himself and the Conservative party from McCarthy's campaign. The ERA saw the French language as one of the greatest threats to the development of Canadian nationalism. It feared that as long as French Canadians, especially those outside of Quebec, were taught in the French language, they interfered with the ERA's plan for a British Canada.

A clear division was emerging between Quebec, which increasingly saw itself under attack from English-speaking Canadians, and the rest of Canada. McCarthy and the ERA fuelled the mistrust. McCarthy had a clear vision of what his Canada should be: cultural conformity, which meant primacy of the English language and the abolition of French-language guarantees where they existed. In January 1890, he tried, unsuccessfully, in Parliament to abolish the use of French in the government and courts throughout the Northwest in 1877, since French had been given equal status with English. McCarthy's campaign attracted little support in Ontario and across Canada; only one candidate associated with the ERA was elected in the 1890 provincial election in Ontario. Yet, when Catholic schools in Ontario and bilingualism in the West became primary ERA targets and McCarthy campaigned for a strong centralized Canada with a predominant English-Canadian nationalism, Quebec was worried. Quebec Premier Mercier called upon French-speaking Canadians at the 1889 Saint-Jean-Baptiste Day celebration to unite to keep Quebec French-speaking and Catholic. One Quebec MLA suggested that a militia be kept at the ready "to defend French Canadian institutions and laws against Anglo-Saxon aggression."[22]

McCarthy vacationed in Manitoba and the Northwest in 1889 and has been inaccurately blamed for rallying Manitobans against French and Catholic education. Although Manitoba entered Confederation as a bilingual and bicultural province in 1870, its cultural duality had been swamped by the arrival throughout the 1870s and 1880s of English-speaking farmers primarily from Ontario. In 1890, the Thomas Greenway government

Manitoba government eliminates Catholic control of education, 1890.

eliminated official bilingualism in Manitoba and created a single public school system funded by the province. The new education system stopped funding for both Protestant and Catholic schools that had been guaranteed in 1870 in favour of public non-sectarian schools. The language of education in the new public schools was to be English. These attacks on Franco- and Catholic-Manitoban institutions were an attempt by English-speaking Protestant immigrants from Ontario to remake the province in their image. The same process was at work in the North-West Territories, where legislation in 1892 brought an end to French-language education after grade three and removed French as one of the official languages in the legislature. However, it was the situation with Manitoba schools that attracted considerable attention and became an important landmark for French-speaking minorities in Canada.

The issue was the loss of French-Canadian and Catholic rights in Western Canada, but the controversy was played out primarily outside the region, especially between politicians in Quebec and Ontario. Catholic bishops demanded that the Government of Canada protect the minority rights of Catholics as they were guaranteed in the *British North America Act*. Even a petition signed by most of the Catholic bishops in Canada calling for federal disallowance of the Manitoba legislation had little impact, although both the Conservatives and the Liberals in Parliament were embarrassed by the treatment of minorities by the provinces. Neither party made the Manitoba schools question an issue in the federal election that was held on March 5, 1891. Each agreed that the best recourse was through the courts, as it generally is with any contentious and divisive issue. The Supreme Court of Canada and the JCPC upheld the validity of the Manitoba legislation but agreed, nonetheless, that Ottawa had the right to restore through remedial legislation the minority rights that the Catholic minority had enjoyed since 1870. The federal government had been able to evade the matter while it worked its way through the courts and had failed to provide leadership on it for more than five years. Once the courts ruled, though, Ottawa was forced to act. It proposed remedial legislation calling for the restoration of separate (religious) schools, but the Manitoba government refused to comply. The province claimed that its new schooling legislation was not based on any religious preference; its new school system introduced in 1890 was to make schooling better for all children regardless of their religion.

There was no easy solution to the controversy, but the best hope lay with compromise and accommodation. Macdonald had managed the issue fairly well as he had with other religious and cultural matters that threatened to divide French-speaking Catholics and English-speaking Protestants within the Conservative party. Unfortunately, Macdonald died on June 6, 1891, and his party—and the Government of Canada—were in disarray for its remaining years in office. Within the Conservative party, the Ontario members did not want the restoration of Catholic schools in Manitoba; Quebec members wanted the Manitoba legislation disallowed. Canada had four different prime ministers in the last five years of Conservative rule: John Abbott (1891–1892), the minister of justice, became the first politician from Quebec to be prime minister; John S. Thompson (1892–1894) from Halifax was the first Roman Catholic to be prime minister; Mackenzie Bowell, former Grand-Master of the Orange Lodges of Canada, served from 1894–1896 and introduced remedial legislation in the House of Commons, promising redress to Manitoba Catholics, but the hugely popular

John A. Macdonald dies, 6 June 1891.

government of Manitoba would not concede easily to Ottawa. Charles Tupper, who replaced Bowell as prime minister on May 1, 1896, had to defend remedial legislation in the 1896 federal election.

Wilfrid Laurier, the leader of the Liberal party, saw little political advantage in the controversy, but before the vote was held on June 23, virtually all of the Liberal candidates in Quebec, including Laurier himself, made a solemn pledge in writing to seek justice for Manitoba Catholics. Although Tupper's Conservatives won more votes than the Liberals and carried half the seats in English Canada, the Liberal landslide in Quebec served to send the first French-speaking prime minister to Ottawa; it also awarded Tupper the dubious distinction of being the shortest-serving prime minister. When Laurier became prime minister, the Manitoba schools question was his to resolve. He had maintained throughout the crisis that a solution had to be found that balanced Manitoba's right to determine its own education system and Ottawa's right to pass remedial legislation to protect religious minorities.

A political cartoon from 1896 with the political rivals Bowell and Laurier having to choose their slippery course concerning the Manitoba schools question.

Source: Library and Archives Canada/C-029623.

Provincial Rights and the Meaning of Confederation

Education and Riel's hanging were not the only issues that highlighted the divisions within Canada in the early years of Confederation. Relations were also strained between the national government in Ottawa and the provinces immediately after Confederation, and it can be argued that tensions in intergovernmental relations have become an integral aspect of Canadian federalism. Political scientists have often described Canada as an example of "dysfunctional federalism," but the country has always managed to survive periods of federal–provincial conflict.

Oliver Mowat, the premier and attorney general of Ontario from 1872 to 1896, was at the centre of the federal–provincial disputes in the first generation of Confederation. Mowat had attended the Quebec Conference in 1864, but he later withdrew from politics for a career as a judge. He was perhaps the only judge in Canadian history to leave his post to become the leader of a political party. As premier, he oversaw a period of rapid urbanization and industrialization but it was tempered by rural depopulation and a general economic crisis across Canada. Mowat was decidedly pro-business, but he also introduced legislation to protect workers. Ontario's first *Factory Act* in 1884, which regulated hours of work for women and children and mandated the first system of safety inspection in Canadian factories, was intended to deal with the changing urban industrial landscape in Ontario. He created a new government department to oversee education in the province and made school attendance compulsory for all children between 8 and 14. He passed legislation protecting a portion of a worker's salary from garnishment for debt, and made employers liable for injuries in the workplace with the *Workmen's Compensation for Injuries Act of 1886*. In the wider field of social welfare, he established children's aid societies to offer a measure of protection to children, reduced the presence of child labour,

Ontario Premier Oliver Mowat—"Father of Provincial Rights Movement."

allowed women to be their children's legal guardians, and established a provincial board of health. He also introduced political reforms to reduce corruption at the ballot box and extended voting rights to all adult males in 1888.

It was Mowat's fight with the Macdonald government in Ottawa that has earned him an important place in Canadian history. Known as the "Father of Provincial Rights," Mowat believed that the *British North America Act* that had created Canada was an agreement between the provinces. He insisted that the provinces had retained in the Confederation agreement the sovereignty and jurisdiction they had prior to union, except for the specific responsibilities surrendered to the federal government. His interpretation gave rise to the compact theory of Confederation, meaning that Confederation arose as an agreement among the provinces and that the Constitution could only be amended with the unanimous consent of all the provinces. Macdonald believed that the provinces had limited sovereignty while the legislative powers of the federal government were extensive. Mowat disagreed, and he was adamant about protecting the jurisdiction and sovereignty of the provinces.

The disputes over the distribution of legislative jurisdiction and power between Ottawa and Ontario in this period should be seen as an attempt by the provinces and the federal government to define and interpret exactly what the delegates thought they had agreed to in Quebec in 1864 when they created the Canadian Confederation. It was the courts that would have the final say in the constitutional disagreements over the division of powers between the provincial and federal governments. The Supreme Court of Canada routinely ruled against Mowat in his attempts to establish provincial sovereignty. The Court, for instance, ruled that the lieutenant-governor of Ontario did not have the jurisdiction to appoint Queen's Counsel, an honorific title bestowed on lawyers to recognize meritorious service in the legal profession. It interpreted the power of the federal government to regulate trade and commerce in the broadest terms while limiting the power of the provinces to legislate in such matters. The Judicial Committee of the Privy Council generally interpreted the Constitution in favour of the provinces, thus supporting a more decentralized view of Confederation.

The role that the courts played in interpreting Confederation can be seen in two cases in the 1880s, both of which had their beginnings with Mowat in Ontario. The first was the case of *McLaren v. Caldwell,* a dispute between two lumber merchants, Peter McLaren and Boyd Caldwell. McLaren, who had improved the waterway to allow the passage of logs, attempted to prevent Caldwell, who had an operation upstream from his, from moving his logs downstream by using the improvements that McLaren had made and without paying. When McLaren won a court injunction against Caldwell, Mowat passed in 1881 *An Act for Protecting the Public Interest in Rivers, Stream and Creeks*, popularly known as the *Rivers and Stream Act*, that allowed Caldwell to move his logs downstream. That McLaren was a Conservative and Caldwell, a Liberal were not unimportant facts, but the federal government disallowed Mowat's legislation, claiming that provinces did not have the authority to legislate in the matter of property rights. Mowat re-enacted the bill twice more and each time Macdonald disallowed the legislation. The Supreme Court agreed with Macdonald, but the Judicial Committee of the Privy Council (JCPC) ruled in favour of the province, establishing the principle of free navigation rights on Canada's rivers and streams.

Mowat's greatest success came in the boundary dispute between Ontario and Manitoba. When Manitoba entered Confederation in 1870, its boundary with Ontario had not been decided, and since the federal government controlled the natural resources of Manitoba, it was in Ottawa's interest to have a generous interpretation of Manitoba's border with Ontario. The present-day border was arbitrated only in 1884, but the dispute continued for several more years as Macdonald insisted that the federal government controlled the natural resources in the region as it had authority to administer all lands reserved for First Nations' occupation. Much of the territory in dispute had been included in Treaty Three negotiated in 1873. Ontario argued that federal jurisdiction was limited to the lands set aside as First Nations' reserves, and the federal government had no authority to issue lumber permits to the St. Catharines Milling Company to cut wood in the area. When it did, Ontario charged the company for cutting wood illegally, and once again, Ottawa and Ontario went to court. In *St. Catharines Milling and Lumber Co. v. the Queen* the JCPC decided that Ontario, and not the federal government, owned the natural resources within the territory awarded to the province in 1884. Even though the JCPC made it clear it was not ruling upon "the precise character of the Indian interest" in the territory, the case was an important one for Aboriginal land rights in Canada. The JCPC ruled that the Crown had title and sovereignty over Aboriginal lands and Aboriginal title was limited to the right to use and occupy the land at the will of the Crown; the First Nations had no right to the timber growing on the land they had given up.[23]

St. Catharines Milling and Lumber Co. v. The Queen, 1888, *an important court ruling for Aboriginal land entitlement.*

Mowat, of course, was not the only premier to confront Ottawa during this period. In Nova Scotia, Premier W.S. Fielding continued to worry about his province's financial position, which he attributed to unfavourable terms of union in 1867. Because 70 percent of provincial revenues came from Ottawa, Nova Scotia demanded a new financial arrangement with the federal government. When Macdonald dismissed the grievances, the provincial legislature passed a motion asking Ottawa to release the province from Confederation. Fielding never pushed the issue of secession because sections of Nova Scotia were benefiting from the tariff provided under the national policy and had no interest in leaving Confederation. Neither did Fielding, really, who later went to Ottawa to join the new Liberal government in 1896.

Quebec Premier Mercier had his own struggles with Ottawa and invited all of the premiers to meet in Quebec City in October 1887 to discuss their lingering grievances against the federal government. This was the country's first interprovincial conference. Fielding's attendance implied he would attempt to work within Confederation rather than try to get out of it. Mowat chaired the meetings, and the premiers agreed upon several resolutions to strengthen the provinces; they particularly wanted to end Ottawa's power of disallowances of provincial legislation. Two provinces, Prince Edward Island and British Columbia (both with Conservative governments), refused to attend, and Macdonald dismissed the conference as the political machinations of his political foes. Because the federal government had lost a number of constitutional battles with the provinces, by the late 1880s Macdonald decided to use the federal power of veto over the provinces more cautiously than he had immediately after Confederation.

By the early 1890s, the provinces had won several important rulings in the courts in areas of resource management, property and civil rights, and education. As a result, the

Map 2.3
Canada in 1900

Source: Reproduced with the permission of Natural Resources Canada 2009. Courtesy of the Atlas of Canada.

federal government began to pay more attention to the items enumerated in section 91 of the *British North America Act*. Mowat would join Laurier after 1896 and remain a proponent of the sovereignty of the provinces, but his tenure as premier of Ontario had demonstrated that the provinces were not subordinate to the federal government. Mowat believed there was a measure of equality between the two orders of government, even if they did not share power equally.

Defending Canadian Interests Abroad and at Home

The *British North America Act* was silent on the issue of foreign policy, though it was understood that Canada was still very much a part of the British Empire after Confederation and the conduct of foreign relations resided with the British government in London, England. While John A. Macdonald recognized this fact and the subordinate position of Canada within the Empire, he hoped the relationship would change over time and the colonial system would be "less a case of dependence on our part, and of over-ruling protection of the part of the Mother Country, and more a case of healthy and cordial alliance. Instead of looking upon us as a merely dependent colony, England will have in us a friendly nation, a subordinate but still a powerful people to stand by her in North America in peace or in war."[24] As Macdonald learned at the negotiations leading to the Treaty of Washington in 1871, as long as Britain was in control of Canada's foreign relations, it would be British rather than Canadian interests that would get priority. Macdonald realized too, of course, that it was important to maintain friendly relations with the United States, and while the Canadian government was preoccupied with consolidating the new nation, foreign affairs might be best left to the British. Nevertheless, Macdonald realized Canada needed a representative in London. All official correspondence between Canada and the British government passed through the British-appointed governor-general. In 1869 Macdonald appointed Sir John Rose, his former minister of finance, as an unofficial representative of the Government of Canada. Although Rose did not receive a salary from the government, his expenses were paid, and he remained in his position until the office of high commissioner was established in 1880, even during the period that Mackenzie was prime minister. Mackenzie made Rose Canada's financial commissioner in London. When he returned to office in 1878, Macdonald wanted to formalize the role of the Canadian representative in London by establishing a "resident minister" in the British capital. This appointment marked the beginning of Canadian permanent representation abroad, but the British government could not simply conceive of Canada having a diplomatic presence in London, which they feared might threaten the unity of the Empire in matters of foreign policy. They relented on the office, but did not want any title that suggested a diplomatic role for Canada.

Canada appoints representatives in London and Paris.

Sir Alexander Galt, an early proponent of a protective tariff for Canada and another finance minister in Macdonald's government, became Canadian high commissioner to Britain in 1880. In 1882, Quebec appointed Liberal Senator Hector Fabre as its agent general to France. To get rid of a Liberal Senate appointment, Macdonald also appointed him Canadian commissaire général to France, a position he held until 1911. These appointments were concerned primarily with promoting Canada's economic interests abroad rather than Canada's wider diplomatic interests. For instance, Sir Charles Tupper, Galt's successor in London, negotiated a trade deal with France in 1892. Formally, the economic arrangement was between France and Britain, but it was negotiated solely by Tupper and represented an important step in Canada managing its own international affairs. In 1894, Canada appointed its first resident commercial agent abroad when John Short Larke was named the Canadian trade commissioner to Australia. This appointment came after the creation of the Department of Trade and Commerce in 1892, and Mackenzie Bowell, the first minister of the new department, led a trade mission to Australia to promote Canadian trade.

Economic considerations, particularly with the United States, remained the basis of much of Canada's foreign relations between the 1870s and 1896. The Conservatives' National Policy was a response to the growing wave of protectionism in the United States and a desire to develop the Canadian economy. Between 1867 and 1896, nearly half a million Canadians fled Canada in search of better economic prospects south of the border, and even Macdonald harboured hopes of a limited free trade arrangement with the Americans—so did the Liberals, though they were divided between commercial union and unrestricted reciprocity. Commercial union essentially meant the establishment of a common market between the two countries and the adoption of identical tariffs with other nations. Many Canadians feared that such an economic arrangement would inevitably lead to political union and the eventual absorption of Canada into the American union. Most Liberals came to understand, too, that many Canadians valued the British connection and might never support commercial union; in 1888, the Liberal party adopted unrestricted reciprocity, or complete free trade, with the Americans instead and made the issue the dominant plank in their 1891 election campaign. Macdonald and his Conserva-

The Old Flag, The Old Policy, The Old Leader. Conservative Campaign Poster, 1891. The poster shows how the Conservatives believed that the National Policy forged an alliance between urban and rural Canada.

Source: M965.34.8, © McCord Museum.

tives responded to the Liberal promise by calling it "veiled treason" that would lead to the destruction of Canada and annexation to the United States. Although Macdonald had attempted to secure a free trade deal with the Americans three years earlier, he uttered one of his most effective and memorable lines from his long political career in 1891: "As for myself, my course is clear. A British subject I was born—a British subject I will die." The campaign, Macdonald's last, saw his party triumph at the polls with an even larger share of the popular vote than it had garnered in 1887. His campaign poster, "The Old Flag, The Old Policy, The Old Leader" proved most effective. Shortly after their defeat, the Liberals quietly dropped their commitment to free trade in time for the 1896 campaign.

While Macdonald was eager to demonstrate his loyalty to the Crown at election time, he was equally determined to keep his distance from those in Britain who wanted dominions like Canada to assume a greater role in defending the Empire. This was much easier for Macdonald in his early years as prime minister because there were few in London who took much interest in the colonies. By the 1880s, however, the Empire entered a new era, marked by economic and territorial competition on a massive global scale that would see a renewed interest in Britain's colonies and mark the end of British apathy towards Canada and the other countries within the Empire. Macdonald wanted nothing to do with any imperial military adventures, and he reminded a British Royal Commission on the Defence of British Possessions and Commerce Abroad in 1880 that he was opposed to a general system of imperial defence. Still, he left little doubt that if Great Britain found itself at war, Canada could be counted on to help: "I think if war were imminent, the spirit of the people themselves would force on the Legislature and the Government of the day the necessity of taking an active part in it."[25] However, when General Lord Wolseley (who had commanded the British forces during the 1870 expedition to Red River) was despatched to the Sudan in Africa to rescue a British expedition led by General Charles Gordon, a British military hero in the Crimean War (1853–1856), who had encountered stiff resistance from local Sudanese insurgents in the region, he recalled how adept the Canadians had been in assisting his troops marching west. He asked that Canadian "voyageurs" be part of his contingent to the Nile River. When the request arrived through Governor-General Lord Lansdowne, Macdonald did not have any objection, as a Canadian Voyageur Contingent would be an imperial initiative and undertaken without any Canadian involvement or support. When those 386 men set sail for Africa, it was Canada's first contribution to a British overseas military operation, but these men were all civilians under six-month contracts for non-combat duties. They did not wear uniforms, bear arms, or participate in any of the skirmishes in which Wolseley engaged. When the situation escalated after the death of General Gordon, Macdonald refused to offer Canadian troops (as the territory of New South Wales in southern Australia had) because he believed the conflict was not in the Canadian national interest. For Macdonald, there would be no automatic Canadian participation in minor imperial conflicts.

Shortly after the incident in the Sudan, the British called the first colonial or imperial conference for 1887 on the occasion of Queen Victoria's Golden Jubilee. Macdonald did not attend. He sent Sir Alexander Campbell, the postmaster general and newly appointed lieutenant-governor of Ontario, and Sandford Fleming, who would give the world standardized time. The British were interested in an imperial system of defence, but Macdonald was not. He saw the conference as a means of discussing postal and telegraphic communications, but at the Jubilee conference and the one that followed in 1894 in Ottawa, the Marquess of Ripon, the British colonial secretary, made it clear that even in commercial and all other treaties, Britain did not see the need for Canadian autonomy. That view would change in a generation when Canada and the rest of the world became embroiled in the first of two major wars.

Conclusion

Creating Canada in 1867 might have been the easy task. As this chapter shows, the nation that was built on accommodation, diversity, and tolerance of minorities was not working as many had hoped. Canada was proving difficult to govern, as Prime Minister Mackenzie claimed in 1878. Minority communities were threatened in New Brunswick, Manitoba, and the Northwest Territories, and the majority was not particularly accommodating on matters such as French-language and Catholic education. As Riel and the First Nations and Métis communities discovered, the tolerance of minorities did not extend very far towards them in this period. Similarly, some migrant groups, such as the Chinese, learned that there would be no accommodation for them in Canada. In politics, the federal and provincial governments quarrelled over the meaning of the Confederation agreement and the respective powers of each order of government as provincial rights emerged as an important issue. Many of these matters frequently became the focus of party politics in the period from 1874 to 1896.

This was also a period of consolidation. The National Policy that combined tariffs, railways, and settlement of the West was launched not merely as an economic objective but also as a nation-building project that would integrate the various regions of the country. The period saw the emergence of embryonic national institutions, such as the Supreme Court of Canada, the National Gallery of Canada, and the blossoming of ice hockey as the nation's favourite pastime. Canada was also showing signs of change as a process of industrialization and urbanization began to alter the fabric of Canada. The nation would soon discover that it was the destination of choice for many people seeking a new life in North America, and that would bring even more profound and lasting change as Canada entered the twentieth century.

Questions to Consider

1. How did Aboriginal peoples respond to the changes in Canada between 1870 and 1885?

2. How would you characterize the ethnic conflict in Canada after Confederation? Was there a solution to those conflicts? Were they avoidable?

3. What was national about Canada's economic position under John A. Macdonald?

4. Why were federal–provincial relations so acrimonious in Canada after Confederation?

5. How was the socioeconomic situation in Canada changing in the period before 1896?

6. How important are cultural and social developments in creating a new nation, such as Canada?

Critical Thinking Questions

1. What are the implications of historians becoming involved in providing "expert" research services to either governments or other groups that might be involved in litigation?

2. Should the governors-general appointed by the British government have been involved in promoting Canadian culture? Why or why not?

3. Was Louis Riel a hero or traitor?

Suggested Readings

General

Bliss, Michael. *Northern Enterprise: Five Centuries of Canadian Business.* Toronto: McClelland & Stewart, 1987.

Friesen, Gerald. *The Canadian Prairies: A History.* Toronto: University of Toronto Press, 1984.

Norrie, Kenneth, Douglas Owram, and J.C. Herbert Emery. *A History of the Canadian Economy.* 3rd edition. Toronto: Thomson Nelson, 2002.

Prentice, Alison, et al. *Canadian Women: A History.* Toronto: Harcourt Brace, 1996.

Romney, Paul. *Getting It Wrong: How Canadians Forgot Their Past and Imperilled Confederation.* Toronto: University of Toronto Press, 1999.

Waite, P.B. *Canada 1874–1896: Arduous Destiny.* Toronto: McClelland & Stewart, 1971.

National Politics

Cook, Ramsay. *Provincial Autonomy, Minority Rights and the Compact Theory 1867–1921.* Ottawa: Queen's Printer, 1969.

Creighton, Donald. *John A. Macdonald: The Young Politician* and *the Old Chieftain,* 2 Vols. Toronto: University of Toronto Press, 1998.

Thompson, Dale. *Alexander Mackenzie: Clear Grit.* Toronto: Macmillan of Canada, 1960.

Underhill, F.H. *In Search of Canadian Liberalism.* Toronto: Macmillan of Canada, 1960.

Waite, P.B. *The Man from Halifax: Sir John Thompson.* Toronto: University of Toronto Press, 1985.

Provincial Politics

Armstrong, Christopher. *The Politics of Federalism. Ontario's Relations with the Federal Government, 1867–1942.* Toronto: University of Toronto Press, 1981.

Beal, Bob, and Rod Macleod. *Prairie Fire: The 1885 North-West Rebellion.* Edmonton: Hurtig Publishers, 1984.

Bercuson, D.J., ed. *Canada and the Burden of Unity.* Toronto: Macmillan, 1977.

Crunican, Paul. *Priests and Politicians: Manitoba Schools and the Election of 1896.* Toronto: University of Toronto Press, 1974.

Evans, A. Margaret. *Sir Oliver Mowat.* Toronto: University of Toronto Press, 1992.

Miller, J.R. *Equal Rights: The Jesuit Estates Act Controversy.* Montreal and Kingston: McGill-Queen's University Press, 1979.

Ormsby, Margaret. *British Columbia: A History.* Toronto: Macmillan of Canada, 1971.

Silver, Arthur. *The French Canadian Idea of Confederation, 1864–1900.* 2nd edition. Toronto: University of Toronto Press, 1997.

Stanley, George. *The Birth of Western Canada: A History of the Riel Rebellions.* Toronto: University of Toronto Press, 1970.

Economy, Society and Culture

Acheson, T.W., D. Frank, and J. Frost. *Industrialization and the Underdevelopment in the Maritimes, 1880 to 1930.* Toronto: Garamond Press, 1985.

Armstrong, Christopher, and H.V. Nelles. *Monopolies Moment: The Organization and Regulation of Canadian Utilities, 1830–1930.* Philadelphia: Temple University Press, 1996.

Bliss, Michael. *A Living Profit: Studies in the Social History of Canadian Business, 1883–1911.* Toronto: University of Toronto Press, 1974.

Bradbury, Bettina. *Working Families: Age, Gender and Daily Survival in Industrializing Montreal.* Toronto: McClelland & Stewart, 1993.

Forster, Ben. *A Conjunction of Interests: Business, Politics, and Tariffs, 1825–1879.* Toronto: University of Toronto Press, 1986.

Kopas, Paul. *Taking the Air: Ideas and Change in Canada's National Parks.* Vancouver: University of British Columbia Press, 2007.

Linteau, Paul-Andre. *The Promoters' City. Building the Industrial Town of Maisonneuve, 1883–1918.* Toronto: University of Toronto Press, 1985.

Macdonald, Norman. *Canada: Immigration and Colonization, 1841–1903.* Toronto: Macmillan, 1966.

Reid, Dennis. *Our Own Country Canada: Being an Account of the National Aspirations of the Principal Landscape Artists in Montreal and Toronto, 1869–1890.* Ottawa: Queen's Printer, 1979.

Sager, Eric, and Gerald Panting. *Maritime Capital: The Shipping Industry in Atlantic Canada, 1820–1914.* Montreal and Kingston: McGill-Queen's University Press, 1990.

Labour and Women

Bacchi, Carole. *Liberation Deferred? The Ideas of the English Canadian Suffragists, 1877–1918.* Toronto: University of Toronto Press, 1983.

Carter, Sarah. *Capturing Women. The Manipulation of Cultural Imagery in Canada's Prairie West.* Montreal and Kingston: McGill-Queen's University Press, 1997.

Cohen, Margorie G. *Women's Work, Markets and Economic Development in Nineteenth Century Ontario.* Toronto: University of Toronto Press, 1988.

Heron, Craig. *The Canadian Labour Movement: A Short History.* Toronto: James Lorimer, 1996.

McDonald, R.J. *Making Vancouver: Class, Status, and Social Boundaries, 1863–1913.* Vancouver: University of British Columbia Press, 1996.

Parr, Joy. *The Gender of Breadwinners: Women, Men and Change in Two Industrial Towns, 1880–1950.* Toronto: University of Toronto Press, 1990.

Foreign and Defence Policy

Berger, Carl. *The Sense of Power: Studies in the Ideas of Canadian Imperialism, 1867–1914.* Toronto: University of Toronto, 1970.

Brebner, John Bartlet. *The North Atlantic Triangle: The Interplay of Canada, the United States, and Great Britain.* New Haven: Yale University Press, 1945.

Hillmer, Norman, and J.L. Granatstein. *Empire to Umpire: Canada and the World into the 21st Century.* Toronto: Nelson Thomson, 2008.

Perin, Roberto. *Rome in Canada: The Vatican and Canadian Affairs in the Late Victorian Age.* Toronto: University of Toronto Press, 1990.

Roussel, Stéphane. *The North American Democratic Peace: Absence of War and Security Institution-Building in Canada–US relations, 1867–1958.* Montreal and Kingston: McGill-Queen's University Press, 2004.

Stacey, C.P. *Canada and the Age of Conflict: A History of Canadian External Policies,* Vol. 1. Toronto: Macmillan of Canada, 1977.

First Nations and Métis Peoples

Carter, Sarah. *Capturing Women: The Manipulation of Cultural Imagery in Canada's Prairie West.* Montreal and Kingston: McGill-Queen's University Press, 1997.

Carter, Sarah. *Lost Harvests: Prairie Indian Reserve Farmers and Government Policy.* Montreal and Kingston: McGill-Queen's University Press, 1997.

Ens, Gerhard J. *Homeland to Hinterland: The Changing Worlds of the Red River Metis in the Nineteenth Century.* Toronto: University of Toronto Press, 1996.

Flanagan, Thomas. *Riel and the Rebellion: 1885 Reconsidered.* Toronto: University of Toronto Press, 2000.

Harris, R. Cole. *Making Native Space: Colonialism, Resistance and Reserves in British Columbia.* Vancouver: University of British Columbia Press, 2002.

Lux, Maureen K. *Disease, Medicine and Canadian Plains Native People, 1880–1940.* Toronto: University of Toronto Press, 2001.

Miller, J.R. *Lethal Legacy: Current Native Controversies in Canada.* Toronto: McClelland & Stewart, 2004.

Stonechild, Blair, and Bill Waiser. *Loyal Till Death: Indians and the North-West Rebellion.* Calgary: Fifth House, 1997.

Notes

1   *The Pic-Nic Speeches Delivered in the Province of Ontario during the Summer of 1877*. Published by the Reform Association of the Province of Ontario, and prepared for the Press by the Secretary, Mr. G.R. Pattullo, of the Woodstock "Sentinel." (Toronto: Globe Printing and Publishing, 1878).

2   David E. Smith, "Party Government in Canada," in R. Kenneth Carty, ed., *Canadian Political System: A Reader* (Peterborough: Broadview Press, 1992), 531–562.

3   P.B. Waite, *Canada, 1874–1896: Arduous Destiny* (Toronto: McClelland & Stewart, 1971), 19.

4   Ben Forster, "Alexander Mackenzie," in *Dictionary of Canadian Biography Online*, http://www.biographi.ca/EN/ShowBio.asp?BioId=40374.

5   Quoted in Ben Forster, "Frederick Temple Blackwood, Marquess of Dufferin" *Dictionary of Canadian Biography Online*, http://www.biographi.ca/009004-119.01-e.php?BioId=40683.

6   Barbara J. Messamore, *Canada's Governors General, 1847–1878: Biography and Constitutional Evolution* (Toronto: University of Toronto Press, 2006), especially 177–213.

7   Quoted in W.S. Wallace, "The Growth of Canadian National Feeling," *Canadian Historical Review* 1, 2 (June 1920): 143–150.

8   Quoted in Waite, *Canada 1874–1896*, 91.

9   Quoted in C.M. Wallace, Sir Leonard Tilley, *Canadian Dictionary Online*, http://www.biographi.ca/EN/ShowBio.asp?BioId=40589.

10 Quoted in Waite, *Canada 1874–1896*, 112.

11 Messamore, *Canada's Governors General, 1847–1878*, 191.

12 Robert M. Stamp, *Royal Rebels. Princess Louise & the Marquis of Lorne* (Toronto: Dundurn Press, 1988), 159.

13 Stamp, *Royal Rebels*, 186.

14 Andrew C. Isenburg, *The Destruction of the Bison: An Environmental History 1750–1920* (New York: Cambridge University Press, 2000), 1–9.

15 The text of the treaties is available at http://www.ainc-inac.gc.ca/al/hts/tgu/index-eng.asp.

16 *Regina v. Johnston*, Saskatchewan Court of Appeal, 17 March 1966, http://library2.usask.ca/native/cnlc/vol06/447.html.

17 The text of Treaty Six can be viewed at http://www.ainc-inac.gc.ca/al/hts/tgu/pubs/t6/trty6-eng.asp. See also, A. Blair Stonechild, "The Indian View of the 1885 Uprising," in J.R. Miller, ed., *Sweet Promises. A Reader on Indian-White Relations in Canada* (Toronto: University of Toronto Press, 1991).

18 D.N. Sprague, *Canada and the Métis, 1869–1885* (Waterloo: Wilfrid Laurier University Press, 1988).

19 Thomas Flanagan and Gerhard Ens, "Métis Lands Grants in Manitoba: A Statistical Study," *Histoire sociale/Social History* XXVII, 53 (May, 1994).

20 J. R. Miller, "From Riel to the Métis," *Canadian Historical Review* LXIX, 1 (1988), p. 7.

21 Maureen K. Lux, *Disease, Medicine and Canadian Plains Native People, 1880–1940* (Toronto: University of Toronto Press, 2001).

22 *Dictionary of Canadian Biography Online*, http://www.biographi.ca/EN/ShowBio.asp?BioId=40390&query=.

23 Full text of the decision can be found at http://library2.usask.ca/native/cnlc/vol02/541.html.

24 Quoted in C.P. Stacey, *Canada and the Age of Conflict: A History of Canadian External Policies, 1867–1921* (Toronto, University of Toronto Press, 1992), 1–2.

25 Quoted in Stacey, *Canada and the Age of Conflict*, 41.

3

Canada's Century: 1896–1914

*I*n 1909, Methodist minister J.S. Woodsworth published a landmark study on immigration to Canada, *Strangers Within Our Gates*. For the preceding two years, as superintendent of the Methodist church's All People's Mission in Winnipeg's north-end slum, he had arranged for English classes, religious instruction, and emergency assistance for newcomers, and was a tireless advocate for measures like compulsory education, more playgrounds, and unemployment insurance.

Still, Woodsworth shared the dominant view that for immigrants to succeed they had to adopt Anglo-Protestant norms and values. Among the groups he highlighted in his book were Russian Jews who, under the Tsar, were denied land, were confined to jobs like peddling, and had faced deadly pogroms, which were mob attacks that authorities allowed and even sometimes arranged. Woodsworth wrote of a Jewish migrant who arrived in Fort Qu'Appelle, Saskatchewan, in 1903. The immigrant's son spoke of letters the father had sent from Canada "full of poetry" about the "green

grass, the fresh air, the woods, the ponds, the birds—and one hundred and sixty acres [of farmland] for ten dollars." The rest of the family, eight in all, followed in 1905. They initially survived on $4 weekly, one-third of that earned by an average urban labourer. However, within a couple of years they had all learned English and boasted a two-storey home, and the lad who spoke of being inspired by his father's letters had obtained work as a messenger boy with the Great North Western Telegraph Company. Woodsworth implored his readers to help such well-intentioned immigrants—in the case of this lad so that he "become[s] a man of high ideals," rather than, in reflecting one stereotype of Jews, "a money-making sceptic."

Introduction

While Canada's early years were marked by a faltering economy and considerable self-doubt about the nation's future, the end of the nineteenth century ushered in a period of rapid growth, expansion, dynamism, and increasing optimism. Between 1896 and 1914, Canada's population increased from 5.1 million to 7.9 million. Internal migration and immigration transformed the West: Between 1891 and 1911 the population of Manitoba rose from 152 000 to 461 000, and British Columbia's, from 98 000 to 392 000. In Saskatchewan and Alberta, where the first census was taken in 1901, the increase by 1911 was from 91 000 to 492 000 and 73 000 to 374 000, respectively. Yet, like immigrants whose experiences ranged from great hopes and success to racism and despair, the Canada of the late nineteenth and early twentieth centuries was a land of increasing complexity and contradictions.

Cities, industry, retail establishments and financial institutions all expanded and modernized at an unprecedented rate, though so too did concerns over resource depletion, urban slums, corporate concentration, class conflict, and moral and social degeneration. It was a period when new captains of industry were held up as heroes, but also one when demands increased for the greater regulation of capital. It was a time when farms mechanized and record output was achieved, but worry abounded in rural Canada over depopulation and anger rose over the perception of urban industrial and financial interests as dominating Canada's political and economic agenda. Canada was expanding and integrating with new provinces, new mass-circulation newspapers, more transcontinental railways, telegraphs, telephones, and the introduction of the wireless radio transmitter in 1901, invented by Italian Guglielmo Marconi. The period also witnessed more intense, defensive, and backward-looking clerico-*nationalisme* in Quebec, and the persistence of strong regional sentiment in the West and the Maritimes. It was a period when imperialists gushed about Canada rising to premier status within the British Empire, but also when the politics of loyalty to Britain brought tremendous division to the country.

This chapter will describe what historians Ramsay Cook and Robert Craig Brown labelled as "A Nation Transformed."[1] It will show why major developments both inspired and concerned Canadians; discuss what groups benefited and suffered; examine the relationship of various trends to emerging social movements, early social welfare, new government regulations, and Canada's external relations; and assess how accelerating change was managed by Canada's political leaders.

Laurier and the New Liberal Era

On June 23, 1896, nearly 20 years of consecutive federal Conservative governments ended when Wilfrid Laurier became Canada's first French-Canadian prime minister. Born in 1841 in Saint-Lin-Laurentides, Quebec, Laurier grew up in a family where politics was a daily staple. His father was a militia lieutenant, justice of the peace, and mayor. Convinced his son needed to know English, Laurier was sent to live with the family of John Murray, a Scottish Presbyterian, in New Glasgow, Quebec, at age 11, where he learned to speak the language with a lilt that later proved highly appealing to Anglo-Canadians. From Murray and his extensive personal library, Laurier also developed a love for the works of literary greats, such as Shakespeare, Milton, and Burns, and the capacity to utilize English with considerable panache. At 13, he was enrolled in the Jesuit-run L'Assomption College, and after went to McGill University, where he graduated with a law degree in 1864.

Politically, Laurier first became linked with the Rouge and opposed Confederation, but by 1871, he accepted Confederation as a *fait accompli*, switched allegiance to the Liberals, and was elected provincially to represent Drummond-Arthabaska in the eastern townships. Soon bored with provincial politics, he ran successfully for the Liberals in 1874 in the same riding for the federal Parliament. In June 1877, in a defining moment of his political career, he made a powerful speech in Quebec City in which he brilliantly dissociated Liberalism—which the Catholic Church still cast as heretical—from European revolutionaries and anti-clerical elements within the Rouge. With Edward Blake losing the 1883 and 1887 elections, the Liberals, in trying to reinvigorate the party, nominated the young, charismatic, and fluently bilingual Laurier as their new leader.

Laurier benefited from a Conservative party that had fallen into disarray following Macdonald's death. Laurier's opponent in the 1896 federal election was the 74-year-old 30-year parliamentary veteran Charles Tupper, who came across as yesterday's man. Laurier promised voters a "sunny" compromise on the still vexing Manitoba school question. By having turned away from free trade to endorse a revenue tariff, which was milder than the National Policy protectionism of the Tories, Laurier made some headway among Montreal and Toronto business interests without alienating the Liberals' freer trade constituency. The Liberals triumphed with 117 seats, compared with 86 for the Conservatives.

June 23, 1896: Laurier elected prime minister.

The new prime minister prioritized national unity. Although sympathetic—especially given his background—to the aggrieved French and Catholic minority in Manitoba, he would not run roughshod over Anglo opinion and provincial control over education. Laurier sent two Quebec MPs—Minister of Public Works Israel Tarte and the 28-year-old Henri Bourassa—to negotiate with Manitoba's provincial Liberal government under Thomas Greenway. The only concession Greenway offered was a half-hour of optional Catholic education at the end of the regular school day. French Catholics were outraged, but Laurier, contrary to Bourassa's recommendation, accepted the offer because he believed nothing more could be obtained at the present time. He also requested that a papal delegate be sent to Canada to assess the situation, hoping that a sympathetic report would subdue Catholic and French-Canadian anger. In March 1897, Monsignor Merry del Val arrived, one of the Pope's closest advisors. Several conversations with Laurier, and a trip west, convinced him that Manitoba's offer was the only realistic option for the time being.

Pope Leo XIII's encyclical *Affari Vos* soon followed in which he wrote that the settlement, though "defective," should not prevent Catholics from accepting "partial satisfaction."[2]

Laurier's desire to find the sweet spot of compromise also became evident with trade policy. He did not pursue significant adjustments to the tariff, a position supported by business and most of Canada's fledgling labour movement, who feared freer trade with America would mean lost jobs. Indeed, in 1897, the U.S. Congress passed the Dingley tariff, which substantially increased rates against most imports in order to protect U.S. jobs. However, Laurier managed to garner positive feedback from free traders and millions of Anglo-Canadians by announcing in 1897 an imperial trade preference as high as 25 percent.

The tariff situation presented Laurier with other challenges. Towards the end of the century, Ontario Liberal governments under Arthur Hardy and then after 1900 under George Ross, being unable to convince Laurier to impose stiff countervailing duties against the Dingley tariff—as Laurier wanted to avoid a trade war—imposed new taxes on exports of unprocessed timber and minerals, with the hope that it would compel processing in Canada. Ontario claimed such action was constitutionally permissible because of its control over resources, but investors demanded that Ottawa disallow the provincial legislation because it invaded federal control over international trade and commerce. Unlike Macdonald, Laurier sought to avoid federal–provincial confrontation and let the legislation stand, which, in the case of timber, did generate more processing and created thousands of jobs, particularly in the Georgian Bay area.

1897: Crow's Nest Pass rate.

Farmers hoping for freer trade remained disgruntled, as they were with the monopoly status still enjoyed by the Canadian Pacific Railway (CPR) throughout large parts of the West. However, in September 1897, Laurier's government agreed to provide the CPR with an annual subsidy of $1100 for each 1.5 kilometres of track for some 563 kilometres through mountainous terrain, and in exchange the railway agreed to lower by approximately 15 percent the price of transporting wheat east and a variety of settler goods shipped west. The arrangement became known as the Crow's Nest Pass rate. Critics said it reinforced the prairies as a producer of raw materials and receiver of processed goods, and thus the region's disadvantaged status within Confederation.

Another source of potential controversy was prohibition. Powerful temperance groups like the Dominion Alliance and the Women's Christian Temperance Union argued that alcohol was the key factor behind social problems, like growing urban crime and venereal disease. During the election campaign, Laurier promised a public vote on the issue. It occurred in September 1898; a razor-thin majority of 51.2 percent supported prohibition. The results were divided on linguistic grounds with every Anglo province in favour, but in Quebec, where wine played an important role in Catholic services, only 18.8 percent voted yes. Laurier refused to take action, using as an excuse the fact that only 44 percent of eligible voters cast ballots. Temperance forces turned their attention to the provincial level, where by 1907 every province had passed legislation to allow communities to prohibit the sale, production, and public consumption of alcohol.

Imperialism, Alaska, and South Africa

Britain's colonial secretary, Joseph Chamberlain, in large part to counter rising German military strength and expanding colonial ambitions, began pushing hard to establish an Imperial Federation that would speak and act as one. Laurier often waxed eloquently, enthusiastically, and—as an admirer of British parliamentary traditions—sincerely about the Empire as advancing civilization, and maintained that if the Mother Country were imperilled, it could count on Canada's help. He also knew, though, that it would be economically and politically disastrous for Canada to automatically commit to every imperial venture.

Imperialist sentiment was ascendant, especially with Queen Victoria's 1897 diamond anniversary on the throne. The jubilee for the Queen in London was a gloriously opulent event with delegations and colour guards coming from around the globe. Laurier basked in its splendour, in hobnobbing with world leaders, and in his private audience with the Queen at Buckingham Palace, where he accepted a knighthood. His grandiloquent speeches heralding the glories of the Empire made him a favourite with the British media and won him many accolades in the Anglo-Canadian press. In spite of this show, in private meetings with Neville Chamberlain and other leaders of the self-governing British dominions, Laurier rejected the idea of an imperial federation.

The same year as the diamond jubilee, in the far-off reaches of the Yukon, at a place called Rabbit Creek, George Carmack, Skookum Jim, and Tagish Charlie discovered gold. Once word leaked, thousands raced north as part of the Klondike gold rush, but the area known as the panhandle (the entry point into the gold fields that stretched south from Alaska down the Pacific coastline) remained disputed. In the fall of 1897, Laurier arrived in Washington with British representative Sir Louis Davies for talks with State Department officials and President William McKinley. The result was an Anglo-American joint commission to settle all outstanding bilateral problems in the north that also included disputes between American and Canadian sealers and fishers.

The commission first convened in Quebec City in 1898. The British delegate, Lord Herschell, proved a strong and effective advocate for Canada. Initially, the Americans offered to lease a strip of land to provide Canada with control over an access route to the gold fields, but when word leaked to the press and produced angry reactions throughout the U.S. northwest, the offer was withdrawn.

With negotiations stalemated, there came calls for, and soon the establishment of, an international arbitration committee. Talks were profoundly affected by Herschell's death in 1899, and two years later by McKinley's assassination, and by his replacement with Theodore Roosevelt, who insisted that Canada did not have a legitimate claim. As U.S. representatives on the arbitration committee, Roosevelt appointed Secretary of War Elihu Root (who was on record as supporting American claims) and Massachusetts Senator Henry Cabot Lodge, who called the Canadian case baseless. Canadian representatives were equally partisan, and Canada expected the new British representative, Lord Alverstone, to be an ally.

1897: Gold discovered in the Yukon.

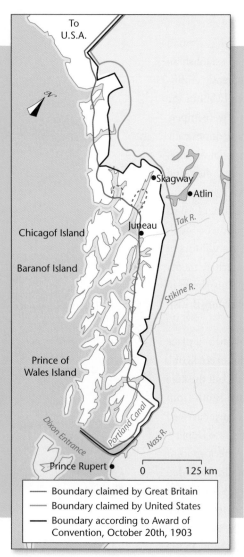

Map 3.1
Competing Claims in Alaska

Boundary claimed by Great Britain
Boundary claimed by United States
Boundary according to Award of Convention, October 20th, 1903

(Map labels: To U.S.A.; Skagway; Atlin; Chicagof Island; Juneau; Tak R.; Baranof Island; Stikine R.; Prince of Wales Island; Dixon Entrance; Portland Canal; Nass R.; Prince Rupert; 0 — 125 km)

October 11, 1899:

Boer War begins.

The belief that Britain would support Canada on the panhandle reflected not only a long and close association between the two but also growing sentiment in English Canada for imperialism. Led by prominent Anglo-Protestants, Canadian imperialists did not speak of Canada as a colony, but as a loyal dominion that would, because of its wide-open space for settlement, vast resources, and vigour of its northern population, eventually rise to a leadership role within the Empire. Imperialists portrayed the United States as coveting Canada and Canada's association with the Empire as keeping the Americans at bay. They also cast French Canadians as loyal to the Crown because they appreciated the rights provided to them as far back as the *Quebec Act*. Through the Empire, it was also maintained, Canada would share in God's plan, and what was called the "white man's burden," to spread civilization and Christianity to inferior peoples. Yet Canada would be treated by Britain as a very junior partner. It was portrayed in popular British literature as a vast, wild frontier, populated by Native savages, fur traders, cowboys, and mounted police, and where high culture was absent. What many Canadians perceived as a British sense of superiority also manifested through the position of the general officer commanding (GOC), a post created in 1880 to which a senior British officer was appointed to manage Canada's military. Most GOCs understandably concluded that Canada's military was in a sad state, something they attributed to underfunding and rampant patronage that resulted in the promotion of well-connected incompetents. In their effort to professionalize Canada's military, several GOCs were fired because they ignored or countermanded directives from Canada's minister of militia and defence, whom they regarded as placing partisan political considerations above achieving military effectiveness.

One of the most contentious GOCs was Major-General Sir Edward Thomas Henry Hutton. Soon after being appointed to the post in 1898, he got into disputes with Minister of Militia and Defence Frederick Borden, who struck down two of Hutton's officer appointees because they were Conservatives. Within a year, Hutton was assigned to South Africa to command troops in the Boer War.

The roots of this conflict lay in Britain's attempts to consolidate its hold over mineral-rich southern Africa, a struggle that for decades had pitted them against the Dutch Afrikaners, or *Boers*, a Dutch word meaning "farmer." A major mineral discovery in 1886 in the Boer-administered Transvaal region drew thousands of British prospectors from the neighbouring Cape Colony. Fearing a loss of control, the Boers denied British newcomers voting rights and more heavily taxed their mining operations. In September 1899, Chamberlain issued an ultimatum to the Boers demanding full equality for British residents. Concluding that war was unavoidable, Afrikaner leader Paul Krugar replied with his own ultimatum, giving Britain 48 hours to withdraw its troops from the Transvaal border or the Boer republics would declare war, which they did on October 11.

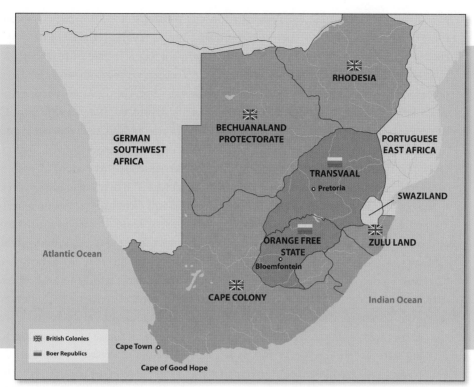

Map 3.2
South Africa at the Time of the Boer War

Source: Canadian War Museum.

Laurier condemned Boer persecution of British settlers but would not declare Canada's willingness to send troops, fearing the costs of conflict, both monetary and human, as well as its potentially deleterious impact on Canadian unity. He initially sought a technical excuse to avoid involvement, stating that Canada's *Militia Act* prohibited participation in a foreign war that did not involve the defence of Canada. Much of French Canada sympathized with the Boers because of their resistance to the British and feelings of kinship with a farming population seeking to retain their culture and homeland in the face of an aggressive outside force. Newspapers like the *Farmer's Weekly Sun* and labour newspapers like the Winnipeg-based *Voice* cast the British as being motivated by greed. Notable opposition to Canadian involvement was also evident in the Maritimes and among Canada's substantial German and Irish-Catholic populations. Pro-war opinion, namely to save the besieged Anglo settlers and to stand by Britain, resonated loudly throughout much of English Canada, particularly in southern Ontario.

On October 3, a week before the war started, Colonial Secretary Chamberlain sent out telegrams to all of the Empire's self-governing dominions, thanking them for their generous offer to send troops. The message was leaked to and printed in the *Canadian Military Gazette* and soon was splashed across newspaper front pages throughout Canada; however, Canada had made no such pledge. The British government was appealing directly to the many Canadians who supported intervention in order to pressure Laurier to send troops.

On October 12, the day after the war began, Laurier faced a divided cabinet. Tarte and Bourassa vigorously opposed participation, while Frederick Borden, Trade and Commerce

Minister Richard Cartwright, and Postmaster General William Mulock demanded Canadian involvement. Laurier offered a compromise: Canada would provide a battalion of 1000 men commanded by a Canadian, though financed and paid for by Britain once arriving in South Africa. Laurier also explicitly stated that this decision was not to be construed as a precedent for Canadian involvement in future imperial wars. The measure was passed as an Order in Council to avoid a divisive parliamentary debate, but not everything could be papered over. Bourassa resigned from the Liberal caucus to sit as an independent and introduced a measure into the House of Commons opposing Canadian participation. Only nine French-Canadian MPs—five Tories and four Liberals—backed it.

Throughout much of English-speaking Canada, there was an overwhelming response to the call for volunteers. In Nelson, British Columbia, only eight men were chosen from 70 applicants. Many men sought to escape from low-paying or humdrum jobs, anticipated an exotic adventure in Africa, and wanted a chance to prove their mettle. Most thought the campaign would be low risk and that British Empire forces would easily crush the Boers. The most common occupations among volunteers were "clerks, grocers, bookkeepers, carpenters, machinists, painters, plumbers, blacksmiths, and electricians."[3] Also, many volunteers were seasonal workers and joining up provided them with employment before the onset of winter shut down activities such as construction. Those with closer ties to England were also more eager to join, as 30 percent of volunteers were British-born at a time when they accounted for 7 percent of Canada's population. By contrast, French-speaking Canadians made up only 3 percent of those who applied to fight in South Africa.

Those accepted for service formed the 2nd Battalion (Special Service), Royal Canadian Regiment. They left Quebec City on October 30 for a month-long voyage to Cape Town on board the *SS Sardinian*, a 25-year-old converted cattle liner designed to carry 700. Once there, they spent the next two months training and coping with insects, extreme heat, and disease, like typhoid fever, which ultimately claimed more lives than Boer bullets.

February 1900: Canadian troops victorious at Paardeberg.

With British casualties mounting against an effective Boer militia, the Canadians were called to action. Their objective was Kimberley, a diamond-mining town on the border between the Cape Colony and the Orange Free State. The Boers made their stand just to the south at Paardeberg Drift. Green Canadian troops, after taking 80 casualties and faltering during the first day's fighting, launched a night-time advance on February 18. Holding hands so they would not stray from each other, they found themselves with an excellent vantage point over the Boers who surrendered. News of the victory sparked celebrations across Canada, including one in Toronto estimated to have had 100 000 people in attendance.

Nonetheless, the Boers continued to have success, especially through the use of hit and run guerrilla tactics. Although the superior British firepower and 400 000 soldiers it committed to the conflict eventually produced victory, the war grew less popular as British losses reached 22 000, and as Britain's military adopted controversial tactics, such as a scorched earth policy, and created concentration camps in which more than 25 000 Boer women and children died, primarily from disease. Morale among Canadian troops declined as the war dragged on, and most men refused to extend their term of service beyond the one-year obligation. By the time the war ended in May 1902, 7368 Canadians had volunteered, with 89 killed in action, 181 dying from disease, and 252 wounded.

A popular depiction of the Canadian victory at Paardeberg drawn by Arthur H. Hilder, which was distributed by the Toronto Globe *as part of a special supplement.*

Having forged a workable compromise on Canadian involvement in the Boer War, and with the Canadian economy on the upswing, Laurier entered the November 1900 federal election in a strong position. His easy-going confidence, personal charm, and eloquence as a speaker contrasted sharply with Tupper, who came across as old and blustering. The Liberals gained 11 seats over 1896, reaching 128 compared with 79 for the Conservatives.

February 1901: Robert Borden becomes Conservative leader.

In February 1901, Tupper retired as Conservative leader and was replaced by Robert Borden. Born in 1854 in Grand Pré, Nova Scotia, Borden's public persona reflected the small agricultural community in which he was raised—unpretentious, hardworking, and reserved. At 20, he read for the bar, but as there was no law school in Halifax, he qualified by apprenticing at the firm of Weatherbe and Graham, where six years later he became a senior partner. Although many considered him too dull for politics, he successfully ran for Parliament in Halifax in 1896 and quickly established a reputation for being effective and fair on parliamentary committees. As Conservative leader, he stayed clear of internal party strife, had few enemies, and initially focused on rebuilding a weakened party organization.

Laurier, too, faced internal party challenges. In autumn 1902, upon returning from an imperial conference in London, he fired his powerful public works minister, Israel Tarte, for openly contradicting recent comments by Laurier that the government was not pursuing free trade with America. The imperial conference had also proven difficult because Chamberlain again sought to tighten the bonds

Robert Borden in 1901.

of the Empire. A coy Laurier said that Canada was ready to discuss imperial federation, but only on the condition of obtaining a meaningful role in directing the affairs of the Empire, something he knew Canadian imperialists wanted but that Britain would not grant. Frustrated with Laurier's manoeuvring, Chamberlain, in private correspondence, called him "the damn dancin' master."[4]

The next year it became evident that Canada could not depend upon Britain to safeguard its interests. With Roosevelt continuing to take a hard line on the Alaska panhandle, London concluded that supporting Canadian claims in the remote north was not worth the risk of worsening relations with America. Secret instructions were sent to Lord Alverstone to forbid a deadlocked report—code for him to side with the Americans if he thought their claim was legitimate. In October, Alverstone did exactly that. Canada's two representatives symbolically resigned from the arbitration committee. Many Canadians spoke of betrayal, but the bonds of loyalty to the Mother Country in English-speaking Canada enabled the imperialist cause to weather the storm.

Cross-Currents in Canada's New Century

Strong opposition to imperialism in Quebec partly reflected an insular and devout Francophone society. The *ultramontaine* creed, which stressed the need for self-improvement through Catholicism, was a major force. The church struggled to deal with modernization; it worried that the scope and pace of industrialization was importing Anglo-Protestant values, namely individualism and an obsession with moneymaking. It also fretted over the flow of French-Canadians to New England for work, such as in timber operations and textile factories. Most clergy supported efforts to promote rural colonization as farming was viewed as godly work and central to Québécois society. The church also endorsed small-scale francophone-run businesses over large corporate enterprises that were usually owned by outsiders and operated in English. Outside the church, Jean-Paul Tardival, the American-born editor of the newspaper *La Verité*, advocated Quebec separatism to protect what he viewed as a French-Catholic "race." More prominent, however, was Henri Bourassa, who in 1903 formed the *Ligue nationaliste* that advocated for a bilingual Canada but that in Quebec emphasized the central role of the Catholic Church in providing moral strength and social stability.

Provincial governments in Quebec—under Liberals Felix Marchard (1897–1900), Napoleon Parent (1900–1905), and Lomer Gouin (1905–1920)—sent mixed messages. They paid homage to the Catholic Church and the province's rural values, yet they also strongly courted foreign investment to create jobs, promote modernization, and build government revenue. American investment poured into pulp and paper operations, which experienced massive growth with an 80 percent expansion in U.S. newspaper circulation between 1870 and 1909. Foreign investment also fuelled new mining operations in gold, copper, asbestos, and bauxite for aluminum (for which in 1902 the company Alcan founded a northern Quebec town that it named after itself).

Across the country, accelerating economic growth generated widespread optimism. In January 1904, in a speech at the recently established Canadian Club in Ottawa, Wilfrid Laurier uttered the most memorable words of his political career, declaring that "as the nineteenth century was that of the United States, so, I think, the twentieth century shall be filled by Canada." That year, Laurier revealed to Parliament plans for a second transcontinental railway. The Grand Trunk was selected for the project, for which it created a subsidiary, the Grand Trunk Pacific, that received subsidies, tax breaks, and land grants. The federal government hoped that the Grand Trunk would cooperate with the western-based Canadian Northern railway. However, the Canadian Northern responded to the new competition by launching its own transcontinental railway, which eventually resulted in an overbuilt and money-losing network.

1904: Grand Trunk Pacific and Canadian Northern announce new transcontinental railways.

With a federal election approaching, Borden sought to hammer Laurier on the railway deal. At the time, most Canadians perceived the new transcontinentals as a sign of growing prosperity, and that November they gave the Liberals an increased majority of 137 seats, compared with 70 for the Conservatives. During the election, Laurier spoke of how recent, and spectacular, growth in the prairies had paved the way for the creation of new provinces. The next year, the Autonomy Bills created Alberta and Saskatchewan. The process was not without controversy, though. One source of debate was the decision to create two provinces rather than one, something that, it was charged, resulted from partisanship. F.W.G. Haultain, who ran the North-West Territories government, had supported the Conservatives in 1904. Some opined that Laurier did not want to place too much power in one large provincial government, very possibly under Haultain's direction. By splitting the territory, it was believed that the Liberals would control at least one province, especially since two Liberals, Walter Scott in Saskatchewan and Alexander Rutherford in Alberta, were asked to form the governments that would call the first provincial elections. Both built political machines that would keep the Liberals in power in Alberta until 1921 and in Saskatchewan until 1929. Anger was expressed because in the new provinces the federal government maintained control over land and sub-surface mineral rights in order to better pursue national projects, such as railway development, and to direct settlement.

Further controversy erupted over state funding for separate and bilingual schools. Under the 1875 *Territories Act*, Protestants or Catholics could tax themselves to create separate, government-supported, schools, but things changed as more non-Francophones moved west. In 1893, monetary support for French education ended, and in 1901 the territorial government gained control over all schools. Laurier sent his Irish Catholic justice minister, Charles Fitzpatrick, and Henri Bourassa, accompanied by papal delegate Monsignor Donato Sbaretti, to the West to negotiate on schools in the territories. The result appeared to return things to the situation under the 1875 legislation; however, Interior Minister Clifford Sifton, Laurier's most prominent Western Canadian MP, resigned from the government when hearing of the deal, as he believed that a common language was essential to building unity, especially with many immigrants arriving in the West. The rift worried Laurier, especially with rumblings that Finance Minister W.S. Fielding might follow Sifton. Although Laurier did not ask Sifton to rejoin the cabinet, as there were rumours of corruption in the Ministry of the Interior, he still asked him to make recommendations on redrafting the education rules, which, as a result, reverted to the 1901 structure. An outraged Bourassa left federal politics.

1905: Autonomy Bills create Alberta and Saskatchewan.

Helping Laurier weather such political storms were the many signs of strong economic growth and modernization. Urban expansion was unprecedented. Between 1891 and 1911, the number of Canadians living in communities of 1000 or more rose from 35 percent to 42 percent of the population. To many, cities were centres of progress, as epitomized by electric street lighting, giant department stores, mass public transportation, and universities. Cities became centres for a wide array of entertainment and recreation. Despite snide commentary about lowbrow influences, people flocked to see the new phenomenon of motion pictures at places like Montreal's ornate 1000-seat Palais Royale, which opened its doors in 1904.

Sports boomed in cities. Numerous communities constructed public swimming pools, gymnasiums, tennis courts, lawn-bowling facilities, and golf courses. Sports were encouraged for young men as a means to stay physically vigorous, given the increasing number of sedentary jobs, and to avoid the troubling temptations of urban life. Sports were also promoted as a way to encourage cooperation and teamwork. Many companies sponsored teams to build employee loyalty and to counter class conflict. Young boys, who were thought to be becoming physically soft in school, were encouraged to participate in sports or to join the Scouts or Cadets (the latter appearing in 1909 as a result of a massive donation from Lord Strathcona, former head of the Hudson's Bay Company and the Canadian Pacific Railway), which were cast as building discipline, loyalty, and patriotism.

Cycling became an urban rage, both for transportation and healthy recreation. Bikes became easier to ride with improvements over the early oversized front wheel design. Between 1893 and 1908, the price of a new bike as advertised in the Eaton's department store catalogue plummeted from $165 to $11.95. Cycling was also accepted as a respectable form of exercise for women. There was growing commentary about the new, more active and public woman, as opposed to the passive and ornamental Victorian ideal. New bicycle fashions and other sportswear for women provided far more freedom of movement than the corsets, hoops, and crinolines of the nineteenth century, such as by incorporating bloomers (essentially baggy trousers) as undergarments. Women participated in a variety of sports, including basketball, ice hockey, tennis, and golf. However, caution was expressed that their activities not become too vigorous, as doctors said that too much exercise would make the pelvic muscles less flexible for childbirth, or lead to "uterine displacement … [that was] associated with dysmenorrheal sterility."[5]

With the cities came the construction of stadiums and arenas and the rise of spectator sports. This was buttressed by mass distribution of newspapers that produced new features to attract readers, one of the most popular being the sports page. Railways began offering special excursions to neighbouring communities to see local teams play. Many expressed the view that sports should remain the realm of amateurs to avoid corruption and poor sportsmanship, but with paying customers, the trend was towards professionalization.

In 1897 the Canadian Intercollegiate Rugby Football Union was formed, centred in Ontario and Anglo-Quebec universities. Interest grew to the point where a new trophy was donated in 1909 by Governor-General Earl Grey that still bears his name for the champion of the Canadian Football League. Ice hockey emerged as Canada's most popular winter sport by 1900. The Stanley Cup, which was donated in 1893 by Lord Stanley of Preston, then Canada's governor-general, was initially a challenge trophy, meaning that any team could compete for it. An example is in 1905 when a squad from Dawson City in the Yukon lost a two-game tournament against the Ottawa Silver Seven by the combined score of 23–2. By 1909, there were two professional leagues: the National Hockey Association and the Pacific Coast Hockey Association, and starting in 1915, only their teams could compete for the Stanley Cup. This privilege was taken over by the National Hockey League in 1926, as the other leagues folded.

In the cities, Canadians were enthralled with technological advances that were presented as promising a better life to all. At Toronto's annual Canadian National Exhibition, the biggest draw was Manufacturers' Hall, a cavernous building where companies displayed their latest innovations. More and more sources venerated businessmen and industrialists as heroes propelling Canada to new heights.

Industrial and manufacturing activity expanded at a record pace, though overall, Canada's economy remained staple-driven, as in 1910 industrial products accounted for 22.5 percent of the country's gross domestic product, which was its annual total value of goods and services. Still, between 1900 and 1912, the number of companies incorporated per year in Canada soared from 53 to 658, and total capitalization of Canadian industry registered an even more impressive rise, going from $12.9 million to $490.6 million. Overwhelmingly, such activity congregated in southern Ontario and southern Quebec because of their larger labour and capital pools, superior transportation networks, and closer proximity to major American markets.

The late nineteenth and early twentieth centuries brought more investment into Canada, as well as foreign ownership. Whereas investment from Britain—still the principal source for Canada—tended to go into bonds, a large percentage of American money went into equity investment (namely shares in companies) and direct investments to establish Canadian-based branch plants of U.S. firms in order to bypass Canada's steep tariffs. By 1909, U.S. investment in Canada reached $254 million, though a year later, British investment in Canada totalled $1.4 billion.

Larger urban markets, rising incomes, and improved transportation reinforced the growing dominance of major department stores, which, despite putting many smaller operations out of business, most Canadians still welcomed for providing greater choice and lower prices. Between 1897 and 1909, Eaton's, which distributed goods across Canada, increased its number of employees from 1600 to 8775. Urban-based financial institutions also underwent massive expansion; between 1901 and 1913, their assets in constant dollars (meaning after inflation was subtracted from the total) nearly tripled to $2.3 billion. Banks consolidated, declining from 37 firms in 1896 to 24 in 1913, but those that remained were stronger and larger, providing 1846 more branches across Canada in 1911 compared with 1900. The Bank of Montreal remained Canada's most significant financial institution, though between 1870 and 1910 its share of total Canadian bank assets dropped from 28.3 to 18 percent, as the Toronto-headquartered Canadian Bank of Commerce and the Montreal-headquartered Royal Bank both gained ground.

Although many people in rural areas worried about the growing influence of urban centres and industrial interests, more farms were doing better than ever. By the turn of the twentieth century, implements such as mechanized manure spreaders, potato diggers, root crop planters, cultivators, hayloaders, and disc harrows had come into widespread use. Over the last two decades of the nineteenth century, the price of a self-binder (an implement that increased wheat productivity 20-fold over manual techniques) was halved to $150. In the West, mechanization, improved farming techniques, better strains of seed (namely faster maturing Red Marquis wheat), and new settlers all played a part in making Canada into a breadbasket for the world. Between 1890 and 1914, seeded areas of wheat rose from 1.1 million to 4.1 million hectares and production from 42.2 million to 161.3 million bushels (1.4 million to 5.6 million cubic metres).

More expensive farmland and industrial jobs, particularly in Ontario, made rural depopulation a major concern. From 1891 to 1901, the province's agricultural districts lost 50 000 people. In Western Canada, farmers claimed that national economic policies, namely high tariffs, were dictated by Central Canadian industrial interests and denied farmers cheaper American products, namely farm implements. Ottawa was also accused, particularly in the West where rail rates were higher, of providing sweetheart deals to Central Canadian railway moguls, conveniently glossing over the fact that lower traffic in the region translated into higher unit costs for rail transport. Grievances also multiplied over the cost of grain storage, especially as the railways owned many grain elevators. Laurier's government established a Board of Railway Commissioners in 1903, a three-judge panel whose job was to ensure fair freight rates. According to historian Ken Cruikshank, the board was even-handed in balancing consumer and railway interests.[6]

Prairie farmers, following the example of those in the American West, created cooperatives, especially for grain storage. The cooperative movement possessed a strong reformist, if not utopian, quality, as its leaders spoke of melding rural, Christian, and sometimes socialist, ideals to produce a truly just society. One of its principal leaders was E.A. Patridge, who in 1906 formed the Manitoba Grain Growers Company, which in six years attracted 27 000 members and handled 28 million bushels (1 million cubic metres) of wheat through its own elevators. Next door, the Saskatchewan Grain Growers Association grew to 1200 locals and 25 000 members by the First World War. In Alberta, the cooperative movement was housed in the United Farmers of Alberta, an advocacy group that, by the end of the First World War, become a highly effective political party.

By no means were all Western Canadians angry, as much of the region was booming. In Winnipeg, Canada's third largest city in 1911 with a population of 150 000, high tariffs had many supporters as nearly 12 000 of the city's workers were employed in manufacturing. All three transcontinental railways went through the city, and in the early twentieth century, Winnipeg trans-shipped more wheat by rail than Chicago. Countless Western Canadian communities promoted themselves as places brimming with opportunities for risk-takers, for those with ingenuity, and for the hard-working. "In forty or fifty years," proclaimed a speaker at the Winnipeg branch of the Canadian Club, "Saskatchewan and Alberta will be greater than Ontario in population, and Winnipeg will have surpassed Toronto and Montreal."[7]

Modernization was also strongly evident in British Columbia. This included in politics where there occurred a trend away from factionalism, in which the province was run almost like a private fiefdom, towards the emergence of more defined, and disciplined, political parties. This was certainly needed, as between 1898 and 1903 British Columbia had five premiers. In 1902, James Dunsmuir, who had made a fortune in coal mining and railway development on Vancouver Island, was forced to resign as premier after trying to arrange for his own railways to benefit from proposed routes on the island. The next year, Richard McBride, who was identified as a Conservative, was appointed by Lieutenant-Governor Sir Henri-Gustave Joly De Lotbinière to take over, and his opponents coalesced into a Liberal opposition. McBride proved an effective leader, remaining in power until 1915. When he took over, British Columbia's debt stood at a crippling $13.5 million. He demanded more money from Ottawa, and the lack of response provided him with a scapegoat for the province's economic problems. After walking out of a 1906 federal–provincial conference, he returned home a hero, and his stand helped him get re-elected later that year. However, also significant was that by that point the provincial economy was rebounding with growing demand and better prices for minerals, lumber, and salmon.

1903: Richard McBride becomes Conservative premier of B.C.

British Columbia's economy largely depended upon primary products. At the outset of the twentieth century, less than 10 percent of its gross provincial product derived from manufacturing. Still, 45 percent of its population lived in communities of 1000 or more, with Vancouver, largely based upon commercial activity, reaching 100 000 residents. The province's dairy and beef cattle farms grew substantially, and between 1881 and 1911, its wheat acreage doubled. During those same years, with the development of refrigerated rail cars, acreage devoted to fruit and vegetable farming expanded six-fold, principally in the Fraser Valley and the Okanagan. British Columbia's salmon canning industry surpassed 1 million cases packed annually in the early twentieth century.

Besides coal on Vancouver Island and the southwestern B.C. mainland, important discoveries of gold and silver were made in the Kootnenays; copper, silver, lead, and zinc in Slocan; and copper in Phoenix. Increasing amounts of B.C. lumber were sent to the prairies for construction, as well as to South America, Asia, and Europe. Foreign investment into British Columbia tripled between 1900 and 1914. Terms for investors were kept favourable, such as 20-year leases on timber limits and low royalties. Whereas in 1900 total investment in B.C. timber was $2 million, by the onset of the First World War it reached $150 million.

While rapid resource development remained high on the province's agenda, moves towards conservation were also growing. New steam-powered machinery, both for cutting and for transporting timber, meant that forests could quickly disappear. As elsewhere in Canada, and across North America, conservation was motivated not only by the desire to preserve nature, which many saw as increasingly threatened by insatiable demand from burgeoning urban centres, but also from the self-interest of capital to scientifically manage a renewable resource. Conservationists were not opposed to development; in fact, many favoured larger corporate enterprises as dominant within the forestry sector. Their reasoning was that larger companies with their more substantial investments would take a longer-term view on resource extraction and practise reforestation, as opposed to smaller companies, which were under great pressure to maximize profits as quickly as possible.

In 1909, Canada participated in the North American Conservation Conference in Washington. Two years later, Clifford Sifton was named to head up a new Commission of Conservation that was to advise the federal government on the management of resources. That same year, Canada signed the Boundary Waters Treaty, which addressed several bilateral concerns, including pollution. Closely related to conservation was increased activity to create national parks, such as Jasper (1907), Elk Island (1913), and Nemiskam (1914) in Alberta, and Mount Revelstoke (1914) in British Columbia.

In the Maritimes, the 1896–1914 period brought a mixed performance. While the populations of Nova Scotia and New Brunswick experienced moderate growth, declining opportunities in Prince Edward Island resulted in a decline from 103 000 to 93 000. Overall, some 100 000 people left the region during the 1890s, which resulted in the Maritimes losing eight seats in Parliament.

Some areas experienced strong economic growth, such as Moncton and Amherst, which were located along the intercolonial railway. Markets for Maritime coal and timber remained strong, in large part to feed industry and urban communities elsewhere. Apple orchards continued expanding in the Annapolis Valley where production topped 1 million bushels (35 000 cubic metres) annually. Maritimers who yearned for the region to be a full participant in industrial modernization often blamed Confederation for its laggard performance. They claimed that the federal government—by creating tariff policies that ignored Maritime industries and by providing poor regional rail subsidies—favoured Ontario and Quebec, where the majority of votes existed. As in the West, such critics largely ignored the fact that compared with Central Canada the Maritimes did not possess the capital, labour pool, or proximity to major North American markets to attract industry. In the 1880s, many of the region's entrepreneurs invested in areas like textiles, sugar refining, and foundries, but they did not have the capital to see them through tough times, with the result being that many went bankrupt or sold their enterprises to Central Canadians, which reinforced regional anger about being dominated, and exploited, by outsiders. The number of branch business outlets in the Maritimes grew from 264 in 1891 to more than 1000 by 1921.

First Peoples

Besides regions, many groups saw themselves as being left behind in the modernizing economy. Not surprisingly, this included the First Peoples. Those who sought to integrate into the white economy were typically employed in low-skilled and low-paying jobs, like in salmon-canning factories in British Columbia. Many performed seasonal work, such as in the logging sector or as hunting guides. Others were reduced to selling hand-crafted trinkets to white tourists.

Indian agents became more arbitrary in directing band life, with the aim of breaking down traditional ways. Through to the First World War, Natives continued to be arrested for partaking in the *potlatch*, a religious ceremony in which gifts were distributed. Natives on reserves who wished to compete in the liberal-capitalist society were frustrated by the Department of Indian Affairs for providing them with tools appropriate for peasant farming. When Natives sought loans for farm machinery, government officials regularly intervened to scuttle the applications, insisting that the Natives were too unreliable to take on debt.

With the arrival of more white settlers and resource development, Natives faced increased pressure to surrender reserve land. Desperate for cash, some bands sold their property; others had little choice about giving up land. Legislation introduced in 1898 empowered the federal government to remove Natives from reserves "next to or partly within a town of 8,000 inhabitants or more."[8] New game and conservation laws impeded the ability of many Natives to support themselves. In 1906, Squamish Chief Joe Capilano travelled to England to present a petition to King Edward VII over federal land policies. Apart from generating some publicity, the effort produced no results because the British maintained that this was an internal Canadian matter.

Native children continued to be placed in church-run residential schools, many of which were boarding institutions located far from their families and bands; the aim was to more effectively root out Native culture. The schools were often overcrowded and the buildings wretched; malnourishment and disease festered, and death rates were incredibly high. Academics were given little emphasis compared with teaching girls "how to become European-style homemakers," and boys "farming and manual skills,"[9] which also saved on costs, as boys chopped wood and performed various farm and building maintenance work and girls cooked food and did the laundry. Children were taught that their traditional beliefs were heathen, they were punished for speaking Native dialects rather than English, they were forced to wear school uniforms, and the boys were required to cut their hair. Physical abuse was common and related not only to the overriding mission to push assimilation but also to the fact that many of the priests and nuns were ill-qualified to teach and some took out their frustrations on the children. In one of many such accounts, at one residential school, a Native boy who spilled too much salt in his oatmeal was told by his teacher, a nun, to eat it. When he refused, she beat him. He ate a spoonful, vomited in the bowl, but was still forced to continue eating. Many Native children ran away, which prompted authorities to move the schools farther from families and bands. There were also several cases of arson, such as at the Mohawk Institute in Brantford, which was destroyed in 1903.

White society expanded to remote northern territories, bringing disease, disruption from alcohol, and, with resource development, interference with wildlife upon which Natives, mostly Inuit, depended for food. In some parts of the north, the combined effects were devastating. In 1902, on Southampton Island in Hudson Bay, an entire band of 68 people perished. Missionaries arrived to educate and to convert, and sought to end Inuit practices like wife-swapping. The federal government maintained that it had no financial responsibilities to the Inuit, as no treaties had been signed with them. It seemed there was little desire to establish treaties, as this gave Ottawa greater latitude to promote resource development, and the Inuit were portrayed as too nomadic to have bona fide claims on particular domains.

New Urban and Workplace Challenges

To the south, rapidly expanding and increasingly complex urban centres generated not only excitement over the prospect of more opportunities and a stronger country but also much hardship and despair. Rudimentary social services were overwhelmed, squalor became more prevalent, and the likelihood for dangerous social unrest seemed to grow more imminent.

Home ownership became more common, but workingmen's homes were commonly just 46 square metres (500 square feet). While electric street lighting replaced kerosene lamps, numerous urban homes remained unwired shacks. Many also lacked internal heating and indoor plumbing, which meant outdoor privy pits, and in most cities, sewer systems and sanitation collection fell far short of demand. More municipal politicians and city elites stressed the need to bring greater professional expertise and rationality to

Source: Library and Archives of Canada, PA-032530.

urban planning. The late nineteenth and early twentieth centuries brought a City Beautiful movement to North America, which emphasized the need for more parks and tree-lined streets, and adorning the urban landscape with statues, arches, and fountains.

Social conditions in many Canadian cities were abysmal. In Montreal, Herbert Brown Ames, a shoe manufacturer, philanthropist, and municipal politician, organized a statistical survey in 1897 that documented a horrid state of affairs for much of Montreal's working class and unemployed who lived in what he called the "City Below the Hill." These neighbourhoods had an infant mortality rate of 20 percent, then the highest recorded figure in North America. In 1911 and 1912, Ottawa saw significant outbreaks of typhus because privies drained into the Ottawa River. Winnipeg, whose civic leaders proclaimed it the "Chicago of the North," had 6000 outdoor toilets in 1905. Middle- and upper-class Canadians increasingly feared poorer neighbourhoods, as they were typically portrayed as places of crime, vice, and general disorder.

Suburban areas expanded, such as Etobicoke outside Toronto, Elmwood outside Winnipeg, and Uplands outside Victoria. Between 1901 and 1914, major cities in Canada doubled in physical space. In part, suburbs grew because of the expansion of streetcar service, the onset of mass production, and the increasing affordability of automobiles. Also key to suburban expansion was the appeal of these areas to those with financial means as a place to get away from congested cities and slums. In the suburbs, one could purchase a semi-rural estate and live in neigh-

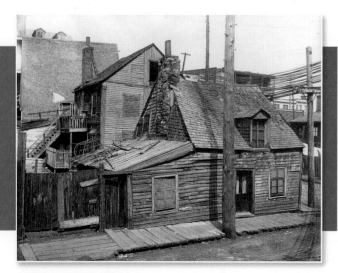

Slum conditions in Montreal, circa 1903.

Source: McCord Museum, II-146539.

bourhoods protected by housing covenants from various religious and racial groups. The suburbs were also viewed as a healthier place to live, both morally and spiritually, as they were largely free of crime and grime, were closer to nature, and had fewer temptations to lead people astray.

The urban workplace—whether it be a factory, retail establishment, or office—was typically growing larger, which meant a less personal relationship between employer and employees. Factories were becoming more mechanized, which increased output and decreased unit costs, thus providing consumers with cheaper prices, but the trend also often meant less reliance on skilled workers and the disappearance of many well-paying jobs. Workplace tasks were increasingly broken down into smaller, simpler components, a trend that, along with tighter shop-floor control by managers over workers, became known as *scientific management*, an approach developed by American engineer and efficiency expert Frederick Winslow Taylor. More workers experienced a loss of pride in their job as it became increasingly rare that they made a product from start to finish. However, the process was not uniform across or even within sectors. For instance, in steel companies, though skilled jobs like moulders disappeared, employers required new skilled and semi-skilled workers with a knowledge of metallurgy and blast furnaces.

Government regulation to protect workers was minimal, in part because of the fear of hurting or driving away business. Wages increased, but not as fast as prices, according to analyses by historians Michael Piva on Toronto and Terry Copp on Montreal.[10] Women and children worked, typically for a third to a half of what men earned. Not until 1907 did the Ontario government pass a law stipulating that children under 16 be limited to a maximum workday of 11 hours.

Social legislation was virtually non-existent. Governments claimed that it bred dependency, though they also lacked the revenue to provide decent social welfare, as income tax did not appear until the First World War. In 1901, Toronto's city council budgeted only five cents per capita for relief. Most support was funnelled through private charities, which provided assistance in the form of food and shelter to those deemed as "deserving poor" because they were clearly unable to work, or, in the case of able-bodied men (as most women were excluded from receiving welfare), performed work like cleaning parks or road building. Usually, assistance was available for only a few days a month, which forced many men to leave their families to search for employment, such as on farms or in timber bush camps.

While corporate profits reached record levels, working-class wages remained low, thus compelling many wives to undertake home-based work, such as tending to gardens and making clothes. Many companies also paid little heed to safety. Between 1904 and 1911, there were 9340 on-the-job fatalities in Canada. Overwhelmingly, employers were hostile to unions, claiming they undermined efforts to run cost-effective operations and were controlled by radicals intent upon fomenting revolution. In 1902, the Canadian Manufacturers' Association called for "concerted action … to resist … unreasonable actions of the various labour unions."[11] Later that year, the Toronto Employers' Association was founded; members pledged to provide assistance to one another—including strike-breakers—to resist unions.

Social Reform

Growing numbers of Canadians spoke out against more evident want and suffering in the midst of greater national wealth. They worried about Canadians turning to "false Gods" like socialism. One response from many churches was to advance the ideas of the social gospel movement, which migrated from Britain and the United States into Canada in the late nineteenth century. It sought to promote Christian activism as a means of addressing a variety of social challenges and ills.

To many, the church seemed in danger of losing its influence. In cities, people were being lured from pews to commercial entertainment, much of which was bemoaned for encouraging morally risky interaction between the sexes, such as at dance pavilions and roller-skating rinks. Threats to the status of the church also came from Charles Darwin's theory of evolution and the growing influence of new social and natural sciences that provided explanations grounded in tangible evidence as opposed to faith.

The social gospel was strongest within Protestant churches, particularly the Baptist and Methodist churches, reflecting their less hierarchical structure and more emotive and participatory services. Social gospellers spanned a wide ideological spectrum. Some advocated socialism as a way to build a Christian society. Generally, they spoke of creating the Kingdom of God on earth. It was a mission that led them to stress the need for social legislation that included things like improving housing, ending child labour, and regulating companies to contain abuses of power. Many leaned to social conservatism as strong emphasis was also placed on moral reform, including practising temperance, sterilizing criminals and the insane, and arresting prostitutes.

Demands for reform also came from an array of urban professionals, academics, and others who presented themselves or were regarded as *progressives*. They spoke of the need for greater order and efficiency and believed that a more rigorous analysis of problems had to be undertaken so as to better understand their roots and scope, and to determine the best means of responding. In part, the rise of progressivism reflected a shift within universities from domains like theology and the humanities, to empirical-based social sciences and natural sciences, as well as a growing faith in professions, such as engineering, to solve the problems of increasingly complex urban-industrial society. The empiricist trend was partially accepted by many churches that created organizations to conduct research, such as the Moral and Social Reform Council of Canada that was established in 1907 by the Methodist Church.

Progressives became involved in a kaleidoscope of causes, such as the need to improve urban housing, regulate utilities, impose rational city planning, pursue urban beautification, and establish non-partisan local governments in which appointed technical experts would have significant power to set the municipal agenda. Many progressives focused on improving public health. Between 1901 and 1914, expenditures by Toronto's Board of Health increased from $51 500 to $292 000. Progressives played a key part in securing passage of a federal *Juvenile Delinquents Act* in 1908, under which young people (who were still tried in adult court and incarcerated in a youth section of a general penitentiary) would be provided with a separate juvenile court and reformatories. While many progressives emphasized the need for social uplift, others linked reforms to preserving

1908: Juvenile
Delinquents Act.

class harmony, because, as one put it: "Out of the slums stalk the Socialist with his red flag, the union agitator with the auctioneer's voice, and the anarchist with his torch."[12]

Many reformers prioritized the need to improve labour relations, as industrialization was accompanied by increasing friction between capital and labour. Among the most prominent figures in this area was William Lyon Mackenzie King, who went on to become Canada's longest-serving prime minister. Born in 1874 in Berlin, Ontario, King was the second of four children to John King, a small-town lawyer, and Isabel Mackenzie, the daughter of rebel leader William Lyon Mackenzie, whom King often cited as an inspiration for him to improve society. At the University of Toronto, where King majored in political economy, he became enthralled with the writings of the British economic historian Arnold Toynbee, who advocated Christian-inspired social reform to humanize modern industrial society, and who established the first university settlement house in London's east end, where students volunteered to help educate the poor. King undertook hands-on work while at the University of Toronto, making frequent visits to the city's red-light district in order to—as he insisted—save prostitutes. In 1896, he left to do postgraduate work, first in Chicago and then at Harvard, eventually earning a Ph.D. While in Chicago, he volunteered at Hull House. Situated in the city's notorious nineteenth ward slum, it provided a day nursery, free lectures, classes, and emergency assistance.

Returning to Toronto in 1897, King, as a summer reporter for the *Mail and Empire*, wrote a series of articles on the city's social problems. Demonstrating political savvy by holding back a story on the post office purchasing uniforms from companies using sweated labour, King ingratiated himself to Postmaster General William Mulock, who soon offered him the management of the federal government's new publication, the *Labour Gazette*. King expressed support for "responsible unions"[13] and the belief that compulsion did not produce effective and lasting labour agreements. Such philosophy was imported into the 1907 *Industrial Disputes and Investigation Act* (IDIA) that King helped prepare, under which the employer or employees involved in a labour dispute could apply for state assistance to help achieve a settlement. Once receiving the request, the government prohibited strikes and lockouts pending investigation and conciliation and the issuing of a non-binding report by a tripartite board. However, Canada's Trades and Labour Congress (TLC), which had initially welcomed the legislation, was soon calling for the IDIA's repeal because the measure had no means to force employers to engage in collective bargaining.

1907: Industrial Disputes Investigation Act.

Unions were becoming a significant player in industrializing Canada, though in 1911 their membership constituted only 5 percent of the total workforce. Bonds within many segments of the working class were strengthened by recreational sporting teams and club activities, or by socializing at workingmen's pubs after the workday ended. Rituals associated with Labour Day, a statutory holiday that debuted on the first Monday of September 1894, also exemplified the growing presence of a distinct working-class culture and the power of labour unions. The day was marked by parades where workers marched in the uniforms of their various trades and displayed floats that, in allegorical form, told spectators of the work they performed, such as one carrying a printing press put together by members of the typographical union.

More Canadian workers joined international unions affiliated with the American Federation of Labor (AFL), seeking the resources and strength of this large U.S. labour body.

By 1900, of the 20 000 unionists belonging to Canada's TLC, 60 percent were linked to the AFL. The AFL prioritized the organization of skilled labour into what were called *craft unions*, rather than joining together skilled and unskilled workers into what were called *industrial unions*. AFL unions also focused on "bread and butter" issues like pay and conditions of work, including controlling the impact of mechanization and shop-floor control by managers, principally to protect craft workers, and shunned radicalism and establishing a political party for labour. They were also among the loudest advocates for limiting immigration over the fear that cheap labour would mean lower wages and the loss of good jobs. Many within the labour movement criticized the approach as exclusivist, as divisive, and as weakening the power of the working class. Yet, as labour historian Bryan Palmer notes, AFL unions did not hesitate to go on strike to achieve a better deal for their members and through such struggles arguably encouraged a growing class consciousness of workers' interests as being diametrically opposed to capital.[14]

To pursue its goals in Canada, the AFL secured the services of John Flett, "a suave, efficient Hamilton carpenter"[15] and a former leader with the Knights of Labor. Flett played a central role in forming more than 100 AFL-affiliated union locals, almost all in Ontario. Nevertheless, growing AFL dominance brought divisions. At the 1902 TLC convention in Berlin, Ontario, delegates from AFL-affiliated unions, who formed a majority, voted out of the TLC any organization simultaneously holding membership in another central labour body, and elected Flett as TLC president.

The migration of workers to AFL-affiliated international unions also reinforced divisions between labour in Quebec and English Canada. In Quebec, the Catholic Church steered Francophones away from international unions, fearing they would inculcate alien ideas and promote strikes, thus undermining the influence of Catholicism and destabilizing Quebec's hierarchical society. In 1907, the first Catholic union was formed in Chicoutimi. With priests acting as councillors, these unions sought greater harmony between labour and capital by pursuing conciliation and arbitration over the use of strikes.

In the Maritimes, the Provincial Workman's Association (PWA), initially the region's principal labour organization, remained separate from the TLC, claiming that its interests would be ignored within a larger, Ontario-dominated, organization. Although the PWA was eventually ousted by its membership because it was viewed as ineffective, this did not end the regional rift. Many Maritimers turned to the radical American-controlled United Mine Workers of America, which condemned craft unions as elitist and in turn was rejected by the TLC for being too "red."

Radical unions became relatively strong in areas where resource extraction dominated, with the most significant concentration in Western Canada. British Columbia had the highest strike rate in Canada, with the coal-mining sector leading the way. One ultimately unsuccessful strike against the Vancouver Coal and Land Company over pay and workplace safety lasted from 1912 to 1914. In such domains, class divisions were particularly stark; there was virtually no middle-class to which workers could aspire to join. Men received abysmal pay, often lived in tents or crude bunkhouses, and, because they were isolated, were often forced to purchase provisions at overpriced company stores. Many workers arriving in the West anticipated starting anew and perhaps even striking it rich, and felt keen disappointment and grew angry over the apparent lack of opportunity. Large proportions of these workers were unmarried and without dependants and therefore were less hesitant about adopting militant tactics.

Socialists, though a minority and plagued by doctrinal divisions, still became a more significant force within Canada's labour movement and on Canada's political landscape. There were four major socialist parties in Canada, each with its own lifespan: the Socialist Labour Party (1894–1910s), the Canadian Socialist League (1898–1903), the Socialist Party of Canada (1905–1925), and the Social Democratic Party of Canada (1911–1920).

In 1906, Toronto's socialist mayoralty candidate gathered an impressive 8600 votes in a second-place finish. The mining district of Springhill, Nova Scotia, was described by historian Ian McKay as "possibly the *reddest* spot on the map of Canada's liberal order."[16] Overall, socialists consistently enjoyed their greatest electoral success in the West and in particular in British Columbia. In 1901, the Socialist Party of British Columbia, the first such party in Canada, emerged in the province's coal-mining districts, and two years later two of its candidates were elected on Vancouver Island. Four years later, socialists were elected provincially in Nanaimo and Newcastle, British Columbia, and in the coal-mining areas of Grand Forks and Rocky Mountain, Alberta.

Mutual hostility developed between the TLC and more radical Western Canadian industrial unions. In 1903, the TLC ordered back on the job its members participating in sympathy strikes to show solidarity with a Western Canadian based walkout by workers seeking membership in the radical United Brotherhood of Railway Employees. In protesting this decision, B.C.-based labour trade councils in Nanaimo, Phoenix, Fernie, and Victoria withdrew from the TLC, and no delegates west of Winnipeg attended the 1903 TLC convention.

Western Canadian workers in particular joined the Industrial Workers of the World (IWW). Established in 1905 in Chicago, the IWW advocated socialism and the use of general strikes to defeat capitalism. Besides tapping into the frustration of many workers, the IWW's appeal derived from providing practical services, such as mail drops and medical depots, to itinerant labourers. Its low initiation fees and dues and transferable membership cards were also well suited to the lives of migratory labourers. The Industrial Workers of the World also produced printed material in several languages, as workers in areas like railway camps came from a wide variety of backgrounds. Condemned as dangerous, the federal government deported IWW organizers who came from the United States and banned IWW meetings on the basis that their camps broke public health regulations, actions that the TLC leadership tacitly endorsed through its silence.

Immigration

Hostility to unions was also grounded in xenophobia. Many longer-settled Canadians feared immigrants, especially from Slavic areas, because they thought these people's beliefs were steeped in radicalism and that they were trying to spread the revolutionary spirit within Canada. In the early twentieth century, Canadian immigration laws were amended to permit the deportation of those promoting "subversion or anarchistic" views. Immigrants also generated concerns about job security and the possibility that their presence

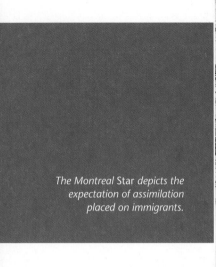

The Montreal Star *depicts the expectation of assimilation placed on immigrants.*

Source: McCord Museum, M2005, 23.236.

could drive down wages. The union movement, including the socialist IWW, supported immigration restriction. Despite these beliefs, Canada needed immigrants to fill the West; they were also needed within growing cities and for the resource sector.

The Laurier years brought an unprecedented boom in newcomers that transformed the country. In 1896, Canada's population stood at 5.074 million, and between that year and 1914 some 3 million newcomers arrived, with the annual figure peaking in 1913 at more than 400 000. This movement was fuelled by falling international shipping rates, rising wheat prices, land shortages in Europe, the closing of the American frontier, improved rail access to the West, and burgeoning job opportunities in urban areas and the resource sector. Although Canada was changed by immigration, its population remained overwhelmingly white, Anglo, French, and Western European. The 1901 census indicated that Canada was 96.2 percent Caucasian, 2.4 percent Native, 0.4 percent Asian, and 0.3 percent black; a decade later, 90 percent of Canadians were of British or French origin.

Quebec sought immigrants from France, but French governments, desiring to retain the country's labour force, especially farmers, discouraged migration by portraying Canada as cold, barren, and primitive. Throughout English-speaking Canada, where the vast majority of immigrants settled, the clear preference was for Protestant Brits and Americans, as they were deemed easiest to assimilate, followed by Northwest Europeans and Scandinavians, while least favoured were Slavs, Southern Europeans, Jews, and visible minorities.

Under the *British North America Act*, immigration was a shared jurisdiction between the provinces and the federal government. During Laurier's time, Ottawa placed its responsibility under the Ministry of the Interior, as it also managed Western Canadian land for settlement. From 1896 to 1905, the interior minister was Clifford Sifton, an ambitious Manitoba businessman who heralded the unlimited potential of the West. Under his direction, the Immigration Department focused on attracting agriculturalists, though it did not exclude others. Its budget was increased from $120 000 in 1896 to $900 000 by 1905, largely to advertise free land. Newspaper publishers from America and Britain were taken on tours of the Canadian West. Canada established an immigration office in central London, as land in Britain was increasingly expensive, many wanted to escape from England's rigid class structure, and numerous people had family, relatives, and friends in Canada. Prospective settlers were also targeted in the United States. Of the possibility of more Americans migrating into southern Alberta, the Lethbridge *Herald* gushed, "this class of immigration is of a top-notch order and every true Canadian should be proud to see it and encourage it."[17] Whereas 1200 people settled in Canada from Britain in 1900, five years later that number reached 65 000, and in 1912–1913, 150 000. American migration to Canada increased from 19 000 in 1900 to 58 000 in 1905 and reached 139 000 in 1912–1913.

Railways also got in on the advertising campaign to attract American farmers and farm labourers to Canada.

Source: Library and Archives of Canada, RG 76 Immigration Records Branch, Vol. 131, file 29480, part 2.

Unable to attract enough immigrants from America and Britain, Sifton turned to the Ukraine and Russia. Between 1891 and 1911, some 500 000 people came to Canada from continental Europe, which also included substantial numbers of Jews, Doukhobours, and other religious minorities. The largest group, 170 000 by the First World War, were from parts of the Ukraine known as Galicia and Ruthenia. These people clamoured to leave places that were characterized by poverty, authoritarianism, and persecution. In the case of Jews in Russia, thousands were killed in state-tolerated or sanctioned *pogroms*.

Sifton spoke of Central Europeans, particularly Ukrainians, as tough and highly motivated, famously, though also condescendingly, describing them as the "stalwart peasant in the sheep-skin coat … born to the soil, whose forefathers have been farmers for ten generations, with a stout wife and a half-dozen children." In the broader Canadian population, they were also stereotyped as unkempt, wild, violent, thieving, and drunkards. Besides farming, many were forced into "less skilled labouring jobs in the yards and around the blast furnaces, coke ovens, and open-hearth furnaces,"[18] or into low-paying railway, mining, or logging jobs. Sifton's successor as interior minister, Frank Oliver, an architect of the Anglo-centric public school system in the former North-West Territories, expressed concern about the impact of such immigrants. "It is not merely a question of filling the country with people who will produce wheat and buy manufactured goods," he said. "It is a question of the ultimate results of the efforts being put forward for the building up of a Canadian nationality so that our children may form one of the great civilized nations of the world, and be one of the greatest forces in that civilization."[19]

Western Canada also became home to significant numbers belonging to autonomist religious communities, the most prominent being the Doukhobours. A German-speaking Christian pacifist sect that rejected modern society, practised communal farming, and avoided outsiders, the Doukhobours, who had faced persecution in Tsarist Russia, started arriving in Canada in the 1890s. Known to be good farmers, they were admitted with the understanding that they would be allowed to retain their traditional ways. As more immigrants settled in the West, the federal government became less tolerant of the Doukhobours, insisting that they adopt individual private property ownership and denying them title to land if they refused to take an oath of allegiance to the Crown, which the Doukhobours considered as incompatible with their covenant to God. To bring attention to their cause, and to demonstrate the purity of their faith, Doukhobours organized nude protest marches, the first in 1902 involving a procession of 1000 parading through the small and scandalized town of Yorkton, Saskatchewan. By the end of the decade, Doukhobours in Saskatchewan had lost more than half their land through government seizures. In 1907, several thousand left the prairies to form a new community in the Grand Forks area of British Columbia on more than 6000 hectares of land purchased by their spiritual leader Peter Verigin.

Many other immigrants experienced a hostile reception in Canada, though very few returned home, determined to build a new life and no doubt unable to afford the return trip. Typically, men who came over by themselves were soon sending for their families. Immigrants established their own religious and cultural institutions. In Winnipeg, Ukrainians, though largely confined to the city's north-end slum, established their own churches, a labour temple, a cooperative society, and a drama club. In 1907, Alberta saw its first Jewish congregation and, soon after, a Hebrew school and a Jewish newspaper. In several cities, Jews opened general stores, clothing, furniture, and jewellery shops, and, in placing great emphasis on education, their children qualified for many professions, enough so that universities placed quotas on the number of Jews that they would accept.

The most intense prejudice was experienced by visible minorities. They were considered impossible to assimilate, as they were thought to be socially, culturally, morally, and genetically inferior to whites and as dragging Canada down. Although Canada sought immigrants from the United States, this did not include African Americans. Black men were portrayed as ruled by savage instincts and as having voracious sexual appetites that endangered white women. Rumours in 1911 that a sizable number of blacks were leaving Oklahoma, bound for Edmonton, resulted in a petition to Ottawa organized by the local Board of Trade listing supporters from 14 percent of Alberta's population demanding that the federal government stop any such movement.

On Canada's west coast, whites spoke of the "yellow peril," meaning the threat of being overrun by hordes of Asians, especially the Chinese. Chinese immigrants started coming to Canada from California in 1858 as part of British Columbia's Fraser River gold rush, where they worked for mining companies as "Coolie" labour, a racist term meaning workers of low status and little skill. Even with the 1885 application of a $50 head tax on each prospective Chinese migrant to Canada, and significant restrictions on Chinese men bringing over their wives and children, by the First World War, Canada's Chinese population reached some 30 000, which was concentrated in British Columbia. Also, by 1908, 5000 Sikhs had arrived in Canada, with a large percentage initially working in B.C. logging camps and lumber mills. Canada's Japanese population reached 14 000 by 1914, with a large proportion making their livelihood in west coast fishing.

Popular stereotypes of the Chinese was that they were dirty and diseased; were responsible for gambling and opium dens; and spread prostitution, including kidnapping and selling women into what was called the "white slave trade." Sikhs and Hindus solicited comments about being unkempt and heathen. The Japanese were portrayed as warlike, as apparently demonstrated by Japan's military incursions into China in the mid-1890s, and its defeat of Russia in 1904–1905, a disquieting event for many whites as it was the first military victory by an Asian country over a European one.

With B.C. politicians lobbying intensely for Asian exclusion and a federal election approaching, the federal Liberals increased the head tax against the Chinese in June 1900 to $100. British Columbia politicians demanded a $500 head tax, which was equivalent to the average annual salary of a labourer. Laurier resisted, as he hoped to expand Canadian trade with China. In 1901, the Dunsmuir government in British Columbia passed an act demanding that Japanese immigrants pass a test demonstrating proficiency in a European language, but Ottawa disallowed it because of treaties between Britain and Japan. With pressure from British Columbia unrelenting, the Laurier government caved in 1903 by introducing the $500 Chinese head tax. The following year, only eight Chinese officially entered Canada, though some were smuggled in from the United States or at remote ports, or gained entry with falsified documents or by bribing immigration officials. Quiet support for this illegal flow came from many employers who still sought cheap Chinese labour.

1903: $500 Chinese head tax.

In 1907, an economic downturn, along with the arrival of more East Asians, touched off a riot in Vancouver that destroyed much of the city's Chinese district, which was the most significant Asian target. The next year, the federal government responded by essentially blaming the victims, as it barred entry to Asian immigrants who did not arrive in Canada via continuous voyage. Although presented as a way to prevent contract Chinese workers in Hawaiian sugar fields from inundating Canada, the ruling practically cut off all Asian migration because there were no direct scheduled voyages between Asia and Canada. Also in 1908, Mackenzie King travelled to Japan to negotiate a separate unofficial "Gentleman's Agreement" on immigration because Britain's treaties with Japan and Britain's authority over Canadian foreign policy technically made Japan exempt from the continuous voyage rule. Desiring to avoid the public dishonour of a formal Canadian quota against its people, Tokyo promised to keep annual migration to Canada to a maximum of 400.

1907: Anti-Asian riot in Vancouver.
1908: Continuous voyage rule; Gentleman's Agreement with Japan.

Women

Several women's groups were among the critics of increased immigration partly because male newcomers, and not women, could gain the right to the vote. Led by middle- and upper-class Anglo- and French-Canadian women, they argued that females would exert a civilizing influence on society through the ballot, but the most widely accepted goals for women were marriage and motherhood. Those who failed at either—unless they were nuns—were pitied or faced scorn. While most women had children, there was panicked talk about Anglo-Protestant "race suicide," especially as non-Anglo immigrants and Francophones had higher fertility rates.

The addition of section 179C to the *Criminal Code* in 1892 added to the pressure to have children by providing up to two years' imprisonment for anyone who offered, sold, or advertised "any medicine, drug or article intended or represented as a means of preventing conception or causing abortion."[20] Many women sent away for sheaths, diaphragms, pessaries, and various contraceptive concoctions advertised under coded phrases like "Every Woman Marvel Whirling Spray." If unable to find or afford the services of an illegal abortionist, some women turned to homemade remedies comprised of ingredients like boric acid, or used a pencil or some other sharp object to abort, which in some cases produced hemorrhaging and death.

Both under Quebec's Civil Code and English Common Law, wives, in many respects, were given the same rights as children and the insane. They could not obtain credit on their own or exert any legal control over joint property. Marriage was sacrosanct, and weddings were to be religious; only in parts of Western Canada were civil unions permitted. As divorce was a federal matter, in most parts of the country it was necessary to obtain a parliamentary decree to secure one, a process that could cost $1000 to complete. In 1900, there were only 11 divorces in Canada, and by 1910 the figure had reached 51. While adultery by a wife was grounds enough for the husband to demand a divorce, before 1925 if the divorce was sought by the wife, adultery by the husband had to be accompanied by desertion, incest, bigamy, or raping another woman.

At home, much of the wife's day was characterized by toil and drudgery. Certainly, there were improvements, such as, in urban areas, access to bakeries and commercial laundries. The early twentieth century also saw the appearance of hand-powered washing machines and better cast iron stoves. Most city homes had running water, though less so in the slums, and working-class homes usually had just one tap, which meant carrying water throughout the house. On farms, things were far more basic. In rural Manitoba shortly after the end of the First World War, 60 percent of homes were still heated by wood stoves, two-thirds had no running water in the kitchen, and most were lit by coal lamps.

Economic necessity compelled numerous women to enter the paid workforce. Many, especially wives and mothers, performed home-based piece work, such as making clothes, for which they earned a pittance because they had to provide their own equipment and material and received little for the products they produced. In 1901, approximately 15 percent of the Canadian workforce was female. Popular attitudes did not favour female work outside the home because it was viewed as threatening the breadwinner status of men and as taking women away from domestic duties and the care of their children. Working women also raised fears because many were young, single, and on their own in cities. With money and free time, and cities offering amusements where the sexes co-mingled—such as nickelodeons (movie theatres that charged a nickel for admission), roller-skating rinks, and dance halls—such women, it was feared, could easily become morally compromised, a worry that prompted groups like the Young Women's Christian Association to establish supervised living quarters for single women.

In the early twentieth century, some 90 percent of women who worked outside the home were single or widowed. This was used to justify lower pay—typically half of what men earned—because it was said that such women had only themselves to support. Married women in the paid workforce were also cast as requiring less money as they were assumed to be simply supplementing their husband's income. Labour unions did little, and usually nothing at all, to organize women workers, viewing the workplace as a male domain.

Overwhelmingly, women were confined to low-paying positions that were perceived as an extension of housekeeping or nurturing. Their most common, though typically least favoured, job before the First World War was as domestic worker, whose annual salary was often less than $100 plus room and board. Many women worked in textile and boot and shoe factories, where their presumed skill at sewing was put to use. In 1911, three-quarters of Ontario textile employees were women, but hardly any were managers. Female employment in clerical jobs increased by 765 percent, or from one-sixth to two-fifths of the total between 1891 and 1911. Many firms viewed young women as brightening up the office. More significant was that the male office generalist was phased out as administrative work was broken down into lower-paid and more repetitive tasks, particularly with the adoption of the typewriter.

In 1900, more than 60 percent of Ontario teachers were female, having tripled as a proportion of the provincial total compared with 1860, as more men withdrew from what they considered an atrociously paid job. Still, men were paid one-third to one-half more than women teaching the same grade. Rural areas, with their smaller tax base, usually hired women with a third-class teaching certificate—the lowest qualification that could be obtained in a few months after completing grade ten—paying them as little as $250 per annum. Most women taught children in elementary schools where their nurturing qualities (supposed because they were female) were considered especially useful.

Technically, women could attend medical school, but few were admitted because the training was considered too intellectually difficult and pressured, and because it was thought that it would create an uncomfortable situation having women work on and have life-and-death control over male bodies. Not until 1903 did Quebec's Legislative Assembly pass a law that allowed Irma LeVasseur to become the first woman doctor to practise in the province. The emerging template was for women to assist male doctors as nurses. Although professionally trained, they were paid on a par with female factory workers. In addition to administering medical care, they were also expected to clean bedpans, prepare meals, and mend hospital clothes. *The Canadian Nurse*, a publication started in 1905 by the Alumnae Association of the Toronto General Hospital School of Nursing, advocated for the creation of a governing body to accredit nurses as a means to professionalize the job and to improve pay and working conditions, but substantive action did not occur until after the First World War.

Besides confining women to certain roles, stereotypes about gender were used by women themselves. They argued that by bringing their (perceived) more compassionate and virtuous qualities and values from the private—or domestic—sphere into the public domain, a better society would result. Many women pursued this link through religion. As historian Ruth Brouwer writes, a significant number of women in English Canada became involved in overseas missions, such as to India and China, where they taught in schools and administered heath care.[21] Closely connected to Protestant churches was the Women's Christian Temperance Union. Its 10 000 members sought to impose prohibition, as well as to stamp out prostitution and obscene literature, sterilize criminals and mental defectives, provide assistance to deserted wives, and gain women the vote so they could use their political influence to better protect families and prevent social and moral decay. In Quebec, between 1901 and 1911, the number of nuns in the province increased from 6629 to 9964 or from 6.1 to 8.0 percent of all single women over the age of 20, an example of the link between religion and women obtaining a means through which they could have an impact upon society. Nuns were permitted to become highly educated and assisted priests in running charities and social services.

Anglo women, led by those from the middle and upper class, also pursued numerous reform causes through groups like the Imperial Order Daughters of the Empire, rural-based Women's Institutes, and the National Council of Women of Canada (NCWC), which was founded in 1893, with Lady Aberdeen, the governor-general's wife, as its first patron. Among the causes such groups advanced, and often spearheaded, were for improvements to education, public health, workplace conditions for women, and the treatment of juvenile delinquents, as well as prison reform and city beautification.

The campaign to obtain the vote for women was central to this first wave of feminism. Dr. Emily Howard Stowe, the second woman licensed by the Ontario College of Physicians and Surgeons (even though she attended medical school in New York because she was first refused acceptance in Canada), was the first major leader in this campaign. As head of the Dominion Women's Enfranchisement Association (DWEA), she and her supporters achieved a breakthrough in 1883 when Ontario provided the municipal franchise to widows and spinsters who owned property. In 1903, her daughter, Dr. Augusta Stowe-Gullen, took over the DWEA, which focused on trying to convince Ontario governments under Liberal George Ross and then Conservative James Pliny Whitney to grant women the provincial franchise. Known for adopting more aggressive tactics, in 1909 Stowe-Gullen organized a march of 1000 women on the provincial legislature. In 1911, she was replaced by Flora MacDonald Denison, and the DWEA was renamed as the more modern-sounding Canadian Suffrage Association. Yet Dennison was even more controversial, as she had separated from her husband and supported easier divorce laws and legalized birth control. In 1912, a rival and more socially conservative Equal Franchise League was formed with support from the NCWC. It insisted that women would use the ballot to achieve a "purifying, civilizing, and stabilizing influence"[22] on society, and not to challenge male authority.

While women took on more public roles by championing progressive causes and by pushing for the vote, which many scholars identify as crucial steps forward towards achieving greater equality, it was also the case that many of these feminists constructed their arguments on the basis of women being "mothers of the nation," an approach that arguably reinforced restrictive stereotypes. Some historians also stress that by focusing on such campaigns, attention has centred on middle- and upper-class women and glossed over the experiences of others, such as rural, working-class, and immigrant women. On farms, women were often responsible for preparing nearly everything for family consumption—such as clothing, soap, preserves, dairy products—and growing vegetables and tending to game. In 1902, black women organized the Coloured Women's Club of Montreal that provided social services and advice on how to cope with racism. There were also women trailblazers in their professional lives such as the journalist "Kit" Coleman, who covered the Spanish-American War from Cuba and described the aftermath of the 1906 San Francisco earthquake for the Toronto *Mail and Empire*.

Opposition to expanded female roles, and especially the right to vote, was most pronounced in Quebec. The Catholic Church and Quebec *nationalistes* like Bourassa portrayed feminism as an attack on the family and Catholicism, and the suffrage campaign as an Anglo-led movement that would import foreign values. For the Roman Catholic Church, there were two acceptable roles for women: as a wife and mother or as a member of a religious order. Associations of laywomen were often treated with suspicion, especially if they sought to move beyond involvement in charity work. The most prominent Francophone group in Quebec, the clerico-nationaliste *Fédération nationale Saint-Jean-Baptiste*, established a women's section in 1907 led by Marie Lacoste Gérin-Lajoie. A self-taught legal expert, Gérin-Lajoie in her 1902 book *Traité de droit usuel* criticized Quebec's Civil Code for its many discriminatory provisions against women. Under her leadership, the women's section became involved in many moral reform campaigns, such as against prostitution and alcohol abuse, and insisted that women would use the vote to reinforce Quebec as a highly moral French and Catholic society. Fearing rebuke from the Catholic Church, it had little contact with groups like the Montreal Suffrage Association, and ultimately Quebec women would not win the provincial franchise until 1940, more than a generation after most other women in Canada.

Creating Culture and State Enterprise

The friction between traditionalism and modernism in Quebec, and persistent difficulties in building greater unity between French and English Canada, continued to be evident in several other areas, including in events that many hoped would build cohesion. Such was the case with the 300th anniversary celebration of Champlain's founding of Quebec City in 1608. *Nationalistes* insisted that the event commemorate the birth of a French-Catholic nation. Laurier's government offered $300 000 for the celebration, but only if the message was that Champlain also established the roots of Canada.

The grand historical pageant stretched over two weeks in July 1908. It involved a cast of thousands and attracted dignitaries from France, American Vice-President Charles Fairbanks, and the Prince of Wales. The *Fédération nationale Saint-Jean-Baptiste* unveiled its own statue of Champlain, while Laurier spoke about how Champlain and New France had established a Canadian nation that joined together the two great European races. The impact of latter-day politics in shaping history was evident in the re-enactment of

Actors posing as British soldiers and French-Canadian militia take part in the historical pageant at the Plains of Abraham.

Source: McCord Museum, MP-1981.94.72.2.

1908: Quebec tercentenary.

1909: Canadian Council of Agriculture formed.

the September 1759 battle on the Plains of Abraham, where actors dressed in the uniforms of the two sides marched and countermarched, but rather than engaging in a mock battle, eventually came together in a show of mutual triumph.

The tercentenary, though manipulated, still spoke to the belief that a sense of shared Canadian identity could be conveyed or created. This was also a challenge because cultural institutions, though emerging, remained in their infancy and were overwhelmingly dependent upon private philanthropy. Orchestras and choirs throughout Canada were comprised of amateurs. In theatre, the most popular draws were British and American touring companies. Art was given its first official home in 1882 when the National Gallery of Canada opened thanks to support from Governor-General Lorne and his wife, Princess Louisa, who was an amateur artist, but the venue initially shared space with the Ministry of Fisheries. It wasn't until 1910 that the National Gallery obtained its first full-time director and its own premises at Ottawa's Victoria Museum. The Gallery emphasized the acquisition of Canadian art, a decision largely attributable to the fact that well-regarded European works were too expensive.

With literature, of all the books listed by the British trade journal *Bookseller and Stationer* as top sellers in Canada between 1899 and 1918, 44 percent were American, 36 percent were British, and just 20 percent were Canadian. Some Canadian authors did obtain a following, including an international one, such as Ralph Connor for *The Man from Glengarry* (1901) and Lucy Maude Montgomery for *Anne of Green Gables* (1908). Rather than conveying a Canadian identity, both were localist in that they described distinct cultures in the Ottawa Valley and Prince Edward Island, respectively.

Besides local identities, regionalism remained very much evident, as did other sources of division. In 1909, farmer organizations, primarily in the prairies, formed the Canadian Council of Agriculture to lobby for greater equity by demanding lower tariffs, railway, and grain storage rates. In 1910, there occurred a record 32 corporate mergers worth $157 million, a trend that forced the federal government to pass *An Act to Provide for the Investigation of Combines, Monopolies and Mergers,* though with numerous loopholes, it resulted in only one successful prosecution after the First World War.

Support grew for the stricter regulation and public ownership of utilities. Several local governments sought to establish maximum rates, though without the power to expropriate, they were ignored by utility magnates, such as Ottawa's Thomas Ahearn and Warren Soper, and Montreal's Henry Holt. Some utility companies were willing to divest their assets to the state given the prospect of regulated rates and meagre profits, like Bell Telephone across the sparsely populated prairies, where between 1907 and 1909 it sold its operations to the three provincial governments.

In Ontario, pressure grew for hydroelectric power to be shifted from private to public control. Far from being radical, the demand was spearheaded by the Waterloo Board of Trade, which charged that private ownership, typically by American firms, resulted in too much energy being sent to the United States or to Toronto because such markets brought greater profits. In 1906, Whitney's Conservative government created the Hydro-Electric Power Commission, which began signing contracts with municipalities to deliver energy over publicly owned transmission lines.

Re-election, Linguistic Divisions, and Laurier's Demise, 1908–1912

Robert Borden anticipated a major breakthrough in the autumn 1908 federal election. The previous year, he had called a national Conservative convention in Halifax that produced a platform revolving around the theme of "purity in politics," emphasizing, for example, the implementation of exams and meritocracy in appointing civil servants. The Conservatives contrasted this approach to charges of Liberal corruption, namely in providing massive tax breaks to the two new transcontinental railways and rumoured graft in the Ministry of the Interior. Yet, Canadians showed that they still remained satisfied with Laurier and his government, providing the Liberals with 133 seats, compared to 82 for the Tories.

Almost immediately after the election, the government faced a crisis over the question of naval defence. Earlier in 1908, Britain announced a program to construct Dreadnought class battleships, the largest and most powerful at the time, to counter a German naval build-up and growing presence in the North Sea. Laurier refused Britain's request to help fund the construction of the vessels. Instead, he promised to build a Canadian navy, which he said would help Britain by freeing up the Royal Navy from Canadian coastal defence responsibilities. Initially, Borden supported Laurier, but things changed dramatically in 1909 when Reginald McKenna, Britain's First Lord of the Admiralty, announced that Germany's aggressive shipbuilding program threatened to overtake the Royal Navy. Australia's new Commonwealth Liberal government promised Britain money for the construction of a Dreadnaught. Anglo-Canadian opinion turned decisively towards supporting cash contributions to Britain, as did Borden.

January 1910: Naval Service Bill.

Laurier responded with a Naval Service Bill that was introduced to Parliament in January 1910 and when passed in May established the Royal Canadian Navy. The legislation announced that Canada would create a force of five cruisers and six destroyers, but in times of emergency Parliament could make these ships available to Britain. The compromise flopped. In English Canada, Laurier was accused of building a "tin-pot navy" that would be useless to Britain against German Dreadnaughts. In Quebec, Bourassa mobilized opposition by arguing that the Naval Service Bill would drag Canada into imperial wars, a view he hammered home in a new newspaper he founded called *Le Devoir*.

Borden remained silent on the naval controversy in Quebec; he left matters to Frederick Monk, who ran what was essentially a separate Quebec wing of the federal Conservative party. Monk formed an alliance with the *nationalistes* to condemn the Naval Service Bill and to defeat Laurier.

French–English relations were further strained by recurring controversies over French-language education, this time in Ontario. Worry had been growing among Anglos over an increasing French population that reached 10 percent of the provincial total in 1901 and had a tendency to send their children to bilingual or French schools. A 1908 report by F.W. Merchant, Ontario's chief inspector of public and separate schools, claimed that Francophone children were failing to learn English. In January 1910, Howard Fergusson, the Conservative representative for Kemptville, introduced a resolution into the Ontario Legislature declaring that English should be the sole language of school instruction. An *Association Canadian-français Education d'Ontario* (ACFEO) was created the same month to defend bilingual and French schools. Premier Whitney ordered another report by Merchant, seeking to defer matters until after another provincial election.

Trouble was brewing elsewhere for Laurier. With the *nationalistes* and Monk's Conservatives coordinating their efforts, the Liberals lost the October 1910 Drummond-Arthabaska by-election, Laurier's old riding that the Liberals had held since 1887. A month later, the first two ships making up new Royal Canadian Navy arrived—aged rust buckets purchased from England that for many Canadians confirmed the "tin-pot" designation. Although they were designed as training vessels rather than for combat, the largest ship, the *HMCS Niobe*, took some 700 men to operate, more than the total number of Canada's naval personnel; on one of its first voyages, it ran aground near Yarmouth, Nova Scotia, and nearly sank.

January 1911: Proposed U.S.–Canada free trade agreement.

At the outset of 1911, the issue of trade catapulted to the political forefront. The U.S. Congress was buckling under pressure to bring down consumer prices by lowering tariffs. Canada was offered an attractive free trade deal that would eliminate duties on a wide range of primary products, and open American markets to Canadian manufactured goods, and did not oblige Canada to immediately reciprocate on tariffs it applied against American industrial and manufactured products. Finance Minister W.S. Fielding triumphantly announced the proposed deal to the House of Commons on January 26. The Conservatives were visibly dejected. Several Liberals urged Laurier to call an election, but instead he left Canada to attend the coronation of George V as England's new King.

Canadian industrial and manufacturing interests began to mobilize opposition. They insisted that America would soon demand that Canada lower tariffs protecting its industry, with the result being U.S. economic domination of Canada, soon followed by its political absorption into America. There emerged a group of prominent men of business and finance (calling itself the *Toronto 18*) who were known as Liberal supporters, but who announced that they would now back the Tories because of the threat posed by free trade.

In June 1911, the proposed free trade agreement passed through the U.S. Congress. However, some remarks made at the time further stoked Canadian opposition. United States President William Howard Taft said that for Canada the agreement symbolized a "parting of the ways" that many Canadians interpreted as leaving behind Britain for America. More to the point was Champ Clark, Speaker of the U.S. House of Representatives, who predicted that Canada would eventually become part of the United States. When the agreement came before Canada's Parliament, the Conservatives initiated a filibuster, meaning that they sought to extend debate interminably as a means of preventing its passage. Convinced that he could sell the free trade deal to Canadians, Laurier had the governor-general dissolve Parliament and call an election for September.

The prime minister opened his campaign in Trois-Rivières, where he declared: "I am branded in Quebec as a traitor to the French and in Ontario as a traitor to the English … I am neither. I am a Canadian."[23] Still, Monk, in alliance with the *nationalistes*, siphoned off support in what had been rock-solid Liberal Quebec. In English Canada, Laurier's stand on free trade and the navy hurt him among imperialists, industrialists, urban workers, and even some sections of agriculture, such as fruit farmers who worried about stronger competition from American growers. The popular vote was close, favouring the Tories 51.6 to 48.4 percent, but the seat count was decisive with 135 Conservatives compared with 85 Liberals. The *nationaliste*–Conservative alliance won 28 of 65 seats in Quebec, while the Tories swept Ontario with 72 of 84 seats.

Continuing Discord, 1912–1914

While remaining relatively quiet about the naval issue during the election campaign, Borden was forced to confront it soon after becoming prime minister. In March 1912, Winston Churchill, Britain's staunchly imperialist First Lord of the Admiralty, presented an alarming picture of German naval strength. In June, Borden left for England to discuss the situation. Upon returning home, he introduced the Naval Aid Bill that proposed to contribute $35 million to Britain to construct three Dreadnaughts. Believing he had been deceived, Monk demanded a plebiscite—a non-binding public vote—on the matter. Rebuffed by Borden, he resigned as public works minister. In December 1912, the Naval Aid Bill was put before Parliament. The Liberals used various procedural points to stall the legislation. After five months of deadlock, an exasperated Borden invoked closure for the first time in Canadian history to end debate and to force a vote on the bill, which the government won by a majority of 33. It was all for nought—two weeks later the Liberal-dominated Senate, in a rare exercise of its power, overturned the legislation.

September 1911: Robert Borden is elected prime minister.

Meanwhile, soon after Whitney's re-election, Merchant submitted his second report, which maintained that French and bilingual schools were failing to properly teach English. The result was *Regulation 17*, which was passed in June 1912. It severely restricted instruction in French past grade one and phased it out completely by grade four in all schools that received provincial funding. All teachers had to be competent in English, and those who were not, or who continued to instruct in French, would be fired. In March 1913, the ACFEO—which condemned *Regulation 17* as a "cruel, arbitrary, unjust, and sweeping denial of … elementary natural, as well as constitutional rights"[24]—started an Ottawa-based newspaper, *Le Droit*, most of whose early editions revolved around denouncing the legislation. *Regulation 17* received wide and damning newspaper coverage in Quebec, where *nationalistes* raised money to start a private French school in eastern Ontario. In the French-speaking Lowertown district of Ottawa, hundreds of students went on strike and their parents occupied the empty schools.

1912: Regulation 17.

Compounding matters was that the economy, after more than a decade of generally strong growth, retracted swiftly and sharply. For example, in 1913, the annual value of building permits issued in Vancouver dropped by half, and then by another 60 percent in 1914. The IWW organized Unemployed Leagues to demand work and social assistance. In Edmonton, jobless protestors occupied several churches frequented by the upper class. Economic troubles also fed xenophobia, as immigrants were viewed as adding to unemployment. Determined to enforce the continuous voyage rule against Asians, in May 1914 Canadian authorities prevented the Japanese steamer *Komogatu Maru* from docking in Vancouver with its passenger manifest of 340 Sikhs, 24 Punjabi Muslims, and 12 Hindus because the vessel had arrived from Calcutta via Hong Kong. The ship remained anchored in the harbour with its crammed human cargo forced to endure sweltering heat and shortages of food. After some five weeks, at 5 A.M. on June 23, in the first official assignment for Canada's new navy, the *HMS Rainbow*, egged on by a small cheering crowd, forced the *Komogatu Maru* out of Canadian waters.

In late July, Borden travelled to the Muskokas for a vacation. His rest was brief. War clouds had been gathering in the Balkans and conflict loomed ominously after a Serb nationalist assassinated the Archduke of Austria and his wife in Sarajevo on June 28. On July 27, Borden read in the newspaper that Austria had declared war on Serbia. That evening, after getting in a round of golf, he received a telegram advising him to return to Ottawa immediately. Europe was cascading towards conflict.

Conclusion

Between 1896 and 1914, Canada became more urban and industrial, technologically advanced, and interconnected. Farms mechanized, food production boomed, millions poured into the prairies, and three railways came to traverse the nation. Expressions of Canadian culture grew more evident and Canada stepped more boldly onto the world stage. Through seeds planted by the social gospel and progressive movements, Canada's social welfare system began to take root, as did the regulatory roles of governments to contain abuses within the capitalist economy. Organized labour emerged as a force, Canada became more multicultural, and women assumed more public roles and demanded greater equality. A young country was appearing to come of age, but these were also years that brought growing worry over corporate concentration, degenerating urban conditions, class conflict and political radicalism; in which regionalism remained potent; where mass immigration generated intensified xenophobia; and where imperialism arguably did more to divide than to unite Canadians.

As prime minister for 15 years, Wilfrid Laurier demonstrated an extraordinary ability to find the sweet spot of compromise. Yet, despite his infectious charm, considerable powers of persuasion, and, when necessary, Machiavellian political tactics, Laurier was eventually consumed by competing interests—namely those of imperialists, Canadian nationalists, and Quebec *nationalistes*—over his solution to the naval dispute and the proposed free trade deal with the United States.

Robert Borden, the outwardly unassuming Halifax lawyer whom many wrote off as too stiff and boring for politics, had finally proven his critics wrong. His first years as prime minister were rough as he faltered on the naval issue and faced an economy that went into a tailspin. His greatest challenge lay ahead, as on August 4, 1914, Canada joined "the war to end all wars."

Questions to Consider

1. What was Wilfrid Laurier's leadership style, and where was this demonstrated?

2. How did the roles, representation, and ambitions of women change during the late nineteenth and early twentieth centuries?

3. How did the Canadian economy change during the late nineteenth and early twentieth centuries?

4. What were the social gospel movement and progressivism? What impact did they have?

Critical Thinking Questions

1. Did Canada really become a more multicultural country during the 1896–1914 period?

2. With the benefit of hindsight, which groups would have likely agreed and disagreed with Laurier's assertion that the twentieth century would belong to Canada?

3. How did imperialism both unite and divide Canadians?

Suggested Readings

General

Armstrong, Christopher. *The Politics of Federalism: Ontario's Relations with the Federal Government, 1867–1942*. Toronto: University of Toronto Press, 1981.

Bélanger, Réal. *Wilfrid Laurier: Quand la politique déviant passion*. Quebec: Les Presses de l'université Laval, 1986.

Bothwell, Robert, Ian Drummond, and John English. *Canada, 1900–1945*. Toronto: University of Toronto Press, 1987.

Brown, Robert Craig, and Ramsay Cook. *Canada, 1896–1921: A Nation Transformed*. Toronto: McClelland & Stewart, 1974.

Hall, David J. *Clifford Sifton*, 2 Vols. Vancouver: University of British Columbia Press, 1981–1985.

Nelles, H.V. *The Politics of Development: Forests, Mines & Hydro-Electric Power in Ontario, 1849–1941*. Toronto: Macmillan of Canada, 1974.

Imperialism and Defence

Berger, Carl. *The Sense of Power: Studies in the Ideas of Canadian Imperialism, 1867–1914*. Toronto: University of Toronto Press, 1970.

Miller, Carman. *Painting the Map Red: Canada and the South African War, 1899–1902*. Toronto: University of Toronto Press, 1993.

Owram, Doug, and R.G. Moyles. *Imperial Dreams and Colonial Realities: British Views of Canada, 1880–1914.* Toronto: University of Toronto Press, 1988.

Ideas and Culture

Berger, Carl. *Science, God, and Nature in Victorian Canada.* Toronto: University of Toronto Press, 1983.

McKillop, A.B. *A Disciplined Intelligence: Critical Inquiry and Canadian Thought in the Victorian Era.* Montreal and Kingston: McGill-Queen's University Press, 1979.

Nelles, H.V. *The Art of Nation-Building: Pageantry and Spectacle at Quebec's Tercentenary.* Toronto: University of Toronto Press, 1999.

Business and Economics

Bliss, Michael. *A Living Profit: Studies in the Social History of Canadian Business, 1883–1911.* Toronto: McClelland & Stewart, 1974.

Cruikshank, Ken. *Close Ties: Railways, Government and the Board of Railway Commissioners, 1851–1933.* Toronto: University of Toronto Press, 1991.

Monod, David. *Store Wars: Shopkeepers and the Culture of Mass Marketing, 1890–1939.* Toronto: University of Toronto Press, 1996.

Nelles, H.V., and Christopher Armstrong. *Monopoly's Moment: The Organization and Regulation of Canadian Utilities, 1830–1930.* Toronto: University of Toronto Press, 1986.

Walden, Keith. *Becoming Modern in Toronto: The Industrial Exhibition and the Shaping of a Late Victorian Culture.* Toronto: University of Toronto Press, 1997.

Social Conditions and Reform

Allen, Richard. *The Social Passion: Religion and Social Reform in Canada, 1914–1928.* Toronto: University of Toronto Press, 1971.

Christie, Nancy, and Micheal Gauvreau. *A Full-Orbed Christianity: The Protestant Churches and Social Welfare in Canada, 1900–1940.* Montreal and Kingston: McGill-Queen's University Press, 1996.

Colpitts, George. *Game in the Garden: A Human History of Wildlife in Western Canada to 1940.* Vancouver: University of British Columbia Press, 2002.

Cook, Ramsay. *The Regenerators: Social Criticism in Late Victorian English Canada.* Toronto: University of Toronto Press, 1985.

Copp, J.T. *The Anatomy of Poverty: The Condition of the Working Class in Montreal 1897–1929.* Toronto: McClelland & Stewart, 1974.

Piva, Michael J. *The Condition of the Working Class in Toronto, 1900–1921.* Ottawa: University of Ottawa Press, 1979.

Sutherland, Neil. *Children in English-Speaking Society: Framing the Twentieth-Century Consensus.* Toronto: University of Toronto Press, 1976.

Valverde, Mariana. *The Age of Light, Soap, and Water: Moral Reform in English Canada, 1885–1925*. Toronto: McClelland & Stewart, 1991.

Labour

Babcock, Robert. *Gompers in Canada: A Study in American Continentalism Before the First World War*. Toronto: University of Toronto Press, 1974.

Belshaw, John Douglas. *Colonization and Community: The Vancouver Island Coalfield and the Making of the British Columbian Working Class*. Montreal and Kingston: McGill-Queen's University Press, 2002.

Craven, Paul. *An Impartial Umpire: Industrial Relations and the Canadian State, 1900–1911*. Toronto: University of Toronto Press, 1980.

Goutor, David. *Guarding the Gates: The Canadian Labour Movement and Immigration, 1872–1934*. Vancouver: University of British Columbia Press, 2007.

Heron, Craig. *Working in Steel: The Early Years in Canada, 1883–1935*. Toronto: McClelland & Stewart, 1988.

McCormack, A. Ross. *Reformers, Rebels, and Revolutionaries: The Western Canadian Radical Movement, 1899–1919*. Toronto: University of Toronto Press, 1977.

Palmer, Bryan. *A Culture in Conflict: Skilled Workers and Industrial Capitalism in Hamilton, 1860–1914*. Montreal and Kingston: McGill-Queen's University Press, 1974.

Immigration and Ethnicity

Avery, Donald. *Dangerous Foreigners: European Immigrant Workers and Labour Radicalism in Canada, 1896–1932*. Toronto: McClelland & Stewart, 1979.

Troper, Harold Martin. *Only Farmers Need Apply: Official Canadian Government Encouragement of Immigration from the United States, 1896–1911*. Toronto: Griffin House, 1972.

Ward, W. Peter. *White Canada Forever: Popular Attitudes and Public Policy toward Orientals in British Columbia*. Montreal and Kingston: McGill-Queen's University Press, 2002.

Zucchi, John E. *Italians in Toronto: Development of a National Identity, 1875–1935*. Montreal and Kingston: McGill-Queen's University Press, 1988.

First Peoples

Kelm, Mary-Ellen. *Colonizing Bodies: Aboriginal Health and Healing in British Columbia, 1900–1950*. Vancouver: University of British Columbia Press, 1999.

Miller, J.R. *Shingwauk's Vision: A History of Native Residential Schools*. Toronto: University of Toronto Press, 1996.

Tough, Frank. *"As Their Natural Resources Fail": Native Peoples and the Economic History of Northern Manitoba, 1870–1950*. Vancouver: University of British Columbia Press, 1996.

Women

Bacchi, Carol Lee. *Liberation Deferred? The Ideas of the English-Canadian Suffragists, 1877–1918.* Toronto: University of Toronto Press, 1983.

Burke, Sara. *Seeking the Highest Good: Social Service and Gender at the University of Toronto, 1888–1937.* Toronto: University of Toronto Press, 1996.

Cook, Sharon. *"Through Sunshine and Shadow": The Women's Christian Temperance Union, Evangelicism, and Reform in Ontario, 1874–1930.* Montreal and Kingston: McGill-Queen's University Press, 1995.

Danylewycz, Marta. *Taking the Veil: An Alternative to Marriage, Motherhood, and Spinsterhood in Quebec, 1840–1920.* Toronto: McClelland & Stewart, 1987.

Kealey, Linda. *Enlisting Women for the Cause: Women, Labour, and the Left in Canada, 1890–1920.* Toronto: University of Toronto Press, 1998.

Myers, Tamara. *Caught: Montreal's Modern Girls and the Law 1869–1945.* Toronto: University of Toronto Press, 2006.

Strange, Carolyn. *Toronto's Girl Problem: The Perils and Pleasures of the City, 1880–1930.* Toronto: University of Toronto Press, 1995.

Notes

[1] Robert Craig Brown and Ramsay Cook, *Canada, 1896–1921: A Nation Transformed* (Toronto: McClelland & Stewart, 1974).

[2] Joseph Schull, *Laurier: The First Canadian* (Toronto: Macmillan of Canada, 1965), 378.

[3] Carman Miller, *Canada's Little War: Fighting for the British Empire in Southern Africa, 1899–1902* (Toronto: J. Lorimer, 2003), 59.

[4] Schull, *Laurier*, 410.

[5] Helen Lenskyj, *Out of Bounds: Women, Sports and Sexuality* (Toronto: Women's Press, 1986), 20.

[6] Ken Cruikshank, *Close Ties: Railways, Government and the Board of Railway Commissioners, 1851–1933* (Montreal and Kingston: McGill-Queen's University Press, 1991).

[7] Brown and Cook, *Canada, 1896–1921*, 53.

[8] Olive Dickason, *Canada's First Nations: A History of Founding People's from Earliest Times* (Toronto: McClelland & Stewart, 1992), 303.

[9] Gerald Frieson, *The Canadian Prairies: A History* (Toronto: University of Toronto Press, 1984), 161.

[10] J.T. Copp, *The Anatomy of Poverty: The Condition of the Working Class in Montreal, 1897–1929* (Toronto: McClelland & Stewart, 1974), Michael Piva, *The Condition of the Working Class in Toronto, 1900–1921* (Ottawa: University of Ottawa Press, 1979).

[11] Ibid., 150.

[12] Sean Purdy, "Industrial Efficiency, Social Order and Moral Purity: Housing Reform Thought in English Canada, 1900–1950," *Urban History Review* 25, 2 (1997): 31.

[13] Charlotte Gray, *Mrs. King: The Life & Times of Isabel Mackenzie King* (Toronto: Penguin, 1997), 138.

[14] Bryan Palmer, *A Culture in Conflict: Skilled Workers and Industrial Capitalism in Hamilton, 1860–1914* (Montreal and Kingston: McGill-Queen's University Press, 1974).

[15] Paul Craven, *"An Impartial Umpire": Industrial Relations and the Canadian State, 1900–1911* (Toronto: University of Toronto Press, 1980), 252.

16   Ian McKay, *Reasoning Otherwise: Leftists and the People's Enlightenment in Canada* (Toronto: Between the Lines, 2008), 129.

17   Valerie Knowles, *Strangers at Our Gates: Canadian Immigration and Immigration Policy, 1540–1997* (Toronto: Dundurn Press, 1998), 90.

18   McKay, *Reasoning Otherwise*, 384.

19   Ibid., 106–107.

20   Angus McLaren and Irene Tigar McLaren, *The Bedroom and the State: The Changing Practices and Politics of Contraception and Abortion in Canada, 1880–1980* (Toronto: McClelland & Stewart, 1986), 9.

21   Ruth Brouwer, *New Women for God: Canadian Presbyterian Women and India Missions, 1876–1914* (Toronto: University of Toronto Press, 1990).

22   Carol Lee Bacchi, *Liberation Deferred? The Ideas of the English-Canadian Suffragists, 1877–1918* (Toronto: University of Toronto Press, 1983), 87.

23   Robert Craig Brown, *Robert Borden: A Biography. Vol. 1, 1854–1914* (Toronto: Macmillan, 1975), 122.

24   Robert Choquette, *Language and Religion: A History of English–French Conflict in Ontario* (Ottawa: University of Ottawa Press, 1975), 163.

4

War *and* Upheaval: *1914–1919*

*N*early a half-century after the First World War ended, retired schoolmaster John Sudbury still vividly recalled the hell of Passchendaele. As part of the 9th Canadian Machine Gun Company, he arrived on October 25, 1917, at a quagmire resulting from weeks of rain and intense shellfire that had churned the earth into a muddy, seemingly impassable bog. Just before sunrise, still under the cover of darkness, he went over the top. Almost immediately, Sudbury heard a thump behind him. Fortunately for him, the mud had absorbed most of the shrapnel, but when he called out to his comrade Stephens, he heard nothing; turning around, he saw only a few chunks of flesh. Sudbury's company continued pushing ahead in "pouring rain and complete darkness," listening for "groans and puffings," so they would not fall over one another. He passed a waterlogged shell hole where he made out two Germans bleeding profusely, boys he judged to be no more than 16. "The look in their eyes I have never been able to forget," he said. "A look of abject fear mingled somehow

Source: Queen's University Archives, A.A. Chesterton Fonds, V007, Box 16-18, Album 2.

with pity."[1] He took a swig from his water bottle, tossed it to his helpless enemies, and continued moving towards his objective, taking cover from enemy and friendly shellfire not properly sequenced with the advance. Suddenly, his leg was jolted by a sharp, searing pain; he had been shot. He found himself alone, crawling through mud, trying to keep his head above the water to avoid drowning. Miraculously, he slithered back a half kilometre until he heard English voices. He was relieved by his "blighty," a term used by troops for a wound serious enough to take them out of action, hopefully back to England, but not permanently disfiguring. He languished for hours as medical personnel tried to cope with the deluge of wounded. Gangrene set in, and after six unsuccessful operations, Sudbury's leg was amputated.

After reading this chapter you will be able to:

1. Appreciate the devastating human impact of the First World War on Canada.
2. Assess how democracy and civil liberties in Canada were compromised by the war.
3. Identify how the Canadian economy was changed by wartime needs.
4. Explain the evolution of Canada's military forces through major campaigns and battles.
5. Understand the ways in which the war was a nation-building experience.
6. Recall major political and social divisions that the war brought to Canada.

Introduction

The First World War still holds iconic status as the most brutal, wasteful, and soul-destroying conflict in modern history. It evokes images of muddy trenches, the killing ground of No-Man's Land, pervasive rats and lice, men hurled *en masse* into storms of shell and machine-gun fire, and a legacy of lost idealism and the death of romanticism. When it was fought, it was called the "Great War for Civilization," a struggle to save the world from Prussian tyranny and militarism. However, historians present a far more complex picture of its origins, tracing them to the emergence of new European states and growing nationalist sentiment, competing economic aims and an arms race between major European powers and rival empires, and a series of alliances that created obligations and suspicions and that seemingly had nations blunder their way into an orgy of destruction.

Under the "Iron Chancellor" Otto von Bismarck and Kaiser Wilhelm II, a newly unified Germany pushed harder throughout the late nineteenth century on industrial, military, and territorial expansion. It decided not to renew treaties with Russia, instead allying with the Austrian-Hungarian Empire and creating a non-aggression pact with Italy in 1881 to create the Triple Alliance. This eventually prompted France and Russia to enter into an alliance to offset Berlin. Britain, fearful of Germany's growing naval strength, established mutual defence agreements with Russia and France. Europe became divided into two camps: the Entente Powers (Britain, France, and Russia) and the Central Powers (Germany, Austria-Hungary, and Italy; though in 1914, with war clouds gathering, Italy negotiated a secret pact with France to stay neutral, and the next year declared Germany the aggressor and joined the Entente).

The spark that set off the powder keg came on June 28, 1914, when Serb nationalists assassinated the heir to the Austrian throne, Archduke Franz Ferdinand. Although the Archduke was not especially popular at home, his murder challenged Austria-Hungary's aim to control the Balkans. The manner by which Austria demanded that the perpetrators be brought to justice essentially denied Serbia's sovereignty; but the purpose was to provoke war so that Austria-Hungary could reassert its dominance in the region. The Germans backed Austria-Hungary despite the possibility of war with Russia because of Russia's strong ties to Serbia. Germany hoped to divide the Entente, believing that France and Britain would not come to Russia's aid. On July 28, Austria-Hungary declared war on Serbia. Russia mobilized its forces, and on August 1, Germany went to war against Russia; France followed on August 3 by declaring war against Germany. Germany invaded Belgium to bypass and encircle France's powerful *Maginot* defensive line on the French-

German border, but this violated Belgian neutrality, which Britain had pledged to defend in a 75-year-old treaty, thus bringing it into the war on August 4.

It was to be the "war to end all wars," an event that initially sparked celebrations across the globe, especially among young men who clamoured to partake in this decisive struggle, and to test their mettle, and who foresaw a great adventure. By the time it ended on November 11, 1918, the war had claimed 10 million military lives and 6 million civilian ones. Canada's 67 000 dead and 172 000 wounded represented 3 percent of its population of 8 million.

In August 1914, Canada was still a colony. When Britain declared war, Canada was committed, but its permanent military numbered just 5000. At the time, Canada's economy was still largely dependent upon the production, extraction, and export of staples. Soon, heavy industry flourished to feed the country's growing war machine. Income and corporate taxes and nationwide social programs debuted. Some 630 000 Canadians, or nearly 8 percent of the country's population, donned a military uniform. Canadian military historians generally agree that Canada's army evolved into one of if not *the* best among the forces fighting against Germany and its allies. Seventy Canadians were recognized with the prestigious Victoria Cross, the British Empire's highest award for bravery. Canada rose in stature within and developed ambitions that extended beyond the realm of the Empire. Indeed, it has become a standard refrain to say that Canada went from "colony to nation" on the basis of its wartime contributions, the collective pride that resulted, and the new international recognition it received. But was this worth nearly a quarter million casualties? Did the war really change Canada's status? By 1914, Canada had already made it clear it would not accept imperial federation. Moreover, the conflict precipitated unprecedented assaults on freedoms and produced deep and long-lasting cleavages based upon language, religion, region, and class. This chapter explores the many ways that the First World War affected Canada and asks readers to weigh its impact on national development.

August 4, 1914: Britain declares war on Germany, thus also committing Canada.

A Glorious Adventure

To Canadians, the Balkans always seemed engulfed in turmoil; thus, when the Austrian Archduke was assassinated, Canadian newspapers took notice but paid more attention to the sensational murder trail of Madame Caillaux, the wife of a former French premier, who shot the editor of the Paris newspaper *Le Figaro* to stop slanders against her husband. Days before Britain declared war, Prime Minister Borden was still vacationing in the Muskokas.

News of Britain's declaration reached Canada on the morning of a Monday bank holiday. With many urban workers enjoying the day off, large crowds gathered outside newspaper offices to hear the latest developments. Newspapers printed multiple editions because people quickly snatched up copies. Technically, Canada's involvement in the war was automatic. Until the Statute of Westminster in 1931 provided Canada and the other British dominions with control over their foreign policy, Britain declared war on behalf of the Empire. However, the level and form of Canada's commitment lay with its own Parliament.

For many Canadians, the answer was clear-cut. Reports from across the country described enthusiastic, celebratory crowds breaking into renditions of "O Canada" and "God Save the King." Certainly, some were worried, but they were not mentioned in newspapers. Although it was known that people died in wars, not since the American Civil

War in the 1860s had North America suffered mass casualties in battle. Also, with a severe economic downturn persisting well into 1915, military service meant a job paying at least $1.10 a day and the means to support one's family, as money that soldiers sent home was supplemented by a government separation allowance and support from the privately run Canadian Patriotic Fund. Young men rushed to recruiting centres, as conventional wisdom held that hostilities would end by Christmas, as many experts said that neither side could sustain total war for more than a few months. Even the *nationaliste* leader, Henri Bourassa, initially said, "It is Canada's national duty to contribute according to her resources."[2]

Canada's Parliament unanimously approved an overseas contingent of 25 000 men, by far the country's greatest military commitment to date, and a war appropriation of $50 million. Ottawa also armed itself with new, and unprecedented, powers to keep Canadians behind the cause. On August 22, the Conservative majority passed the *War Measures Act*, and made its powers retroactive to the beginning of the war, thus establishing criminal conduct before it was defined as such. The Act permitted Ottawa to impose a command economy, namely one run by the government and not market forces, to intern suspected dissenters, and to censor all means of communication. Those contravening the Act were liable to receive a $5000 fine—about six times the average annual salary—five years in jail, or both.

Two days after Canada went to war, Minister of Militia and Defence Sam Hughes dispatched telegrams to the commanders of the country's 226 militia units instructing them to send men to a new military base he had ordered constructed at Valcartier, a barren and sandy expanse of land located 30 kilometres north of Quebec City. There were many other existing and suitable training sites, but they would not suit Canada's highly driven, charismatic, but also impulsive and overbearing, militia minister. Hughes sought to create an army of citizen soldiers whom he hoped to personally lead into battle. Reflecting his longstanding passion for the militia, whose members he portrayed as more adaptable than those belonging to the permanent force, whom he characterized as "professional loafers," he went so far as to send one of Canada's two permanent force battalions, the Royal Canadian Regiment, to Bermuda for garrison duty, thus robbing green recruits of highly capable trainers. To his credit, Hughes would spot and promote good militia commanders, namely Lieutenant-Colonel Arthur Currie, whom he put in charge of the 2nd Brigade. However, he also championed less competent friends and supporters, as well as his son Garnet who was widely regarded as a poor military leader but made second-in-command in the 3rd Brigade (though it was Garnet who convinced Currie to accept his father's offer of command, as Currie, a Victoria land developer, considered staying in Canada to raise money to pay back $10 000 in regimental funds he had transferred to cover for bad investments).

By September, Hughes's unrelenting efforts resulted in the appearance of a tent city at Valcartier housing in what had grown to be 33 000 members of the Canadian Expeditionary Force (CEF). The chaotic process of development generated many troubling questions, especially about cost overruns, such as for medicine, binoculars, and horses that seemed ready for the glue factory. Hughes also insisted on having men equipped with the Canadian-made Ross rifle. A decade earlier, he had convinced Laurier to adopt it for the militia, a sales job made easier since Charles Ross agreed to place his rifle factory in the prime minister's home riding of Quebec East. The Ross was accurate and powerful but could fire only five rounds a minute, one-third the rate of the Lee-Enfield, the standard issue for British soldiers. The Ross was also expensive to manufacture; was too long for the confines of trench warfare; had defective sites; and easily jammed. Besides equipment problems, some two-thirds of the original CEF were British-born men who were eager to assist their homeland, but this portended future recruitment problems as the number of these expatriates dwindled.

Initially, it seemed everyone wanted to demonstrate patriotism. Soon after Canada joined the war, department store owner John Eaton donated $100 000 for armoured cars equipped with Colt machine guns. By the end of August 1914, the Imperial Order Daughters of the Empire (IODE) raised $100 000 to establish a hospital ship. Several businesses, no doubt anticipating a short war, continued paying the salaries of employees who enlisted to their families. Toronto's municipal government contributed 100 horses to the army, continued paying its employees who enlisted, and provided them with a life insurance policy, a gesture it quietly dropped in 1915. The first nationwide appeal for the Canadian Patriotic Fund at the end of August 1914, which was to provide money to the dependants of servicemen, quickly exceeded its $6 million target. Canadians responded to the rallying cry that if one could not "fight," then they should "pay" to help those at home who had sacrificed through the enlistment of a loved one. Yet, to keep the fund solvent and to promote certain conduct, only women who demonstrated financial need, acted frugally, and remained beyond moral reproach received support. Assistance ranged from $10 to $20 a month and when added to money garnished from a soldier's pay to send home and the government separation allowance, the support provided was roughly equivalent to the salary of an unskilled male worker. Although Canadians responded well to periodic drives to replenish the Patriotic Fund, it struggled to meet the need as the number of recruits grew and wartime inflation mounted, and thus required increased government contributions. In the Second World War, the Patriotic Fund was dropped in favour of a government-financed dependants' allowance, whose monthly minimum was raised to $35.

Torontonians pitch in to raise money for the Canadian Patriotic Fund.

Source: Library and Archives of Canada, PA-042857.

The Enemy Within

As Canada's first total war, many Canadians worried about spies and saboteurs, especially with a neutral United States containing millions of German Americans. Up to 16 000 Canadian militia personnel patrolled the international border and guarded arsenals and critical infrastructure. Soon after the war started, Canadian militiamen near Niagara Falls killed two American hunters; the jittery and inexperienced soldiers feared that the Americans were scouts for a hostile force. With time and no attacks, anxiety eased, though fears were periodically stoked by newspaper accounts of nefarious schemes afoot, such as in early 1915 when two German Americans were arrested in Detroit for plotting to destroy buildings in Windsor and Walkerton, Ontario. The February 1916 fire that demolished the House of Commons, which was caused by a combination of careless smoking, piles of paper lying about, and highly oiled pine desks, chairs, and panelling, was initially blamed in screaming newspaper headlines on German-American saboteurs. Parliament was transferred to the nearby Victoria Natural History Museum, where some joked that the "fossils were moved out and a new batch moved in."[3] Also in spring 1916, the majority Anglo population in the southwestern Ontario community of Berlin led a successful name-changing campaign to Kitchener to commemorate the late British minister of war. During the contest, soldiers with the 118th battalion stole a bust of Kaiser Wilhelm I from the German Concordia Club, dumped it into Victoria Lake, and sacked the premises, ignoring the fact that the club had ceased operations for more than a year and that almost half its members had volunteered to fight for Canada.

One thing most German Canadians had going for them was that their long-settled status in Canada made them British subjects. This was not the case with some 60 000 more recently arrived Ukrainians from the Austrian-controlled province of Galicia, who were classified as enemy aliens. Canada's federal government promised them equal treatment so long as they obeyed the laws of the land, yet, within a month of the war starting, Sir William Otter, the first Canadian-born general officer commanding, was convinced to come out of retirement to become the director of internment operations. Authorities noted that in August 1914 the Western Canadian Ukrainian spiritual leader, Bishop Nicholas Budka, advised his followers "to support the peace-loving [Austrian] Emperor Franz-Joseph." Within a week, Budka recanted, insisting that all Ukrainians were "faithful citizens of … the British Empire."[4] Understandably, many considered the second comment dishonest, but it was assumed that numerous Galicians would follow Budka's initial, and subversive, advice.

Enemy aliens were ordered to register their location with authorities. Those who tried to leave the country, such as to find work in the United States, were interned, as it was assumed they were attempting to get home to fight for the enemy. Canada interned 8579 individuals, though if the 3100 German reservists and the 800 prisoners-of-war sent to Canada by British authorities are subtracted, the remaining 4679 comprised about 8 percent of potential enemy aliens.

Twenty-four internment stations were established in British Columbia, Alberta, Ontario, Quebec, and Nova Scotia. Living facilities for the inmates included tents, railway cars, bunkhouses, armouries, barracks, forts, exhibition buildings, and factories. In Kingston, German POWs were housed in Fort Henry, a stone garrison built in the 1830s to defend

October 1914:
Internment of Ukrainian
Canadians commences.

Canada from an American invasion that never happened. Others, especially Ukrainians, were sent to remote places, such as Kapuskasing in northern Ontario and Spirit Lake in northern Quebec, as well to work in Canada's emerging national parks, such as Banff, where they built roads with pick-and-shovel, setting the groundwork for what politicians predicted would be a post-war tourist boom. Some 100 prisoners died from illnesses, and six were killed, including for trying to escape. In 1916, as Canada's labour surplus transformed into a shortage, most Ukrainian internees were paroled, though only if they accepted certain work, such as farm labour.

Into the Breach

In the first month of the war, German forces advanced rapidly, all the way to the outskirts of Paris. They were turned back in early September at the Battle of the Marne. Both sides then literally dug in, starting the construction of a trench network that would snake its way through France and Belgium all the way from the Swiss border to the North Sea. However, the Germans maintained control over higher ground and built their trenches on the reverse side of hills or slopes, which provided better protection against artillery fire.

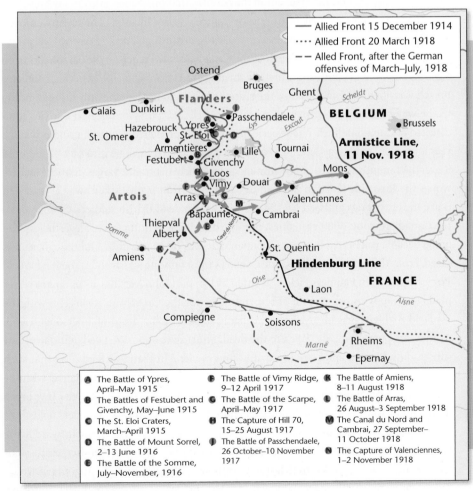

Map 4.1
The Western Front and Major Canadian Engagements, 1914–1918

Source: Veterans Affairs Canada.

On October 15, 1914, cheering crowds in Plymouth, England, greeted the first Canadian troops to arrive. Known as the 1st Division, its members were to continue training at Salisbury Plain, a plateau in south-central England. After a week of pleasant weather, rain came, and came—the rain fell for 89 out of 123 days, creating massive flooding as the chalky terrain could not soak up the water. Tents leaked, uniforms became sodden, Canadian-made boots disintegrated in the swamp-like conditions (which brought accusations of shoddy work and profiteering), and there resulted a massive influenza rate and an outbreak of cerebrospinal meningitis. Responding to growing outrage among the Canadians, a British division was moved from their huts at Shorncliffe camp near Dover to make room for them.

In February 1915, the 1st Division moved to France under the command of British General Edmund Alderson, who had experience leading Canadian troops in the 1899–1902 Boer War. They joined the British at Neuve Chapelle, where the Canadians experienced their baptism by fire from March 10 to 12. The British had borne the brunt in the sector, taking nearly 13 000 casualties over a much longer period, compared with only 100 for Canada.

April 22–May 3, 1915: 2nd Battle of Ypres.

But this was the proverbial calm before the storm, as in late April there came the 2nd Battle of Ypres. With Germany occupying nearly all of Belgium, the allies were determined to hold a 20 square kilometre salient in the country that protruded into enemy lines. The Canadians arrived on April 14 to relieve France's 11th Division. The enemy enjoyed superior firepower and was determined to make a breakthrough. April 22 dawned warm and sunny, but things soon turned ghastly as the Canadians saw French territorial soldiers from Algeria retreating in panic, some literally turning green from chlorine gas. A six kilometre breach was opened up in the allied lines, and the Canadians were the only thing standing in the way of a major German advance. On April 24, cylinders released a toxic cloud directed at Canadian lines. As the eerie green mist approached, Canadian soldiers, still a year away from receiving decent gas masks, were ordered to urinate into a cloth and hold it over their mouth and nose, as the ammonia would help neutralize the gas. To make matters worse, the Ross rifle failed in the heat of battle. Men frantically kicked away at its seized bolts; the lucky ones grabbed Lee-Enfield rifles from dead British soldiers. Over 16 days, the Canadians took 6000 casualties, one-third of their fighting force. Nevertheless, the battle became celebrated because Canadian defences ultimately held and the salient was saved. From this clash there also came Canada's most famous words about the First World War: the poem "In Flanders Fields." Written by Captain John McCrae, its poignant verses made the poppy into a symbol of remembrance for the Great War. A surgeon with the 1st Field Artillery Brigade, McCrae was badly shaken by the death of a personal friend. At first, his poem laments: "We are the dead. Short days ago / We lived, felt dawn, saw sunset glow / Loved and were loved, and now we lie / In Flanders fields." So that such sacrifice not be given in vain, McCrae implores readers to "Take up our quarrel with the foe / To you from failing hands we throw / The torch; be yours to hold it high / If ye break faith with us who die / We shall not sleep, though poppies grow / In Flanders fields."

Troops generally followed six- to seven-day rotating shifts between the forward firing line, support, and reserve trenches. Life at the front was often vile: Men frequently went without bathing for weeks; trenches were often waterlogged, and the dugouts in which men slept were usually ledges dredged into the dirt walls; rotting food, wet uniforms,

Canadian soldiers draining trenches on the Western Front, July 1916.

Source: Library and Archives of Canada, PA-000396.

open-pit latrines, and sometimes decomposing bodies produced an indescribable stench; rats fed off corpses and army rations; lice infested uniforms, laying their eggs in the seams; and enemy shelling often seemed relentless. Even in a relatively minor battle like Neuve Chapelle, more shells were fired than during the entire Boer War. In many sectors, men dared not look over the trenches, lest a sniper pick them off. Thousands were immobilized with shell shock or what some military authorities sarcastically called "hysterical sympathy with the enemy." Medical personnel often implemented electro-shock therapy to ferret out fakers, to prevent others from following suit, and to force men to conquer their fears. Men were sustained by close relationships forged with their comrades. They also coped by developing a sardonic sense of humour, as expressed in raunchy songs and in regimental and battalion newspapers that poked fun at authority figures and the sorry predicament of the "poor bloody infantry."

Compounding difficulties was that Germany enjoyed air superiority during the first half of the war. Canada had no air force at the war's outset because its leaders did not view the country as prone to aerial attack. The navy wasn't much better. Canadian vessels were few, poorly armed, and obsolete. Soon after the war started, British Columbia's government, fearing an attack on its unguarded coastline, bought two small and unarmed submarines from a Seattle company; the cost amounted to two times the federal government's 1912–1913 budget for the navy.

Rallying the Home Front

Long casualty lists were countered by inspirational press coverage. Most journalists were eager to do their bit. Canada's most significant figure in providing battlefield accounts was William Maxwell Aitken, who, in March 1915, was appointed as the official *eyewitness* for the Canadian press. After making a fortune in Canada by selling industrial bonds and by arranging corporate mergers, Aitken pursued broader horizons in England. By the outset of the First World War, he had obtained a controlling interest in the Rolls Royce Company and a substantial piece of the London *Daily Express*, and ran successfully for Britain's Parliament. Keen to promote Canada within the British Empire, he helped bankroll the creation of the Canadian War Records Office (CWRO), which was to collect documentation about Canada's war effort, and became its director in January 1915. He also established Canada's official war art program that seconded British and Canadian painters (including several who in the 1920s formed Canada's renowned Group of Seven), as Aitken envisaged such work as becoming a central piece of a future Canadian war museum. Based largely on his work for Canada, which also involved the production of photographic and film propaganda, in 1916 he was appointed to oversee the creation of newsreel propaganda for Britain, in 1917 was given a peerage as the 1st Baron of Beaverbrook, and in 1918 was made Britain's minister of information.

June 1915, office of the chief press censor created in Canada.

In Canada, the leakage of some sensitive news early in the war, such as troopship departure times, convinced Ottawa to create in June 1915 the position of chief press censor, who received authority to prohibit sources "preventing, embarrassing, or hindering the successful prosecution of the war."[5] The chief censor banned 253 printed sources, with 222 coming from the United States and 164 written in a foreign language, particularly those of Canada's enemies. Historian Jeff Keshen argues that Canadian civilians remained well sheltered from knowing the gruesome realities of war, not only because of censorship but also as a result of Canada's great distance from the battlefields of Europe. However, in his intensive study of Toronto newspapers, historian Ian Miller counters that civilians did read truthful, and sometimes graphic, accounts of battles, which were underlined by long casualty lists and honest letters sent home from Canadians fighting overseas.[6]

Given that before the war, Germany was a leading force in the development of art, music, literature, and other areas linked to an advanced civilization, much of the earlier discourse blamed its aggression and militarism on the ambitions of Kaiser Wilhelm II, but the message soon changed to indict all Germans. Starting in late 1914, information emerged reporting on German atrocities against Belgian civilians, which sparked the creation of citizen-run Belgian Relief Committees across Canada. Many accusations, such as Belgian women and babies being killed and mutilated, were issued and given legitimacy by the British government's 1915 Bryce Commission, though after the war they were shown to be based upon fabricated testimony by Belgian refugees.

In May 1915, the British passenger ship *Lusitania* was sunk, with a loss of 1198 lives, including 170 Canadians. Berlin's assertion that the vessel carried munitions, which was likely true, was denounced as a vicious lie spread by a brutal enemy accused of striking a medal to honour those who committed the monstrous deed. The Germans became called "Huns" after the fifth-century marauding warriors under Attila the Hun and were said to be motivated by the ethos of *kultur*, namely a belief in their superiority and their right to impose their will on others.

In Canada's churches, a common message became that Britain and its allies were providing "Christ's soldiers." Young Canadians were fed a steady diet of pro-war propaganda. New books on Ontario's high school curriculum included *How Britain Strove for*

Peace and *Germany's Swelled Head.* The war also inspired some 300 patriotic tunes written by Canadians. For example, in Harry Taylor's "We'll Love You More When You Come Back Than When You Went Away," a young man's mother and his wife urge him to perform his duty to King and country.

Grassroots volunteer initiatives to support the war effort enveloped communities. Women, particularly those from the upper and middle class, who had more free time, influence, and connections, led numerous campaigns. The IODE, whose membership grew by one-third to 40 000 during the war, sent supplies to military hospitals and millions of books, magazines, and cigarettes to soldiers. In Ottawa, the Women's Canadian Club started a tea shop and second-hand store that raised thousands of dollars for various war charities. The volunteers the club recruited, including the wives of Prime Minister Borden and Opposition Leader Laurier, helped staff major retail stores, which, on specified days, turned over a portion of their profits to support the war effort. As well, fundraising efforts organized by the Local Council of Women included variety shows using local talent.

In the first third of the war, military recruitment remained strong. By early 1915, Canada had raised a 2nd Division, which, when arriving in England in September to join the 1st Division, resulted in the creation of the Canadian Corps. Prior to September 1915, 69 of 71 infantry battalions authorized by Ottawa attained full strength. In many cases, men were drawn into regiments on the basis of ethnic background, like the Toronto Scottish. There were Sportsmen or Pals Battalions promoting combat as a comparatively safe and manly game. Imperialistic sentiment was used, such as by Ottawa's 207th, which in one of its recruiting posters showed an officer pointing to the Union Jack that he proclaimed, "stands for liberty." Reflecting current conceptions of manliness and duty, the Niagara-based 98th Battalion advertised that to shirk military service was "to live in humiliation."[7]

During the earlier part of the war, it often seemed that men volunteering for military service were trying to join an exclusive club. Deluged with applicants, Toronto's Queen's Own Rifles said it would accept only those with militia experience. In August and September 1914, more than 5000 Canadian men were rejected for military service on medical grounds and through to 1916, the rejection rate was 25 percent, with the principal reasons being

- failure to meet height (5 foot 4 inches or 1.63 metres) and expanded chest (34 inches or 86 centimetres) requirements
- bad teeth (as men overseas often had to subsist on hard tack)
- flat feet
- varicose veins
- poor hearing or eyesight
- low intelligence
- tuberculosis and venereal disease

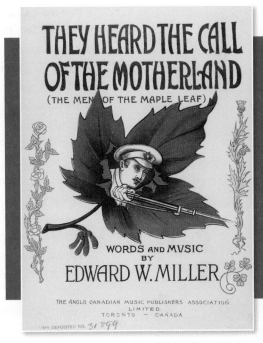

Canada's loyalty to Britain was a theme in numerous war songs.

Source: Library and Archives of Canada, Sheet Music from Canada's Past. Edward W. Miller, *They Heard the Call of the Motherland* (Toronto: Anglo Canadian Music Publishers Assn., 1916).

Married men were required to get their wives' written permission to enlist, a policy advocated by Sam Hughes, who insisted it was a man's duty to properly provide for his dependants. Realizing that rejected men, in looking outwardly healthy, would likely face public scorn, the government issued a lapel pin with the initials A.R. meaning "applied, rejected."

As the war dragged on, recruiting problems became evident, and the pressure to enlist intensified, especially in English Canada. Citizen recruiting committees visited employers to identify men who could or should be pressed into uniform, and then arranged for follow-up appeals by military recruiters. Patriotic rallies turned into recruiting drives. At one massive gathering in Toronto's Riverdale Park in the summer of 1915, where the crowd was estimated at 200 000, a number of women walked through the throng with a torn pillow, placing chicken feathers on men in civilian clothes to shame them into service. Convinced of the unique ability of women to influence men to join up, the commanding officer of the Toronto-based 124th Overseas Battalion, Lieutenant-Colonel W.B. Kingsmill, implored women to shun those who refused to don a uniform: "Bar them out, you women. Refuse their invitations, scorn their attentions. For the love of heaven, if they won't be men, then you won't be women. Tell them to come in uniform. Tell them to join the colours while they can still do so with honour."[8] In Toronto, one estimate concluded that two-thirds of those who were eligible ultimately volunteered for military service, though this was in a city whose population was four-fifths Anglo and Protestant.

By contrast, many Francophones saw the First World War as Britain's conflict. Native-born Anglo-Canadians demonstrated less inclination to enlist compared with British expatriates. Lower recruitment in the Maritimes—9.96 percent of those aged 18 to 45, compared with 14.42 percent in Ontario and 15.52 in the Prairies—reflected less enthusiasm among Acadians, a long-settled Anglo population, and an economic boom in port cities, which meant more well-paying jobs in a region that had long suffered from a declining economy. Also in many Central Canadian urban centres, recruitment was hurt by expanding opportunities for decently paid war jobs, while in rural Canada young men were increasingly needed on farms to meet the growing demand for food. By the end of 1915, Canada had recruited nearly a quarter million volunteers for military service, but rising casualties, especially by Britain, which implemented conscription in January 1916, intensified pressure on Canada to do more. On New Year's Day 1916, Robert Borden publicly committed Canada to the lofty and symbolic (but also, many military leaders said, unrealistic) goal of raising a voluntary army of half a million men.

The greatest challenge with recruitment was in Quebec. Hughes, supremely confident to the point of self-delusion, brushed aside his membership in the Orange Order and support for *Regulation 17*, and believed that his Huguenot ancestry would rally Québécois to his side. When the war started, he had an opportunity to change negative perceptions of himself and the belief among Francophones that Canada's military was an Anglo institution, as, for instance, in 1912 only 27 of 254 Canadian officers were Francophones. This also meant that there were few French-Canadian officers to lead regiments and to help with recruitment. With French Canada initially demonstrating some enthusiasm for the war, enough Québécois volunteered for the 1st Division to start a French-speaking regiment, but Hughes, seeking to create a unified Canadian military, dispersed Francophones into Anglo-dominated battalions. Only with considerable pressure from prominent French-Canadian politicians, and a $50 000 donation from the Montreal doctor and militarist Arthur Mignault, was the French-commanded and French-speaking 22nd Battalion created within Canada's 2nd Division. To fill the ranks of the 22nd, it was necessary to recruit Francophones from across Canada.

The fact that French Canadians married younger and more often had families to support hurt their recruitment. Many were needed on farms, while in urban areas, particularly Montreal, well-paying industrial war jobs were a stronger attraction than $1.10 a day as a private. Ontario's *Regulation 17* continued to sow bitterness and further damaged French-Canadian recruitment, especially as it generated well-publicized flashpoints. In October 1915, two French-speaking teachers were fired from Ottawa's Guigues School for not instructing in English. They re-established classes at a nearby private home, and Francophone students boycotted the provincially appointed replacements at Guigues. Francophone school commissioners, who had also been fired by the provincial government for defying *Regulation 17*, orchestrated an invasion of Guigues. Parents stormed the school and for several days women held off the police with long hatpins. In Quebec, many claimed that the real Prussians were next door in Ontario, not overseas. A petition from Quebec bearing 600 000 signatures demanded the repeal of the legislation. In Parliament, Laurier, so as not to alienate his Anglo supporters and MPs (who were starting to grumble about his opposition to conscription), had Ernest Lapointe, who since 1904 had represented the rural Quebec riding of Kamaouraska, introduce a resolution in Parliament asking that the Borden government urge Ontario to rescind *Regulation 17*. The federal government maintained that schooling fell under provincial jurisdiction, and, with its parliamentary majority, soundly defeated the Lapointe proposal.

Economic Expansion

Rising demand for food, both in growing and increasingly industrialized Canadian cities and to feed troops and civilians overseas, provided for a major upsurge in agriculture. Canadian cheese and pork exports reached record levels. Between 1914 and 1919, the price of wheat tripled because of enormous demand, yet problems also emerged through a combination of overexpansion (to take advantage of high prices) and the federal government strongly encouraging Western farmers to solely emphasize wheat, a situation that soon tied the prairie economy more strongly to one crop and made it highly susceptible to a major downturn, which is what happened when wheat prices tumbled after the war.

Canadian farms had to deal with growing labour shortages as young men joined the military or took better-paying urban war jobs. Also in the West, there were complaints that the federal government overwhelmingly directed war contracts to Central Canada, bypassing Winnipeg, then Canada's third largest city. Ottawa claimed that its sole consideration was efficiency and that industries in Central Canada were larger, more mechanized, and had better access to labour, capital, and transportation. Playing a key role in developing the federal government's industrial mobilization strategy was Solicitor-General Arthur Meighen, who represented the Manitoba riding of Portage La Prairie.

By March 1915, 200 Canadian firms were involved in war production. Ontario produced 60 percent of munitions in Canada. Although out-migration occurred from the Maritimes as people took war jobs in Central Canada, the value of exports passing through Halifax soared from less than $20 million in 1915 to $140 million two years later, while Cape Breton experienced a major upsurge in coal production in large part to feed war industries.

Initially, war contracts were arranged through the federal government's Shell Committee, but it was grossly mismanaged under Colonel J. Wesley Allison, an old militia friend of Sam Hughes. Complaints multiplied over defective products, including an abnormally high proportion of shells that were duds. The committee signed contracts for items whose price seemed exorbitant, and accusations multiplied about war profiteering and committee members being on the take. By the end of 1915, the British government became so disgusted with the state of affairs that it threatened not to purchase any more Canadian shells.

December 1915: Imperial Munitions Board established.

In December 1915, the Imperial Munitions Board (IMB) replaced the Shell Committee. Technically, the IMB was an arm of the British government, but in Canada a Canadian, Joseph Flavelle, president of the massive William Davies meat packing company, ran it. Under the IMB's direction, Canada became a significant arms producer and supplier, and did so with contracts that set down strict quality control, delivery deadlines, and maximum profits, typically in the 5 percent range. By 1917, Canada was producing nearly 30 percent of the ammunition used by Britain. Some 600 factories and 25 000 workers became linked to the IMB, which quickly evolved into Canada's largest corporate enterprise, which included chemical factories, shipyards, submarine construction at Canadian Vickers in Montreal, and aircraft production at the IMB's Canadian Aeroplanes Limited plant in Toronto.

Still, the IMB was not free from controversy. Its relations with labour were strained. Flavelle rejected a "fair-wage clause," fearing that if it were linked with the IMB, it would become a goal in every labour dispute and the additional costs could hurt war production. In 1916, Hamilton munitions workers at an IMB-affiliated company went on strike, which Canada's chief censor ordered newspapers not to report. Also, the IMB suffered a public relations disaster when Canada's new cost-of-living commissioner reported that William Davies made an 85 percent profit in 1916, partly from injecting water into bacon to exaggerate its weight. Flavelle became an object of scorn, sarcastically nicknamed "His Lardship" or the "Baron of Bacon."

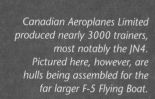

Canadian Aeroplanes Limited produced nearly 3000 trainers, most notably the JN4. Pictured here, however, are hulls being assembled for the far larger F-5 Flying Boat.

Source: Library and Archives of Canada, PA-025197.

Increasing Professionalism Overseas

In March 1916, Canada's still largely untested 2nd Division arrived at St. Eloi, just to the south of Ypres. On March 27, the British set off six massive mines underneath German trenches and advanced some 300 metres. The Canadians joined the battle on the night of April 3, but their communications broke down and large numbers could not locate themselves on maps because the terrain was so altered. They lost much of the British-captured ground, a failure that cost General Alderson his command.

Alderson's replacement was Britain's Lieutenant-General Julian Byng. He had commanded Canadians in the Boer War and in May 1915 supervised the successful British withdrawal from the doomed Gallipoli mission against Turkey. Nicknamed "Bungo" in his early years, some expressed doubts about Byng, who, it was said, got his breaks because his father, the Earl of Strafford, was a friend of the Prince of Wales. As head of the Canadian Corps, Byng proved to be a "cool and effective field commander"[9] and, with a friendly demeanour, was popular among the men; however, his first battles in June at Sanctuary Woods and at Mount Sorrel were disappointments. The Canadians fell back 700 metres, suffered 8500 casualties, and eight of Byng's battalion commanders were incapacitated with shell shock.

For the allies, the war reached a low point in mid-1916. To relieve pressure on the French, who were suffering massive casualties at Verdun, and convinced that German defences could be broken and the stalemate on the Western Front ended, Britain's Commander-in-Chief, Douglas Haig, prepared for a massive attack at the Somme. The Germans knew it was coming. Nearly 2 million shells were fired off in advance, but they failed to destroy well-fortified dugouts where the enemy waited. On July 1, British troops, many of whom were over-laden with equipment, struggled over trench parapets. Slowly advancing towards German lines, they were slaughtered, suffering 56 470 casualties, 19 240 of which were fatal, the bloodiest single day ever for the British military. That day, along with the entire Somme campaign that lasted until late November, came to personify for many the utter futility and carnage of the Great War, as over those five months the British advanced only 10 kilometres at the cost of 420 000 casualties, along with 200 000 casualties for the French and 500 000 for the Germans. Among those decimated on July 1 was the Newfoundland Regiment. In just half an hour at Beaumont Hamel, of 830 who went over the top, more than 700 became casualties, about half of whom were killed. Over the course of the Somme campaign, Canada suffered 24 000 casualties, including 8000 dead.

July 1, 1916: Battle of the Somme starts.

In spite of everything, Canadian forces learned, adapted, and improved. Training became more specialized, incorporating the bloody lessons of battle. The movement towards building a more professional army was further helped along by the declining influence of Sam Hughes as a result of recruitment problems and his worsening relations with Borden. Also reflecting the trend of professionalization, as well as the growing determination of the Canadian government to have a greater say over the use of the country's troops, was the creation of Canada's London-based Ministry of Overseas Military Forces in autumn 1916. It was to better coordinate with the British on standardizing and improving training, and to ensure that better-prepared Canadian officers took on broader leadership roles.

Canadian tactics and leadership became more effective. General Arthur Currie, who had risen to command the 1st Division, after having proven himself cool under fire and whose strategy at 2nd Ypres was key in turning back the German offensive, developed "bite and hold" infantry tactics in coordination with rolling artillery barrages that became a central feature in Canadian advances. In September, Canadian forces pushed forward 3000 metres to capture the village of Courcelette, the longest sustained advance by the allies in the Somme campaign. The battle became known for the first major use of tanks, something played up in newsreels, including in the CWRO film, *The Battle of Courcelette*, which had bilingual subtitles and toured extensively in Quebec, accompanied by two wounded French veterans because of the major role played by the 22nd Battalion in the advance. The *land ships*, as tanks were initially called, were presented to theatregoers as certain to crush the Germans, especially since the enemy was slow to develop them. While later versions of the tank were moderately effective, the Mark I, the model shown in this movie, moved only as fast as a man walking and also provided enemy artillery with an easy target because of its propensity to break down.

Canadian troops were acquiring a fierce reputation for trench raiding. These night-time operations involved a group of riflemen, bombers, and wire-cutters to attack a portion of the enemy lines to create fear, inflict damage, and gather information, including by capturing the enemy. Between November 1916 and the end of March 1917, the Canadians launched 60 raids, 48 of which managed to reach German trenches and take 338 prisoners. Also, though not publicized in Canada because of its association with German fiendishness, Canadians became proficient in the use of poison gas like phosgene. Moreover, better coordination was being achieved between artillery and advancing infantry; intelligence gathering became more effective; an expanding service corps that between 1916 and 1918 doubled to five metric tons the amount of shells delivered daily to the front was better supplying Canadian troops; and mass linear assaults that consistently produced high casualties were being replaced by synchronization between self-contained platoons of bombers and riflemen.

Looming Crises at Home

Borden's announcement of a half-million man military initially inspired more enlistments: 29 185 in January, 26 658 in February, and 34 913 in March 1916. However, in no month after June 1916 did more than 10 000 men volunteer, and in the 13 months before the first call-up of conscripts in January 1918, not one infantry battalion achieved full strength. Hughes's political stock plummeted with waning recruitment and allegations of corruption involving the Shell Committee, which were confirmed by a 1916 Royal Commission. Hughes also openly denounced Borden's decision to establish the Ministry of the Overseas Military Forces, which he saw as openly challenging his management of Canada's military. He was convinced that he could bully Borden—whom he regarded as genial but weak—into reversing his decision. The gamble backfired, and on November 9 Hughes was fired and replaced by the more low-key, but competent, Toronto industrialist Edward Kemp.

As the demands of the war intensified, it created conditions for modest social change. In August 1914, the Red Cross established 100 spots for Canadian women to go overseas as nurses. Nurses were typically portrayed in terms that denied their professionalism by tapping into traditional notions of womanhood, namely the belief that women were selfless, self-sacrificing "angels of mercy" that was even reflected in their quasi-religious uniform of a white nun-like dress. More than 6000 women applied, eager to contribute, show their patriotism, travel, grow within their profession, and experience adventure. All told, 2504 Canadian nurses, and roughly 2000 less-trained members of Voluntary Aid Detachments who performed medical, clerical, and driving duties, served in England, France, and the Eastern Mediterranean in Gallipoli, Alexandria, and Salonika. Unlike their British counterparts, Canadian nursing sisters were commissioned with the rank of lieutenant, though they did not have any power over males of subordinate rank. Many worked at casualty clearing stations, performing triage and administering basic care, sometimes within range of enemy artillery. Thirty-six Canadian nursing sisters died during the Great War while serving outside of Canada—15 at sea, 15 from disease, and 6 from enemy shell fire.

Women took an array of jobs to release more men for overseas service and to meet growing demands at home. Some 35 000 were hired in munitions plants, almost all in Ontario, and 6000 in an expanding wartime civil service, overwhelmingly in clerical positions. Women also assumed new roles as bank tellers, streetcar conductors, and as police matrons. However, convinced that female labour was temporary, many companies did not bother to create decent separate facilities. In 1918, the Ontario government distributed circulars telling women workers that they should prepare to leave their wartime jobs to make room for veterans.

The war also affected race relations. Aboriginal peoples were initially kept out of uniform because it was said that the enemy would not accord "savages" civilized treatment. The ban was never fully enforced and in December 1915 was formally removed, and 3500 Natives enlisted. Some saw enlistment as a means to escape poverty on reserves, others as a way to earn respect and better treatment for their people, and some perceived it as reflecting their treaty status in which they swore allegiance to the Crown in exchange for certain rights and privileges. Overseas, some Natives fought alongside whites, but large numbers were segregated into labour and forestry battalions that, though having the advantage of suffering lower casualties, were perceived as less important.

In Canada, the *Indian Act* was amended to make it easier for the federal government to take over or lease reserve land for war needs. However, later in the war, Natives claimed they could not legally be conscripted since they were not citizens and did not have the right to vote; and in January 1918 they were granted exemption from conscription, as were Asians because they too were denied the franchise. Native leaders hoped that loyal service would win greater rights for their people, but soon after the war, Fred Loft, a Mohawk veteran who rose to the rank of lieutenant, realizing that virtually nothing had changed, started the Pan-Canadian League of Natives, an initiative that spoke to growing frustration and activism among Aboriginals.

Chinese and East Indians were also initially excluded from the Canadian military, though enforcement was often lax, especially in areas where recruitment shortages became more serious. With Japan as a wartime ally, the Japanese were admitted into Canada's army and many saw combat. Many black Canadians sought to enlist with the expectation that it would bring greater equality. Some were accepted into combat units, like the Black Watch of Montreal, but many more were rejected in what they were told was a "white man's war." In April 1916, the No. 2 Construction Battalion was created, an all-black and white-

April 1916:
No. 2 Construction
Battalion established.

commanded formation located in Nova Scotia. Attached to the Forestry Corps in France, its members worked as loggers and in lumber mills, and performed construction and shipping work, including the building and repairing of trenches. Although they worked alongside white soldiers, they remained segregated when it came to non-work activities.

By the time Canada's forces reached four divisions in 1916, it required 75 000 recruits per year to maintain its fighting strength. With rising casualties making the enlistment shortfall more critical, the military softened enlistment rules. In 1915, a married man no longer required his wife's written permission to enlist. The April 1915 creation of the Canadian Army Dental Corps meant that recruits with bad teeth could be admitted; for many men it was their first trip to a dentist. In July, the minimum height for infantrymen was lowered to 5 foot 2 inches (1.57 metres), and to 5 feet (1.52 metres) in early 1917, and the chest measurement was dropped to 33 inches (84 centimetres). In late 1915, minimal eyesight requirements were lowered, and the next year those with flat feet were admitted because of the recent development of corrective boots. Later in 1916, men were being admitted with varicose veins, partial deafness, and even missing fingers, so long as it was determined by doctors that they could still perform their duty.

Nevertheless, the growing crisis with enlistment led to more finger pointing, particularly at Quebec. By mid-1916, 27 percent of Canadians lived in Quebec, but only 14 percent of recruits came from the province, and a large number of those were from Quebec's Anglo minority. In April 1916, the Hamilton Recruiting League, a citizen-run organization, became the first of its type to formally demand the implementation of conscription, declaring it essential if Canada was to reach its goal of a 500 000-man army. They declared it was the fairest system because it exacted the same sacrifice from all those deemed eligible to fight. Soon, scores of organizations were pushing for conscription, as were newspapers, though they were overwhelmingly Anglo.

Some attempted to calm the mounting discord in French–English relations. In June 1916, John Milton Godfrey, a prominent Toronto lawyer and Liberal, but also an imperialist who was president of the Canadian National Service League (which was started in April 1916 to help Canada reach its target of 500 000 military volunteers), and Arthur Hawkes, a journalist and publicist for the Canadian Northern Railway, started the *Bonne Entente*, whose first meeting was at Toronto's prestigious National Club. The group contacted prominent French Canadians to create a public dialogue and better understanding, especially in light of a growing campaign in Quebec to boycott Ontario goods. In Quebec, Premier Lomer Gouin and Georges Garneau, chairman of the National Battlefield Commission, assumed the leadership of *Bonne Entente*. Thousands attended a number of travelling conferences, but things never got beyond platitudes, and the movement quickly faded. In February 1917, Godfrey formed the Win the War movement that endorsed conscription and promoted the creation of a coalition government to ensure its implementation.

In Quebec, some prominent Francophones tried to save the recruitment situation. The most public effort was that of Captain Talbot Papineau, the well-known and charismatic grandson of the *patriote* leader, Louis-Joseph Papineau, and Henri Bourassa's cousin. In August 1914, he joined as an officer with the Princess Patricia's Canadian Light Infantry and two years later was awarded the Military Cross for bravery at St. Eloi. Before that battle, he sent an open letter to Bourassa that appeared in newspapers across Canada. Designed to boost recruitment in Quebec—though curiously written in English—it stressed the grave threat posed by Germany, Canada's legal obligation and sense of duty to Britain, Quebec's moral responsibility to help France, and the unique opportunity the war presented to French Canadians to demonstrate their love of Canada and to forge a new sense of unity with their Anglo brethren. Bourassa was unmoved and so were most Québécois. Besides questioning Papineau's authorship—"A brave and active officer as he is has seldom the time to prepare and write such long pieces of political eloquence"[10]—Bourassa's published reply argued that by not rushing into uniform, French Quebecers were showing themselves as most attached to Canada, not Europe, a recruitment pattern he said was also evident among long-settled Canadian-born Anglos.

With options narrowing to reach enlistment targets, the government moved closer to conscription. During the last week of 1916, Ottawa's new National Service Board launched a Canada-wide survey of available labour. When pressed, Borden refused to promise that the survey would not be used to help identify conscripts, but the Board's director, R.B. Bennett, made such a pledge, especially in Quebec.

December 1916: National Service Board established.

International Recognition and Military Success

Canada's expanding contributions to the war strongly affected its external relations. From 1915 onward, Canada was borrowing greater sums from U.S. money markets to help finance the war. With the United States joining the conflict in April 1917, there came coordination in hemispheric defence, namely with naval patrols. Also in 1917, Canada sent its own representative to Washington, who worked out of the British embassy to better coordinate on resource allocation to maximize military production, and in February 1918, expanded this role by creating the Washington-based Canadian War Mission.

Although remaining tightly tied and loyal to Britain, frustration mounted in Ottawa over a lack of consultation, including on the use of Canadian troops. Borden was furious when British Prime Minister Herbert Asquith told him that sharing too much information could result in security breaches. Borden wrote, but after further reflection decided not to send, a letter to Canada's high commissioner to share with the British government in which he threatened: "It can hardly be expected that we shall put 400,000 to 500,000 men in the field and willingly accept the position of having no more voice and receiving no more consideration than if we were toy automata."[11]

Besides Canadian efforts to exert more control over the use of its troops, such as by establishing the Ministry of Overseas Military Services, important changes that affected Canada's influence occurred in the British government. In December 1916, 102 British Liberals, frustrated by Britain's lack of success against Germany, deserted Asquith and joined with opposition Conservatives to make War Minister David Lloyd George prime minister. Seeking greater mobilization of Empire resources, Lloyd George established an Imperial War Cabinet to involve the dominions in a consultative role. Borden arrived in London in March 1917 for initial meetings, and the next month—with Canada's prime minister claiming much of the credit—the Imperial War Cabinet passed Resolution IX declaring the dominions as "autonomous members of the Empire."

March 1917: Resolution IX of the Imperial War Cabinet. Canadian autonomy recognized within the Empire.

The trends towards greater recognition, influence, and autonomy were bolstered by success on the battlefield, particularly at Vimy Ridge, Canada's most celebrated clash in the First World War. Here, Canada's four divisions fought together for the first time. Although assisted by French and British forces, Canada took the brunt of the battle in capturing a position that had been in German hands since October 1914 and that previous attempts by the Europeans to retake had failed. The ridge was not especially high, 110 metres at its peak, but it was steep in certain areas and provided an excellent vantage point. Five German regiments—about 8000 men—were dug in where they had established a defensive fortress with "caves, tunnels, concrete machine-gun positions, fire trenches, and deep and elaborate dugouts."[12]

Generals Byng and Currie had meticulously prepared Canadian forces, in many cases for months, for the massive attack. Practice fields were created, and men were assigned recognizable targets to capture, not lines on a map. The Canadians, expressing confidence and growing pride, began referring to themselves as "Byng's Boys." For two weeks prior to the attack, 350 000 shells were fired to soften up German defences. The Canadians knocked out more than two-thirds of enemy guns by using aerial photography and a new cathode ray detection device (a forerunner of radar) developed by Colonel Andrew McNaughton, a graduate of physics and engineering from McGill University.

April 9, the day of the attack, was miserable, as sleet and snow fell during the night. The two sides exchanged furious artillery barrages; then, as dawn approached, Canadian guns fell silent to lull the Germans into resting. At 05:30, with some cover still provided by darkness, 1000 large Canadian guns opened up and 40 000 Canadians went over the top in precisely timed sequence. They followed closely behind an intense creeping barrage; many men simply put their head down and moved forward as if going through a hailstorm. In some sectors, the fury and accuracy of Canadian firepower was so overwhelming that the Germans barely managed to return fire. Canadian casualties mounted quickly, nonetheless, as enemy troops were experienced, well disciplined, and skilled, and their third major defensive line had time to compose itself. Canadian stretcher-bearers were so overwhelmed with wounded in some sectors that German POWs were forced to assist. Private William Green saw a shell tear off the head of a machine gunner a few metres away from him and the headless body with blood gushing out of the top still staggering forward a few steps.

The ridge was captured that first day and over three days the Canadians surged forward 4000 metres, the longest sustained advance by the allies to that point in the war. The victory gave the allies a commanding vantage point over the Douai plain. The French referred to Vimy as "Canada's Easter gift to the Allies." King George V sent a congratulatory message to Canada, and news of the victory was carried on the front page of major newspapers, including the *Times* of London and the *New York Times*, where the United States had just declared war on Germany on April 2.

In later British historical accounts, Vimy typically received short shrift, cast as one part of the larger and much longer Battle of Arras. In Canada, it continued to be portrayed as a nation-building event that earned the dominion international respect and recognition. One newspaper, under the headline "Makers of Canada," printed an illustration of Canadian troops charging up the ridge while underneath was the well-known painting of the Fathers of Confederation at the 1864 Charlottetown conference, a symbolic analogy

April 9–12, 1917:
Battle of Vimy Ridge.

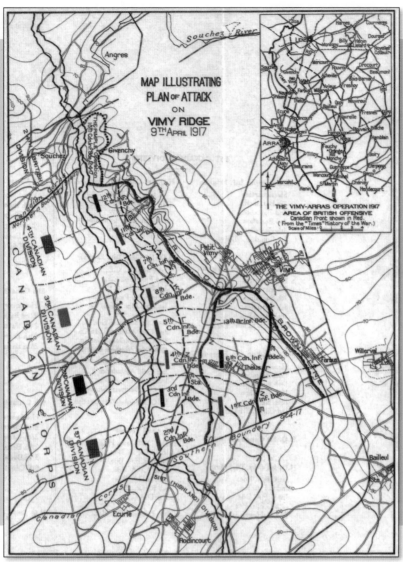

Map 4.2
The Order of Attack by Canada's
Four Divisions on Vimy Ridge

Source: Library and Archives Canada, nmc-111121-1.

reinforced by the upcoming 50th anniversary of Confederation, even though official celebrations of the event were postponed because of the war.[13] The costs of capturing Vimy were steep: 10 602 Canadian casualties, including 3598 dead, losses that pushed the country closer to implementing the very divisive policy of conscription.

Victory at Vimy resulted in Byng's promotion to lead Britain's 3rd Army. Command of the Canadian Corps finally went to a Canadian, Arthur Currie, whom Byng had groomed for the position. The pear-shaped Currie did not look like a commander and he wasn't overly popular with Canadian troops. He was far more comfortable around fellow officers than ordinary soldiers, wasn't an inspirational speaker, and believed in strict discipline. Some men griped that Currie drove the Canadians too hard and produced high casualties, presumably for his own glory, though, in fact, he always devised plans to minimize

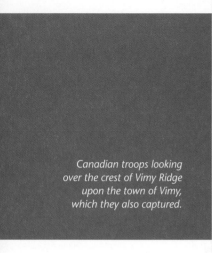

Canadian troops looking over the crest of Vimy Ridge upon the town of Vimy, which they also captured.

Source: Library and Archives of Canada, PA-001446.

casualties, and on a percentage basis Canadian losses moved steadily downward. Currie ran his headquarters like a CEO, soliciting and weighing options presented by his commanders. He demanded competence and results, and upon taking over the Corps, he refused to give Garnet Hughes command of the 1st Division because he believed he had failed as a leader at Ypres and in the Somme campaign. Hughes was offered command of the yet-to-be created 5th Division, whose members would later be dispersed throughout the army. The two former friends became bitter enemies, as did Currie and Sam Hughes, something that played out after the war as Sam Hughes, until his death in 1921, continued to attack Currie's reputation. The personal vendetta was carried on by Garnet Hughes and in 1927 resulted in Currie launching a $50 000 libel suit against the Hughes-controlled Port Hope *Evening Guide* for charging that he had needlessly wasted Canadian lives by attacking Mons on November 11, 1918, the last day of the war, a case that netted Currie only $500 and exacted a great personal toll.

In mid-August, Currie had the Canadian Corps attack Hill 70, near Vimy. Artillery barrages and the release of chlorine and phosgene gas preceded the offensive, which was launched at 04:25 on August 15, securing the high ground that morning and the remaining objectives the next day. Over the following three days, the Germans counter-attacked 21 times, and released as many as 20 000 mustard gas shells, before finally conceding defeat.

Douglas Haig next focused on Passchendaele, which became known as the 3rd Battle of Ypres. He remained determined to achieve a major breakthrough. Enmity was growing between Haig and Lloyd George over lack of progress, and it was essential to provide some relief to battle-weary French forces, who were reported near mutiny in several areas. Millions of shells were directed against German lines to prepare for the thrust, but they destroyed the irrigation system on the low-lying ground; that and record rainfall turned the terrain into sludge where, in many parts, the muddy water was waist deep.

The quagmire that was Passchendaele. Sometimes it took as many as eight stretcher-bearers to carry a wounded soldier through the mud.

Source: Canadian War Museum, 19930013-509.

Haig tasked the Canadians with capturing the village of Passchendaele and the surrounding ridge. Currie resisted; he wanted to proceed to Cambrai and leave the Germans in the muck. He viewed the battlefield as a death trap and predicted, almost precisely as it turned out, 16 000 Canadian casualties. The Germans were well encased in concrete pillboxes, which were difficult to locate in the mangled terrain, even for observers in low-flying aircraft. The Canadians were given only two weeks to prepare their attack. Currie's plan was to overrun the ridge in four set-piece "bite and hold" offensives, because, unlike Vimy or Hill 70, conditions made it impossible to secure the objectives in one fell swoop. The Canadians also did not have the element of surprise as the Germans did from their higher vantage points where they could view Canadian preparations.

On October 26, the Canadians attacked, and over the 12-day battle, their artillery fired off an astonishing 1 453 056 shells. The Canadians lost 8400 men for every kilometre gained and in total suffered 15 654 casualties. Some called Currie a butcher, though Canada's casualty rate was far lower than at 2nd Ypres, and his strategy, combined with the battlefield proficiency of Canadian soldiers, brought victory. Out of this hellhole, Canadian troops began referring to the Corps as if it were a sacred institution, as they came to believe in its invincibility. Among the allied countries, Canada's army was becoming viewed as "shock troops" to be used in the more difficult cases. However, the gap between battlefield losses and enlistments at home continued to widen—totalling 115 170 and 60 418, respectively, from January to November 1917—a trend that moved Borden and his government towards implementing conscription.

Although the ground war remained the major dimension of Canada's military effort, its contributions to aerial combat also expanded notably. In Canada, airstrips were enlarged and new ones were constructed for training purposes, such as the one at Barrie. Even still, nearly 5000 prospective Canadian pilots took training in Texas because of superior facilities and more good flying days. In all, 22 812 Canadians served with Britain's flying

November 1917:

Battle of Passchendaele.

services, the overwhelming majority with the Royal Flying Corps. Of 13 160 who were aircrew, 1388 were killed, 1130 were wounded, and 377 became prisoners of war. Whereas Canadians composed 6 percent of British flying casualties in 1915, that figure reached 16.8 percent by 1918. Canadian airmen were perceived by the public as "knights of the sky," romanticized winged warriors who enjoyed celebrity status as they engaged in aerial dogfights in the wild blue yonder.

Eleven of 27 Empire aces that downed 30 or more enemy aircraft were Canadian. Some attained great fame, such as William Barker and Raymond Collishaw, with 50 and 60 air victories, respectively, though none more so than William Avery "Billy" Bishop of Owen Sound, Ontario, with 72 victories, second in the Empire, and third among all the allies (France's René Fonck had 75 kills and Britain's Edward Mannock had 73, though Germany's Manfred von Richtofen had 80). Historian Brereton Greenhous insists that Bishop exaggerated his record, as many of his kills were not witnessed, though such a charge could also be made against most aces.[14] On the basis of its airborne contributions, Canada successfully pressured the British into accepting the creation of two separate Canadian squadrons, a development that, on September 19, 1918, was formalized into the creation of the Canadian Air Force.

The war at sea became significant to Canada. In October 1916, Germany's U-53 arrived at Newport, Rhode Island, demonstrating that its armed submarines could cross the Atlantic. After leaving Rhode Island, the U-53 sank five allied steamers in international waters, thus raising fears over similar activity off the Maritime provinces and in the mouth of the St. Lawrence. The Canadian government ordered the construction of small anti-submarine vessels and ratcheted up that demand in early 1917 as Germany adopted unrestricted U-boat warfare to starve Britain into submission. However, Canadian vessels engaged in detection and avoided engagement; of modest size and often with wooden hulls, they were no match for the Germans. Starting in 1917, American vessels patrolled off Nova Scotia's southern shore and in the Bay of Fundy. Convoys protected by American and British naval vessels were organized from several Maritime ports, especially Halifax. The convoys were highly successful because U-boats had to surface to attack, and the flotillas were well armed. In spring 1917, 25 percent of merchant vessels leaving North America for Britain faced a U-boat attack, but between May 1917 and October 1918, that figure plummeted to 0.5 percent.

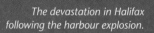
The devastation in Halifax following the harbour explosion.

Source: Library and Archives of Canada, C-019950.

December 6, 1917:
Halifax explosion.

Sharply increased port activity in the Maritimes brought many jobs to a region that had experienced declining economic prospects for decades, but in Halifax, the largest and most significant port, rapidly increased activity combined with slipshod procedures for handling the extra traffic, also brought disaster. On the morning of December 6, 1917, the Belgian relief ship *Imo* collided with the *Mont Blanc*, a French munitions vessel carrying 600 barrels of aviation fuel and over 2700 metric tons of TNT. The result was the greatest human-made explosion to that point in history. Damage extended some 16 kilometres inland; buildings shook in New Glasgow 125 kilometres away; and the explosion was heard in North Cape Breton 360 kilometres away. Out of a population of 45 000, 2000 Haligonians were killed, 9000 were injured, and 10 000 were left homeless, and the city's north end and large parts of Dartmouth were levelled. Flying glass was responsible for killing and injuring many of those people. Aid poured in from across Canada, as well as from Newfoundland, Britain, and the United States, but it was delayed by a major winter storm the next day that dumped 40 centimetres of snow on the city, which left homeless survivors, and those in windowless accommodation, freezing.

Intensifying Demands at Home

Canadians were not simply being asked to sacrifice more; their federal government would play an increasing role in extracting contributions. By the winter of 1916–1917, there were fuel shortages from soaring demand from war industry, and labour shortages were taxing the poorly paid mining sector. Brownouts came to Ontario as the province's hydro-electric generating capacity struggled to meet demand from factories on both sides of the international border. In June 1917, the federal government appointed a fuel controller who was given the power to enforce cuts in public consumption. Buildings deemed non-essential, such as theatres, were forced to close an extra day per week. Across Ontario, streetlights were turned off between 5 P.M. and 8 P.M., and every second light remained on for the rest of the night. A sense of duty, or fear of fines or public shaming, convinced most Canadians to respect heatless Mondays during February and March 1918 by not burning coal, turning instead to sources like wood stoves.

The federal government also appointed a food controller in June. Between 1913 and 1917, France's wheat crop plunged by 57 percent, and Germany's U-boat campaign forced Britain to implement coupon rationing. Canadians faced moderate restrictions, namely meatless days in restaurants and fines for hoarding. Many who lived in urban areas responded to calls to grow "war gardens" in their yard or in designated city lots. Urban Canadians helped out on farms to try to compensate for labour shortages, though farmers sometimes hesitated to accept the volunteers, viewing them as too soft and inexperienced. The federal government, and several provincial and municipal ones, provided a week's paid holiday to their employees if it was used to provide farm labour. Young people pitched in as *Soldiers of the Soil*, a federal–provincial farm labour program that in 1918 attracted 20 000 high school boys and 2500 young women.

Financing the war became more challenging. Defence expenditures rose from $13 million in 1913 to $311 million in 1916 and continued to climb. Adding to costs was the federal government's purchase in 1917 of the heavily indebted Grand Trunk, Grand Trunk Pacific,

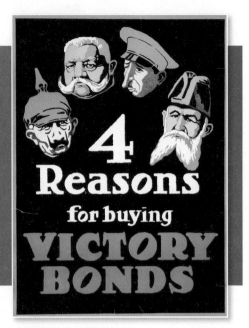

Stereotypes of militaristic and unsavoury enemies were used to inspire contributions to the 1918 Victory Bond drive.

Source: Archives of Ontario, I0016191.JPG.

and Canadian Northern railways to create the Canadian National Railway, a reorganization that took five years to complete. Finance Minister Thomas White was advised to borrow from Canadians, but he feared draining what he saw as a small domestic financial market. In November 1915, the federal government tested the waters by seeking $50 million through the sale of war bonds offering 5 percent tax-free interest. The result far exceeded expectations, raising $100 million from corporations and $79 million from individuals. In February 1916, another war bond drive topped its goal of $250 million, which was 10 times more than what was raised through a new, albeit modest, Business Profits Tax introduced that same year. In 1917, Ottawa added a new "temporary" tax on personal incomes, though it did so cautiously in a country that had never before had such a levy. At a time when the average income was $600 per year, only single people making more than $2000 a year and families earning more than $5000 a year would pay income tax.

With war bonds, caution was thrown to the wayside. A National Executive Committee based in the Department of Finance arranged for banks, along with stock and bond houses, to receive a 0.5 percent commission on each bond sold. A Dominion Publicity Committee that also operated through the Department of Finance organized public appeals. Branches of the committee supervised by prominent individuals were established in each province, city, and town of worthwhile size. The Committee signed agreements with the Canadian Press Association to publish upbeat stories about Victory Bond drives. Commencing six weeks prior to the Victory Bond issue date, and especially during the three-week purchasing period, it became virtually impossible for citizens to open a newspaper or magazine, or walk down the street, without confronting posters and advertisements telling them that duty, honour, and loyalty—to King, country, and Canada's sons sacrificing overseas—compelled them to purchase a bond. For those moved by more narrow concerns, propaganda also reminded them that at 5 percent interest, government securities constituted a better investment than putting one's money in the bank. The results were extraordinary: In November 1917, 820 000 Canadians loaned Ottawa $398 million, and in November 1918, more than 1 million people provided $660 million.

Moral and Social Reform

To numerous Canadians, the spirit of duty and self-sacrifice that had evidently manifested in millions of citizens was viewed as proof that the war was divinely guided in that good was vanquishing evil and civilization was moving forward. Many in the adoption of prohibition saw further evidence of that process. Abstinence became linked with patriotism and the spirit of sacrifice. Prohibition would save grain, allow distilleries to be converted to war production (such as for making shell propellants and disinfectants for the Medical Corps), and, with people forced to give up drink, they could better commit their full mental and physical abilities to the war effort. Ontario's Methodist Church gathered signatures from 64 000 mothers pleading with the federal government to protect young men in uniform from the corrupting influence of drink, which many linked to rising venereal disease rates, by allowing only dry canteens—a suggestion that produced angry responses from soldiers. In early 1916, Saskatchewan adopted prohibition following a strong endorsement in a public plebiscite (a non-binding vote), and the other Prairie provinces quickly followed suit. Nova Scotia joined in late 1916, with the exception of Halifax, which had long enjoyed a lucrative liquor trade to serve garrisoned military personnel. In 1917, New Brunswick and Newfoundland went dry, and Prince Edward Island strengthened its 1901 prohibition legislation. That same year, the *Ontario Temperance Act* was passed shortly after the provincial government received a petition with 825 000 signatures demanding prohibition. Quebec moved more slowly in part because wine played a role in Catholic mass. In early 1918, its legislature abolished retail sales of spirits, but still allowed wine, light beer, and cider. On April 1, 1918, the federal government settled matters by declaring Canada dry for at least one year after the war ended.

Growing support for female suffrage was also in part premised on a link between the war and social uplift. More Canadians warmed to the idea that women would use the vote to produce a better post-war world; women's many contributions to the war effort helped this cause. The Canadian Suffrage Association, like its British counterpart, created a war auxiliary and declared that its first priority was to help achieve victory. In 1916, Robert Borden declared that women had raised $50 million for the war.

The first breakthrough for women in attaining provincial suffrage was in Manitoba, where rural women had proven themselves as indispensable on farms; where women had long participated in politics through their own auxiliaries of groups like the Grain Grower's Association; and where Nellie McClung had emerged as a major leader in the suffrage movement. McClung was part of the Ontario migration to the West, arriving in Manitoba in 1880 at age seven. She became a best-selling novelist and was widely known as "rip-roaring public speaker."[15] Rejecting the idea of women's lives being biologically destined to revolve around family, and as subordinate to men, she expressed the hope that "the time will come … when women will be economically free, and mentally and spiritually independent enough to refuse to have … food paid for by men; when women will receive equal pay for equal work, and have all avenues of activity open to them." As head of the Women's Political Equality League, which focused on improving conditions for working-class women, McClung said that women would use the vote as "a tool to … elect candidates interested in … a minimum wage law, mothers' allowances …women factory inspectors … [and] prohibition,"[16] as she was also a long-time member of the Women's Christian Temperance Union, who saw male drunkenness as bringing great hardship to women and children.

Before the outbreak of the war, McClung effectively lampooned Conservative premier Rodmond Roblin, a strong opponent of female enfranchisement, in a satirical play called *The Parliament of Women* that warned against the perils of giving men the vote. With the May 1915 election of the Liberals under T.C. Norris, who had gone on record as supporting female enfranchisement, in January 1916 Manitoba women received the provincial vote. The other Prairie provinces followed suit later that year. In 1917, a provincial plebiscite extended the vote to women in British Columbia. Ontario's Conservative government, in

September 1917:
The Wartime Elections
Act *provides the federal*
franchise to women,
21 or older, with a
husband, brother, son,
or father in the military.

trying to appear more progressive than the opposition Liberals, also came on board that year. The Maritimes were more cautious: Nova Scotia gave women the vote in 1918; New Brunswick, in 1919 (but did not allow women to run for provincial office until 1934); Prince Edward Island, in 1922; and Newfoundland, in 1925. In Quebec, where the powerful Catholic Church portrayed female enfranchisement as threatening family stability, women were denied the provincial vote until 1940.

In September 1917, the die was cast for women to obtain the federal franchise. Two months before a federal election, the Borden government forced the *Military Voters Act* and the *Wartime Elections Act* through Parliament. The first provided nursing sisters with the vote, and the latter did the same for the wives, widows, mothers, sisters, and daughters of servicemen. The government enfranchised women whom, it logically figured, would support its policy of conscription. Soon after being re-elected, Borden's government passed the *Women's Franchise Act* that extended the vote to all female British subjects aged 21 and older. Canada acted before Britain and the United States, though Asian and Aboriginal Canadian women had to wait until after the Second World War before receiving the vote.

Conscription

While women's suffrage was controversial, the campaign to implement conscription that played a key role in providing them with the federal vote was even more divisive. While in London in the spring of 1917 to participate in meetings of the Imperial War Cabinet, Borden was presented with a gloomy situation. In March, Russian Czar Nicholas II abdicated following widespread rioting in Petrograd, the capital. The economy was in freefall, and starvation was spreading with some 15 million Russians having left farms. Social Democrats under Alexander Kerensky established a provisional government and agreed to back the allies, but Russia's military was also in disarray, with many defecting to the Bolsheviks, under Vladimir Lenin, who were rapidly gaining strength. At the same time, Italy's army was collapsing before Austrian forces, and mutinies were spreading among French soldiers. America's entry into the war on April 2 offered great hope, but its mobilization would take months. Many military analysts predicted the war would continue until the end of 1919. Visiting wounded Canadians while in England, Borden wrote in his memoirs about being moved by the experience and becoming more determined that Canadian soldiers be provided with the support they needed.

May 1917: Military
Service Act *introduced.*

Canada remained short of its target of a 500 000-man army. The National Service Board survey suggested that some 300 000 men were still available for military service. Upon returning to Canada in May, Borden instructed Solicitor-General Arthur Meighen to prepare a *Military Service Act* (MSA). Presented to Parliament on May 18, it demanded that all single men and childless widowers age 20 to 32 register for possible compulsory service. Certain groups, however, were provided with exemptions: those whose military service would produce great hardship to their family, those whose civilian work was deemed essential for Canada, and those recognized as conscientious objectors, namely clergy, and Mennonites or Doukhobors, whom the Canadian government had officially excluded from military obligations in 1873 and 1898, respectively.

Borden appealed for national unity and bipartisan support of the MSA. Stating it was essential that political partisanship be cast aside in the prevailing crisis, he offered to form a coalition government with Laurier. A year earlier, Laurier had agreed to extend the government's term for a year beyond the legal five-year mandate to avoid a wartime election, but this time he rebuffed Borden. Besides his personal conviction against compulsion, Laurier feared that if he joined Borden, it would hand over French and Liberal Quebec to Bourassa's *nationalistes*, with the fallout being more intense French–English discord, the potential for violence, and irreparable damage to the Canadian federation. Some Liberals believed their party had an excellent chance of defeating Borden in an election. The Conservatives had lost several recent federal by-elections in part because of corruption connected to the Shell Committee, the fiasco of the Ross Rifle (which was officially dropped as the standard issue for Canadian troops in mid-1916 in favour of the Lee-Enfield), the open political warfare between Borden and Hughes, and rising wartime inflation. Some Liberals were also convinced that conscription would not be an easy sell, even in English Canada. Many farmers opposed conscription, given mounting labour shortages, while most of organized labour, though urging patriotism and counselling against wartime strikes, stressed the need—and fairness—of truly conscripting wealth as well as men, namely in the form of taxes. The TLC resolved only not to actively "resist the implementation of the *Military Service Act*,"[17] though more radical unions, especially in Western Canada, advocated open defiance of conscription.

When the MSA came up for vote in Parliament, Quebec Liberals unanimously opposed the bill and were joined by nine Quebec Tories. By contrast, Ontario Liberals supported the MSA 10–2. It became law on August 28, but implementation was largely delayed until after the December federal election. In Quebec, some young men joined a paramilitary group called *Les Constitutionelles,* and in the summer of 1917, a bomb that the group targeted for the pro-conscription owner of the Montreal *Star,* Hugh Graham, killed Graham's chauffeur.

Before dropping the election writ, Borden's government imposed closure on Parliament to ensure passage of the *Military Voters Act* and the *Wartime Elections Act.* The former, besides enfranchising nurses, empowered the government to distribute, as it saw fit, the ballots cast by military personnel—logically considered as overwhelmingly pro-conscription—in provincial constituencies where servicemen did not indicate their riding. The latter stripped the vote from conscientious objectors and those of enemy background naturalized after March 31, 1902. As nearly all these immigrants came to Canada while Laurier governed, they, like conscientious objectors who opposed conscription, were assumed to be Liberal supporters.

Numerous Liberal MPs in English Canada agonized over whether to stand by Laurier, as they believed in conscription or were convinced that their constituents favoured it. Realizing that many Liberals were ready to defect, Borden reconstituted his Conservatives into the Union party just before Parliament dissolved for the December 17 election, a change he cast as being in the spirit of non-partisanship. By November, many Liberals became Union candidates, including Manitoba's former premier Arthur Sifton and Ontario's Liberal leader, Newton Rowell. Of the Unionists who were elected, 115 were Conservatives and 38 were former Liberals, the latter all being Anglophones.

The election was arguably the nastiest and most divisive in Canadian history, with the Unionists setting the tone, even portraying Laurier as a friend of the Kaiser. Nearly all

Francophone newspapers reiterated support for the war but also portrayed conscription as breaking previous promises and as trampling their rights. On the other side of the linguistic divide, the usually Liberal-aligned Manitoba *Free Press* said that Quebec had "failed Canada," while the Conservative Toronto *Mail and Empire* cast the prospect of Laurier's election as "pleasing to the Kaiser."[18] In Toronto, there were several incidents of soldiers breaking up meetings of Laurier supporters, while in Quebec, Union candidates had to have police escorts. To solidify its hold on English Canada, Unionists promised that conscription would not be applied to families that already had a man in uniform. Seeking to improve prospects in rural areas, Borden pledged that those needed on farms would not be conscripted. Organized labour was promised more representation on government war boards. The TLC gave only tepid support to independent labour and Liberal-Labour candidates, not one of whom was elected.

The Unionists won 151 seats to the Liberals' 82. The breakdown of support pointed to a fractured country and was the greatest threat to national unity until the 1980 Quebec referendum on sovereignty association. The Liberals took 62 of 65 seats and nearly 73 percent of the popular vote in Quebec. The only Unionists elected in Quebec—Justice Minister Charles Doherty in St. Ann, Herbert Brown Ames in St. Antoine, and Naval Minister Charles Ballantyne in St. Lawrence-St. George—represented Montreal ridings with a heavily Anglo population. The Maritimes returned 21 Unionists and 10 Liberals, compared with 19 Liberals and 16 Conservatives in 1911. Liberal support remained strongest in ridings with a significant Acadian presence, like Restigouche-Madawaka in New Brunswick, and in areas where port activity, and hence good civilian jobs, had grown substantially, like Inverness and Lunenburg in Nova Scotia. In Ontario, the Unionists took 74 of 82 seats, with 63 percent of the vote, and in some Toronto ridings they topped 80 percent. The Liberals retained some strength in parts of eastern Ontario, like Prescott and Russell, where Franco-Ontarians were concentrated. In Western Canada, where a large number of recent immigrants were stripped of the right to vote, 54 of 56 seats, and 71 percent of ballots, went Union.

December 1917: Union government elected.

Ultimately, some 125 000 men were conscripted, 47 049 went overseas, and 24 132 were taken on strength in France—hardly enough, as J.L. Granatstein and J.M. Hitsman argue, to tip the scales against Germany, and, as such, not worth the grief and division brought to the country. If forcing an equal sacrifice from Quebec constituted a major aim, then the government came up short. Only 23 percent of those conscripted were French-speaking, as most Québécois, particularly those from agricultural areas, successfully convinced conscription tribunals of their need at home. Historian J.M. Willms contends that critics of conscription are reading history with the benefit of hindsight. He points out that when Borden implemented the MSA, Canada's casualty rate far exceeded new recruits, and the best intelligence predicted nearly two more years of bloodletting.[19]

The implementation of conscription proved as difficult as its passage. On January 19, 1918, the day after the first conscripts reported for duty, representative J-N Francoeur proposed to the Quebec Legislature that the province secede from Canada. Of those conscripted, 6.7 percent in the West, 9.3 percent in Ontario, and a whopping 40.8 percent in Quebec did not report for duty despite a possible five-year jail term. Federal authorities raided places like theatres, dance halls, pool halls, and roller-skating rinks, arresting young men without exemption papers. By March 6, 3085 had been apprehended, with the largest number, 605, located in Montreal. In Sherbrooke, a military policeman was found guilty of manslaughter after shooting a man trying to evade arrest. The most serious incident occurred over the Easter weekend in Quebec City. It started with the arrest of a conscription resister named Mercier, which precipitated a large protest rally in the working-class district of Saint-Roch. A Dominion Police station was set ablaze, as well as the offices of the Quebec City *Chronicle* and *L'Evenement*, both of which supported conscription. The army was called in and the mayor read the *Riot Act*. On Easter Sunday, the two sides confronted each other. Rioters threw snowballs, ice, rocks, and chunks of pavement, and there were reports of gunshots being fired at the soldiers. Troops fired into the crowd and the cavalry charged, leaving five civilians dead and more than 50 wounded.

Of those who reported to conscription boards, 93.7 percent sought an exemption, and 87 percent were successful, being able to show that their absence would bring great hardship to their family or that military service would take them from a job essential to the home front. Still, local boards were sometimes inconsistent in their application of the rules and in some cases applied a heavy hand to force men into uniform. Some members of religious denominations unfamiliar to conscription tribunals—like Plymouth Brethren—were rejected for exemption. Because many Mennonites were not baptized until 21, and thus not full-fledged members of the faith, they too sometimes faced problems obtaining exemptions. In Winnipeg, Jehovah's Witnesses who refused service were taken to the Minto Street barracks, stripped naked, and sprayed with ice cold water to compel them to change their mind; the account made it into newspapers after several had to be hospitalized. By the end of the war, 117 conscientious objectors were behind bars.

Outside of Quebec, dissenters received little backing and much condemnation. Support for conscription remained solid, bolstered by difficulties that the allies continued to have overseas. By early 1918, British casualties had reached the point where 18-year-olds were being conscripted, but the situation in Germany was growing desperate with labour unrest, riots, and tens of thousands dying from starvation. German generals planned for a massive push to turn the tide. Preceded by a colossal bombardment and the release of poison gas, and using what remained of its best fighting formations, Germany launched its last major offensive on March 21. Within three days, it had recaptured virtually all its losses on the Somme, and once again threatened to take Paris. However, German supply lines were badly overstretched, and within weeks, the offensive collapsed. Initially, the thrust generated much alarm among the allies, so much so that on April 19 Borden's government cancelled conscription exemptions, including for those working on farms, a decision that prompted 5000 farmers from Ontario and Quebec to march on Parliament in protest.

As the war against Germany moved into its final phases, the threat perceived from Bolshevism became far more ominous. In October 1917, Bolsheviks seized power in Petrograd. On March 3, 1918, Russia signed the treaty of Brest-Litovsk with Germany, which took Russia out of the war and allowed Germany to devote more resources to the Western Front. Canada became involved in attempts to re-establish anti-communist forces, first in early 1918 by sending 40 officers and men to Archangael, near Murmansk,

April 1918: Anti-conscription riot in Quebec City.

as military trainers. In October, Canada contributed some 4000 soldiers to a more substantial allied intervention in Siberia to support the Czech Legion that had seized control of the Trans-Siberian railway and had set out for Vladivostok where anti-communists remained in control under the brutal dictatorship of Alexandr Kolchak. The Canadians saw very limited action. In late 1918, two Canadians were killed in a battle against some 600 Bolsheviks by the Dvina River near Archangael. In Vladivostok, the Canadians did not lose any men in battle, as they were mostly assigned to patrols and labour fatigues, but three died in accidents and 16 from disease. The overall mission was a failure: Kolchak grew increasingly unpopular; the allies could not agree on strategy; and there was little popular support for the intervention in Canada after the war in Europe ended. In April 1919, Borden pulled the plug, and by June the troops were home.

The decision to get involved reflected mounting fears over the potential export of Bolshevism to Canada. Communists held important positions in many unions, particularly in Western Canada. Anger was being fed by growing inflation; between 1916 and 1918, Canada's cost of living rose by 42 percent. Conscription drew considerable criticism from the labour movement, as did the continuing absence of legislation guaranteeing unions collective bargaining rights. In July 1918, the federal government announced a policy giving workers the right to organize, but at the same time it outlawed strikes and lockouts for the duration of the war.

Labour militancy was on the rise. In April of that same year, there occurred an illegal walkout by Winnipeg civic employees and in the summer a nationwide strike by letter carriers. In July, Albert "Ginger" Goodwin, the socialist vice-president of the British Columbia Federation of Labour and secretary of the Mill and Smeltermen's Union in Trail, was shot and killed by a Dominion Police officer while resisting arrest for evading conscription. The officer claimed self-defence and was never charged, which, in August, touched off a 24-hour general strike in Vancouver.

Division within Canada's labour movement between radicals and moderates was coming to a head. At the September 1918 TLC convention in Quebec City, more Central Canadian delegates defeated every militant resolution put forward, nearly all by Westerners. Tom Moore, a Niagara Falls carpenter and well-known moderate, was elected as TLC president. Before departing from Quebec City, Western delegates met as a caucus and agreed to reconvene the next year separately from the TLC. The federal government moved to clamp down on radicalism. In autumn 1918, an Order in Council banned more than a dozen communist and socialist organizations and stipulated that anyone advocating, teaching, advising or defending "the use of force, violence, or physical injury to person or property in order to accomplish governmental or economic change"[20] could face five years in jail.

Autumn 1918: Influenza epidemic in Canada.

In the final months of the war, Canada's home front also confronted an unseen, but far deadlier, invasion from the Spanish influenza epidemic. Historians Mark Humphries and Esyllt Jones link its spark, and nationwide spread, to soldiers transported across Canada for service in Vladivostok.[21] In this pre-antibiotic period, the flu killed an estimated 25 million people worldwide, and in Canada some 50 000, with a shockingly high proportion between the ages of 20 and 40. It also hit Aboriginals particularly hard. For example, in Norway

House, a largely Cree and Métis community in northern Manitoba, one-fifth of the population died within six weeks of the epidemic hitting. City theatres and other public venues closed down, and public events, including church services, were cancelled. Rural residents were also hard hit because they were isolated from health services and often from neighbours who could help them. In Saskatchewan, the province's Bureau of Public Health received reports of livestock left untended and entire families found dead in their homes.

Triumph and New Trials

Canadian troops played a decisive role in the final push to victory, which became known as the "last 100 days." Starting at Amiens, and over the following 12 days, the Canadian Corps reclaimed 173 square kilometres, liberated 27 villages, and captured 9000 Germans. Currie continued to forge ahead to prevent the enemy from regrouping. Casualties and battle exhaustion rates rose, but the Canadians still broke through German defences at Drocourt-Quéant and Canal du Nord and then led in the liberation of Cambrai and Valenciennes. On November 7, they crossed into Belgium and four days later symbolically ended the war at Mons, from where the allies had fled at the outset of hostilities in August 1914. During those final 100 days, the Canadian Corps reclaimed 1300 square kilometres; liberated 228 villages, towns, and cities; and captured 623 heavy guns, 2842 machine guns, 336 trench mortars, and 31 537 Germans. It was a remarkable feat, but the butcher's bill was high—from August 8 to November 11, the Canadian Corps sustained 45 835 casualties, almost one-eighth the losses suffered by British forces, but Canada had one-fiftieth the number of troops in the field.

November 11, 1918: Armistice ends the First World War.

Canadians awoke on November 11 to news of the Armistice. Celebrations continued throughout the day and into the night with fireworks, street dancing, and Kaisers burned in effigy. Canadians rightfully took pride in their country's contributions towards achieving victory. Befitting its accomplishments and sacrifices, Borden demanded that Canada have a separate signature on the Treaty of Versailles that formally ended the First World War and a separate seat at the new League of Nations, an international intergovernmental organization created by the Treaty of Versailles and based in Geneva. Britain was opposed to separate Canadian status, arguing that the Empire, to retain its international clout, had to speak with one voice. Borden was offered a spot among the five British representatives at Versailles; in this capacity, he was to represent all the dominions (as Canada was the senior dominion), but he declined. The United States argued that separate Canadian representation would mean an extra voice for British interests; Borden shot back by saying that proportionately Canada had done more than the United States to defeat Germany. It was finally decided that at Versailles, Canada, Australia, and South Africa would each be allowed two representatives—the same as Belgium—and New Zealand one representative at the conference's plenary sessions and a signature on the treaty. It was a change in international status from the pre-war period, though it was generally known that the most important decisions were being made in private by the leaders of the four principal powers: Great Britain, the United States, Italy, and France. Canada also obtained its own seat at the League of Nations, though this, too, was granted to other self-governing dominions like Australia and New Zealand.

There was a growing sense that Canada's role in the war had given birth to a new national spirit. In describing the return home of the 19th Battalion, the Hamilton *Spectator* dwelt upon a "path of glory ... across the craters of St. Eloi, over the shell-swept areas of the Somme basin, up the scarred heights of Vimy Ridge and the slopes of Hill 70, through Passchendaele's slough and mud and blood to the epic days of 1918 ... which released the world from the yoke of Prussian militarism."[22] Millions of Canadians flocked to a series of post-war battle trophy shows to see items captured by Canadian soldiers. At Toronto's Canadian National Exhibition, the best-attended pavilion, attracting over 200 000 people in ten days, was a war trophy display billed by the Toronto *Star* as "living evidence of Canadian valour in France and Flanders."[23]

But the joy of victory, and the national pride that manifested, did not mean the end of difficulties and divisions linked to the war. There was the immediate and formidable challenge of transitioning Canada from war to peace. Some 400 000 servicemen had to be reintegrated. Tens of millions were spent on veterans' programs—an unprecedented amount for social welfare—but it was still not enough. Although stressing its commitment to care for those who had fought for Canada, the federal government operated with minimal tax revenues, feared adding significantly to a war debt of $1.3 billion, and, still harbouring the perception of welfare as something that should be discouraged as too costly and for sapping people of initiative, suggested that ex-soldiers, as Canada's best and strongest, could get back on their feet with minimal help.

Back in 1915, the federal government created the Military Hospitals Commission to provide medical care and pensions for wounded veterans. In early 1918, it became part of the new Department of Soldiers' Civil Re-establishment that administered a broader range of programs. On paper, Canada provided the most generous pensions among allied countries for wounded veterans, but only 5 percent of claimants obtained the top-paying category, compared with more than 50 percent who received remuneration in the bottom 20 percent of the award structure. Pension commissioners, most of whom were not veterans, tended to approach their job as guardians of the public purse rather than as advocates for veterans. Veterans were disqualified from retraining programs if it was felt they could return to their pre-war line of work. At training facilities, there were numerous complaints by veterans over poor equipment and ill-qualified instructors. Under the Soldier Settlement scheme, veterans received assistance to buy a farm each: The deal was that they would provide a 10 percent down payment and could borrow up to $4500 for property that would be amortized over 20 years at 5 five percent interest. By the end of 1921, the program had placed more than 25 000 veterans on farms, but their failure rate was very high because of declining crop prices, the government's unwillingness to ease repayment terms, and men assigned land in remote areas with poor access to markets. Within five years, 80 percent of veterans who participated in the farm program went broke.

Discord from the war also continued to reverberate from rural Canada; for some farmers, though, things had improved. The war brought record demand for numerous commodities and good prices. By the end of the decade, some 150 000 farms had a car, and nearly 50 000 a tractor. Between 1911 and 1921, improved farmland in Canada rose from 19.5 million hectares to 28.7 million hectares. Still, many farmers remained angry over the government's decision to cancel conscription exemptions for agricultural labour. The nationalization of bankrupt railways resulted in the Crow's Nest Pass rate being suspended as a cost-saving measure. In the closing months of the war, the Canadian Council of Agriculture demanded that Ottawa adopt its "New National Policy," whose planks included lower tariffs, steeper progressive taxes, and, in reflecting growing distrust towards major political parties, the introduction of a system of direct democracy under which voters could initiate and ratify legislation and recall representatives seen as no longer serving the people's interests. Also rankling was the federal government's regulation of wheat prices. Towards the end of the war, as the price of wheat reached a record high, the federal government created a Board of Grain Supervisors to control prices and over-see distribution. Soon after the war, it became the Canada Wheat Board, but it was dis-mantled as grain prices began tumbling. Farmers demanded that the Wheat Board be re-implemented to guarantee a minimum price but were rebuffed. Following a Union government budget in June 1919 that failed to deliver tariff concessions as previously promised, Manitoba's T.A. Crerar, the minister of agriculture, and eight other Union MPs from the Western provinces defected to sit as independents.

The trend among farmers towards creating their own political movement quickly gained momentum. In autumn 1919, farmers, though not yet having decided upon a name for their emerging party, won federal by-elections in Assiniboia, Saskatchewan, and in the rural New Brunswick constituency of Victoria-Carleton. In October, farmers in Ontario achieved a remarkable breakthrough when their former lobby group, the United Farmers of Ontario (UFO), decided to contest the 1919 provincial election. Ontario farmers were mobilized not only by lingering anger over the elimination of conscription exemptions, as well as by high tariffs and railway rates, but also by growing fears over a loss of power brought on by accelerated urbanization during the First World War. The UFO won only 22 percent of the popular vote, but this translated into 44 seats in a legislature of 111 because of rural overrepresentation. To form a government, the UFO joined forces with 11 Labour representatives whose strong showing in the 1919 Ontario election reflected yet another source of discontent.

More workers were drawing motivation from the idea that the war had been fought to defend freedom and advance civilization and that this should include full rights for workers. Such ideals were evident in the March 1919 Reconstruction Program of the New Brunswick Federation of Labour, which demanded collective bargaining rights, an eight-hour workday, freedom of speech and assembly, public ownership of utilities and resources, public housing, better educational opportunities, and cooperatives to protect workers from profiteers.

A growing segment of labour was coming to the conclusion that social justice would result only from the destruction of capitalism and the establishment of a communist or socialist government. For those who believed in revolution, never before did it seem so possible. Communist forces consolidated in Russia and in the chaos and despair of post-war Germany, the radical leftist Spartacus League threatened to seize power. In Australia, a sizable segment of organized labour became part of a single One Big Union, whose power, it was said, would bring capitalists to their knees. Strikes spread across North America, in

October 1919:
United Farmers of Ontario
form a government.

Canada totalling a record 2.1 million workdays in 1919. In most cases, strikers were trying to catch up to high inflation. As well, with union membership more than doubling during the war from 143 000 to 249 000, and peaking at 378 000 in 1919—with more people employed and labour shortages making workers less fearful of joining a union—many new labour organizations were trying to prove their worth to workers who, now that the war was over, did not feel the same pressure to stay on the job.

In March 1919, Western Canadian unionists met separately at Calgary's labour temple. Although many delegates hoped to remain affiliated with the TLC, a larger number of radicals were determined to create a new, separate, and more militant labour body. Delegates endorsed having a 30-hour workweek, allowing general strikes, and establishing One Big Union, and declared themselves as favouring "proletarian dictatorship."[24] On May 1, Winnipeg metal trade workers went on strike to achieve union recognition, something for which they had battled for more than a decade. The next day, building and construction trade workers who sought better wages joined them. On May 6, both groups appealed to the Winnipeg Trades and Labour Council for support. Influenced by the success of sympathy strikes to back Winnipeg municipal workers the previous year, the result (announced on May 13) saw trade council members endorse a general strike by an overwhelming margin of 11 000 to 500.

May–June 1919: Winnipeg General Strike.

The walkout started at 11 A.M. on May 15 and within 24 hours, 22 000 workers left their jobs and Winnipeg ground to a halt. Federal authorities feared that the strike could inspire a revolutionary wave, as smaller walkouts developed across Canada to show solidarity with Winnipeg workers and to address local labour grievances. Walkouts occurred in some 25 Canadian communities, including Halifax, Montreal, Toronto, Calgary, Edmonton, and Vancouver.

Winnipeg manufacturers, lawyers, and bankers formed a Committee of 1000 to help maintain basic services and order. While the provincial Liberal government of T.C. Norris, which was elected on a reform platform—and in 1916 introduced workman's compensation and minimum wage legislation—generally kept out of the dispute, municipal and federal politicians, particularly Canada's chief lawmaker, acting Minister of Justice Arthur Meighen, cast the strikers as intent on seizing power and establishing a Bolshevist government. Foreign radicals were blamed for the strike despite its Anglo leadership. The Manitoba *Free Press* referred to strikers as "bohunks" and the Winnipeg *Tribune* told its readers: "Remember, behind … this strike is a group of revolutionaries—its most active followers are undesirable aliens."[25]

After five weeks, a dawn raid by authorities nabbed the eight principal strike leaders. Four days later, on June 21, there came *Bloody Saturday*. It started with a rally by strikers against the resumption of streetcar service. When the crowd failed to disperse as ordered, the mayor read the *Riot Act*. Mounties on horseback with revolvers drawn charged into the crowd, leaving two strikers dead. Fearing another, and deadlier, confrontation, the strike committee ended the walkout on June 26. Seven of the eight arrested strike leaders were convicted of "seditious conspiracy" and received jail sentences ranging from six months to six years. Still, the federal government was convinced that existing legislation did not provide an adequate enough deterrent.

In June, the government added section 41 to the *Immigration Act* that made the deportation of radicals easier, including those from Britain, though the measure was applied only against Slavs and Finns. The next month, section 98 was added to Canada's *Criminal Code.* Its severity exceeded any wartime attack on free expression as it established a maximum penalty of 20 years' imprisonment against anyone who printed, published, wrote, edited, issued or sold "any book, newspaper, periodical, pamphlet, picture, paper, circular, card, letter, writing, print, publication, or document of any kind in which it is taught, advocated, advised or defended ... that the use of force, violence, terrorism or physical injury be used as a means of accomplishing any governmental, industrial, or economic change."[26]

July 1919: Section 98 added to Canada's Criminal Code.

A New Liberal Leader

On February 22, 1919, 50 000 people, half of Ottawa's population, lined city streets to pay their final respects to Sir Wilfrid Laurier, who died five days earlier at the age of 78. Although vilified in English Canada for opposing conscription, in death Laurier attained iconic status, as he had sat in Parliament for 45 years, served as Liberal leader for more than three decades, and had been prime minister for 15 years. However, his party had been out of power since 1911. The Liberals began a process of renewal by announcing a national leadership convention to take place in Ottawa in August. It was to be the first of its kind to reflect a new democratic spirit coming out of the war. Similar to modern political conventions, some 1000 delegates were to be selected from constituencies across Canada to choose the next leader, rather than using the past practice where the party's parliamentary caucus made the choice behind closed doors.

The Liberals would turn to William Lyon Mackenzie King. To many, he was an odd choice: a podgy, balding bachelor, who was rather stiff, standoffish, and socially awkward, and had a penchant for using platitudes and cloying flattery towards those he wanted to win over. In an era before television and image-makers, this mattered less than the fact that King was a master political tactician with an astonishing ability to read the public mood, build coalitions, impress the right people, make the right friends, and demolish his enemies.

First elected in 1908, King served as minister of labour, but was defeated in the 1911 Tory sweep of Ontario. He established himself as a labour relations expert and made a great deal of money by spending most of the war years in the United States working for the famous multi-millionaire John D. Rockefeller, Jr. He helped resurrect Rockefeller's image and established labour peace—though by creating a company-controlled workers' association—following the April 1914 Ludlow Massacre, when, in a union recognition fight against the Rockefeller-owned Colorado Fuel and Iron Company, 20 men, women, and children evicted from company housing were killed by private guards.

Throughout his years in the United States, King maintained ties with the Liberal party, though the distance enabled him to evade public commentary on the contentious issue of conscription, which he opposed. As the 1917 election approached, he returned to the political fray. He considered jumping to the Union party, but decided to stay loyal to Laurier, whom he considered his political mentor and because like Laurier he feared the consequences of conscription on French–English relations. Nevertheless, King tried to stake out a more nuanced position than Laurier, claiming that he did not reject conscription in principal, but for reasons not entirely clear, opposed the specific legislation advanced by Borden's government. King lost the riding of North York, just outside Toronto, by 1000 votes, but did better than most Liberals in the area.

At the Ottawa convention, the Liberals were looking for a fresh start, for someone who could project an image of reform and heal bitter rifts left from the war, as many had bolted from the party to the Unionists. Anglo members were determined that the leadership go to one of their own after 28 years of Laurier at the helm. King trumpeted his reform past—his personal lineage to rebel leader William Lyon Mackenzie and his long involvement in progressive causes—and the fact that he was a labour relations expert, which meant he could present himself as a conciliator who could build bridges between opposing forces. At 45 years old and with a boyish face, he also came across as youthful, at least when compared with the initial front-runner, 70-year-old William Fielding, the former premier of Nova Scotia and federal finance minister, who many considered a man of the nineteenth century, and whom numerous Liberals never forgave for abandoning Laurier and supporting the Unionists on conscription. In his convention address, King, while avoiding specifics, declared his support for the right of workers to organize unions and for the creation of government unemployment, old age, sickness, and disability insurance programs. He also presented himself as favourable to freer trade—though not to the extent to completely alienate high-tariff supporters—and won favour for having stuck by Laurier in 1917, especially among Quebec's 297 delegates, 207 of whom backed King. It took five ballots to make King the new leader, and in that final vote, he barely squeaked in over Fielding by a count of 467 to 439.

*August 1919:
William Lyon Mackenzie
King becomes federal
Liberal leader.*

Conclusion

The impact of the First World War on Canada was profound and multi-faceted. Canada's annual defence budget soared from $72 million (29.3 percent of total government expenditures) in 1914 to $439 million (59.3 percent) in 1918. The government managed the lives of Canadians as never before, establishing new taxes, imposing compulsory military service, implementing food and fuel control, curtailing basic freedoms, and introducing the first nationwide social welfare program for veterans. Organized labour grew more powerful, aggressive, and to many, threatening. Women gained the vote. Prohibition triumphed. Canada's contributions to the war effort generated tremendous pride and nationalism and considerably raised the country's profile and international status.

It has become almost axiomatic to state that during the First World War Canada transformed from "colony to nation." Yet, by 1914, was it not already moving from the Empire? Did Canada gain anything denied to other dominions, such as Australia and New Zealand? Was the war truly nation-building? Contrasting with the triumph at Vimy, Canada's decisive role in the last 100 days, and the innumerable contributions and sacrifices made at home were the divisions caused by conscription, the persecution of ethnic minorities and political dissenters, the manipulation of the voting system, and nearly a quarter million Canadians killed or wounded and countless others psychologically scarred for the rest of their lives.

In many ways, the road ahead for Canada did not seem as clear in 1919 as compared with the heady and enthusiastic days of August 1914. Growing disenchantment during the war played a key role in the genesis of third-party politics and in a larger segment of organized labour moving towards radicalism. By the November 1918 armistice, French and English Canada were more divided than at any other time since the 1837 rebellion. Throughout the 1920s, legacies from the First World War would continue to reverberate loudly on Canadian society and culture, politics and the economy, and Canada's relations with the outside world.

Questions to Consider

1. How did the First World War affect civil liberties?
2. How did the First World War impact French-English relations?
3. How did the First World War affect Canada's economy?
4. To what extent did the First World War change Canada's relations with Britain?

Critical Thinking Questions

1. How well did Canada's military perform in the First World War?
2. Did Canada emerge from the First World War as a stronger country?
3. What Canadians might have been left disillusioned by the First World War?

Suggested Readings

General

Gwyn, Sandra. *Tapestry of War: A Private View of Canadians in the Great War.* Toronto: HarperCollins Publishers, 1992.

Legault, Roch, and Jean Lamarre, dirs. *La Première Guerre mondiale et le Canada: contributions socio-militaires québécoises.* Montreal: Méridien, 1999.

MacKenzie, David, ed. *Canada and the First World War: Essays in Honour of Robert Craig Brown.* Toronto: University of Toronto Press, 2005.

Morton, Desmond, and J.L. Granatstein. *Marching to Armageddon: Canadians and the Great War, 1914–1919.* Toronto: Lester & Orpen Dennys, 1989.

Politics

Brown, Robert Craig. *Robert Laird Borden: A Biography*, 2 Vols. Toronto: Macmillan of Canada, 1975, 1980.

English, John. *The Decline of Politics: The Conservatives and the Party System, 1901–20.* Toronto: University of Toronto Press, 1977.

Morton, Desmond. *A Peculiar Kind of Politics: Canada's Overseas Ministry in the First World War.* Toronto: University of Toronto Press, 1982.

Home Front

Armstrong, John Griffith. *The Halifax Explosion and the Royal Canadian Navy: Inquiry and Intrigue.* Vancouver: University of British Columbia Press, 2002.

Jones, Esyllt W. *Influenza 1918: Disease, Death, and Struggle in Winnipeg.* Toronto: University of Toronto Press, 2007.

Miller, Ian Hugh Maclean. *Our Glory and Our Grief: Torontonians and the Great War.* Toronto: University of Toronto Press, 2002.

Rutherdale, Robert. *Hometown Horizons: Local Responses to Canada's Great War.* Vancouver: University of British Columbia Press, 2005.

Thompson, John Herd. *The Harvests of War: The Prairie West, 1914–1918.* Toronto: McClelland & Stewart, 1978.

Dissent and Civil Liberties

Keshen, Jeffrey A. *Propaganda and Censorship during Canada's Great War.* Edmonton: University of Alberta Press, 1996.

Shaw, Amy. *Crisis of Conscience: Conscientious Objection in Canada during the First World War.* Vancouver: University of British Columbia Press, 2009.

Socknat, Thomas Paul. *Witness Against War: Pacifism in Canada, 1900–1945.* Toronto: University of Toronto Press, 1987.

Labour and Women

Bercuson, David. *Fools and Wise Men: The Rise and Fall of the One Big Union.* Toronto: McGraw-Hill Ryerson, 1978.

Heron, Craig, ed. *The Workers' Revolt in Canada, 1917–1925.* Toronto: University of Toronto Press, 1998.

Kealey, Linda. *Enlisting Women for the Cause: Women, Labour, and the Left in Canada, 1890–1920.* Toronto: University of Toronto Press, 1998.

Marshall, Debbie. *Give Your Other Vote to the Sister: A Woman's Journey into the Great War.* Calgary: University of Calgary Press, 2007.

Naylor, James. *The New Democracy: Challenging the Social Order in Industrial Ontario, 1914–1925.* Toronto: University of Toronto Press, 1991.

Social Policy and Culture

Cook, Tim. *Clio's Warriors: Canadian Historians and the Writing of the World Wars.* Vancouver: University of British Columbia Press, 2006.

Morton, Desmond. *Fight or Pay: Soldiers' Families in the Great War.* Vancouver: University of British Columbia Press, 2004.

Morton, Desmond, and Glenn Wright. *Winning the Second Battle: Canadian Veterans and the Return to Civilian Life, 1915–1930.* Toronto: University of Toronto Press, 1987.

Tippett, Maria. *Art at the Service of War: Canada, Art, and the Great War.* Toronto: University of Toronto Press, 1984.

Vance, Jonathan. *Death So Noble: Memory, Meaning, and the First World War.* Vancouver: University of British Columbia Press, 1997.

Army

Cook, Tim. *At the Sharp End: Canadians Fighting the Great War, 1914–1916.* Toronto: Penguin, 2007.

Cook, Tim. *No Place to Run: The Canadian Corps and Gas Warfare in the First World War.* Vancouver: University of British Columbia Press, 1999.

Cook, Tim. *Shock Troops: Canadians Fighting the Great War, 1917–1918.* Toronto: Penguin, 2009.

Crerar, Duff. *Padres in No Man's Land: Canadian Chaplains and the Great War.* Montreal and Kingston: McGill-Queen's University Press, 1995.

Dancocks, Daniel. *Sir Arthur Currie: A Biography.* Toronto: Methuen, 1985.

Haycock, Ronald Graham. *Sam Hughes: The Public Career of a Controversial Canadian, 1885–1916.* Waterloo: Wilfrid Laurier University Press, 1986.

Iarocci, Andrew. *Shoestring Soldiers: 1st Canadian Division at War.* Toronto: University of Toronto Press, 2008.

Morton, Desmond. *When Your Number's Up: The Canadian Soldier in the First World War.* Toronto: Random House of Canada, 1993.

Nicholson, G.W.L. *Canadian Expeditionary Force, 1914–1919: Official History of the Canadian Army in the First World War.* Ottawa: Queen's Printer, 1962.

Rawling, Bill. *Surviving Trench Warfare: Technology and the Canadian Corps, 1914–1918.* Toronto: University of Toronto Press, 1992.

Schreiber, Shane B. *Shock Army of the British Empire: The Canadian Corps in the Last 100 Days of the Great War.* Westport: Praeger, 1997.

Vennat, Pierre. *Les «poilus» québécois de 1914–1918: Histoire des militaires canadiens-français de la première guerre mondiale.* Montreal: Méridien, 1999.

Air Force and Navy

Hadley, Michael L., and Roger Sarty. *Tin-Pots and Pirate Ships: Canadian Naval Forces and German Sea Raiders, 1880–1918.* Montreal and Kingston: McGill-Queen's University Press, 1991.

Vance, Jonathan. *High Flight: Aviation and the Canadian Imagination* Toronto: Penguin, 2002.

Wise, S.F. *Canadian Airmen and the First World War.* Toronto: University of Toronto Press, 1980.

Internment and POWs

Morton, Desmond. *Silent Battle: Canadian Prisoners of War in Germany, 1914–1919*. Toronto: Lester Publishing, 1992.

Swyripa, Frances, and John Herd Thompson, eds. *Loyalties in Conflict: Ukrainians in Canada during the Great War*. Edmonton: Canadian Institute of Ukrainian Studies, 1983.

Vance, Jonathan F. *Objects of Concern: Canadian Prisoners of War Through the Twentieth Century*. Vancouver: University of British Columbia Press, 1994.

Waiser, Bill. *Park Prisoners: The Untold Story of Western Canada's National Parks, 1915–1946*. Saskatoon: Fifth House, 1995.

Memoirs and Novels

Bird, Will R. *Ghosts Have Warm Hands*. Toronto: Clarke, Irwin, 1968.

Cowley, Deborah, ed. *Georges Vanier, Soldier: The Wartime Letters and Diaries, 1915–1919*. Toronto: Dundurn Press, 2000.

Harrison, Charles Yale. *Generals Die in Bed*. London: N. Douglas, 1930.

Roy, Reginald, ed. *The Journal of Private Fraser, 1914–1918: Canadian Expeditionary Force*. Victoria: Sono Nis Press, 1985.

Notes

[1] J.L. Granatstein and Norman Hillmer, eds., *Battle Lines: Eyewitness Accounts from Canada's Military History* (Toronto: Thomas Allen Publishers, 2004), 161–162.

[2] Toronto *Globe*, 10 August 1914, 13.

[3] Lita Rose Betcherman, *Ernest Lapointe: Mackenzie King's Great Quebec Lieutenant* (Toronto: University of Toronto Press, 2002), 3.

[4] Joseph Boudreau, "The Enemy Alien Problem in Canada, 1914–1921," Ph.D., University of California, Berkeley, 1965, 45–46.

[5] Ottawa, Government of Canada, *Order in Council, PC 1330*, 10 June 1915.

[6] Jeff Keshen, *Propaganda and Censorship during Canada's Great War* (Edmonton: University of Alberta Press, 1996); and Ian Hugh Maclean Miller, *Our Gory and Our Grief: Torontonians and the Great War* (Toronto: University of Toronto Press, 2002).

[7] Metropolitan Toronto Library, Baldwin Room, *World War One Broadside Catalogue*, n.p.

[8] Miller, *Our Glory and Our Grief*, 119.

[9] J.L. Granatstein and Desmond Morton, *Marching to Armageddon: Canadians and the Great War, 1914–1919* (Toronto: Lester & Orpen Dennys, 1989), 112.

[10] http://www.thesacredvoicegallery.com/papineau2.htm.

[11] Granatstein and Morton, *Marching to Armageddon*, 135.

[12] Tim Cook, *At the Sharp End: Canadians Fighting the Great War 1914–1916* (Toronto: Penguin, 2007), 97.

[13] Ottawa *Journal*, 30 June 1917, 5.

[14] Brereton Greenhous, *The Making of Billy Bishop: The First World War Exploits of Billy Bishop, VC* (Toronto: Dundurn, 2002).

[15] Alison Prentice, Paula Bourne, Gail Cuthbert Brandt, Beth Light, Wendy Mitchinson, and Naomi Black, *Canadian Women: A History* (Toronto: Harcourt Brace Jovanovich, 1988), 198.

16   Mary Kinnear, *A Female Economy: Women's Work in a Prairie Province, 1870–1970* (Montreal and Kingston: McGill-Queen's University Press, 1998), 85.

17   Desmond Morton with Terry Copp, *Working People: An Illustrated History of the Canadian Labour Movement* (Ottawa: Deneau, 1984), 111.

18   Elizabeth Armstrong, *The Crisis of Quebec, 1914–1918* (Toronto: McClelland & Stewart, 1974), 207–208.

19   J.L. Granatstein and J.M. Hitsman, *Broken Promises: A History of Conscription in Canada* (Toronto: Oxford University Press, 1977), Chapter 2; A.A. Willms, "Conscription: A Brief for the Defence," Carl Berger, ed., *Conscription 1917* (Toronto: University of Toronto Press, 1970).

20   Ottawa, Government of Canada, *Order in Council, PC 2384*, 28 September 1918.

21   Mark Osborne Humphries, "The Horror at Home: The Canadian Military and the 'Great' Influenza Pandemic of 1918," *Journal of the Canadian Historical Association* 16 (2005): 235–260; Esyllt W. Jones, *Influenza 1918: Disease, Death, and Struggle in Winnipeg* (Toronto: University of Toronto Press, 2007).

22   Hamilton *Spectator*, 9 May 1919, 1.

23   Toronto *Star*, 3 September 1919, 3.

24   Gerald Friesen, *The Canadian Prairies: A History* (Toronto: University of Toronto Press, 1984), 360.

25   Manitoba *Free Press*, 17 June 1919, 2.

26   *Revised Statutes of Canada*, 10 George V, Chapter 146, 7 July 1919.

5

*T*he Turbulent Twenties

*B*utch Caroll's after-school job paid more than what was earned by a full-time farmhand in Saskatchewan. Every afternoon he visited a warehouse and loaded up liquor for transport. Sometimes he drove there, always careful not to speed to avoid attracting attention. He headed south to a secret rendezvous point near the international border. There he met contacts that smuggled the stash into the United States where, since January 1920, prohibition had been the law of the land. He dealt with the likes of "Doc" Riley who had once nearly beaten a Mountie to death for trying to double-cross him after taking a bribe.

Butch's employer was the king of Canada's liquor trade, Harry Bronfman. Back in 1899, a dirt-poor Harry arrived with his brother, Sam, in the Saskatchewan hamlet of Wapella, having fled from the Czarist pogroms that killed thousands of Russian Jews. The brothers scraped together enough money to purchase the Balmoral hotel in Yorkton. From this inauspicious beginning, they built an empire by taking advantage of loopholes in Canada's temperance legislation. After the First World War, they obtained a licence to start the Canada Pure Drug Company, which allowed them to sell alcohol for medicinal purposes. Not too long after, the Bronfmans created a

series of heavily guarded liquor warehouses (popularly known as boozoriums) near the American border that shipped as many as 10 000 cases of alcohol a month into the United States and cleared as much as $400 000 profit monthly. But this invited cutthroat competition. In late 1922, their brother-in-law was gunned down in broad daylight in the Bienfait, Saskatchewan, railway station. Shaken by the murder, the Bronfmans relocated to Montreal, where liquor production was legal. There they created an even more profitable distillery that eventually became known worldwide as Seagrams.

After reading this chapter you will be able to:

1. Assess the impact of and controversies relating to prohibition.
2. Understand the rise and different outcomes of regional political protest.
3. Appreciate the degree to which the 1920s roared economically, witnessed sexual liberation, and encouraged greater equality for women.
4. Identify and explain the contours of post-war Canadian foreign policy.
5. Recall expressions of a more robust Canadian culture.
6. Explain the extent to which Canada become a haven for immigrants.

Introduction

The bootleggers, mobsters, and masses of people who winked at the law to visit speakeasies (establishments that illegally sold alcoholic beverages) were all part of the image the "roaring '20s." In popular lore, it was a time when people cast aside the propriety of the pre-war period to live fast and loose, reacting to a war that had taught them to live for the day because there was no certainty of tomorrow. It was a period of prosperity and get-rich-quick schemes; of fads, like mah-jong; of crazy, and garish, styles like long raccoon coats; of nonsensical sayings like "twenty-three skidoo"; of flappers who conveyed sexual liberation; of frenetic dances like the Charleston; and of fast-paced jazz. To sum it up, it was an exciting, youthful, noisy, risqué, party-like decade. No doubt, such images were partly constructed on the basis of what came before—a pre-war depression and more than four years of bloodletting—and after the 1920s: the most severe depression in modern times. This chapter seeks to critically assess what actually changed and examines these questions: Did looser moral standards take hold? Did Canadian society become more accepting of differences? Did women enjoy greater liberation? Did the country become more independent? Did the '20s roar economically? And what did the period reveal, or affirm, about politics and effective political leadership?

Factionalism and a Faltering Economy, 1920–1921

By 1920, Robert Borden was desperate to leave office. His Union government was despised in French Canada and was bleeding support among the workers and farmers. Even much of the business community was upset over the wartime decision to nationalize the railways. In February, the Western Canadian MPs that had resigned from his government the previous year organized themselves into a distinct parliamentary group called the Progressives. After nine years as prime minister, Borden was exhausted, especially after having taken the country through the tumult of war. He wanted Finance Minister Thomas White to replace him, but White too was worn out and ready to retire. On July 10, 1920, Borden handed over the job of prime minister to the energetic, ambitious, and brilliant 46-year-old Arthur Meighen.

July 1920: Arthur Meighen becomes prime minister.

Born in Manitoba in 1874, the same year as his rival Mackenzie King, Meighen studied at the University of Toronto, earning a degree in mathematics but also qualifying as a teacher and a lawyer. Elected to Parliament in 1908 to represent Portage la Prairie, five years later, with the Tories in power, he was appointed solicitor-general and before becoming prime minister held the positions of secretary of state, minister of the interior, minister of mines, minister of Indian affairs, and minister of justice. Although physically slight, Meighen commanded a considerable presence as a result of his keen intellect, supreme self-confidence, exceptional oratory, and biting—though often cruel—wit. However, to many, he came across as aloof, cold, and uncompromising. He was remembered and hated in French Canada for his role in implementing conscription and by many in the labour movement for crushing the Winnipeg General Strike. In the face of profound opposition from rural Canada, he remained steadfast in his belief for higher tariffs, insisting that protectionism would ensure vibrant urban-industrial markets for Canadian farm products.

Meighen became prime minister as the economy nose-dived. High wartime inflation continued into peacetime, hitting a combined 27 percent in 1919–1920. Many firms overproduced, which soon precipitated rapid deflation and a sharp contraction in production. In 1921, the price level dropped by 28 percent and manufacturing output by one-third. Whereas Canada experienced 900 bankruptcies in 1919, that figure climbed to 2451 in 1921. The cost of nationalizing the railways—a process not completed until 1922—was staggering and compromised the ability of the federal government to undertake other large projects, namely, to reduce unemployment, which reached 15 percent. In 1922, the federal government's railway debt, at $160 million, exceeded its 1913 budget.

Pressure grew on the federal government to take action to alleviate suffering. As a fiscal conservative who opposed debts and viewed welfare as encouraging dependency, Meighen responded cautiously. In December 1920, his government announced it would make $500 000 available over that winter to provide up to one-third of relief costs to municipal and provincial governments.

Political discontent festered in many parts of the country. In July 1921, the United Farmers of Alberta (UFA) won power with 38 seats in a provincial assembly of 61. Disgruntlement also mounted out east. Although New Brunswickers re-elected the Liberals with 24 of 48 seats in October 1920, they also voted in nine members of the new United Farmers of New Brunswick and for the first time two Labour members. With the recovery of European and Scandinavian fleets, employment in the Maritime fishing sector declined from 17 583 in 1919 to 12 395 by 1923. The completion of the Panama Canal in 1914 and its large-scale use after the war to transport west-coast timber to Europe hurt the Maritime forestry sector. The expansion of hydroelectric power in Central Canada, and new and more accessible coalmines in places like Pennsylvania, cut mining jobs in Cape Breton by 25 percent. Consumer demand slackened, and manufacturing jobs in the Maritimes plummeted from 46 004 in 1919 to 27 855 in 1921.

People in the region directed much of their anger against the federal government. They griped over reduced tariff protection for Maritime coal and steel, and the federal government's decision in August 1918 to incorporate the Maritime-based and Maritime-managed intercolonial railway into the new nationalized system, which shifted control from Moncton to Montreal and eliminated rail subsidies ranging from 20 to 50 percent.

Arthur Meighen was among the most effective parliamentary debaters in Canadian history. He held King in contempt for supposedly lacking conviction, but to many, Meighen came across as arrogant and inflexible.

Source: Library and Archives of Canada, C-005799.

Business interests formed a Maritime Board of Trade to campaign for better tariff and rail rates, improved port facilities, increased subsidies, and improved links between Prince Edward Island and the mainland. Meighen cast their demands as excessive; King expressed empathy but avoided making specific promises.

Outside of Canada, Meighen was intent on building stronger Anglo-American cooperation, and for this purpose had Canada play the role of what historian J.B. Brebner called a "linch pin."[1] This became evident at the June 1921 imperial conference where the principal issue was whether or not to renew the Anglo-Japanese treaty. Australia and New Zealand were strongly in favour—arguing that Japan had been an important wartime ally and that it was imperative for the Empire to maintain good relations with this major Pacific power—and Britain leaned in the same direction. However, the United States expressed opposition, viewing its substantial financial interests in China as threatened by an expansionist Japan. Meighen supported Washington and stressed the importance of establishing close ties between Britain, its Empire, and America. Meighen stood firm against formidable political veterans like Australia's William Hughes, letting it be known that Canada would not consider itself as bound by a renewed treaty. Fearing an open breach in the Empire, the treaty was left in limbo until the 1922 Washington Conference replaced it with a 5-5-3 ratio on American, British, and Japanese naval strength and a four-power accord involving the United States, France, Japan, and Britain, whose governments pledged to respect one another's rights in the Pacific.

June 1921: Meighen scuttles the Anglo-Japanese treaty.

A New Political Landscape

Meighen called an election for December 6, 1921. He attacked the Liberals as free traders who would bring about Canada's absorption into the United States and denounced the Progressives for promoting class warfare. King made only vague references to tariff reform because of his need to keep protectionist forces in Quebec on side. Anger in the agricultural West rose as the price of wheat dropped from $2.78 per bushel (0.04 cubic metre) in September 1920 to $1.76 in April 1921. Many parts of the prairies, namely the short-grass plains, had experienced droughts from 1917 to 1921. Winnipeg also suffered as the widespread use of the Panama Canal decreased east–west rail traffic in which the city was a major hub. King continually reminded Quebec voters of Meighen's close association with conscription; when visiting the province, Meighen required extra security.

The Liberals captured 117 seats, one shy of a majority (though they could count on support from one independent Liberal and one Labour-Liberal MP), while Meighen's Liberal and Conservative party (that reverted to just Conservative after the election) finished with just 50 seats. Canada's French–English divide remained starkly evident, as the Liberals took all 65 seats in Quebec, with more than 70 percent of the vote, while Meighen's best showing was in Ontario, where his party won 36 seats with less than 40 percent of the vote. The results shattered Canada's two-party political tradition with the election of 65 Progressives: 38 (of 43 available seats) from the Prairies, three from British Columbia, 21 from Ontario, and one from New Brunswick.

The rise of the Progressives reflected longstanding rural grievances and suspicions of urban and financial power (especially in Toronto and Montreal), wartime challenges and hardships,

December 1921: King elected prime minister; Progressives elect 65 members.

and the post-war collapse of wheat prices. Central planks in their platform included tariff reductions, the nationalization of railways and utilities, progressive income and corporate taxes, and more direct forms of political participation, such as referenda, to introduce and approve legislation and to recall representatives judged as failing to serve the will of constituents. The Progressives also supported more equal rights for women, prohibition, and the establishment of citizen-run cooperatives to buy and sell goods, planks that reflected their declaration to build a more moral society that they presented as derived from superior rural ethics.

King created an initial cabinet that balanced between region, religion, and language. Ontario and Quebec each received six cabinet posts, Nova Scotia two, and all the other provinces, except Manitoba, one. Francophones, Anglophones, Catholics, and Protestants were all represented. His government stuck to current economic orthodoxy by pursuing a balanced budget. Although having expressed sympathy for unemployment insurance when running for the Liberal leadership, King now claimed his hands were tied because such an initiative fell under provincial constitutional jurisdiction. Over the winter of 1921–1922, he adopted Meighen's policy of offering limited federal matching funds to support local relief efforts, a program his government discontinued the following spring to save money and did not renew during the winter of 1922–1923.

King sought to court the Progressives, classifying them as "Liberals in a hurry." He asked T.A. Crerar, the Progressives' leader, to closely consult with, or even to join, his cabinet. He continued talking about tariff reform, though his protectionist wing from Quebec, led by Justice Minister Lomer Gouin, the former premier of the province, left him with little manoeuvrability.

King benefited from divisions within Progressive ranks. One faction, led by Crerar, that garnered most of its support from Manitoba and Saskatchewan, wanted to make the Progressives into a political party that could work effectively within Parliament and to broaden out its base of support beyond farmers. A smaller, more doctrinaire group, who had most appeal in Alberta and Ontario, countered them. Inspired by those such as Henry Wise Wood, president of the UFA, and J.J. Morrison, secretary of the United Farmers of Ontario (UFO), they rejected the need for party unity and broadening out, claiming it would dilute Progressive ideology and turn them into just another political party that placed obtaining power above principles. They advocated that each MP should vote according to the wishes of their constituents and that Group Government, where representatives would be chosen to represent different occupations, replace the prevailing party system.

The Progressives didn't have much in the way of centralized organization, and their putative leader, T.A. Crerar, had little authority. Lack of cooperation between the two factions prevented the Progressives from assuming the role of official opposition. In November 1922, a frustrated Crerar resigned as leader and was replaced by Robert Forke, a former municipal politician from Brandon, Manitoba, who was described by many as more of a chairman of the board.

Political action by farmers at the provincial level had mixed results. The United Farmers of Manitoba, first elected in 1922 under John Bracken, moved to work more closely with the Liberals with whom they formed a coalition in the 1930s. The UFA remained in power until 1934, though it increasingly adopted orthodox economic policies, demanded party unity, and rejected Group Government. The UFO faltered because of division between Premier E.C. Drury, who favoured broadening out, and J.J. Morrison's supporters. The UFO's alliance with Labour representatives dissipated over issues such as farmer opposition to a maximum workweek at regular pay (farmers insisted they always worked until the job was done), and its popularity also plummeted as the economy continued to falter. In 1923, Ontarians voted the Tories back into power with an overwhelming majority of 75 out of 110 available seats.

Tough Times

Resource extraction played a major role in the Western Canadian economy, in some areas compensating for the post-war economic downturn. In Manitoba, the potential of northern development, especially with mineral extraction, continued to fuel construction of the Hudson Bay railroad. By the end of the decade, it reached Churchill on the shores of the Hudson Bay, helping to increase the white population in the province's northern territory from 20 402 in 1921 to 30 669 a decade later. In British Columbia, mining, timber, fishing, and agriculture drove the provincial economy. Vancouver overtook Victoria as the major metropolis, in part because the Panama Canal made it easy to ship from Canada's west coast to the east, including to Britain and Europe. The province's economy grew faster than most other parts of Canada, with the net value of production expanding by 30 percent during the 1920s to reach $331 million. Diversification into manufacturing became significant, rising from $28 million in 1922 to $134 million in 1928.

Tough times persisted on Canada's east coast, though; there was the widespread sense that things had gotten worse. Out-migration from the Maritimes, namely to the northeastern United States and Western Canada, continued strong. The number of seats held by the Maritimes in Parliament declined from 33 to 31 to 30 in the elections of 1917, 1921, and 1925. The early1920s saw a growing fascination with traditional Maritime folk society and culture, a trend fed by the sharp post-war downturn and a belief in a simpler and supposedly better past, and because the promotion of folk culture offered a means to encourage tourism to improve the laggard economy.

Many Maritimers felt that King had deceived them by suggesting sympathy for their grievances while running for prime minister. Under the rallying cry of *Maritime rights*, sentiment once again began growing for Maritime union or even for secession from Canada. The Tories benefited from this anger. In 1923, they ousted the Liberal government in Prince Edward Island and won a federal by-election in Kent, New Brunswick, a riding that had been held by the Liberals since 1896.

Canada's working class also experienced tough times. A 1921 analysis in Toronto concluded that a family of five required a minimum $25.43 a week to survive, but the average male wage in the city was only three-quarters of that figure. High unemployment made many workers fearful of trying to start or join a union lest they lose their job—and it remained the case that governments did virtually nothing to help the jobless. The prevailing attitude was that unemployment was a personal failing and that those willing to work could find jobs.

The early 1920s saw a concerted effort by employers to roll back wages, bust unions, and blacklist union organizers. Union membership plummeted from 376 000 in 1919 to 240 000 in 1924. In a sign of the times, Labour Day parades (once a source of pride for workers and unions) disappeared from numerous communities. More workers and unions turned to May Day celebrations to commemorate the successful revolution that established the communist Soviet Union. Although Canada recognized the Soviet government in 1924 (nine years before the United States), it broke off relations later that year after allegations came from Britain that the Soviet trade mission in London was being used for espionage. In Toronto, May Day celebrations, organized in large part by Canada's Communist Party, formed in 1921, drew crowds of up to 25 000, where participants demanded jobs and social services.

There were outbreaks of labour militancy, but the results rarely favoured workers. One hot spot was the Maritime coal mines where dismal working conditions and growing pressure on labour to accept lower wages and fewer shifts prompted many to join the United Mine Workers (UMW), an international union known for militancy. District 26 of the UMW, with 13 000 members in Nova Scotia and New Brunswick, was being steered towards radicalism under the leadership of the firebrand socialist James B. McLachlan. In 1922, many members of the UMW were up for a new contract, but coal companies, led by the newly formed conglomerate, the British Empire Steel Corporation (BESCO), demanded a 30 percent wage cut. District 26 declared a strike. An agreement was hammered out in which many cuts were averted, but McLachlan and his supporters spoke of a sell-out. The next year, McLachlan convinced many members of District 26 to stage a wildcat walkout to support striking Sydney steelworkers. More than 1000 troops were sent to the area and clashes occurred. John L. Lewis, president of the UMW in the United States, fired McLachlan and his executive for the illegal walkout. The steelworkers' strike collapsed, union activists were blacklisted, McLachlan was jailed for making seditious remarks, and more moderate figures took over District 26. Still, this did not prevent another strike two years later against a proposed 20 percent wage cut by BESCO during which one miner was killed.

In general, working class radicalism was in decline. Strike activity dropped from 3.4 million days in 1919 to 800 000 the next year, and bottomed out at 152 000 in 1927, though there were anomalies like 1.5 million strike days in 1922. Despite some large May Day gatherings, there was less talk of revolution, and a result was the disintegration of the Western Canadian–based Socialist Party of Canada and the national Social Democratic Party. The trend among labour was to seek measured, and generally more moderate, adjustments through the prevailing political system.

The post-war period produced more success at the polls for worker candidates whose emphasis on improving labour rights and social welfare was patterned after Britain's Labour party. In the November 1919 municipal election in Winnipeg, labour candidates won the districts composing the city's working class north end. The same year, 11 Independent Labour party candidates won seats in the Ontario election. In 1920, Manitoba's Dominion Labour party and Independent Labour party won 11 seats in a legislature of 55, and in British Columbia three labour representatives were elected in a legislature of 47. In the 1921 federal election, two labour representatives attained office: William Irvine in Calgary and James Shaver (J.S.) Woodsworth in Winnipeg North, a seat he held until his death in 1942.

1922: First major strike by District 26 of the UMW.

Linguistic and Social Strains

Canada's post-war labour movement experienced more pronounced divisions on the basis of language and religion. Reflecting still palpable resentment towards English Canada from the First World War, as well as fears, especially from within the Catholic Church, over initial post-war radicalism and alien values being inculcated by American-controlled international unions—to which three-quarters of unionized Quebecers belonged—the clergy intensified efforts to link with the Francophone working class by creating the *Confédération des travailleurs catholiques* (CTCC) in 1921. Initially, with a membership of 18 000, its affiliates installed Catholic priests as counsellors and as the final authority in labour negotiations. Promoting the idea of Catholic social relations, the CTCC pursued improvements for labour by trying to establish more harmonious relations with capital, namely by advocating conciliation and arbitration over strikes.

The early 1920s also brought new challenges to Quebec relating to the quickening pace of urbanization and industrialization. The province's Liberal government, whose control of the legislature stretched back to the turn of the century, followed an approach that sought to bridge modernism and respect for tradition. Louis-Alexandre Taschereau, whom Gouin had hand-picked to succeed him as premier in the summer of 1920, continued efforts to try to attract large-scale investment that increasingly brought the provincial economy under Anglo-Canadian and American control. He also praised the influence of the Catholic Church and traditional rural society for establishing a higher moral standard in Quebec. His government increased funding to Quebec's Department of Colonization to assist more Francophones in taking up farming. Although the Catholic Church did not completely trust his commitment to traditionalism, Taschereau's Liberal party triumphed in the 1923 provincial election with 64 out of 85 seats and 55 percent of the vote.

Conservative nationalism stressing *La survivance* of traditional Quebec society became more prominent during the early 1920s under the leadership of Abbé Lionel Groulx, a cleric, historian, author, and educator, who was the central figure in establishing *L'Action française*, an intellectual movement transplanted from France. Its rise was clearly a reaction to the implementation of wartime conscription and the attack on French-language rights in Ontario. As Anglophones had rejected Henri's Bourassa's vision of a bilingual and bicultural Canada, Groulx's idea of a Quebec- and Francophone-based nationalism resonated. *L'Action française*'s membership, though small, was influential, attracting leading French Canadians from law, education, journalism, and the church. They insisted that education for Francophones infuse Catholic values; presented traditional pursuits, namely farming, as instilling a higher ethical standard and as creating a vigorous population; and used history to buttress their cause by portraying New France as a devout, ordered, and idyllic rural society. Groulx embraced the idea of two solitudes between English and French; though not explicitly calling for Quebec's independence, he presented Confederation as artificial and Canada's unravelling as inevitable.

Another persistent problem related to the ongoing mistreatment of Canada's First Nations. Natives accused governments and businesses, such as timber enterprises, of seizing land that they had never surrendered by treaty. Native parents were still being coerced—by threats of cutting off government aid, for example—to send their children to church-run boarding schools off reserves, where they were forced to speak English and dress like whites, and where physical abuse to achieve such ends was common. In Western Canada, authorities intensified efforts to enforce bans on traditional Native dances at venues like fairs and stampedes. An amendment in 1920 to the *Indian Act* provided the federal franchise only to Natives who moved off reserves, which removed them from the band list and any claims to reserve land. During the 1920s and 1930s, only about 2400 natives—some 2 percent of status Indians—were enfranchised. Historian Robin Brownlee wrote that assimilation remained the goal, as the Indian mode of life was perceived as characterized by "lack of ambition, idleness, and unreliability."[2]

There was also more active opposition. In 1923, the Ontario-based Six Nations took a case for home rule to the League of Nations in Geneva. Some smaller countries that had battled for independence—such as Estonia, Ireland, and Panama—offered support, but with Britain backing Canada, the League agreed it was an internal Canadian matter. Three years later, the federal government imposed an elective system upon the Six Nations, abolishing its hereditary-based council, which also reduced the influence of Native women who did not have a vote but under the traditional system had often received appointments to tribal councils. The Six Nations continued efforts for more autonomy, even symbolically issuing a declaration of independence in 1928, though Ottawa and London ignored it.

Canada maintained, and in many ways strengthened, its determination to remain a white, Christian, and British country, a trend reinforced by an initially weak post-war economy and worry that immigration would bring rising unemployment. Lingering wartime anger had Germans, Austrians, and Hungarians barred from Canada until 1923. The same applied to Hutterites, Doukhobours, and Mennonites for having preached pacifism, and because many spoke a German dialect and rejected mainstream Canadian society by living in self-contained collectives. Pressure to assimilate intensified upon such groups, namely to send their children to public schools, enough so that during the early 1920s some 2000 Mennonites left Canada for Mexico and Paraguay. In 1923, the Chinese head tax was replaced by changes to the *Immigration Act* that virtually barred Chinese migration to Canada. Between 1923 and 1947, when the federal government finally allowed Chinese-Canadian males to bring over their wives and children under 18, only 44 Chinese were admitted into Canada. Canada's Japanese population grew over the decade from 15 000 to 21 000, through natural increase and the few hundred permitted in annually under the 1908 Gentleman's Agreement. The B.C. government drastically cut fishing licences to the Japanese because they were viewed as fierce competitors, particularly in the fishing sector, thus forcing many to work for low wages in salmon canning factories, where they joined large numbers of Aboriginals.

A Fireproof House

Although Canada had battled for a signature on the Treaty of Versailles and a seat at the League of Nations, under King it pulled back from involvement in international affairs, especially if presenting the possibility of binding commitments. Highly sensitive to opinion in Quebec, from where the Liberals obtained more than half their parliamentary seats, and seeking to build upon heightened Anglo-Canadian nationalism out of the war, King sought greater Canadian autonomy from the Empire. More than Borden or Meighen, King recoiled from Article X of the League of Nations covenant, the provision providing for collective security, meaning that League members would commit militarily if necessary to prevent unwarranted aggression by one nation against another. Often, King would speak rather piously about how Europe could learn from North America, where more than a century of peace had prevailed.

Concerns about Canada becoming heavily embroiled in international conflict were moot because it had practically jettisoned its military. The rapidity of post-war disarmament was established under Borden and Meighen. After the war, plans were announced to add six squadrons to the new Canadian Air Force. However, with the post-war economic downturn, these plans were scuttled. Canada took some 100 older surplus aircraft from Britain, which were managed by the new Canadian Air Board and used mainly for civilian operations, such as surveying, supplying remote areas, and watching for forest fires. The Air Board also operated refresher training courses for the Canadian Air Force, which in April 1924 had the term "Royal" added to its title, though by that point, the Canadian government had even sold off most of the country's training aircraft. Disarmament under King gained momentum. In 1922, as a cost-cutting measure, the Department of Militia and Defence and the Air Board were amalgamated into a new Department of National Defence, and that year's federal budget allocated the military a meagre $1.46 per capita.

1924: Royal Canadian Air Force created.

King's determination to avoid Canadian involvement in controversial foreign ventures was evident in the September 1922 Chanak crisis. Located on the Turkish side of the Dardanelles Strait, Chanak was guarded by a British garrison under the terms of the 1920 Treaty of Sèvres. A Turk nationalist movement under Mustapha Kemel rejected the treaty, and his forces, some 80 000 strong, approached Chanak demanding control. Britain sought a show of support from the Empire. Cables were dispatched asking for assistance that the British leaked almost immediately. An annoyed King first heard about Britain's request from a Toronto *Star* reporter. Meighen, sensing the opportunity to make a major breakthrough in English Canada, declared to a meeting of Toronto businessmen that when the Mother Country asked for help the only proper response was "Ready, Aye, Ready, we stand by you." King believed that the massive casualties and domestic divisions wrought by the First World War had made Anglo-Canadians less jingoistic. The Progressives, with their focus on domestic issues, like the tariff, also opposed participation, and nearly every Quebec MP rejected Canadian involvement. Still, wary of publicly snubbing the British for fear of angering Anglo-Canadians, King said Canada's Parliament would decide the country's response, realizing that it would take time to recall MPs and debate the issue. King's strategy proved brilliant, because in October, before Parliament could deal with the matter, Britain and Turkey signed an armistice.

September–October 1922: Chanak crisis.

A North American Nation

While Canada recoiled from engagements abroad, closer to home it further integrated with the United States. By 1921, 45.6 percent of exports and 69 percent of imports tied Canada to its southern neighbour. During the early 1920s, American investment into Canada exceeded that from Great Britain, a pattern that never reversed; British investment went mostly into stocks and bonds, and investment from the United States was largely direct investment to establish enterprises. With the high tariff remaining a central feature of Canadian economic policy—averaging 16 percent—this encouraged the creation of more Canadian-based branch plants of American businesses in order to avoid paying duties. Between 1918 and 1930, the number of U.S. branch plants in Canada rose from 466 to 1107. By 1922, Ford had established four auto assembly plants in Ontario and one in Montreal; Chrysler, Dodge Brothers, and Studebaker soon followed.

By mid-decade, the last Canadian-owned car company, McLaughlin, located in Oshawa, Ontario, merged with General Motors (GM), and by the end of the decade, Ford and GM were producing a quarter-million cars annually in Canada. American capital controlled 68 percent of Canadian-based electrical factories, 42 percent of machinery shops, and 41 percent of chemical plants by 1930. A large portion of U.S. investment went into primary production, which also meant limited processing in Canada. One key area was pulp and paper in order to serve a massive increase in U.S. newspaper circulation from 61 million copies at end of the war to 93 million in 1929. Over the 1920s, Canadian newsprint production tripled and Canada became the world's largest papermaker, though 80 percent of the production went to the United States.

Reflecting the significance of the U.S.–Canada relationship, King travelled to Washington in 1922 to meet with American President Warren Harding, the first official summit between leaders of the two countries. The next year, Canada signed a foreign treaty for the first time without British involvement when Ernest Lapointe, Canada's fisheries minister, signed the Halibut Treaty with the United States to better regulate dwindling Pacific fish stocks. Britain wanted to be a co-signatory, but Canada maintained that the agreement did not involve any imperial interest. King also got the British to back down by threatening to open a Canadian legation in Washington to replace the prevailing structure of a Canadian representative operating out of the British embassy, a change that would have been a more open breach in the Empire. Historian C.P. Stacey called the Halibut Treaty "a minor landmark in the country's development as an international person,"[3] though it hardly raised any notice in the U.S. Congress that had to provide its ratification.

1923: U.S.–Canada Halibut Treaty.

Later that year, King travelled to London to attend his first imperial conference. In the wake of Chanak, Britain wanted to reassert its leadership and achieve greater unity within the Empire. It had support from Australia and New Zealand, who, being more isolated, coveted the protection provided by the Royal Navy. King approached the gathering with trepidation. He viewed the Empire as a force for good and as a counterweight against too much American influence, but he also knew that Canada's association with imperialism and British wars had brought great division.

The British sought to charm the new Canadian leader with one social engagement after another, including a private dinner with the King and Queen. King revelled in such flattery and pomp, as it appealed to his enormous and equally fragile ego, but it did not convince him to change his position against centralization. For King, the goal was to replace the Empire with a "Co-operative Commonwealth" in which members would be linked on the basis of shared ideals, values, and histories, not binding commitments. The conference dragged on for six weeks; King rejected every joint communiqué suggesting closer imperial ties. An exasperated British Foreign Secretary Lord Curzon commented privately: "the obstacle has been Mackenzie King … who is obstinate, tiresome, and stupid."[4] Seeking to present some show of unity, South Africa's leader, Jan Smuts, came up with a compromise final communiqué, which reasserted the idea of autonomy within the context of the Empire by stating rather circuitously: "This … is a conference of representatives of the several Governments of the Empire; its views and conclusions on Foreign Policy … are necessarily subject to the action of the Governments and Parliamentarians of the various portions of the Empire."[5]

To better pursue its foreign interests, Canada began to professionalize its Department of External Affairs. At the time, the elderly Sir Joseph Pope, who had served as under secretary since the creation of the department in 1909, managed a small staff that focused on passport work and matters of protocol. The department's legal counsel, Loring Christie, was an effective advisor, but King considered him suspect because he had served Borden and Meighen. King turned to Oscar Douglas (O.D.) Skelton to serve as his principal advisor on foreign policy, and he went on to replace the 72-year-old Pope in 1925 after Pope was given a generous retirement package.

King first heard Skelton speak in January 1922 at the Ottawa Canadian Club against the idea of a united Empire foreign policy. He found him compelling and his views similar to King's own. Brilliant and highly driven, Skelton became dean of arts at Queen's University at just 30 years of age. He served as an advisor to King at the 1923 imperial conference, helping him stave off British pressure for centralization. Of his counsel, the prime minister wrote: "With every line … I am in heart and entire accord."[6] Skelton remained King's most trusted advisor on foreign policy until Skelton's death in 1941.

In 1924, Skelton reinforced King's decision to reject the proposed Geneva Protocol to reinvigorate the principle of collective security at the League of Nations. An initial delegation King sent to Geneva in September 1922—that included Ernest Lapointe—argued that a proviso should be added to Article X of the League covenant stating that no country could be compelled into an act of war without the approval of its government. France opposed this. It pushed for a collective security provision with strength following the devastation of the First World War, which was largely fought on its territory. Canadian representatives helped bring forward a resolution before the League's General Assembly, which stated: "It is for the constitutional authorities of each Member to decide … in what degree … [it] is bound to assure the execution of this obligation by employment of its military force." The opposition to it coalesced into 22 abstentions or absences and one negative vote from Persia. Canada interpreted this as a victory against collective security, though technically

1924: Failure of the Geneva Protocol.

unanimity was needed to change Article X. The Geneva Protocol sought to establish an arbitration system under a Permanent Court of International Justice and for signatories to protect victims of aggression, though with the proviso that any "obligations were limited by their geographic positions and the state of their armaments."[7] This constituted too much commitment for Canada. Senator Raoul Dandurand, Canada's representative at the League, explained his country's rejection of the protocol by comparing Canada to a "fireproof house" whose distance protected it from the flames of war that so often seemed to engulf Europe.

Although Canada minimized its obligations to the League of Nations, its membership remained a source of national pride. Once the Geneva Protocol failed, King did not oppose Dandurand's selection as president of the League Assembly, a compromise choice between England and France. In 1926, Canada secured one of the three-year revolving seats on the League of Nations Security Council, its more powerful inner body where the major international powers had permanent representation. King was initially leery, fearful that this membership could imply more commitments, but was convinced otherwise by Ernest Lapointe.

In other respects, Canada's presence abroad continued to grow. In 1925, the federal government spent an unprecedented $1.3 million to acquire a neoclassical mansion in Trafalgar Square to serve as the new home of its high commissioner in Britain. With Skelton becoming under secretary of state that year, External Affairs became a beehive of activity. He put out a call to professors teaching in postgraduate university programs, like history and political economy, to encourage their top students to apply for careers in the foreign service. Government exams were administered both in Canada and overseas to acquire the best candidates; Skelton often marked the exams and conducted lengthy personal interviews. He assembled a highly impressive team, many of whom were Rhodes Scholars and who went on to shape Canadian foreign policy over the next three decades, including future prime minister Lester Pearson, who was recruited from Oxford.

On the Move

Back home, during the first half of the 1920s, the numbers of Canadians living in urban areas—meaning communities of at least 1000 people—surpassed those in rural areas. By mid-decade, at a time when the country's population stood at 9 million, Toronto reached 600 000 people, a 50 percent increase compared with a generation earlier. Vancouver doubled its population to 233 000 between 1911 and 1931, surpassing Winnipeg to become Canada's third largest city. Montreal, Canada's largest urban centre, grew from 750 000 to 1 million over the 1920s. More Canadians were moving to new suburban areas, such as Outremont in Montreal, Rosedale in Toronto, and Point Grey in Vancouver. Land on the fringe was cheaper, more people could afford cars, and in many cities streetcar service extended to outlying areas. Cities expanded their physical size, annexing surrounding boroughs, townships, and villages. Suburban areas were especially popular among the middle class. Many were inspired by the idea of a semi-rural estate as opposed to increasingly congested cities. The suburbs provided segregation from poorer Canadians, and especially immigrants, who were often excluded through housing covenants. In Westdale, a suburb of Hamilton, developers promised to keep out "Negroes, Asiatics, Russians, Serbs, Rumanians, Turks, Armenians … [and] Jews."[8]

Canadians were becoming more mobile and by the mid 1920s, the automobile was considered more of a necessity than a luxury. Between 1920 and 1924, the average price of a car dropped 38 percent—dipping below $700—and dealers offered finance plans that brought cars within the financial reach of many members of the working class. By the end of the decade, Canadians owned some 1.2 million automobiles, resulting in road construction struggling to keep pace with demand. At Long Branch along the two-lane Toronto–Hamilton highway, the number of cars counted per day increased from 269 in

1914 to 8236 in 1922. Cities transformed with the appearance of traffic signals, rounded corners, gas stations, and new playgrounds to keep children off more hazardous streets, though at least those streets became less polluted with horse manure. While cars were advertised as giving people more freedom, new speeding laws, parking rules, and other traffic laws became part of an increasingly regulated—and congested—urban landscape.

Cars made for a more fast-paced life, though they also gave urbanites greater means to seek tranquility in the surrounding countryside, and they broke down the isolation of many rural areas, though farmers often did not welcome the increased interchange. Cars also provided Canadians with more vacation options. By the 1920s, civil servants were entitled to one or two weeks' paid leave annually, as were employees in about 200 private companies. In 1925, more than half of the 104 000 visitors to Rocky Mountain Park—later renamed Banff—arrived by car. The decade introduced the new urban middle-class leisure activity of auto-camping, which was served by roadside campsites and cabins. The 1920s also brought a tourist boom to Niagara Falls, including from U.S.-based car traffic. To attract more visitors, Niagara Falls repackaged itself "into a modernized 'jazz age' tourist town marked by dance pavilions, bowling alleys, autocamps, and from 1925 onwards, the nightly multi-hued illumination of the waterfall."[9]

The increasing mobility of society and the notion of the 1920s as a "restless, inquisitive, thrill-seeking age"[10] were also evident in the expansion of air travel, which had advanced in sophistication and reliability during the war. Very few Canadians had the opportunity to fly, but there was tremendous interest in developments. At Toronto's Canadian National Exhibition in 1920, 100 000 gathered to watch First World War aces William Barker, Billy Bishop, and Forde McCarthy perform a series of mock dogfights. A notable number of ex-pilots of the First World War purchased trainers and turned to stunt flying, including mid-air wing walking, or gave rides to earn money. Flying clubs opened up across Canada and by the end of the decade, the country had 539 licensed commercial pilots.

In 1920, the Canadian Air Service Association was established in Calgary, and the next year the Commercial Air Pilots' Association of Canada was created. However, early commercial aviation was not a great money maker; the number of airline companies dropped from 30 to eight over the first four years of the decade. Canada's post office inaugurated air service in 1927, starting with Rimouski (where trans-Atlantic liners often docked) to Montreal. There were also opportunities for bush pilots to serve remote areas, namely mining and timber operations, and to survey land. Between 1924 and 1930, federal government aerial surveys in northern territories covered 415 000 square kilometres. In 1920, the Quebec-based timber company Price Brothers established air patrols to map out its assets in the Lac St-Jean area, to dust against parasites and to guard against fires and in 1921 became the larger Laurentide Air Service. Because of competition from the Ontario Provincial Air Service, it went out of business in 1925. By the end of the decade, the Ontario Provincial Air Service had 33 aircraft and patrolled 50 million hectares of forests. In 1926, Western Canada Airways was created, mostly serving remote communities in northern Manitoba and Ontario; in 1930, it became Canadian Airways Limited after purchasing some small eastern airlines and emerged as a major carrier of freight and passenger service.

1926: Western Canada Airways created.

Cultural Cross-Currents

Canadians embraced a stronger consumer ethos during the 1920s. Canada's major department stores, Eaton's and Simpson's, expanded their production and mail-order departments. By the end of the decade, Eaton's had grown to 47 retail outlets and 100 mail-order offices, and employed 26 700. Canadians became enamoured with American products, clamouring for the latest car model or appliance, linking it to modernity. American cultural exports inundated Canada and Canadians accepted it more and more. For every home-grown magazine Canadians bought, eight were imported from the United States, the most popular being the *Ladies' Home Journal,* the *Saturday Evening Post,* and *McCall's.* By 1923, 98 percent of the motion pictures seen by Canadians were American-made.

The advent of radio broke down the isolation of many Canadians, linking them to a broader mass culture, but that culture was often American. The first U.S. radio station, KDKA in Pittsburgh, began broadcasting in November 1920. Only a month later in Montreal, the Marconi Company started station XWA. Canada had 30 radio stations by 1923, and that doubled by the end of the decade as Canadian radio purchases soared from 10 000 in 1923 to 297 000 in 1929. However, most Canadian stations had weak signals and could broadcast for only a few hours a day because they shared six frequencies. The large number of Canadians who lived near the international border typically tuned into American radio stations that carried slickly produced comedy, drama, and variety shows. New American radio networks, starting with the National Broadcasting Corporation in 1927, acquired many Canadian affiliates that wanted better access to popular U.S. shows. By the end of the 1920s, about 80 percent of the programs broadcast on Canadian stations were American in origin.

1928: Royal Commission on Broadcasting.

The federal government appointed a Royal Commission on Broadcasting in 1928. Although chaired by a pillar of free enterprise, Bank of Commerce president Sir John Aird, the commission drew upon European examples, particularly the British Broadcasting Corporation, to recommend a public monopoly over broadcasting. Soon after the commission reported, Canada entered the Great Depression and there was little appetite to spend large sums to create a public broadcasting network. What resulted was a hybrid system: the creation of a public broadcaster along with the maintenance of privately owned stations, which, it was said, would bring radio coverage to the maximum number of Canadians at the lowest possible cost.

1924: Boston Bruins become the first American-based NHL team.

Americanization also impacted sports in Canada, particularly ice hockey. In 1924, Boston millionaire Charles Adams paid $15 000 as a franchise fee to establish the Bruins, the first U.S.-based National Hockey League (NHL) team. With the Bruins drawing as many as 10 000 a game, others were enticed. In 1925, the Pittsburgh Pirates joined the league, and in New York City, millionaire bootlegger William "Big Bill" Dwyer paid what was then considered the astounding price of $75 000 to move Hamilton's NHL squad to the just-completed Madison Square Garden, where they became the New York Americans. Their success at the box office produced a second New York team in 1926, the Rangers. Before the decade ended, the Chicago Black Hawks and Detroit Cougars joined the NHL, thus making it a league of six American and four Canadian teams (the Montreal Canadiens, Montreal Maroons, Ottawa Senators, and Toronto Maple Leafs). Toronto sportswriter Leslie Roberts lamented what he saw as a new obsession with filling arenas, something he attributed to a growing tendency to "tak[e] our cues from our cousins beyond the border,"[11] though the trend also reflected spectator sports becoming a more popular urban leisure activity.

The 1920s became the age of the professional—and particularly American—sports hero whose exploits received tremendous coverage in the mass media. Canadians, as much as Americans, knew what New York Yankees baseball star Babe Ruth looked like and were familiar with all the catchy nicknames of U.S. sporting stars, like the "Galloping Ghost" (footballer Red Grange) and the "Manassa Mauler" (boxer Jack Dempsey). The ethos of the sporting celebrity also came to hockey. In 1924, the newly created Montreal Maroons made a media splash by buying Hooley Smith for $22 500, at a time when a labourer commonly made $500 per annum.

Canadian football was also becoming Americanized, with the adoption of the forward pass and the football shrinking from rugby size to be more in line with the American pigskin. In baseball, in 1928, the Montreal Royals joined the International League with Baltimore, Newark, Buffalo, Reading, Toronto, Rochester, and Jersey City, and the higher calibre of play attracted crowds as large as 20 000. Baseball was especially popular in the Maritimes, a product of strong influences from the New England states. Every small community seemed to have a team, and local leagues and rivalries flourished. Although amateurism remained dominant, in 1923, teams in Halifax, Dartmouth, and Kentville started a short-lived professional league, but it soon became too costly to run, as competition resulted in the importation of higher-priced players from the United States. Sports in the Maritimes also linked to the United States through yachting competitions. The launching of the *Bluenose* at Lunenburg in 1921 ushered in an unprecedented period of popularity for yachting as the ship won numerous head-to-head competitions against American schooners for the *Halifax Herald* International Fisherman's Trophy, an award that the newspaper established in 1920.

Although culture was becoming more continental, Canadian content projected more boldly in several areas. The *Canadian Bookman*, a literary review founded in 1919, promoted domestic works, as did the Canadian Authors Association started two years later. Canadian art began attracting more notice and respect with the appearance of the Group of Seven. Several members—such as Frank Varley, Arthur Lismer, and A.Y. Jackson—had been official Canadian war artists. The catalogue to their first show held in May 1920 in Toronto stated that their aim was to "paint Canada in a new way."[12] To do so, they applied the techniques of European impressionism and post-impressionism to express the harsh beauty of the Canadian Shield as symbolizing the country's strength and grandeur. Granted, it was largely an Ontario-centric vision of Canada, and one that excluded First Nations, immigrants, visible minorities, and even urban areas, though in the mid-1920s several members of the Group of Seven were hired by the railways to paint scenes from places like Banff to encourage tourism to Western Canada. It also took some time for the Canadian public to warm to these unique works. Those running Canada's national gallery preferred more traditional art, though they still purchased and displayed many of the Group's works because they were far cheaper than those of well-known European artists.

Social Change and Anxiety

The 1920s brought much commentary over declining moral standards. The decade witnessed the decline of the church-based social gospel movement. More Canadians joined secular service clubs like the Rotarians and Foresters, through which, besides contributing to the community, they could make useful contacts and obtain services like life insurance. As well, the rise of university-based social sciences brought academics to the lead in several campaigns for social reform. Some criticized the social gospel for having attracted political radicals. Many reformers became disillusioned after the war, which brought heightened class conflict and severe economic decline rather than a renewed, uplifted society.

In an effort to reinvigorate Protestantism and the social gospel spirit, thousands of Methodist, Congregationalist, and Presbyterian churches merged in a new United Church that was formally founded on June 10, 1925, with 693 000 members and instantly became Canada's largest Protestant denomination. The move also brought division, as nearly 2 million members of these faiths remained separate. In the Maritimes and Central Canada, many withdrew into a Presbyterian General Assembly. Distrust was voiced over the "theological liberalism"[13] and more active social agenda of the United Church. There was also fear that, given its size, the United Church would seek to wield the power of a state church.

1925: United Church of Canada is established.

Many also saw moral decline in the collapse of prohibition. Federal prohibition ended in early 1919, leaving the question of enforced temperance to the provinces. Before the year ended, Quebec legalized the sale of beer and light wine. Although charges for drunkenness dropped dramatically under prohibition, large numbers of Canadians ignored temperance legislation, no longer motivated by wartime need. Between 1920 and 1929, the annual number of Canadians convicted under liquor control acts grew from 10 000 to 19 000. In 1922, an estimated 40 percent of Alberta's pool halls and a third of its cafés sold liquor illegally. With liquor consumption permitted for medicinal purposes in most jurisdictions, Canadians turned to doctors and pharmacists who were often accused of behaving like bootleggers.

With the United States maintaining prohibition until 1933, many Canadian and U.S. gangsters became involved in rum running to America. The legendary American mobster Al Capone had booze stashed in secret tunnels in Moose Jaw, Saskatchewan. Moderation leagues emerged in every province to promote government liquor sales, arguing that this would undercut criminal activities and massively raise public revenues. In an October 1920 plebiscite, two-thirds of Quebec voters approved government-owned liquor stores. The next year, voters in British Columbia and the Yukon followed, as did Manitoba in 1923, Alberta in 1924, and Saskatchewan and Newfoundland in 1925. Ontario's deeply religious attorney general, W.F. Nickle, remained steadfast for prohibition, but his more pragmatic boss, Conservative Premier Howard Ferguson, believed it was not working, wanted the revenue, and saw the issuance of liquor licences as an excellent means of establishing patronage-based loyalty. In 1925, Ferguson allowed the sale of 4.4 percent light beer. With little outrage over the measure, Ferguson announced as the December 1926 election approached that if he was returned to power he would approve government liquor sales, cleverly making the issue one of many for voters. With another Tory majority, Ontario's first liquor store opened its doors in Toronto on June 1, 1927. Before the end of the decade, New Brunswick and Nova Scotia had legalized liquor. Although Prince Edward Island stayed dry until 1948, the taxes it collected on liquor-based medical prescriptions continued to be a major source of revenue.

The American government accused Canada of not seriously trying to stem the flow of liquor south. However, given the number of people tempted by the potential riches in bootlegging and the massive expanse of the international border, controlling contraband trade was well beyond the capacity of customs officers in both countries. Speedboats, and in winter automobiles, crammed with liquor zipped across places like the St. Lawrence and the Detroit Rivers. Fleets of Maritime schooners set sail for the Caribbean or St. Pierre and Miquelon where legal trade, principally in rum and whiskey, flourished. Then they anchored by "rum row" just outside the 19-kilometre limit of America's coastal waters. At night, they transferred their cargo onto small boats that brought the liquor ashore. By the mid 1920s, an estimated 50 percent of Maritime ships were involved in the liquor trade.

With Quebec ending prohibition earlier than any other place in North America, bars and nightclubs thrived in Montreal, establishments that also became famous for their chorus lines of scantily dressed young women. During the 1920s, Montreal acquired a reputation as North America's sin city, a place to which Americans flocked to escape the restraints of prohibition.

The notion of the '20s as the Jazz Age also took hold in Montreal. Many Canadians saw jazz as an evil influence, linking its faster and less structured rhythmic qualities, and roots in black America, to savage behaviour and sexual licentiousness. Montreal, like many places, had white-run establishments that played commercial jazz to exclusively white audiences. For those who wanted the "real thing," they headed to the city's black district in St. Antoine, where there was Rockhead's Paradise and the Café St. Michel, where jazz greats, such as Oscar Peterson, made their reputation, though such places also generated concerns over race mixing.

Moral concerns also focused upon Canadian adolescents. They were staying in school longer, as besides compulsory attendance—with the notable exception of Quebec until 1943—high school entrance exams and fees were waived. Keeping young people out of the work world longer encouraged the appearance of a more distinct youth culture with its own tastes, styles, and conduct. While often entertaining and titillating, there also emerged the image of *flaming youth*. The press carried sensationalist accounts of girls wearing flapper-type dresses, bobbing their hair like starlets, and applying makeup to look older, and of boys joining gangs, drinking alcohol, and turning to crime. In 1922, *Maclean's* carried an exposé about adolescent "fussing parties"[14] characterized by liquor, smoking, jazz, and sex.

Young Canadians were strongly encouraged to join clubs and associations that promoted character building, healthy outdoor activities, and Christian values, such as the YMCA and YWCA, Boy Scouts, Girl Guides, and—exclusively for Protestants—the Tuxi Boys and Canadian Girls in Training, most of which grew in membership. To control those who went awry, there was broader application of the 1908 *Juvenile Delinquents Act*, which authorized the creation of "juvenile courts and probation programs." Although more progressive than trying youth in adult courts and incarcerating them in special wings of penitentiaries, still, those running juvenile courts were provided with "wide discretionary powers for defining, regulating, and controlling … delinquents."[15] Boys were most often arrested for property crimes and efforts to reform them focused on creating the ideal working-class male, which meant teaching them to be law-abiding, punctual, and respectful of authority, and to learn a trade. A high proportion of girls were arrested for sexual misconduct, and their reform program emphasized the need for self-restraint and training in domestic roles.

Among many women, there was the hope of building upon obtaining the vote to establish more broadly based equality. In British Columbia, a group called the New Era League encouraged women to use the franchise to secure improvements in "child welfare, education, and recreation."[16] In the 1921 federal election, only five women ran for office and one was successful, Agnes Macphail, a 31-year-old school teacher who represented the Progressives in the Ontario constituency of South Grey by Georgian Bay. In Parliament, she focused on agrarian and labour issues, but the media often dwelt upon the fact that she was not married and defied convention by not wearing a hat and gloves in public.

Agnes Macphail, Canada's first woman MP.

Source: Library and Archives of Canada, PA-127295.

1921: Agnes Macphail becomes the first woman elected to Canada's House of Commons.

At the provincial level, women gained little presence in politics and only in Western Canada. Louise McKinney was elected to the Alberta legislature in 1917 for the short-lived Non-Partisan League, a predecessor of the UFA, for which Irene Parlby won as a candidate in the 1919 provincial election. In British Columbia, Mary Ellen Smith, a Liberal, won a 1918 Vancouver by-election, succeeding her late husband. Nellie McClung sat as a Liberal member of the Alberta legislature from 1921 to 1926.

In Quebec, women were still trying to obtain the provincial vote. Opposition from the Catholic Church prompted the *Fédération Nationale Saint-Jean-Baptiste* to abandon its support for women's suffrage in 1920. Two years later, Marie Lacoste Gérin-Lajoie, president of the *Fédération*, formed the Provincial Franchise Committee, with one English and one French section, the latter of which she led. Archbishop Paul-Eugene Roy denounced the initiative, saying that suffrage was an Anglo-led movement that would divert women from their primary roles as producers and protectors of the French-Canadian family. Gérin-Lajoie took her appeal to the International Union of Leagues of Catholic Women in the hope of getting papal support, but the authority of the Quebec church was reaffirmed. The *Fédération* withdrew its support for the Provincial Franchise Committee, and Gérin-Lajoie resigned her presidency.

During the 1920s, more young women were attending high school, but classes in domestic science, typing, stenography, and bookkeeping accompanied this trend. Female university undergraduates nearly doubled over the decade from 3716 to 7428, or from 16.3 percent to 23.5 percent of Canada's university population. More than 80 percent of females were enrolled in arts programs, compared with less than 50 percent of men. Women made up less than 2 percent of medical students and less than one-quarter of 1 percent of those in law. Gender-segregated courses also existed, such as math and English classes at the University of British Columbia.

The 1920s conveyed some liberation for women through fashion. Corsets and bloomers went out of style. Skirts still went to the ankle, though the look was slimmer and more form fitting, suggestive of the more independent and active woman. Hollywood presented women

Montreal Star *cartoonist Arthur George Racey finds amusement in the local controversy caused by women wearing the latest bathing suit style.*

Source: McCord Museum, M2005.23.119.

as more liberated and sexual, as personified by the movie star Clara Bow, who adopted the clothing and short bobbed hairstyle of the flapper. The movie trade press promoted her as the "It girl" because she had the indescribable "magnetic force of it," meaning the charisma of sex appeal.

The importance of beauty became more prominent with the rise of mass advertising for face creams, cosmetics, mouthwashes, and deodorants, which also helped spark the new phenomenon of beauty parlours. More active women were expanding their presence in sports, which was helped tremendously by dress reform that gave them more freedom of movement, including in the water, where bathing suits, though remaining modest, lost their dress-like appearance. Both lawn tennis and softball became more popular for women, and at universities they participated in a wide variety of intramural sports. The Edmonton Grads, a girls' high school basketball team, did much to popularize the sport in Canada. Formed in 1915, over the next quarter century they compiled an incredible record of 502 wins and 20 losses, becoming the women's world champions in 1923 and representing Canada at Olympic Games from 1924 to 1936. Fanny "Bobbie" Rosenfeld, whose nickname referred to her short bobbed hair, became a top-ranked world female athlete in the 200-metre, long jump, shot-put, and discus, and in 1928 captured Canada's first Olympic track and field medal, a silver. She also gained notoriety as Toronto Grass Court Tennis Champion, as a baseball player, and as a star centre in women's ice hockey, which, however, was dogged by demands that it should eliminate all body checking. It was still commonly believed that athletic women were too masculine, risked their reproductive organs, and had puny babies. At the first British Empire Games, held in Hamilton in 1930, there were 33 events for women in track and field, but this did not include the 800-metre race and the broad jump because they were considered too strenuous for women.

Contrasting with the notion of the 1920s as a period of sexual liberation was the abundantly clear expectation that unmarried women retain their purity, that marriage remain monogamous, and that divorce was unacceptable. Throughout the decade, the divorce rate hovered between 5.6 and 8.2 per 100 000, compared with more than 60 by the end of the Second World War. Couples seeking a divorce in Quebec, Ontario, and Prince Edward Island had to obtain a parliamentary decree. Justice Minister Ernest Lapointe advised King that any Quebec MP who voted to loosen the divorce laws could kiss their political career goodbye. Women arrested for prostitution or deemed at high risk of becoming "fallen" could find themselves incarcerated at places like Toronto's Mercer Reformatory where they were involuntarily tested and treated for venereal disease and subjected to a regimen of work, moral instruction, and training for jobs, such as domestic service.

Consternation mounted over women having fewer children. Between 1921 and 1931, the fertility rate of women aged 15 to 49 dropped from 128.1/1000 to 99.5/1000. This was primarily due to a declining infant mortality rate and the fact that in growing urban areas (as opposed to farms) children rarely contributed to, but nearly always drained, the family income. Many people believed that careerism was threatening women's commitment to the family, as between 1921 and 1931, the total number of working women rose from 490 150, or 15.4 percent of the labour force, to 665 859 or 16.9 percent. However, their participation rate was inversely related to age, standing at, in 1921, 39.8 percent of women 20 to 24 versus 12 percent of those 35 to 64; in other words, married women, and especially mothers, were far less likely to take paid employment outside the home.

Every Canadian province introduced a minimum wage for women, starting in 1917 and ending in 1930. Supporters said it would stop women from endangering their health by working more than one job and prevent many from turning to prostitution to make ends meet. The minimum wage, besides being atrociously low, was easily circumvented, such as if an employer claimed it was necessary to make special provisions to accommodate women workers. Key areas of female employment, such as domestic service, were not covered, and there seemed little will by governments to enforce the legislation. In Ontario, only one employer was charged for violating the minimum wage law between 1920 and 1925.

Employment options for women mostly remained entrenched within gender-based stereotypes. The vast majority were secretaries, sales clerks, teachers, nurses, waitresses, textile workers, and domestics. In 1921, 82 percent of Canadian teachers were women and nearly all of them were instructing in the lower-paid elementary grades, where it was said that their natural, nurturing qualities would be of greatest use. Women's poor pay as teachers reflected the reality that a large percentage of female teachers had a third-class certificate that required only a grade ten education and a four-week teacher training course. Even when their qualifications were identical to men's, women came up short, as in Nova Scotia during the mid-1920s where men with a first-class teaching certificate averaged $1557 per annum compared with $816 for women.

Nursing made gains towards achieving greater professional recognition, in large part because of the contributions made by nurses during the First World War. By 1922, every province had enacted legislation specifying educational requirements to become a nurse and provided provincial nursing associations with the power to determine who was properly qualified. Still, nurses earned about the same as an unskilled male labourer.

About 13 percent of women who worked were self-employed and the 1920s saw the establishment of business and professional women's clubs. For large numbers of women, self-employment meant cleaning, cooking, or doing laundry for different clients. Some established more significant enterprises, albeit ones typically reflecting stereotypes of natural feminine roles, like fashion designing, selling clothes, running restaurants, and establishing girls' schools.

Marriage and motherhood remained portrayed as the most important roles for women. In the early 1920s, *Maclean's* started a Bride's Club section whose message was that true happiness was found in the home, though in countless households little had changed in the daily drudgery. A 1922 Manitoba survey of nearly 450 farm women taken by the *Grain Grower's Guide* revealed a life of "unrelenting physical labour,"[17] as only 10 percent had access to electricity and about 30 percent to running water. In urban areas, the use of modern appliances expanded, though as late as 1948 fewer than half of Canadian households had an electric stove and fewer than a third had replaced the icebox with an electric refrigerator. Those with more modern conveniences often faced the expectation of keeping a cleaner home and of being able to complete more tasks daily.

Women confronted increased pressure to follow advice from a growing number of health-care professionals, especially when it came to babies and child care. The early twentieth century witnessed significant strides forward in the quality and availability of medical care. More women were delivering babies in hospitals—for example, half in British Columbia by the end of the decade—and those babies were more likely to survive. Between 1921 and 1929, Canada's infant mortality rate dropped from 135 per 1000 to 76 per 1000. Many women welcomed the professional guidance, though the dominant message was that no one was knowledgeable enough to ignore the professional advice and that to do so was irresponsible. The federal government encouraged the trend, spurred on by the desire to ensure a strong future generation following the devastation of the First World War and the 1918 influenza pandemic. In 1919, Ottawa created the Division of Child Welfare and placed it under the direction of Dr. Helen MacMurchy, who in 1910 had been hired by the Ontario government to make recommendations on strategies to reduce infant mortality. Through reams of pamphlet literature, particularly *The Canadian Mother's Book*, the division disseminated advice on household hygiene and achieving rapid success in everything from breastfeeding to baby bowel movements to ensuring children's healthy emotional development.

While plenty of advice was dispensed, other forms of support, particularly for mothers with financial need, remained inadequate. Mothers' allowances were introduced, starting in 1916 in Manitoba where they were strongly advocated by Nellie McClung and supported by the reform administration of Liberal T.C. Norris. They were to assist mothers who had children under 15 and whose husbands had died, or were incapacitated, incarcerated, or placed in an asylum. With widows of servicemen receiving pensions, this created momentum to help other mothers left destitute through no fault of their own. Saskatchewan followed in 1917 and Alberta in 1919—again reflecting strong feminist leaders on the Prairies—Ontario and British Columbia in 1920, and by the end of the decade, mothers' allowances had expanded to all parts of Canada except Prince Edward Island. The average support of $40 a month was less than half of a war widow's pension, and only one-third of what a 1923 budget drawn up by the Toronto *Mail and Empire* said was essential for a family of four.

In most provinces, applicants for mothers' allowances had to have a minimum of two children, and only naturalized British subjects were eligible. A mother was certain to be denied support if she was divorced, if caring for a child born out of wedlock or, quite commonly, if she had been deserted by her husband (because this raised suspicion that she was of low moral character). Most jurisdictions reversed the exclusion of deserted women, as it was realized that it was often the husband who had acted immorally, though such a change was not implemented in Nova Scotia until 1930, in Quebec until 1937, and in New Brunswick until 1943. In making decisions on who received support, local boards often relied upon field agents, some of whom were trained social workers, especially in large cities, though many investigators were "middle-class snoops,"[18] women who were prominent in their church, the YWCA, or some other such service organization. Word of child neglect, a dirty house, consumption of alcohol, familiarity with men, or frivolous spending often resulted in a rejected application or funding being terminated. Charlotte Whitton, the socially conservative head of the Canadian Council on Child Welfare, spoke for many by insisting that those who received public support had to be morally deserving.

"King" of Politics, 1924–1926

While worry spread about the destabilizing impact of social change, in the realm of politics Prime Minister King continued to grow more skilled in managing contending forces and maintaining power, even when it was apparently slipping from his grip. To hold Quebec, he increasingly relied upon advice from Ernest Lapointe who, in 1924, moved from fisheries minister to justice minister after Gouin's resignation because of deteriorating health. Until his death in 1941, Lapointe served as King's Quebec lieutenant, sitting next to the prime minister in Parliament.

1924: Ernest Lapointe becomes minister of justice.

Lapointe sought to increase French-Canadian representation in the government and civil service. In 1923, the *nationaliste* newspaper, *Le Devoir*, caused something of a stir in Quebec through an exposé on federal departments that revealed, for instance, that of the 229 income tax collectors in Montreal, 150 were English, and that 21 English and three French Canadians made up those earning the top salary bracket in the federal finance department. Lapointe sought to reduce the influence of those whom he regarded as having anti-French attitudes. There was rampant speculation he was responsible for derailing Justice Lyman Duff's bid to become chief justice of the Supreme Court because he was regarded as insensitive to French Canada. Lapointe's friendly demeanour and ability to inspire a crowd enabled him to connect with ordinary folks. He was inclined to support limited social legislation, and, like King, was more pragmatic than ideologically driven. For example, to bolster the strength of the Liberal government outside Quebec, particularly in the Prairies, and because he was less tied than Gouin to Montreal's business interests, he was flexible on the matter of tariff reductions.

In the 1924 Speech from the Throne, the Liberals promised fewer taxes, a balanced budget, and lower tariffs. Robert Forke said he would work with the government to produce the details. That year's budget did indeed make several tariff reductions, including on imports of agricultural machinery. Things became complicated after J.S. Woodsworth proposed an amendment to reduce tariffs on necessities of life and to make up any lost government revenues as a result of lower duties by implementing a steeper progressive income tax, a graduated inheritance tax, and a levy on unimproved land. These measures reflected stated Progressive policies, but Forke and his supporters feared that if they backed Woodsworth, the Tories, despite favouring protectionism, would join them to defeat the Liberal budget and force an election (as the defeat of a budget was tantamount to a successful motion of non-confidence).

Forke's decided to support the Liberals, which drew fire from more doctrinaire Progressives who accused him of placing politics over principle and thus corrupting the Progressives. Fourteen Progressives, almost all from Alberta, broke ranks, not just to support Woodsworth but also to form a separate parliamentary bloc they called the "Ginger Group," named after slain conscription resister Albert "Ginger" Goodwin.

1924: Formation of the Ginger Group.

With his budget approved and the Progressives imploding, King stepped up appeals to farmers, namely by reintroducing the Crow's Nest Pass rate in 1925. He also promised

Progressives who supported him that he would make good on a 1922 pledge to return lands taken from the Prairie provinces in 1905 to entice railway development and homesteaders. Ottawa had paid the provincial governments an annual subsidy, but with more natural resources discovered, the potential riches from the confiscated land were considered far greater. A Natural Resources Bill, which was an agreement with Alberta, was tabled in the House of Commons, but it ran into problems when Henri Bourassa demanded that any change to the province's status include public financing for French-language and separate schools. Unable, or unwilling, to deliver, because education fell under provincial jurisdiction and because of strong opposition in the West to such schools, King backed off on the Natural Resources Bill for fear that he would be portrayed as selling out French rights for the purpose of reaching a deal with the West.

King also faced continuing political challenges in the Maritimes where there was the widespread belief that he had done little to address their concerns. In June 1925, the Liberals received a shock in Nova Scotia, a province it had governed for 43 years and where the Tories held only three seats. Running on a "provincial rights" platform, the Conservatives reversed the tally, winning 40 of 43 seats. In August, New Brunswick replaced a Liberal government that held 24 of 48 seats with a Conservative one that won 37 ridings.

Several advisors warned King to delay a federal election, though he remained confident because the Liberals had won six recent federal by-elections. However, the Liberals were plagued by poor party organization in Ontario, where they had gone through three provincial leaders over the past four years. Seeking to improve his prospects in Western Canada, King tried to convince Saskatchewan's popular Liberal premier, Charles Dunning, to run federally, but he declined, not being confident enough of the national party's chances. In the Maritimes, King blundered on the campaign trail by declaring: "What are Maritime Rights? Let us know what they are so that we may fight for them."[19] Although meant to be accommodating, the comment reinforced the perception that he was oblivious to the region's grievances.

On election night, October 29, the Conservatives took 116 seats and 46.5 percent of the popular vote, compared with 99 Liberals with 39.9 percent. The badly fractured Progressives dropped to 24 seats, with all but two coming from the Prairies. King lost his own riding of North York, and eight members of his cabinet were defeated. Quebec remained the Liberals' lifeline, giving the party 60 of its 65 seats. The Tories triumphed in Ontario, winning 68 of 82 seats, and they benefited from anger in the Maritimes, taking 23 of 30 seats. In responding to this seeming political disaster, King would prove that beneath his rather dull exterior lay a "bold and … daring tactician."[20] Soon after the election, he met with Canada's governor-general, Lord Julian Byng. The former Canadian Corps commander still saw himself as a simple, honourable soldier, and for him King's honourable course of action was to hand over power to Meighen. Initially, King said he intended to do so but insisted to Byng that if Meighen could not command the confidence of Parliament that he be given a chance to govern before an election was called. Upon further reflection, King decided not to hand over power; instead, he would let Parliament decide the fate of his government, banking on the Progressives supporting the Liberals rather than the high-tariff Tories.

Parliament convened on January 7, 1926. The Liberals remained the governing party, as they had yet to lose the confidence of the House. The Speech from the Throne was a clear play for Progressive support—it promised to create a non-partisan Tariff Board to establish fair rates, to reduce freight rates, and to complete the construction of the Hudson Bay railway to provide better international trade outlets for Western Canada. For the Maritimes, the government said it would appoint a Royal Commission to investigate the region's grievances. King also sought to gain support from Parliament's two labour MPs, J.S. Woodsworth and A.A. Heaps, by pledging to create an Old Age Pension scheme.

Old Age Pensions existed in several European countries and even in Newfoundland since 1911, though in Newfoundland the payments were tiny and available only to those 75 or older at a time when life expectancy was a little less than 60. King declared his support for Old Age Pensions at the 1919 Liberal party convention but ignored them after being elected as prime minister. The situation for many elderly Canadians without financial means or private insurance was desperate. Many were forced into places such as the Ontario County Refuge, where, even as late as the early 1940s, 96 seniors slept in the attic, nine in hallways, and 16 in the basement. Children had a legal responsibility to financially support their elderly parents, but this was difficult to enforce and often ignored.

The political challenges confronting King went beyond the need to build linkages with other parliamentary parties and factions. In January 1926, allegations surfaced that numerous customs officials, including several high-ranking ones, had been complicit in smuggling liquor to the United States. With the Progressives dedicated to establishing a higher moral standard in government, King knew they would not look the other way.

King bought time by authorizing a parliamentary committee to investigate the scandal. In the interim, he tried to shore up support. In February, he won a by-election in Prince Albert, Saskatchewan, thus making up for his loss in North York in the 1925 election. In March, he convinced Charles Dunning to run in a federal by-election in Regina, a seat the other parties did not contest. Dunning was immediately put into the cabinet as minister of railways and canals, and became recognized as the leader of the Liberals' Western Canadian bloc.

There was better news for King on the economic front as 1925 brought a bumper wheat crop and improved grain prices. By the first quarter of 1926, industrial employment had rebounded to its highest level in six years. The April 1926 federal budget introduced tax cuts and tariff reductions. In spring, the Old Age Pension Bill passed through Parliament and the Tariff Board was created, though disputes over membership delayed its functioning. As well, the Royal Commission on the Maritimes was appointed under the respected British jurist Sir Arthur Rae Duncan.

In June, the parliamentary committee examining the customs scandal issued a damning report, citing widespread graft and recommending the dismissal of nine senior employees and the arrest of former customs minister Jacques Bureau. Realizing that Progressive support for his government was now gone, King asked Byng to dissolve Parliament and to call an election. Byng refused, insisting that Meighen should be given a chance to govern, especially since the Tories held a plurality of seats. King said this was not Byng's decision to make; rather, according to King, Byng's role was to simply execute the prime minister's wishes, and to do otherwise was to effectively throw Canada back to the time before it achieved responsible government and was ruled by the decree of governors.

On June 28, King resigned and Byng asked Meighen to form a government. Meighen jumped at the opportunity, despite having no support from the Progressives. His government lasted three days. Meighen then asked Byng to call an election, and with no other possible government, the governor-general agreed. To King, the sequence of events demonstrated Byng's contempt for Canada's Parliament, his favouritism for the Tories, and his willingness to treat Canada like a colony. The Progressives were widely assailed for their central role in defeating both the Liberal and the Tory governments and forcing Canadians back to the polls so soon.

In the campaign leading up to the election on September 14, all other issues, including the customs scandal, faded next to King's fight with the governor-general. King presented himself as protecting Canadian rights and as embodying emerging post-war Anglo-Canadian nationalism, and Meighen as Britain's and Byng's candidate. The Liberals triumphed with a renewed majority government of 116 seats, compared with 91 Conservatives. A dejected Meighen asked the Tories to find a new leader, while the Progressives, left with just 11 seats, spiralled towards political oblivion, though they had set an important precedent—soon to be repeated—by establishing a viable third-party alternative.

Cautious Internationalism

The new Liberal government was sworn in on September 26; a week later, King travelled to London to attend another imperial conference. It was a gathering he approached with more confidence than three years earlier, both because of his new mandate and because Britain, in the lead up to the conference, no longer pressured for a common imperial foreign policy or defence arrangement, no doubt realizing that it was a non-starter. This was again underlined the previous year when King's government said that Canada would not be bound by the Locarno Treaty under which the signatories, including Britain, agreed to defend the borders of France, Belgium, and Germany, including the demilitarized Rhineland, as established by the Treaty of Versailles.

O.D. Skelton, who accompanied King to London, favoured an unequivocal statement of Canadian independence, but King thought this was too extreme. King found himself in the unfamiliar role of trying to preserve a continuing imperial structure, though, fresh from his battle with Byng, he also sought an agreement with the British on formally changing the role of the governor-general. Anti-British sentiment was strong in the new Irish Free State and in South Africa under the Afrikaner nationalist J.B.M. Hertzog, who threatened to break from the Empire without an unequivocal affirmation of equality. Australia and New Zealand, as they had in 1923, largely for security reasons, remained supportive of a more centralized imperial structure. King worked closely with Herzog to redefine the relationship between Britain and the dominions. Their ideas appeared in the *Balfour Report* (named for Britain's Colonial Secretary who chaired the conference), which spoke of "communities within the British Empire" equal in status, and "freely associated as members of the British Commonwealth of Nations," this being the non-binding structure that King had long advocated. King also obtained agreement that Britain would establish a High Commission in Canada through which government-to-government interchanges would proceed and in the process formalized the governor-general's role as a largely ceremonial representative of the British sovereign; however, "the umbilical chord with the mother country was not completely severed."[21] It would take another five years for Canada's control over its foreign policy to be officially sanctioned by Britain. Canada could still not amend its constitution. Though the Canadian government had the power to abolish appeals to the Judicial Committee of the Privy Council, King refrained from implementing such a change because of strong opposition from several provincial governments who saw Canada's Supreme Court as inclined towards supporting federal powers.

No longer prepared to project the façade of being part of an imperial structure that spoke with one voice on foreign policy, Canada established its own diplomatic representation in Washington in 1927. It was a legation, which, in the diplomatic pecking order, stood one wrung below an embassy, but for Canada this was a major development and as such its government spent the hefty—and controversial—sum of $500 000 to acquire a mansion in the heart of Washington's diplomatic quarter. King chose Vincent Massey as Canada's first representative. The head of Canada's largest agricultural implement manufacturer and one of the country's wealthiest men, Massey, a graduate of Oxford, was known as worldly and charming, as a patron of the arts, and for his significant philanthropic work. He had briefly entered King's cabinet as minister without portfolio but was defeated in the 1925 election.

In Washington, Massey faced an uphill battle to get Canada noticed. Massey made headway through the social circuit, as the gatherings he and his equally charming and urbane wife, Alice (daughter of the well-known author, George Parkin, and educated in Canada, England, and Switzerland), hosted at the legation quickly became popular among Washington's elite, especially as the Masseys were personal friends with, and thus able to secure the attendance of, several of the capital's power brokers. In 1927, Canada's federal government convinced the United States to reciprocate by establishing a legation in Ottawa.

The following April, Sir William Clark, formerly comptroller general of Britain's Department of Overseas Trade, was named the first high commissioner to Canada. To maintain balance between French and English Canada, in September, Canada's Office of the Commissioner General in Paris, which was established in 1882, was upgraded to a legation. Two months later, France reciprocated with the same level of representation in Ottawa. In 1929, Canada added another legation in Tokyo. Its purpose was to better regulate migration to Canada; to encourage trade (as by 1929, Japan was Canada's fourth largest customer, importing $38 million worth of goods and material); and to turn the page on the sometimes difficult relations as exemplified in the 1908 Gentleman's Agreement to restrict Japanese immigration to Canada and Canada's leading role in scuttling the renewal of the Anglo-Japanese treaty.

Although Canada expanded its presence abroad, it continued to reject any version of collective security. The only international treaty the King government enthusiastically endorsed was the 1928 Kellogg-Briand Pact. Initiated by the United States and France, it substituted arbitration for sanctions and sought to outlaw war as an instrument for settling international disputes, an agreement that many sarcastically labelled a "big international kiss." Yet, the mood in Canada grew more conducive to the principles of the pact. As in Britain and the United States, about a decade after the war ended, there came several books from Canadian Great War veterans reflecting upon the gruesome, and soul-destroying,

1927: Canada and the United States establish independent diplomatic relations.

The National War Memorial in Ottawa. The design by Vernon March of England came from a 1925 competition open to all British subjects. Twenty-two figures representing all parts of Canada's military march through an arch under the allegorical representations of peace and freedom and through which they experience resurrection. Delayed for many years because of disputes over its exact location and the death of its sculptor, the memorial was finally unveiled in the spring of 1939 by King George VI and Queen Elizabeth.

Source: Perry Mastrovito/
Creatas/Picture Quest.

1927: R.B. Bennett becomes Conservative leader.

aspects of the conflict, the most notable being *All Else Is Folly* in 1929 by Peregrine Acland, a former major with the First Division, and *Generals Die in Bed* in 1930 by Charles Yale Harrison, previously a machine gunner with the Royal Montreal Regiment.

Historian Thomas Socknat argues that by the late 1920s, pacifism had gained a considerable following in Canada, expanding from a small cadre of social gospellers and labour radicals to include many who belonged to farm, women's, students', church, and mainstream labour organizations. Across North America, the conspiracy theory spread that the Great War was precipitated and lengthened by profit-seeking international arms manufacturers. Historian Jonathan Vance argues that Canada's commemoration of the war throughout the 1920s—in memorials, service rolls, stained glass church windows, art, and popular literature—continued to convey reverence for those who sacrificed, pride in the country's battlefield accomplishments, and that the struggle to defeat Germany was essential because it preserved freedom and advanced civilization.[22] Vance classified the pacifists as a notable minority, but still a minority, who carried on their campaigns through minor publications and at small gatherings. In 1928, the Armistice Ceremonial Committee of Canada was formed. Led by prominent politicians, religious leaders, and other well-known figures, it campaigned to give Armistice Day (later renamed Remembrance Day) greater prominence because it was initially joined with Thanksgiving. Three years later, it was changed to November 11, the date the war ended, despite opposition from many businesses about another statutory holiday. The day brought prayers for peace, but was primarily about remembrance and the commemoration of noble sacrifice, not the promotion of pacifism.

Better Times

On July 1, 1927, a buoyant Prime Minister King presided over ceremonies at Parliament Hill to commemorate Canada's diamond jubilee, a celebration meant to replace Canada's cancelled 50th birthday party, which was viewed as inappropriate during the war. The Prince of Wales attended, as did the Duke of York, and Britain's Prime Minister Stanley Baldwin. The Prince dedicated a new memorial chamber in Parliament's Peace Tower containing a Book of Remembrance listing the names of all Canadians killed in the First World War and unveiled a statue of Sir Wilfrid Laurier on Parliament Hill.

King would soon face new opposition in Parliament. In October, the Tories gathered in Winnipeg to replace Meighen. Like the Liberals had done in 1919, the Conservatives selected delegates from across the country to make this decision rather than leaving it in the hands of their parliamentary caucus. The Tories went for R.B. Bennett of Calgary, the only Conservative elected from the Prairies in 1926. First elected to the assembly of the North-West Territories in 1908, seven years later, at age 35, Bennett became the first leader of Alberta's Conservative party. Profoundly self-assured, often overbearing, and with an incredible capacity for work, Bennett was so determined to succeed that he even chose to eat six meals a day because he believed he required a more physically imposing presence for politics. Elected to the federal Parliament in 1911 to represent Calgary, five years later he assumed the position of director of the National Service Board. Passed over for a cabinet post by Meighen, he resigned in 1921. Before returning to Parliament four years later, he amassed a vast personal fortune through shrewd investments and by inheriting a principal share in the E.B. Eddy paper company. An effective, though somewhat frenetic public speaker, "Bonfire" Bennett, as he was nicknamed, was once clocked at 220 words a minute. King was unfazed, dismissing his new opponent as inexperienced and bombastic. Undeniably, King was thrilled to see Meighen go because he always seemed to best him in parliamentary debate.

Other political challenges, such as the persistence of provincial rights, emerged. With expanded revenues, such as from liquor sales and gasoline taxes, aggregate spending by provincial governments as a proportion of federal expenditures grew from 19.2 percent in 1921 to 40.3 percent in 1929. This brought more overlap of services, competing intergovernmental ambitions, and increased potential for disputes. In Ontario and Quebec, there was growing concern that King was trying to grab control over hydroelectric power on international waterways, an ever-more lucrative source of revenue and engine of economic development. In November 1927, King convened a dominion–provincial conference, then the largest such gathering in Canadian history. By that time, Ontario's Howard Ferguson and Quebec's Alexandre-Louis Taschereau had formed an alliance to resist Ottawa. At the conference, they rallied the other premiers to reject any constitutional amending formula that would enable repatriation of the *British North America Act* from England for fear that this would give Ottawa the means to more easily change the Constitution to increase its powers. The provinces also unanimously opposed conditional federal grants, insisting that money provided to them by Ottawa should come without any strings attached. Still, King had reason to feel optimistic. Besides enjoying a majority government, the economy continued its upswing. By 1927, unemployment dipped below 3 percent, but for millions, making ends meet remained a struggle. In 1929, the average annual salary had risen to $1200, but the Department of Labour estimated that $1430 was necessary to maintain a family in a "minimum standard of health and decency."[23]

Nonetheless, a buying frenzy took hold on Canadian stock markets, fuelled by rising employment and income, very low margin requirements for purchasing stock, and stock prices whose continued rise seemed to hold out the promise of easy money. While major stock exchanges in Montreal and Toronto did record business, unprecedented activity also came to newer markets in Vancouver and Calgary that specialized in penny stocks of start-up companies, particularly in the resource sector, many of which had virtually no capital but hoped to strike it rich in places like Alberta's Turner Valley where oil had been discovered in 1914. Everyone with a little extra cash seemed to be dabbling on the stock market, oblivious to the fact that stocks were increasingly overvalued. Even usually cautious voices joined the upbeat chorus, such as banker Sir John Aird who, just weeks before the great stock market crash of October 1929, declared that "the barometer of our prosperity is steadily rising."[24]

Even though the Taschereau–Ferguson alliance brought friction to the Canadian federation, it also helped to eliminate a longstanding barrier to national unity: Ontario's *Regulation 17*, which was of benefit to King. Ferguson realized that the legislation complicated

1927: Regulation 17 repealed in Ontario; 1928: L'Action française disbands.

1927: Duncan Royal Commission reports.

1927: Old Age Pensions introduced.

his ability to form a common front with Quebec. Toning it down or even quashing it was made easier because Anglophone Canadians, in the wake of the Great War, had grown more distant from a British-Canadian identity. In 1923, some 100 leading Anglo-Ontarians, including several former school inspectors, established a Unity League whose reports emphasized that students in private bilingual schools spoke and wrote English as well as those in unilingual public schools. Ferguson appointed a Commission of Inquiry to examine bilingual schools in 1925, whose favourable report on their quality resulted in the repeal of *Regulation 17* in 1927. This hastened the end of *L'Action française* in 1928, because the most prominent symbol of Anglo intransigence was removed, though also explaining the organization's demise were internal divisions and fears created by its rhetorical flirtations favouring Quebec's secession from Canada.

The federal government also achieved some *rapprochement* with the Maritimes as a result of the Duncan Royal Commission, which issued its report in 1927. King was pleased that the commission did not personally blame his government for regional problems and rejected the theory that Confederation was long-stacked against the Maritimes. But the three commissioners, who heard from hundreds of witnesses, agreed that the region was unduly suffering and recommended substantial increases in federal subsidies, lower freight rates, and improvements to rail, ferry, and port services. King's government responded with some relief on rail rates, new subsidies to assist Maritime coking plants, port improvements in Halifax and Saint John, and money for a second ferry to Prince Edward Island.

The Liberals presented themselves as responding to social need with the first distribution of Old Age Pension cheques in 1927, a milestone in the development of Canada's social welfare system. The number of state-supported pensioners grew from 2712 in 1928 to 42 553 by 1930. Initially, only Canada's four Western provinces joined the shared-cost scheme, followed by Ontario in 1929. The Maritimes and Quebec came on board after 1931, when the federal government increased its share of funding from 50 percent to 75 percent. Only British subjects aged 70 or older with an annual income of less than $125 qualified for the maximum $20 monthly pension. Applicants received nothing if they had access to more than one dollar a day, and in assessing assets their children's income was counted. Upon a pensioner's death, the provincial government could seek repayment of its contributions with 5 percent interest from the pensioner's estate, a practice that was not completely phased out until the late 1940s.

Outside its borders, Canada continued to build autonomy. The imperial conference of 1926 had authorized the establishment of an "expert committee" to recommend concrete measures to achieve the principal of equality within the new Commonwealth. Canada's team was headed up by Justice Minister Lapointe and included O.D. Skelton, both of whom strongly advocated Canadian autonomy. Most of the committee's work was done in 1929, leading up to an October conference in London focusing upon the external application of dominion legislation, as Britain still technically set foreign policy for the Commonwealth. The deliberations set the stage for an imperial conference in 1930 that resulted in the *Statute of Westminster*, which removed this vestige from Canada's colonial past.

New Canadians and Women Become Persons

In 1925, with Canada's economy recovering and requiring more labour, the federal government established an agreement to pay the country's major railways, which were also in the steamship business, to bring over immigrants. The arrangement, which lasted until 1931, brought 370 000 people to Canada, a large percentage of whom came from Central and Eastern Europe. Racism spiked as a result of increased immigration, a trend that included the migration into Canada of a racist American organization—the white-robed and hooded Ku Klux Klan (which, after the First World War, experienced massive growth in the United States, particularly in the Midwest, as a reaction against increased immigration and urbanization, which were cast as destroying core values).

Three Klan organizations emerged in Canada: the Ku Klux Klan of Canada, the Kanadian Ku Klux Klan, and the Ku Klux Klan of the British Empire. Their strongest presence was in southwestern Ontario (focused against Catholics and blacks), British Columbia (against Asians), and Alberta and Saskatchewan (against Eastern and Central European Catholics and Jews). The spectacle of cross burnings came to Canada, which the Klan used to strike fear into their targets and to proclaim their commitment to keep the country white and Protestant. For instance, in Oakville, some 40 kilometres west of Toronto, an estimated 75 hooded Klan members descended on a home where a black man cohabitated with a white woman. A cross was burned on the front lawn and the man was warned that if he was "ever seen walking down the street with a white girl again," the Klan "would attend to him."[25]

Ku Klux Klan members participate in a cross-burning ceremony near Kingston, Ontario, in August 1927.

Source: Archives of Ontario, #21329.

In Saskatchewan, Klan membership was estimated as high as 40 000 out of a population of 900 000. In the June 1928 Saskatchewan election, the Tories, led by J.T.M. Anderson, partly campaigned on a promise to demand that Ottawa cut immigration and worked closely with the Klan to rally support. Technically, the Liberals won the election with 28 seats and 45.5 percent of the vote compared with 24 Tories with 36.5 percent, but 11 Progressives and independents, determined to rid Saskatchewan of Liberal machine-style politics, threw their support behind Anderson.

For women, the struggle for equality yielded better results, at least symbolically. Seeking to build on the election of women to the House of Commons and provincial legislatures, pressure grew over the 1920s for women to be declared as eligible to sit in Canada's appointed Senate. This had been denied because section 24 of the *BNA Act* identified a qualified "person" for the Senate by using the pronoun "he." Five prominent Alberta women—Emily Murphy, Nellie McClung, Louise McKinney, Irene Parlby, and Henrietta Muir Edwards—launched the *Person's Case*, as it became popularly known. Among their accomplishments, in 1916, Murphy became the first female police magistrate in the British Empire, and Edwards, the oldest member of the group, was a founder of the National Council of Women of Canada and the Victorian Order of Nurses.

Murphy was the catalyst. Having made a name for herself by successfully pressuring the Alberta government to pass the *Dower Act* in 1916, entitling wives to one-third of their husband's estate, Murphy was made a magistrate to hear cases in a woman's police court. Soon, she was challenged by a male lawyer who said she was unqualified to sit on the bench because she was not a "person" as specified by the use of the pronoun "he"—a challenge Murphy successfully countered. Although a champion for women's rights, Murphy, and the four other complainants in the *Person's Case*, shared prejudices common to white, middle- and upper-class, Anglo-Canadian society. In her 1922 book, *The Black Candle*, Murphy cast Chinese males as spreading opium dens, and, along with blacks, as a threat to the purity of white women. Concerns over societal degeneration also had Murphy support a 1922 UFA resolution for the forced sterilization of "mental defectives," which became law six years later and established a Eugenics Board that, until it was disbanded in 1972, enabled the sterilization of 2822 men and women.

On five occasions between 1920 and 1927, the federal government refused demands to change the eligibility for the Senate to include women partly because it feared a backlash from Quebec where the Taschereau government was on record as opposing liberalization. However, Murphy discovered that under the *Supreme Court of Canada Act*, five people, acting as a unit, could petition the Supreme Court on interpretations of the Constitution, and that the federal Department of Justice would cover the costs of the case if the issue was deemed to be of national importance. Justice Minister Lapointe, who sympathized with the Alberta women, backed their challenge to section 24. In April 1928, the Supreme Court ruled against the women. Adopting a strict interpretation of the *BNA Act*, it concluded that if the term "person" was meant to include women, the framers of the Constitution would not have specifically linked it to the pronoun "he." The case was appealed to the Judicial Committee of the Privy Council, which delivered its verdict in October 1929. Lord Sankey, speaking for the Council, compared the *BNA Act* to "a living tree capable of growth and expansion within its natural limits,"[26] meaning it considered the Supreme Court's interpretation of a "person" as too narrow and anachronistic, and thus overruled it.

1929: Women declared "persons" under the BNA Act.

Although an important victory, when it came time to choose the first female senator, Prime Minister King rejected both Murphy and McClung. Instead, he selected Carinne Wilson, the bilingual daughter of a former Liberal senator, wife of a Liberal MP, and founder of the National Federation of Liberal Women, who had been active with several volunteer groups traditionally associated with women, such as the Red Cross. Wilson turned out to be no political wallflower. She went on to become president of the League of Nations Society of Canada (1936–1942) and chair of the Canadian National Committee on Refugees (1938–1948), a position from which she caused some grief for King by publicly castigating his government for refusing to accept Jewish refugees trying to flee Nazi Germany.

Conclusion

The 1920s often seem portrayed in terms of how they contrasted to what came before and after. As a reaction to the First World War, people were depicted as cutting loose and living for the day, and when juxtaposed against the Great Depression, the '20s certainly "roared" economically. But the roar could also be characterized as symbolizing the political and social turbulence of the decade, one in which the currents of change moved in many, and often contradictory, directions.

Canada grew more autonomous, urban, industrial, and North American in its economy, culture, and outlook. Good times, consumerism, and eventually a stock market buying frenzy took hold, though only later in the decade and after a deep recession. Although often presented in popular lore as a period of freewheeling capitalism, the decade also saw important, though limited, breakthroughs with social welfare, such as Old Age Pensions.

More independent, active, and sexually liberated women gained prominence, though not until the end of the decade were Canadian women accepted as "persons" under the law. While Canadians celebrated the triumph of democracy and the advance of civilization with the defeat of Germany, the 1920s also brought intense xenophobia, the busting of unions, and contrasting interpretations on the meaning and legacy of the First World War. Stronger expressions of Canadian nationalism were accompanied by lingering French–English discord, more pronounced regionalism, the rise of third parties, and increased economic and cultural integration with the United States. While Canada became an independent actor on the world stage, it used its voice to weaken the League of Nations and sought retreat within what it hoped would be a fireproof house.

The decade began with Arthur Meighen as prime minister. Although unequalled as a parliamentary debater, his determination to stand by principles often made him appear too rigid and headstrong. He regarded King with contempt, as making policy according to the whims of public opinion, but it was King who remained prime minister for 90 percent of the decade. By balancing between often contending interests, King effectively directed the ship of state through the turbulence of the post-war period. As the decade drew to a close, he wrote in his diary that "much has been accomplished … I have everything to be grateful for."[27] But even this master political practitioner, who managed to hold on to power after seemingly losing it in 1925, could not cope, at least initially, with the Great Depression that defined the 1930s.

Questions to Consider

1. What economic changes occurred in Canada during the 1920s?

2. How did the 1920s affect women and immigrants?

3. How did Canada's relations with Britain and the United States change during the 1920s?

4. Why did the Progressives rise and ultimately fail as a political party?

Critical Thinking Questions

1. What accounted for King's success as a politician during the 1920s? How was his approach different from Meighen's?

2. Were the 1920s a time of moral decline? Explain.

3. What accounts for the lasting image of the 1920s as "roaring"? Is this a useful term for understanding the decade?

Suggested Readings

General

Bothwell, Robert, Ian Drummond, and John English. *Canada, 1900–1945.* Toronto: University of Toronto Press, 1987.

Gray, James. *The Roar of the Twenties.* Toronto: Macmillan of Canada, 1975.

Thompson, John Herd, and Allen Seager. *Canada 1922–1939: Decades of Discord.* Toronto: McClelland & Stewart, 1985.

National Politics

Angus, Ian. *Canadian Bolsheviks: The Early Years of the Communist Party of Canada.* Montreal: Vanguard, 1981.

Graham, Roger. *Arthur Meighen: A Biography*, 2 Vols. Toronto: Clarke, Irwin, 1960–1965.

Laycock, David. *Populism and Democratic Thought in the Prairies, 1910 to 1945.* Toronto: University of Toronto Press, 1990.

McNaught, Kenneth. *A Prophet in Politics: A Biography of J.S. Woodsworth.* Toronto: University of Toronto Press, 1959.

Morton, W.L. *The Progressive Party in Canada.* Toronto: University of Toronto Press, 1950.

Neatby, H. Blair. *William Lyon Mackenzie King, Vol. 2: The Lonely Heights, 1924–1932.* Toronto: University of Toronto Press, 1959.

Owram, Doug. *The Government Generation: Canadian Intellectuals and the State, 1900–1945.* Toronto: University of Toronto Press, 1986.

Provincial Politics

Badgley, Kerry. *Ringing in the Common Love of Good: The United Farmers of Ontario, 1914–1926.* Montreal and Kingston: McGill-Queen's University Press, 2000.

Bock, Michel. *Quand la nation débordait les frontières: les minorités françaises dans la pensée de Lionel Groulx.* Montreal: Hurtubise HMH, 2004.

Forbes, Ernest. *The Maritime Rights Movement, 1919–1927: A Study in Canadian Regionalism.* Montreal and Kingston: McGill-Queen's University Press, 1979.

Johnston, Charles Murray. *E.C. Drury: Agrarian Idealist.* Toronto: University of Toronto Press, 1986.

Oliver, Peter. *G. Howard Ferguson: Ontario Tory.* Toronto: University of Toronto Press, 1977.

Trofimenkoff, Susan Mann. *Action Française: French Canadian Nationalism in the Twenties.* Toronto: University of Toronto Press, 1975.

Vigod, Bernard L. *Quebec Before Duplessis: The Political Career of Louis-Alexandre Taschereau.* Montreal and Kingston: McGill-Queen's University Press, 1986.

Economy and Society

Comacchio, Cynthia R. *Nations Are Built of Babies: Saving Ontario's Mothers and Children, 1900–1940.* Montreal and Kingston: McGill-Queen's University Press, 1993.

Comacchio, Cynthia R. *The Dominion of Youth: Adolescence and the Making of a Modern Canada, 1920–1950.* Waterloo: Wilfrid Laurier University Press, 2006.

Heron, Craig. *Booze: A Distilled History.* Toronto: Between the Lines, 2003.

Morton, Suzanne. *At Odds: Gambling and Canadians, 1919–1969.* Toronto: University of Toronto Press, 2003.

Traves, Tom. *The State and Enterprise: Canadian Manufacturers and the Federal Government, 1917–1931.* Toronto: University of Toronto Press, 1979.

Foreign and Defence Policy

Eayrs, James. *In Defence of Canada, Vol. 1: From the Great War to the Great Depression.* Toronto: University of Toronto Press, 1964.

Hilliker, John. *Canada's Department of External Affairs, Vol. 1: The Early Years, 1909–1946.* Montreal and Kingston: McGill-Queen's University Press, 1990.

Stacey, C.P. *Canada and the Age of Conflict, Vol. 2, 1921–1948. The Mackenzie King Era.* Toronto: University of Toronto Press, 1981.

Labour, Women, and Social Policy

Christie, Nancy. *Engendering the State: Family, Work, and Welfare in Canada.* Toronto: University of Toronto Press, 2000.

Crowley, T. A. *Agnes Macphail and the Politics of Equality.* Toronto: J. Lorimer, 1990.

Hall, M. Ann. *The Girl and the Game: A History of Women's Sport in Canada.* Peterborough: Broadview Press, 2002.

Heron, Craig, ed. *The Workers' Revolt in Canada, 1917–1925.* Toronto: University of Toronto Press, 1998.

Hobbs, Margaret, and Joan Sangster, eds. *The Woman Worker, 1926–1929.* St. John's: Canadian Committee on Labour History, 1999.

Little, Margaret. *"No Car, No Radio, No Liquor Permit": The Moral Regulation of Single Mothers in Ontario, 1920–1997.* Toronto: University of Toronto Press, 1998.

Morton, Suzanne. *Ideal Surroundings: Domestic Life in a Working-Class Suburb in the 1920s.* Toronto: University of Toronto Press, 1995.

Naylor, James. *The New Democracy: Challenging the Social Order in Industrial Ontario, 1914–1925.* Toronto: University of Toronto Press, 1991.

Sangster, Joan. *Regulating Girls and Women: Sexuality, Family and the Law in Ontario, 1920–1960.* Toronto: Oxford University Press, 2001.

Snell, James G. *The Citizen's Wage: The State and the Elderly in Canada, 1900–1951.* Toronto: University of Toronto Press, 1996.

Strong-Boag, Veronica. *The New Day Recalled: Lives of Girls and Women in English Canada, 1919–1939.* Toronto: Copp Clark Pitman, 1988.

Nativism and First Peoples

Avery, Donald. "*Dangerous Foreigners*": *European Immigrant Workers and Labour Radicalism in Canada, 1896–1932.* Toronto: McClelland & Stewart, 1979.

Backhouse, Constance. *Colour-Coded: A Legal History of Racism in Canada, 1900–1950.* Toronto: The Osgoode Society for Canadian Legal History by the University of Toronto Press, 1999.

Ray, Arthur. *The Canadian Fur Trade in the Industrial Age.* Toronto: University of Toronto Press, 1990.

Sandlos, John. *Hunters at the Margin: Native People and Wildlife Conservation in the Northwest Territories.* Vancouver: University of British Columbia Press, 2007.

Tough, Frank. *As Their Natural Resources Fail: Native Peoples and the Economic History of Northern Manitoba, 1870–1930.* Vancouver: University of British Columbia Press, 1996.

Culture

Crowley, Terry. *Marriage of Minds: Isabel and Oscar Skelton Reinventing Canada.* Toronto: University of Toronto Press, 2003.

Hill, Charles. *The Group of Seven: Art for a Nation.* Ottawa: National Gallery of Canada, 1995.

McKay, Ian. *The Quest of the Folk: Antimodernism and Cultural Selection in Twentieth Century Nova Scotia.* Montreal and Kingston: McGill-Queen's University Press, 1994.

Tippett, Maria. *Making Culture: English-Canadian Institutions and the Arts before the Massey Commission.* Toronto: University of Toronto Press, 1990.

Vance, Jonathan. *Death So Noble: Memory, Meaning, and the First World War.* Vancouver: University of British Columbia Press, 1997.

Vipond, Mary. *Listening In: The First Decade of Canadian Broadcasting.* Montreal and Kingston: McGill-Queen's University Press, 1992.

Notes

[1] John Bartlett Brebner, *The North Atlantic Triangle: The Interplay of Canada, the United States and Great Britain* (New Haven: Yale University Press 1945).

[2] Robin Jarvis Brownlie, "'A Better Citizen Than Lots of White Men': First Nations Enfranchisement—An Ontario Case Study, 1918–1940," *Canadian Historical Review* 87, 1 (2006): 48.

[3] C.P. Stacey, *Canada and the Age of Conflict, The Mackenzie King Era. Vol. 2: 1921–1948.* (Toronto: University of Toronto Press, 1984), 56.

[4] R. MacGregor Dawson, *William Lyon Mackenzie King: A Political Biography, 1874–1923* (London: Methuen & Co Ltd., 1958), 477.

[5] Stacey, *Canada and the Age of Conflict*, 69.

[6] John Hilliker, *Canada's Department of External Affairs, Vol. 1: The Early Years, 1909–1946* (Montreal and Kingston: McGill-Queen's University Press, 1990), 95.

[7] Stacey, *Canada and the Age of Conflict*, 58.

[8] Richard Harris, *Creeping Conformity: How Canada Became Suburban, 1900–1960* (Toronto: University of Toronto Press, 2004), 88.

[9] Karen Dubinsky, *The Second Greatest Disappointment: Honeymooning and Tourism at Niagara Falls* (Toronto: Between the Lines, 1999), 121.

[10] Jonathan Vance, *High Flight: Aviation and the Canadian Imagination* (Toronto: Penguin, 2002), 75.

[11] Kevin Jones, "Sports and Games from 1900–1920," in Maxwell Howell and Reet Howell, eds., *History of Sport in Canada* (Champaign: Stipes Publishing Company, 1985), 266.

[12] Peter Mellen, *The Group of Seven* (Toronto: McClelland & Stewart, 1970), 98.

[13] N.K. Clifford, "Interpretations of the United Church of Canada," *Church History* 46, 2 (1977): 213.

[14] Cynthia Comacchio, *The Dominion of Youth: Adolescence and the Making of Modern Canada, 1920–1950* (Waterloo: Wilfrid Laurier Press, 2006), 64.

[15] Bryan Hogeveen, "'Impossible Cases Can Be Cured When All the Factors Are Known': Gender, Psychiatry and Toronto's Juvenile Court, 1912–1930," *Canadian Bulletin of Medical History* 20, 1 (2003): 48.

[16] Jean Barman, *The West Beyond the West: A History of British Columbia* (Toronto: University of Toronto Press, 1991), 230.

[17] Mary Kinnear, "'Do You Want your Daughter to Marry a Farmer': Women's Work on the Farm, 1922," *Canadian Papers in Rural History* VI (1988): 139.

[18] Alvin Finkel, *Social Policy and Practice in Canada: A History* (Waterloo: Wilfrid Laurier University Press, 2006), 102.

[19] Ernest R. Forbes, *The Maritime Rights Movement, 1919–1927: A Study in Canadian Regionalism* (Montreal and Kingston: McGill-Queen's University Press, 1979), 146.

[20] Dawson, *William Lyon Mackenzie King*, 77.

[21] Lita Rose Betcherman, *Ernest Lapointe: Mackenzie King's Great Quebec Lieutenant* (Toronto: University of Toronto Press, 2002), 127.

[22] Thomas Socknat, *Witness Against War: Pacifism in Canada, 1900–1945* (Toronto: University of Toronto Press, 1987); Jonathan Vance, *Death So Noble: Memory, Meaning, and the First World War* (Vancouver: University of British Columbia Press, 1997).

[23] Desmond Morton with Terry Copp, *Working People* (Ottawa: Deneau, 1980), 138.

[24] John Herd Thompson and Allen Seager, *Canada 1922–1939: Decades of Discord* (Toronto: McClelland & Stewart, 1985), 193.

[25] Constance Backhouse, *Colour-Coded: A Legal History of Racism in Canada, 1900–1950* (Toronto: The Osgoode Society for Canadian Legal History by the University of Toronto Press, 1999), 174.

[26] John T. Saywell, *The Lawmakers: Judicial Power and the Shaping of Canadian Federalism* (Toronto: University of Toronto Press, 2002), 192.

[27] H. Blair Neatby, *William Lyon Mackenzie King, Volume II, 1924–1932: The Lonely Heights* (Toronto: University of Toronto Press, 1963), 299.

6

The Great Depression

For more than a decade, Ted Bates, who folks in the central Saskatchewan hamlet of Glidden described as "big, jolly, outgoing and cheerful," had run a successful butcher shop. Ted had been drawn from England to Saskatchewan in1914 by advertisements from Canada's Immigration Department. Seven years later, he married Rose Slatter, another British émigré, and in 1924, they had a son, "the sunshine of their home," whom they nicknamed Nipper.

The Depression destroyed their world. People could no longer afford meat. In 1933, Ted sold the shop and the family left for Vancouver, hoping for brighter prospects. But the money for the shop never materialized, there was no work in Vancouver, and Ted did not meet the residency requirement to qualify for relief. Ted was told that the only place he could qualify for relief was in Glidden, and both he and Rose were determined not to return to their hometown as paupers. Rose pawned her jewellery to rent a car and to buy gas, and the family started to make their way back to Saskatchewan.

Middle-aged, broke, and seeing only a bleak future, they made a fateful decision. In Perdue, Saskatchewan, some 60 kilometres west of Saskatoon, with only a few dollars remaining, Ted bought a few litres of gas. That night, he parked the car by an abandoned shed and handed Nipper a book to read. Ted attached a hose to the exhaust, started the car, and filled it with deadly fumes. However, he and his wife awoke the next morning; they had not been able to afford enough gas to kill

them. But it had been enough to claim their beloved son. Distraught and panicked, Ted foraged through his suitcase for the tools of his trade: his butcher knives. Later that day, the couple were found in a pool of blood, but still alive, having been too groggy and weak to successfully kill each other. They were charged with murder, but residents in their hometown, who learned of their tragic story, rallied around them. A mass meeting was called where it resolved that the Bateses had been victims of the Great Depression. Money was raised to pay for their legal costs and for Nipper's funeral. A jury in Biggar, Saskatchewan, agreed that the Bateses were victims and acquitted them. Ted died in 1954, after which Rose returned to England. They never had another child.[1]

> **After reading this chapter you will be able to:**
>
> 1. Identify the events that triggered a worldwide economic depression.
> 2. Appreciate the profound human impact of the economic crisis on all Canadians.
> 3. Evaluate government attempts to resolve the economic crisis.
> 4. Explain the impact of the Depression on party politics and federal–provincial relations.
> 5. Specify progressive legislative changes that occurred during the decade.
> 6. Recall the government's approach to the mounting threat of another world war.

Introduction

The Great Depression left an indelible mark on Canadians and Canada. At its peak, nearly one-third of Canadians were unemployed. Throughout the West, farms literally dried up and were blown away in what became known as the *dust bowl*. In their desperation to find answers, Canadians turned to new, unorthodox, and sometimes extreme political solutions. Many of those who lived through the "dirty thirties" were forever marked by the experience. They carried away a profound sense of insecurity, marked by the beliefs that it was critical to spend prudently, save assiduously, and to steer clear of debt to avoid the abject poverty that they had experienced or certainly knew others had endured. But with so many people unable to find work, perceptions of the unemployed as being shiftless and lazy began changing, as did the expected responsibilities of government to assist those in need.

This chapter explores the human impact of the Depression; the effectiveness of political leaders in meeting the crisis; the influence of this economic disaster in changing Canada's political landscape; and its relationship to foreign and defence policy, especially as the threat of another world war grew more ominous.

October 29, 1929: Wall Street stock market crash.

Crisis Strikes

On October 29, 1929, the Wall Street stock market in New York crashed, in what became known as "Black Tuesday." Hundreds of millions of dollars in assets evaporated. The event simultaneously spread to Canadian markets, given the close economic ties between the two countries. On Toronto's Mining Exchange, the value of shares plummeted from $710 million in 1929 to $140 million a year later, while in Vancouver over the same period, the drop in the annual number of shares traded went from 143 million to 9 million.

The stock market crash was symbolic of deeper structural problems in the economy and was compounded by the poor responses of governments that were still too attached to minimal economic regulation. Over the later half of the 1920s, stock speculation became rampant, and the shares of numerous companies were grossly overvalued. In the United States in 1929, new investment in companies totalled $3.2 billion, compared to an $87 billion increase in the value of their shares traded on stock markets. Speculation and overvaluation had also become widespread on Canadian markets, with many brokerage houses knowingly selling grossly inflated stocks and pushing up prices through insider trading. Soon after the crash, Ike Solloway, who ran Toronto's largest brokerage house, received a $225 000 fine and four months in jail for fraud.

Before the crash, the economy was starting to slow down. Wheat prices, which made up one-third of Canadian exports, were steadily declining from 1927 onwards—with record yields, overproduction, grain elevators jammed, Argentina and Australia dumping wheat on world markets, and the recovery of French and Belgian fields from the First World War. By the time of the Depression, many Western Canadian wheat pools were on shaky financial ground and with the stock market crash began to collapse. Whereas in 1928 net farm income on the Prairies was $363 million, in 1932 it had actually declined to *minus* $3.1 million.

Government policy exacerbated the initial downturn. In 1928, the United States raised interest rates to contract the money supply to try to cool off the stock market and to get people to put their money into safer investments like bonds. Over the course of 1929, the tight money policy began to slow down activity in other areas like home construction. Consumer spending declined and unemployment began inching upwards. When the stock market crashed, already "skittish"[2] consumers reacted by retracting their spending significantly, thus magnifying the impact. The crash was also compounded by the decision of the American Federal Reserve Board not to re-inflate markets to keep credit flowing. This decision was based upon attachment to the gold standard (meaning that money, and hence its total supply, had to remain convertible into gold at a set price, though that price would rise from US$20 to US$35 an ounce (30 grams) between 1929 and 1930 to allow more money to be printed), as well as the perception that government should play a limited role in the operation of markets. Although Republican President Herbert Hoover was not a traditional conservative—having initiated massive government intervention in the First World War as food controller—he remained guided by the notion that the market was self-correcting. To protect jobs, the United States Congress, again turning to orthodox responses, markedly raised tariffs with the implementation of the 1930 *Smoot-Hawley Act*. This sparked similar protective responses by other governments, including Canada's, thus producing a dramatic drop in global trade. This was a particularly catastrophic scenario for Canada, whose economic health greatly depended upon international commerce. In 1929, 22 percent of gross national expenditures on Canadian goods came through foreign purchases, compared with 5 percent in the case of the United States, and one-third of total Canadian exports went to the United States. When the trade contraction came, it was quick and massive. Whereas the value of Canadian exports in 1928 was $1.3 billion, by 1932 it had fallen to $0.5 billion.

Governments were woefully unprepared, both in practice and in philosophy, to deal with the collapse. They provided few social services and those offered were miserly, which reflected limited state revenues, traditionally modest roles for government, and the general determination to keep taxes low. Local governments still provided the bulk of welfare, namely through modest make-work projects. Furthermore the still prevalent view was that the unemployed could find jobs if they really wanted, such as by working on a farm.

In January 1930, a gathering of Western Canadian mayors in Winnipeg made a collective plea to the federal government to provide money for public works. However, Prime Minister King remained convinced that the decline was a temporary downturn in the business cycle and that it was not necessary or prudent for the government to assume additional costs. Canada's two labour MPs, J.S. Woodsworth and A.A. Heaps, proposed that the federal government establish an unemployment insurance program. The Conservatives,

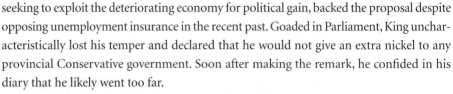

July 1930: Richard Bedford Bennett elected prime minister.

seeking to exploit the deteriorating economy for political gain, backed the proposal despite opposing unemployment insurance in the recent past. Goaded in Parliament, King uncharacteristically lost his temper and declared that he would not give an extra nickel to any provincial Conservative government. Soon after making the remark, he confided in his diary that he likely went too far.

As the July 1930 federal election approached, King felt optimistic about his chances against the untested Richard Bedford Bennett, but King had said little to convince Canadians that he had any answers to turn the economy around. Bennett conveyed the message that, as a tremendously successful businessman, he knew how to create wealth and that he had a plan, namely to "blast" Canada out of the Depression by raising tariffs to protect Canadian markets and jobs. Although protectionism would ultimately worsen the downward cycle, at the time Bennett offered hope, proclaiming, prophetically (as it turned out) that the "Conservative party is going to find work for all who are willing to work, or perish in the attempt."[3]

During the six-week campaign, Bennett travelled more than 22 000 kilometres by rail and road and delivered nearly 200 speeches. Many of his rallies attracted thousands and they were carried over radio, a medium for which his booming voice and lively cadence were well suited, especially when compared with King, whose airtime performances were flat, scripted, and lacked excitement because they were delivered in a studio. The results of the election indicated that the popular vote remained close, favouring the Tories by 48.8 to 45.2 percent, but when it came to parliamentary seats, the Conservatives triumphed decisively with 134, compared with 91 Liberals, 11 Progressives, and 2 Labour representatives. King had lost and Bennett was the new prime minister.

Hard(er) Times

Bennett selected an Ontario-centric cabinet. He gave five junior portfolios to Quebec despite 25 Conservatives having been elected in the province. He also micro-managed, convinced that he knew best. Soon circulating among the press corps was a joke about Bennett walking down the corridors of Parliament talking to himself, with the punch line being that he was holding a cabinet meeting.

1931: Statute of Westminster.

In early 1931, Bennett left for England. The trip was initially undertaken to sign the *Statute of Westminster*, which formalized the complete control by Canada and the other self-governing dominions over their foreign policy. Bennett sought to use the visit to try to achieve freer trade among Commonwealth members. However, no side was willing to make major concessions for fear of giving others an advantage. Upon returning home, Bennett delivered on his promise to raise tariffs. His government ratcheted up rates on some 130 items by as much as 50 percent. Rather than blasting Canada out of the Depression, the new tariffs contributed to the protectionist trade war and, as outlined in Figure 6.1, the downward cycle of Canadian commerce. For example, in British Columbia, exports dropped from $238 million in 1929 to $100 million by 1934.

Philosophically, Bennett believed in the importance of self-reliance, thrift, and hard work and that welfare bred dependency—he had risen from very modest circumstances on a New Brunswick farm to become one of Canada's richest men. He responded cautiously to the call for more government assistance, especially since the federal government had

Source: Library and Archives of Canada, C-009076.

Prime Minister Bennett, surrounded by his cabinet, speaks by telephone to Sir George Perley, Canada's representative to the British Empire Trade Fair in Buenos Aires, Argentina, March 1931.

limited revenues. At the time, Ottawa largely kept out of direct taxation, which was a shared jurisdiction with provincial governments, and, according to the *British North America Act*, most social welfare, including care for the unemployed, was a provincial responsibility.

In 1930, Bennett's government offered $20 million in emergency aid to the provinces, but on a shared-cost basis with federal funds capped at one-third of total relief expenditures. Bennett was motivated by the desire to minimize budget deficits in accordance with economic orthodoxy. To control its own costs, the federal government laid off thousands of civil servants, cut the salary of many more, and delayed numerous public works projects. Bennett insisted that his government would not accept the dole—a direct payment to the unemployed—and that able-bodied men had to perform work to receive relief. Within a couple of years, though, he went back on that strategy because make-work projects cost far more than a straight payment to the jobless. Several significant public works projects were initiated; for example, Winnipeg built a new hockey arena, the Saskatoon City Hospital underwent a major renovation, and many communities undertook long overdue road construction and repair. Most public works jobs, however, were basic manual labour, which included cleaning parks and shovelling snow.

Provincial governments, badly strapped for cash, continued to download half or more of relief costs on to municipalities, even though property taxes,

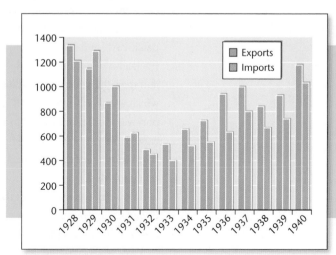

Figure 6.1
Canadian International Trade, 1928–1940 (millions of dollars)

Source: F.H. Leacey, ed., *Historical Statistics on Canada* (Ottawa: Statistics Canada, 1983), series G-381-385.

the major source of local government revenue, was pretty much exhausted, as homeowners strongly resisted any rate increase, and many people had lost their homes. To maintain social peace and to prevent people from starving, municipalities went into deep debt—and in some cases bankruptcy—to provide assistance and begged senior levels of government for more help. Even with the tight-fisted approach, Bennett's government would ultimately spend an unprecedented $200 million through matching relief grants, and whereas relief expenditures by all levels of government stood at $20 million in 1930, they reached $173 million in 1935.

By 1931, more than half a million Canadians were looking for work, and by 1933, unemployment peaked at some 30 percent of the potential workforce. For many, being on welfare was humiliating, a personal failing, and a disgrace. Many men saw it as a surrender of their manhood, such as "their right to be a husband and sit at the head of the table and carve the roast."[4] Numerous men refused assistance no matter their circumstances, thus often forcing their wives to apply. Even with rapidly increasing numbers of unemployed, the idea strongly persisted that the jobless were lazy. For instance, convinced that there existed wastage in the distribution of relief, Bennett demanded that provincial and municipal governments work harder to cut off support to those deemed capable of finding work or else Ottawa would reduce its matching financial contributions.

The process of applying for public assistance reinforced the sense of shame. People had to prove their need to local boards that, in many cases, demanded they sell all luxuries (their car, radio, jewellery, or anything else that was deemed unnecessary or frivolous), and to give up their liquor permit—which, following prohibition was issued to those eligible to buy booze—as many viewed the unemployed as shiftless and slothful. Relief often came in the form of vouchers for fuel or for the cheapest basic food staples (the most common voucher handed out). No leeway was made for personal preferences or religious and cultural dietary laws and customs. Many found the use of the vouchers embarrassing and stigmatizing, as well as difficult, as not all vendors accepted them because they did not want to wait, or go through bureaucratic hoops, to get reimbursed by the government.

There was no standardization between locales as to who got what, which reflected a patchwork, and arguably chaotic, system of support. Relief payments often depended on the health of a locale, though a common denominator was that assistance was temporary and sporadic, very often less than a week per month. For example, in Amherst, Nova Scotia, which was relatively better off and where there existed a tradition of labour militancy, support was $5.70 monthly, but in Sydney and Glace Bay, it was $4 monthly, which was not even enough for food. Generally, when it came to relief, the married were favoured over the single, those with children over the childless, and British subjects over recent immigrants. Local relief boards often excluded those who had not lived in a community for a specified period of time and frequently cut off those deemed as morally undeserving. In communities across Canada, people lined up at soup kitchens, often run by churches, where, to minimize costs, "heavy reliance was placed upon … hash and cereals"[5] that were slopped onto metal plates.

Lives were shattered, and more people lost all hope during the Great Depression. The recorded number of suicides increased from 593 in 1928 to 805 in 1931. Canadians were marrying later because they could not afford their own place to live, and they were having fewer children. Between 1929 and 1933, the marriage rate per 1000 declined from 7.7 to

6.0, and the total number of births per annum dropped from 250 355 in 1930 to 228 296 in 1934. More husbands and fathers, unable to provide for their families, or whose home life had become poisoned by poverty, deserted their families. In Edmonton, for example, the number of females listed as heads of households rose from 978 in 1921 to 2653 in 1931. The problem of husbands abandoning their families became so significant that in Ontario in 1934 the government reduced from five to three years the length of time necessary to qualify for a mother's allowance in the case of desertion. To control costs, rejected applications for mothers' allowances in Ontario grew from 458 in 1930–1931 to 1259 in 1935–1936, as investigators, faced with far more applicants and limited revenues, undertook more exacting analyses, such as of existing assets and the mother's behaviour.

Men went door to door seeking out odd jobs. It became common to see them, depending upon the season, pushing around a lawnmower or carrying a snow shovel and knocking on doors. During these difficult economic times, more people seemed to be helping each other out, although this could be a sentiment most likely enhanced over time when viewed through the pleasing lens of nostalgia. With record numbers of Canadians strapped for cash, bartering came back into vogue. Many doctors, particularly in rural areas, often accepted food for services, as there was no public health insurance, and fewer people could afford private medical plans.

Pressure built during the Depression to dismiss women from the paid workforce so more men could perform the breadwinner role, a trend helped along because more men were willing to accept lower wages. Quebec's legislature nearly passed a measure that would have required a woman to show financial need to take a job other than as a farm cook or domestic servant. All family members tried to pitch in. More wives and mothers worked as domestics, which was deemed as an acceptable role. One woman recalled that she "worked two days a week for a neighbour, an elderly gentleman and his blind son … I did the washing, ironing, mending, baking, and washed floors for the sum of $1 a day." More women turned to home-based employment, but here too things were harder during the Depression. One analysis concluded that whereas the price received for sewing a dozen dresses in 1929 was $5.00, by 1934 it was just $1.35.

At home, women tended to boarders, grew vegetables, and became experts at recycling. One woman recollected the 98 pound (44.5 kilogram) sack of flour she used to buy with the "bold coloured lettering across it" indicating that it was "either Cream of the West or Robin Hood," but that "a good soaking in suds … and much scrubbing on the zinc washboard would remove the lettering completely," thus allowing her to use the unbleached cotton to make "pillowcases, tea cloths, mattress covers, almost everything."

Children wore more hand-me-downs, family members cut each other's hair, and meals contained less meat. One man who grew up near the CPR railway recalled that as a child "one of my daily duties was to go and pick up a basket of coal along the tracks," while another said, "I'd scrounge around to find bleach bottles and clean quart baskets that paid me 1 cent each."[6] More children were forced to leave school to contribute to the family income, such as by selling newspapers or by working as full-time babysitters.

The Depression also worsened the situation for Canada's already long-suffering First Nations and Métis. By the end of the decade, their life expectancy was half that of non-

Natives. In 1930, in recognition of climbing death rates among Natives, the federal government began funding some on-reserve nursing stations but also, to save money, disbanded medical clinics in many remote First Nations communities. In 1931, Ottawa drastically cut medical assistance to the Inuit in the northern Quebec area of Ungava, claiming that this was a provincial responsibility. Quebec disagreed, arguing that the status of the Inuit were like other Natives, namely as wards of the federal government, despite there being no formal treaty that had established this. While the governments bickered, the Inuit waited, suffered, and sometimes starved, as their hunting grounds grew more depleted of caribou, seal, and fox. Not until 1938 did the courts rule that responsibility for Inuit fell to Ottawa.

Across Canada, non-status Indians (meaning they lived off reserves) and Métis could rarely afford medical services; this included an estimated 90 percent of Alberta Métis who had tuberculosis. A 1934 provincial commission headed up by Alberta Supreme Court Justice Freeman Ewing concluded that for the Métis, the best means of raising their status was by adopting white ways. For humanitarian reasons, the commission recommended that farm colonies be set up for the Métis "on good agricultural land, near lakes with plentiful stocks of fish and with access to timber for building," a recommendation that resulted in the *Métis Population Betterment Act*, which according to historian Olive Dickason, was the "most advanced legislation in Canada relating to the Métis."[7]

The Depression prompted more Canadians to seek out scapegoats for their misery, and one favourite were Jews. Anti-Semitism was fuelled by the opposing stereotypes of Jews as wealthy financiers and manipulators of the money system who benefited from the suffering of others, or as political radicals intent on exploiting the current economic catastrophe to create disorder. As a result, fascism began gaining popularity. In Quebec, its emphasis on the need for order and its defence of traditional moral values resonated with parts of the Catholic Church. Indeed, like much of the Catholic Church in Italy, that in Quebec expressed admiration for fascist leader Benito Mussolini, who was heralded for providing Italy with greater stability and for combating socialism. In 1932, Quebec's Adrien Arcand, Canada's most prominent fascist, founded *Le Goglu*, a publication that promoted French-Canadian racial purity and the need to protect Quebec from excessive liberalism, materialism, and communism, behind which, it said, was the Jew. An *Achat chez nous* movement urged Québécois to boycott Jewish merchants. Outside Quebec, Swastika clubs emerged in Toronto during the early 1930s that comprised mostly jobless and disaffected young males who held rallies in the city's Beach district, where posters appeared declaring "No Dogs or Jews Allowed."

With rising unemployment, immigration, as outlined in Figure 6.2, was reduced to a trickle. Whereas Canada accepted 144 983 immigrants in 1929, by 1935 it was merely 11 277. One of the beliefs of the times was that immigrants stole jobs. In 1931,

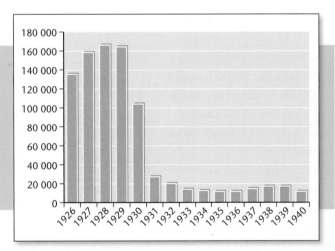

Figure 6.2
Immigration to Canada, 1926–1940

Source: F.H. Leacey, ed., *Historical Statistics on Canada* (Ottawa: Statistics Canada, 1983), series A-350.

Bennett's government banned immigrants, others than farmers, who were not of British stock. A concerted effort was made to deport immigrants considered as inclined towards Bolshevism. If people who were "politically suspect" lost their job, they were arrested because it was simple and fast to deport someone for vagrancy or for becoming a charge on the state. Over the first four years of the Depression, some 20 000 people were deported, with the trend line moving upwards from 1964 in 1929 to 7647 in 1932.

Immigrants were not the only source of fear over the spread of Bolshevism. The Communist party gained strength, both from the anger and the desperation created by the Depression and because it organized marches and demonstrations by the unemployed despite the threat of violent responses from authorities, or the possibility of being jailed for 20 years, as stated in section 98 of the *Criminal Code.* The Workers' Unity League, a union body created in 1929 by the Communist Party of Canada, grew to 40 000 members by the early 1930s. Several labour disputes turned violent, especially as employers sought to break unions and roll back wages, often to deal with their own declining profits. One of the most notable struggles was in 1931 at Estevan and Bienfait, Saskatchewan, where 600 miners confronted six companies supported by the provincial Conservative government and the RCMP. The battle ended on September 29 after authorities confronted a large march by strikers, with the result being three workers shot and killed, whose tombstones were inscribed with the epitaph, "murdered by the RCMP."

August 1931: Communist party headquarters raided.

Prime Minister Bennett declared his intention to put the "iron heel" to communists. Working with Ontario's attorney-general and local law enforcement authorities, on August 11, 1931, a raid was launched on Communist party headquarters in Toronto. Eight men, including the party's leader, Tim Buck, were charged under section 98 and received jail terms ranging up to ten years, which effectively outlawed the Communist party (though ultimately all the men were released within three years).

Continuing Retrenchment Abroad

Canadian foreign policy continued to be largely guided by the desire to avoid the possibility of costly and divisive military engagements, as it had been during the 1920s. Bennett's approach reflected a population that focused inward on the country's growing economic malaise, as was evident in September 1931, when Japan invaded the Chinese territory of Manchuria in a blatant effort to expand its access to minerals and political influence throughout Asia. The invasion was a set-up, launched in response to a section of the South Manchurian Railway being blown up that Tokyo blamed on China but was actually perpetrated by Japanese officers. Japanese military forces seized major strategic points within 24 hours and within a week controlled most of central Manchuria.

The League of Nations met in emergency session to discuss its response. Bennett's government adopted a wait-and-see approach, though press opinion in Canada—then the only barometer of public opinion—was overwhelmingly opposed to applying collective security, arguing that Canada had no vital interests at stake. Considerable pro-Japanese sentiment was expressed. *Saturday Night* magazine reminded its readers that Japan had been an ally during the First World War and was an effective counterweight to the Soviet Union.

Things grew more problematic when Japan threatened Shanghai, which contained significant Western business interests. In March 1932, the League called for an immediate ceasefire. Canada criticized Japan, though in decidedly temperate terms, which also reflected Britain's approach so as not to isolate Tokyo. Unfazed by the League, Japan proceeded to establish the new puppet state of Manchukuo in what had been Manchuria. In October, the League recommended non-recognition of Manchukuo and urged the two sides to work out an agreement. Canada's message in the League was non-committal and in some respects criticized China as much as Japan for the crisis. In reacting to the criticism it did receive, Japan quit the League, not fearing any retribution. Canada maintained cordial relations with Japan, continuing its full range of bilateral trade and commented no further on events in Manchuria.

The Depression reinforced the trend from the previous decade of significant cuts to Canada's military. During the early 1930s, the permanent army was capped at a few thousand personnel. Militia funding dropped from $11 million in 1929 to $1.6 million three years later. In 1932, the federal government proposed an annual budget of $422 000 for the navy, which was not even enough to cover its fixed costs. However, the threat of resignation from the navy's chief officer, Commodore Walter Hose, convinced Ottawa to return the figure to the 1931 budget level of $2 million.

The Depths of Despair

In 1932, Bennett hosted a summit of Commonwealth leaders in Ottawa to try to rekindle efforts to create freer trade among member countries. There was plenty of pomp and press coverage as Canada had never before hosted such a large and prestigious international gathering. A few export items were given a Commonwealth preference, but once again, the overall results were marginal. Behind closed doors, frustration mounted. Bennett thought Britain's Prime Minister Stanley Baldwin condescending, while his British counterpart regarded Bennett as pigheaded and considered leaving the conference early.

Although the Depression deepened, by no means did all Canadians suffer. Those with skills and good jobs arguably did better in terms of their buying power. As labour historian Bryan Palmer notes, "between 1929 to 1933 wages declined by 14 per cent, but the cost of living fell by almost 22 per cent."[8] One man in Winnipeg recalled that finally he was able to purchase that "snazzy 1929 Auburn roadster" he always wanted because, a few years into the Depression, it sold for just $100 down and $15 monthly and the dealer was "glad to take it." But such good fortune was built upon widespread suffering. Besides the unemployed, countless workers took wage cuts, afraid of losing their jobs. At the Mohawk Handle Company in New Westminster, British Columbia, where 15 cents an hour was being paid to men who painted handles, and where there were rumblings of a walkout, one former employee remembered: "The directors called a meeting about all this strike business and the superintendent told them, 'Let 'em all quit! I can replace 'em all by tomorrow morning if they do.' … We stayed on the job and kept getting fifteen cents an hour. That was the Depression for you."[9]

Between 1928 and 1933, Canadian manufacturing output dropped by 48 percent, retail sales by 44 percent, and investment in durable assets by businesses by an incredible 82 percent.

Overall, between 1929 and 1933, Canada's gross national product—the total annual value of goods and services—contracted by 42 percent. In 1933, unemployment peaked at 1.35 million, or 30 percent of the workforce. An estimated 100 000 men were "riding the rods," meaning that they were hoping on rail cars and moving from place to place in search of work. They took up temporary residence in what were called *hobo jungles* on the outskirts of cities and towns by the railway tracks, places that were composed of "crude huts made from tin sheets, packing crates, boxes, and other debris hauled from garbage dumps."[10] In such places, there developed a sense of comradeship in shared hardship, with residents often helping each other out by sharing what food they had, for example.

The Depression united the country in misery. In Ontario and Quebec, manufacturing production dropped by half between 1929 and 1933. In British Columbia, production declined from $331 million in 1929 to $149 million in 1932. In Vancouver, a city lot listed at $1500 in 1929 sold for $50 in 1935. On the opposite side of the country, in the Maritimes between 1929 and 1933, timber production plunged by 75 percent, fishing by 47 percent, and coal mining by 45 percent. In Newfoundland, in August 1932, an angry mob of unemployed men gutted the legislature. With Newfoundland on the verge of financial collapse, Britain established a commission to examine options to help save the floundering island. It recommended that a British-appointed Commission government replace island self-rule. With Britain agreeing to finance Newfoundland's debt, the island reverted to colonial status in February 1934.

Elsewhere in the country, much of the Prairies were devastated. In 1932, the price of wheat bottomed out at 34 cents a bushel (0.04 cubic metre), less than 20 percent of its 1928 value. Between 1931 and 1941, an estimated 250 000 people left the region, many heading for British Columbia because at least there the more pleasant weather made it easier to survive. Across much of the Prairies, the scale of devastation was biblical, with droughts, high winds, and blinding dust storms destroying once fertile topsoil. The first such episode came in 1931 following a brutally cold winter but with virtually no snow, which was followed by a hot and dry summer, thus making the soil like dust, a cycle that repeated every year in large parts of the southern Prairies until 1937. In Moose Jaw and Regina, white clothes took on a permanent tinge of grey, roads and sidewalks always remained "gritty" and homes "perennially dusty."[11] Highways often became impossible to navigate because of dust storms that reduced visibility to but a few centimetres. Hot dry weather also brought plagues of grasshoppers. Clouds of hoppers would suddenly appear, blacken the sky, and descend to devour all vegetation. In Winnipeg, grasshopper invasions in 1932 left every golf course unplayable, and in Regina one hopper blizzard was so intense that when rain came, the storm sewers became clogged with the insects.

In Saskatchewan, the value of production dropped by an unbelievable 78 percent between 1928 and 1932. In August 1931, the Canadian Red Cross sent out a nationwide appeal to help an estimated 125 000 farm people in Saskatchewan. Churches served as depots for food and clothing, and the outpouring of generosity filled 249 rail cars. Over the course of the Depression, one-fifth of Saskatchewan's population moved elsewhere, thus ending its status as Canada's third most populous province. Auctions of farm machinery, animals, and other items became common. With their remaining cash, many farmers in

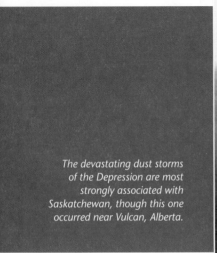

The devastating dust storms of the Depression are most strongly associated with Saskatchewan, though this one occurred near Vulcan, Alberta.

Source: Glenbow Museum, NA-2685-86.

1934: Dionne Quintuplets born.

southern Saskatchewan, where conditions were worse, hoisted their home onto a trailer and moved to better land in the north, or settled in the cities. In Alberta, ranches dried up and cattle perished in such numbers that in 1935 the federal government agreed to buy 15 000 half-starved livestock to prop up the market and to prevent a further exodus of ranchers to places like Edmonton and Vancouver to find work.

With the Depression being a global phenomenon, Canada suffered a dramatic drop-off in tourism, especially from the United States. Between 1930 and 1933, the annual number of visits by Americans was nearly halved from 13 million to 7 million. Canada's net revenue from tourism dropped from $300 million in 1929 to $120 million in 1933. Canada's Senate was tasked with establishing a commission to make recommendations on reversing the trend, but it was unable to produce any effective answers.

One of the few bright spots with tourism, but whose experiences left a legacy of controversy, was the Dionne Quintuplets, who were born in May 1934 to dirt-poor Francophone farmers in the northern Ontario hamlet of Corbeil, just outside North Bay. The first quintuplets ever to survive, their births were called a miracle, especially as they were administered by a country doctor, Allan Roy Dafoe. Their births were splashed across newspapers throughout North America, as it was an uplifting story of survival against the odds in the midst of so much bad news. Chicago promoters who wanted to put the babies on display at the city's Century of Progress Exposition approached the parents, who agreed on the basis of getting one-quarter of the gate receipts. The press vilified the parents, especially since the babies were still extremely fragile.

The provincial government of Mitchell Hepburn stepped in to take over custody. Within two months of being born, decisions about the quints' upbringing went to a board of guardians that did not include their parents. At five months, the babies were placed in

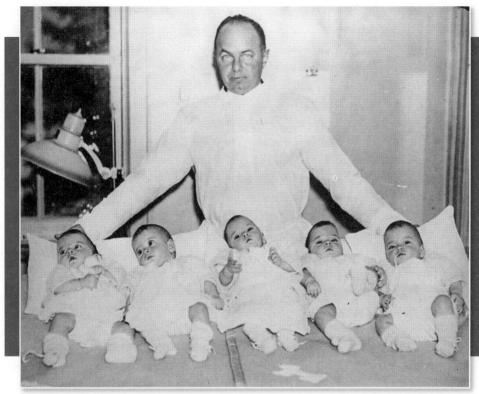

Source: Library and Archives of Canada, C-019533.

Premier Hepburn poses with the Dionne Quintuplets. Not until 1938 did the parents, who accused the government of trying to sever the children from their Francophone heritage, regain some control over their upbringing.

a government-built facility, part hospital and part nursery, where their upbringing was governed by doctors and other heath-care professionals working under the direction of Dr. William Blatz, director of the Institute of Child Psychology at the University of Toronto. Located in Callendar, near North Bay, the Dafoe Hospital, nicknamed *Quintland*, was also developed as a tourist site. Visitors flocked from across North America—including Hollywood stars like Jimmy Stewart and Bette Davis—and stood behind large windows to view the babies as they went about their daily routines that were planned down to the minute; this carried on well into their toddler and childhood years. The showing of the Dionne Quintuplets pumped millions of dollars into the northern Ontario economy.

As the Depression worsened, Prime Minister Bennett became an object of scorn. Canadians sarcastically spoke of *Bennett buggies* (a car pulled by a horse because its owner could not afford the gas), *Bennett barnyards* (abandoned farms), and *Bennett coffee* (boiled grain). Because Bennett considered charity a religious obligation and a private matter, few Canadians realized that he sent thousands of dollars of his own money to people who wrote him about their hardships. "I suppose I am silly to write," went one such letter from an Alberta farmwoman, "but I haven't any one else … so am going to hope and pray that you will read this yourself and help me or us, rather." She told of having five small children for whom she had been unable to afford milk or vegetables for months. "Please help me by lending me some money and I will send you my engagement ring and wedding ring as security,"[12] she wrote pleadingly, to which Bennett responded by sending her five dollars in the mail.

Despite his private charitable nature, Bennett projected a tough exterior. His rotund physical stature and wealthy background increasingly came to symbolize the image of a plutocrat. Though his government had spent record sums on welfare, its approach still reflected the belief in a limited role for the state to control deficits and discourage personal dependency. In mid-1932, the federal government introduced a plan under which it would provide up to one-third of personal costs to a maximum of $200 to help urbanites resettle on farms, where, it was thought, they could at least feed themselves. However, much of the land chosen, in part for cost savings, was remote, and many participants lacked adequate agricultural experience. In Hearst and Kapuskasing in northern Ontario, the failure rate among participants was 70 percent. In Quebec, where the provincial government provided more support for colonization, as farming was viewed as the cultural and moral backbone of French Canada, the results were somewhat better, though failure rates, depending upon the district, still ranged between 25 and 67 percent.

In part to restore faith in the capitalist system, governments initiated efforts to reform stock markets. In 1930, in Ontario, George Drew, a well-known Conservative, former mayor of Guelph, and who then held the quasi-judicial post of master of the Supreme Court of Ontario, was appointed by the provincial Tory government of George Henry to head up a board to enforce a new *Securities Fraud Prevention Act*. The next year, it became the Ontario Securities Commission under whose direction, in 1934, the Toronto Stock Exchange was merged with the more volatile and less respected Standard Stock and Mining Exchange. Although Drew wanted to avoid a level of regulation that could discourage investment, the Securities Commission did investigate major fluctuations in stock prices and demanded up-to-date and audited reports by companies listed on the stock exchange. In 1934, Algonquin Mines was delisted for failing to supply such information, as was Arni Mines after its shares shot up from 8 to 20 cents, and then quickly fell back to 4 cents. Also in 1934, Ottawa passed a *Companies Act* that required firms that fell under federal jurisdiction "to file … detailed prospectuses and copies of sales literature before offering securities to the public."[13]

There was growing concern, keenly felt by Bennett, that the deepening economic crisis was threatening the stability, and perhaps even the survival, of the capitalist system. Bennett expressed anxiety over Canada's growing transient population, a group that was largely young, male, and single. With fewer responsibilities and often feeling themselves unwanted and shunned by society, it was feared that radical agitators could influence these men.

To try to keep such men occupied and under control, Bennett latched on to an idea suggested by his chief of the general staff, General Andrew McNaughton, that work camps be established, administered by the Department of National Defence, where these men would contribute to civilian infrastructure projects and rebuild crumbling military facilities. The first camp was opened in October 1932, and by 1934 nearly 60 had emerged. The largest concentration was in British Columbia, where 53 camps were established, followed by Ontario with 37, and more than 115 000 men participated in the work camp scheme. Several important projects were completed, such as by 1935 in Ontario, four aerodromes, 24 landing strips, three air stations, and three military barracks. Across Canada, men worked on 40 highway projects, including in national parks, like Banff, to make them more accessible for tourism.

However, the camps soon exacerbated discontent. Most were placed in remote areas, often too remote to receive radio signals, an intentional decision in part so that any radicalism among participants would be quarantined and to isolate camp workers from outside agitators. Many saw themselves as banished. They received free transport, food, and accommodation, though with cost control being a major consideration, they often slept in tents or dilapidated bunkhouses, and their pay was 20 cents a day, which they considered insulting. With bitter sarcasm, they commonly referred to themselves as the "royal 20 centers." They received a tobacco allowance, but it was a mere 1.45 cents a day, which meant that it was necessary to work a week for one pack. Authorities gave virtually no consideration to establishing recreational facilities because the camps were considered temporary. Many camps lacked supplies, such as boots and warm clothing. The work was often backbreaking and purposefully assigned with primitive equipment to keep men occupied longer at the lowest possible cost.

Anger festered. At Lac Suel, near the Manitoba–Ontario border, where men were assigned to clear the shoreline of marketable timber for a planned hydroelectric project, one camp worker said: "We were slaves, what else would you call a man who is given twenty cents a day and is expected to believe their bullshit that he is an important part of the country?"[14] Men complained about the military running facilities like boot camps as the *King's Orders and Regulations*, the basic military legal system, was applied. Worker committees were prohibited and anyone involved in a protest could be kicked out of the camp and forced to make his own way home. Even with such restrictions, the camps experienced 359 strikes, and 17 391 men were dismissed for disciplinary breaches. As historian Pierre Berton aptly concluded: "McNaughton's scheme for staving off revolution had the seeds of revolution inherent in it."[15]

New Answers or New Threats?

More Canadians were coming to the conclusion that mainstream politicians had no answers to reverse the crippling effects of the Depression. They began turning to others advocating sweeping change. In 1932, some 100 farmers, workers, academics, socialists, Labour party representatives, and former Progressives gathered in Calgary to form the Co-operative Commonwealth Federation (CCF). The CCF spoke of working towards implementing socialism through democratic means, while in the short term pursuing better social welfare programs. Its first leader was former Methodist minister J.S. Woodsworth, who had represented the largely working-class and immigrant federal riding of Winnipeg North since 1921. Although committed to parliamentary institutions and peaceful change, and though rejecting overtures made by communists to form a common front, the CCF was still portrayed as a radical organization. In part, this was its own making, as in 1933 it released the *Regina Manifesto* that, in setting out the party's purpose and platform, not only advocated initiatives such as comprehensive crop insurance and a national labour code but also ended with the declaration that "no CCF government will rest content until it has eradicated capitalism and put into operation a full program of socialized planning."[16]

The CCF achieved virtually no presence in Quebec where the Catholic Church condemned it as socialist, alien, and atheist. Not until 1940 did it win its first seat in the

August 1932: CCF founded in Calgary.

Maritimes. In the 1934 Ontario election, it won just one seat and 7 percent of the popular vote. In British Columbia, where labour militancy was pronounced in mining districts, in the 1933 provincial election the CCF won 31.5 percent of the popular vote, though this translated into only seven of 47 seats. The next year in Saskatchewan, where the Depression arguably hit the hardest, the party took 24 percent of the popular vote but only five of 55 seats. In its first federal election in 1935, the CCF attracted 9.3 percent popular support, but only seven MPs in a Parliament of 245. However, among those seven was Tommy Douglas. A former Baptist minister, Douglas was elected in the Saskatchewan constituency of Weyburn, and would, in 1944, form Canada's first CCF government in Saskatchewan.

Between August 1933 and July 1935, five provincial Conservative governments lost power. In the Maritimes, Tory administrations fell to moderate reform Liberals under Angus Macdonald in Nova Scotia, A. Alison Dysart in New Brunswick, and Walter Lea in Prince Edward Island. The only provincial government to retain power throughout the Depression was Manitoba's centre-left Liberal-Progressive coalition under John Bracken, though it was reduced from majority to minority status in 1936.

In British Columbia, Fraser Tolmie's Conservative government became torn by internal dissent as the Depression portended doom for its electoral prospects. Tolmie faced T.C. "Duff" Pattullo, who became Liberal leader in May 1930. Pattullo had migrated from Ontario, drawn west by the Klondike gold rush. He settled in Prince Rupert, where he became a prominent businessman and mayor. Charismatic and colourful, he came across, as historian Jean Barman writes, "as immensely self-confident, dapper, even a bit flamboyant."[17] He rebuilt the party organization, bought radio time with his own money and gave as many as 20 public speeches a day. Casting Tolmie as a puppet of business interests, Pattullo, despite his entrepreneurial background, spoke of the need for "socialized capitalism," meaning that the government had to "recognize both the duty and the desirability of giving larger consideration to the needs and welfare of society generally."[18] Also, with the election of Franklin Roosevelt as U.S. president and his introduction of the New Deal in 1933, which largely revolved around implementing massive public works projects, Pattullo promised a similar strategy should he be elected as premier, which happened that November as his Liberal party captured 34 of 47 seats.

Pattullo pleaded with Bennett for more federal money. He played the regional card, claiming that Confederation was not working for British Columbia because he said that between 1926 and 1931 Ottawa took out $20 million more from the province than it put back into it. Pattullo did deliver some reforms, such as raising the minimum wage and imposing an eight-hour workday and 49-hour workweek, put more money into education, and funded some public works projects, including construction of a bridge over the Fraser River to connect Vancouver and New Westminster. The provincial debt increased, though expenditures were offset somewhat by better royalties from rising mineral prices, especially for gold. When it came time for Pattullo to face the voters again in 1937, enough people agreed that his government was moving in the right direction to provide his Liberals with a slightly reduced majority of 31 out of 48 seats.

The politics of reform was also evident in Saskatchewan, where in June 1934 the Tories under J.T.M. Anderson lost to the Liberals, whose leader, James Gardiner, ran on a platform

November 1933: Liberal T.C. "Duff" Pattullo elected B.C. premier.

advocating unemployment insurance, drought relief, and easier credit for farmers. That same month, Mitchell Hepburn brought the Liberals back to power in Ontario after a 28-year drought. An onion farmer by background, the hard-drinking and combative Hepburn sold himself as a champion for ordinary, hard-working folks and the downtrodden, even though his property was valued at $150 000—50 times as much as the average Ontario farm. Once in power, Hepburn forged strong ties with the business community, particularly those involved in resource development. His government provided them with generous tax breaks and argued that such risk takers represented the best hope to lift Ontario out of the Depression, though it was also from this source that his Liberal party received hefty donations.

June 1934: James Gardiner elected Saskatchewan premier and Mitchell Hepburn elected Ontario premier.

The next year, a more radical change occurred in Alberta with the election of the Social Credit party under William "Bible Bill" Aberhart, an event considered so unique that it made the front page of the *New York Times*. Born in Perth County, Ontario, in 1878, Aberhart initially trained as a teacher. After earning a B.A. through correspondence courses offered by Queen's University, he moved to Calgary in 1910 and became a school principal. Passionate about his Baptist religion, he devoted much of his time to bible study and in 1927 became dean at the Protestant fundamentalist Calgary Prophetic Bible Institute. A gifted speaker, he obtained widespread fame as a preacher, especially from his broadcasts of the *Back to the Bible Hour* over CFCN, a Calgary radio station whose powerful signal blanketed the Prairies and the northwest United States, and from which Aberhart drew a weekly audience of some 350 000.

Aberhart spoke of his conversion to Social Credit after a former student committed suicide, a tragedy he blamed on the Depression. Developed by a Scottish engineer, C.H. Douglas, Social Credit theory advocated greater state control over the monetary system to correct the problem of under-consumption, something that Douglas, a virulent anti-Semite, blamed on profit-seeking Jewish financiers. Although anti-Semitism permeated Social Credit in Alberta, Aberhart publicly avoided the screed. Also, to the dismay of Douglas, Aberhart advanced a highly simplified version of Social Credit monetary theory, but it was easily understood by the masses, particularly the *A + B Theorem* that spread like a prairie wildfire. With *A* being total salaries and wages, *B* other costs of production and profits, and *C* being the total price charged for goods, under-consumption was explained by the gap between the values of *A* and *C*. Aberhart's solution was to contribute to *B* so that when added to *A*, the total would equal *C*, thus solving under-consumption. This plan would be accomplished by the province distributing a dividend that Aberhart said Social Credit experts had calculated at $25 monthly. Economists warned of hyperinflation, jokes were told about "funny money," and it was pointed out that the provincial government had no constitutional authority to print money. But Albertans took hope from Aberhart's message; they believed in him as a man of God, and his promise of free money was like manna from heaven.

The governing United Farmers of Alberta (UFA) could no longer sell itself as populist, having implemented traditional responses to offset the Depression; indeed, many former supporters now cast it as being run by lawyers and agricultural elites. Disaster also struck the UFA in 1933 when a jury convicted Premier John Brownlee of seducing a government

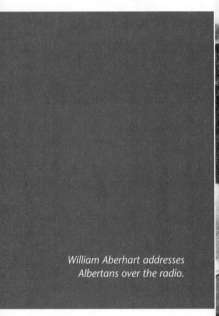

William Aberhart addresses Albertans over the radio.

Source: Glenbow Archives, NA-2771-2.

August 1935: William "Bible Bill" Aberhart elected Alberta premier.

employee who was a minor. Although overturned on appeal, salacious press coverage of the trial destroyed Brownlee's career, prompting him to resign in July 1934.

By the time Aberhart announced his intention to run for premier in early 1935, an army of supporters belonging to 1600 Social Credit study groups in the province were primed to pitch in. Aberhart ran the show, though, personally vetting and choosing all the Social Credit candidates. During the campaign, he relentlessly attacked the banks and promised to wrestle power from the "Fifty Big Shots" running the country that Albertans understood to mean the barons of Toronto's Bay Street and Montreal's St. James Street, Canada's main financial districts. In August 1935, Social Credit swept Alberta, winning 56 of 63 seats.

As premier, Aberhart initially followed a safe, traditional course, as he feared disinvestment from the province if Social Credit monetary policy was immediately implemented. His government emphasized debt reduction, though in some domains it was reformist—for instance, making modest improvements to health services and education. But this cautious approach brought mounting criticism. Douglas, who was not one to mince words, accused Aberhart of selling out to the financial interests. Several MLAs who considered themselves Social Credit purists threatened to resign. In 1937, Aberhart introduced legislation authorizing the provincial government to print scrip, or promissory notes, and in a companion piece of legislation sought to deny court appeals by banks over such currency production. However, the federal government challenged the measures, and in March 1938 Canada's Supreme Court quashed them. Aberhart blustered against federal intrusion but did not initiate an appeal; instead, he demanded greater provincial powers and blamed Ottawa for Alberta's continuing economic woes. Moreover, to contain attacks on his government, he introduced the *Accurate News and Information Act* that gave it the power to compel the publication or correction of a story and to force a reporter to reveal a source. Some accused Aberhart of behaving like a dictator. Alberta newspapers fought back, won their case in court to overturn the legislation, and collectively received the prestigious Pulitzer Prize, the first time it was awarded to a non-American source.

Banishing Bennett and Re-crowning King

Although assailed as heartless, Bennett's government had spent more on public assistance than any previous one and had also made noises about implementing an unemployment insurance plan. With the national debt hitting $135 million in 1934, he ended up moving in the opposite direction by cutting grants for relief to the provinces by 20 percent. British economist John Maynard Keynes's theory that governments should spend their way out of a depression and then pay down the debt in better times, was gaining more adherents (especially after Keynes published *The General Theory of Employment, Interest and Money* in 1936), but the prevailing orthodoxy remained that governments should pursue balanced budgets and minimize interference with the market economy. To deal with the crisis in Prairie agriculture, Bennett's government introduced the 1934 *Prairie Farm Rehabilitation Act* under which funds were made available for large-scale re-seeding, drought resistant grasses, and new methods of tillage to preserve moisture and to protect soil. With federal assistance, water-catching dugouts were constructed on 50 000 farms, and some 800 000 hectares of marginal land was transformed into community pastures. The same year, in an effort to provide greater stability to the financial sector and more coordinated economic planning, the government created the Bank of Canada, which would set interest rates and establish minimum reserve requirements for all Canadian chartered banks. To promote public education, unity, and nationalism and to counteract American influence, the federal government established the Canadian Radio Broadcasting Corporation in 1932, which four years later became the Canadian Broadcasting Corporation (CBC).

1934: Bank of Canada created. 1936: Canadian Broadcasting Corporation created.

Overworked and nearing nervous exhaustion, Bennett contemplated retirement. His Conservative party was also splintering, as Bennett and his well-known minister of trade and commerce, H.H. Stevens, had a very public political divorce. A small businessman by background, Stevens sometimes proved antagonistic towards major capitalists because he believed they abused power to destroy competition. Aware of Stevens's growing popularity as a "people's champion," Bennett appointed him to head up a parliamentary Price Spreads Commission. Many of its findings were shocking, such as the Eaton's department store paying a home-based female worker 9.5 cents for each dress she produced and then selling them for $1.59. Before releasing his report, Stevens publicly accused top executives at the retailing giant Simpson's of milking $10 million out of the firm. With Simpson's threatening legal action, Bennett ordered Stevens to apologize, but he refused. Bennett responded by changing the parliamentary commission into a Royal Commission and removed Stevens, which prompted him to resign and create the Reconstruction party three months before a federal election. The party gathered 8.7 percent of the popular vote—and a single seat for Stevens—with most of those votes being siphoned from the Conservatives.

1934: Price Spreads Commission.

January 1935: Bennett's New Deal broadcasts.

For a while it seemed that Bennett might snatch victory from what appeared to be an impending certain defeat. In January 1935, without warning his caucus, he went over national radio (in airtime he purchased himself) to outline a Canadian version of Roosevelt's New Deal. In five 30-minute broadcasts, Bennett, who boldly declared to listeners that the "old order is gone,"[19] promised to implement a broad range of reforms, including a national minimum wage, unemployment insurance, maximum hours of work, collective bargaining rights for labour, better old age pensions, and public health insurance.

Although stimulating a broader debate on the responsibilities of government to assist those in need, Bennett's New Deal soon appeared as ill-conceived and deceitful, designed solely to help him win an upcoming election. The promises were placed in the Tory's Throne Speech; Bennett expected a short debate in which the Liberals would oppose the plan, thus allowing him to run for re-election as the voice of reform. But King outmanoeuvred Bennett, moving quickly past the Throne Speech to demand that the Tories detail their legislative package. The only thing the Conservatives could provide was an unemployment insurance plan that they had quickly cobbled together. The Bill only committed the federal government to provide one-fifth of the funding, with the rest coming from equal contributions by employers and employees into an unemployment insurance fund. Furthermore, only those who had contributed to the fund for a minimum period of time could collect benefits. Less than 60 percent of Canadian workers were covered; seasonal and part-time workers were excluded. Length of coverage was tied to how long one had worked before losing a job and payments were miserly, ostensibly to discourage dependence on the state. With the Conservatives looking like amateurs, or frauds, by proposing a New Deal for which they had virtually no legislative proposals, fracturing over the Price Spreads Commission, and still being unable to reverse the crippling effects of the Depression, the Liberals were able to run an election campaign that made few specific promises and that presented the choice to Canadians with the memorable catchphrase of "King or chaos."

Symbolically underlining Bennett's failure to deal with the Depression, King campaigns in Saskatchewan in a Bennett buggy.

Source: Library and Archives of Canada, C-000623.

The idea of chaos spreading under Bennett grew more prevalent as the election approached. Anger continued to mount in the McNaughton work camps. Starting in late 1934, in British Columbia's interior, about half of the 7000 camp workers organized by a new Relief Camp Workers Union voted to go on strike. With no response from the federal government, they converged on Vancouver, where they occupied buildings like the municipal museum and the main library. Because they left the camps, Bennett maintained that they had become a provincial responsibility, and as the two levels of government bickered over who should respond, this further poisoned the atmosphere among the strikers. Their principal leader was Arthur "Slim" Evans. A dedicated communist, member of the Workers Unity League, and a veteran of numerous strikes as a leader in the United Mine Workers, Evans still carried a limp from being shot 20 years earlier during a strike at the Rockefeller mines in Ludlow, Colorado.

Evans's plan was to organize the strikers for a pilgrimage to Ottawa. Vancouver officials, including Mayor Gerald Grattan McGeer, allowed the strikers to raise money for the trip so that they would vacate the city as soon as possible. In April 1935, about 1000 strikers departed by boarding in and on top of boxcars for what became known as the "On-to-Ottawa trek." Initially, the federal government ignored them, believing their stunt would fade away once the cold and snow of the Rocky Mountains were reached. But the opposite happened: The trek took on the aura of a crusade against Bennett's policies towards the unemployed, and their numbers grew as they moved through each community. By Medicine Hat, Alberta, they were 1500 strong. In several places they received a sympathetic reception and were allowed to raise money through a "Tag Day," though this was also permitted so that they would minimize their stay. The trekkers maintained strong discipline; their leaders forbade panhandling and established a system of fines, such as for drunkenness, so that the movement would come across as comprising responsible young men who simply wanted decent work.

Bennett feared that if the trekkers reached Winnipeg, the "centre of western Canadian radicalism,"[20] their numbers could grow to dangerous proportions. He instructed the country's two major railways, the Canadian National and Canadian Pacific, to complain that the trekkers were trespassing on their property. In response, his government declared the trek as illegal and halted it in Regina, where the RCMP directed the trekkers to the Regina fair grounds. Two negotiators—Minister of Railways Dr. Robert Manion and Minister of Agriculture Robert Weir—were sent West. It was agreed that a delegation, including Evans, would be allowed to meet with Bennett in Ottawa. When that happened, Bennett was condescending and hostile, accusing the trek leaders of fomenting revolution; he warned them that his government would do "whatever is necessary to maintain law." Determined to show that he was not intimidated, Evans shot back by telling Bennett that he was not fit to be the "premier of a Hottentot village."[21]

Things started to come to a head on June 27, two weeks after the trekkers arrived in Regina. When they refused to move to another location, and began initiating plans to continue the trip east by trucks, authorities were ordered to end things. The Relief Camp Workers' Union was declared an illegal organization, and warrants were issued for the trek leaders under section 98 of the *Criminal Code*. On July 1, nearly 4000 trekkers and

The On-to-Ottawa Trek.

Source: Library and Archives of Canada, C-029399.

July 1, 1935: Regina Riot.

their supporters gathered in Regina's Market Square. When the leaders started to address the crowd, tear gas canisters were set off and the police pounced with clubs swinging. The strikers fought back. It took three hours for authorities to gain full control, and by that time one detective was dead, a dozen police were wounded, half a dozen civilians had been shot, one later died, more than 100 trekkers were injured, and eight of their leaders and 76 others had been arrested.

Premier Gardiner, who had opposed such heavy-handed tactics, appointed a Regina Riot Inquiry Commission. Bennett challenged its legitimacy, saying it was motivated by political partisanship. The federal government proceeded to prosecute 38 cases. Armed guards were placed at the courthouse where the three main leaders—including Evans—were being tried. With an election approaching, Bennett trumpeted his determination to protect Canada from communism. Having made bail, Evans went on a speaking tour and received plenty of press coverage, including for his claim that the riot was a set up. He argued, with some effectiveness, that he could have been arrested far more easily and without violence rather than having authorities go after him at a mass rally. King avoided discussing the trial, saying that the court would decide matters, but he did portray the work camps as a failure and section 98 as too draconian, and promised that if elected he would end both, which he did do the following year.

Ultimately, in 1936, eight trekkers received sentences of 6 to 12 months, though all the others, including Evans, evaded conviction. On May 16, 1936, the Regina Commission reported and actually justified the decision to halt the trek in Regina, largely because communists led it. Although the commission raised questions about the decision to arrest the trek leaders at a public gathering, it also cast law enforcement personnel as courageous and placed much of the blame for the riot on the trekkers, though by this time such words of support were small consolation for Bennett.

October 1935: King returns as prime minister.

Besides having to cope with deteriorating domestic conditions, in the immediate lead up to the federal election on October 14, 1935, Bennett faced a foreign crisis that reflected badly on the image of his government to manage difficult situations. On October 3, fascist Italy, whose dictator, Benito Mussolini, spoke in terms of reviving the glory of ancient Rome, used a border dispute involving its colony in Somalia to invade neighbouring and resource-rich Abyssinia (Ethiopia today). The League of Nations met in emergency session to determine its response. Few considered military intervention, but economic sanctions were on the table. Bennett said that Canada's Parliament would decide the country's response once it was recalled after the election. King, however, better sensing the public mood, rejected any possibility of Canadian intervention. He was convinced that few Canadians were willing to fight, and possibly die, to defend Abyssinia, an attitude largely grounded in racism. As one prominent French-Canadian intellectual put it, why should Canadians take up arms "to rescue a certain tribe of Negroes?"[22] King also realized that risking possible hostilities against Italy, and its large military, conjured fears of conscription, especially in Quebec, where Mussolini enjoyed some popularity for having established a workable relationship with the Vatican and for his efforts in bringing greater order to Italy, a country that had been engulfed by political and social turmoil following the First World War.

With events unfolding rapidly, including proof that Italy was using poison gas against the Abyssinians, Canada's representatives at the League of Nations convinced Bennett to give them some latitude in responding. Advisory Officer W.A. Riddell was especially appalled by Italy's aggression. In a League Economic Sub-Committee tasked with recommending sanctions, Riddell, before properly checking with Ottawa, proposed that Italy be denied imports of coal, copper, iron, steel, and most crucial of all, oil, as estimates indicated Italy had about a three-month supply of petroleum to fight its war. Many were alarmed with Canada's apparent willingness to take the lead against Italy, a position that further sealed Bennett's fate.

The election, which took place during the Abyssinian crisis, saw the Liberals crush the Tories, taking 173 out of 245 seats. A dejected Bennett expressed his willingness to step aside, but the Conservatives did not replace him as leader until 1938 with the 30-year parliamentary veteran Robert Manion, whose former cabinet posts included the Department of Soldiers Civil Re-establishment and Railways and Canals. Bennett retired to England, where he died in 1947 and remains Canada's only prime minister buried on foreign soil.

In one of his first actions as prime minister, King recalled Riddell from the League of Nations in Geneva for acting without government authorization and then backpedalled from possible sanctions. Closer to home, he pursued Canadian interests through foreign policy by seeking freer trade with the United States, arguing that Bennett's policy of protectionism had been an economic disaster. He also travelled to Washington to meet President Roosevelt. In his diary, King gushed about forming a special bond with the famed American leader because Roosevelt told King to phone him whenever he thought it was necessary. Although Roosevelt regularly played up to the ego of visiting leaders, there was chemistry between the two, as well as results, namely a modest move to freer trade despite strong protectionist sentiment in the U.S. Congress.

King proceeded cautiously in developing domestic economic policy. He chose C.A. Dunning as his finance minister, a fiscal conservative who opposed adding to the national debt. Initially, the Liberals cut relief grants to the provinces, justifying this on the basis of a modestly improving economy. King announced the creation of the National Employment Commission (NEC), but to control costs, made it solely an advisory body rather than one that would help with job creation or unemployment relief. He also sent Bennett's unemployment insurance legislation off to the courts to test its constitutionality, a move that many criticized as a delay tactic.

Reviving a "Golden Era" in Quebec

In late 1935, King called a dominion–provincial conference to improve intergovernmental relations, but recent federal cuts to relief payments soured the meeting. In the case of Quebec, federal–provincial relations also grew more strained with the election of Maurice Duplessis.

A lawyer from Trois Rivières, Quebec, Duplessis was first elected to the provincial legislature in 1927 and six years later became leader of the province's Conservative party. In 1935, he formed an alliance with *L'Action Libéral Nationale* (ALN). Led by Paul Gouin, the son of former Quebec premier Lomer Gouin, ALN followers were renegade Liberals who broke ranks from Liberal Premier Alexandre Louis Taschereau, whom they cast as too close to the business community and too focused on attracting American investment, as lacking commitment to the maintenance of French-Catholic society and culture, and as backing policies that were failing to combat the Depression. In the 1935 provincial election, the Conservative–ALN alliance promised to bust corporate monopolies, increase wages, provide state-run hydro, and create a progressive labour code. The Liberals, who had run Quebec since 1897, held on—but just barely—by a margin of 47 to 42 seats.

Over the ensuing months, Duplessis spearheaded a relentless attack on government mismanagement and corruption, revealing that Taschereau's brother had deposited interest on money belonging to the legislature into his personal account, which prompted the premier to resign. Another election was called for August 1936. The ALN–Conservative alliance ran under the banner of the Union Nationale, though Gouin had been squeezed out of the new party and few ALN members were candidates. Presenting itself as a force for reform, the Union Nationale triumphed with 76 out of 90 seats.

As premier, Duplessis largely abandoned social reform, allied with big business, and courted foreign investment. Still, he connected to French-Catholic Quebec. Folksy, charismatic, and comfortably paternalistic, he promoted a popular defensive nationalism that stressed the need to protect a traditional and highly moral Québécois culture and society. He backed continuing church control over social services and the education of French Catholics; emphasized the need to strengthen the rural sector because of the strong values agricultural life supposedly inculcated; zealously protected Quebec's powers within the federation; and pursued an unrelenting campaign to crush "godless" radicals. In 1937, following the repeal of section 98 of the *Criminal Code*, Duplessis's government passed an

August 1936: Maurice Duplessis elected as Quebec's premier.

Act Respecting Communist Propaganda. Known as the Padlock Act, it gave the provincial government the power to close for up to one year any place used "to propagate communism or bolshevism by any means whatsoever." When asked by one member of the Liberal opposition how communism would be defined, Duplessis replied that it could be "felt." Within a year, Quebec police had initiated over 120 raids. Besides suspected communists, Jehovah's Witnesses, who church leaders like Cardinal Villeneuve cast as "heretics,"[23] were targeted.

Social and Political Change, 1936–1938

The Depression played a fundamental role in generating other and, by latter-day standards, progressive legislative change. One was the move to legalize the dissemination of birth control information and devices, which under the *Criminal Code* still carried a maximum penalty of two years' imprisonment. Prior to the First World War, such information spread surreptitiously, though the birth control campaign became more public in the 1920s, including through Canadian speaking tours by well-known birth control advocates Britain's Marie Stopes and America's Margaret Sanger.

Legalizing artificial birth control faced strong opposition. Eugenics-based arguments from Protestant Anglo-Saxon leaders, including many female leaders, warned of "race suicide" and of larger immigrant families degenerating the gene pool. The Vatican continued to prohibit birth control for Catholics. Francophones were told that a low birth rate would mean even more Anglo domination. Only the United Church of Canada accepted birth control, justifying its position on the basis that it would foster more stable marriages and families. Overall, the message from most churches was that artificial birth control was a sin because it destroyed life and encouraged sexual promiscuity.

Nevertheless, the Depression compelled more Canadians to limit family size. Law enforcement authorities were turning a blind eye to clinics that disseminated birth control information in several communities in Ontario, British Columbia, and Manitoba. Those associated with such clinics seemed less motivated by women's rights as opposed to ensuring better breeding and social order. Rising unemployment generated concern over parents being unable to care for their children, with the anticipated results being overwhelming strain on state resources, rising crime, disorder among youth and, based upon eugenics theory, social degeneration.

Among those subscribing to such a doomsday scenario was A.R. Kaufman of Kitchener, the owner of a rubber company that made rain ware, not condoms. In 1932, he founded the Canadian Birth Control League. Four years later, one of his employees, Dorothea Palmer, was arrested in the heavily French-Catholic community of Eastview, outside of Ottawa, for distributing League literature. She was acquitted in her initial trial and subsequently before the Ontario Court of Appeal as the judges declared that in some circumstances birth control was a social good, namely by reducing the number of children among the poor and unemployed, a verdict that essentially ushered in the legalization of artificial means of birth control.

June 1937: Acquittal of birth control advocate Dorothea Palmer upheld by the Ontario Court of Appeal.

Pressure for social change mounted from organized labour, which later on in the Depression became more powerful. This was particularly the case in Ontario where the American-based Congress of Industrial Organizations (CIO) focused its efforts. Since its creation in 1935, the CIO achieved remarkable success in organizing American workers in major industries, such as auto, rubber, and steel. It became known for using the sit-down strike, meaning its members occupied a work site to prevent operations from continuing, a method denounced by opponents as an illegal and radical attack on private property, but that often produced positive results for strikers.

In December 1936, the CIO launched a campaign to organize 4000 General Motors' (GM) autoworkers in Oshawa, Ontario. Mitchell Hepburn waded into the battle, casting the CIO as filled with communists whose invasion from America would undermine Ontario's economic recovery. A union recognition strike began at GM on April 8, 1937. Hepburn wired federal Justice Minister Ernest Lapointe warning of the potential for violence and demanding that RCMP personnel be dispatched to augment local police. Lapointe authorized sending one detachment, though King was dubious and rejected Hepburn's demand for a second detachment because of the prime minister's desire to avoid alienating labour and, more personally, because of his growing distaste for Hepburn, whose heavy drinking and carousing ways he considered boorish, and because Hepburn, despite being a fellow Liberal, was fast becoming a champion for provincial rights.

Hepburn accused the federal government of treachery and publicly stated he was "no longer a Mackenzie King Liberal." The premier ordered the Ontario Provincial Police to the GM plant and authorized the recruitment of a temporary constabulary force that the strikers nicknamed "Hepburn's Hussars or Sons of Mitches." After a few weeks, GM made it clear that it wanted the dispute settled. In a face-saving compromise for Hepburn, GM workers were allowed to organize a union as long as it was not accredited as being part of the CIO. What resulted was CIO in all but name—a formality soon rectified—and the strikers won a 44-hour workweek and a seniority system. By the end of 1937, some 65 000 Canadian workers were CIO members, and compared with 1932, total union membership in Canada had increased by one-third to 385 000.

The Depression dragged on. After a few years of modest economic recovery, October 1937 brought another major downturn on stock markets, followed rising unemployment. King remained cautious in responding. Ottawa created a youth training program, but funded it at only $1 million rather than the $10 million recommended by the NEC. Under a new *Municipal Improvement Assistance Act*, the federal government made $30 million available at 2 percent interest for public works projects, but it was known that most locales could not afford to take on extra debt.

On the face of things, Ottawa seemed off the hook when it came to primary responsibility for the unemployed. In June 1936, Canada's Supreme Court rejected Bennett's unemployment insurance scheme, claiming that such an initiative fell under provincial jurisdiction. The federal government appealed the case to the Judicial Committee of the Privy Council (JCPC). Lord Chancellor Sankey, as evident in his "Living Tree" argument in the *Person's Case,* was inclined towards "progressive constructionalism."[24] But he had been recently replaced with a change of government in Britain from Labour to Conservative. Lord Aiken now presided over the JCPC, was not in favour of loosely interpreting federal powers, and upheld the Canadian Supreme Court's decision to disallow Bennett's legislation.

The JCPC's verdict brought widespread criticism that it was out of touch with Canadian needs and produced many demands that future appeals to the JCPC be prohibited. A

April 1937: General Motors strike in Oshawa.

significant number of legal scholars opined that the distribution of powers between the federal and provincial governments had to be changed so that Ottawa could effectively deal with the Depression.

1937: Royal Commission on Dominion–Provincial Relations.

In 1937, the King government appointed a Royal Commission on Dominion–Provincial Relations to analyze "the economic and financial basis of Confederation and the distribution of legislative powers in light of economic and social developments of the last seventy years."[25] One of the commissioners was Newton Rowell, then chief justice of Ontario. Formerly leader of the Ontario Liberals, Rowell had been one of the principal voices advocating that the party move further away from the *laissez-faire* approach. The other commissioner was Dr. Joseph Sirois, a well-known Quebec notary. Several provincial governments, namely those in the Maritimes that were more dependent on federal largess, indicated a willingness to consider a revised power-sharing structure if Ottawa assumed responsibility for the unemployed, provided them with greater subsidies, or gave them exclusive control over some direct tax fields. However, Pattullo and Aberhart were leery about the Royal Commission and Duplessis and Hepburn were hostile, fearing a federal power-grab. At hearings held in provincial capitals, Duplessis kept the commission waiting for an hour; Hepburn presented a brief that was in large part a personal attack against King; and, according to deputy commissioner Wilfrid Eggleston, the Alberta legislature "formally voted to have nothing to do with us." But the public wanted results, and criticism mounted towards "strident provincialism."[26]

Pursuing Peace and Appeasing Aggressors, 1936–1938

Tensions continued mounting outside Canada as Nazi Germany became more aggressive in pursuing its ambitions. In Canada, more people began worrying about the possibility of another world war—this included King, who recalled the massive losses and longstanding divisions, especially between French and English, that came to Canada as a result of the First World War. King stuck by his longstanding approach to foreign policy, namely that it not undermine national unity, and as such, he stressed that every effort had to be made to retain peace.

There were dissenting voices, and among the most prominent was J.W. Dafoe, publisher of the Winnipeg *Free Press*. Despite a long and close association with the Liberal party, Dafoe criticized King for adopting the policy of appeasement and weakening the ability of the League of Nations to deal with the growing Nazi threat. In March 1936, King did not protest Germany's remilitarization of the Rhineland, despite this being a blatant violation of the 1925 Locarno Treaty. France sought a tough response, but King, like most world leaders, chose to put faith in Hitler's offer of a 25-year non-aggression pledge.

The next year, the Liberals implemented the *Foreign Enlistment Act* to prevent Canadians from joining the Spanish Civil War. Those who broke the law faced up to two years in jail. Some 1500 Canadians fought in Spain. Nearly all joined the Mackenzie-Papineau battalion, Canada's contribution to the International Brigades that comprised some 35 000 volunteers from 22 countries. Most, including from Canada, were communists, and they fought alongside the Spanish Republicans against Francisco Fanco's Nazi-supported Nationalists. Ill-trained, ill-equipped, and poorly led, nearly 50 percent of the Canadians who battled in Spain were killed.

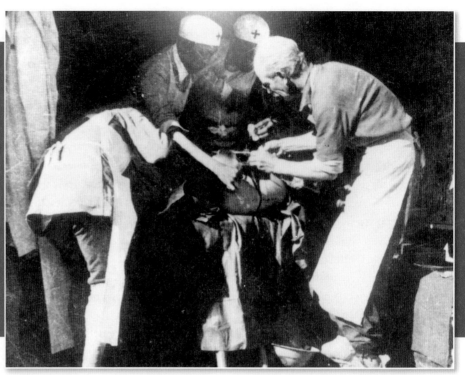

Source: Library and Archives of Canada, PA-114795.

Among the Canadians drawn to Spain was thoracic surgeon and ardent communist Dr. Norman Bethune. In 1938, with Franco on the verge of victory, Bethune left Spain to join Mao Tse-Tung's communist forces in China, a country in which he remains revered as a hero. In November 1939, Bethune cut himself while operating, contracted blood poisoning, and died shortly thereafter.

June 1937: King meets with Hitler.

King fervently believed he could negotiate a lasting peace in Europe. In his diary, he wrote of a séance in which the ghosts of his mother and British foreign secretary Lord Grey told him that he was chosen for such a noble service. Arrangements were made for King to meet Hitler in June 1937. The easily flattered King dwelt upon the fact that in personal meetings Hitler gave him twice the time initially allotted. Impressed or seduced by Hitler, King described him as "a calm, passive man" whose eyes had "a liquid quality … which indicates keen perception and profound sympathy," and that he "could see particularly how humble folk would come to have a profound love [for him]."[27] King expressed willingness to consider German claims in Europe but made it clear that Canada would fight if Britain was attacked.

While in Germany, King said nothing about the persecution of Jews, even though since the 1935 Nuremberg Laws they were forced to wear a prominent yellow Star of David in public. Although sometimes writing in his diary with sorrow about their increasingly desperate plight—such as following orchestrated attacks on November 9–10, 1938, known as *Kristallnacht*, in which some 100 synagogues were destroyed and nearly 100 Jews were murdered—ultimately for King the question of whether or not to help Jews by accepting more into Canada was a political one, and he concluded that opening the doors a little wider would gain him few, and likely cost him many, votes. Between 1933 and 1939, 4000 European Jews were permitted into Canada compared with 200 000 into the United States, 70 000 into Britain, 50 000 into Argentina, and 27 000 into Brazil. In January 1939, a petition against Jewish migration organized in Quebec by the *Societé St-Jean Baptiste*, which

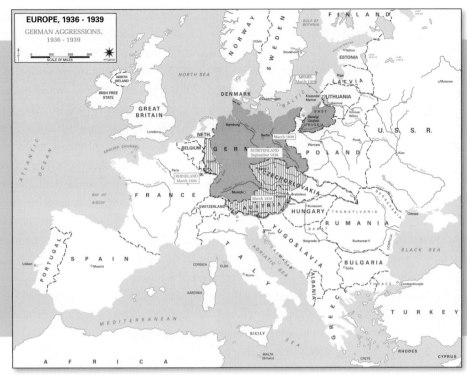

Map 6.1
*Nazi Expansion in Europe,
1936–1939*

Source: United States Military Academy.

cast it as a threat to the province's French and Catholic society, and presented to Parliament by Wilfrid Lacroix, the member for Quebec-Montmorency, contained 127 364 names.

Ottawa claimed that its approach towards Jewish migration was motivated by the desire not to add to unemployment. Yet, in the late 1930s, Canada allowed entry to Sudeten Czech refugees fleeing from the Nazis. It justified the difference by portraying Sudetens as highly desirable agricultural people as opposed to the more urban, and less employable, Jews. More odious, though perhaps more truthful, was Canada's top civil servant responsible for immigration, F.C. Blair, an avowed anti-Semite, who warned his elected superiors that to let in additional Jews would encourage a flood tide that would threaten Canada's Christian character.

King, like most world leaders, remained committed to appeasing Hitler. He remained silent over the *Anschluss*, Germany's 1938 military occupation of Austria. Soon after, the majority German-speaking population in the Czechoslovak region of Sudetenland demanded incorporation into Germany. Britain's Prime Minister Neville Chamberlain urged the Czech government to negotiate with the Nazis. King supported Chamberlain, characterizing the issue as one of Sudeten self-determination. In September, Chamberlain, following a third meeting with Hitler in Munich, triumphantly returned to London declaring that he had achieved "peace for our time" by agreeing (without consulting the Czech government) to transfer Sudetenland to Germany. King immediately wired Chamberlain to express his "unbounded admiration at the service you have rendered mankind."[28] Sensitive to public opinion, he also cabled Ernest Lapointe, then on board the *Queen Mary* on his way home from the League of Nations, to declare: "Great rejoicing [in] Canada today."[29]

March 1938: Anschluss.
September 1938: Munich
*agreement gives Germany
Sudetenland.*

Meanwhile, in Asia, in July 1937, Japan launched a brutal campaign to further expand its presence in China. Shanghai was attacked, which threatened foreign interests and lives, including 250 Canadians living in the city. Regardless, Ottawa opposed economic sanctions against Japan, once again. In fact, between 1937 and 1939, Canada did record business in metal exports to Japan—namely nickel, copper, aluminum, lead, and zinc—which helped feed Japan's military. On December 12, Japan's army entered Nanking and over the next six weeks raped 20 000 women and killed 40 000 civilians. At the League of Nations, New Zealand urged comprehensive sanctions against Japan, a position that reflected its proximity to and fear of Japanese aggression. Canada maintained that nothing could be accomplished unless the major powers took the lead, which they were unprepared to do, but Canada's stance reflected the fact that there was virtually no support among the public to get involved.

King moved slowly on re-arming Canada, fearful of sending a message that he was preparing the country for war. In 1936, he rejected a British request to create a Canadian-based Commonwealth air training scheme. Mindful of gathering war clouds, in 1937 his government voted against a CCF parliamentary resolution stating that if war came, Canada would remain neutral. Also that year, Canada's defence budget was increased from $20 million to $36 million, though military leaders estimated that a minimum of $57 million was needed to achieve a decent level of preparedness.

In assessing King's foreign and defence policies, historian James Eayrs used the terms "low" and "dishonest." He accused the prime minister of placing his own narrow political interests, such as retaining support in Quebec, over properly preparing Canada for a war that any reasonable person would have realized was coming. Eayrs also castigated King for naïveté in his dealings with Hitler, for coddling the fascist dictators, and for working to undermine the strength of the League of Nations. However, J.L. Granatstein and Robert Bothwell portrayed King's strategy in a much more positive light, arguing that King pursued peace until every possible avenue was exhausted, enabling him to bring a united country into the Second World War—a country whose population had come to accept that there was no other option.[30]

On the Cusp of a New Order

As the decade drew to a close, there were still 900 000 Canadians officially registered with public agencies as unemployed out of a non-agricultural workforce of 3.8 million. In May 1938, more than 1000 homeless men in Vancouver occupied the city's main post office, the municipal art gallery, and the Hotel Georgia. On June 19, the police attacked the last holdouts at the post office, releasing tear gas and clubbing the men as they fled the building, producing more than 100 wounded and 22 arrests.

Governments remained reluctant to assume the costs of caring for the jobless, and the perception of welfare as encouraging slothfulness remained strong. But it had also become clear that the scope and length of the Depression had changed the views of many. Practically everyone knew people who had lost their job and that it was not easy to obtain another. With millions of Canadians having received relief during the 1930s, the idea of this being shameful was dissipating, and demands grew louder that governments had to do more to help those in need.

At the end of 1937, a member of the NEC informed King that it would soon issue a report recommending that the federal government create an unemployment insurance scheme. King instructed Minister of Labour Norman Rogers to pressure the NEC's chair to quash the recommendation, claiming it was not financially feasible. Rogers resisted, for he too believed that Ottawa had to do more. As a compromise, King accepted a recommendation to hand over the question of unemployment insurance to the Royal Commission on Dominion–Provincial Relations. In the short term, he agreed to establish a parliamentary committee under Rogers to make recommendations on increases to public welfare. Rogers soon advised spending an extra $75 million, but in caucus Finance Minister Dunning, who remained wedded to balanced budgets, opposed him. King's cabinet leaned towards Rogers, who threatened to resign if no action was taken. King split the difference, authorizing an additional $40 million for public relief in the 1938 budget. Although amounting to only 7.2 percent of total government expenditures and falling far short of need, some historians cast the initiative as a significant shift towards the deficit-financing strategy of John Maynard Keynes to stimulate the economy.

That summer, with the threat of war becoming more ominous, U.S. President Roosevelt, in a speech at Queen's University in Kingston with King by his side, assured Canadians that if they were attacked the United States would provide protection. While the need to improve hemispheric defence was a growing concern, Roosevelt's pledge also made King uneasy because the president emphasized the vulnerability of, and America's willingness to shore up, Canada's west coast against the possibility of a Japanese attack. Determined to safeguard Canadian autonomy, King ordered that some naval vessels in Halifax be sent to British Columbia.

Canada's 1938 budget allocated an extra $60 million to the military, though to many this was only a down payment on what was needed after years of neglect and the increasing speed and scope of Germany's military build-up. Even after two years, the federal government had failed to select a Canadian manufacturer to produce 7000 Bren light machine-guns ordered by the British. Faced with the prospect of losing the contract, an agreement was signed later that year with the Toronto-based John Inglis Company. In its haste to settle matters, the government failed to put out a general call for tenders, an omission that generated rumblings of a corrupt inside job. Fearing the image of having created another Shell Committee—the federal government's initial purchasing agency of military items in the First World War that was discredited for mismanagement and fraud—King ordered the creation of a Royal Commission to investigate for improprieties in the Inglis contract. The commission cited no scams, but in responding to procedural lapses that its report identified, the federal government created a new Defence Purchasing Board that implemented such a cumbersome approval process for military contracts of more than $5000 that many companies decided not to make a bid.

On January 16, 1939, the opening day of that year's parliamentary session, King, in seeking to prepare the public for the possibility of conflict, quoted Laurier's comment made at the outset of the First World War that "when Britain is at war, Canada is at war." The comment drew widespread criticism from Quebec, horrified Lapointe, and soon prompted King to pledge that if war did come, he would not implement conscription.

In March 1939, Germany effectively tore up the Munich agreement by expanding its occupation of Sudetenland into the rest of Czechoslovakia. Britain renounced the policy of appeasement and provided defence guarantees to Poland and Romania. However, King urged continued negotiations with Hitler and privately criticized Chamberlain for drawing a line in the sand. In Montreal and Quebec City, sizable anti-war rallies were organized, and the *nationaliste* newspaper *Le Devoir* predicted that many French-Canadian MPs would abandon King if Canada went to war. Given the latest developments overseas, even Lapointe changed his message, indicating that Canada could not simply stand on the sidelines should France and Britain go to war.

May–June 1939: Royal tour of Canada.

That spring, feelings of loyalty to Britain were stoked by a month-long visit to Canada by King George VI and Queen Elizabeth, the first ever visit to Canada by a reigning British monarch. On May 17, both King and Lapointe donned ceremonial civilian uniforms known as Windsor Dress to greet the royal couple in Quebec City. Across the land, thousands lined railway tracks to wave and catch a fleeting glimpse of the British monarchs. In late May, 100 000 people waited in drizzle in Regina, and a few days later the population of Melville, Saskatchewan, swelled from 4000 to 60 000 to cheer the royals.

September 10, 1939: Canada enters the Second World War.

Regardless of such feelings of kinship with Britain, King sent Hitler correspondence pleading for renewed discussions and for him and the German dictator to meet again, as King believed that his negotiating skills could prevent the world from descending into another bloodbath. He received a reply on July 21 proposing some friendly student and officer exchanges, and the possibility of another summit. Tentative plans were made for King to visit Germany in November, but it was not to be. On September 1, Germany invaded Poland. Two days later, Britain declared war on the Third Reich. A week later, Canada joined the battle, following a symbolic parliamentary debate to demonstrate its independence; however, it was hardly an intimidating belligerent. Its navy had merely 2000 personnel and 13 fighting ships; its air force 3000 personnel and 37 debatably combat-ready aircraft; and its permanent army 5000 personnel with only two light tanks and four anti-aircraft guns.

Conclusion

In 1939, Canada's federal government spent $317.2 million on social assistance, $100 million more than was spent in 1926. When considered as a percentage of the country's gross national product, both years produce a figure of around 6 percent. Government support may have consistently failed to meet need, but this does not mean that things remained consistent. Over the course of a decade-long and devastating Depression, a growing number of Canadians from all walks of life grew ready, and indeed eager, for change—and often radical change—to more effectively redress the economic malaise. Fewer people were blaming the economic hardship suffered over that decade on personal failure or indolence. Governments would spend record sums on welfare, assumed unprecedented and often crippling debts, and by the end of the decade, Prime Minister King was dabbling with Keynesian economic planning.

Canadian foreign policy reflected a population willing to fight a *just* war, but also one that had shed much of the militarist and romanticist perspective on combat that had been prevalent before the First World War. There was a resolve, especially in Quebec, that Canada not be dragged into another European, or British, conflict not in keeping with Canadian interests. Like most of the free world, Canada arguably abdicated moral international responsibilities in the face of tyranny. Yet King's strategy of pursuing peace until the last possible moment, while slowly re-arming, would bring a mostly united, and at least marginally prepared, country into the Second World War. For the most part, the country's population had come to accept that using force was the only plausible option to deal with the threat posed by the Axis powers.

Responses to the Great Depression laid significant groundwork for important changes in the roles and responsibilities of governments. The 1930s also marked Canada's long journey from isolationism and appeasement to help confront the scourge of fascism. These and other changes to Canada's political, social, cultural, and economic landscape would pale in comparison with the transformative impact and legacy of the Second World War.

Questions to Consider

1. What was the economic impact of the Depression in different parts of Canada?

2. How was social welfare administered, and how well did it meet the needs in Canada during the Depression?

3. How did the Depression impact women, First Nations, and immigrants?

4. What factors influenced the pattern of Canadian foreign policy during the 1930s?

Critical Thinking Questions

1. How did the Depression impact Canada's military?

2. How did the Depression impact Canada's political system?

3. What were the similarities and differences between Bennett and King as prime minister? Did this account for their relative success?

Suggested Readings

General

Broadfoot, Barry. *Ten Lost Years, 1929–1939: Memories of Canadians Who Survived the Depression.* Toronto: Doubleday, 1985.

Gray, James. *Red Lights on the Prairies.* Saskatoon: Western Producer Prairie Books, 1986.

Neatby, H. Blair. *The Politics of Chaos: Canada in the Thirties.* Toronto: Macmillan of Canada, 1972.

Owram, Doug, and Kenneth Norrie. *A History of the Canadian Economy.* Toronto: Harcourt Brace Jovanovich, 1991.

Safarian, A.E. *The Canadian Economy in the Great Depression.* Toronto: McClelland & Stewart, 1970.

Thompson, John Herd, and Allen Seager. *Canada, 1922–1939: Decades of Discord.* Toronto: McClelland & Stewart, 1985.

National Politics

Bacher, John. *Keeping to the Marketplace: The Evolution of Canadian Housing Policy.* Montreal and Kingston: McGill-Queen's University Press, 1993.

Finkel, Alvin. *Business and Social Reform in the Thirties.* Toronto: J. Lorimer, 1979.

Glassford, Larry A. *Reaction and Reform: The Politics of the Conservative Party under R.B. Bennett, 1927–1938.* Toronto: University of Toronto Press, 1992.

Horn, Michiel. *The League for Social Reconstruction: Intellectual Origins of the Democratic Left in Canada, 1930–1942.* Toronto: University of Toronto Press, 1980.

Mills, Allen. *Fool for Christ: The Political Thought of J.S. Woodsworth.* Toronto: University of Toronto Press, 1991.

Neatby, H. Blair. *William Lyon Mackenzie King, 1932–1939: The Prism of Unity.* Toronto: University of Toronto Press, 1976.

Owram, Doug. *The Government Generation: Canadian Intellectuals and the State, 1900–1945.* Toronto: University of Toronto Press, 1986.

Peers, Frank. *The Politics of Canadian Broadcasting, 1920–1951.* Toronto: University of Toronto Press, 1969.

Struthers, James. *No Fault of Their Own: Unemployment and the Canadian Welfare State, 1914–1941.* Toronto: University of Toronto Press, 1983.

Young, Walter. *The Anatomy of a Party: The National CCF, 1932–1961.* Toronto: University of Toronto Press, 1969.

Provinces

Black, Conrad. *Render unto Caesar: The Life and Legacy of Maurice Duplessis.* Toronto: Key Porter Books, 1998.

Finkel, Alvin. *The Social Credit Phenomenon in Alberta.* Toronto: University of Toronto Press, 1989.

Fisher, Robin. *Duff Pattullo of British Columbia.* Toronto: University of Toronto Press, 1991.

Hesketh, Bob. *Major Douglas and Alberta Social Credit.* Toronto: University of Toronto Press, 1997.

Irving, John. *The Social Credit Movement in Alberta.* Toronto: University of Toronto Press, 1959.

Lipset, Seymour Martin. *Agrarian Socialism: The Cooperative Commonwealth Federation in Saskatchewan. A Study in Political Sociology.* Berkeley: University of California Press, 1950.

Quinn, Herbert. *The Union Nationale: A Study in Quebec Nationalism.* Toronto: University of Toronto Press, 1963.

Saywell, John T. *Just Call Me Mitch: The Life of Mitchell F. Hepburn.* Toronto: University of Toronto Press, 1991.

Stingel, Janine. *Social Discredit: Anti-Semitism, Social Credit, and the Jewish Response.* Montreal and Kingston: McGill-Queen's University Press, 2000.

Struthers, James. *The Limits of Affluence: Welfare in Ontario, 1920–1970.* Toronto: University of Toronto Press, 1994.

Vigod, Bernard. *Before Duplessis: The Political Career of Louis Alexandre Taschereau.* Montreal and Kingston: McGill-Queen's University Press, 1986.

Waiser, W.A. *Saskatchewan: A New History.* Calgary: Fifth House, 2005.

Foreign and Defence Policy

Drummond, Ian, and Norman Hillmer. *Negotiating Freer Trade: The United Kingdom, the United States, Canada, and the Trade Agreements of 1938.* Waterloo: Wilfrid Laurier University Press, 1989.

Eayrs, James. *In Defence of Canada*, Vols. 1, 2. Toronto: University of Toronto Press, 1964.

McFarland, John. *Ernest Lapointe and Quebec's Influence on Foreign Policy.* Toronto: University of Toronto Press, 1999.

Meehan, John D. *The Dominion and the Rising Sun: Canada Encounters Japan, 1929–1941.* Vancouver: University of British Columbia Press, 2004.

Stacey, Charles Perry. *Canada and the Age of Conflict*, Vol. 2. Toronto: Macmillan of Canada, 1981.

Women

Baillargeon, Denyse. *Making Do: Women, Family and Home in Montreal during the Great Depression.* Waterloo: Wilfrid Laurier University Press, 1999.

Lévesque, Andrée. *Making and Breaking the Rules: Women in Quebec, 1919–1939.* Toronto: McClelland & Stewart, 1994.

Strong-Boag, Veronica. *The New Day Recalled: Lives of Girls and Women in English Canada, 1919–1939.* Toronto: Copp Clark Pitman, 1988.

Labour

Endicott, Stephen Lyon. *Bienfait: The Saskatchewan Miners' Struggle of '31.* Toronto: University of Toronto Press, 2002.

Patrias, Carmela. *Relief Strike: Immigrant Workers and the Great Depression in Cowland, Ontario, 1930–1935.* Toronto: New Hogtown Press, 1990.

Waiser, W.A. *All Hell Can't Stop Us: The On-to-Ottawa Trek and Regina Riot.* Calgary: Fifth House, 2003.

Nativism and First Peoples

Abella, Irving, and Harold Troper. *None Is Too Many: Canada and the Jews of Europe, 1933–1948.* Toronto: Lester & Orpen Dennys, 1982.

Delisle, Esther. *The Traitor and the Jew: Anti-Semitism and the Delirium of Extremist Right-Wing Nationalism in French Canada from 1929 to 1939.* Montreal: Robert Davies Publishing, 1993.

Roberts, Barbara. *Whence They Came: Deportation from Canada, 1900–1935.* Ottawa: University of Ottawa Press, 1988.

Robin, Martin. *Shades of Right: Nativist and Fascist Politics in Canada, 1920–1940.* Toronto: University of Toronto Press, 1992.

Waiser, Bill. *Who Killed Jackie Bates?* Calgary: Fifth House, 2008.

Notes

[1]   Pierre Berton, *The Great Depression, 1929–1939* (Toronto: McClelland & Stewart, 1990), 185–189.

[2]   Doug Owram and Kenneth Norrie, *A History of the Canadian Economy* (Toronto: Harcourt Brace Jovanovich, 1991), 391.

[3]   Larry A. Glassford, *Reaction and Reform: The Politics of the Conservative Party under R.B. Bennett, 1927–1938* (Toronto: University of Toronto Press, 1992), 77.

[4]   Barry Broadfoot, *Ten Lost Years: Memories of Canadians Who Survived the Depression* (Toronto: Doubleday, 1985), 70.

[5]   James H. Gray, *The Winter Years: The Depression on the Prairies* (Toronto: McClelland & Stewart, 1966), 147.

[6]   Elizabeth St. Jacques, *Survivors: The Great Depression, 1929–1939* (Sault Ste. Marie: Maplebud Press, 1991), 59–60.

[7]   Olive Dickason, *Canada's First Nations: A History of Founding Peoples from Earliest Times* (Toronto: Oxford University Press, 2002), 350.

[8]   Bryan Palmer, *Working-Class Experience: Rethinking the History of Canadian Labour, 1800–1991* (Toronto: McClelland & Stewart 1992), 233.

[9]   Broadfoot, *Ten Lost Years*, 2, 224.

[10]   Laura Sefton MacDowell, "Relief Camp Workers in Ontario during the Great Depression of the 1930s," *Canadian Historical Review* 76, 2 (1995): 208.

[11]   Gray, *Winter Years*, 106.

[12]   http://www.thestar.com/News/Canada/article/602625.

[13]   Christopher Armstrong, *Blue Skies and Boiler Rooms: Buying and Selling Securities in Canada, 1870–1940* (Toronto: University of Toronto Press, 1991), 218.

[14]   Bill Waiser, *All Hell Can't Stop Us: The On-to-Ottawa Trek and Regina Riot* (Calgary: Fifth House, 2003), 35.

[15]   Berton, *Great Depression*, 159.

[16]   "The Regina Manifesto," http://www.saskndp.com/assets/file/history/manifest.pdf.

[17]   Jean Barman, *The West Beyond the West: A History of British Columbia* (Toronto: University of Toronto Press, 1991), 254.

[18]   Robin Fisher, *Duff Pattullo of British Columbia* (Toronto: University of Toronto Press, 1991), 215.

[19]   John T. Saywell, *The Lawmakers: Judicial Power and the Shaping of Canadian Federalism* (Toronto: University of Toronto Press, 2002), 203.

[20]   Palmer, *Working Class Experience*, 246.

[21] Waiser, *All Hell Can't Stop Us*, 134, 138.

[22] H. Blair Neatby, *William Lyon Mackenzie King, 1932–1939: The Prism of Unity* (Toronto: University of Toronto Press), 139.

[23] Ibid., 235.

[24] Saywell, *Lawmakers*, 216.

[25] "Dominion-Provincial Relations: Royal Commission on," http://www.thecanadianencyclopedia.com/index.cfm?PgNm=TCE&Params=A1ARTA0002349.

[26] Lita-Rose Betcherman, *Ernest Lapointe: Mackenzie King's Great Quebec Lieutenant* (Toronto: University of Toronto Press, 2002), 236; John Herd Thompson and Allen Seager, *Canada, 1922–1939: Decades of Discord* (Toronto: McClelland & Stewart, 1985), 298.

[27] J.L. Granatstein and Norman Hillmer, *For Better or for Worse: Canada and the United States to the 1990s* (Toronto: Copp Clark Pitman, 1991), 142.

[28] Neatby, *William Lyon Mackenzie King*, 293.

[29] Betcherman, *Lapointe*, 251.

[30] James Eayrs, "'A Low Dishonest Decade': Aspects of Canadian External Policy, 1931–1939," in H.L. Keenleyside, ed., *The Growth of Canadian Policies in External Affairs* (Durham: Duke University Press, 1960): 14–34; J.L. Granatstein and Robert Bothwell, "'A Self-Evident National Duty': Canadian Foreign Policy, 1935–1939," *Journal of Imperial and Commonwealth History* 3 (1976): 212–233.

7

War *and* Upheaval, II: *1939–1945*

*I*n September 1939, Laura Haferkorn eagerly anticipated her fourth birthday. Hers was a happy, safe, quiet, and structured childhood in the southwestern Ontario village of Centralia, where her father served as a United Church minister. But when Hitler's army invaded Poland, and Britain declared war on Nazi Germany, "Dad decided it was his patriotic duty to enlist." Two years later, he went overseas as a pastor for Canadian troops. To save money and to provide support for her mother, Laura, her baby brother, and her mom left for the "noise and bustling … streets" of Toronto, where they moved in with her mother's elderly parents. The war came to define Laura's childhood. At school, she and her classmates put together ditty bags—containing a washcloth, a cake of soap, a tube of toothpaste, a chocolate bar, and chewing gum—for Canadians serving overseas. Outside of school, she collected scrap, mainly metal and rubber items, for salvage drives and saved quarters to purchase War Savings Stamps. It was an exciting, but also difficult and fearful, time in her life. As soon as she was able to read, she "scanned the newspapers for familiar names," including that of her father's, in columns listing the dead, wounded, or missing. She struggled to find the right words to fill weekly letters she was obliged to send to her dad, a man who had become a stranger to her. Still, every night she dutifully prayed for his safe return and for a family life she had come to idealize. On VE-Day, May 7, 1945,

chapter 7

Source: Library and Archives of Canada C-017291.

the PA system at her school rang out: "The war in Europe is over! The war in Europe in over!" Her classmates cheered, many jumped on their desks, though Johnny, whose father had been killed the previous winter, remained sullen. Arriving home, she found her mother crying from both joy and worry as soon she would be reunited with a man she had not seen for four years. Initial happiness turned sour. Laura recalled, "Dad wasn't used to children and said we got on his nerves." His faith shaken by what he had witnessed overseas, "Dad decided to leave the church." But new opportunities beckoned, as the Department of Veterans Affairs gave him a free university education, where he eventually retrained as a social worker.[1]

After reading this chapter you will be able to:

1. Show how the war transformed the Canadian economy and the roles of government.
2. Explain the connection of the war to more extensive social welfare.
3. Understand Prime Minister King's strategy of balancing war needs with domestic challenges.
4. Assess Canada's military contributions to the war.
5. Evaluate the degree to which the war changed the status of women.
6. Recall how Canada dealt with perceived threats to internal security.

Introduction

The war transformed Canada as much as the lives of Canadians like the Haferkorns. From a population of 11.5 million, more than 950 000 Canadian men and 50 000 women donned a military uniform. Millions whose lives were ravaged by the Depression found well-paying jobs in the bustling war economy. For this highly mechanized conflict—whose costs claimed as much as 50 percent of Canada's gross national product (the total value of all goods and services over a year) compared with 10 percent in the First World War—Canada created the allies' third-largest navy, fourth-largest air force, and fourth-largest army. During the war, the modern interventionist federal government emerged, as did the basics of Canada's modern welfare state. New fundamental rights appeared for labour, as did new, though arguably less profound and permanent, opportunities for women. Canada gained new international stature from its contributions to the war, emerging from the conflict as a self-proclaimed middle power more committed to internationalism and collective security rather than pre-war isolationism and appeasement, though its economic and military ties to the United States grew far tighter. Canada's far north was accessed as never before, and Newfoundland was brought further into its orbit. For those who fought and survived, unprecedented opportunities appeared, courtesy of Canada's new Department of Veterans Affairs.

Renowned military historian J.L. Granatstein calls the Second World War "Canada's War."[2] American historians Studs Terkel wrote of *The Good War* and Michael Adams *The Best War Ever*.[3] These characterizations also reflect the fact that allies (those countries fighting against the Nazis and fascists) saved democracy from the totalitarian and expansionary Axis powers (Germany, Italy, and Japan) and, in the case of the Germany's Third Reich, a regime determined to commit genocide against Jews, Gypsies, people with mental or physical disabilities, and others deemed genetically inferior. Also, in North America, the war would supplant an economic depression with an economic boom, ushering in the longest sustained period of prosperity in the twentieth century. But the question remains: Can one speak of war in such terms? What of the 40 000 civilians incinerated in the allied firebombing of Dresden, the 200 000 Japanese obliterated by the atomic bombs dropped on Hiroshima and Nagasaki, the allied prisoners of war (POWs) starved and tortured in Japanese POW camps, Russia's 20 million war dead, and the 6 million Jews systematically slaughtered in the Holocaust? For Canada, more than 42 000 people were killed, more than 55 000 were wounded, and untold thousands were scarred psychologically. Canada interned thousands—certainly many Nazi and fascist supporters and sympathizers, but also communists, pacifists, and anti-conscriptionists—and 23 000 Japanese Canadians were forcibly evacuated from coastal areas. In this chapter, we will outline the myriad, modernizing, destructive, and transformative impacts of the Second World War on Canada.

Gearing Up, 1939–1940

Throughout the 1930s, the Western powers had tried to appease Hitler, but with each concession, the German dictator pushed harder. Between 1936 and 1939, Germany expanded into the Rhineland, Austria, the Sudetenland, and Czechoslovakia. Starting in 1936, Britain began re-arming, though it was not until March 1939, with Hitler effectively tearing up the September 1938 Munich Agreement (that ceded to Germany the area of Czechoslovakia known as the Sudetenland) by invading all of Czechoslovakia, did Britain threaten war should the Nazis invade Poland or Romania.

Prime Minister King desperately wished to avoid war. He spoke of the death and suffering that it would again inflict upon millions as immoral, and as a politician he feared the threat to national unity and the fortunes of his Liberal party in Quebec, as a world war would most certainly raise the spectre of conscription. King also knew that if Britain went to war, Canada could not abstain. Very slowly, so as not to create alarm, his government started re-arming Canada's feeble military during the late 1930s. Among Western leaders, King stuck most resolutely to the need to negotiate with Hitler. In August 1939, only weeks before the World War started, and months after Chamberlain had abandoned negotiations with Hitler, King recommended that England's King and Queen visit Germany to try to restart discussions, and in response to an invitation from Hitler, which King had solicited, he planned a second visit to Germany in November. As noted in chapter six, historians disagree on King's actions: some classify him as naïve, as motivated by the desire to retain support in Quebec, and as irresponsibly failing to properly prepare Canada for war, though others portray King as a clever strategist who demonstrated he had exhausted every possibility for peace and thus was able to bring a relatively united nation into war.

On September 1, 1939, Germany invaded Poland. Two days later, Britain declared war on Germany. Canada did not declare war for another week, a nod to its newly acquired control over foreign affairs, though it also provided some time to more easily obtain war-related goods from the United States, whose *Neutrality Act* (which America soon ignored) prevented it from supplying such items to nations at war. On September 1, the federal government declared the *War Measures Act* in effect, and, two days later, under its provisions, introduced the Defence of Canada Regulations (DOCR). The DOCR enabled the federal government to

- intern enemy aliens;
- prohibit organizations deemed subversive;
- imprison those "mak[ing] statements intended or likely to prejudice the recruiting, training, discipline, or administration of any of His Majesty's forces";
- suspend jury trials and habeas corpus (meaning that those arrested could be held incommunicado with no right to appear before a court);
- and censor all media.[4]

By 1941, 35 associations were banned in Canada, principally for being pacifist, fascist, or anti-British. Among these was the National Union party, headed up by Canada's self-proclaimed Furher, Adrien Arcand, who advocated the relocation of Canadian Jews to Hudson Bay. The Communist Party of Canada (CPC) was declared illegal in June 1940, as it supported the August 1939 Nazi-Soviet Non-Aggression Pact and Russia's invasion of Finland, and denounced the allies for waging an imperialist war of aggression. By the end of 1940, the number of internees had reached 1200. Many were sent to remote locations, such as Petawawa, Ontario, where they planted trees and built rifle ranges, or to Kananaskis, Alberta, where they worked in national parks. About half were German nationals and German Canadians. After Canada declared war on Italy on June 10, 1940, hundreds of Italians labelled as supporters of Mussolini were interned. The federal government refused to legalize the CPC after the Soviet Union became an ally following the May 1941 Nazi invasion of Russia, or even after the Soviet Union established an embassy in Ottawa in October 1942. Only in 1943 was the CPC allowed to re-emerge as the Labour Progressive party, and it met with some success, electing two candidates in the 1943 Ontario election and one, Fred Rose, in a federal by-election.

By late 1941, 325 print sources were banned in Canada: More than half came from enemy countries, while most of the rest were small-circulation, enemy-language, pacifist, fascist, or socialist sources from a neutral United States or from Canadian organizations banned under the DOCR. Some mainstream Canadian publications were fined—mostly as warnings—for printing stories deemed damaging to the war effort, such as, in early 1942, a $200 penalty applied against the Ottawa-based French-language newspaper *Le Droit* for alleging that allied air raids on occupied France had killed women and children besides damaging industry.

Canada's Parliament convened on September 8, 1939, to vote on Canada's entry into the war. Only two Quebec MPs expressed opposition, as did the leader of the Co-operative Commonwealth Federation (CCF), J.S. Woodsworth, a committed pacifist, who, because of this position and his deteriorating health, was replaced as leader in 1940 by M.J. Coldwell. On September 10, 1939, Canada joined the fight to crush the Nazis.

September 3, 1939: Britain declares war on Germany. Canada follows a week later.

Prime Minister King initially spoke of Canada fighting a war of "limited liability," meaning one where the contribution of material, not manpower for combat, would dominate. His goal was to minimize casualties and to prevent the need for conscription, something King had pledged to Quebec three times in 1939 that his government would not implement.

Caution was also evident in initial defence planning, namely with the British Commonwealth Air Training Plan (BCATP). Britain first proposed a Commonwealth air training scheme in 1936 to prepare for the possibility of war. Canada was considered an ideal location because of its vast open space, access to America's large air industry, relative safety from enemy attack, and closer proximity than Australia for ferrying planes to England. But King did not want to give the impression that Canada was eager to re-arm. Canadian negotiators also pushed Britain to bear most of the costs despite Canada reaping the lasting benefits through the construction of airfields. After protracted negotiations, which stretched into November 1939, Canada agreed to contribute $313 million; Australia, $97.4 million; New Zealand, $21.6 million; and Britain, $218 million.

Source: Library and Archives Canada, PA-200350.

Prime Minister King (seated at left) and Undersecretary of State for External Affairs O.D. Skelton (standing at right) at the signing of the British Commonwealth Air Training Plan agreement, December 16, 1939.

King and the Liberals soon faced political challenges that had the potential to compromise Ottawa's ability to plan Canada's war effort. In Quebec, Premier Maurice Duplessis called a snap election in autumn 1939 to obtain a strong mandate to resist what he predicted would be a wartime power grab by the federal government. King, realizing that the war would likely soon heat up, and that Ottawa would require more powers, wanted Duplessis removed from office. To accomplish this, King's key cabinet ministers from Quebec—Justice Minister Ernest Lapointe, Public Works Minister P.J.A. Cardin, and Minister of Pensions and Health Charles "Chubby" Power—publicly threatened to resign if Duplessis was re-elected, the implication being that this would produce greater Anglo control in Ottawa and increase the likelihood of conscription. The tactic worked, as on October 25, Liberal Adelard Godbout became premier with a whopping 54 percent of the popular vote and 70 of 85 seats in the Quebec legislature.

October 1939: Godbout defeats Duplessis in Quebec.

King, though entering the fifth year of his mandate as prime minister, initially obtained agreement from the Conservative leader, Dr. Robert Manion—a First World War hero—to delay a federal election until late 1940. However, King knew his electoral prospects were much better if a vote occurred before the war in Europe started to intensify, especially given his opposition to conscription. His opportunity came on January 18, 1940, when George Drew, leader of the Ontario Conservative party, made a speech to the provincial legislature that was highly critical of Ottawa's limited war effort. Premier Mitchell Hepburn, whose relationship with King had become characterized by mutual loathing, introduced a motion into the legislature regretting that "the Federal Government … has made so little effort to prosecute Canada's duty in the war."[5] King seized upon this statement to call an election as a referendum on his war leadership.

March 1940:

Liberals re-elected.

Manion was caught unaware. Searching for a strategy, the Conservative leader called for a "national unity" or coalition government that would harness the "best brains." Compared with the Liberals, the Conservatives, having been politically decimated during the Depression, appeared short on talent, and in Quebec the idea of a coalition government conjured memories of Robert Borden's Union government (where Manion got his start), which was created in large part to ensure the passage of conscription. The result on March 26 was the most lopsided to date in a federal election, with the Liberals winning 181 seats, the Tories 40, Social Credit 10, the CCF 8, and independents 6. An embittered Manion retired and died three years later. He was replaced by R.B. Hanson, formerly the trade and commerce minister under Bennett, as interim leader.

From Phoney to Total War at Home, 1940–1942

After the 1940 election, the lull in combat known as the Phoney War, following Germany's brutal month-long campaign to conquer Poland, abruptly ended. On April 9, 1940, the Nazis invaded Norway and Denmark utilizing *blitzkrieg*, or lightning quick, offensive tactics. The next month, they sliced through the European low countries—Belgium, the Netherlands, and Luxembourg—and by June 23 had conquered France, thus gaining control over Western Europe. In August, the Battle of Britain commenced with the *Luftwaffe* pummelling England from the air in preparation for Operation Sea Lion, the planed invasion of England.

In Canada, the war became far more serious and frightening. In mid-1940, air raid blackout drills (that had initially been confined to coastal areas) moved inland as far as Calgary and Toronto. Canada could have considered itself a prime target, as between the fall of France and the Soviet Union joining the allied cause following Operation Barbarosso (the Nazi invasion of Russia launched on June 22, 1941), Canada was Britain's most powerful ally.

As in the First World War, Canadians at home became involved—and often consumed—in myriad volunteer activities to support the war effort. Millions of women knitted warm garments for Canadians in uniform and civilians in allied countries in need. Over the course of the war, the Imperial Order Daughters of the Empire collected and distributed 1 404 831 books and 13 364 226 magazines for Canadian servicemen. Thousands assisted the Canadian Red Cross, which was made responsible for providing relief packages consisting of biscuits, butter, cheese, chocolate, tinned meat, jam, powdered milk, prunes, raisins, sardines, salmon, salt, pepper, sugar, soap, and cigarettes to POWs from Commonwealth countries. At its peak, the Canadian Red Cross churned out 40 000 such parcels weekly and a remarkable grand total of 16 310 602 during the war.

Far more than during the First World War, Canada's federal government became involved in encouraging and directing voluntarism. In mid-1940, the Department of National War Services started registering and operating through designated "citizen committees" to coordinate and optimize the impact of volunteer groups. It declared the YMCA, Salvation Army, Knights of Columbus, and Canadian Legion as official auxiliaries for Canada's military, providing them collectively with as much as $13 million annually. Operating under the Directorate of Auxiliary Services within the Department of National Defence, the YMCA was to focus on providing servicemen with sporting activities; the

Source: Library and Archives of Canada, e-010695744.

Propaganda also played upon fears and stereotypes to promote Victory Bond purchases.

Salvation Army on recreational huts; the Knights of Columbus on social functions; and the Legion on educational services.

Canadians also invested their money in the war effort. War Savings Certificates began selling in May 1940, paying back, tax-free after seven years, $5 for every $4 invested, and raised more than $300 million. Many certificates were obtained by purchasing 16 War Savings Stamps for 25 cents each, a program popular among school children. Of far greater significance were the ten wartime and one post-war Victory Bond drives that raised $12.5 billion. The federal government spent more than $30 million to promote Victory Bonds in posters, direct mailings, movie trailers, radio spots, and advertisements in virtually every major daily, weekly, business, labour, and ethnic newspaper and magazine. The appeals were many and varied. "A drop in the bucket?" asked one advertisement. "Even one $100 bond will pay for two complete flying outfits or 3,000 bullets … or … half a ton of bombs to drop on Berlin!"[6] People were told that each dollar put into Victory Bonds would expedite the return home of loved ones. One advertisement portrayed a teary-eyed young girl pleading on behalf of Victory Bonds so that she could soon be reunited with her daddy.[7]

On June 21, 1940, Canada's Parliament passed the *National Resources Mobilization Act* (NRMA). It took a census of all available labour, both male and female, 16 and older, and established conscription for home defence for single men, aged 19 to 45, initially for one month, but increased it to four months in February 1941 and in April possibly for the entire war. In August 1940, Camelien Houde, the colourful, populist mayor of Montreal, was interned, ultimately for four years, for advocating that men not register for home defence.

August 1940: Creation of Permanent Joint Board of Defence.

May 1940: Release of the Rowell-Sirois *Commission Report.*

The fall of France and Britain's precarious situation also moved Canada closer to the United States, which reflected both Canadian defence needs and concern in Washington over the security of North America. In August 1940, American President Franklin Roosevelt invited King to Ogdensburg, New York, about a two-hour drive from Ottawa, where the president was inspecting troops. What resulted was the creation of the Permanent Joint Board of Defence. With equal representation from both countries, it was the first-ever bilateral defence pact to provide for the security of North America.

Within Canada, the growing demands of the Second World War affected the division of powers between federal and provincial governments. Ottawa needed more money to fight the war, and taxes were a key source. The problem was that taxation was a joint constitutional jurisdiction. To address this situation, the Liberals turned to the *Rowell-Sirois Report*, the release of which King delayed until after the 1940 federal election because of its sweeping, and controversial, recommendations. Given its mandate to examine the failings of governments to combat the Depression, the Rowell-Sirois Commission did not actually refer to the war; its report pointed out that over the previous generation, social welfare demands had increased well beyond the capacity of municipal and provincial governments. Its answer was to provide the federal government with exclusive control over income, corporate, and inheritance taxes, in exchange for Ottawa creating a national unemployment insurance scheme, a national adjustment grant to ensure all parts of the country meet a minimum standard in areas like education and health, and to assume up to 40 percent of the combined municipal–provincial debt.

Momentum to implement the report was buttressed by the need to empower the federal government to meet the rising demands of the war. Some argued that the intent of the Fathers of Confederation was being subverted. Historian Paul Romney argues that constitutional centralists became more powerful during the Depression, especially after the Judicial Committee of the Privy Council struck down Bennett's New Deal legislation, thus supposedly undermining the ability of the federal government to ease the plight of the jobless. In setting up the Rowell-Sirois Commission, King received much of his advice from Labour Minister Norman Rogers, who admired Roosevelt's New Deal, and from Winnipeg *Free Press* publisher J.W. Dafoe, a strong opponent of the Compact Theory of Confederation. One of the major background studies on the "Origins of Confederation" (upon which the commission based its recommendations) was by the prominent Toronto historian Donald Creighton, a strong admirer of John A. Macdonald and his belief in the necessity of a strong central government so that Canada would avoid the divisions that had plunged the United States into civil war, and in establishing a government that would enable Ottawa to build a national economy and a united country stretching from the Atlantic to the Pacific Ocean.[8]

In July 1940, the federal government introduced an unemployment insurance fund into which employers, employees, and the federal government would contribute. Although Mitchell Hepburn, Duff Pattullo, and William Aberhart espoused provincial rights, they agreed to a constitutional amendment to allow the new scheme to be passed. The Godbout government in Quebec, somewhat beholden to the federal Liberals for its recent victory, said little. With the jobless rate plummeting, the unemployment fund quickly built up a large surplus. A person had to work 180 days to qualify, only 42 percent of workers were eligible, and the benefit was tied to previous income. Nevertheless, Ottawa had delivered, and, as such, demanded taxing powers.

The King government called a dominion–provincial conference for January 1941. Hepburn attended under protest and tried to rally Aberhart and Pattullo to form an oppositional front. King's stern finance minister, J.L. Ilsley, declared that if a deal was not reached, Ottawa might unilaterally raise income and corporate taxes as a wartime emergency measure and provide no monetary compensation to the provinces. Hepburn remained rigid—at one point even calling King a Nazi—but found himself increasingly isolated and portrayed as hurting the war effort. Forced to relent, Hepburn was humiliated and resigned as premier. The result of the conference was the 1942 *Dominion–Provincial Taxation Agreement Act*, which saw the provinces rent their tax fields to Ottawa, at least for the war's duration, on the basis of recommendations made by the Rowell-Sirois Commission.

Tax rates soared to record levels to pay rapidly rising war costs, including for an unprecedented expansion of the federal bureaucracy from 46 000 in 1939 to more than 115 000 in 1945, mostly to manage the war effort. Annual corporate taxes collected in Canada rose from $85 million in 1939 to $850 million in 1944, and income taxes from $142 million in 1939 to $977.7 million in 1945.

To run the war, King assembled what was arguably the most capable cabinet in Canadian history. In April 1940, he moved Clarence Decateur (C.D.) Howe from the Department of Transport where, among other accomplishments, he created Trans-Canada Airlines, to head up the new Department of Munitions and Supply. The next month, Colonel J.L. Ralston, a veteran of the First World War, assumed the post of minister of national defence, following Norman Rogers's death in an air crash; Rogers had assumed the defence portfolio in 1939. Angus Macdonald resigned as premier of Nova Scotia to become minister of national defence (naval services). J.L. Ilsley transferred from national revenue to finance; the Saskatchewan power broker and former premier Jimmy Gardiner headed up the department of agriculture; and following Ernest Lapointe's death from cancer in November 1941, brilliant Quebec corporate lawyer Louis St. Laurent was made justice minister and became King's Quebec lieutenant.

These ministers came to increasingly rely upon civil service mandarins. Educated at elite institutions like the London School of Economics and Harvard, many were very familiar with, and generally sympathetic to, the latest economic theories, namely those of John Maynard Keynes, the British economist whose advocacy of government intervention, notably increased spending rather than reliance on a self-correcting free market to alleviate downturns in the business cycle, had gained much popularity during the Depression. Among these newly prominent experts was Cyril James, an economist and the principal of McGill University, who, in 1941, was asked to head up a new federal Advisory Committee on Reconstruction to make recommendations on post-war planning so that the economic and social difficulties following the First World War would not be repeated.

Under Ottawa's guidance, Canada was moving towards a command economy, in which the federal government imposed an increasing array of regulations, in part to avoid repeating problems that emerged during the First World War. Such was evident in the creation, and rapid expansion, of the Wartime Prices and Trade Board (WPTB). Many recalled that hyperinflation during the First World War generated considerable economic and social strain. The WPTB was given the power to set prices and wages, and manage the distribution of scarce items. By mid-1940, sharply rising demand from war industry and the military prompted it to set maximum prices on several commodities, namely basics, such as coal, wool, butter, and sugar. In autumn 1941, the WPTB established a rental rate freeze as people flocking to cities for war jobs faced severe accommodation shortages and a spike in rents. At the same time, it imposed a freeze on wages and prices, a measure that most came to consider a resounding success, for whereas the cost of living rose by 17.8 percent from August 1, 1939, to October 1, 1941, it rose by only 2.8 percent between October 1, 1941, and April 1, 1945.

While the WPTB focused on controls, the Department of Munitions and Supply fixated on production to provide for an army that grew from 5000 to 700 000, an air force from 3000 to 230 000, and a navy from 2000 to 100 000. As outlined in Figure 7.1, expenditures on the war claimed an overwhelming share of the federal budget. Canada produced 400 naval and 391 cargo ships, 50 000 tanks, 16 000 military aircraft, 850 000 military vehicles, 1.5 million rifles and machine guns, 72 million artillery and mortar shells, and 4.4 billion rounds of small arms ammunition. To generate such numbers, C.D. Howe cut through red tape, sending letters of intent to firms so they could get moving on war production and then quickly following up with formal contracts. He also recruited "dollar a year" men to advise on war production, experts and major figures from industry whose salaries continued to be paid by their company. The process was not without its critics, however. Organized labour expressed anger over being excluded from such advisory roles. There were charges of conflict of interest as advisors were drawn from the same sector they were asked to regulate, like the B.C. lumber baron H.R. Macmillan who was made timber controller.

To quicken the transition of industries to war production, they were provided with accelerated depreciation allowances as a tax write-off—amounting to $514 million between 1940 and 1945—and low-interest and long-term loans. In some regions, Howe was criticized for favouring large companies for government war contracts, nearly all

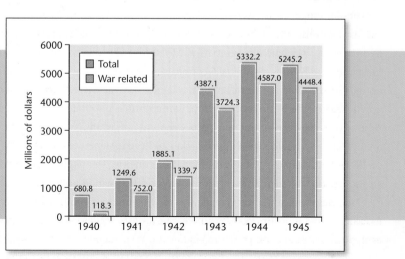

Figure 7.1
War-Related Expenditures as a Portion of Total Government Spending, 1940–1945

Source: *Canada Year Book,* 1948–49, 973.

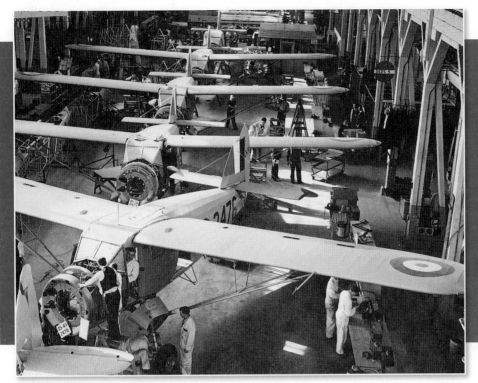

Noorduyn Norseman aircraft roll off the production line in Montreal for the Royal Canadian Air Force, 1941.

Source: Library and Archives of Canada, C-085214.

of which were located in Central Canada. But for Howe, an engineer and businessman by background, this was a matter of efficiency because he determined that bigger firms with a larger labour market at their disposal were in a better position to deliver what was necessary for the war effort. Moreover, the demand for efficiency cut both ways. For instance, National Steel Car in Malton, Ontario, which Howe considered inefficient, was taken over by Munitions and Supply in October 1942 and run as a Crown corporation (a government-owned enterprise) called Victory Aircraft. In all, Munitions and Supply created 28 Crown corporations, such as Polymer (that produced synthetic rubber), Citadel Merchandising (machine tools), Defence Industries Incorporated (armaments), and Research Enterprises Limited (optics, radar, and other technologically advanced items with a military application).

Even with war production concentrating in central Canada, the war-generated economic boom spread across Canada. In Montreal, the gross value of industrial and manufacturing production went from $483 million in 1939 to $1.2 billion in 1944; in Toronto, the corresponding figures were $482 million to $1 billion. Although there was grumbling in the Maritimes about shipbuilding being done by the Great Lakes and along the St. Lawrence, a record 75 000 in the region found employment in the sector, especially in Halifax, which became the principal Canadian launching point for westbound North Atlantic convoys. In British Columbia, some 39 000 obtained jobs in shipbuilding, and whereas industrial employment in Vancouver stood at 39 205 in 1939, it reached 88 938 in 1944, with thousands migrating to the city from across the Prairies. In many parts of the

Prairies, though, the BCATP promoted growth. One hundred and thirty-seven facilities were opened to train pilots, navigators, bombardiers, gunners, and wireless operators; Canadians made up 72 835 of the program's 131 553 graduates. Bases appeared in all parts of Canada, as indicated in Map 7.1, but given its wide-open and flat land, the Prairies, and particularly Saskatchewan and southern Alberta, benefited most. The Northwest Staging Route opened up remote areas in northern Alberta and British Columbia and in the Yukon. Established in late 1941 in cooperation with the United States to help supply the Soviet Union with food, materiel, and aircraft, the Staging Route, which ended in Fairbanks, Alaska, consisted of a line of 13 small airports, 11 of which were on Canadian soil.

Canada's rapidly expanding war effort presented the federal government with major financial challenges beyond the need to raise taxes. Besides funding Canada's military needs, there was growing demand from Britain, with whom Canada ran a trade surplus. But Britain was forced to pour all its financial resources into a desperate fight for survival and could no longer pay its debt to Canada, which reached $795 million by March 1941. That money was needed by Canada to pay its trade deficit with the United States, a situation that threatened to produce a currency crisis. Ottawa established a Foreign Exchange Control Board to contain the out-migration of funds, prohibit the importation of non-essential goods from the United States, and encourage exports and discourage imports. The value of the Canadian dollar went from roughly par with the American dollar to 90.9 cents.

To assist a nearly broke Britain, in March 1941, the U.S. Congress ratified the Lend-Lease program that initially provided 50 First World War vintage destroyers to England in exchange for 99-year leases on British bases in the West Indies and Newfoundland. Ottawa worried that Lend-Lease would worsen Canada's financial situation because Britain, soon given access to a $7 billion Lend-Lease account in the United States, would be able to decrease its Canadian purchases. In April 1941, at a meeting at Hyde Park, New York, King told Roosevelt, with whom he felt he had established a special, close, relationship, that by the end of the year, the currency situation would damage Canada's economy and its ability to fight the war. Roosevelt agreed that the present world crisis necessitated a

Map 7.1
Location of BCATP Bases across Canada

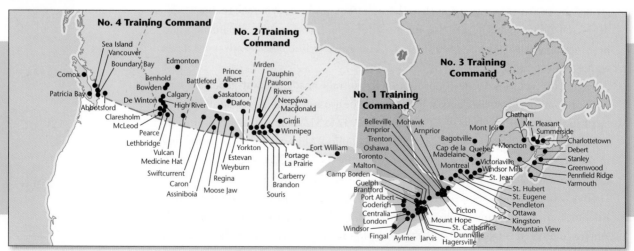

Source: Map published with permission from Lester and Orpen Dennys and Key Porter Books. Copyright © 1989 Jonathan Gladstone.

strong and stable Canada, and he realized that Canadian import controls hurt American business. In the resulting Hyde Park Declaration that was announced on April 20, 1941, the United States agreed to increase its purchases of war materiel in Canada and to allow Britain to use a portion of its Lend-Lease account to do the same (an amount that rose from $220 million in 1941 to $311 million in 1944). This solved the currency crisis but also entwined Canada's economy more closely with its southern neighbour.

April 1941:
Hyde Park Declaration.

Canadians in Uniform, 1940–1942

Overseas, on June 12, 1940, several thousand Canadian soldiers in Britain were rushed to Brest, France, as part of the 2nd British Expeditionary Force in a desperate attempt to retain a portion of northwest Europe from which a counter-attack could be launched against the advancing Nazis. After only two days, and before encountering the enemy, the plan was abandoned because it was considered a suicide mission. Canadian soldiers settled in Britain to protect the island from a possible Nazi invasion. By 1943, as the First Canadian Army, their presence had grown to three infantry and two armoured divisions, as well as two armoured brigades, with more than 250 000 men.

News stories sent to Canada portrayed these soldiers as serving the crucial and much appreciated role of defending the Mother Country from a Nazi invasion, the possibility of which, however, largely dissipated by mid-1941 as the German military turned east to attack the Soviet Union. Nevertheless, Canadian servicemen performed many valuable tasks, such as helping to harvest crops, mine coal, douse fires, and dig people out from the rubble following bombing raids. But as they stayed on in England, many became bored and restless and, to the disgust of locals, imbibed heavily whenever the opportunity presented itself. Canadian soldiers grew angry towards British military instructors whom, they said, treated them as incompetent colonials, but the fact was that Canadian soldiers were not well prepared for combat, especially since most of their initial commanders were old and thought in terms of First World War tactics.

While Canadian soldiers in Britain impatiently waited for action, the story with the Royal Canadian Air Force (RCAF) was much different. By December 1939, Canadian airmen were assisting in Royal Air Force attacks on German naval vessels. The next year they participated in the Battle of Britain. Over the summer and autumn of 1940, No. 1 RCAF Squadron lost 16 Hawker Hurricanes but was credited with somewhere between 30 and 38 kills. In 1941, RCAF fighter squadrons were tasked with escorting British bombers on daytime raids into France and Belgium. Although played up in the press as delivering effective blows to the Nazis, the fact was that in these missions the allies, fighting far from base and with generally inferior aircraft, lost three fighter planes for every one they shot down.

At sea, in mid-1940, the few destroyers then largely composing the Royal Canadian Navy (RCN) sailed across the Atlantic to help defend Britain. Over the latter half of 1940 and into 1941, German U-boats operating out of occupied bases in France, Belgium, and the Netherlands enjoyed increasing success in destroying naval and cargo vessels faster than they could be replaced. Canada would soon play a leading role in meeting this threat, namely through its use of the Corvette. A mid-sized escort ship, it was relatively simple, quick, and inexpensive to construct and repair, important factors given Canada's tiny navy at the start of the war and, at least initially, the limited capacity of its shipyards.

Expanding commitments abroad meant greater efforts to get men into uniform. To release more men for active service, the federal government created three female military services:

June 1941:
CWAC is established.

1. The Canadian Women's Army Corps (CWAC) on June 27, 1941, whose strength reached 21 624
2. The Canadian Women's Auxiliary Air Service on July 2, which in February 1942 was renamed as the Women's Division of the RCAF (RCAF–WD) and reached 17 101 personnel
3. The Women's Royal Canadian Naval Service (WRCNS), established on July 31, 1942, whose numbers reached 6781

Pressure mounted to conscript for overseas service. Defence Minister Ralston cast conscription as the fairest and most efficient system to meet military need. R.B. Hanson's caution on the issue contributed to his quick departure as interim Conservative leader and replacement by former prime minister and unabashed pro-conscriptionist Arthur Meighen. Canada's ability to avoid conscription for overseas service was made possible because its army was late in becoming actively involved in combat. Its early, and limited, engagements were disastrous, starting at Hong Kong. The British had assured the Canadians that the Japanese were poor soldiers and would not attack Hong Kong and risk conflict with the Empire. Canada agreed to send troops in October 1941, but all its A and B formations—meaning those considered ready for action—were unavailable but not those in the C category belonging to the Royal Rifles of Canada and Winnipeg Grenadiers, who required more training. To make matters worse, they went with no radios, no mortars, and no mechanical transport. On December 8, 1941, the Japanese, only hours after attacking America's Pacific fleet at Pearl Harbor, Hawaii, landed en masse in Hong Kong, where a Canadian force of 96 officers and 1877 other ranks were garrisoned. Although demonstrating great tenacity, the 1689 Canadians who survived surrendered on Christmas Day and were condemned to spend the rest of the war in Japanese slave-labour POW camps. They regularly put in 14-hour days in mines, steel mills, and shipyards, and in building airport landing strips with pick and shovel. Beatings, torture, and mock executions were common. Their diet consisted of "weeds, flowers and other unidentifiable greens"; rice that often reeked of gasoline because of the barrels in which it was cooked; and seaweed and fish heads. Malnutrition produced swelling and burning of the feet and left POWs highly susceptible to diphtheria, beriberi, pellagra, parasitic worms, dysentery, and what they nicknamed "Hong Kong balls," which caused their testicles to enlarge sometimes to the point where they could no longer walk.[9]

December 8–25, 1941:
Battle of Hong Kong.

Evacuation and Northern Development, 1942–1943

The attack on Hong Kong profoundly affected Canada's Japanese population, especially since it resulted in Canada declaring war on Japan. No other population connected to the enemy faced the same suspicions and mistreatment. Canada had a long record of prejudice against the Japanese, who were stereotyped as aggressive, militaristic, and impossible to assimilate. Soon after the Second World War started, many British Columbians rediscovered Hilda Glynn Ward's 1921 book *The Writing on the Wall*, which warned against Japanese plans to conquer North America.

Japan's attack on Pearl Harbor threw many British Columbians into a panic. Blackouts continued for three nights along Canada's west coast and radio stations went off the air so that their signals could not attract Japanese planes. Some 40 Japanese nationals were immediately interned. Those naturalized as Canadians after September 1, 1922, were to report to authorities for photographing and thumb printing. The RCMP and military intelligence had kept Japanese Canadians under general surveillance since Japan's 1937 invasion of China but had uncovered no fifth column or clandestine activity. Rumours circulated that in Hong Kong, many *Issei* (first-generation Japanese settlers) had helped invading Japanese forces, which by early 1942 had conquered the Philippines, Malaya, Singapore, and Burma. Fear, racism, and economic self-interest spread the theory that the 1200 fishing boats registered to Japanese Canadians, who had long presented formidable competition to white British Columbian fishers, would be used to help guide in the enemy. The Vancouver *Province* claimed that the secret, and highly effective, attack on Pearl Harbor was certainly abetted by treachery from within the local Japanese population and added that among the Japanese in Canada, there could be no doubt that some were loyal to the Japanese Emperor.

The usually charitable Victoria Kiwanis Club resolved that since it was impossible to distinguish between loyal and disloyal Japanese, it was prudent that a general internment be implemented. Japanese schools were closed, Japanese cultural associations were shut down, Japanese newspapers were banned unless they printed in English, and Japanese fishing vessels were impounded. King initially said that loyal Japanese would be provided with full protection of the law, but pressure mounted from British Columbia, namely the charge that the federal government was not protecting Canada's west coast. Vancouver City Council portrayed the 25 000 Japanese in the province as a "potential reservoir of voluntary aid to our enemy."[10] Similar commentary came from B.C.'s lieutenant-governor, its attorney general, and its commissioner of Provincial Police. Eight federal MPs from British Columbia, including six Liberals, demanded that all the Japanese be moved at least 160 kilometres inland. On January 8, 1942, a Conference on Japanese Matters convened in Ottawa, chaired by the minister of pensions and national health, Ian Mackenzie, who represented the riding of Vancouver Centre. A past president of the Vancouver Great War Veterans Association and former minister of national defence, Mackenzie, though having previously supported the enfranchisement of Japanese veterans of the First World War, now expressed the view that many Japanese Canadians were loyal to Japan because they thought in racial, not national, terms. The federal government also felt compelled to act after the American government on February 20, 1942, ordered its Japanese population evacuated from coastal areas. Four days later, Canada followed suit, and on February 27, the federal government established the British Columbia Security Commission to govern the evacuation process.

Japanese Canadians in British Columbia were to be moved at least 160 kilometres from the coast; those who refused faced internment and forced labour. Families were sometimes given only a few hours' notice to pack up and leave; each adult was permitted

Source: Library and Archives Canada, PA-037467.

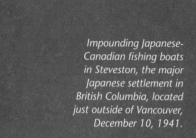

Impounding Japanese-Canadian fishing boats in Steveston, the major Japanese settlement in British Columbia, located just outside of Vancouver, December 10, 1941.

to take 68 kilograms of items, and each child 34 kilograms. Federal authorities sold off confiscated Japanese property, often at bargain-basement prices. For example, 542 Fraser Valley farms owned by Japanese Canadians and assessed at more than $1 million were sold for two-thirds of that amount. Some Japanese of financial means bought properties inland, if they were allowed. In Lillooet, British Columbia, the Japanese were told that they were welcome, as they were viewed as providing a needed economic stimulus, but once arriving, they were forced to build log cabins (that had no access to electricity and running water) in the dry sagebrush outside of the town, and were allowed into town only in daylight and only to do business. Calgary, Medicine Hat, and Lethbridge were among the many communities that refused to accept Japanese evacuees. Thousands of Japanese were left with no choice but to live in quickly constructed government housing complexes, the largest, with a population of 4000, in Slocan, British Columbia. The average cost to build such accommodation was $146 per unit, less than 5 percent the price of a modest urban house, as they were approximately 37 square metres; constructed of "tar paper and rough green lumber";[11] used oil lamps; and were heated by wood.

Despite a booming war economy, it was difficult for the Japanese to obtain jobs. Many took seasonal employment in lumbering and agriculture, typically for lower wages than whites were paid. Although not interned, their travel was strictly controlled: In British Columbia, it was limited to 75 kilometres from home, and in Alberta, to 20 kilometres. To most Canadians, such actions seemed justified in light of events following shortly after the evacuation. In late May, Japanese forces attacked Dutch Harbor, Alaska, and on June 3 occupied the outer Aleutian islands of Attu and Kiska. Also in June, a Japanese submarine shelled Santa Barbara, California, points in Oregon, and the remote outpost of Estevan Point on Vancouver Island.

Fear of a Japanese attack would also transform Canada's north through the construction, mostly by the American military, of the Alaska Highway, whose immediate purpose was to quickly transport troops and supplies in the event of a Japanese invasion from

April–November 1942: Construction of the Alaska Highway.

the north. It was built in rough form between April and November 1942, and stretched more than 2500 kilometres from Dawson Creek, British Columbia, to Fairbanks, Alaska, with all but 400 kilometres located in Canada. Its construction involved 14 000 military personnel from the U.S. Army Corps of Engineers, 77 civilian contractors, and 6000 civilian employees, and cost $130 million.

Linked to the highway was the CANOL (short for Canadian Oil) pipeline project. It was to transport crude oil from Norman Wells on the Mackenzie River to Whitehorse in the Yukon, where it would be refined and used at different points along the highway. However, the pipeline was not effectively designed for cold weather conditions, and its 2600 kilometres took nearly two years to complete. It pumped oil for only 16 months; considered a money loser, Imperial Oil abandoned it two years after the war ended.

Some 33 000 American military personnel were stationed in Canada, nearly half of whom worked on the Alaska Highway. Some Canadians expressed concern over the country's sovereignty, but the highway also meant thousands of well-paying civilian construction jobs. Several remote communities experienced an unprecedented boom, though they also struggled to cope. Dawson Creek, a community of 728 before the coming of the highway, soon totalled 9000. There, and in several other northern communities, the Americans built water mains, sewage facilities, telephone lines, roads, and other infrastructure. Media accounts said that new economic opportunities extended to Aboriginal peoples, though their involvement in better-paying jobs was minimal; typically, they served as guides. Unfortunately, the arrival of whites spread disease, such as measles and whooping cough, to Aboriginal peoples, which often proved fatal because little previous contact with whites meant they had not built up immunities against such ailments.

Rising Demands and Strains at Home, 1942–1943

By the time the Alaska Highway was completed in rough form, the federal government concluded that an attack upon Canada was very remote. It largely cancelled air raid drills by the end of 1942. Still as the war overseas intensified, Ottawa demanded more sacrifices of Canadians. Taxes continued rising, and in 1942 the federal government introduced a compulsory savings program that was garnished from paycheques as an anti-inflation measure. Targets established for the semi-annual Victory Bond drives became more ambitious, reaching $1.2 billion by November 1943. People worked longer in large part to produce for the war effort. Whereas in 1939, 61 067 Canadians laboured between 55 and 64 hours per week, in 1943 that figure reached 176 730.

In mid-1942, the National Salvage Committee, fairly dormant since its creation in November 1940, kicked into high gear. Nationwide publicity campaigns beseeched Canadians to collect and donate, among other items, metal and rubber products, and fats and bones, so that they could be transformed into tanks, planes, and explosives. By mid-1942, Canadians had to cope with a variety of shortages. Assembly lines stopped producing cars for civilian use. In April 1942, ration coupon books were issued entitling drivers to only 545 litres of gasoline per year, enough for about 1930 kilometres. A month later, strict restrictions were placed on tire sales, as Japan's expansion throughout Southeast Asia cut off rubber supplies. Canadians also adjusted to lower house temperatures because of limits imposed on coal made available for civilian use. They faced less selection with clothing (a measure needed to save cloth), as manufacturers were prohibited from producing certain items, such as evening dresses, double-breasted suits, pleats, pant cuffs, epaulets, shoulder pads, and extra pockets. In 1942 and 1943, sugar, tea, coffee, butter, and meat were rationed because imported products became more difficult to obtain and to accommodate rising demand from troops and civilians overseas, especially in Britain.

In 1942, Canada supplied 82 percent of Britain's imported wheat, 99 percent of its imported flour, and 72 percent of its imported bacon. The arrival of a shipment of Mexican bananas was rare enough to warrant a story in the Hamilton *Spectator*. Liquor rationing was introduced to maximize labour supply for sectors important to the war effort and because alcohol could be converted for use as an explosive propellant and as a medical disinfectant. Government propaganda told Canadians that they were being asked to sacrifice little compared with the burdens borne by soldiers and civilians overseas, such as in England, where in 1943 people were entitled to only one-third as much butter and one-tenth as much meat as Canadians. As hard as the rationing was, polls showed that more than three-quarters of Canadians supported rationing. Many grew their own food in backyard Victory Gardens or followed recipes printed in newspapers that used more plentiful items. However, black marketing and hoarding produced thousands of arrests annually, and with their healthier wartime incomes, Canadians spent 80 percent more on food than during the Depression, including by eating out at restaurants far more often.

By 1942, more than 350 000 men had volunteered for military service, but as in the First World War, the greatest challenge was in Quebec. As of October 1941, voluntary enlistment there stood at 41.6 percent of Ontario's total, whereas Quebec's population was 85.5 percent of Ontario's. Following the fall of France, authorities worried that the French population in Quebec appeared to have greater sympathy for the Vichy government that represented Nazi-occupied France than for the "Free France" forces under Charles de Gaulle that urged resistance to the Nazis. This tendency reflected the great esteem in which many Québécois held the Vichy leader Marshall Pétain, a hero of the First World War, and the Vichy program that advocated steering France away from the secularism of the Third Republic and back to a more traditional, corporatist order, based in large part upon the Papal Encyclicals of Pius XI. One poll taken in July 1942, four months before Canada broke off relations with the Pétain government, revealed that among French Canadians in Quebec, 66 percent rejected the idea of a war against Vichy. Also disturbing in that poll was the finding that only 33 percent believed that "Canada would be fighting this war if she were completely independent and not part of the British Empire."[12]

It was becoming increasingly important that enlistment in different parts of Canada be balanced against rising domestic labour needs. In early 1942, the federal government created the National Selective Service (NSS) within the Department of Labour. It was tasked with estimating the need for and ensuring, through compulsion if necessary, the availability of adequate labour for war-related industry. Although generally meeting wartime demands, historian Michael Stevenson argues that because King feared a political backlash, namely from labour, NSS was not allowed to adequately exercise its powers, which allowed worker shortages to persist in several sectors—including agriculture, mining, and meat packing—and prompted the resignation of its first director, Elliott Little.

Most of King's cabinet did not support—or at least did not yet actively push for—conscription, though divisions were emerging. Besides Ralston, King's two other cabinet ministers from Nova Scotia, Angus Macdonald and J.L. Ilsley, advocated conscription and claimed that King was too concerned with losing Quebec. King's stance provided Meighen with the possibility of picking up support in English Canada, especially with major newspapers like the Toronto *Globe and Mail* endorsing conscription. Meighen was scheduled to run for Parliament on February 9, 1942, in a by-election in the Toronto constituency of York South, which, despite large numbers of working-class voters, had elected a Tory in every federal election since 1904. The Liberals did not run a candidate, a decision they presented as a courtesy to Meighen, but their goal was to avoid splitting the anti-Tory vote. King also undercut Meighen by announcing in the January 22 Throne Speech, which opened the parliamentary session, that his government would hold a plebiscite (a nonbinding vote) in April asking Canadians if they would release the government from its pledge of "no conscription for overseas service."

Meighen's opponent was schoolteacher Joseph Noseworthy, who had run in York South in the 1940 federal election. With strong trade union support, and emphasizing the need for the federal government to start planning for the post-war period so that the economic turmoil following the First World War was not repeated, Noseworthy crushed Meighen by nearly 4500 votes. For King, there remained the dicey matter of the plebiscite. "Non" forces in Quebec were being mobilized by *La Ligue pour la defence du Canada*, headed up by the well-known *nationalistes* André Laurendeau, co-founder of the *mouvement de jeunesse nationaliste Jeune-Canada*, and Paul Gouin, formerly of *L'action liberale nationale*. Thousands joined the Ligue, which also received support from the many chapters of the *Societé St-Jean Baptiste*. The results were potentially catastrophic for the country. In Quebec, 72 percent voted "Non," but in the rest of Canada nearly 80 percent said "Yes," thus producing an overall majority of 65 percent willing to release King's government from its pledge of "no conscription for overseas service." Given the breakdown of the results, the prime minister decided not to proceed with conscription.

King's response to this vote was Bill 80. Introduced into the House of Commons on May 8, it permitted conscripted service anywhere in the Western Northern Hemisphere. It was not conscription for overseas service, but it opened the door a little more to the possibility, enough so to prompt the resignation of Public Works Minister P.J.A. Cardin. Only four French-speaking Liberals voted for Bill 80, though the rest abstained, thus ensuring its passage. To better defend Quebec's interests, *La Ligue* transformed itself into the *nationaliste* political party *Le bloc populaire canadien*. For Ralston, Bill 80 did not go far enough and he handed in his resignation, but as a former militia colonel who prided himself on honourable conduct, he would not leave his post until given permission by his superior, and King refused the resignation.

Noseworthy's victory demonstrated that Canadians were thinking beyond the prevailing conflict and were concerned over the possibility of difficult economic times returning after the war. Growing numbers wanted the federal government to initiate economic

April 1942: Plebiscite on releasing the King government from its pledge of "no conscription for overseas service."

plans and social welfare programs to offset an anticipated post-war downturn, a trend that drew more support to the CCF. In the April 1941 B.C. election, the CCF won 12 of 48 seats to become the official opposition to the Pattullo government. The next year, the CCF established formal links with the Canadian Congress of Labour (CCL), which had been formed in 1940 out of an alliance between the All Canadian Congress of Labour and the Congress of Industrial Organizations, and was highly critical of King's government for failing to introduce legislation guaranteeing the right of a union to obtain recognition and bargain collectively if securing a majority of support from workers.

Following Meighen's defeat, the Tories realized they had to change direction. In August 1942, 159 Conservative policymakers and intellectuals gathered in Port Hope, Ontario, where they endorsed measures like the need for assistance to Maritime fishers, national collective bargaining legislation, low-cost housing, and a national public health insurance scheme. At the party's national convention in Winnipeg in December, John Bracken, Manitoba's premier for the past 20 years and who was first elected under the Progressive party banner, was made the Tories' new leader. As an overture to Bracken, and to underline the party's new direction, the Conservatives renamed themselves as the Progressive Conservatives, and in his acceptance speech Bracken did not mention conscription. Bracken did not run for Parliament until the 1945 federal election, perhaps wary of suffering Meighen's fate. This lowered his profile and permitted Tory hard-liners on the issue of conscription to continue to take the lead in the House of Commons.

The divisive results of the 1942 plebiscite, and the increasing demands that the war was placing upon Canadians, prompted the federal government to take a more active approach towards managing information. In September, a far more comprehensive Wartime Information Board replaced a rather low-key Bureau of Public Information. The Board consulted with advertising agencies and academics in forming propaganda strategy. It commissioned numerous surveys from the newly created Canadian Institute of Public Opinion to gauge support for various government war policies and to identify the most effective means of mobilizing people. It also closely coordinated with the National Film Board (NFB). Established in 1939 with one assistant, two secretaries, and a production supervisor, by war's end the NFB had a staff of 787 and had produced more than 500 films, the majority celebrating Canada's war effort. Canadians also received information about the war through carefully censored Canadian Broadcasting Corporation radio reports. The upbeat nature of news was evident in information conveyed on the disastrous raid by Canadian soldiers on the French coastal community of Dieppe in August 1942. The first stories, filed by correspondent Rooney Pelletier, proclaimed: "It's been a wonderful day. I don't think there's a Canadian … whose heart didn't pound a little faster today."[13]

Military Developments, 1942–1943

The assault on Dieppe was designed to test Combined Operations' procedures and German defences in Europe, in preparation for an eventual full-scale invasion. The Americans, and especially the Soviets who were taking massive casualties, were clamouring for the creation of a Western European front. General H.D.G. Crerar, then acting commander of the Canadian Corps in England, pushed for major Canadian involvement, arguing it would raise troop morale, especially since many were growing frustrated, as they saw American soldiers, whose country declared war on Germany on December 11, 1941 (four days after doing so against Japan), playing a more active role in ground campaigns.

The Dieppe raid, codenamed Rutter, was slated for July but was cancelled because of bad weather, thus perhaps producing dangerous leaks from among those selected to participate. Many historians lay much of the blame for what happened at Dieppe on Admiral Lord Louis Mountbatten, King George VI's cousin, who was appointed Britain's chief of Combined Operations. A poor tactician but exceptional self-publicist, Mountbatten was determined to push ahead with what he saw as a high-profile venture. He brushed aside concerns expressed by military subordinates and in intelligence reports and ensured that the Dieppe raid, now renamed Jubilee, was remounted for August 19.

August 19, 1942: Raid on Dieppe.

At Dieppe, the Germans had constructed a formidable defensive network. The Canadians had lost the element of surprise after an attacking flotilla ran into a German coastal patrol. During the raid, allied naval and air support was inadequate; many troops were delivered late and to the wrong landing spot. They stormed ashore in full daylight onto pebble beaches where footing was difficult and there was no cover from nearby cliffs from where the Germans opened up a deadly barrage. Of the 4963 Canadians who participated, 907 were killed, 586 were wounded, and 1946 were taken prisoner.

While Canada's army was removed from action following Dieppe, its navy and air force continued to expand their roles. The RCN patrolled along Canadian and British coastlines, off India and Africa, and in the Caribbean and Mediterranean. The sea war also came close to Canada as German U-boats stationed themselves off the east coat and penetrated the St. Lawrence, coming within a few hundred kilometres of Quebec City. Over the later half of 1942, mainly in the gulf area of the St. Lawrence, two small naval vessels and 19 merchant ships were sunk, and in September, the St. Lawrence was closed to cargo and convoy traffic.

The most prominent role for the RCN was in the northwestern Atlantic, where by midsummer 1942, it was protecting 40 percent of convoys that went between Canada and Britain. All told, the RCN successfully escorted 25 343 cargo vessels across the Atlantic. Convoys of as many as 100 cargo ships and their military escorts gathered, principally in Bedford Basin (Halifax's massive ice-free natural harbour) for journeys that went as far north as Cape Farewell, located at the southern tip of Greenland. The convoys had to travel at the speed of the slowest ship to protect all vessels, and all types of decrepit ones were called into service to transport supplies overseas. Besides German U-boats, the weather was a potentially deadly foe. In rough seas, waves crashed over the deck and semi-submerged vessels. Frigid conditions presented the threat of icing, which could capsize a ship in a matter of hours; to fall into the frigid North Atlantic brought death in a matter of minutes.

The role of sea and air power, both Canadian and American, was, by the early 1940s, also dramatically affecting Newfoundland. Convoys sailed from St. John's and the American navy acquired bases under Lend-Lease at Argentia and Stephenville. Ferry Command, which started in late 1940, flew some 11 000 military aircraft to Britain from airfields in Gander, Newfoundland, and Goose Bay, Labrador. Gander and nearby Botwood served as RCAF bases from which seaplanes were dispatched to help protect convoys. At its peak in 1943, some 6000 Canadian and 20 000 American military personnel were stationed in

Newfoundland. Determined that Newfoundland not become part of the United States, the Canadian government established a high commission in St. John's in 1941.

Canadian airmen also came to play a major role in Bomber Command, a division of Britain's Royal Air Force. Placed under Air Marshall Sir Arthur Harris in February 1942, Bomber Command sought to pummel Germany into submission through mass raids on urban areas to knock out industry and transportation, and to destroy civilian morale. Many came to question the morality of this approach (in light of events like the February 1945 1300-plane raid on Dresden, where incendiary bombs and strong winds produced a firestorm that literally incinerated some 40 000) and its effectiveness (given that even after two years of the bombing campaign, German military production peaked in mid-1944). In spite of this, it is important to ask what German output would have been if these raids had not occurred.

Canada supplied 15 squadrons and 25 percent of personnel to Bomber Command, and suffered 9919 fatalities. The missions left many survivors psychologically scared for life. Mostly involved in night-time raids, RCAF personnel, once over targeted cities, confronted hundreds of powerful searchlights to guide German anti-aircraft fire and fighter pilots. Anti-aircraft gunners put up a "box barrage" of flak to fill a section of the air through which some planes had to fly. In many ways, the question of survival was a matter of chance. In 1942 and 1943 an average of almost 5 percent of planes were lost in every raid launched by Bomber Command.

January 1, 1943: No. 6 Bomber Group formed.

Canada's major role in Bomber Command, and the belief among many Canadian air force personnel that they were not receiving due recognition from the British, such as for promotion, prompted Ottawa to demand a separate, Canadian-staffed and -led section of Bomber Command. The British resisted, claiming this was impractical and would compromise efficiency; the Canadians refused to relent, and on January 1, 1943, No. 6 (Canadian) Group was formed. Based in Yorkshire, it was the only non-British group in Bomber Command.

In the summer of 1943, Canada's army finally became heavily involved in combat. On July 10, some 30 000 Canadian soldiers stormed ashore near the town of Pachino, Sicily. Advancing Canadians had to traverse mountains via steep, narrow, and winding goat paths often blocked or booby-trapped by the enemy. They also endured Sicily's desert-like terrain, excruciating summer heat, and the threat of disease; for instance, some 1200 Canadians in Sicily contracted malaria. They soon confronted battle-seasoned German troops with the 15th Panzer Division and the Hermann Göring Division. The enemy, fighting a well-executed rear-guard action, inflicted more than 19 000 allied casualties, of whom 2310 were Canadian, including 522 Canadian dead.

On September 3, 1943, Canadian troops joined Britain's Eighth Army in crossing the Strait of Messina into Italy. Of the 92 757 Canadians sent to Italy, 5764 were killed, 19 486 were wounded, and 1004 were captured. Only the beginning of the campaign was relatively easy as the Germans drew back to establish defensive positions. In October, the 1st Canadian Infantry Division met stiff resistance at Campobasso, located some 100 kilometres northeast of Naples. The next month, the Division moved northeast to cross the Sangro River, advancing in cold and sleet and through mud-soaked terrain, and on December 6, encountered heavy German resistance at the Moro River, which came to be called the "river of blood." Late December brought the clash at Ortona where the Canadians battled

December 1943: Battle of Ortona.

Canadian Armour Passing Through
Ortona, *as depicted by the official
Canadian war artist, Charles Comfort.*

Source: Canadian War Museum, CN 122451.

against two well-seasoned and well-entrenched German paratroop battalions. Fighting proceeded room-by-room as the Canadians blasted their way through walls adjoining row houses, some of which were booby-trapped.

Political and Social Developments, 1942–1944

Given Canada's very substantial wartime contributions and sacrifices, its federal government lobbied for more international recognition, especially when it coincided with Canadian interests. Demands were made for representation on a number of allied boards helping to conduct the war effort, something resisted by Britain and the United States. In making its case, Canada advocated something it called the Functional Principle. Typically credited to Hume Wrong, then assistant to Canada's ambassador in Washington, the Functional Principal proposed that in certain areas, or functions, Canada was a leading power, and thus warranted representation.

Canada first met with disappointment, as in March 1942 it was unsuccessful in securing membership on the Allied Munitions Assignment Board; Canada ranked third in allied war production, but that translated into only 5 percent of the total. Canada also sought representation on the Combined Food Board. The British were opposed and the Americans suggested that Canada should be satisfied with membership on the less powerful Combined Production and Resources Board. Ottawa persisted, and ultimately, based on Canada's massive agricultural output, achieved success, though to do so, Canadian officials made implied threats about not being as generous in future with the terms of war loans to Britain.

Canada remained a secondary player among the allies. Such was evident at the September 1944 Quebec City Conference between Roosevelt and Britain's Prime Minister Winston Churchill, where King obtained no more than a photo-op with the two allied leaders. Nonetheless, Canada's ambitions and the perspective of its citizens had shifted with respect to the future direction of the country's foreign policy. Appeasement and isolationism were largely rejected. A public opinion poll in November 1943 revealed that 78 percent of Canadians (56 percent in Quebec) felt that Canada should assume a more prominent post-war role in maintaining international order, even if it meant using Canadian troops. Canada strongly supported and actively participated in the United Nations Relief and Rehabilitation Administration that was formed by the allies in 1942 to provide aid to devastated areas, and to the formation of the United Nations (UN), a term that the allies used to describe themselves by 1943, which had its founding convention in San Francisco in March 1945, with Canada as a charter member. Historian Adam Chapnick argues that King, despite heading up the Canadian delegation to San Francisco, remained determined—as he had with the League of Nations—that membership would not involve binding commitments. He had Canada participate because of overwhelming public support (as much as 90 percent) for UN membership; strong pressure from influential internationalists in the Department of External Affairs, such as Lester Pearson, who thought in terms of Canada having become a "middle power" that could have an impact outside of its borders; and the possible opportunities that could be created through the UN for enhanced post-war trade. What King categorically rejected was the suggestion made in early 1944 by Lord Halifax, Britain's ambassador to the United States, before a Tory audience in Toronto, that the Commonwealth should develop a united post-war foreign policy to obtain more international clout.

Hope and ambition juxtaposed against trepidation and anxiety. These themes were also linked to social changes that the war accelerated within Canada, namely to potential challenges to the traditional social order as a result of the 370 000 women who, between June 1939 and the beginning of 1944, obtained employment in areas directly connected to the war effort, often in roles that had been the exclusive domain of men. The number of women with jobs outside the home grew from 22.7 to 33.1 percent of the eligible female workforce, aged 14 and older. Many of the jobs they undertook were relatively well paid, skilled, and physically demanding. Record numbers of working women were married and had children. In mid-1942, to meet the rising demand for labour, the federal government introduced income tax breaks for working couples and passed legislation to provide joint federal–provincial funded child-care facilities. Some historians, such as Jeff Keshen, emphasize social progress and long-term contributions to gender equality as a result of the new wartime roles women successfully undertook; others, however, such as Ruth Pierson and Janet Stephens, underline the persistence of traditionalism. For instance, NSS initially recruited women aged 20 to 24 for war jobs in order to target the single and mobile, and not until July 1943 did it actively seek to include wives and mothers. The NSS's Women's Division, established in early 1942 under Fraudina Eaton of the prominent department store family bearing her name, concerned itself with the moral side of women workers. It stressed the need of those who were single and coming for jobs from out of town to have access to wholesome recreational activities, such as at the YWCA, so that they not descend into immoral conduct. It praised companies like John Inglis in Toronto for hiring a female welfare supervisor and a female recreational supervisor, and for arranging for women employees to have free access to a nearby community swimming pool and gymnasium.

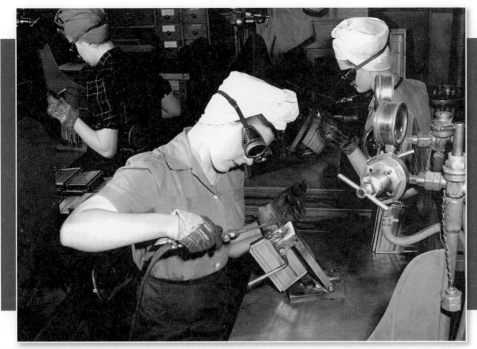

Women at the John Inglis plant in Toronto weld magazine clips for Bren Guns.

Source: Library and Archives of Canada, WRM 4468.

Ottawa stipulated that 75 percent of government subsidized daycare spaces be reserved for the children of "war workers." Ontario and Quebec, both centres of war production, were the only provincial governments to participate in the jointly funded scheme. Ontario opened 28 daycare facilities, though the 1085 spaces met perhaps 20 percent of the need among mothers in war industry. In Quebec, only six facilities opened, offering fewer than 200 spots in Montreal. Working mothers also prompted widespread public discussion about child neglect and delinquency, and emotionally detached children being raised in "sterile" and "unloving" institutional settings.

Government propaganda and press commentary often conveyed the message that women workers had taken wartime jobs solely out of patriotism in order to release men for military action and would return to domestic life once victory was attained. Yet, several news accounts, especially those written by female columnists, heralded the workplace contributions of women and spoke favourably of this being the basis for more permanent change. Lotta Dempsey, a future editor-in-chief with *Chatelaine*, then the most widely circulated magazine geared to Canadian women, wrote in 1943: "This was the time and the place it really started, the honest-to-goodness equality of Canadian women. It began to happen that hour when Canadian girls left desks and kitchens ... stepped into overalls and took their places in the lines of workers at lathes and drills."[14]

At the wartime workplace, men still dominated higher-prestige and higher-paid jobs and virtually monopolized positions of authority. Many women spoke of being changed by their work experience, often in ways that portended ambitions extending beyond traditional female roles. They were proud of having coped with long hours and physically demanding tasks, from successfully performing "men's" jobs and from earning their own paycheque.

In early 1943, a ten-woman subcommittee was established within the federal government's Advisory Committee on Reconstruction to examine employment issues of particular concern to females. Chaired by Margaret Stovel McWilliams, a former journalist and Winnipeg alderman, its report, delivered in November, asserted: "Whatever field of employment women have entered they have proved themselves competent, conscientious workers."[15] The subcommittee endorsed vocational training programs for women, equal pay for equal work, government-subsidized daycare, and a 14-week maternity leave. The report was not well received in Parliament; most members simply ignored it. Regardless of how it was received, it nonetheless spoke to the conviction among many women that they were making substantial contributions in the workplace, were proving themselves equal to men in numerous and previously exclusive male domains and, as such, deserved greater workplace rights, including the right, no matter their marital status, to obtain decent employment in peacetime.

Controversy also accompanied women into the CWACs, RCAF-WD, and WRCNS. The government presented these enlistments as a temporary emergency measure. Canadians were assured that precautions were in place to prevent femininity from being compromised in the rough military world. For example, the government announced that it had hired top fashion experts to design female military uniforms. It also sought to counter what became known as the "whispering campaign" about military women being man-hungry, prostitutes, or lesbians, such as by telling Canadians that all women in uniform attended a weekly church parade.

Initially, women who enlisted earned two-thirds the male pay rate. They were mostly confined to lower-grade jobs that reflected gender stereotypes. As of March 1945, 62 percent of CWAC personnel were administrative clerks and 8 percent were cooks, yet overall, women qualified for more than 50 trades, including radar operator, mechanic, and air traffic controller. To attract more female recruits, in July 1943, their basic pay was raised to 80 percent of the male rate, and raises for achieving trade qualifications were provided on an equal basis with men. Despite facing discrimination, internal military surveys revealed that most servicewomen found military life agreeable. They spoke of gaining satisfaction from "learning to cope" with difficult situations and from developing "greater self-discipline."[16] Some journalists—mostly female ones—predicted permanent change from women's military experience. Rita McLean Farquharson, the *Canadian Home Journal*'s associate editor, said that though many servicewomen dreamed of "a man ... a home [and] a baby," they also had become more independent and would "not wait" with bated breath "for a Prince Charming to come riding by."[17]

The war also shaped the lives of Canadian children. Those old enough partook in patriotic activities. By the end of 1944, Ontario students had raised nearly $800 000 for the Red Cross. For salvage campaigns, children foraged through attics, garages, and barns, and then transported items by wagon or in six-quart fruit baskets to depots that were often located on school grounds. But the war also generated much concern about young Canadians. With so many fathers in the military, or both parents working, it was assumed that too many children were not receiving proper guidance. There was talk of an emerging crisis with delinquency, as court appearances by juveniles rose from 9497 in 1939 to 13 802 three years later. One reaction was increased pressure upon working mothers to return home as soon as the war ended, though there were other, and arguably more progressive, responses. All levels of government became more active in providing recreational facilities and programs and within schools, a variety of responses occurred. One was a reaction against child-centred progressive education, which was criticized for being too permissive. Other responses, however, included more emphasis on hiring guidance counsellors and improving the qualifications and pay of teachers as schools were severely handicapped during the war by the departure of thousands of poorly paid teachers into the military or better-paying war jobs.

The war brought other types of challenges more to the forefront, such as from rural Canada. In part this was because many commodity prices had been low when Canada entered the war and farmers claimed that they had not been given adequate time to rise before the WPTB price freeze took effect. Added to this was the difficulty of securing adequate farm labour. By 1944, some 500 000 Canadians from farms and small towns had donned a military uniform, and 300 000 had migrated to cities for work. Many farmers asked—to no avail—that military recruiters ease off in agricultural districts or that Ottawa allow commodity prices to rise so that farmers could afford to pay the wages necessary to retain experienced labourers. Numerous sources of labour were mined in what often became a desperate attempt to deal with deficiencies. For example, more than 100 000 high school and university students participated in farm labour programs, but many farmers hesitated to accept such help because they thought the participants were capable of performing only the simplest tasks and were not up to the rigours of agricultural life.

The Canadian Federation of Agriculture (CFA), formed in 1935, emerged as a strong campaigner for the nation's farm interests. Farmers demanded better prices and a more substantive role in agricultural policymaking. Historian Ian MacPherson argues that the war years saw the transition of farmer organization from an agrarian protest movement to an economically oriented lobby.[18] Effective lobbying by the CFA played a part in establishing government subventions for several commodities to stimulate production and to make up for lower prices.

Organized labour also presented new challenges. In many ways, workers were better off during the war. Unemployment evaporated and between 1938 and 1943 the average annual pre-tax salary rose from $956 to $1525. Countless workers were determined not to let down the country during this crisis. They clocked in record hours and produced to their absolute limit. Both the Trades and Labour Congress and CCL leadership officially discouraged strikes. Nonetheless, grievances mounted. Early in the war, the King government ignored union demands to provide compulsory collective bargaining rights. Many workers were also angered by mandatory wage controls, claiming that their pay had not risen adequately since the Depression.

Labour's potential strength increased as worker shortages helped the cause of unionization, since people became less fearful about losing their job if they supported a union. That fact, along with a burgeoning industrial workforce, resulted in an explosion of union membership from 358 967 in 1939 to 724 188 by 1944. Despite pledges from many of Canada's union leaders to avoid wartime strikes, organized labour began flexing its muscles. In 1943 there were 401 strikes and 1 041 198 days lost, more than five times the number of strike days in 1939. Many Canadians demanded the internment of strike leaders, but King chose the path of conciliation. In the spring of 1943, his government tasked the recently established National War Labour Board to undertake a comprehensive investigation of labour relations. Its report was received in August, but not made public until early 1944, and concluded that improvements in collective bargaining rights for labour were justified.

Although Ottawa stalled, action occurred at the provincial level. As an election approached, the Ontario Liberals, under the leadership of Harry Nixon, who replaced Hepburn's hand-picked successor, George Conant, tried to win back the working-class support that Hepburn had squandered for the Liberals years earlier with his actions against the CIO (see Chapter 6). Nixon proposed legislation guaranteeing unions collective bargaining rights if obtaining a majority of support from workers. However, the Ontario Tories, like the national party under Bracken, shifted to the left under George Drew, who also enjoyed public appeal as a First World War hero.

For the August 1943 provincial election, the Conservatives ran on the 22 Point Platform, which, among other planks, endorsed improved pensions for the unemployed; construction of public housing; increased funding for public education; and legislation guaranteeing collective bargaining rights for labour. Drew's main challenge came not from the Liberals but from the CCF, led by former Rhodes Scholar and lawyer Edward (Ted) Jolliffe. Labour's vote swung behind the CCF.

The Tories, saved by the rural and small-town vote, squeaked into office with 37 seats, three more than the CCF, which the CCL officially endorsed and 19 of the CCF's victorious candidates were trade unionists. Drew accepted the 1943 *Collective Bargaining Act* under which an Ontario Labour Court was established as a division of the Supreme Court of Ontario. The next year it was replaced by a Labour Relations Board because the cost of settling matters in court were too costly, and judges wanted to avoid becoming arbiters in labour disputes. Besides Ontario, in 1943, the Pattullo government in British Columbia amended the *Conciliation and Arbitration Act* to require an employer to enter into collective bargaining with a union when the provincial minister of labour was satisfied that the union held a majority of support among workers. In 1944, the Godbout government in Quebec passed the *Loi des relations ouvrières*, which facilitated successful unionization drives for thousands of workers.

The message was becoming clear to the federal Liberals: The time had arrived to take more substantive action to demonstrate a clear commitment to post-war planning, social security, and better labour relations. According to a September 1943 national poll, CCF support stood at 29 percent compared with 28 percent each for the Liberals and the Progressive Conservatives.

That year, the Advisory Committee on Reconstruction established a subcommittee to examine social security. Its research director was Leonard Marsh, the director of social research at McGill University, who was widely considered a leading expert on employment and social policy. His 1943 *Report on Social Security* advocated family allowances, better unemployment insurance and old age pensions, a public health insurance program, sickness benefits, and death benefits for dependants of the deceased. King balked at accepting such a sweeping range of proposals. He worried about the price tag and a backlash from provincial governments over excessive centralization and the invasion of their constitutional jurisdiction.

True to form, King staked out a middle position. In the January 1944 Throne Speech, he committed his government to provide family allowances the following year, a payment for each child up to the age of 16. When passed by Parliament on August 1, the *Family Allowances Act* established Canada's first universal social program and it came with an annual price tag of $200 million. In many cases, it added 20 percent to a family's income, though the government refused to index it to inflation. Besides directly helping families, the federal government saw the allowance as providing a spending stimulus to counter a post-war economic downturn, as forestalling demands for major wage increases, and as easing the transition of women out of the post-war workforce to make room for veterans. Allowance cheques were made out to mothers to signify their fundamental role in caring for the family. The program was immensely popular, especially in Quebec, where families were larger, averaging four children per couple.

Among other social policies, a new *National Housing Act* was passed in 1944 to deal with chronic housing shortages; though rather than making funds available for public housing, the Act encouraged private construction by providing buyers with easier down payment requirements. In a direct overture to labour, on February 17, 1944, the federal government introduced PC 1003 (an Order in Council) that provided workers under federal jurisdiction with union recognition if their chosen union received a majority of support. The importance to the survival of the King government of introducing such social policies was underlined by the June 15, 1944, election of the first CCF government in Canada when former Baptist minister Tommy Douglas became Saskatchewan's premier, with 53 percent of the popular vote and 90 percent of the seats.

February 1944: PC 1003 introduced.

Completing Canada's War, 1944–1945

While King battled at home to keep political opponents at bay and the country united behind the war effort, Canadian soldiers overseas widened their fight to finish off the enemy. In Italy, in 1944, just to the north of Ortona, the Canadians confronted major German defensive lines, starting with the Gustav Line, which consisted of mine belts up to 91 metres deep, pillboxes, tank turrets embedded in concrete, and anti-tank ditches. Starting on May 14, I Canadian Corps battled for three days to break through its section. The Germans then fell back to the even more formidable Hitler Line. The Canadians attacked on May 23, and that day Canada's 2nd Infantry Brigade took 543 casualties, a record for such a formation during the Italian campaign.

I Canadian Corps continued its slow, grinding, and often deadly, advance northward. In August 1944, it pierced the Gothic Line—stretching from Pisa on the Ligurian Sea to Pesaro on the Adriatic Sea—at the cost of 4000 casualties, one-quarter of which were fatal. Fighting for the Canadians continued into Rimini, Bologna, the Po Valley, Coriano, Romangna, the Savio and Senio Rivers, and the area north of Florence. Starting in February 1945, I Corps was moved from Italy to join II Corps in northwest Europe in a campaign that involved 237 000 Canadians, more than 44 000 of whom became casualties, a number that included more than 11 000 killed.

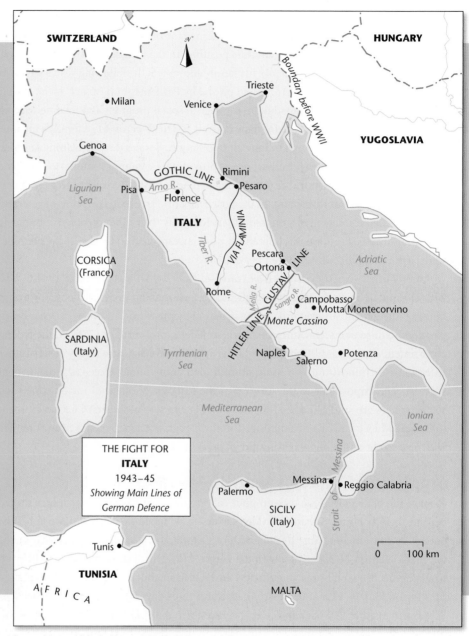

Source: Maps published with permission from Lester and Orpen Dennys and Key Porter Books.
Copyright © 1989 Jonathan Gladstone.

June 6, 1944: D-Day.

Map 7.2
Principal Battles and the Main German Defensive Lines in the Italian Campaign, 1943–1945

The northwest European campaign started on D-Day—June 6, 1944. Some 15 000 mostly untested Canadian troops stormed ashore at Juno Beach—stretching some five kilometres from Saint-Aubin-sur-Mer on the east to Courseulles-sur-Mer on the west—as part of Operation Overlord, the invasion of Normandy, the largest-ever amphibious assault, involving 160 000 allied troops that landed at five sectors. D-Day brought the Canadians 914 casualties, including 340 dead, though pre-invasion estimates had predicted up to double that number. On that first day, Canadian forces advanced further than any other allied army.

The Germans soon regrouped, and within five days Canadian losses reached 1017 dead and 1814 wounded, rates that corresponded to some of the worst fighting on the western front during the First World War. Throughout the Normandy campaign the Germans occupied excellent defensive positions, often taking advantage of high ground, waterways, and other natural terrain features. It would take 33 days for Canadian and British forces to capture Caen, a port city that Field Marshall Bernard Montgomery, Britain's highest-ranking officer, said was possible to take by the end of D-Day. On August 21, the Canadians and other allied forces closed the Falaise-Argentan Gap through which the Germans were retreating, thus stranding large numbers of the enemy and ending their resistance in Normandy. But victory came at a steep price: During the Normandy campaign, Canada took 18 444 casualties, including 5021 dead, losses that almost matched those suffered over the entire 18-month Italian campaign.

Defenders of Canada's battlefield performance, such as historian Terry Copp, argue that the pace of the Canadian advance reflected the intensity of their opposition and difficulty of the terrain.[19] Their main tank, the Sherman, also handicapped Canadians because

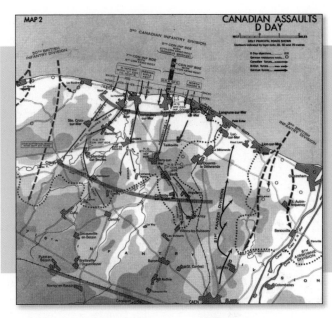

Map 7.3
The Canadian Attack on Juno Beach, June 6, 1944

Source: Library and Archives Canada NMC 188128.

Sergeant Gordon D. Petty of the Canadian Army Film and Photo Unit taking newsreel footage beside a shell-damaged building near Hoogerheide, Netherlands, 15 October 1944.

Source: Library and Archives Canada Mikan Number: 3204448.

its high silhouette projected a prominent target and it had lighter armour and less firepower than German Panzer and Tiger tanks. Copp asserts, though, that the Canadians always gave as good as they got, proof of which was seen in their notable contribution to the half million German casualties in Normandy. To critics, such as historian and Army Colonel John English, the allied victory was primarily the result of superior numbers and firepower that eventually wore the enemy down. English cast Canadian military leadership as lacking imagination, as too often adopting orthodox and very costly frontal assaults, sometimes with inadequate artillery and air support.[20] He pointed out that Montgomery had little confidence in Canadian military leadership, including in Canada's highest-ranking general, H.D.G. Crerar, who the British leader characterized as "prosy and stodgy,"[21] reflecting Crerar's long stint in bureaucratic positions. Montgomery most respected Canadian General G.G. Simonds, who was widely regarded as tactically innovative, though he also devised plans that were so complex that they often faltered among inexperienced troops and less capable commanders. Simonds, rather than changing his approach, fired a division commander, six of nine brigadiers, and 14 of 24 battalion commanders in July and August of 1944.

Following victory in Normandy, in September Canadian forces assumed the left flank of the allied advance and were assigned to capture the French channel ports. By October, Le Havre, Boulogne, Calais, and—most symbolically—Dieppe were in allied hands. However, these port facilities were badly damaged and too small and distant to handle the magnitude of supplies required by the allies. Only the Belgian port of Antwerp, located 80 kilometres inland from the North Sea along the Scheldt River, could fill the bill. It had been captured undamaged by Britain's Second Army on September 5, but not the surrounding area. The Canadians were tasked with clearing the Germans from the series of waterways and islands to the north of Antwerp that formed the Scheldt estuary. Advancing in cold and sleet, the Canadians had to traverse rivers, canals, water-filled ditches, flooded fields, and badly exposed roadways. Reflecting their growing battlefield proficiency, they prevailed, but only after a month of bloodletting that produced 6367 casualties, more than 1800 of which were fatal.

October–November 1944: Battle of the Scheldt.

The next major drive, launched in February 1945, saw the First Canadian Army (now composed of I and II Corps) move west to take Nijmegen in the south-central Netherlands, and south, to neutralize the enemy between the Maas and Rhine rivers in Germany. Late that month, II Corps drove east to take the ancient Rhine town of Xanten. Twelve days of fighting produced 3638 Canadian casualties. In late March, both I and II Corps drove north to liberate the Netherlands and advanced into northwestern Germany. During this final phase of operations, extending from March 24 to May 5, the First Canadian Army, though having evolved into a "superb … fighting force,"[22] still suffered 6298 casualties, 1482 of which were fatal.

Rising casualties intensified pressures to implement conscription, but King continued to resist. Signals from Quebec were becoming more worrisome. On August 8, 1944, Maurice Duplessis returned to power. Godbout's government had initiated several progressive measures—the vote for women in 1940, compulsory education until age 14 in 1943, and establishing the basis for Hydro-Quebec in 1944—but many viewed it as too closely aligned and beholden to the federal Liberals and not outspoken enough against conscription. Ten days after Duplessis's election, Camelien Houde, just released from his internment, was greeted by a cheering crowd of 50 000 Montrealers and soon won back the job of mayor, though he kept out of the conscription debate.

Defence Minister Ralston became far more outspoken about the need for conscription after visiting troops overseas in autumn 1944, where it was noted that several battalions were below strength. With Ralston no longer willing to relent—because he believed that battlefield efficiency was being compromised and that this cost lives—King accepted the defence minister's two-year-old resignation offer. King's decision, made without warning and before the entire cabinet, stunned its members and temporarily quieted other critics on the conscription issue. To replace Ralston, King appointed General A.G.L. McNaughton, a popular figure among Canadians. Few realized McNaughton had been sent home from England because of several botched training exercises, to prevent him from commanding Canadians in action as he wanted, and because of his absolute determination to resist any British plan to divide up Canadian forces. McNaughton's new assignment was to convince a notable proportion of the 68 000 men then conscripted into the home defence force to accept overseas service. Within weeks, McNaughton admitted he could not succeed. In cabinet, support for conscription grew, with powerful ministers like Howe now on board, and there were rumblings of resignations should King not act.

November 1944: Mackenzie King authorizes conscription for overseas service.

In late November 1944, King relented, but in doing so he still pursued a compromise. He authorized the conscription for overseas service of 16 000 men serving under the NRMA, a figure the Army's Chief of Staff identified as bare minimum. In Parliament, the measure was supported by fewer than half of the French-Canadian Liberals and it prompted Air Minister Power's resignation because he had pledged his opposition to conscription to his Quebec City constituents. There were demonstrations by some 2000 in Montreal and smaller protests in places that included Quebec City and Chicoutimi. Overall, the response in Quebec was far less violent than the reaction to conscription in the First World War because King, unlike Borden, was viewed to have resisted for as long as possible. In English Canada, many resented King for holding out for so long against conscription, but ultimately by taking some action, he avoided a political catastrophe.

The Liberal government also held support because by 1944 it was starting to implement not only social welfare measures but also substantive planning to try to ensure a smooth transition to peacetime. That year, C.D. Howe was moved from the Department of Munitions and Supply to the newly created post of minister of reconstruction. At his urging, firms received more than $250 million in accelerated depreciation tax write-offs between November 1944 and January 1946 to assist with their conversion from war-related to civilian production.

For many Canadians, returning to normalcy meant getting women, and particularly wives and mothers, out of full-time employment and back home to take care of husbands, raise families, and make room in the post-war workplace for veterans. Many women accepted the message that their employment had been an emergency wartime measure; some had come to loathe their wartime jobs and yearned for an easier and, they hoped, more stable and tranquil life. Women with children often felt guilty—or were made to feel guilty—for not spending more time at home. After nearly six years of war, many single women worried that time was of the essence if they wanted to avoid spinsterhood.

To encourage the trend towards domesticity, the federal government ended its financial support for daycare and cut income tax exemptions for married women from a wartime high of $750 to $250 as of January 1, 1947. The Women's Division of NSS directed women who wanted to stay in the workforce into low-paying and typically female jobs like "laundry work, household labour, or, for the better educated, low-paying clerical work."[23] No protection was extended to women as many employers restructured the gender composition of their workforce. Typical was the story of one woman who had worked for the Canadian National Railway and bitterly recalled a foreman who, soon after the war, approached her and commented sarcastically, "You look like a good-looking man," before firing her.[24]

By the end of 1944, plans were well underway to eliminate the CWAC, the RCAF-WD, and the WRCNS. Two years earlier, Ottawa established a committee to examine the Special Problems of Discharged Women. Geared in large part to attract more female recruits, its recommendations served as the basis for honourably discharged servicewomen becoming eligible for veterans' benefits, including free university education and vocational retraining. But when it came to the administration of these programs, counsellors with the Department of Veterans Affairs (DVA)—mostly male—steered servicewomen towards accepting cash payouts in lieu of job retraining and to settle into domestic life, or to pursue employment in areas widely perceived as "female," including through a Home Aide program to train them to become more professional, and hopefully better-paid, domestic servants, an option that few women veterans took. Although female veterans trained for 85 different occupations—journalism, commercial art and photography, and various mechanical, laboratory, and technical posts, for example—some 90 percent became stenographers and typists, hairdressers and beauticians, and textile workers. Captain (Dr.) Olive Ruth Russell, the senior woman administrator in the DVA, pushed for the right of servicewomen to receive veterans' benefits, though she also said that women accepted that the main priorities were to re-establish male veterans who had done the actual fighting, and to protect family life.

The retention of long-held attitudes also continued to have its uglier side. As the war drew to a close, Japanese Canadians were forced to choose between dispersal within Canada east of the Rockies or repatriation to Japan. By mid-August 1945, 10 397 Japanese Canadians, a number that included 3484 children, opted for repatriation. By the end of the year, 4720 officially requested that their decision be revoked, as many came to realize that Japan was utterly devastated. Ottawa announced that it would accept re-applications to stay in Canada if they had been made before September 2, 1945, the official date of Japan's surrender, but would treat other requests on a case-by-case basis. In all, 3964 returned to Japan. Unable to adjust, many applied to come back to Canada, but only 174 cases were successful.

While efforts were being made to disperse or expel the Japanese, Canadians awaited with much anticipation, and trepidation, the return home of 500 000 servicemen. Determined to avoid mistakes made with veterans of the First World War, the federal government had started very early on to plan for repatriation. In October 1939, when Canada's 1st Division was still preparing to depart for England, an Order in Council created a Cabinet Committee on Demobilization and Re-establishment; in October 1941, the federal government announced the Post-Discharge Re-establishment Order. Under its provisions, those honourably discharged would receive a tax-exempt gratuity payment of $7.50 per month for time they served in the Western Hemisphere, and $15 per month for time overseas. For veterans who did not claim other benefits, such as retraining, more cash was available, up to a level matching the gratuity in the form of a tax-free Re-establishment Credit intended to help veterans purchase, furnish, or equip a home or business.

Several other pieces of legislation soon followed. The 1942 *Reinstatement in Civil Employment Act* affirmed healthy veterans the right to resume their pre-military job, or a comparable post with their former employer, at a rate of pay equivalent to what they would have earned had they not enlisted. Grants and subsidized loans were made available to those who wanted to start their own business, to enter commercial fishing, or, under the 1942 *Veterans Land Act*, to farm full-time or to start a maximum 8100 square metre hobby farm. The 1942 *Vocational Training Co-ordination Act* provided living allowances to any veteran who decided to retool at the government's expense, an opportunity that, after the First World War, was made available only to those whose injuries significantly compromised their likelihood of finding work. Qualified veterans could obtain free university education with a living allowance for a period equivalent to the time they spent in the military, and provision was made for others to participate by obtaining a high school diploma in as little as six months under a special accelerated program. In March 1944 the DVA was created, with Ian Mackenzie, who was popular among veterans, appointed as minister, to better coordinate these and other programs, including pensions and medical care. Veteran benefits dwarfed all other federal social welfare costs, accounting for, between 1944 and 1948 inclusive, expenditures of $1.842 billion out of $3.621 billion.

As the next federal election approached, King remained concerned. His limited response to conscription left the Tories with room to gain ground. This was evident in February 1945 when his newly appointed minister of national defence, A.G.L. McNaughton, lost to the Conservative candidate, Garfield Case, in the Grey Bruce by-election.

Before dissolving Parliament for an election scheduled on June 11, King's government declared its support for a White Paper on Income and Employment commissioned by the Department of Reconstruction. The Paper advocated that Ottawa use its new taxing and, hence, spending powers to maintain "a high and stable level of employment." In the June 1945 election, the Liberals ran on the slogan: "A New Social Order" for Canada, especially with family allowance cheques scheduled to be mailed out on July 1. Also critical—and very fortunate—for King was the luck of timing, as on May 8, 1945, Germany surrendered. Besides spreading a joyous mood across the country, the defeat of the Nazis neutered the contentious issue of conscription, which had the greatest potential to help the Conservatives. Japan was not defeated until August 15, but Canada had committed few resources to the Pacific campaign. CCF prospects were compromised by recent Liberal social policies and the government's commitment to comprehensive post-war planning. Also of significance was the 1945 Ontario election, which occurred one week before the federal vote. Ten days before Ontarians went to the polls, Jolliffe accused Premier Drew of having created a "Gestapo" to spy on the CCF. However, Jolliffe could not prove the charge, which made the CCF look desperate and unprofessional, especially since a confident Drew promised to appoint a commission to investigate the accusation. The commission

May 8, 1945: VE-Day as Germany surrenders; June 11, 1945: Liberals re-elected.

corroborated some of Jolliffe's charges, but that came after the Tories triumphed with 68 seats, compared with 11 for the Liberals and 8 for the CCF.

The 1945 federal election results saw Quebec overwhelmingly remain Liberal, delivering the party 53 of its 65 seats. In Ontario, the Tories took 48 seats, compared with 34 for the Liberals, as there was lingering resentment over King's delays on conscription. The Liberals stayed level in the Maritimes compared with 1940, but lost ground in the West, in part because of the commodity price freeze and what many in the region saw as indifference to farm labour shortages. Military voters generally disliked King because of his delays on conscription, but comprehensive veterans' programs made them optimistic about their post-war prospects. Although the soldiers' vote was a key factor in King losing his own Prince Albert constituency, post-election polls indicated that the Liberals took 35 percent of the military vote, compared with 32 percent for the CCF and 26 percent for the Progressive Conservatives. Overall, the Liberals retained a majority, though a razor-thin one, winning 125 of 243 seats, compared with 65 for the Progressive Conservatives, 28 for the CCF, and 13 for the Social Credit.

As the war drew to an end, many challenges and uncertainties lay ahead. Numerous veterans would have great difficulty reintegrating back into civilian life. One indication of possible future turmoil involving veterans was the VE-Day riot in Halifax. More than 1000 naval personnel led in the looting of some 500 stores and produced $5 million in damages, three civilian deaths, and 211 arrests. The riot was not simply, as some concluded, triggered by early closings on VE-Day that prevented servicemen from obtaining a celebratory drink or meal. It also derived from a desire among servicemen to reap revenge on a city towards which resentment had been building for years, as wartime Halifax, beset by extreme overcrowding, witnessed strained relations between civilians and servicemen.

Throughout urban Canada there remained severe shortages of decent and affordable accommodation, a shortfall the federal government estimated at 600 000 homes. Many also fretted over organized labour as a threat to post-war economic, political, and social stability. In 1945 days lost to strikes topped 1 million, as new unions sought to establish themselves and labour battled to make up for wages frozen since late 1941.

Conclusion

Questions and concerns swirled as Canadians prepared for peace:

- Could Ottawa fulfill its commitment to provide comprehensive post-war planning and decent social welfare? Both George Drew and Maurice Duplessis made it clear that they wanted taxing powers returned to the provinces.
- Had Canada exchanged its recent colonial relationship with Britain for subservience to the United States?
- What role would Canada assume in the new United Nations?

The war brought many questionable policies that historians still debate. Was there justification for outlawing political groups like the Communist Party of Canada and pacifists like Jehovah's Witnesses? In 1988, the Canadian government offered an official apology and $21 000 to each surviving Japanese Canadian who was evacuated. Hysteria and racism affected the treatment of Japanese Canadians; yet, in the context of war, was there reason for concern and action? Many thought King acted without principle on the matter of conscription, placing the political interests of the Liberals in Quebec over the need to properly reinforce Canadian troops. But King did manage to keep Quebec *nationalistes* at bay, avoided the violent anti-draft riots of the First World War, and kept the country reasonably united. Social policies introduced by the Liberals were not nearly as comprehensive as Leonard Marsh advised, and despite King's reformist credentials, his actions were no doubt motivated, and limited, by what was deemed necessary to undercut the CCF and to stimulate the post-war economy. Still, his government provided Canadians with ground-breaking policies, such as family allowances, the *National Housing Act*, PC 1003, and the Veterans Charter.

Numerous Canadians suffered tremendously during the war and would look back upon this time with sadness, bitterness, and anger. Lives were destroyed by death, wounds, internment, and forced evacuation. Still if there is such a thing as a "Good War," perhaps the Second World War qualifies. Its cause to crush Nazism and Fascism was unassailable. For Canada, these years saw

- an economic depression supplanted by an economic boom;
- timid isolationism replaced by a commitment to engaged internationalism;
- governments assuming unprecedented responsibilities for the welfare of Canadians;
- new roles for women;
- isolated areas accessed and integrated as never before;
- the stage set for the addition of a tenth province.

Compared with 1939, Canada emerged from the trials and horrors of the Second World War as stronger, more internationally respected, and harbouring confidence in its ability to meet the challenges of the post-war world.

Questions to Consider

1. In what ways did the Second World War create new opportunities for Canadians?
2. How did the war change the responsibilities of Canada's federal government?
3. Did the war alter the status of women?
4. What were the major contributions of Canada's three military branches to the war effort?
5. How did the war impact Canada's relations with the United States?
6. How did the war affect federal–provincial relations?

Critical Thinking Questions

1. Was King an effective wartime leader?
2. Is it appropriate to use terms like "The Good War" or "Canada's War"?
3. Should Canadians feel shame in their treatment of Japanese Canadians?

Suggested Readings

General

Bercuson, David. *Maple Leaf Against the Axis: Canada's Second World War*. Toronto: Stoddart, 1995.

Granatstein, J.L., and Desmond Morton. *A Nation Forged in Fire: Canadians and the Second World War, 1939–1945.* Toronto: Lester & Orpen Dennys, 1989.

Keshen, Jeffrey. *Saints, Sinners and Soldiers: Canada's Second World War.* Vancouver: University of British Columbia Press, 2004.

Stacey, Charles Perry. *Arms, Men and Government: The War Policies of Canada, 1939–1945.* Ottawa: Department of National Defence, 1970.

Politics

Chapnick, Adam. *The Middle Power Project: Canada and the Founding of the United Nations.* Vancouver: University of British Columbia Press, 2005.

Granatstein, J.L. *Canada's War: The Politics of the Mackenzie King Government, 1939–1945.* Toronto: Oxford University Press, 1975.

Granatstein, J.L. *How Britain's Weakness Forced Canada into the Arms of the United States.* Toronto: University of Toronto Press, 1989.

Granatstein, J.L., and J. Murray Hitsman. *Broken Promises: A History of Conscription in Canada.* Toronto: Oxford University Press, 1977.

Stevenson, Michael D. *Canada's Greatest Wartime Muddle: National Selective Service and the Mobilization of Human Resources during World War II.* Montreal and Kingston: McGill-Queen's University Press, 2001.

Economic, Social, and Scientific Impact

Avery, Donald. *The Science of War: Canadian Scientists and Allied Military Technology during the Second World War.* Toronto: University of Toronto Press, 1998.

Bothwell, Robert, and William Kilbourn. *C.D. Howe: A Biography.* Toronto: McClelland & Stewart, 1979.

Coates, Ken, and W.R. Morrison. *The Alaska Highway in World War II: The U.S. Army of Occupation in Canada's Northwest.* Toronto: University of Toronto Press, 1992.

Granatstein, J.L., and Peter Neary, eds. *The Veterans Charter and Post-War Canada.* Montreal and Kingston: McGill-Queen's University Press, 1998.

Hatch, F.J. *The Aerodrome of Democracy: Canada and the British Commonwealth Air Training Plan.* Ottawa: Directorate of History, 1983.

Marshall, Dominique. *Aux Origines Sociales de l'État-Providence—Familles Québécoises Obligation Scolaire et Allocations Familiales, 1940–1955.* Montreal: Les Presses de l'Université de Montréal, 1998.

Zimmerman, David. *The Great Naval Battle of Ottawa.* Toronto: University of Toronto Press, 1989.

Civil Liberties

Abella, Irving, and Harold Troper. *None Is Too Many: Canada and the Jews of Europe, 1933–1948.* Toronto: Lester & Orpen Dennys, 1982.

Kaplan, William. *State and Salvation: The Jehovah's Witnesses and Their Fight for Civil Rights.* Toronto: University of Toronto Press, 1989.

Kordan, Bohdan. *Canada and the Ukrainian Question, 1939–1945.* Montreal and Kingston: McGill-Queen's University Press, 2001.

Roy, Patricia, J.L. Granatstein, Masako Iino, and Hiroko Takamura. *Mutual Hostages: Canadians and Japanese during the Second World War.* Toronto: University of Toronto Press, 1990.

Sunahara, Ann Gomer. *The Politics of Racism: The Uprooting of Japanese Canadians during the Second World War.* Toronto: James Lorimer & Company, 1981.

Ward, W.P. *White Canada Forever: Popular Attitudes and Public Policy Toward Orientals in British Columbia.* Montreal and Kingston: McGill-Queen's University Press, 1978.

Army

Copp, Terry. *Fields of Fire: The Canadians in Normandy.* Toronto: University of Toronto Press, 2004.

Copp, Terry, and Bill McAndrew. *Battle Exhaustion: Soldiers and Psychiatrists in the Canadian Army, 1939–1945.* Montreal and Kingston: McGill-Queen's University Press, 1990.

Delaney, Douglas E. *The Soldiers' General: Bert Hoffmeister at War.* Vancouver: University of British Columbia Press, 2005.

English, John. *The Canadian Army and the Normandy Campaign: A Study of Failure in High Command.* Westport, CT: Praeger, 1991.

Granatstein, J.L. *The Generals: The Canadian Army's Senior Commanders in the Second World War.* Toronto: Stoddart, 1993.

Granatstein, J.L. *Canada's Army: Waging War and Keeping the Peace.* Toronto: University of Toronto Press, 2002.

Greenhous, Brereton. *"C" Force to Hong Kong: A Canadian Catastrophe, 1941–1945.* Toronto: Dundurn, 1997.

Nicholson, Lt.-Col. G.W.L. *The Canadians in Italy, 1943–1945.* Ottawa: Queen's Printer, 1956.

Stacey, Charles Perry. *Official History of the Canadian Army in the Second World War,* 3 Vols. Ottawa: Department of National Defence, 1955, 1960, 1966.

Villa, Brian Loring. *Unauthorized Action: Mountbatten and the Dieppe Raid.* Toronto: Oxford University Press, 1994.

Zuehlke, Mark. *Ortona: Canada's Epic World War II Battle.* Toronto: Stoddart, 1999.

Zuehlke, Mark. *Juno Beach, Canada's D-Day Victory: June 6, 1944.* Vancouver: Douglas & McIntyre, 2004.

Air Force and Navy

Douglas, W.A.B. *Official History of the Royal Canadian Air Force*, Vol. 2. Toronto: University of Toronto Press, 1985.

Douglas, W.A.B., Roger Sarty, Michael Whitby, Robert Caldwell, William Johnston, and William Rawling. *A Blue Water Navy: The Official Operational History of the Royal Canadian Navy in the Second World War, 1943–1945*, Vol. II, Parts 1 and 2. St. Catharines, ON: Vanwell, 2002, 2007.

Greenhous, Brereton, Stephen Harris, William Johnston, and William Rawling. *The Crucible of War: The Official History of the Royal Canadian Air Force*, Vol. 3. Toronto: University of Toronto Press, 1994.

Milner, Marc. *North Atlantic Run: The Royal Canadian Navy and the Battle for the Convoys*. Toronto: University of Toronto Press, 1985.

Sarty, Roger. *Canada and the Battle of the Atlantic*. Montreal: Art Global, 1998.

Tucker, Gilbert Norman, *The Naval Service of Canada: Its Official History*, 2 Vols. Ottawa: King's Printer, 1952.

Prisoners of War

Auger, Martin F. *Prisoners of the Home Front: German POWs in Southern Quebec, 1940–1946*. Vancouver: University of British Columbia Press, 2005.

Dancocks, Daniel. *In Enemy Hands: Canadian Prisoners of War, 1939–1945*. Edmonton: Hurtig Publishers, 1983.

McIntosh, Dave. *Hell on Earth: Aging Faster, Dying Sooner. Canadian Prisoners of the Japanese during World War Two*. Toronto: McGraw-Hill Ryerson, 1997.

Women and Children

Bilson, Geoffrey. *The Guest Children: The Story of the British Child Evacuees Sent to Canada During World War II*. Saskatoon: Fifth House, 1988.

Dundas, Barbara. *A History of Women in the Canadian Military*. Montreal: Art Global, 2000.

Galloway, Patricia, ed. *Too Young to Fight: Memories from Our Youth During World War II*. Toronto: Stoddart, 1999.

Pierson, Ruth. *They're Still Women After All: Canadian Women and the Second World War*. Toronto: McClelland & Stewart, 1986.

Stephen, Jennifer A. *Pick One Intelligent Girl: Employability, Domesticity, and the Gendering of Canada's Welfare State, 1939–1947*. Toronto: University of Toronto Press, 2007.

Toman, Cynthia. *An Officer and a Lady: Canadian Military Nursing and the Second World War*. Vancouver: University of British Columbia Press, 2007.

Notes

1. Janine Roelens-Grant, ed. *Fighting for Home & Country: Women Remember World War II* (Guelph: Federated Women's Institutes of Ontario, 2004), 94–95.

2. J.L. Granatstein, *Canada's War, The Politics of the Mackenzie King Government, 1939–1945* (Toronto: Oxford University Press, 1975).

3. Studs Terkel, *The Good War: An Oral History of World War Two* (New York: Pantheon Books, 1984); Michael C.C. Adams, *The Best War Ever: America and World War II* (Baltimore: The Johns Hopkins University Press, 1994).

4. Canada, *Order in Council*, PC 882, Oct. 13, 1942.

5. Granatstein, *Canada's War*, 76.

6. *Saturday Night*, April 19, 1943, 19.

7. Ibid., Oct. 30, 1943, 20.

8. Paul Romney, *Getting It Wrong: How Canadians Forgot Their Past and Imperiled Confederation* (Toronto: University of Toronto Press, 1999), 170.

9. Jonathan Vance, *Objects of Concern: Canadian Prisoners of War Through the Twentieth Century* (Vancouver: University of British Columbia Press, 1994), 221–225; Dave McIntosh, *Hell on Earth: Aging Faster, Dying Sooner. Canadian Prisoners of the Japanese during World War Two* (Toronto: McGraw-Hill Ryerson, 1997), 250–255, 258.

10. Patricia Roy, J.L. Granatstein, Masako Iino, and Hiroko Takamura, *Mutual Hostages: Canadians and Japanese during the Second World War* (Toronto: University of Toronto Press, 1990), 91.

11. Ibid., 120.

12. Library and Archives of Canada (LAC) Wartime Information Board records, RG36, Series 31, Vol. 13, File 8-7A, Confidential Report of a Recent Survey of Public Opinion Among French-Canadians in the Province of Quebec Conducted by the Canadian Institute of Public Opinion, July 6, 1942.

13. Raj Ahluwalia, *We Interrupt This Program: The News Broadcasts That Kept Us Tuned In* (Toronto: Winding Star Press, 2000).

14. *Women at War* (Toronto: Maclean-Hunter, 1943), 10.

15. Gail Cuthbert Brandt, "'Pigeon-Holed and Forgotten': The Work of the Subcommittee on the Post-War Problems of Women, 1943," *Histoire sociale/Social History* 15, 29 (1982): 241.

16. Department of National Defence, National Defence Headquarters, Directorate of History and Heritage, 156.2A 34009(D2), Unit Morale Report, CWAC, MD #13, Oct. 1944.

17. *Canadian Home Journal*, March 1945, 14.

18. Ian MacPherson, "An Authoritative Voice: The Reorientation of the Canadian Farmers' Movement, 1935 to 1945," *Historical Papers* (1979): 164–181.

19. Terry Copp, *Fields of Fire: The Canadians in Normandy* (Toronto: University of Toronto Press, 2004).

20. John English, *The Canadian Army and the Normandy Campaign: A Study of Failure in High Command* (Westport, CT: Praeger, 1991).

21. J.L. Granatstein, *The Generals: The Canadian Army's Senior Commanders in the Second World War* (Toronto: Stoddart, 1993), 183.

22. J.L. Granatstein, *Canada's Army: Waging War and Keeping the Peace* (Toronto: University of Toronto Press, 2002), 307.

23. Jennifer A. Stephen, *Pick One Intelligent Girl: Employability, Domesticity, and the Gendering of Canada's Welfare State, 1939–1947* (Toronto: University of Toronto Press, 2007), 102.

24. LAC, Tape R-8548, Interview with Irene Wheeler.

8

Consensus *and the* Cold War: *1945–1957*

*O*n April 4, 1957, E. Herbert Norman, Canada's ambassador to Egypt, leapt to his death from the ninth floor of a Cairo apartment building. He was a casualty of the Cold War. Norman first studied the works of Karl Marx as a teenager and by the time he embarked on postgraduate work at Cambridge, was a devotee of communism. Completing a Ph.D. at Harvard, he became a leading expert on modern Japan, publishing two books that were among the first in the Western world to use Japanese sources. Brilliant and highly driven, in August 1946, he was appointed head of the Canadian legation in Tokyo. But as the Cold War became more intense, concerns grew in the U.S. Congress over Norman having access to sensitive documents, concerns that were made public in autumn 1950 and produced a formal RCMP investigation. Norman was cleared but was reassigned as Canada's high commissioner to New Zealand, a post that one former colleague described as "exile ... for someone of [his] calibre." Six years later, he returned to the diplomatic limelight as Canada's ambassador to Egypt, one of the world's most prominent trouble spots. Only days after Norman arrived in Cairo, Egypt became embroiled in a war against Israel, Britain, and France, and all were pressured into accepting a United Nations' (UN) international peacekeeping force, a solution Norman helped negotiate. The U.S. Congressional Subcommittee

chapter 8

Source: Glenbow Museum, NA-5600-7760a.

on Internal Security fretted over Norman being ambassador to a country then perceived as a Soviet proxy and once again made public innuendos about his communist sympathies. Norman slipped into depression, spoke of people out to "destroy him," and dreaded the prospect of once again facing "question after question."[1] His suicide occurred a few months before a Canadian federal election and hurt the Liberal government of Louis St. Laurent, which many Canadians saw as too closely aligned with the United States, a nation accused of hounding a man to his death.

After reading this chapter you will be able to:

1. Understand why the post-war period ushered in a strong sense of optimism.
2. Identify the degree to which fear of communist expansion shaped Canadian foreign policy.
3. Evaluate the extent to which anti-communism impacted upon Canadian democracy and civil liberties.
4. Assess the degree to which women's roles conformed to the domestic ideal.
5. Specify the degree to which immigration patterns changed after the war.
6. Explain why Canadians unexpectedly elected John Diefenbaker in 1957.

Introduction

Herbert Norman's tragic fate reflected the profound impact of the Cold War on post-war Canada. Although many condemned the United States for its role in Norman's suicide, the desire to safeguard the Western way of life from the Soviet Union also reinforced ties between Canada and the United States, guided much of Canada's foreign policy, and generated intolerance and repression at home. Popular opinion in the early post-war period would also constrain women and children within more traditional roles and maintained strong pressure on immigrants and Aboriginals to assimilate. Nevertheless, the notion of a post-war consensus built upon widely shared views, values, and assumptions also drew strength from the belief that there was much to celebrate.

At the end of the Second World War, Canadians faced a future that seemed rich in possibilities. Democracy had triumphed over totalitarianism. Canada emerged from the conflict as a respected middle power, with more international influence—it had become a significant industrial nation, though there was unease about what the future held. The dropping of atomic bombs on Hiroshima and Nagasaki on August 6 and 9, 1945, had not only produced celebrations over Japan's surrender on August 16 but had also horrifically demonstrated the catastrophic consequences of another world war. Many feared a steep post-war economic slump as had occurred following the First World War. There was worry that Canada's labour movement, whose membership had doubled during the war, would prove a threat to social order. There was the immediate challenge of reintegrating hundreds of thousands of veterans. But as things turned out, the period between the end of the Second World War and the defeat of the Liberal government of Louis St. Laurent in 1957 (which brought 22 years of Liberal dominance to an end) came to be widely regarded as prosperous and socially stable.

Between 1945 and 1960, Canada's population grew from 12.1 million to 17.9 million, a figure that included some 350 000 added from Newfoundland, which became Canada's tenth province in 1949. Canada's urban population reached 60 percent of the nation's total, with greater Montreal climbing to nearly 2 million people and Toronto to 1.2 million. In Toronto in 1954, the first major phase of its underground subway system was launched, stretching some nine kilometres north–south from the downtown Union train station to the city's outskirts, which was then Eglinton Avenue. Pervasive became the picture of most Canadians joining a burgeoning middle class, whose members owned their own homes and cars, and enjoyed a happy, stable, and traditional family life. In many ways, it did appear that Canadians were doing better than ever, but many questions remained:

- To what extent did dissatisfaction and dissent manifest?
- Were women happy with their lot?
- How did immigrants fare?
- How did Canadians react to the country's closer ties with the United States?
- Did they share the same fear of communism as their southern neighbour?

This chapter explores the extent of post-war prosperity, optimism, and consensus, and the experiences of those who challenged or rejected widely perceived norms.

Re-establishing Civilian Society

Although many of Canada's Second World War veterans struggled to re-establish themselves into civilian life, overall, they were less embittered than veterans had been after the First World War. Through what became known in 1945 as the Veterans Charter, some 100 000 men retrained for more than 100 vocational trades, 75 000 obtained full-size or hobby farms, and nearly 54 000 qualified for free university education, peaking at 40 percent of Canada's university population. "Where would I have been if there hadn't been a war?" remarked one veteran who, with government assistance, went on to become a lawyer. "[Maybe] ... a two-bit clerk ...with no future."[2]

After nearly six years of war, record numbers of Canadians rushed to the altar, eager to settle down, start a family, and enjoy the fruits of peace. Canada's marriage rate rose from 9.0 per 1000 in 1945 to 10.9 the following year, and the fertility rate per 1000 women climbed from 24.3 in 1945 to a post-war peak of 28.9 in 1947.

There were pressing challenges as the country shifted to peace. Canada's housing supply remained critically short. In 1945, the Wartime Prices and Trade Board introduced emergency regulations prohibiting civilians from migrating to Vancouver, Victoria, Winnipeg, Hamilton, Toronto, Ottawa, and Hull unless they had a formal job offer and a special government permit.

On the labour front, unions continued their battle for acceptance and to gain workers a bigger piece of the pie. Many launched a peacetime offensive for significant salary hikes to make up for ground seen as lost during the wartime wage freeze. Though having recently won substantive collective bargaining legislation, there remained the issue of compulsory check-offs or mandatory union membership. Many labour leaders feared that returning servicemen, in reacting against wartime strikes, would help employers decertify unions by refusing membership. In 1945, days lost to strikes topped 1 million and in 1946 reached an all-time record of 4.5 million. Among the most prominent disputes was a bitter 99-day strike over compulsory check-offs and pay, starting on September 12, 1945, at the Ford plant in Windsor, Ontario. The RCMP warned about communist influence, but the federal and Ontario governments appeared to realize that union leaders were seeking improved conditions, not to impose a radical agenda. The federal government appointed Supreme Court Justice Ivan Rand to settle the dispute at Ford. The resulting Rand Formula did not compel union membership but did require that everyone covered by a collective agreement pay union dues because all shared in any benefits won, which constituted another significant breakthrough for labour. Between 1945 and 1948, industrial wages in Ontario rose from 69.4 to 91.3 cents per hour. A post-war "peace formula"[3] took hold in which

September 1945: Ford strike in Windsor.

unions opted for legal legitimacy and steady workplace improvements over broader, class-based campaigns, such as to gain shop-floor control.

Canada's political left was modest. Its only CCF government, in Saskatchewan under Tommy Douglas, downplayed socialist doctrine and rhetoric and instead focused on implementing practical initiatives to assist ordinary people. Fulfilling a 1944 campaign promise, on January 1, 1947, the CCF introduced a plan for free universal access to hospital care, a measure that protected many from bankruptcy and whose popularity sparked new, though less generous, programs in British Columbia and Alberta, where hospital care became subsidized. With the passage of a progressive *Trade Union Act*, union membership in Saskatchewan soared by 118 percent between 1944 and 1948. In 1946, the CCF expropriated the Prince Albert Box Company because it did not abide by the provisions of the *Trade Union Act*. However, the government sought to ensure that this enterprise (for which it paid fair market price), and other provincial Crown corporations, turned a profit, and Douglas's government held the line against raising taxes.

Canada's post-war economy quickly came to inspire confidence and optimism. Unemployment increased in 1945, as Canada shifted from a war footing to peacetime production, but, based upon the experience after the First World War, it was not nearly as bad as many feared, with unemployment climbing from 0.7 to 3 percent. After years of doing without during the Depression and the war, Canadians were anxious to spend, and at the end of the conflict they held $6.5 billion in accumulated savings.

Ottawa was by all appearances effectively handling the economic transition to peacetime. Under the 1945 *National Emergency Transition Powers Act*, which was administered by C.D. Howe's Department of Reconstruction, the federal government maintained control over the price of items until it was believed that their supply had reached a level at which removing the ceiling did not risk generating significant inflation. By February 1946, about 300 items had their price decontrolled, and by early 1948 the process was complete. In 1946, consumption rose by 11 percent in constant dollars (meaning after inflation was subtracted from the total), and inflation peaked at 14 percent in 1949 but soon settled back to between 2 and 3 percent.

Public support remained strong for the federal government to pursue more extensive planning and to provide social programs to ensure greater stability. Most Canadians remembered the Depression and feared that a hands-off approach would bring its return. Bolstered by the Rowell-Sirois Commission and public opinion, and having committed itself in the later stages of the conflict to implementing more extensive welfare and Keynesian economic strategy, Ottawa was poised, and determined, to carry on as the dominant level of government within the federation. However, premiers George Drew of Ontario and Maurice Duplessis of Quebec had different ideas. With the emergency of war now over, they demanded that Ottawa relinquish the taxing powers it had assumed.

The King government called a dominion–provincial conference for August 1945. It spelled out its intentions in a document called the *Green Book*, which sought to institutionalize the recent transfer of powers and responsibilities between the two levels of government. Drew and Duplessis, determined to resist a loss of power and money (as the bulk of taxes were collected in central Canada), formed an oppositional alliance, though they received support only from Angus Macdonald, who in September 1945 returned as premier of Nova Scotia, having completed his post as federal minister of defence (naval services), with no love lost for Prime Minister King, who he thought had acted irresponsibly by resisting conscription for so long. Finally, in 1947, with Finance Minister Ilsley threatening to proceed unilaterally, the federal and provincial governments hammered out a five-year agreement (renewed until 1957) under which Ottawa retained its wartime taxing powers in exchange for transfer payments. Ontario and Quebec refused to sign, and in 1947, Ontario began its own modest income and corporate tax system. With far more revenue at its disposal, Ottawa spent twice as much as all the provincial governments combined.

Early Post-war Foreign Policy

The post-war period soon become largely defined by the Cold War. In Canada, the United States was cast as the leader in defending the "free world" against the Soviet Union, which was portrayed as determined to spread godless communism across the globe. For Canada, the Soviet Union had been a critically important, though never trusted, wartime ally. The Communist Party of Canada, which was banned in 1941 (though allowed to run as the Labour Progressive party in 1943), would not reappear until 1959.

September 1945: Igor Gouzenko defects.

One of the first major events that touched off the Cold War occurred in Canada. On September 5, 1945, Igor Gouzenko, a cipher clerk at the Soviet embassy in Ottawa, defected after learning that he and his family were to be sent home. Gouzenko sneaked out more than 100 secret documents exposing Soviet attempts to steal information about the atomic bomb, which was then solely in American hands, and to establish a network of sleeper agents across North America. This information ultimately led to the arrest of 22 local agents and 15 Soviet spies.

In early 1946, the federal government created the Kellock-Taschereau Royal Commission to investigate and interrogate many of those named by Gouzenko. Its recommendations resulted in the establishment of a federal security panel, with military and RCMP representatives, to identify communists in sensitive positions. Canada's lone Labour-Progressive Member of Parliament, Fred Rose, who was elected in a 1943 by-election in the Montreal working-class riding of Cartier, and re-elected in 1945, was charged with violating the *Official Secrets Act*. Expelled from Parliament, he was jailed for more than four years and then left for voluntary exile in Poland. Canada's National Film Board (NFB) had its funding slashed and almost ceased to exist because John Grierson, its commissioner until 1945, was named by Gouzenko as a communist sympathizer, something many were prepared to believe because of the NFB's wartime films praising the Soviet Union.

Although the Gouzenko affair placed Canada in the maelstrom of the early Cold War, it tried to gear its foreign policy towards building international cooperation and linkages. While Prime Minister King remained leery about international commitments—and thus strongly supported Article 44 of the new UN Charter permitting members to opt out of collective security—key figures in Canada's Department of Foreign Affairs saw the country as an important middle power with a substantive role to play on the international stage. Because of its rich uranium deposits, Canada was the only non-superpower to have representation on the UN Atomic Energy Commission, and Lester B. Pearson was named the first chairman of the UN Food and Agricultural Organization. Canada also increased its recognition and respect abroad, as between the end of the war and 1960 it established formal diplomatic ties with 36 countries.

Canada was also shedding the last vestiges of its colonial past. On January 1, 1947, the *Canadian Citizenship Act*, came into effect and ended the status of Canadians as British Subjects. Pressure built to end appeals to the Judicial Committee of the Privy Council (JCPC), a campaign that started during the Depression but was suspended during the war. Several provincial governments resisted given the JCPC's record of defending provincial rights, but in 1946 the JCPC itself agreed that the 1931 *Statute of Westminster* negated this right of appeal. Prime Minister King delayed; he was worried about a backlash from Canada's still powerful pro-British constituency, especially with rising sentiment to appoint a Canadian-born governor-general, talk of producing a new distinctly Canadian flag to replace the British Red Ensign, and the likelihood that King would be succeeded by his Francophone justice minister Louis St. Laurent. But once St. Laurent succeeded King and was re-elected as prime minister in June 1949, the bill ending appeals to the JCPC was passed into law and given royal ascent on December 10, 1949. Three years later, Vincent Massey, Canada's former ambassador to the United States, became the first Canadian-born governor-general since the Marquis de Vaudreuil-Cavagnal was appointed to represent the French Crown in 1755.

Despite its commitment to internationalism and maintaining an independent voice, Canada was operating in a world dominated by the American–Soviet rivalry. It agreed with the United States that the Soviet Union was a serious threat to freedom and peace. In the first two years after the war, the Soviet Union came to control governments in Poland, Romania, Yugoslavia, Albania, Bulgaria, and East Germany, partly as empire building and to spread communism, but also to establish a buffer area so that, after suffering 20 million dead in the Second World War, any future conflict would not be fought on its territory. In 1947, King signed a Joint Statement for Defence Collaboration that spoke of improving U.S.–Canada military cooperation, but it made no concrete commitments. The Soviets accused Canada of being a puppet of America, an attack to which Ottawa responded by closing its embassy in Moscow.

Economics drew Canada closer to the United States during the early post-war period. A devastated Europe could not pay Canada for the goods it required, funds that Canada needed to pay its perennial trade deficit with the United States. With a liquidity crisis looming, Ottawa applied controls against American imports and the outflow of currency. Canada sought access to the funds the United States was making available to Europe under the 1947 Marshall Plan, a massive aid program to assist Europe with its post-war recovery. Several American politicians were angered by Canada's discriminatory legislation, but once the import controls were lifted, the United States allowed the Europeans to use up to $300 million per year they received under the Marshall Plan to purchase Canadian goods.

Several high-ranking officials on both sides of the border advocated further U.S.–Canada integration, namely by establishing a comprehensive free trade pact. King authorized secret negotiations and a tentative deal was reached in February 1948 for the wholesale removal of duties over a five-year period, but he grew worried, recalling the disastrous political impact of free trade for the Liberals in the 1891 and 1911 elections. While contemplating the issue in his library, he came across a copy of Sir Richard Jebb's 1905 book *Studies in*

Colonial Nationalism. In his diary, King wrote of the book mysteriously opening up to a chapter entitled "The Soul of Empire," something that the spiritualist in King interpreted as supernatural forces warning him that free trade would again be seen by the public as threatening to sever Canada's links to Britain and bringing about its absorption into the United States. As a result, he jettisoned the plan.

Politics and Economics: The Early St. Laurent Years

November 1948: Louis St. Laurent becomes prime minister.

Canada's ties with the United States grew closer, especially with King's retirement in November 1948, one month shy of his 74th birthday, and his replacement with the more openly pro-American and stridently anti-communist Louis St. Laurent. Born in Compton in Quebec's Eastern Townships in 1882 to a French-Canadian father and Irish mother, the fluently bilingual St. Laurent entered King's government in 1942 to replace Ernest Lapointe as justice minister and soon became the prime minister's Quebec lieutenant, his most important advisor on French Canada. Detesting political gamesmanship, St. Laurent, a prominent corporate lawyer before entering politics, ran his government like a business, treated his cabinet like a board of directors, and demanded efficiency and results. Initially, political handlers worried that his keen intellect, considerable wealth, and reserved nature would make him appear too aloof, but he demonstrated great ease conversing with Canadians, projected a genial grandfatherly image, and became affectionately known as "Uncle Louis."

Seven months after being appointed as King's replacement, St. Laurent and his Liberal party faced the electorate in June 1949. The government pointed to a buoyant economy. The Liberals had established an excellent campaign organization, and, with strong ties to the business community, had accumulated plenty of cash for the campaign. The Progressive Conservatives, by selecting the well-known George Drew to succeed John Bracken as their leader in 1948, anticipated a political revival. However, St. Laurent came across as far more likeable than the rather stiff and overly combative Drew. Many regarded Drew as too Ontario-centric (having been premier for the past five years), as anti-Quebec because of his recent comments that the baby bonus (family allowance) was a bribe to French Canadians because they tended to have larger families, and as too unbending in his previous power struggles against the federal government, which also made it seem ironic that he was now trying to become prime minister. The Liberals triumphed with 49 percent of the popular vote and 193 of 262 seats.

The Liberals continued to benefit from a booming economy. Inflation, unemployment, and taxes remained low. The influential C.D. Howe moved from the Department of Reconstruction—which closed down operations in 1948—to become minister of trade and commerce, where he strongly

Prime Minister "Uncle Louis" St. Laurent's reads comic strips to his grandchildren.

Source: Library and Archives of Canada, PA-125907.

encouraged foreign investment, particularly from the United States, through various incentive programs. By 1950, American investment constituted 75 percent of the total coming into Canada. American ownership became more dominant in several sectors, such as 60 percent of both Canadian mining and oil and gas production. Responding to those who spoke about a sell-off of Canada, Howe maintained that the greatest threat to sovereignty was a poor economy.

Canada's strong economy and the ability of its federal government to afford social programs like family allowances and unemployment insurance were key in convincing Newfoundland to join Confederation. Britain, which had been forced to take over the governance of Newfoundland when the island went broke during the Depression, wanted it to become part of Canada. A 1944 estimate concluded that the island needed some $100 million in assistance. In early 1946, Britain's House of Commons announced the creation of a National Convention in Newfoundland to make recommendations for a referendum on the island's future. It convened on September 11, 1946, though initially there was little discussion among the 45 delegates about joining Canada. One man, though, changed the agenda: Joseph R. Smallwood. A native Newfoundlander, Smallwood in earlier years had used his marvellous oratorical skills and considerable personal charm to achieve success as a union organizer, newspaper journalist, and radio commentator. He argued that union with Canada would bring Newfoundland social programs well beyond the ability of what its current government could afford. Convention delegates still decided to keep Confederation with Canada off the referendum, but a petition organized by Smallwood that obtained 50 000 signatures demanded it and Britain ensured that it appeared.

Smallwood worked out a draft agreement with Ottawa that promised Newfoundland full access to federal social programs, funds to improve its antiquated railway and to upgrade the Gander airport, and the federal government's assumption of Newfoundland's debt. His presence dominated the campaign at rallies, over the radio, and as editor of the newly established *Confederate* newspaper. The Responsible Government League (RGL) opposed Smallwood, warning Newfoundlanders that their distinctiveness, self-determination, and tax dollars would all disappear if they became a part of Canada. Many Catholics on the island feared that, as part of Canada, they would lose their right to send their children to separate denominational schools. Commercial interests on the Avalon Peninsula (the most populated part of the island in the southeast where St. John's is located) fretted over increased competition from the mainland.

Opponents to Confederation lacked unity, as there also emerged the Economic Union party (EUP), which advocated tighter relations with the United States. The campaign was bitterly fought; in his memoirs, Smallwood said that he received death threats. On June 3, 1948, 45 percent of Newfoundlanders voted for independent responsible government, 41 percent for joining Confederation, and 14 percent for maintaining the current British-controlled commission government. A second referendum was slated for July 22 in which commission government was dropped as an option. Anti-confederates remained divided and lacked funds, and a tenuous alliance between the EUP and RGL generated fears about Newfoundland becoming part of the United States. The result revealed a deeply divided community, but Confederation squeaked in with 52.3 percent, and on March 31, 1949, Newfoundland officially became Canada's tenth province.

March 31, 1949: Newfoundland joins Canada.

Source: Library and Archives of Canada, PA-128080.

Joseph Smallwood becomes a Father of Confederation by signing the terms of union with Canada.

The Cold War Grows Chillier

Breaking from King's more cautious approach, St. Laurent spoke of the need to remain vigilant against communist expansion. In 1948, a Soviet-sponsored coup brought communists to power in Czechoslovakia; in response, England, France, Belgium, Holland, and Luxembourg signed the Treaty of Brussels, which established a mutual defence pact. On April 4, 1949, Canada joined the United States, the nations belonging to the Brussels pact, and other European states, in forming the North Atlantic Treaty Organization (NATO), a military alliance whose members agreed to provide collective defence. Besides selling NATO to Canadians as a means of containing the Soviet Union and its communist allies, Canada's government pointed out that as a multilateral rather than as a bilateral pact, no one nation, namely the United States, would dominate NATO. Canada also promoted NATO as an association of democracies dedicated to advancing freedom, and as an organization that would encourage trade among it members, an economic aim that Canada got inserted as Article II in NATO's Charter. When presented to Parliament, only two votes opposed Canada's membership in NATO.

April 1949: NATO created.

Fear of communist expansion kept Canadian support for NATO very strong, especially with the success of the communist revolution in China that saw the fall of Nanking on April 21, 1949, and the Soviets successfully testing the atomic bomb in August, which American President Harry Truman made public on September 23. Quickly, though, Canadian policy-makers came to understand that their influence within NATO was quite limited. The United States dominated, while Britain and France were the principal secondary powers. Article II was forgotten, as was the idea of NATO being an exclusive association of democracies, as its charter members included Portugal's military dictatorship under Antonio Salazar, because the United States sought access to air bases in the Portuguese-controlled Azores islands.

In November 1951, as part of NATO, Canada sent a brigade of about 6000 soldiers to northwest Germany, its largest ever commitment to a non-combat military venture. In 1952, Canada's federal government established a record peacetime defence budget of $2.4 billion, nearly five times as great as two years earlier. Most of that increased expenditure came as a result of Canada joining the American-led and UN-sanctioned "police action" to enforce collective security in Korea. Following the Second World War, with Soviet forces occupying the northern half of Korea and other allied troops in the south, the UN decided that for administrative purposes the country would be temporarily partitioned along the 38th parallel until elections would be held to unite it under a single government. But North Korea's leader, Kim Il Sung, and his Soviet supporters, had a different idea. In December 1948, Kim became the first premier of the Democratic People's Republic of Korea (an austere, militaristic, communist regime); Kim was determined to unify Korea under his rule. Signals came from America that Korea was not vital to its strategic interests, though the United States did not expect an invasion. With a green light from Moscow, on June 25, 1950, 110 000 North Korean soldiers poured across the 38th parallel and overwhelmed far weaker South Korean forces.

June 1950:
Korean War begins.

The United States sought UN approval to apply collective security against North Korea. Support came because the Soviets were boycotting the UN because of its refusal to officially recognize the new communist People's Republic of China. Although the mission was UN sanctioned, the Americans commanded it and supplied more than 90 percent of the international force. The St. Laurent government, seeking to show its support while also hoping to avoid high casualties, announced in July that Canada would provide three outdated navy destroyers and a Royal Canadian Air Force squadron comprising propeller-driven Vampire fighters to assist with logistics and communications. With the war going badly for the United States, Washington called on its friends to do more. With Britain, Australia, and New Zealand committing ground forces, Canada promised a brigade on August 7. Some historians, such as Robert Prince, argue that Canada's primary concern was holding back the communist tide, though others, like Denis Stairs, insist that Canadian policymakers hoped that more significant participation would provide Canada with the influence to constrain the United States from transforming this into a wider conflict.[4] Participation also brought economic benefits through a new U.S.–Canada Industrial Mobilization Committee, where Canadian industry was given access to U.S. military orders, something that generated $300 million worth of business between April 1951 and December 1952.

Ottawa authorized the creation of a 10 000-strong volunteer force for the Korean War. In September, the need for Canadian troops appeared to decline after the Americans landed behind enemy lines at Inchon, prompting a rapid North Korean retreat. However, U.S. Supreme Commander General Douglas MacArthur pursued the North Koreans across the 38th parallel, with the apparent aim of reuniting Korea under non-communist control. Although Canada quietly questioned MacArthur's strategy, it supported a UN resolution justifying the incursion into the north. In light of American success, Canada scaled back its commitment to half a brigade, and because all that was expected of these men was occupational duty rather than combat they were despatched to Korea before being fully trained.

On their way over, things changed dramatically. MacArthur ignored warnings from Peking not to approach the Yalu River, China's border with Korea, and in late-November

1950, waves of Chinese troops poured into Korea, throwing the badly outnumbered Americans into a desperate retreat. The Canadians were pressured to join the fray, but their commander, Lieutenant-Colonel J.R. Stone, insisted on the eight weeks' training that they were promised. In battle, the Canadians acquitted themselves well. On April 23 and 24, 1951, at Kapyong, located 40 kilometres northeast of Seoul, they suffered 10 dead and 23 wounded, but played a key role in thwarting a Chinese attack that could have struck deep into central Korea. Those serving with the 2nd Battalion of the Princess Patricia's Canadian Light Infantry won the American Presidential Unit Citation, the first Canadian formation ever so honoured. Nonetheless, there were morale and discipline problems. Canadian troops considered Korea cold and dirty and many developed contempt for local civilians, referring to them by the racist term "gook." Once the Americans recovered from the Chinese attack, the conflict became a grinding stalemate until an armistice signed on July 27, 1953, essentially returned things to the way they were before the war started, with Korea once again being partitioned along the 38th parallel. Supporters of the intervention stressed that it had contained communism in Asia, though at the cost of 516 Canadian lives, losses that were the fifth largest among the 23 UN combat participants, after the Republic of (South) Korea, (137 889 killed), the United States (35 516), the United Kingdom (1109), and Turkey (721).

April 1951:
Battle of Kapyong.

East–West relations did not start to tentatively improve until the Russian dictator Joseph Stalin died on March 6, 1953. Soon after, Canada restored diplomatic relations with the Soviet Union. Canada initially expressed apprehension over Stalin's successor, Nikita Khrushchev, who often seemed unpredictable and openly belligerent. Trade possibilities with the Soviet Union were explored, but only with non-strategic products like wheat. Canada continued to play a role in seeking to destabilize the Soviet-dominated Eastern European bloc (that in 1955 formed a military alliance called the Warsaw Pact), by pursuing relations with Yugoslavia, whose leader, Josep Broz Tito, broke from the Soviet Union in 1948. Participation in early international aid, namely the 1950 Colombo Plan, was in part predicated on Canada's desire to help steer the developing world away from communism. At the urging of the United States, Canada became part of the International Commission for Supervision, joining Poland and India in enforcing the 1954 Geneva Accords under which Vietnam was to be temporarily partitioned following the defeat of the French colonial forces by the Vietminh communists. Political scientist Thakur Ramesh says Canada initially followed its stated intention to impartially apply the accords. However, with Poland, a Soviet satellite state, consistently taking the side of the Vietminh, and India moving in this direction as an outgrowth of its anti-colonial struggle that brought it independence from Britain in 1947, Canada gravitated towards advancing Western interests by increasingly backing non-communist South Vietnam.[5]

Map 8.1
Major Battles of the Korean War

Source: Major Battles of the Korean War Invasion and Counter Stroke, 25 June–26 November, 1950 National Defence. Reproduced with the permissions of the Minister of Public Works and Government Services 2010.

Measures to neutralize communism continued in Canada. Between 1951 and 1958, Canada allowed the United States to construct three northern radar lines to protect North America against a possible Soviet air attack: the Pine Tree Line at 50 degrees latitude, the Mid-Canada Line at 54 degrees latitude, and the Distance Early Warning Line at 70 degrees latitude. Although Canada did not have the televised show-trials of suspected communists like America did, many lives were still shattered, such as when the RCMP visited an employer to "advise" on an employee's political leanings. Emphasis focused on those considered as influencing public opinion, such as employees of the Canadian Broadcasting Corporation (CBC). Among those targeted at the CBC was the Academy Award–nominated screenwriter Ted Allen, who ended up moving to England because his earlier association with the Young Communists made it impossible for him to find steady work in Canada in his chosen profession.

Many groups were closely monitored, such as the Canadian Peace Council, the Association of Ukrainian Canadians, and the United Jewish Peoples Order. In April 1951, the St. Laurent government passed an amendment to the *Criminal Code* increasing the penalty from two to seven years' incarceration for belonging to an organization that advocated the overthrow of constituted authority by force. By 1956, the RCMP was carrying out nearly 75 000 security checks annually to identify communists or their sympathizers. It also conducted wiretaps, including against suspected homosexuals, many of whom were fired from federal government jobs if they had access to sensitive documents because it was felt that their sexual orientation, considered deviant, would make them susceptible to blackmail by Soviet agents. To better detect homosexuals, the government eventually approved experimentation with a machine that measured the dilation of pupils in response to various images, with the assumption being that homosexual men would focus on pictures of the male physique.

Anti-communism percolated throughout the general population. A May 1953 public opinion poll showed that 62 percent of Canadians felt that communists should be denied freedom of speech. Fear spread over the potential consequences of associating with communists. In part to retain support, and arguably their continued existence, Canada's union movement undertook internal purges of communists throughout the late 1940s and 1950s. It was also steered in this direction by American-controlled international unions, which then dominated both the Canadian Congress of Labour (CCL) and the Trades and Labour Congress (TLC). America's 1947 *Taft-Hartley Act* banned communists from holding any union office, and this put pressure on Canadian locals of U.S.-based international unions to follow suit. Communists were purged from the executive of several CCL-affiliated unions, including the United Auto Workers, Mine-Mill, and the Shipyard Workers Union.

In 1949, the American Federation of Labor (AFL) successfully pressured the TLC to expel the Canadian Seamen's Union (CSU) because of communist links among the CSU's leadership. Both the AFL and the TLC supported raids on the CSU's membership by the conservative Seafarers' International Union (SIU) despite the SIU being led by Hal Banks, who had served a four-year prison term in the United States for forgery and who had escaped prosecution for murder because the only witness had disappeared. With both the CCL and the TLC buying into the anti-communist Cold War milieu, and the division between craft and industrial unions becoming less relevant in large and modern industries, Canada's two major labour bodies, following the 1955 merger of the AFL and the Congress of Industrial Organizations in America, joined forces in 1956 to form the Canadian Labour Congress. Canada's labour movement expanded its organizational links with an increasingly moderate CCF, which in 1956 released the Winnipeg Declaration that, unlike the earlier Regina Manifesto, made no mention of eradicating capitalism and endorsed a social democratic mixed economy.

Continental Canada

Integration with the United States also continued at the cultural level. In 1951, American magazines sold 86 million copies in Canada, compared with 42 million Canadian magazines sold. Canada possessed few major home-grown cultural institutions, such as ballet troupes, theatre companies, or orchestras. As the 1949 federal election approached, St. Laurent's handlers warned him that he would lose votes if he were perceived as dismissive of Canadian culture. Days before calling the election, his government established the Royal Commission on National Development in the Arts, Letters and Sciences under Vincent Massey, who was then chancellor of the University of Toronto. The Massey Commission, as it became known, heard from some 1200 people between August 1949 and July 1950, nearly all of whom emphasized the need for greater government support for the arts and higher education. Its 1951 report established the basis for the Canada Council—though it took another six years to appear—a federal government agency that supported more than 1500 annual university scholarships, pumped more than $40 million annually into other university initiatives, provided money for a new National Library, and funded numerous cultural bodies, such as the Winnipeg Ballet created in 1950, and the Stratford Shakespeare Festival, which debuted in a giant tent in 1953.

Even with these great strides being made to develop a Canadian-centred culture, Canadians nonetheless remained mass consumers of American culture. Hollywood films dominated in Canadian cinemas. In 1952, the first Canadian television stations went on the air: CBFT in Montreal and CBLT in Toronto, and within seven years that number reached 47. Canadians did watch some home-grown products, such as the Maritime musical show *Don Messer's Jubilee*, and *Hockey Night in Canada* became a Saturday-night institution. But even on the CBC, the most popular programs were U.S. ones, such as *I Love Lucy* and *The Jackie Gleason Show*.

American direct investment into Canada continued rising, from $3.58 billion in 1950 to $8.33 billion in 1957. The U.S.–Soviet arms race bolstered this trend; for instance, the Canadian Crown corporation Eldorado sold as much as $300 million worth of uranium per year to the United States, most of which was used to build nuclear weapons.

Good Times

Canada's economy hummed along, with industrial production, congregated in southern Ontario, leading the way. Over the course of the 1950s, industrial output grew by some 50 percent. In several areas, expansion was extraordinary, such as with the production of electrical items, whose value tripled between 1945 and 1960. Firms were becoming more mechanized and efficient. Between 1945 and 1957, the number of manufacturing establishments rose by 30.6 percent to 378 751; the number of employees, by 21.5 percent to

1.36 million; but the value of production went up by a whopping 161.3 percent to $4.82 billion. In the West, the energy sector expanded, sparked by a major oil strike in Leduc, Alberta, in February 1947. Annual crude oil production in Alberta went from 10 889 barrels in 1948 to 113 278 in 1958, while natural gas produced in the province rose from 875 cubic metres in 1941 to 3994 cubic metres in 1956. The fishing sector, a bellwether of the Maritime economy, saw moderate growth in the value of exports, from $99.5 million in 1949 to $123.4 million in 1957.

Across Canada, farms modernized. Rural electrical customers nearly doubled from 1.98 million households in 1945 to 3.645 million a decade later, or from 38 to 69 percent. Tractors and other major farm machinery disseminated widely. With wheat, between 1945 and 1960, seeded areas grew from 930 000 to 1 million hectares, but the number of bushels produced from that land skyrocketed from 316.3 million to 514.3 million. In the first decade after the Second World War, total farm income in Canada rose from $851.7 million to $1.174 billion.

Unemployment remained low, hovering between 2.8 and 5.9 percent between 1945 and 1957. Canadians were earning more: between 1945 and 1960, the average annual salary nearly doubled from $1649 to $3176; between 1945 and 1955, the hourly industrial wage went from 69 cents to $1.45, and in construction, from 74 cents to $1.52. However, in the service sector, where women were employed in large numbers, the increase was from 43 to 86 cents. Pay also varied considerably between regions. In 1950, whereas the average Canadian weekly salary was $45.08, it stood at $38.17 in the Maritimes, $42.09 in Quebec, $46.58 in Ontario, $43.83 in the Prairies, and $47.70 in British Columbia. Throughout the 1950s, union membership stayed at about one-third of the non-agricultural workforce and strikes remained low, ranging between 500 000 and 750 000 days per year, the result of better salaries and the fear among some unions of being labelled as radical.

Canada's housing market remained red hot, fed by rising incomes, easier down payment requirements, low mortgage interest rates, and affordable prices. The 1944 *National Housing Act* halved the down payment requirement to 10 percent and the Central Mortgage and Housing Corporation (CMHC), a federal Crown corporation established in 1945, helped keep mortgages fixed for as long as 25 years, up to five times the pre-war standard, and at rates as low as 4 percent. For several years after the war, demand outstripped the supply of homes, as housing starts had dramatically declined during the Depression and the war. Nearly 368 000 homes were constructed between 1945 and 1949, and in practically every year throughout the 1950s, more than 100 000 new residential homes were built. Whereas the value of residential construction was $1.04 billion in 1945, a decade later, in constant dollars, it reached $2.78 billion.

One million Canadians settled in suburban communities between 1945 and 1960, a trend reinforced by expanding car ownership and road construction. New, massive, planned communities emerged, such as Don Mills, north of Toronto, on 810 hectares of farmland that was largely bankrolled by financier E.P. Taylor. Former hamlets—such as Scarborough and North York outside Toronto, and Burnaby and Coquitlam outside Vancouver—exploded in population; in the case of North York, growth was 1075 percent between 1941 and 1961.

New housing in the north-west Toronto suburb of Rexdale in the 1950s. Much of the farmland was purchased by developer Rex Heslop who believed that the new 401 highway, started in 1952, and the city's expanding international airport located nearby at Malton, would bring strong demand for housing.

Source: City of Toronto Archives, Series 497, Item 845010.

Large builders used standardized designs, most typically for small one-storey bunga-lows or larger ranch-style homes. The CMHC sold blueprints for many such homes for as little as $10. Builders used pre-assembled parts and drywall rather than plaster, because it was fast and cheap, though new suburban homes included modern conveniences, such as central heating, flush toilets, baths, showers, and carports. Some criticized these new suburban developments for the uniformity of housing, for establishing bland neighbour-hoods, and, as some later postulated, for subliminally reinforcing societal conformity. Yet countless Canadian families were thrilled to leave overcrowded city centres for new, affordable, and child-friendly neighbourhoods with large backyards, parks, safe streets, and modern household conveniences. Home ownership grew at an unprecedented rate, rising from 57 to 65 percent of households between 1941 and 1951, and it's no wonder because houses started for as little as $3000. An important development that made much of this possible was the construction of new highways that connected the suburbs to city centres.

With their rising incomes, Canadians were on the move more than ever. People clamoured for cars, which were difficult to purchase until the late 1940s when supply finally began to catch up with demand. Car registration among Canadians rose from 1.16 million in 1945 to 4.1 million in 1960. There came the new phenomena of motels for car travellers, their number in Ontario more than tripling from 151 in 1951 to almost 500 three years later. With tourism, 10 times as many Canadians visited the United States as compared with Americans who came to Canada. More Canadians were travelling by airplane, as its technology and safety advanced notably during the Second World War, and air routes expanded with the government-owned Trans-Canada Airlines being joined by the privately owned Canadian Pacific Airlines in 1942. Although air travel remained relatively expensive, total passengers grew from 81 600 in 1946 to 429 700 thousand in 1955.

Consumerism took greater hold as Canadians had more disposable income—and more stores issued credit cards. In the suburbs, retail malls with car parking lots became the trend, growing from 64 in 1956 to 231 four years later. Total retail sales increased from $4.57 billion in 1945 to $13.47 billion in 1955. Canadians sought the latest items, like cars with a convertible roof; electric ranges and automatic clothes dryers; and gadgets, like transistor radios. The television quickly became a household staple, with sales rising from 325 in 1948 to more than 100 000 by 1953, as mass production and demand brought falling prices. For instance, whereas a 1948 16-inch (40-centimetre) Freed-Eiseman tabletop black-and-white model cost $795, a 1954 17-inch (43-centimetre) RCA black-and-white model listed for $189. Modern conveniences also came in the form of new, and very popular, ready-made or instant food products, like TV dinners, Kraft Dinner, and Jell-O.

Government spending helped fuel the post-war boom. Ottawa led the way with major infrastructural projects. In 1948, it provided $150 million for the Trans-Canada Highway. It forged ahead with plans for the St. Lawrence Seaway, prodding the United States to share the costs—which for Canada reached just less than $1 billion between 1955 and 1959—by threatening to proceed on its own and thus manage the waterway. Several essential services experienced massive expansion. Money spent on hospital construction went from $18.9 million in 1945 to $130 million a decade later. In education, the value of construction on university campuses went from $5.1 million to $22 million, as the 40 000 veterans who attended university sparked a new trend in enrolment, which increased from 64 731 in 1945 to 113 729 in 1955. Over that decade, university operating budgets rose from $30.5 million to $100.2 million, in part to support hiring more faculty, whose numbers across Canada went from 4503 to 5992. But the process was not without controversy.

In 1951, much of the new money for universities came from federal sources. Quebec refused the money, as Premier Duplessis considered it a way for Ottawa to interfere with provincial control over education. Also, though an expanded university system broadened opportunities for Canadians, historian Paul Axelrod points out that because new corporate and even government money often came with strings attached, such as setting the direction of research, the potential increased for compromising the independence of universities.[6] Far more construction occurred with elementary and secondary schools, as enrolment exploded from 2.04 million in 1945 to 4 million in 1960. In the first post-war decade, school construction costs rose from $12.9 million to $171 million, and operating budgets rose from $139 million in 1945 to $902 million in 1960, in large part to pay a teaching corps whose numbers nearly doubled over those 15 years, from 84 114 to 163 578. All levels of government pitched in: Over the 1950s, federal contributions (even though schooling fell out of its jurisdiction) went from $12.2 million to $51.4 million; provincial support, from $128.5 million to $541.9 million; and municipal contributions, from $199 million to $652.5 million.

With Canada's strong economy, its federal government made moderate improvements to social programs without raising taxes or taking on significant debt. In 1952, the income-based means test for Old Age Pensions was removed for those 70 and older, and applied to those 65 to 69, who now became eligible for this benefit. Pension rates, though far from lucrative, doubled from 1927 to 1950 to reach $40 monthly and were further supplemented with modest payments made by every provincial government except Ontario, Prince Edward Island, and New Brunswick. In 1957, the federal Liberal government introduced the *Hospital Insurance and Diagnostic Services Act*, under which the federal government began to work out shared-cost agreements with the provinces—which were completed by 1961—to provide Canadians with free hospital care and laboratory and radiological diagnostic services. Polls showed that as many as 80 percent of Canadians endorsed some type of public health insurance scheme, as approximately one-third had no insurance, and private schemes were expensive and did not cover many treatments and services.

Several other social welfare initiatives were not as well received. The federal government strongly resisted providing subsidized public housing, opposition it had long held, believing it would sap individual initiative, damage a critical domain of the private sector, and bring the country too close to socialism. In a 1947 speech, then–Justice Minister St. Laurent declared: "No government of which I am a part will ever pass legislation for subsidized housing."[7] The 1949 *National Housing Act* deviated from this position by offering to fund up to 25 percent of the costs for public housing, but the gesture was immediately criticized by public housing advocates for being grossly inadequate, especially in light of continuing federal control over income and corporate tax fields. Also, under the 1949 legislation, public housing initiatives had to go through some 80 steps before being approved. As housing historian John Bacher observed, "only where political demands were strongest"[8] did construction result. Between 1949 and 1963, a mere 11 000 subsidized units were built with federal assistance. The most substantial initiative was a slum redevelopment project in the Toronto neighbourhood of Regent Park. Started in 1947 and completed in 1959, and primarily funded by municipal money, it was a series of three- and six-storey walk-up structures that together took on the appearance of a concrete fortress. The project's goal was to achieve low per-unit building costs, but there was also the intent that public housing not look appealing so that people would want to save for their own home and, ideally, move into something better. In Regent Park, and in later public housing developments, the designs often physically separated residents from the surrounding community and inherently stigmatized them.

The idea of bringing back government-funded daycare drew criticism for encouraging women to choose paid work over raising their children. In Toronto, the city government partially funded some daycare centres in the early post-war period but quickly abandoned the practice, especially when it was discovered that communists were among those lobbying for more extensive public support. Many of those who required daycare could not afford it; in Toronto, the rates increased as much as sixfold between 1948 and 1951. In 1952, in British Columbia, there were only 277 licensed daycare spaces. It wasn't until the 1970s that daycares became regulated and started receiving public funds to create subsidized spaces for those with great financial need.

With the public generally supportive of Ottawa's stronger role, federal–provincial disputes remained low-key, at least in English Canada. In Ontario, in 1948 the outwardly amiable Leslie Frost—whose self-proclaimed small-town values and longevity in office, lasting until 1961, earned him the affectionate nickname of "Old Man Ontario"—succeeded the combative George Drew as premier. Frost understood that when it came to federal–provincial relations, Ontarians wanted greater consensus, which they viewed as contributing to effective planning and continuing prosperity. In 1952, his government agreed to a five-year tax rental agreement with Ottawa in which Ontario largely ceded control over income and corporate taxes in exchange for a larger subsidy, a minor share in inheritance duties, and the federal government's abandonment of its right to participate in some smaller direct tax fields.

Elsewhere, the expression of regional grievances remained relatively quiet as growth continued strong. In Alberta, the province's Social Credit government moderated its doctrines under Ernest Manning, who took over after William Aberhart's death in 1943, and would remain premier for a quarter century. Manning openly denounced anti-Semitic elements within Social Credit and made moves to purge the party of such extremism, though critics, such as historian Janine Stingel, argue that this prejudice was still quietly tolerated.[9] The Manning government focused on courting investment, providing price supports to farmers, and followed a fiscally conservative approach, such as on debt reduction. Manitoba's economy benefited from increased mining activity and the development of hydroelectricity in the north. In several northern areas of Saskatchewan, uranium mining created boom conditions. In British Columbia, lumbering rapidly expanded to meet record demand for homes and furniture. Liberal Byron "the Boss" Johnson, who became British Columbia's premier in 1947, forged ahead with an ambitious $90 million transportation plan, as much of the province, even relatively close to Vancouver, was cut off and remained in frontier-like conditions.

Rural electrification in British Columbia intensified, and a new pipeline was built to the Alberta oil fields. Investment was courted, particularly for resource development. In 1951, the Aluminium Company of Canada signed an agreement to construct a massive smelter 110 kilometres southeast of Prince Rupert in what would become the town of Kitimat. The same year, the H.R. MacMillan Export Company merged with Bloedel, Stewart and Welch Ltd. to form the lumbering giant MacMillan Bloedel, the largest corporate merger in the province's history. In 1952, the colourful W.A.C. Bennett, a former Conservative who turned to Social Credit after twice failing to become British Columbia's Conservative leader, won the premiership in part by tapping into the substantial support for Social Credit among the 20 percent of the province's population who had come from the Prairies. Although casting himself as an outsider and not beholden to vested interests, "Wacky" Bennett, as he became affectionately (or derisively) known over two decades as premier, eagerly courted foreign investment, heralded the free market but did not oppose massive corporate mergers, and controlled budget deficits. Enriched by booming mining, timber, and pulp and paper sectors, his government launched an aggressive province-building campaign under which, by 1958, more money was spent on roads than during the entire history of the province. Fights would come with Ottawa over the control of waterways for hydroelectric development, but not until the early 1960s.

Pas Comme les Autres (Not Like the Others)

In Quebec, Maurice Duplessis's Union Nationale government, despite aggressively court-ing Anglo and American investment, used French-Canadian nationalism to build support, including in combating federal power. In 1948, Duplessis symbolically adopted the *fleurs-de-lys* as Quebec's flag. Three years later, his government rejected federal funding for universities and in 1954 imposed its own tax on incomes to force the federal government to scale back its control in this area. In 1953, the Union Nationale established the Quebec Royal Commission of Inquiry into Constitutional Problems. The five-volume report that was released in 1956 presented Confederation in 1867 as a pact between the English and French that inherently gave Quebec special status to protect and promote the French language and culture.

Despite his substantial ties to corporate interests, Duplessis managed to project a folksy charisma that endeared him to ordinary Francophones, especially those living in rural areas for whom he cast himself as protector. *Le chef*, or the chief, as he became widely known, commanded a dominating presence in Quebec, where many were convinced that he was the only one capable of running the province. To others, however, he was demagogic and authoritarian and his government was corrupt. Widespread was the belief that only those areas that voted Union Nationale would receive decent government service, something that helped keep rural Quebec, which required electrification, strongly behind the Union

"Drums Along the Ottawa." The 1954 income tax fight between the federal and the Quebec provincial government as depicted by the Montreal Gazette's political cartoonist John Collins.

Source: McCord Museum, M965.199.7902.

Nationale. For Quebec dairy farmers, Duplessis refused to authorize the sale of margarine, whose 1886 ban in Canada was overturned by the courts in 1950, but it would not appear in Quebec until 1961, two years after Duplessis died. Support from rural areas paid off handsomely because with the government dragging its feet on electoral readjustment, rural Quebec (as late as 1951) held 55 percent of the seats in the provincial legislature despite having only one-third of the province's population.

Duplessis preached a backward-looking form of Quebec nationalism, describing the province as possessing a morally superior society based upon its agricultural and Catholic nature. Much of the Roman Catholic Church, which had some 8000 priests across the province in the 1950s, strongly backed Duplessis, especially since his government permitted the church to retain control over schools and most social services for Francophones, a practice that also saved the provincial government a great deal of money. The church also firmly endorsed Duplessis's efforts to repress the political left—which it cast as promoting social disorder, violence, and atheism—as well as Jehovah's Witnesses for their denunciations of Catholicism and the Pope.

Financial backing for the Union Nationale came from Anglo and American big business, which enjoyed low taxation and faced little or no obligation to process resources in Quebec. In 1949, 92.8 percent of minerals were exported from Quebec in raw form. Between 1953 and 1959, total U.S. investment in Quebec doubled to $4 billion, and Americans dominated in areas that included industry and resource development. The government maintained it was collecting substantial revenues from royalties and that investment created many good jobs. On the one hand, between 1944 and 1959, aggregate payments to Quebec workers grew by 154.7 percent, but on the other, with most large firms operating in English and favouring those of Anglo background, Francophones were confined to the lower rungs, earning, on average, two-thirds of their English-speaking counterparts, and by the end of the decade, only 5 percent of company directors in Quebec were Francophone. In presenting himself as a man of the people, Duplessis meant it in a paternalistic way; he had little tolerance for protest. He was strongly anti-union, claiming he was protecting the province from outsiders and communists. His government barely tolerated the *Confédération des travailleurs catholiques du Canada* (CTCC), despite its heavy church involvement and advocacy of joint committees of labour and management, rather than strikes, to settle disputes.

Forces for change were brewing in Quebec, but it would take Duplessis's death to unleash the process. While Duplessis's power base was rural Quebec, the province's urban majority continued to grow. Federal government programs like unemployment insurance and family allowances started to cut into church power over social services. As well, Quebec's church-run classical colleges and universities were increasingly portrayed as failing to equip Francophones for success in Quebec's urban and industrial society because of their tendency to steer students into the liberal professions. More Quebecers expressed frustration with the economic power exerted in the province by Anglos and Americans. The new mass media, particularly television, was making Quebecers more aware of the fact that compared with other parts of Canada they were not doing as well in terms of personal financial wealth. Some reformist elements in the Catholic Church cast Duplessis's government as corrupt because of its vast use of patronage and reliance on corporate contributions. Organized labour, including the 100 000-strong CTCC, became more hostile to the Union Nationale. This became plainly evident during the five-month long strike starting on Valentine's Day 1949 by some 5000 of Canada's poorest paid, and overwhelmingly Francophone, workers led by the National Federation of Mining Industry Employees and the CTCC against the American-owned Johns Manville Corporation and three other smaller Anglo- and American-owned companies near Asbestos and Thetford Mines in Quebec's Eastern Townships. Chaplains in the area backed the strikers and dismissed the government's claim that communists were fomenting class conflict. Archbishop Charbonneau of Montreal was among those who condemned the employers, and he helped raise funds for the strikers; soon rumours circulated—though never proven—that Duplessis pressured the Vatican to transfer Charbonneau to the Diocese of Victoria, British Columbia. The provincial government declared the strike illegal and sent in the police to protect replacement workers. The dispute ended after strikers trying to close the mines clashed with police who, after the *Riot Act* was read, threatened to open fire.

Numerous Quebec intellectuals expressed the need for fundamental change. In 1948, the modernist artist Paul-Émile Borduas released the widely read *Refus global* that beseeched Quebecers to reject stultifying orthodoxies, namely those imposed by the church and the provincial government, and to embrace outside influences, which for Borduas prompted him to leave Quebec permanently. Among intellectuals on the scene at Asbestos was Pierre Trudeau, then a young left-wing lawyer, academic, and intellectual. In a book of essays he organized and edited in 1949 collectively entitled *La grève de l'amiante*, Trudeau cast the strike as a seminal event in the awakening of Francophones against a repressive provincial government and to the need for major change to achieve greater economic and social justice. It was a message that he and a number of social scientists, primarily at Laval University, began disseminating in 1950 by establishing a small-circulation, but soon influential, publication called *Cité libre*. While Trudeau promoted an inclusive pluralistic society linked by a common civic nationalism, others who advocated against Duplessis advanced an ethnic-based *nationalisme* of Quebec for *les Québécois* as a way to open up opportunities for Francophones. The two groups attempted to join forces by creating the *Rassemblement* in 1956 as a left-of-centre alternative to the Union Nationale. Internal dissent kept its membership below 500, and the partnership dissolved by the end of 1957, thus setting the stage for a battle between two alternative reformist visions for Quebec's future.

Newcomers and Natives

Demographically, Canada was becoming more diverse; immigration was once again changing the face of the nation. After slowing to a trickle since the early 1930s, immigration became a major source of population growth in the post-war period. Between 1946 and 1952, Canada provided refuge to 164 000 displaced persons (DPs) from war-torn Europe. Newsreels of the chaos, suffering, and starvation left by the war moved Canadians. Of those classified as DPs, 23 percent were Poles; 16 percent, Ukrainians; 11 percent, Germans and Austrians; 10 percent, Jews; 6 percent, Latvians; 6 percent, Lithuanians; 5 percent, Hungarians; 4 percent, Russians; 3 percent, Czechs; and 3 percent, Dutch. Immigrants were selected based on their occupational skills, particularly skills in which Canada had shortages; selection was also based on who would not significantly alter Canada's white and Christian character. Of the 250 000 Jewish survivors of the Holocaust, Canada accepted only 8000 by the end of 1948, the same year Israel was created, which provided an outlet for European Jewry.

In 1947, in an official Statement on Immigration, Prime Minister King talked of Canada's "absorptive capacity," meaning its need not only to keep the number of newcomers to a level that would not add notably to unemployment and strain social services, but also to prevent immigrants from altering Canada's racial character. Of the Chinese, many of whom clamoured to leave a homeland then ravaged by civil war and persistent and widespread squalor, King remarked in Parliament: "Any considerable Oriental immigration would … give rise to social and economic problems … that might lead to serious difficulties."[10]

As noted in Table 8.1, immigration continued to grow during the 1950s, fuelled by labour shortages in several sectors, namely in construction, industry, forestry, and, for women, domestic service. Canada continued to give priority entry to immigrants from Britain, 800 000 of whom arrived between 1946 and 1967, because of economic difficulties at home, family ties in Canada, and the perceived ease of cultural adaptation. Canada accepted virtually no black immigrants from the various Commonwealth nations, though. As noted in Table 8.2, the principal origins of Canada's population on a percentage basis changed little. The aggregate population of other Europeans grew significantly, namely from Germany (many of whom were skilled workers) and Italy (a large percentage of whom went into the building trades). For instance, between 1951 and 1961, 230 000 Italians arrived in Canada, 90 000 of whom settled in Toronto, making them the city's largest non-British ethnic group.

Table 8.1
Immigration to Canada by Year, 1945–1957

Year	Number
1945	22 722
1946	71 719
1947	64 127
1948	125 414
1949	95 217
1950	73 912
1951	194 391
1952	164 498
1953	168 868
1954	154 227
1955	109 966
1956	164 857
1957	282 252

Source: F.H. Leacey, ed., *Historical Statistics on Canada* (Ottawa: Supply and Services, 1983), series A-35.

Table 8.2
Canada's Population by Origin, 1941–1961

Year	Total	British	% British	French	% French	Other European	% Other European	Other	% Other
1941	12 152 655	5 715 904	47	3 483 038	28.7	2 943 926	24.2	9 787	0.1
1951	13 618 190	6 709 685	49.3	4 319 167	31.7	2 553 722	18.7	35 616	0.3
1961	17 651 785	7 996 669	45.3	5 540 346	31.4	4 026 850	22.8	88 190	0.5

Source: F.H. Leacey, ed., *Historical Statistics on Canada* (Ottawa: Supply and Services, 1983), series A-125–163.

Open racism became far less acceptable in the post-war years, especially as the Holocaust became widely known. The UN Charter that Canada signed denounced racism. In 1944, Ontario's government outlawed workplace discrimination on the basis of race and in 1951 did the same with housing covenants designed to keep certain groups out of neighbour-hoods; however, a high burden fell upon the complainant to prove that racism was the intent of those that they charged. The same year as King's Statement on Immigration, the federal government rescinded the 1923 Chinese exclusion legislation and permitted Chinese men with Canadian citizenship to bring over their wives and children under 18. Also in 1947, Chinese and East Indians received the provincial franchise in British Columbia, and two years later the Japanese were given the federal and British Columbia vote and were re-qualified for possible immigration to Canada. As with previous generations of immigrants, it took time and often more than one generation, for newcomers to start climbing the social ladder. By the end of the 1950s, Italians composed 33 percent of Toronto's general labourers, but only 2 percent of its professionals, and Italian men earned 60 percent of the average male income in the city. Within a decade, though, most Italian families had saved enough money to purchase their own home and a large number sponsored other family members to settle in Canada. There were numerous other success stories, such as that of A.J. Frie-man, a Jewish immigrant who rose from peddling rags to become the owner of Ottawa's largest department store. As depicted in the chapter-opening photo, in 1954, Violet King became the first black woman admitted to the bar and the first to practise law in Canada. In 1957, Douglas Jung became Canada's first Chinese MP, elected in Vancouver Centre.

Canada was still a country where many social clubs and neighbourhoods remained restricted to white gentiles, where universities continued to impose restrictive quotas, particularly against Jews, and where racial segregation was practised. In November 1946, Viola Desmond was fined $20 and sentenced to 30 days in jail for sitting in the "White Only" section of a movie theatre in New Glasgow, Nova Scotia, and the law under which she was charged was not repealed until 1954. Instilling Canadian values was also sometimes pursued by harsh means, as in British Columbia in 1953 when the provincial government forcibly removed 170 Doukhobor children from their homes, made them wards of the state, and placed them in boarding schools to ensure that they followed the provincial curriculum, a policy that prompted a Doukhobor sect called the Sons of Freedom to start a campaign of arson that destroyed scores of schools in British Columbia. Not until 1962 did Canada's *Immigration Act* eliminate racial considerations for applicants, namely the likelihood of them adapting to Canada's cold climate, something used to disqualify blacks because they typically came from warmer areas.

Much concern was voiced over the large number of Central Europeans coming to Canada, specifically how well they would assimilate and if they harboured sympathy for communism. Social workers, schools, and government agencies, including the NFB that made films geared to newcomers, stressed the need to learn English and to embrace Canadian civic and family values. Groups like the YMCA, the YWCA, and the Rotarians set up classes to teach newcomers Canadian customs, including eating habits and typical modes of dress. The Department of Citizenship and Immigration praised such efforts, though also to build positive relations and to promote some local colour, worked with ethnic organizations to assist with "international music nights, parades and pageants, craft shows, and folk societies."[11] It also pushed to establish more elaborate citizenship ceremonies; disseminated literature extolling the superiority of Canadian democracy, especially over communism; surveyed the ethnic press for signs of communist sympathy; provided support to anti-communist ethnic associations; and published accounts of tyranny in Soviet-dominated areas and heroic stories of escape, something that reached a peak following Canada's decision to accept 30 000 refugees from the failed 1956 Hungarian uprising against Soviet control (a decision that some government officials privately questioned because of fears that the Soviets would plant spies within such a large group).

While many immigrants, or their children, ascended the social latter, things remained dismal for Canada's longest-settled population—its Aboriginal peoples. Most reserves still did not have running water. The post-war economic boom essentially passed Natives over. Such was the unmistakable conclusion conveyed in two federally commissioned surveys placed under the direction of Harry Hawthorne, the founder of the University of British Columbia's anthropology program, an expert on coastal Aboriginal peoples and who, along with his wife and academic colleague, Audrey Hawthorne, was a driving force behind the creation of the B.C. Museum of Anthropology. The first report, released in 1955 (and whose conclusions were echoed in the second report in 1966), emphasized the precarious, and often pitiable, economic status of Aboriginal peoples. Of those in British Columbia, the 1955 report said that their employment was "confined almost entirely to a few primary industries, particularly fishing, logging, trapping, farming … farm labour,"[12] and in salmon canaries, all of which was low-paid. They also remained wedded to reserves largely because they had become dependent upon the scarce government assistance provided through federal Indian agents.

Many Aboriginals hoped for better lives out of the Second World War, perhaps none more so than Native veterans who sought benefits for their service to the country. However, they were excluded from numerous government programs, such as loans to start a business or a farm, because they were judged as lacking the competence or sense of responsibility to deal with debt repayment. Aboriginal children, as wards of the state, were still being forced into residential schools if it was felt that they were not receiving proper schooling or care at home.

Not everything remained in stasis, though. In 1946, a Select Joint Committee of the Senate and House of Commons was established to explore changes to improve the *Indian*

Act. Of the 136 briefs the Committee received from First Nations, 126 concerned schooling, and of those, only five were positive. Many submissions asked for less church involvement and less emphasis upon assimilation, and heavily criticized residential boarding schools for separating children from their parents and communities. There was growing recognition that the present educational system for Aboriginals was not working. Too many priests were not properly trained as teachers, it was becoming more difficult for churches to attract people to do educational missionary work, and the residential school system had grown more costly to maintain because many buildings had fallen into disrepair during the Depression and had to be replaced. The new trend was to place Native children in public schools, though once there they were commonly segregated from white children, experienced cultural and social shock, and grew disillusioned and angry as they came to better understand their dreadful economic circumstances compared with whites.

Native voices did play a role in effecting change. In 1951 the *Indian Act* was amended to formally legalize the *Potlatch*, the ceremonial distribution of gifts, and Natives were now permitted to consume alcohol in public places. In reclaiming their heritage, the Kwakiutl people who lived in northeastern Vancouver Island, after three decades of lobbying, managed to repatriate 600 of their ceremonial items from two British Columbia museums.

Social Conservatism

Despite rapid change, in many ways post-war Canadian society projected itself as more traditional and socially conservative. To some commentators, both contemporary and historical, this reflected a reaction to the perception of greater moral laxity and challenges to conventional gender roles in wartime. But things were, in fact, not so clear-cut. For instance, more Canadians identified themselves as churchgoers in the 1950s, but religious leaders complained about irregular attendance and a lack of devoutness.

One popular image of the 1950s was that the lives of women became more overtly connected to traditional aspects of femininity, such as the primacy of domestic and family life and the importance of glamour and beauty. In the world of high fashion, in a reaction against wartime austerity that simplified clothing and saw women don garb appropriate for the factory, in 1947 the internationally known and trend-setting French designer Christian Dior came out with his New Look, which was characterized by full skirts, cinched waists, and exaggerated bust lines, all to accentuate feminine curves. Swimwear became more provocative, as the French bikini also debuted in 1947. In popular entertainment, such as Hollywood movies, strong and resourceful wartime heroines were gradually replaced by "wholesome and pretty" women, like Doris Day and Audrey Hepburn, or by sex kittens, such as Jayne Mansfield, Rosalind Russell, and Marilyn Monroe. Family-oriented women also assumed more prominence in the post-war media. One analysis of Canadian magazine advertising observed that portrayals of women in the role of housewife rose from a 40 percent average between 1939 and 1943 to a figure close to 70 percent in 1950.[13] Newspaper and magazine stories carried titles such as "I Quit My Job to Save My Marriage."[14]

Post-war women were to devote themselves to marriage and motherhood. Romance and passion were portrayed as important but only in the context of having a successful monogamous marriage. In the years following the Second World War, Canadians married younger, a trend bolstered by the strong economy and the belief they could support a family. Between 1945 and 1958, the average age of brides dropped from 25.3 to 24.8 and of grooms from 29 to 27.7. There was concern about rising divorce rates, especially in the period soon after the war, as long absences and the strains and traumas of combat destroyed many marriages. The number of divorces peaked at 8213 in 1947, nearly tripling the pre-war figure. However, marriage remained the overwhelming norm, with the divorce rate reaching only 65.6 per 100 000 Canadians (one-third the rate a little more than quarter century later) and it remained less than 40 per 100 000 throughout the 1950s. Divorce continued to be viewed as shameful and scandalous, and couples were expected to stick it out, especially if they had children.

The relative affordability of suburbia made it possible for more women to stay at home, where they could focus on raising their children. This was not a choice available to many working-class and immigrant women, who were forced into low-paying jobs, such as domestic service, waitressing, and working in the textile industry. During these years, Canadians were having plenty of children. The fertility rate per 1000 women aged 15 to 49 stood at 87 in 1941, 109 in 1951, and 117 in 1956. The post-war period ushered in what became known as the baby boom, a trend that extended until the early 1960s. Between 1946 and 1957, the number of babies born per year went from 300 547 to 469 903, and the total over that period exceeded 4.8 million. More than 80 percent were born in hospitals, and by 1953, Canada's infant survival rate was three times as high as in the previous decade. Compared with 1931, males born at the end of the 1950s could expect to live eight years longer to 68.3 and women, 12 years longer to 74.2.

A new army of child psychologists, public health nurses, and other experts dispensed advice—principally to women—on child-rearing through books, magazines, and newspapers, and on radio and television. The most widely sold work, the *Common Sense Book of Baby and Child Care*, by American Dr. Benjamin Spock, first appeared in 1946 and quickly went through multiple editions, ultimately selling 50 million copies worldwide, bested in sales only by the bible. Spock's emphasis on the need for a "steady, loving person"—whom most assumed to be the mother—as a continual presence and "promise of security"[15] for the baby and child was a message especially well received after years of instability during the Depression and the Second World War. Canadians also joined this emerging group of celebrity child-care experts, the most prominent being William Blatz of the University of Toronto's Institute of Child Study, who had directed the care of the Dionne quintuplets, and Samuel Laycock, professor of child psychology at the University of Saskatchewan. In print and over the airwaves, they espoused an essentially conservative vision of what constituted normal and successful family life, emphasizing the "entrenchment of traditional gender roles."[16] The Cold War reinforced pressures to create strong and stable families to bolster democratic society against the insidious attempts of communists to spread their creed—a belief more strongly articulated in the United States but also evident in Canada.

Women who did not have children were often portrayed as selfish or pitiable. Even new home designs reinforced women's family-centred role: Large kitchens attached to most other rooms in a free-flowing open design, not only to maximize space in small bungalows but also to make it easier for children to be supervised while their mother went about her household routines.

Numerous women chaffed against being homebound or having their social life revolve around visits with other stay-at-home moms, trips to the park, group shopping excursions, mah-jong and bridge games, shepherding their children to various activities, and joining the local parent–teacher association. A 1956 study by three sociologists entitled *Crestwood Heights* that focused on an outlying upper-middle class section of Toronto shed some much-needed light on the reality of women's lives at the time. While many of the housewives interviewed expressed satisfaction with their life, several used words like "humdrum" and "monotony" to describe their daily routine.[17]

Few women went on to higher education; their percentage of Canada's university population at 20.9 percent in 1955 was slightly lower than in 1925 when it stood at 21.3 percent. Women were also heavily congregated in general arts, teacher training, and nutrition; by contrast, in 1950, there were 9588 males and 48 females enrolled in engineering, 948 males and 6 females in dentistry, 4135 males and 274 females in medicine, and 2365 males and 274 females in law.

It took a generation after the end of the Second World War for Canada's female job participation rate to reach its 1944 peak. However, by the late 1940s, the aggregate number of women in the paid workforce was greater than until 1943, and the total number of married women in Canada's paid employment market rose from 85 600 in 1941 to 349 000 in 1951. The notion of domestic life defining the lives of post-war Canadian women is also challenged in historian Valerie Korinek's analysis of *Chatelaine*. She points out that the magazine, in seeking to maximize its readership, published material to appeal to the broadest possible spectrum of women readers, and, as such, provided articles sympathetic to "the stay-at-home mother with children, through to the working wife, the childless couple, [and] the single career girl."[18]

The employment of single women was widely perceived as temporary until marriage, and the earnings of wives and mothers as simply supplementing the income brought in by the male "breadwinner," not in terms of building a career. Mothers regularly delayed participating in the paid workforce until their children were in school, and then, to accommodate their children's schedule, worked part-time, thus receiving fewer benefits and opportunities for advancement. Women often remained trapped in poorly paid job ghettos. In 1951, 96.4 percent of stenographers and typists, and 88.9 percent of sewing machine operators, were women. As outlined in Table 8.3, women continued to be paid little more than half of what men earned. Men also earned more for doing the same job. At a time when a male sewing machine operator made $1.20 an hour, the pay received by a woman was 80 cents.

Nevertheless, some progress in the workplace was evident. The National Council of Women of Canada and the Canadian Federation of Business and Professional Women, though still largely run by elites, openly allied with women trade unionists in a campaign for equal pay for equal work. On April 5, 1951, Ontario's government passed the *Female Employees Fair Remuneration Act*. By the end of the decade, eight other provinces followed suit, as did the federal government in 1956 with the *Female Employees Equal Pay Act*. However, the statutes contained numerous loopholes, such as ambiguity on what constituted equal work, and assumptions about greater male strength that enabled them to perform jobs better regularly nullified the equal pay provision.

April 1951: Passage of the Ontario Female Employees Fair Remuneration Act.

Table 8.3
Average Weekly Pay in Canada, by Gender, 1945–1957

Year	Men ($)	Women ($)
1945	35.04	19.84
1947	41.35	23.11
1949	47.38	27.14
1951	56.46	32.27
1953	62.71	35.07
1955	66.86	37.52
1957	72.23	39.49
1959	79.20	43.36

Source: F.C. Leacey, ed., *Historical Statistics on Canada* (Ottawa: Supply and Services, 1983), series E-60–68.

Youth also garnered far more attention as the baby boom generation matured. The 1950s witnessed the generalized use of the term "teenager." As children stayed in school longer rather than entering the workforce, a separate youth culture—with its own lingo, musical tastes, and magazines, and to which a bevy of consumer products were marketed— became far more noticeable and a source of societal titillation and anxiety.

Much of the media conveyed socially conservative messages about youth. In popular American television families, such as those in *Father Knows Best* and *Leave It to Beaver*, children were well behaved, always respected authority, and were clean-cut. As historian Mona Gleeson writes, a great deal of public discourse relating to youth stressed the theme of conformity to well-defined behavioural codes presented as "normal" and hence, desirable.[19] In part, this was a reaction to the perception of too many ill-governed youth in wartime and was now reinforced by the Cold War, in which morally upright youth, just like the stable patriarchal family, were viewed as a bulwark against the spread of communism. In magazines, school lessons, numerous films, and on television, a common message was for youth to seek acceptance over individuality and to respect adult authority. Good kids dressed conservatively: slacks, a shirt, and perhaps a jacket for boys, and a long skirt and a respectably fitting sweater for girls. Dating was important; those who did not were pitied. Popular teenage pastimes included attending sock hops (dances in high school gymnasiums where youths had to remove their shoes to protect the varnished wood floor), hanging out at the soda or malt shop, and "cruising," often by borrowing their parents' car. Many adults fretted over such activities, and the greater independence youth seemed to enjoy, as sexual self-restraint was expected until marriage; such social situations made it difficult to uphold these expectations of virtue.

Girls who had a boyfriend proudly displayed their status by wearing his class ring or jacket, as if it was a form of marriage; girls who went "too far" sexually more often tried to hide the fact than brag about it, lest they be considered easy and spoiled for marriage. Boys were expected to work especially hard in school as a means of getting ahead and to prepare for their role as sole income earner for their soon-to-be families. Girls, though presented with more career possibilities than were their mothers, were to remain lady-like and not show too much intelligence, lest they scare off potential suitors. Parents were bombarded with advice on how to raise normal children. In books and newspaper and magazine articles, and over radio and television, child psychologists and a variety of other self-described child experts advised parents to work at retaining a positive and stable home environment by not arguing excessively and by demonstrating cooperative decision making, with the caveat that ultimate authority lay with the father.

Socialization, though also expanding opportunities for youth, was evident in a rapidly growing post-war school system. This included many new large rural schools—serving consolidated school districts—that replaced more often dilapidated than quaint one-room schoolhouses. The rapid expansion of rural roads and bus service made this possible and largely ended the situation where rural youth were forced to live somewhere else if they wanted to go to high school. Although several areas resisted consolidation because it meant loss of local control, including over tax rates to support education, more people accepted the fact that larger schools offered rural youth a far greater array of subjects, modern equipment, and services like guidance counsellors, and helped to reduce drop-out rates. Across Canada, average daily attendance at schools rose from 85.4 percent in 1945 to 92.4 percent in 1955, compared with 77.3 percent in 1925. To promote good conduct, school boards intensified education in citizenship.

School boards were pressured to offer more structured learning and expunge any adoption of child-centred progressive education, which was blamed by many for failing to instil adequate discipline and not teaching the basics to children. One widely read critique, *So Little for the Mind*, written in 1953 by the Saskatchewan history professor Hilda Neatby, skewered progressive education for producing "self-indulgence and mediocrity."[20] Such reactions were being fed by the fear that too many young people were going awry. Court appearances by juveniles rose from 7304 in 1950 to 16 009 by 1960, though in large part this was due to demographics as the maturation of the baby boomers created a massive teenage population. As historian Mary Louise Adams observed, the fact that young people continued to go bad when, after the war, in economic and social terms, so "much [appeared] to be right ... was one contradiction ... that threw optimistic visions of a tranquil, democratic future into question."[21]

During the late 1940s *zoot suiters*—who wore outlandish outfits that included a long and loose-fitting jacket and high-waisted baggy trousers—garnered widespread media coverage despite their small number. The zoot suit was emblematic of freedom and rebelliousness, characteristics attributable to youth. In 1949, Toronto City Council passed a resolution demanding that zoot suits be outlawed. The next decade, the leather-jacketed "hoodlum" became prominent in public consciousness. Among official inquiries into delinquency were a 1950 Mayor's Committee in Toronto and a provincial commission in 1958 organized by Ontario's attorney general. Several culprits were identified: working mothers, "single parenthood, evidence of alcoholism,"[22] dilapidated housing, and other problems cast as threatening family stability.

Popular entertainment aimed at youth was also attacked. Crime and horror comic books and pulp fiction novels bearing titles such as *Tales from the Crypt* were one such

True Crime Cases *was one such magazine published by the Norman Book Company and Superior Publishers of Toronto during this period.*

Source: http://strawresearch. mcgill.ca/printculture/gallery1/ index.html.

source. A growing legion of critics vehemently denounced such sources for breaking obscenity laws and for perverting young minds by glamorizing violence, including violence against women in images where women were typically drawn with exaggerated breasts and buttocks and often in suggestive or skimpy clothing. Championing the campaign against such sources was Davie Fulton, the rookie federal Conservative member representing Kamloops, British Columbia, and future federal justice minister in the Diefenbaker government. Among his many supporters were the Federated Women's Institutes, the Federation of Home and School Associations, the Ontario Teachers' Federation, Parent-Teacher Federations, and the Imperial Order Daughters of the Empire.

In December 1949, Fulton introduced a Private Member's Bill that quickly passed through Parliament and the Senate to ban the importation into Canada of "any magazine or book ... devoted to the pictorial presentation of crime" and "any publication a dominant characteristic of which is the undue exploitation of sex, or of sex and any one of the following subjects, namely, crime, horror, cruelty and violence."[23] Seizing an opportunity based on the implications of the Bill, several Toronto-based publishing houses began producing salacious material.

During the 1950s, movies eclipsed comic books and pulp fiction as a source of concern regarding negative influences upon youth. To counteract declining movie attendance that came with the spread of television, movie producers and theatre owners undertook several initiatives: widescreen epics, 3-D films, drive-ins (which many saw as encouraging promiscuous behaviour among teenagers), and movies aimed at an expanding adolescent market. Many films were innocent or purposefully silly—like *I Was a Teenage Frankenstein*—but others were criticized for providing sympathetic or glamorized treatment of alienated, defiant, and delinquent youth. Among those that stood out was *Rebel Without a Cause.* Released in 1954 and starring teen idol James Dean, it revolved around misunderstood teenagers from middle-class suburban homes. It garnered tremendous attention because of Dean's own reputation as a rebel and his death later that year in a high-speed automobile accident; among the film's scenes was the death of a teenager in a "chicken run" drag race with stolen cars. That year also brought the release of *Blackboard Jungle.* Set in a high school in a low-income area, its scenes included teenage hoodlums attacking a female teacher and trying to terrorize a new male teacher. Its soundtrack included tunes like "Rock Around the Clock" by Bill Haley and the Comets, and newspapers reported on youths wildly dancing in theatre aisles.

Purveyors of rock and roll music were also blamed for corrupting youth. With its roots in black American rhythm and blues, rock music was cast by many as a racial and sexual threat, as "cannibalistic and ritualistic" and as "work[ing] on a man's emotions like the music of the heathen in Africa." Its loud and rhythmic quality and the audacious style of many performers was thought to encourage sexual revolt, none more so than in the case of its first white superstar, Elvis Presley, who to many sounded "too black" when he sang, and with his on-stage pelvic gyrations threw female spectators into fits of sexually charged frenzy. In Ottawa, several teenage girls at a Catholic school who attended one of Presley's three Canadian concerts in 1957—his first tour outside the United States that also included shows in Toronto and Vancouver—were suspended. Giving voice to numerous Canadian parents, Toronto *Telegram* columnist Frank Tumpane started an "Elvis Suppresley Fan Club."[24]

Changing the Guard, 1956–1957

Despite evidence of dissent from dominant practices and ideas, at the national political level few Canadians in the mid-1950s would have predicted defeat for the federal Liberals. The economy remained strong, the government appeared as effective managers, the Liberal party was well organized and financed, and St. Laurent enjoyed far more popularity than opposition leader George Drew. In 1953, the Liberals were re-elected with a whopping majority of 172 seats, compared with 51 for the Tories, 23 for the CCF, and 15 for the Social Credit. But by the mid-1950s, there was a growing sense that the Liberals had grown accustomed to power and were becoming aloof and arrogant. As well, though Canada continued to court American investment, there was mounting unease that the country was relinquishing too much sovereignty.

One major spark of controversy came from the decision to build an oil pipeline from Alberta to Ontario. In early 1956, C.D. Howe arranged for two rival groups—one American and one Canadian—to partner on constructing the project under the name of Trans-Canada Pipelines. In May, the new company said it needed $80 million in emergency financing by June 7 to buy pipe and to keep things on schedule, especially as the onset of winter would slow construction. Only Parliament could authorize the funds. However, the CCF wanted a Canadian Crown corporation to build the pipeline, the Conservatives demanded that Canadians be the senior partner in the project, and both political parties expressed doubts that the loan would be repaid. The opposition began a filibuster—a series of lengthy speeches designed to paralyze Parliament—to which the Liberals responded with closure that put a deadline on debate. The opposition effectively portrayed the Liberals as subverting Parliament's authority and the democratic process for the purpose of serving American corporate interests. Although the Liberals were later vindicated by a royal commission that said closure was the only option left to keep the pipeline on schedule, and though the pipeline was completed on time and the loan was repaid, any satisfaction for the Liberals was bittersweet, as it came after the next federal election.

Concern about growing American influence was also expressed in the Royal Commission on Canada's Economic Prospects. Placed under economist and future federal finance minister Walter Gordon, who would later gain notoriety for his staunch Canadian nationalism, the commission's report, released shortly before the 1957 election, identified increasing American dominance over the Canadian economy as a significant problem. With the United States controlling, for example, 70 percent of Canadian petroleum production and 43 percent of Canadian manufacturing, the report concluded that this led to an excessive outpouring of profits to the United States rather than their reinvestment to keep Canadian-based enterprises modern and competitive. The report also attracted attention because Canada's economy was starting to falter. In 1956, annual inflation jumped from 1.5 to 3.2 percent. It was cut in 1957 by raising interest rates to dampen spending, but this strategy also meant reduced aggregate demand and rising unemployment.

Other points of friction were developing in U.S.–Canada relations. By the mid-1950s, it was becoming better known that Canada, which had engaged in some agricultural trade with the People's Republic of China, believed that the communist government should be recognized and given a seat in the UN. Canada quietly pursued a two-China policy in which the Chinese Republic, which was ousted from the mainland in 1949 and confined to the island of Taiwan, would also continue to be recognized. However, the United States insisted on continuing to isolate the communist government, which did not gain entry into the UN until October 1971, when it also became a permanent member of its exclusive and more powerful Security Council. There was growing distaste in Canada over the American show-trials of suspected communists, many of whom were badgered and threatened by congressional committees with contempt and jail time if they did not name suspected communists. Although the ringleader of this strategy, Wisconsin Republican Senator Joseph McCarthy (after whom the term *McCarthyism* was coined), was officially censured by the U.S. Senate in 1954 for portraying the American military as infiltrated with communists, Herbert Norman's 1956 suicide brought a flurry of condemnations from Canadian politicians, the media, and the public over obsessive, devious, and dangerous means employed by the United States to track down communists. Even though many Liberals joined this chorus of criticism, including Minister of Foreign Affairs Lester B. Pearson—who was a friend of Norman and whose name had been mentioned in 1951 by a U.S. congressional subcommittee as possibly sympathetic to communism—the Liberals were still hurt by the Norman incident because they were seen as most friendly to the United States.

The Liberals also hurt their popularity in English-speaking Canada by their response to the autumn 1956 Suez crisis. The roots of the crisis lay in the rise of Arab nationalism after the Second World War and the fact that Egypt was turned down by Britain and the United States for aid to build the Aswan Dam about 1000 kilometres up-water from Cairo on the Nile River because of Egypt's strong ties to the Soviet Union. Egyptian President Gamal Nasser responded by nationalizing the Suez Canal, a 162-kilometre waterway that had been financed by private British and French interests and constructed by 30 000 Egyptian labourers from 1859 to 1869, a key trade and transportation route that connected the Nile River to the Mediterranean Sea and that remained under lease to the Europeans. The Europeans rejected Egypt's offer of monetary compensation, and there was rising concern that Nasser, to get his way, would close the canal. Factoring into the emerging crisis was that Egypt, in a move against its archenemy Israel, blocked the Straits of Tiran, Israel's only outlet to the Red Sea, and permitted Palestinian fighters to attack Israel from Egyptian territory.

October 1956: Suez Crisis.

On October 29, 1956, Israeli forces, as prearranged with Britain and France, crossed into the Sinai Peninsula, the area of Egypt that connected to Israel's southern border. The Israelis quickly defeated the inferior Egyptian military and moved towards the canal. The next day, the British and French governments, utilizing a UN resolution calling for an immediate ceasefire, said that they would occupy a zone around the canal and establish a 15-kilometre buffer between the Israelis and Egyptians. As expected, Nasser rejected this proposal, and on October 31, the British and French responded by attacking Egyptian forces by air. The Soviet Union upped the ante by threatening to intervene to protect

Egypt. Fearing that events were spiralling out of control, the Americans demanded that the invading forces withdraw. U.S. President Dwight David Eisenhower was incensed that the Europeans had planned the intervention in secret. Eisenhower, whose re-election bid for president against Democrat Adlai Stevenson was occurring a week later, wanted attention focused on the Soviet intervention in Hungary, not on division between the Western allies.

St. Laurent was also miffed, namely at British Prime Minister Anthony Eden for publicly stating that he hoped England could count on Canada's support. St. Laurent made it clear this was not forthcoming and, adding what many Canadians considered an insult, publicly stated that Britain's day of acting like the "superman" of Europe had passed; however, Canada would make a major contribution to diffusing the Suez crisis. It enjoyed excellent diplomatic links to both the United States and Britain, and Pearson could deal effectively with Nasser, having had con-

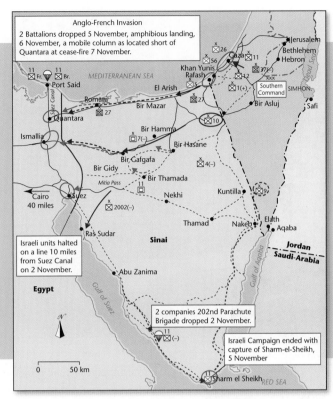

Map 8.2
Major Military Movements in the Suez Crisis, November 1956

Source: Map courtesy of the Department of History, United States Military Academy.

structive discussions with him the previous year on regional issues and Egypt's relations with the Soviet Union. Pearson proposed and helped shepherd through the UN the establishment of a multinational "emergency force" under an integrated UN command (named UNEF I) to monitor a cease-fire and the withdrawal of foreign forces from Egypt, an initiative that won him the 1957 Nobel Peace Prize. Although garnering considerable praise for his role, which eventually became a symbol upon which Canada would define itself as a "peacekeeper nation," initially the reactions were far from unanimously positive.

Canada was soon embarrassed because the troops it selected for UNEF I that came from the Queen's Own Rifles were rejected by Egypt because of overt references to British heritage, in both the regiment's name and the uniform style. Ultimately, Canada was permitted to participate, but its contribution of 1000 soldiers, which made up one-sixth of the UN force, was kept to background roles in communications and logistics. Many Anglos charged that Canada had deserted the Mother Country to do America's bidding by helping push Britain out of Egypt. One poll showed that 43 percent of Canadians supported Britain's actions in Suez compared with 40 percent who were opposed.

The Liberals faced tougher political opposition in Canada. On December 14, 1956, the Progressive Conservatives turned from an ailing George Drew, who had proven a disappointment as leader, to select John George Diefenbaker as their new chief. Born in 1895 in Neustadt, Ontario, Diefenbaker was raised in modest circumstances on a 65-hectare homestead wheat farm near Prince Albert, Saskatchewan, that his schoolteacher farther had purchased for $10. He initially made his mark as a trial lawyer, often taking on unpopular

John Diefenbaker demonstrates his oratorical skills in Canada's Parliament, 1948.

Source: Library and Archives Canada/C-080883.

June 1957:
John Diefenbaker elected.

cases to support people with few resources. Made leader of the Saskatchewan Conservative party in 1938, he personified what political scientists came to label as a Red Tory, meaning that he supported the market economy but also government intervention to protect collective needs and to ensure decent social conditions, a philosophy that, for example, prompted Diefenbaker during the Depression to support the creation of an unemployment insurance scheme.

A strong civil libertarian, in part because his Germanic name had brought his family prejudice, Diefenbaker had been one of the few MPs to oppose the forced evacuation of the Japanese Canadians during the Second World War. Elected to the House of Commons in 1940, and outwardly ambitious, Diefenbaker ran unsuccessfully for the party's national leadership in 1942 and 1948 before finally attaining success at the Progressive Conservative's 1956 convention. An exceptional, though some thought blustering, speaker, he projected the image of a crusading populist who approached issues with a sense of righteousness. His hero was John A. Macdonald, a nation-builder, who, he said, steadfastly protected Canada from American economic and political domination and remained loyal to Britain.

The Liberals were pleased with Diefenbaker's selection because he was not the choice of the Tory establishment, who saw him as unpredictable and as less friendly to business than his main leadership rival, Donald Fleming (who Diefenbaker later made his finance minister) and thus as hurting Conservative fundraising prospects. A January 1957 public opinion poll placed the Liberals comfortably ahead at 48 percent, compared with 31 percent for the Progressive Conservatives. However, on the hustings (political campaigning) leading up to the federal election on June 10, Diefenbaker proved to be an outstanding and tireless campaigner, criss-crossing the country by train and feeding off the energy of ever-larger crowds who enthusiastically responded to his self-proclaimed outsider status and his campaign themes of Liberal arrogance, subservience to American interests, and ties to big business, as opposed to his own pledge to stand up for Canada and ordinary Canadians. St. Laurent remained personally popular, but at 75 years old he appeared tired and sometimes cranky when compared with the vigour and optimism that Diefenbaker brought to the contest.

On the eve of the election, *Maclean's* magazine, convinced that the Liberal juggernaut remained too powerful, initially went to press with a lead story about yet another victory for St. Laurent. The Liberals narrowly won the popular vote, with 40.9 percent compared with 38.9 per cent for the Tories, but when it came to parliamentary seats, the Progressive Conservatives achieved a minority government with 112, compared with 105 Liberals and 48 for the other parties.

Conclusion

Canada was about to embark on a new direction. Diefenbaker would be less pro-corporate and less pro-American. Growing turmoil would also mark his years in office, as the 1960s witnessed more intense political, social, and cultural change. Canada during the late 1940s and most of the 1950s was increasingly prosperous; more Canadians were coming to share in the good life, becoming part of a mushrooming middle class. Optimistic about the future, they married younger and produced record numbers of children. Canada discarded the last vestiges of its colonial past—developing its own citizenship, ending references to the JCPC, and appointing a Canadian governor-general —and its federal government invested millions to support Canadian culture. As an increasingly confident and engaged middle power, it expanded its presence abroad and made important contributions at the UN. There was widespread agreement among Canadians that the Soviet Union and its communist allies were bonafide threats to freedom, that sacrifice was essential to keep them at bay abroad, and that some curtailment of rights at home was necessary to prevent their fellow travellers and other sympathizers from carrying out sinister plans to destabilize Canada. Unions appeared less militant and the political left more moderate. Louis St. Laurent, who ran his government, and arguably the country, like a business and exuded a quiet confidence and comforting grandfatherly image, seemed in many ways to personify the era.

Still, there were many cracks in the supposed consensus. Numerous Canadians were left untouched by the country's growing prosperity, several provincial governments tried to oppose Ottawa's growing power, many disliked Canada's closer ties with the United States, and condemned, or themselves suffered from, the Cold War campaigns to root out communists. Pressure, and sometimes coercion, played a role in keeping women to the domestic sphere, compelled youth to conduct themselves with restraint, persuaded immigrants to shun their traditional ways, and convinced Canadians to recoil from any possible association with communists. Much of the basis for what followed in the 1960s—such as Quebec's Quiet Revolution, more contentious Canada–U.S. relations, more boisterous Canadian nationalism, and more outspoken protest from women, youth, and ethnic and racial minorities—not only represented a reaction against many social conventions promoted during the 1950s but also could be traced to dissatisfaction evident during the early post-war years.

Questions to Consider

1. What were the major trends with Canada's economy after the Second World War?

2. What factors and goals defined Canadian foreign policy during post-war period? What were the consequences? Did Canada achieve its aims?

3. What impact did the Cold War have within Canada?

4. What conventions were expected of women and children? Were they followed?

5. What factors accounted for Diefenbaker's victory in the 1957 federal election?

Critical Thinking Questions

1. To what extent is it appropriate to use the word "consensus" to describe post-war Canada?

2. To what extent did Canada become more modern during the post-war period?

3. To what extent did post-war Canada become more multicultural?

Suggested Readings
General

Bothwell, Robert, Ian Drummond, and John English. *Canada Since 1945: Power, Politics and Provincialism.* Toronto: University of Toronto Press, 1989.

Creighton, Donald. *The Forked Road: Canada, 1939–1957.* Toronto: McClelland & Stewart, 1976.

Thomson, Dale. *Louis St. Laurent: Canadian.* Toronto: Macmillan of Canada, 1967.

Whitaker, Reginald. *The Government Party: Organizing and Financing the Liberal Party of Canada, 1930–58.* Toronto: University of Toronto Press, 1977.

Provincial Politics, Social Policy, Economy

Behiels, Michael. *Prelude to Quebec's Quiet Revolution: Liberalism versus Neo-Nationalism, 1945–1960.* Montreal and Kingston: McGill-Queen's University Press, 1985.

Black, Conrad. *Render Unto Caesar: The Life and Legacy of Maurice Duplessis.* Toronto: Key Porter, 1998.

Blake, Raymond. *Canadians at Last: Canada Integrates Newfoundland as a Province.* Toronto: University of Toronto Press, 1994.

Finkel, Alvin. *The Social Credit Phenomenon in Alberta.* Toronto: University of Toronto Press, 1989.

Finkel, Alvin. *Social Policy and Practice in Canada: A History.* Waterloo: Wilfrid Laurier University Press, 2006.

Graham, Roger. *Old Man Ontario: Leslie M. Frost.* Toronto: University of Toronto Press, 1990.

McLeod, Thomas H., and Ian McLeod. *Tommy Douglas: The Road to Jerusalem.* Edmonton: Hurtig, 1987.

Mitchell, David. *WAC Bennett and the Rise of British Columbia.* Vancouver: Douglas & McIntyre, 1983.

Trudeau, Pierre Elliott. *The Asbestos Strike.* Toronto: James Lewis & Samuel, 1974.

Foreign Policy and the Cold War

Bothwell, Robert. *Alliance and Illusion: Canada and the World, 1945–1984.* Vancouver: University of British Columbia Press, 2007.

Chapnick, Adam. *The Middle Power Project: Canada and the Founding of the United Nations.* Vancouver: University of British Columbia Press, 2005.

Eayrs, James. *In Defence of Canada, Vol. 4: Growing Up Allied.* Toronto: University of Toronto Press, 1980.

Glazov, Jamie. *Canadian Policy Towards Khrushchev's Soviet Union.* Montreal and Kingston: McGill-Queen's University Press, 2002.

Hewitt, Steve. *Spying 101: The RCMP's Secret Activities at Canadian Universities, 1917–1997.* Toronto: University of Toronto Press, 2002.

Jockel, Joseph. *No Boundaries Upstairs: Canada, the United States, and the Origins of North American Air Defence, 1945–1958.* Vancouver: University of British Columbia Press, 1987.

Muirhead, Bruce. *Dancing Around the Elephant: Creating a Prosperous Canada in an Era of American Dominance, 1957–1973.* Toronto: University of Toronto Press, 2007.

Richter, Andrew. *Avoiding Armageddon: Canadian Military Strategy and Nuclear Weapons, 1950–1963.* Vancouver: University of British Columbia Press, 2003.

Smith, Denis. *Politics of Fear: Canada and the Cold War, 1941–1948.* Toronto: University of Toronto Press, 1988.

Whitaker, Reginald, and Gary Marcuse. *Cold War Canada: The Making of a National Insecurity State, 1945–1957.* Toronto: University of Toronto Press, 1994.

Military

Bercuson, David. *Blood on the Hills: The Canadian Army in the Korean War.* Toronto: University of Toronto Press, 1999.

Johnston, William. *A War of Patrols: Canadian Army Operations in Korea.* Vancouver: University of British Columbia Press, 2003.

Maloney, Sean. *War Without Battles: Canada's NATO Brigade in Germany, 1951–1993.* Toronto: McGraw-Hill Ryerson, 1997.

Stairs, Denis. *The Diplomacy of Constraint: Canada, the Korean War and the United States.* Toronto: University of Toronto Press, 1974.

Watson, Brett. *Far Eastern Tour: The Canadian Infantry in Korea, 1950–1953.* Montreal and Kingston: McGill-Queen's University Press, 2002.

Labour and Immigration

Abella, Irving. *Nationalism, Communism and Canadian Labour: The CIO, the Communist Party and the Canadian Congress of Labour, 1935–1956.* Toronto: University of Toronto Press, 1973.

Hawkins, Freda. *Canada and Immigration: Public Policy and Public Concern.* Montreal and Kingston: McGill-Queen's University Press, 1988.

Iacovetta, Franca. *Such Hardworking People: Italian Immigration in Post-War Toronto.* Montreal and Kingston: McGill-Queen's University Press, 1992.

McInnis, Peter S. *Harnessing Labour Confrontation: Shaping the Post-war Settlement in Canada, 1943–1950.* Toronto: University of Toronto Press, 2002.

Whitaker, Reginald. *Double Standard: The Secret History of Canadian Immigration.* Toronto: Lester and Orpen Dennys, 1987.

Gender, Youth, Suburbanization

Adams, Mary Louise. *The Trouble with Normal: Post-war Youth and the Making of Heterosexuality.* Toronto: University of Toronto Press, 1997.

Axelrod, Paul. *Scholars and Dollars: Politics, Economics and the Universities of Ontario, 1945–1980.* Toronto: University of Toronto Press, 1982.

Fahrni, Magdalena. *Household Politics: Montreal Families and Postwar Reconstruction.* Toronto: University of Toronto Press, 2005.

Gidney, R.D. *From Hope to Harris: The Reshaping of Ontario's Schools.* Toronto: University of Toronto Press, 1999.

Gleason, Mona. *Normalizing the Ideal: Psychology, Schooling and Family in Post-War Canada.* Toronto: University of Toronto Press, 1999.

Harris, Richard. *Creeping Conformity: How Canada Became Suburban, 1900–1960.* Toronto: University of Toronto Press, 2004.

Korinek, Valerie J. *Roughing it in Suburbia: Reading* Chatelaine *Magazine in the Fifties and Sixties.* Toronto: University of Toronto Press, 2001.

Loo, Tina, and Carolyn Strange. *True Crime, True North: The Golden Age of Canadian Pulp Magazines.* Vancouver: Raincoast Books, 2004.

Owram, Doug. *Born at the Right Time: A History of the Baby Boom Generation.* Toronto: University of Toronto Press, 1996.

Parr, Joy. *Domestic Goods: The Material, the Moral and the Economic in the Post-War Years.* Toronto: University of Toronto Press, 1999.

Porter, Ann. *Gendered States: Women, Unemployment Insurance, and the Political Economy of the Welfare State in Canada, 1945–1997.* Toronto: University of Toronto Press, 2003.

Tillotson, Shirley. *The Public at Play: Gender and the Politics of Recreation in Post-War Ontario.* Toronto: University of Toronto Press, 2000.

Culture

Litt, Paul. *The Muses, the Masses, and the Massey Commission.* Toronto: University of Toronto Press, 1992.

Rutherford, Paul. *When Television Was Young: Primetime Canada, 1952–1967.* Toronto: University of Toronto Press, 1997.

Notes

1. Roger W. Bowen, ed., *E.H. Norman: His Life and Scholarship* (Toronto: University of Toronto Press, 1984), 60–68.

2. Barry Broadfoot, *The Veterans' Years: Coming Home From the War* (Vancouver: Douglas & McIntyre Ltd., 1985), 192.

3. Peter McInnis, "Planning Prosperity: Canadians Debate Post-war Reconstruction," in Greg Donaghy, ed., *Uncertain Horizons: Canadians and Their World in 1945* (Ottawa: Canadian Council for the History of the Second World War, 1996), 253.

4. Robert Prince, "The Limits of Constraint: Canadian-American Relations and the Korean War, 1950–51," *Journal of Canadian Studies* 27, 4 (1992–93): 129–152; Denis Stairs, *The Diplomacy of Constraint: Canada, the Korean War and the United States* (Toronto: University of Toronto Press, 1974).

5. Ramesh Thakur, *Peacekeeping in Vietnam: Canada, India, Poland, and the International Commission* (Edmonton: University of Alberta Press, 1984).

6. Paul Axelrod, *Scholars and Dollars: Politics, Economics and the Universities of Ontario, 1945–1980* (Toronto: University of Toronto Press, 1982).

7. Michael McMahon, *Metro's Housing Company: The First 35 Years* (Toronto: Metropolitan Toronto Housing Company Limited, 1990), 11.

8. John Bacher, *Keeping to the Marketplace: The Evolution of Canadian Housing Policy* (Montreal and Kingston: McGill-Queen's University Press, 1993), 185.

9. Janine Stingel, *Social Discredit: Anti-Semitism, Social Credit and the Jewish Response* (Montreal and Kingston: McGill-Queen's University Press, 2000).

10. Alan G. Green, *Immigration and the Post-War Canadian Economy* (Toronto: Macmillan of Canada, 1976), 17, 21.

11. Franca Iacovetta, *Gatekeepers: Reshaping Immigrant Lives in Cold War Canada* (Toronto: Between the Lines, 2006), 76.

12. Jean Barman, *The West Beyond the West: A History of British Columbia* (Toronto: University of Toronto Press, 1991), 308.

13. M. Susan Bland, "Henrietta the Homemaker and Rosie the Riveter: Images of Women in Advertising in *Maclean's* Magazine, 1939–1950," *Atlantis* 8, 2 (1983): 72.

14. Joan Sangster, "Doing Two Jobs: The Wage-Earning Mother, 1945–70," in Joy Parr, ed., *A Diversity of Women: Ontario, 1945–1980* (Toronto: University of Toronto Press, 1995), 104.

15. Doug Owram, *Born at the Right Time: A History of the Baby Boom Generation* (Toronto: University of Toronto Press, 1996), 33.

16. Mona Gleason, "Psychology and the Construction of the 'Normal' in Post-War Canada, 1945–1960," *Canadian Historical Review* 78, 3 (1997): 445.

17. Veronica Strong-Boag, "Home Dreams: Women and the Suburban Experiment in Canada, 1945–1960," *Canadian Historical Review*, 77, 4 (1991): 503.

18. Valerie J. Korinek, "Roughing it in Suburbia: Reading *Chatelaine* Magazine, 1950–1969," Ph.D., University of Toronto, 1996, 35.

19. Mona Gleason, *Normalizing the Ideal: Psychology, Schooling and Family in Post-War Canada* (Toronto: University of Toronto Press, 1999).

20. Owram, *Born at the Right Time*, 126.

21. Mary Louise Adams, *The Trouble with Normal: Post-War Youth and the Making of Heterosexuality* (Toronto: University of Toronto Press, 1997), 51.

22. Ibid., 57.

23. Augustine Brannigan, "Mystification of the Innocents: Crime Comics and Delinquency in Canada 1931–1949," *Criminal Justice History* 7 (1986): 111.

24. Owram, *Born at the Right Time*, 156.

9

*U*ncertainty
and Conflict:
1957–1967

*J*oan Johnson was a beautiful young woman barely out of technical college when she landed her first job in the office of a Toronto private investigation firm. Several times each month she would leave work early for a visit to the beauty salon. After a shampoo and style, she rushed to her apartment to change into her evening wear and then headed to one of the crowded bars in downtown Toronto. There, it had been arranged for her to meet a married man. He would never know her real name. She always tried to strike up a conversation with the stranger, but most times he was not interested in idle chatter. After some awkward moments and perhaps a drink, they headed to a shabby motel room.

Joan knew the script well. Once they were in the motel room, she slipped out of her dress and hurried under the covers. After he removed his trousers, there would be a loud pounding at the door. When he opened it, the motel manager, a private detective, the distraught wife, and, sometimes, a lawyer all rushed into the room with a photographer who came to record the visual evidence of an adulterous scene. In 1960, adultery was the only grounds for divorce in Canada, and for helping to stage such events, Joan Johnson earned $100.[1]

Joan Johnson's shady life came to the attention of Canadians in a CBC television interview in June 1960. June Callwood, a young journalist with the national network, caused an uproar when her interview with Johnson—who was dubbed the "Shady Lady"—was aired; the CBC had concealed Johnson's identity and she was shown only in silhouette on the television screen. A day after the interview aired, the Ontario attorney general ordered an investigation into her story and the methods used by

Canadians to obtain a divorce. When the police began a search to find the Shady Lady, Johnson said her interview with Callwood was a hoax. Callwood insisted that Johnson had been telling the truth. Other reporters, including Pierre Berton, reported that detective agencies did a brisk business in providing evidence of adultery in divorce cases. The attorney general's office also ordered an investigation into divorce records to see whether Mrs. Johnson's pictures appeared in the files of co-respondents. No pictures of her were found. The attorney general even tried to prevent Mrs. Johnson's own divorce, arguing that adultery had not occurred in her own marriage. For those trapped in bad marriages, there was no easy way out. Seven years later, in 1967, the Canadian government would introduce amendments to the *Criminal Code* to change the archaic laws governing divorce—as well as homosexuality, abortion, and other social issues—that made such antics as those performed by Johnson unnecessary.

> **After reading this chapter you will be able to:**
>
> 1. Describe the major features of Quebec's Quiet Revolution.
> 2. Assess the state of federal–provincial relations in Canada.
> 3. Understand Canada's evolving relationship with the United States.
> 4. Explain attempts to deal with persistent regional economic disparity in Canada.
> 5. Evaluate the changes occurring in Canada during this period.
> 6. Consider the importance of Canadian nationalism.

Introduction

Marriage was only one of many institutions that Canadians would reconsider as a trend towards a more secularized and liberal state gathered momentum in the decade from 1957 to 1967. In 1957, Canada had a divorce rate of 40.3 per 100 000 people—a three-fold increase from the rate in 1936, but a mere fraction of the 124.3 divorces per 100 000 two years after the new divorce laws were introduced in the House of Commons in 1967. The sanctity of marriage disappeared in a society that was outwardly marked by change, and it was only one of the signs of a changing nation as Canadians came to value individual choice and the pursuit of individual happiness. A new Canada seemed to be emerging. Quebec, Aboriginal peoples, English-speaking citizens, and new immigrants seemed to be searching for a new role and identity. Disadvantaged citizens and regions also clamoured for the redress of their predicament as social and economic unrest became hallmarks of Canadian society.

Despite this, the decade from 1957 to 1967 would be marked more by uncertainty than by fundamental institutional change. Questions were raised not only about social Canada but also about economic, cultural, and political Canada, but, at the end of the decade, the change would be minimal, though instability seemed to replace stability in politics, the economy, and society overall. Severe strains would be exerted on the fabric of the nation, but at the end of the decade when Canada celebrated its centennial, the nation was still remarkably like it was when the decade began.

In many ways, this chapter presents the idea that if the initial post-war period could be characterized as consensus concealing conflict, then the period from 1957 to 1967 portrays the opposite. Was this the case? Did changing social mores, Quebec's Quiet Revolution, rising anti-Americanism, competing visions of Canadian nationalism, and a growing aura of protest among a wide cross-section that considered the system unjust provide evidence of mounting discord that would fundamentally change Canada? Or was it simply a reflection of the uncertainty that had always pervaded the nation and the continuation of the problems and issues that had, in many ways, always defined Canada?

A New Government and a New Beginning?

On the surface, Canada was doing very well and Canadians appeared happy when they went to the polling stations on June 10, 1957. There seemed to be no reason why the Liberals would not win their sixth majority government. However, Canadians gave the Conservatives a minority government—an indication that many were dissatisfied with much more than a national government that had held power for more than two decades.

Many historians and political commentators who have studied the late 1950s have laboured to explain why the Liberals lost in 1957. Their attention has been misplaced. What they have failed to understand was that Diefenbaker's victory reflected a level of discontent and uncertainty across the country. The result was not so much about the Liberal party as it was about Canadians and why they turned on the government that had guided them successfully through the Second World War and had ushered in a post-war boom. The opinion makers, however, continued to focus on the Liberals even in defeat; the *Maclean's* cover story following Diefenbaker's victory was on Lester B. Pearson—who would eventually replace Louis St. Laurent as leader of the Liberal party—and not on the new Progressive Conservative leader or the obvious discontent that had made the Conservative victory possible.

1957: Royal Commission on Canada's Economic Prospects acknowledges economic disparity across Canada.

The Royal Commission on Canada's Economic Prospects certainly recognized the discontent in the nation, but its report had arrived too late to help the Liberal government that had appointed it. Chaired by Walter Gordon, a Canadian businessman with close ties to the Liberal party, its final report came five months after Diefenbaker became prime minister, and its message was dire, warning that all was not well in the nation. Despite the riches that abounded in the general prosperity following the war, Canada was poor in too many ways, and it was evident everywhere. Many of the cities and towns lacked the necessary infrastructure and amenities for social, cultural, and economic well-being, despite the rapid pace of urbanization in recent years. The royal commission found huge numbers of Canadians with incomes insufficient for their needs, families unable to care decently for their children, and elderly citizens living in abject poverty. It also uncovered serious tensions throughout the land. The diversity of Canada, best characterized by the two historic communities of French- and English-speaking Canadians and usually celebrated as contributing to the richness of the country, made managing the affairs of state difficult, and Gordon warned of troubles ahead. Moreover, there were tensions between regions, particularly between the economically challenged areas of the Atlantic and the Prairies and the prosperous centre, between various ethnic and economic groups, and between capital and labour. Gordon noted metaphorically that we "could do with fewer level-crossings and more museums."[2]

Diefenbaker understood this, and he promised a new national policy for Canada. He had earned a reputation for defending the traditionally disadvantaged and those familiar with despair and disappointment and he brought this approach to government. Those who were disenfranchised (or considered themselves as such) shared his belief that Canada was not living up to its potential. He realized that even those who had shared greatest in the post-war economic boom were disillusioned that their nation did not seem to have any great national purpose. For those whom the prosperity had passed over, they simply wanted in. Diefenbaker believed that the farmers of Western Canada had been victimized by the business and financial interests of Central Canada and that the economically depressed regions of Canada resulted from an uncaring state. He was concerned that many rural citizens had been left behind in the general national prosperity. His goal as prime minister was not merely the reconciliation of English- and French-speaking Canadians but the inclusion of other ethnic groups within the Canadian nationality. At his party's leadership

John Diefenbaker.

*1957: Ellen Fairclough
becomes first woman
cabinet minister.*

convention in 1956 he had broken with tradition: Instead of having his nomination moved and seconded by a French- and English-speaking party member, he had Premier Hugh John Fleming of New Brunswick nominate him and Colonel G.R Pearkes of British Columbia second the nomination. The symbolism was immense: Diefenbaker would be no establishment or Central Canadian toady—he wanted a new Canada.

Diefenbaker and his wife, Olive, made their own way to Ottawa a few days after the election in 1957. They carried their own luggage and boarded a regular Trans-Canada Air Lines flight from Saskatoon; the prime ministerial plane was busy flying Liberal cabinet ministers— many of whom had gone down to defeat—back to Ottawa to clean out their offices. John G. Diefenbaker became Canada's 13th prime minister on June 21, 1957, and held the position until 1963. In his six years of power, he never lived up to his promise or the optimism he had initially inspired in Canadians.

By the time Diefenbaker became prime minister, seven of the ten provinces had Conservative governments; those under Liberal control were Prince Edward Island, Manitoba, and Newfoundland, and only the last remained happy with the federal Liberals. Prince Edward Island had been locked in a bitter dispute with the previous Liberal government. Ottawa had demanded that P.E.I. repay the extra revenue it had received when the federal government miscalculated P.E.I.'s share of the revenue under the existing tax rental agreement, and in 1959 it would elect a Progressive Conservative government led by Walter Shaw. In Manitoba, the farmers were angry (as they were across the country) that the Liberal government continued to insist that Canadians never had it so good, even as farm income dropped sharply throughout the 1950s. The most popular politician in Manitoba was Duff Roblin, the newly crowned Conservative leader and soon to be premier. He had worked hard to get Diefenbaker elected. So, too, had Leslie Frost, the well-respected premier of Ontario, who had his own fight with the Liberal government in Ottawa for a greater share of the revenue that it collected from his province. Fleming from New Brunswick and Robert Stanfield, the reform-minded premier of Nova Scotia, were also Diefenbaker allies, and even Maurice Duplessis in Quebec saw the Conservatives—traditionally stronger proponents of provincial rights—as an improvement over the Liberals. Premier Joseph R. Smallwood in Newfoundland, which had been solidly Liberal since joining Canada in 1949, ran his province as a personal fiefdom and remained outside the Conservative fold.

Even before Parliament met, the cabinet, which included Ellen Fairclough as the first woman federal cabinet minister, had been busy. It had given federal employees a pay raise, provided assistance to coal mines in Nova Scotia, dispatched officials to Europe to find markets for Canadian grain, and provided price support for Canadian turkeys. The torrid pace that the Diefenbaker cabinet set during the summer continued after Queen Elizabeth II came to Ottawa on October 14, 1957, to be the first monarch to open the Canadian Parliament. The government appointed a royal commission to investigate the energy sector, raised old age pensions, provided a cash-advance of $150 million to farmers for grain held in storage, changed the *Unemployment Insurance Act* to remove the discriminatory provisions against married women, introduced a series of tax cuts to help lower-income Canadians, amended the *Criminal Code* to ensure the humane slaughter of animals, and passed a host of other measures. Canadians were not accustomed to such an active Parliament and neither was the Liberal party of St. Laurent.

St. Laurent resigned as Liberal leader and a leadership convention selected Lester B. Pearson, the former secretary of state for external affairs and Nobel Laureate, as his replacement. Acting on rather foolish advice on his first day on the job, Pearson presented a motion in the House of Commons calling upon Diefenbaker to do the only honourable thing possible and turn the government back to the Liberals without even another election. Pearson immediately realized the terrible blunder he had committed. Before the new opposition leader took his seat, Diefenbaker was on his feet in full rhetorical form, fuming at Liberal arrogance. Within days, he had dissolved Parliament and called new elections.

Ellen Fairclough in the House of Commons.

Source: Library and Archives Canada. Credit: Duncan Cameron/Library and Archives Canada/PA-129249.

The campaign was all about Diefenbaker. He emerged as Canada's first charismatic twentieth-century leader, and in him, Canadians found a new nationalist. Diefenbaker invoked a vision of Canada as a nation of the North that would develop northern resources and create equality of opportunity for all. He invited Canadians to join his vision of one Canada so that the nation could realize its great potential. Thousands braved the bitter February winter in 1958 to attend Conservative rallies. They congregated along the railways lines to get a glimpse of their prime minister. Even Quebec's Premier Maurice Duplessis, who had discreetly used his influence in the 1957 election to help a few Conservatives, turned his Union Nationale political machine to Diefenbaker's cause. Not even *Maclean's* could misjudge the temper of the nation this time. Diefenbaker scored the largest victory in Canadian history to that point, winning 208 seats, including 50 from Quebec, where the Liberals had been ensconced since the days of Sir Wilfrid Laurier; he captured 53.7 percent of the popular vote, the highest ever recorded in any peacetime federal election.

A New National Policy in a Recession

Diefenbaker swept into office promising a new national economic policy, but the economy slowed considerably just as the Conservatives moved into Ottawa. The economic downturn cannot be attributable to Diefenbaker and the Conservatives; the Liberals knew in 1957 that the country faced uncertain economic times. Of course, they made no mention of it during the campaign, and later they successfully blamed the recession on the Conservatives.

1957: Canada enters a recession.

After the Second World War, the Canadian economy had grown remarkably, largely because of the demand for natural resources. American investment in the resource sector had fuelled much of that boom, as Canadian resources found a ready market, particularly in Europe and the United States, as part of the international recovery throughout the 1950s. The Korean War had also fuelled the demand for Canada's resources. By 1956, the demand was weakening, however, and economic indicators pointed to potential trouble ahead. By 1957, the recession was in full swing, marked by a sharp rise in the unemployment rate from 3 to 8 percent; it would remain around 7 percent until 1962.

Exports declined in 1957 and 1958 and did not return to their pre-recession levels until 1961. Similarly, consumer demand stagnated and increased to the rate experienced in the immediate post-war boom only after 1961. New investment in Canada dropped from 18 percent in 1956 to 6 percent in 1957 and continued to decline further each year until 1962. The resource boom in commodities such as oil and gas, nickel, and uranium was over for the moment, and this added to the severity of the economic downturn in Canada. Economic growth would remain depressed until the early 1960s.

The new government was unprepared for the recession. Towards the end of 1957, welfare and social assistance offices across Canada saw the return to their doorsteps of men and women who were able and willing to work but either could not find employment or had exhausted their unemployment insurance payments. Post-war employment prosperity had come to an end. The introduction of the *Unemployment Assistance Act* by the federal government in 1956 had permitted all provinces to reform their policies governing social assistance for unemployed workers and establish fairly similar benefits across the country. In Ontario, for instance, the government had modernized its *Unemployment Relief Acts* of 1930 and introduced the *General Welfare Assistance Act* in 1958 to provide public assistance to unemployed employables—a phenomenon that Canada had not seen since 1940.

Diefenbaker tried a variety of measures to deal with the recession. First, he attempted to stimulate the economy through various Keynesian policies, such as income support and investment in infrastructure. He had a vision of Canada as a northern nation and placed great stock in the development of the North. The government spent more than a $100 million on what he called a great national program of public works (or an infrastructure program) to open up the vast economic potential of the North and other underdeveloped regions of Canada through such programs as his "Roads to Resources" initiative. The new highways constructed through the Yukon and the Northwest Territories and the construction of the South Saskatchewan River Dam, which was completed in 1967, turned out to be important investments, but they could not bring the country out of recession. Other stimulus plans included loans totalling $150 million to builders and home owners to reinvigorate the housing market.

Diefenbaker also proved willing to increase income security. The government expanded the feature of the unemployment insurance plan that covered workers who had exhausted their benefits to receive a special seasonal benefit to reflect the seasonality of work in Canada. When the special feature was first introduced in 1950, it ended each year in mid-March, but it was extended to mid-May for 1957 and to the end of June in 1958. Pension benefits were also increased for the elderly, people with vision impairments, and those with other disabilities. Interest-free advances were extended to farmers for farm-stored grains when the Canadian Wheat Board, the sole purchaser of wheat in Canada, could not purchase any more wheat because their granaries were full. Ottawa amended the federal–provincial tax-sharing arrangement with the provinces to give them an additional $87 million in revenue to spend on economic recovery programs, and it increased transfers to the provinces for health insurance. For its stimulus package, the government incurred a deficit in 1958–1959 of $1.4 billion as government spending increased by 32 percent.

Second, the government attempted to slay the recession and strengthen the economy for the future by increasing economic productivity and efficiency, normally referred to as supply-side economic policy. An essential component of this approach for the Diefenbaker government was to recognize the changes in Canada's labour market. Government came to believe that workers no longer had the proper skills or qualifications that were needed for the new Canadian economy. It was necessary, therefore, to upgrade human capital through increased access to post-secondary education and skills training. Ottawa had begun in 1951 to provide financial aid to universities and colleges across Canada, though Quebec refused to accept the money until 1960. Diefenbaker introduced the *Technical and Vocational Assistance Act* (TVTA) in 1960 to fund investment in technical and vocational education. The program allowed the provinces to construct educational institutions that were designed to change the nature of Canada's workforce by training young people for stable, long-term employment in technological fields. Another initiative was the Winter Works Program, first instituted in 1958. Designed as a short-term federal measure, the program was an attempt to solve local unemployment problems through shared-cost programs between the federal and provincial governments. It was also hoped that the projects would not simply create employment but would encourage the construction industry, for instance, to continue operation year-round and cease being a seasonal industry.

Monetary policy was the third way that the government attempted to deal with the recession. It had to confront rising unemployment and rising inflation, a phenomenon that economists later called *stagflation*. As the government struggled to align its fiscal policy—its decisions on taxation, borrowing, and spending—to deal with the recession, it eventually understood that the country's monetary policy was too restrictive, which only exacerbated the economic difficulties the country faced. Monetary policy is the decisions a government makes to control the amount of money in circulation, usually to control the level of inflation. In Canada, monetary policy is controlled by the Bank of Canada, a Crown corporation that operates independently of government, but it is, ultimately, accountable to Parliament.

James Coyne, the governor of the Bank of Canada, had been appointed by the Liberal government and the Conservatives did not trust him. After all, the Conservatives had no tradition and practice with governing, having sat so infrequently in the government benches in Ottawa. They held office for only 11 of the previous 61 years, and not since 1935. They came to Ottawa in 1957 with not a single MP who had any experience in running the country. Because the Liberal party had become the natural governing party in Canada, a Conservative government always assumed that no civil servants could be trusted, including the governor of the Bank of Canada—and perhaps with some justification: Diefenbaker faced each day in the House of Commons a number of former civil servants, including Lester B. Pearson, Mitchell Sharp, Jack Pickersgill, and others, who had also left the civil service for the Liberal party. Diefenbaker did not think the Bank of Canada's governor was much different.

The matter was made much worse because Coyne thought he knew what was best for Canada's economy, and his view conflicted with the government's. Coyne pursued a policy of tight money, which meant that he kept interest rates high to control inflation. It also increased the costs of borrowing money. High interest rates also increased the value of the Canadian dollar against other currencies and encouraged Canadians to borrow capital in the cheaper American markets, which, in turn, forced up the Canadian exchange rate, making Canadian exports even more expensive, and further limiting economic recovery. Canadian economists and the public alike called for Coyne's dismissal, but when the government asked him to step aside, he refused to go. Coyne might have gone a few months before his term ended, but the Diefenbaker government released details of his lucrative pension, which incensed the governor. Coyne eventually resigned, but only after the whole episode created considerable uncertainty in Canadian financial markets and made the government look silly and incompetent. The fiasco with the governor of the Bank of Canada, together with the government's decision to fix the exchange rate for the Canadian dollar at 92.5 American cents, raised serious questions about Diefenbaker's ability to manage the nation's financial and economic affairs.

1962: Canada fixes value of Canadian dollar at 92.5 American cents.

As the episode with the Bank of Canada shows, the Conservatives were often their own worst enemies. The devaluation of the dollar might have provided good political ammunition for the Liberals, but when they were returned to power, they kept the Canadian dollar where Diefenbaker's government had pegged it until 1970—and the devaluation helped the economy recover. In 1962, real GNP grew by 7.1 percent, compared with the average of 2.9 percent between 1957 and 1961, and it would continue to expand until 1973. A devalued Canadian dollar gave Canadian exporters a definite advantage in the expanding American economy.

Diefenbaker holding up 91-cent Diefendollar, 1957. The Liberals distributed thousands of "Diefendollars" or "Diefenbucks," linking the beleaguered Canadian dollar to Tory mismanagement.

Source: M999.66.1.1.
© McCord Museum.

Confronting Regional Economic Disparity

Although the government had to deal with short-term economic problems, Diefenbaker had promised to deal with the long-term structural challenges of Canada's regional economies. Since Confederation there had been vast differences in the fiscal capacity of the provinces, but the Gordon Commission of 1957 noted that there were also vast differences in the opportunities for growth among the provinces and regions of Canada. Whether measured in levels of income (see Figure 9.1), gross provincial product per capita, or rates of unemployment, there were considerable differences among the various provinces, and between some of the provinces and the national averages. These economic differences were known as the *disparity gap*, and it had become clear that even in periods of economic prosperity, the economic disparities between the rich and poorer provinces did not disappear.

There was a growing expectation among Canadians in the disadvantaged regions that the state had to address their predicament. The Diefenbaker government made the reduction of regional economic differences and the improvement of struggling regional economies a priority. Diefenbaker realized, however, that he could not rely on existing government departments and regular transfers from Ottawa to the provinces to foster economic growth in depressed rural areas. He launched a series of initiatives aimed at eliminating regional

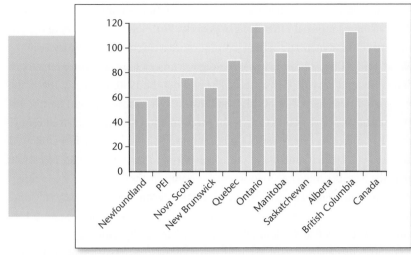

Source: Adapted from Statistics Canada, National Income and Expenditure Accounts: Annual Estimates, 1926–1986, 13-531-XPB 1986001. April 1, 1989, Table 36.

Figure 9.1
Index of Per Capita Personal Income, 1964

Diefenbaker begins series of government programs to address regional economic disparity.

economic disparities, and successive national governments since have realized that if regional disparity is to be eliminated, the depressed regions need special policies that will allow them to expand at faster rates than the more prosperous regions of the country.

One of the most obvious signs of regional disparity was rural poverty, and Diefenbaker vowed to fix it through a series of initiatives that would be modified and expanded by successive governments well into the 1990s. He began with the Atlantic Provinces Adjustment Grants, a payment in addition to the regular equalization transfers that allowed the provinces to undertake large-scale capital projects, such as hydroelectric development. Another of his early national attempts to rebuild rural economies in Canada came through the *Agricultural Rehabilitation and Development Act* (ARDA) in 1961. It was a federal–provincial initiative designed to address the plight of those living on marginal farmland and those in resource sectors who were struggling to make a decent living. Ottawa also created in 1962 the Atlantic Provinces Development Board. Staffed by federal officials from various government departments, it was the first attempt to develop a comprehensive regional development strategy aimed at improving the basic infrastructure of a region. Its $186 million budget was aimed primarily at highway construction, water and sewage projects, the creation of industrial parks, and the generation and transmission of electrical power.

Later, when the Liberals were returned to power, they built upon Diefenbaker's initiatives. The *Agriculture and Rural Development Act* then turned its focus on development in non-agricultural and resource sectors to absorb the surplus labour from farming and fishing. In 1966, the government created the Fund for Rural Economic Development (FRED), which focused on five areas of Canada (Gaspé Peninsula in Quebec, two regions in New Brunswick, all of Prince Edward Island, and parts of northern Manitoba) with particularly low incomes and little hope of private-sector investment to develop both infrastructure and economic investment opportunities.

The provinces were also involved in the attempt to spur economic development in economically depressed areas within their jurisdictions. When Stanfield was elected premier of Nova Scotia in 1956, he realized that many of the small rural communities that depended on agriculture, fishing, and coal often lived in poverty. With low productivity and often using antiquated equipment, many in those communities were struggling to survive in the modern world. One of his solutions was to lend government funds to entrepreneurs to establish industries and provide factory jobs. Throughout the 1950s and early 1960s, the Nova Scotia government helped establish small textile, fish-processing, and hardboard plants with financial support from a Crown corporation known as the Industrial Estates Limited, but it had mixed success. Many of the economically challenged provinces followed Nova Scotia's lead and created similar lending agencies to loan funds to facilitate economic development: the New Brunswick Development Corporation, the Manitoba Development Fund, and the Newfoundland and Labrador Corporation. While these agencies had some spectacular failures (such as Nova Scotia's expenditure of millions of dollars to lure Clairtone, an innovative hi-fi and colour television firm founded by Canadians Peter Munk and David Gilmore, to Stellarton, Nova Scotia), there were also some successes, such as the establishment of the Michelin tire plant in Bridgewater, Nova Scotia.

There has been considerable debate on the various government schemes to stimulate economic growth in the economically challenged regions of Canada. Some have argued governments wasted millions of dollars with limited success, while others maintain that people have a right to live in the parts of the country they have always called home and, moreover, it is the state's responsibility to help them do so. If nothing else, government expenditure in the depressed regions allowed citizens to earn a higher level of income than would have been possible without state intervention.

What did become clear with Diefenbaker was that not all regions and not all Canadians shared in the nation's wealth, and governments could no longer ignore the problem; they had to be proactive in finding a solution. However, the federal programs of the 1950s and 1960s were designed and implemented to deal with specific problems and lacked an overall strategic approach. The lack of coordination between the federal and provincial governments remained a major problem, but more troubling was the lack of an integrated plan among various federal departments. Each new initiative seemed to be planned and implemented without much consideration of what was happening elsewhere. By the end of the 1960s, there emerged a consensus that regional disparity could not be adequately addressed without a centralized federal agency with the necessary authority to coordinate all federal regional development efforts and a mandate to work cooperatively with the provinces.

National Standards and Federal–Provincial Revenue Sharing

The share of revenue that was collected by the federal and provincial governments had always caused major strains in federal–provincial relations, but there emerged a consensus that all Canadians should share equally in the national revenue in the late 1950s. In 1957, the taxation agreements that had been negotiated during the Second World War were renewed and all provinces, apart from Quebec, participated. Quebec was the only province, then, collecting all of its taxes. In exchange for collecting all the personal and corporate taxes and succession duties for the participating provinces, Ottawa transferred to each of those provinces a percentage of the actual revenue collected in the province, although Ontario participated only in personal income tax collection with Ottawa. Provinces received 10 percent of personal income taxes collected in the province; 9 percent of the corporate income taxes; and 50 percent of succession duties. Because some of the provinces were much wealthier and had a larger tax base than others, the revenue available to some provinces was much greater than that of others. This meant that a poorer province, such as New Brunswick, would have much less revenue than would a wealthier province, such as British Columbia or Ontario. This disparity raised the issue of equity among Canadians because the level of public services that might be provided in a wealthier province was much greater than that in the economically disadvantaged provinces.

The solution to the fiscal imbalance was found in a formal equalization program in 1957. The equalization grants were given by Ottawa to the provinces out of its general revenues to spend as they saw fit. The principle of equalization became so accepted by the provinces and Canadians that it was enshrined in the Canadian Constitution in 1982. The concept of equalization had first been raised in the Rowell-Sirois Commission that was appointed during the Great Depression of the 1930s to study the federal–provincial fiscal arrangement. By the late 1950s, the federal government had become increasingly worried that the provinces would demand their constitutional rights and levy their own direct taxes, which would create ten tax regimes across the country. An equalization program was designed to provide a reasonable measure of equality of services across the country that otherwise the poorer provinces would not have been able to afford. It guaranteed that the revenue for each province would be raised to the per capita level of that of the wealthiest two provinces and it brought a measure of financial stability to all provincial governments. Equalization payments were paid out of the general revenue that Ottawa collected and wealthier provinces did not contribute directly to an equalization program.

1957: Equalization principle established.

The equalization formula has always been complicated and has always been a major point of irritation in federal–provincial relations, though it became more complicated in the 1962 revisions to the agreement. In that year, revenue from natural resources was included in the agreement for the first time, largely because resource-rich Alberta was receiving equalization payments. The Diefenbaker government moved away from the top-two province standard in favour of a national average. The revisions represented a major change in federal–provincial fiscal relations, as tax rental or tax sharing agreements were replaced by tax collection agreements. The federal government did not seek to rent the three major taxes from the provinces in 1962, which meant that the provinces would have given up the collection of some taxes in exchange for a fixed sum on money from Ottawa; instead, the federal government allowed each province to set its own personal and corporate income tax rates. Ottawa reduced its tax rates to allow the provinces to set their own rate of taxation to keep the taxation level near rates existing at the time. The federal government agreed to collect provincial taxes if the provinces set their rates as a percentage of basic federal rates. Provinces could, of course, collect their own taxes, and Ontario chose to have Ottawa collect only its personal income tax; Quebec remained outside of the scheme. None of the provinces were satisfied with the revenues they collected and they all demanded a greater share of taxation revenue, but the system remained in place, with minor modifications, until 1977.

Medicare

A new development of the late 1950s and early 1960s was the proliferation of shared-cost agreements between the federal and provincial governments. These were programs that the federal government offered to the provinces but were conditional on the provinces contributing usually 50 percent of the cost of the program. This approach often allowed the federal government to set national priorities, but it was also an attempt to meet the social needs of all Canadians, regardless of where they lived in the country. In 1953–1954, Ottawa's expenditure on such programs was $75 million, but it rose to more than $935 million a decade later. Diefenbaker established 15 new shared-cost programs, but several programs were especially expensive, particularly the hospital insurance plan that had been introduced in April 1957. It cost nearly $400 million annually. Still, Canadians demanded that the state deal with existing injustices and inequalities in Canada, and Ottawa's answer was often through shared-cost agreements. Most Canadians wanted a national health plan and although there was little agreement on what form it should take, it was eventually provided through the shared-cost arrangement.

The drive for a national system of publicly administrated and state-funded medicare in Canada began in Saskatchewan when it introduced a comprehensive medical insurance program in 1961. Premier Tommy Douglas, who had led his Co-operative Commonwealth Federation (CCF) party to victory in Saskatchewan in 1944, announced in 1959 his plans for a prepaid compulsory medical-care program for the province that would provide universal coverage and high-quality service for all residents. By the time the *Medical Care Insurance Act* passed the provincial legislature and was to become law on July 1, 1962, Douglas had been recruited to lead the New Democratic party, which had emerged from a union of the CCF and the Canadian Labour Congress. Woodrow Lloyd became the premier of Saskatchewan and he had to deal with an assault from the province's doctors who opposed the plan for state-run medicine.

1962: Saskatchewan introduces free medical services, or medicare.

On the day the legislation was to be put into effect, Saskatchewan's doctors went on strike, claiming that "socialized medicine" would ruin healthcare; they wanted patients covered by private insurance, with the government paying premiums for those that could not afford them. The deadlock lasted for nearly a month during which time a baby from the Yorkton area died of meningitis while his parents searched for medical help while the strike was on. The doctors finally capitulated in the face of growing animosity and agreed to the government's promise that they could work in private clinics on a fee-for-service basis. Canada had its first universal medical insurance program that gave medically necessary services to many people who would have otherwise been without healthcare. Medicare would become one of the major victories for social justice and equality of the period.[3]

Spurred by the public interest and apparent widespread support for the historical legislation in Saskatchewan, the federal government began to consider creating a plan to cover all Canadians. As a first step, the Diefenbaker government appointed Supreme Court Justice Emmett Hall to head a Royal Commission on Health Services. When he issued his report in 1964, Diefenbaker was no longer prime minister, but Hall recommended publicly funded, comprehensive universal insurance not only for doctors' services but for prescription drugs and home care, as well as dental and optical services for some groups.

Search for Balance: Canadian–American Relations

During Diefenbaker's years as prime minister, Canada's relationship with the international community was marked by great uncertainty. Many in Canada were particularly concerned about the growing interdependence of Canada and the United States, but there was no easy way to set Canada and Canada's priorities apart from those of the Americans. This was a period of great homogenization and no matter how hard some Canadians tried to keep their country apart, the United States exerted—usually without much effort—a profound influence on Canada.

Diefenbaker never had an easy relationship with the Americans, but it is important to remember that when he became prime minister, the Cold War was still the most important factor in Canadian foreign policy. In a March 1951 *Maclean's* article entitled "If the Russians Attacked Canada," a defence analyst projected that an invading Soviet bomber fleet would target nine Canadian cities from Halifax to Vancouver, and the destruction would be massive. The Canadian government had learned firsthand from the Gouzenko Affair (discussed in Chapter 8) that the Soviet Union was not to be trusted, and Diefenbaker harboured deep suspicions about its totalitarian system. He realized, as did the Liberals before him, that the Soviet Union was the new enemy. With the technological advances in long-distance bombers, the Arctic was no longer a shield against nuclear warheads falling on Canada. The period after the Second World War demonstrated a gradual march towards increased defence cooperation between Canada and the United States. It was only with the long protracted war in Vietnam in the late 1960s that many in Canada began to question Canada's military alliance with the United States, and even then, few advocated standing too far from their American neighbour.

After the Soviet Union developed the capacity to strike North American targets with nuclear weapons in the mid-1950s, the joint defence of North America became extremely important. The Canadian government had initially hoped that the huge sums of cash it had given to A.V. Roe Canada, a division of the British aerospace company Hawker Siddeley, would produce an "all-Canadian" interceptor. The AVRO CF-105, or AVRO Arrow as it was known, might offer a measure of protection from the Soviets. It would also stimulate the

AVRO Arrow RL-201.

Source: Courtesy of AVRO Museum.

*1957: North American
Air Defense Command
is established.*

Canadian aviation and high-tech industry. Until the AVRO Arrow went into production, the government had to rely on American interceptor jets, and it cooperated with the U.S. military to build early warning radars across the Canadian North.

Shortly after Diefenbaker became prime minister, he signed the North American Air Defense Command (NORAD) Agreement to provide continental air defence for North America under American control. There has been much debate surrounding this decision; it has been suggested that Diefenbaker did not know what he was doing, as the agreement integrated continental defence. He had approved NORAD without consulting either his cabinet or the Department of External Affairs and without parliamentary debate. Moreover, the agreement meant that Canada would have a subordinate role in the defence alliance based on nuclear deterrence. By throwing Canada's defence in with the United States, Canada had to acquire nuclear weapons. Diefenbaker maintained that the Canadian military and the St. Laurent government had both approved of the plan. It is interesting that the furor that NORAD aroused in Parliament in 1958 was not over the decision to create the alliance, but rather the process through which it was done. The threat from a Soviet bomber was real in 1958, and NORAD seemed to be a logical military development for a Cold Warrior like Diefenbaker. It should be noted, however, that Diefenbaker was flexible when it came to trading with communist countries, especially in the export of Canadian grains. He authorized the sale of wheat to Russia, China, and Cuba, but still disliked the regimes immensely.

By the time NORAD was fully functioning, surface-to-air missiles, such as the Bomarc-B, had become the major defence against incoming bombers, not interceptor jets. This development made the expensive AVRO Arrow obsolete even before it went into production. Canadians remain attached to the Canadian-designed and -built delta-wing supersonic interceptor, which was the subject of a 1997 CBC docudrama—*The Arrow*, starring Dan Aykroyd. It does not seem to matter to many Canadians that when the Diefenbaker government cancelled the plane it was far behind schedule, far over budget, without a market, and obsolete. Some 14 000 highly skilled workers engaged in the project were immediately laid off; many of them went to the U.S. space program. Diefenbaker ordered the planes, models, and even blueprints destroyed, and bought 56 nuclear Bomarc missiles from the United States to provide for the defence of Canada. The government might have made the right decision to scrap the AVRO Arrow, but Diefenbaker paid a high political price for it.

By 1962, Diefenbaker was wavering on his commitment to continental defence because the anti-aircraft Bormarc missiles, already installed in Canada, had to be armed with nuclear warheads. Earlier, in 1957, Diefenbaker had thrown his lot to the nuclear side. At a NATO heads of government meeting, he had endorsed the policy of the alliance adopting nuclear weapons, but Diefenbaker was surprised when many Canadians took to the streets to protest such weapons. At the time, even though public opinion polls were showing that most Canadians agreed that Canada should have nuclear arms, the letters that poured into his office convinced Diefenbaker that the views of those ordinary Canadians who took the time to write to him did not agree with the survey results. He was also becoming increasingly worried about U.S. President John F. Kennedy's aggressive behaviour towards the communists, and in his cabinet, there was a split over the nuclear issue. When Diefenbaker eventually decided not to accept nuclear warheads, his minister of defence resigned. The Liberals, while they were in opposition, opposed Canada having nuclear weapons (only to accept them when Pearson became prime minister). Canada's wavering on arming the Bormarcs worried the Americans as they believed it left the United States vulnerable to Soviet attack.[4]

1962: Diefenbaker quarrels with Kennedy during the Cuban Missile Crisis.

Canada had another major disagreement with the United States during the Cuban Missile Crisis in October 1962. Some Canadians have seen this dispute as evidence of Diefenbaker's nationalism, and others have seen it as the failure of Canadian leadership. Diefenbaker maintained that he had to protect Canada from American military control. Others have seen the quarrel as simply an indication of Diefenbaker's personal animosity with a popular U.S. president whom he had come to detest.

The crisis occurred when the Americans discovered that Soviet missiles were being deployed in Cuba. Kennedy imposed a naval blockade as a way to force the Soviets to withdraw their weapons. Before he told Americans in a television broadcast on October 22 of his decision to confront the Soviets, Kennedy sent a special envoy to Ottawa to inform Diefenbaker and ask that the Canadian forces within NORAD be put on alert in case of a Soviet military response to the U.S. action. Diefenbaker learned quickly that the 1958 agreement he had signed with former President Dwight Eisenhower had serious consequences for Canadian sovereignty. He did not take kindly to the American order; he had expected to be consulted on North American defence and not merely told what the Americans were planning. President Kennedy and his advisors concluded that the Canadian government did not understand the threat posed by the Soviets and grew increasingly angry with Diefenbaker. For three days, Diefenbaker refused to bow to American pressure and the photographic evidence they had given him of the Soviet presence in Cuba before finally authorizing the use of the Canadian military if it became necessary. In the meantime, Diefenbaker called for a UN inquiry into the Cuban situation as a way of resolving the crisis. After the Soviets backed down, Kennedy was hailed as a hero even within Canada, and Diefenbaker was made to look foolish and indecisive even in the face of imminent danger. Some Canadian nationalists have suggested that after the Cuban Missile Crisis, the Kennedy administration worked to get rid of Diefenbaker.

Diefenbaker and Civil Rights

Society was showing signs of chafing under the accepted modes of behaviour in the late 1950s, but there was no rebellion in Canada in the decade that followed. Many of the children born as part of the baby boom after the Second World War came of age as Diefenbaker settled into Ottawa, but social and cultural values changed only slowly. Still, inequalities were challenged; Diefenbaker himself was concerned about inequalities in Canadian society. Although his Bill of Rights has been superseded by the Charter of Rights and Freedoms that came in 1982, Diefenbaker had committed his government to protecting fundamental freedoms. Growing up in Saskatchewan, he had memories of discrimination against French Canadians, Aboriginal peoples, Métis, and European immigrants, and he vowed to make human rights a priority if he ever realized his dream of being prime minister. In 1960 he introduced a Bill of Rights, which included fundamental freedoms for all Canadians, but the Bill had its limitations as it applied only to matters

*1960: Diefenbaker
introduces Canadian
Bill of Rights.*

under federal jurisdiction. However, it was the first attempt by the Government of Canada to establish basic rights in Canadian society and laid the foundation for the 1982 Charter of Rights and Freedoms. Diefenbaker believed that he would never get the provinces to agree to a constitutional amendment to enshrine the Bill into the Constitution, but his list of human rights and freedoms found greater permanence in the 1982 Charter.

Diefenbaker continued his human rights crusade into the discussions with the Commonwealth, particularly with the apartheid regime in South Africa. The Canadian government had always refrained from interfering in the internal affairs of member nations in either the Commonwealth or the United Nations, but Diefenbaker insisted that South Africa must provide equal opportunity for all people, regardless of race, colour, or creed, when it applied for entry into the Commonwealth in 1961. South Africa withdrew its application for membership, remaining outside the reach of the Commonwealth, although it would be another Canadian prime minister that would play a pivotal role in having the Commonwealth impose sanctions against the racist regime in South Africa in the 1980s.

Immigration

Diefenbaker would not tolerate discrimination in Canadian immigration policy, either. Immigration policy during the period was also marked with considerable uncertainty. Economic factors remained important and the traditionally preferred groups remained at the top of the list of newcomers, but the government showed humanitarian concern for displaced persons and worked to remove colour from Canada's immigration policy. During the 1957 campaign, Diefenbaker had promised to overhaul the *Immigration Act* in favour of a new approach to immigration. As a first step, Ellen Fairclough, the new immigration minister, granted an amnesty to all illegal alien residents in Canada. In March 1959, the government moved to restrict admission of non-dependant relatives through the family sponsorship program, ostensibly to allow more qualified immigrants to enter Canada. The decision angered Italian, Greek, and Portuguese Canadians and their organizations, forcing the government to back down, showing that certain ethnic groups could influence government policy. The government also dramatically amended Canada's refugee program and took measures to ensure that political refugees were legitimate and not trying to jump the queue. Not surprisingly, the number of refugees admitted declined, just as the country slipped into recession. Over the course of two years (1959–1960), during World Refugee Year, Canada relaxed its policy on refugees.

Canada remained a desirable destination for many people seeking a better life, but Canada did not want just any immigrants. The state began to focus on long-term labour market trends and sought educated and skilled people; these changes were controversial and alienated many in the immigrant communities. The traditional source of Canada's immigrants in continental Europe and the United Kingdom was also drying up, and Canada had to look elsewhere for its immigrants. In 1962, Fairclough introduced major reforms to Canada's immigration policy to reflect the country's new priorities. She also eliminated the overtly racist features of Canada's immigration laws by eliminating national preferences and hence racial discrimination, although European immigrants retained the right to sponsor a wider range of relatives than others. Three years later, the Department of Immigration was created, and in 1967 a formal points system was introduced.

*1962: Canada eliminates
race from immigration
regulations.*

Diefenbaker Government in Trouble

The bloom quickly faded from the Diefenbaker rose, but voters were never sure what to do with their vote through much of the 1960s. The uncertainty of the decade was perhaps best reflected in its politics. Although Diefenbaker's national vision captivated voters in 1958, he seemed to age quickly in office and he never lived up to the expectations Canadians had for him. Within four years, he had squandered the vast support he had garnered and was reduced to a minority government when Canadians voted on June 18, 1962. He was able to hold on to much of the West and a majority of seats in Atlantic Canada, perhaps because of his attempt to address their grievances. The industrial heartland of Ontario and Quebec deserted him, as the Liberals attempted to blame him for the country's economic woes and for such unpopular decisions as the cancellation of the AVRO Arrow.

The Liberals were unable to claim victory because of the emergence of the Social Credit in Quebec. It began in Canada under William Aberhart in Alberta in 1935 and in 1952 in British Columbia, but Social Credit was never a force in national politics until it won 30 seats in 1962. Twenty-six of these came in Quebec where Réal Caouette's brand of conservative rhetoric appealed to rural Quebecers who were unsure of what was happening in their own province. The CCF never lived up to expectations. After the party's dismal performance in the 1958 election that saw them win just eight seats, party leadership sought an alliance with organized labour. It won 19 seats in 1962, but it never became a factor in national politics throughout the decade.

Diefenbaker struggled in the minority Parliament in 1962 and saw his party's support drop even further amid a growing economic crisis, a dispute with the United States over nuclear weapons, and the Cuban Missile Crisis. Even his own party turned against him and attempted to have him replaced as leader. Despite all of the Conservative woes, voters did not trust the Liberals under Pearson enough to give them clear control of the government when Canadians went to the polls again on April 8, 1963.

1963: Pearson becomes prime minister.

Even as Liberals sought to re-invent their party and their leader—Pearson dropped his trademark bow-tie, for instance, and the party recruited a number of younger candidates who favoured progressive social legislation—they could not sway enough voters to give them a majority government. When Pearson went to the polls again in 1965, he could do no better, even though by then Diefenbaker was so badly mauled by his own party that Pearson's failure to win decisively speaks volumes not only about how Pearson failed to captivate the imagination of the country but also about the uncertainty of the period. Canadians did not consider either of the two major parties as having the necessary vision for the nation and they were not willing to venture into the unknown with any of the newer parties. Only two years apart in age, neither Pearson nor Diefenbaker seemed right for the nation.

Expansion of the Welfare State

Pearson demonstrated that a minority government operating from a centrist position and depending on the left for support can produce successful and progressive legislation. He never seemed to govern with the caution one expects from a minority Parliament. As Diefenbaker attempted to deal with some of the nation's structural economic problems, Pearson focused on the creation of a new social Canada. During two minority governments over the span of five years, Pearson implemented new social legislation, including a universal system of medical insurance (despite the opposition of some of the provinces and the insurance companies), a national contributory pension plan, the extension of family allowance benefits to 16- and 17-year-olds to keep them in school, interest-free loans in 1964 to make post-secondary education more accessible for lower-income Canadians, and funding half the operating costs of colleges and universities. Pearson also understood the growing tensions in Quebec and appointed a royal commission to study bilingualism and biculturalism. Reluctantly, he appointed a commission to study the conditions facing women in Canada, and he enthusiastically promoted new Canadian symbols.

It might be argued that Pearson never envisioned the social programs Canada ended up with in the 1960s. During the 1963 election campaign, Pearson had promised free medical services only to children under 16 and to persons over 65. All others would have to pay the first $25 of any medical visits. When the Hall Commission recommended that the federal government pay 50 percent of any provincial medicare program that provided universal coverage, Pearson was forced to rethink his plans. The New Democrats—whose support the Liberals needed to govern—immediately endorsed Hall's recommendation. So, too, did Canadians, but Pearson and the government moved forward cautiously.

One reason for Pearson's caution was that the provinces disagreed about the form the healthcare system should take. While they all agreed that medical health insurance was, in itself, beneficial for all citizens, they could not agree upon how it should be administered. Quebec, for instance, insisted that it would not participate in any shared-cost or conditional programs that was designed and controlled by the federal government. Alberta wanted a program that allowed user fees and provided a role for private insurance companies. British Columbia, Manitoba, and Ontario all insisted that the provincial government knew better than Ottawa the health needs of their citizens and argued that the provinces should be allowed to design their own programs without interference from Ottawa. They believed that the federal government should simply provide the financial resources necessary for the provinces to implement their own systems. The other provinces were happy to have Ottawa contribute to programs they could not afford to implement on their own.

In the 1965 federal election campaign, Pearson finally committed his party to a Hall-style medicare system, but it would be another three years before Canada would have a national universal medicare program. On July 1, 1968, when Ottawa finally made funds available to the provinces for a national health insurance program, often referred to as medicare, it was not a single national plan. Rather, it was 12 provincial and territorial health insurance plans that agreed to adhere to a set of national principles in exchange for federal funding: The principles of medicare in 1968 included universality of coverage; portability of coverage when people lived outside their home province; comprehensive coverage of physician's services; public administration of the provincial plans; and accessibility without user fees.

If the provinces adhered to these national standards, they were eligible to claim 50 percent of the cost of their medicare programs. Between 1968 and 1972, all ten provinces and the two territories negotiated agreements with Ottawa, agreeing to provide universal public coverage for hospital and physician care, in exchange for access to federal funding.

Healthcare soon became one of the largest expenditures for governments but also one of the defining characteristics of social citizenship in Canada.

The federal government improved other social programs as a way of responding to the tensions within the country. It was believed that a common set of social rights, shared and available to all citizens, would enhance a wider sense of community and social cohesion. Because of the redistributive nature inherent in some of these social programs, they strengthened the level of attachment to the nation and encouraged citizens to see themselves as members of a single community, enjoying a common set of rights and sharing a common set of obligations. In Canada, as in other Western nations, the development and expansion of social programs in the 1960s encouraged a sense of social citizenship. Medical care, like education and other public goods, became a right of Canadian citizenship.

The 1960s also saw Canada establish a national contributory pension plan. The federal government had first introduced a cost-shared pension plan with the provinces in 1927. It had assumed full responsibility for pensions for persons over 70 in 1951 and maintained a cost-shared pension for those aged 65 to 69. These were non-contributory pensions, meaning that Canadians received those pensions whether or not they worked outside the home. Diefenbaker had introduced an initiative in 1962 that allowed Canadians employed outside the home to save for a pension and even appointed a commission to investigate a contributory pension plan for Canadians. Pearson continued the initiative and, after long and protracted negotiations with the provinces, the Canada and Quebec pension plans were introduced in 1966. These were self-supporting plans financed with contributions from employees and employers.

1966: Canada and Quebec Pension Plans are established.

One of the best examples of *cooperative federalism*—the term given to Pearson's negotiations with the provinces to avoid a constitutional crisis over jurisdiction of social policy in the 1960s—was the establishment of the Canada Assistance Plan (CAP) in 1966. Ottawa helped fund the cost of many provincial programs, but such arrangements were often haphazard; CAP was an attempt to bring some order to federal involvement in these initiatives by establishing a comprehensive financial arrangement between the federal and provincial governments. The federal government agreed to share equally with the provinces the cost of such programs as old-age assistance, assistance for people with disabilities, pensions for people who were blind, and unemployment assistance. This program was an attempt to allow the provincial government to manage an array of social programs, but it also allowed the federal government to set certain national standards. Because CAP had not set any limit on provincial spending on their social programs, Ottawa soon realized that public spending could quickly get out of control.

Canadian–American Relations

Pearson got on better with the Americans than Diefenbaker had, but just barely. He never seemed sure how to handle Canada's relationship with the United States. After becoming prime minister, he and U.S. President Lyndon Johnson asked Arnold Heeney, a former Canadian ambassador to the United States, and Livingston T. Merchant, a former American ambassador to Canada, to prepare a report on the bilateral relationship between the two countries. The Merchant-Heeney report called for a return to quiet diplomacy. It also recommended that Canada accept American leadership even as the Canadian government attempted to defend its national interest.

The report came at a time when there was a growing nationalist movement in Canada. Pearson, the liberal internationalist and former diplomat, favoured the report's recommendation to avoid public disagreement on important issues. At the same time, he continued many of Diefenbaker's policies to deal with the tensions within Canada. He also pursued new policies to strengthen Canadians' sense of national identity. His government introduced legislation to protect Canada's fledgling magazines, but he undermined his own legislation by providing exemptions for both *Time* and *Reader's Digest*, the two American giants that dominated the Canadian marketplace. He severely criticized Diefenbaker for accepting nuclear weapons in Canada only to change his mind after he became prime minister. He attempted to limit American control of the Canadian economy in his 1963 budget but eventually fired his minister of finance and removed all proposals to limit foreign investment in Canada. Pearson clearly forgot about the Merchant-Heeney insistence on quiet diplomacy when he went to Temple University and suggested that the United States halt its bombing of North Vietnam in favour of negotiations. President Lyndon Johnson, who assumed the presidency after Kennedy's assassination, was so angry with Pearson that according to journalist Lawrence Martin, Johnson grabbed Pearson by the shirt collar, lifted the prime minister off the floor, shouted, "You pissed on my rug!" and told him to keep his nose out of American affairs.

By the late 1950s, Canadians were worried that much of the investment in Canada was concentrated in the hands of foreign capitalists, particularly from the United States. After the Second World War, the Canadian government had invited foreign capital to develop the resource sector and, within a decade, U.S. capital had come to control important sectors of the economy. Although the government had strict rules over the control of financial institutions and utilities, 75 percent of the oil and gas sector, 60 percent of mining, and 60 percent of the manufacturing sector resided with American investors.

Both Diefenbaker and Pearson were worried about the level of foreign ownership. Diefenbaker announced during the 1957 election campaign that he would divert a portion of Canada's trade away from the American to British markets. He had little success, as Britain was increasingly looking towards Europe and membership in the European Economic Community, and saw little advantage of increased trade with Canada. Nor was Canada particularly supportive of the attempts to liberalize international trade that might have reoriented exports away from the United States. In the 1964 negotiations over the General Agreement on Trade and Tariffs, which had been initially introduced in 1947 to liberalize international trade, Canada refused to participate in the general lowering of tariffs. Rather, it favoured a product-by-product scheme, arguing that any general lowering of the tariff unfairly hurt resource-export nations and those dependent on manufactured imports, like Canada.

Despite the Canadian rhetoric about multilateralism, Canada preferred bilateral treaties when it came to trade. The best example of this was the Auto Pact signed between Canada and the United States in January 1965. The auto sector was a microcosm of Canada's economic relationship with the United States. Canada had lost its auto industry in the 1920s when all of the Big Three U.S. companies—Ford, General Motors, and Chrysler—formed strategic alliances with Canada's struggling auto manufacturers that saw the American car companies assemble in Canada numerous models for the Canadian and Commonwealth market behind a 17.5 percent protective tariff wall. Like the Americans, Canadians

1965: Canada and the United States sign Auto Pact.

loved their cars, and Pearson wanted to keep some of the high-paying jobs in automobile production in Canada. The Auto Pact integrated the North American car and auto parts industries, while protecting a share of the continental market for Canadian producers. The Canadian government was able to guarantee minimum production levels in Canada. The Auto Pact also created thousands of high-paying and skilled manufacturing jobs in Canada, but the limited free trade agreement was another step in the economic integration of Canada and the United States.

It is ironic that Prime Minister Lester B. Pearson, who began his tenure as prime minister as an economic nationalist, created a single North American auto zone—after all, Pearson had appointed Walter Gordon, a noted Canadian nationalist, as his minister of finance. Gordon had warned in his 1957 royal commission report of the dangers of foreign direct investment in Canada; Diefenbaker had ignored his recommendations and even created a North American energy market (to secure markets for Western oil producers), but there was reason to think that Pearson's government would be different. In his first budget in June 1963, Gordon proposed a 30 percent tax on foreign takeovers of Canadian businesses and a series of measures designed to limit foreign control of the Canadian economy. Because of pressure from the United States and especially from the Canadian business community, Gordon withdrew the measures and was eventually fired. Pearson, at Gordon's urgings once again, amended the *Canadian Bank Act* in 1967 to limit foreign control of Canadian banks to 25 percent and appointed a task force headed by Mel Watkins in 1967 to review foreign direct investment in Canada. The *Watkins Report* subsequently served as a rallying call by Canadian nationalists, but as Pearson discovered, Canada's economic interests might best be served as part of a North American economy.

Quebec and the Quiet Revolution

Governing Canada has never been easy, and in the 1960s both the Diefenbaker and the Pearson governments had to deal not only with rising expectations among the nation's citizens but also with demands from the provinces for greater autonomy. The history of intergovernmental relations in Canada in the 1960s has focused largely on the relationship between Quebec and the federal government; the relationship between the other provinces and Ottawa has been largely ignored, but it is important to remember that the emergence of provincial governments as the articulators of regional and provincial interests—rather than powerful ministers in the federal cabinet, which had been the case for much of the twentieth century—included more than the province of Quebec. Still, what happened in Quebec in the 1960s is important because a generation of Canadians grew up trying to understand and deal with Quebec's place in Canada. Like the other provinces, the state in Quebec finally came to play a major role in all aspects of society, culture, and the economy. "The Quiet Revolution" is the phrase used to describe this period in Quebec's history (1960–1966, corresponding to the time that the Liberals held office in Quebec) in which much changed, quite rapidly, within the province. During this period, French-speaking Quebecers improved their economic position in the province and developed the self-confidence not only to change their society and become more like the rest of North America but also to see themselves as constituting a nation that wanted greater control over its sovereignty. It is believed the phrase was coined by a *Globe and Mail* writer who was observing these changes taking place, changes that were revolutionary on the one hand, yet quiet on the other: hence, the Quiet Revolution.

Starting the chain of events was the death of Quebec Premier Maurice Duplessis in 1959, followed several months later by the death of his successor, Paul Sauvé. Their party, the Union Nationale, which had ruled the province for nearly a generation, was defeated by the Liberal party shortly thereafter. Like all of the other provinces, Quebec had changed enormously over the previous two decades, but the election of the Liberals in 1960 marked a revolution of sorts in the province. While Duplessis had worked with the Roman Catholic Church and other elites to perpetuate the myth of a rural agrarian society, the Liberal government of Jean Lesage challenged the traditional, conservative rural-oriented values of Quebec society. As he embraced modernity, Lesage severed many of the links between church and state and created an interventionist state; he enacted a series of policies that created a secular and modern society in Quebec.

The changes in Quebec were championed by a new middle class that had emerged in the 1950s. They had found employment in the vast bureaucracy of the Catholic Church in the generation after the end of the Second World War. Many wanted to dismantle the traditional nationalism of Quebec but, in fact, they were merely replacing it with a new form of nationalism through the establishment of a modern state. The new middle class viewed state intervention as a positive development, and the church was unable to mount an offensive against such state involvement even if it wanted to. The Catholic Church in Quebec—like other established churches across Canada—started to lose its control over society, reflected most obviously in a rapid decline of those attending mass; many women and men left the religious orders and the number of new recruits dwindled. Another indication of the change in Quebec was that the birth rate from 1959 to 1969 was practically cut in half.

For the decade following the 1960s, the Quiet Revolution was seen as an event of mythological proportions and it gave a simple interpretation of modern Quebec history: It "pitted *la grande noirceur* of the Duplessis era against the so-called *enlightenment* of the Quiet Revolution."[5] The historiography of the Quiet Revolution remains fiercely contested, especially among Quebec historians. Some continue to insist on the revolutionary nature of the 1960s, criticizing those who attempt to find the origins of the Quiet Revolution in the earlier post-war period as merely attempts to rehabilitate the conservative and traditionalist Duplessis regime as a liberal one. Others have placed the origins of the Quiet Revolution within modern liberal capitalism that had its beginnings in the nineteenth century rather than in the post-war period, suggesting that Quebec was not radically different from other parts of North America when it came to industrialization, urbanization, and the embracing of other elements of modernization. Others, such as Jocelyn Létourneau, who holds a Canada Research Chair in the History of Contemporary Quebec at Laval University, has pointed out that the origins of the Quiet Revolution stemmed from the new middle class of technocrats, academics, intellectuals, and bureaucrats that emerged in the 1960s and came to dominate Francophone society. As they imposed their version of modernity on Quebec society, it was their culture and their history that became the Quiet Revolution.

1960: Quiet Revolution begins in Quebec.

All of these interpretations have one element in common: There is an agreement that the Catholic Church and Catholicism were relatively unimportant in the process. However, historian Michael Gauvreau has recently argued that the Catholic Church was, in actuality, an important impetus for the Quiet Revolution. By focusing on individuals working within the church, he concludes that the Quiet Revolution might be seen as a "sustained attempt to enhance and strengthen, rather than weaken and ultimately sever, the relationship between Catholicism and Quebec society." Recent scholarship on the Quiet Revolution, particularly from Gauvreau and Létourneau, shows that the origins of the Quiet Revolution lie in the cultural and economic—and not simply the political and intellectual—history of Quebec.[6] Thanks to the recent scholarship on Quebec, we now know that the changes in Quebec society did not begin with the election of Premier Jean Lesage, a former cabinet minister in St. Laurent's government in Ottawa, nor end with the defeat of his provincial Liberal party at the hands of a renewed Union Nationale in 1966. Despite their insistence that it was time for change in the 1960 election campaign, the Liberal party, it should be recalled, had each of its candidates state their connections to the Roman Catholic Church just as the old Union Nationale had done.

Some of the most profound changes came in education, but change was not a sure thing when the Liberals were first elected. When the suggestion first arose in his government that Quebec follow North America's lead for a secular state-run public school system, Lesage steadfastly refused to create a ministry of public education. When he first relented, it was only to allow Monseigneur Alphonse-Marie Parent, the vice-rector of Université Laval, to study education in Quebec. Parent recommended a single and secular education system for the province, but there would be no secular educational system for Quebec. The legislation that created a provincially administered system also created a Superior Council of Education that gave bishops considerable control over the religious content taught in the school system. To catch up with the rest of North America, the school-leaving age in the province was raised to 16 and all children were guaranteed access to all secondary schools and new junior colleges that were established.

The Quiet Revolution also saw the emergence of a new strategy for economic development. Duplessis had long worked with foreign capital to exploit the province's resource sector and to establish a manufacturing sector, but after 1960 the province turned to state capital as a source of economic development—the same strategy that had been employed in many of the other provinces. Most of the provincial premiers of the period realized that the state could be a useful agent of economic development. Quebec was different from the other provinces only in that state capitalism in Quebec became intertwined with language. For many Quebecers, state capitalism was a means not only of limiting the control of capital coming into the province but also of ensuring that all new jobs created by the state within its economic realm would be filled by French-speaking Quebecers.

One of the best-known events of the Quiet Revolution was the nationalization of hydroelectricity in Quebec, though one prominent historian has noted that "the process was neither quiet nor revolutionary."[7] Hydro-Quebec, which has come to symbolize the Quiet Revolution, was created in 1944, when then premier Adélard Godbout expropriated the electricity and gas assets of the Montreal Light, Heat and Power Company, a powerful

1962: The nationalism of hydroelectricity with Hydro-Quebec.

During the debate over the nationalization of hydroelectric power in Quebec, the Liberal party published a manifesto with the cover "Maintenant ou jamais!—Maître chez nous [Now or never! Masters in our own house]," and in September 1962 an election was called on this issue.

Source: http://montrealconflict. files.wordpress.com/2007/12/ maitrechez-nous.jpg.

1962: Maîtres chez nous *becomes mantra of Quebec Liberal party.*

monopoly in Montreal; he created a provincial Crown corporation to run the utility. When the Lesage government was elected, it gave Hydro-Québec control over all of the sites that had potential for hydropower that were not held by private interests and began the process of changing the language of work at the corporation's head office and all of the work sites. French-speaking engineers had begun work on the massive hydroelectric projects on the Manicouagan and Outardes Rivers in 1959. These engineering projects were important for the new government, as French was the language of the projects and they spawned the creation and expansion of Quebec-based consulting and engineering firms.

In February 1962, René Lévesque, the provincial minister of natural resources, criticized the private power companies for the lack of electricity throughout the province and the small number of management positions open to Francophones in the various utilities, and he announced his plan to complete the process that began a generation earlier to nationalize all power companies in the province. The province was divided on the issue, and Lesage called a snap election to let the people decide. The election was no contest: The Liberals presented the nationalization of the power companies as a means of ending economic colonialism by kicking the foreign companies out of the province. The Liberals chose *maîtres chez nous* (masters in our own house) as their slogan and easily won re-election. The government proceeded and bought, for $604 million, 80 companies involved in the private generation of electricity to make Hydro-Québec what it has become today—the world's largest hydroelectric generating company.

Hydro-Québec was not the only instance of state capitalism at work in the province. In 1961, Lesage created an economic planning council that examined the province's economic potential and the role the government should play in developing it. It created a provincially administered corporation in 1964, the *Société générale de financement*, to fund Quebec companies with plans to invest in the province. It also dispatched bureaucrats throughout the province to help with economic development, as the federal government had done for the nation as a whole. All these initiatives, together with health, education, and social expenditures, were costly undertakings, and the provincial debt soared as government expenditures increased dramatically. Some have argued that Quebec considered its own pension plan as a way to fund economic development in the province. After the Quebec Pension Plan was created, the government established the *Caisse de depot et de placement* to oversee the pension plan and invest the fund in the best interests of the province. It has become one of the largest institutional investors in Canada.

The Quiet Revolution was also marked by the desire Quebecers had to deal with their place in Canada. Historian Ramsay Cook has noted that what was happening in Quebec was a case of "the government being pushed by a nation on the march towards a progressive new society."[8] Quebec had rarely seen itself as just another of the provinces that made up Canada, and it disliked the injustices it saw in its own society. At the time, few Canadians saw where the new Quebec was heading, and most certainly did not realize that it would shake the very foundations of Confederation and threaten the unity of the country within a generation.

Lesage established a ministry of federal–provincial relations to deal with Ottawa, and those that followed him in the office of premier clearly saw themselves as the equal of the prime minister of Canada. Quebec was rapidly beginning to act as a nation, and it wanted greater power, greater financial resources, greater autonomy, and less federal involvement in Quebec, except for the unconditional transfer of funds from Ottawa. A new nationalism was developing in Quebec and many there saw their province as their state. For many intellectuals they had to end the colonization that they believed had existed since the conquest in 1763, and for many of them that process could succeed only if Quebec wrestled control of social programs from Ottawa.

Family allowances provided one example of Quebec's increasingly aggressive position in relation to Ottawa. Family allowances had been one of the most important social programs in Canada for nearly half of a century. They began as a universal social program in 1945 under Prime Minister William Lyon Mackenzie King and paid benefits to all families with children. The federal government liked family allowances for a variety of reasons, not least because in a diverse and increasingly multinational state such as Canada, where the lines of regional and ethnic cleavage have been particularly strong, the program was one way of maintaining social cohesion and national unity.

When René Lévesque became Quebec's family and social welfare minister in 1965, he announced that he wanted to control all federal social security programs in his province and limit federal involvement to funding the programs. He maintained that Quebec City knew better than Ottawa the particular needs of his province, a claim initially made in the 1963 *Rapport de la Quebec Comité d'Etude sur l'Assistance Publique* (the *Boucher Report*), which recommended that the federal government withdraw from a variety of joint programs and simply provide the provinces with the financial resources it allocated to these programs. Quebec believed that only with total control of its social security program could it deal effectively with the poverty within its provincial boundaries, and that could not happen if Ottawa continued to manage such programs as family allowances. Lévesque's own plan for social security reform in Quebec depended, in large measure, on getting his hands on the $180 million that the family allowance program paid to families in Quebec.

In 1966, Lévesque demanded that Ottawa either radically reform the family allowance program to meet the priorities of Quebec or, barring that, transfer funds for the program to the provinces. He insisted on using the word "repatriation" in his demand, suggesting that the province was taking back the program that was constitutionally within the jurisdiction of the province. Of course, the reforms that Lévesque enunciated followed closely the masters-in-our-own-house rhetoric of a more autonomous Quebec. While the province had opted out of several federal–provincial programs throughout the 1960s, most notably the Canadian Pension Plan and Youth Allowances, the withdrawal from family allowances was particularly troubling for the federal government. Ottawa had established family allowances as a purely federal initiative as part of its national social security program immediately following the end of the Second World War. If Quebec opted out of the program, which was seen, in part, by federal political leaders as an important aspect of Canadian citizenship, it would represent the strengthening of provincialism, particularly in Quebec, and an erosion of the strong central government that had emerged during and immediately following the Second World War. In the case of family allowances, the federal government refused, but in other areas Quebec had more success, as with the Quebec Pension Plan.

The Liberal government in Quebec had learned that the state could be used to build a new kind of Quebec nationalism, but it did not pay enough attention to the political map of the province. In the 1966 provincial election, the Liberal party captured 47 percent of the popular vote, compared with just 40 percent for the Union Nationale, but the Liberals lost the election, as many of the seats remained in rural Quebec. Still, the election of Daniel Johnson (who died in 1968) did not reverse the demands from Quebec for special status in Confederation. A year before the provincial election, Johnson had raised the possibility of independence for Quebec in *Égalité ou Indépendance* (Equality or Independence), which became his party's campaign slogan. Once in office, he pushed hard for constitutional change to recognize Canada as the union of two nations rather than ten provinces. He changed the name of the Legislative Assembly of Quebec to the National Assembly of Quebec as part of redefining Quebec's collective identity. Another important part of the new nationalist movement was the replacement of the term *French-speaking Quebecers* with *Québécois* to describe the people of Quebec.

During the Quiet Revolution there emerged in Quebec a pro-independence movement. At first, it was a small group led by Pierre Bourgault's *Ressemblement pour l'indépendence nationale* (RIN) and the *Ralliement national* (RN), which, together, captured 9 percent of the popular vote in the 1966 provincial election. The RIN had come to prominence for its violent protest during the visit of Queen Elizabeth in 1964, but the independence movement became a real political force when René Lévesque left the Quebec Liberal party after he became convinced that it would never demand sovereignty for Quebec. He created the *Mouvement Souveraineté* (MSA) in 1968 and a year later the Parti Québécois (PQ), dedicated to the creation of a sovereign state for Quebec. Even supporters of the federalist parties in Quebec—the label attached to those committed to Quebec remaining in Canada—made special status within the Canadian federation one of their primary goals. The notion of Quebec as merely one of the ten provinces was gone, as Quebec came to see itself in the 1960s as a state within Canada, one that was distinct from the other provinces.

Political parties campaigning for independence of Quebec participate in 1966 provincial election.

Pearson: Confronting the New Realities

When the Liberals returned to power in 1963, they realized that Canada was a different country from what it had been when they last sat in the government benches. The Liberals knew that they had to continue enlarging the social welfare state. Pearson also recognized that something profound was happening in Quebec, and in the 1963 campaign, he promised a new deal for the province. He realized that Ottawa had to deal with the new Quebec, though Pearson, like most people in English-speaking Canada, looked at Quebec with bewilderment, wondering what Quebec really wanted. Pearson, the former diplomat, began a process of dealing with Quebec's place in Canada that was to dominate the national political agenda for much of next generation. He chose a path of pragmatic accommodation with Quebec, often with the support of Ontario Premier John Robarts, but his agenda of cooperative federalism with Quebec would not survive his departure from the political scene.

Pearson's first task was to try to understand what was happening in Quebec. To do that, he appointed the Royal Commission on Bilingualism and Biculturalism with two co-chairs: André Laurendeau, a leading Quebec journalist who convinced Pearson to take separation seriously, and Davidson Dunton, the president of Carleton University. The royal commission's goal was to study and report on the state of bilingualism and biculturalism in Canada. The commission travelled across the country to raise the consciousness of ordinary citizens to the fact that Canada was a bilingual and bicultural nation. While the commission recommended that French and English should be the two languages of the federal government, it also made a large number of citizens, primarily immigrants, aware of the fact that they were members of neither historical community but were undoubtedly Canadian, nonetheless. Even by the early 1960s it was clear that Canada was no longer a bicultural and bilingual nation, but a multicultural one: One in four Canadians could not trace their ancestry to either French or British origins. Of course, the French–English dichotomy had always ignored Canada's Aboriginal and Métis peoples.

There were a number of intellectuals and union leaders in Quebec who were extremely worried about what was happening in their province. They harboured contempt for those who wanted to distance Quebec from the rest of Canada and were concerned with the brand of nationalism being pursued by the provincial government. Three middle-aged men have come to represent this group, and they all played a major role not only in Quebec policies and society but also that of Canada as well. Pierre Trudeau had long fought Duplessis, but he refused to enter the political arena and spent his time carping from the sidelines. Two others, journalist Gérard Pelletier and labour leader Jean Marchand, shared Trudeau's concern about what was happening in Quebec, and they believed that Quebec's interest could be best served if they joined the federal government in Ottawa. When Pearson asked them to run for the federal Liberals, they agreed, but they did not agree that the way to deal with Quebec was through the policy of accommodation that Pearson had pursued since 1963. They refused to accept the premise of the Quebec provincial government that Quebec was the "homeland" of French-speaking Canadians; they believed that the development and protection of French was a responsibility of the federal government and that French-speaking Canadians could be at home in any part of Canada.

At the time, Canadians were looking for someone who understood Quebec. Many had hoped that the Quiet Revolution would make the province like all of the others (though they were never sure what that would be), but clearly that was not happening. What Canadians witnessed in Quebec was troubling, especially the violence that seemed to be engulfing the province. On May 31, 1963, *Time* magazine ran a headline "Bombs in the Quiet Land" that spoke of a reign of terror in Quebec. Over an 11-week period, a series of explosions had killed a security guard and injured several others, including a bomb specialist with the army. All of the targets were Government of Canada buildings, such as army-recruiting centres and other offices of the Canadian military. Mailboxes were

1963: Royal Commission on Bilingualism and Biculturalism appointed to study French–English relations.

Source: © National Archives of Canada/Credit: Duncan Cameron/National Archives of Canada, C-025003.

*Left to right:
Marchand, Trudeau,
and Pelletier.*

*1967: Growing violence
in Quebec and French
President Charles de
Gaulle incites crowds
in Montreal.*

also a target in both Montreal and Quebec City. Much of the violence was attributed to the Front de libération du Québec (FLQ), which *Time* described as "a lunatic fringe of violent nationalists whose aim is the secession of French-speaking Quebec from the rest of English-speaking Canada."[9] In 1964, the Fédération Libérale du Québec cut all ties with the federal Liberal party to become an autonomous provincial party, and large and violent demonstrations greeted the Queen on her visit to the province. Perhaps the most troubling event occurred during French President Charles de Gaulle's visit to Quebec during the 1967 Centennial. Quebec had opened Maison Québécoise in Paris in 1961 and de Gaulle had even said that Quebec would become a separate state. Pearson and his officials were worried about de Gaulle's visit but did not really think he could encourage Quebec independence during his visit; however, he did precisely that. Speaking to a large enthusiastic crowd in Montreal, de Gaulle shouted, *"Vive la France! Vive le Quebec! Vive le Quebec libre!"* which brought a thunderous response from those assembled below the balcony of the Montreal City Hall. Pearson was outraged. De Gaulle hastily departed Canada after Pearson cancelled their meeting, and many in Canada were left wondering what was happening in Quebec and where it would all end.

The Persistence of Regionalism

Quebec was not the only province undergoing profound change or quarrelling with the federal government. The Atlantic provinces never received much respect in Confederation after the end of the nineteenth century, and by the late 1950s, it was clear the region had fallen

Source: CHUCK MITCHELL/CP Images.

far behind the rest of the country. Per capita income for all four provinces was well below the national average. Nova Scotia, the economic leader of the region, could claim a per capital income that represented only 75 percent of the national average; Newfoundland's stood at 54 percent, whereas Ontario's per capita income as a percentage of the national average was 120 percent. In the early 1960s, 38.5 percent of new homes built in the Atlantic provinces did not have flush toilets, compared with just 8.7 percent in Ontario. Diefenbaker was the first prime minister to make regional inequalities in Canada an election issue, and by the 1960s, Ottawa had finally come to realize that some regions were suffering gravely after the provincial governments there had made it clear that they were not prepared to accept the status quo. They sought to stimulate their provincial economies and transform their provincial societies.

Louis Robichaud becomes the first Acadian premier of New Brunswick in 1960.

In New Brunswick, the first Acadian elected premier, Louis Robichaud, led his Liberal party to victory on the promise of change. His Equal Opportunity Program attempted to improve the lives of rural citizens through improvements in education, health, and social services. In Nova Scotia, CBC television captured the agony of the region when in October 1958 an accident at Springhill resulted in the death of 74 miners. Premier Robert Stanfield promised educational change and economic development, and he created the Industrial Estates Limited, as noted earlier, with Frank Sobey—best known for the chain of grocery stores across Canada—as president to bring manufacturing to the provinces. Similarly, Joseph R. Smallwood, one of Canada's most colourful premiers, attempted to create an industrial revolution in Newfoundland. He managed to convince Ottawa to participate in funding the resettlement of several hundred small and isolated fishing communities, such as Pushthrough on the southwest coast of Newfoundland, to larger towns that were designated as growth centres. Although the promised jobs never materialized in those centres, most of the families that relocated found themselves with much better social services and amenities, including schools, medical facilities, running water, and electricity. In Nova Scotia, there was also relocation of people, most notably people from the Halifax suburb of Africville. It was one of city's oldest and largest black neighbourhoods, but through years of neglect and racism it became one of the worst slums in the country. In the rush of urban renewal sweeping North America, the Halifax city council relocated the citizens of Africville to another part of the city. At the time urban planners across North America praised the relocation, but the citizens of Africville saw it as the destruction of their vibrant community and as an overt act of racism. Peter Kelly, the mayor of Halifax, apologized to the people of Africville and their descendents in February 2010 for the decision and provided $3 million in compensation to build a church and interpretative centre at the site of the former community. None of the Atlantic provinces met with much economic success greater than they had in the immediate post-war period, but as with the resettlement communities in Newfoundland, there were substantial improvements in living standards, income levels, and social services, even if much of the improvement resulted from government spending and transfers to individuals.

Like Atlantic Canada, the Western provinces of Manitoba, Saskatchewan, and Alberta often saw themselves as disenfranchised from Confederation, as did British Columbia. British Columbia has always elected colourful politicians and none more so that W.A.C. Bennett. He led his Social Credit party to victory and remained in office for two decades. During that time, British Columbia flourished, but it, too, quarrelled with Ottawa, especially over natural resources. One area of disagreement was ownership of offshore resources that would also become a major source of disagreement with the Atlantic provinces. Beginning in the 1950s, the international community turned its attention to the continental shelves off their coasts. With the discovery of oil and gas, nations were quick to extend their territorial control over the traditional five-kilometre limit. In 1960, Canada established a 19-kilometre limit along its coastline and told fishing nations to stay outside that line. The United Nations attempted to bring some order to the chaos and established the Law of the Sea Conferences that would last for nearly two decades before an international agreement emerged on territorial waters, but that process did little to settle the issue of who controlled the offshore resources—the provinces or the federal government.

Ottawa maintained that it controlled all off-shore waters and it, alone, would control access to all mineral, oil, and gas deposits on the continental shelf. When Shell Oil announced its plan to drill for oil off British Columbia in 1961, it applied only to the federal government for a permit. British Columbia was outraged, and in 1962 it took the matter to court, but the federal government imposed a moratorium to prevent crude oil tankers from travelling through the pristine and fragile coastline of British Columbia, effectively delaying further exploration. A similar constitutional dispute occurred on the east coast when oil companies began to explore for oil off Newfoundland in 1966. The matter dragged on between the two levels of government until the early 1980s.

Yukon and the Northwest Territories: Canada's Northern Colonies

When Britain transferred the 10.1 million square kilometres that make up the Arctic archipelago to Canada in 1880, it was only with reluctance that Canada agreed to accept it. The size of the territory was immense: Even Baffin Island, admittedly one of the large islands, was twice the size of the United Kingdom. Periodically, as historian Ken Coates points out, Canadians have been fired up with enthusiasm about the North, but the excitement never had much staying power. In the late 1950s, Diefenbaker encouraged Canadians to develop their northern regions as part of a new national policy. The North—although often mythologized and included by Canadians as a defining characteristic of their identity—had been largely ignored until the Second World War, when its military and strategic importance became apparent.

During the 1950s and 1960s, the North remained a colony for Canada. The region was very much under the control of the federal government and was run by outsiders. Until the mid-1960s, Ottawa was the territorial capital of the Northwest Territories, and federal administrators wanted to remake the Northwest Territories and the Yukon, the other northern territory, in the image of southern Canada. Diefenbaker's vision of the North was in many ways just another development project in that it was to use the resources of the North for the economic well-being of southern Canada. For a few years, through strong federal support in the form of subsidies and tax incentives, the region enjoyed an economic boom as the search for resources moved into high gear.

As was the case with much of rural Canada, there was growth in the level of services available throughout the North. Schools were established and parents who had traditionally been migratory were encouraged to remain in their communities so that their children could be educated and, hence, assimilated into the mainstream culture. For parents in more remote locations, residential schools were established. Hospitals and an array of medical services were provided in the larger centres, and when facilities did not exist, persons needing medical attention were flown south. To diversify the local economy, Ottawa promoted the establishment of cooperatives as a form of regional economic development. Some of these later played important roles in promoting Inuit art for markets in southern Canada and Europe.

The region remained sparsely settled throughout this period, though the population doubled between 1951 and 1976. Of the Northwest Territories' 42 000 inhabitants in 1976, about 27 000 were First Nations, Métis, and Inuit; in the Yukon, slightly more than one-third of the 20 000 people were Aboriginal. In the North, as was the case throughout Canada, Aboriginal rights started to emerge in the late 1960s, as a new generation of leaders began to reassert their authority over the region and challenge the assimilationist policies of the federal government and control of their regions by outsiders.[10]

Aboriginal Canadians: Laying the Foundation of Change

Change in Aboriginal societies rivalled that of any other group or province during the 1960s. The civil rights movement in the United States and the resistance of colonized peoples throughout the world spurred much of the reconsideration of Aboriginal peoples in Canada. The prolonged post-war economic prosperity had had little impact on Canada's Aboriginal communities, and many Canadians were shocked by the deplorable conditions in which Indigenous people lived. Diefenbaker took an important step in the 1960s when he permitted Aboriginal people to vote without surrendering their status and their treaty rights, which had been a precondition of their attaining the franchise since Confederation. This was largely a symbolic move, as many Aboriginal people chose not to cast their ballot.

1960: Aboriginal people are given the right to vote.

Source: Library and Archives Canada/Credit: Nick Nickles/Canada Dept. of Indian Affairs and Northern Development Collection /PA-123915.

After the Diefenbaker government extended the franchise to Status Indians in 1960, the first reserve Indians to vote federally were those of the Rice Lake Band near Peterborough, Ontario, in a by-election on October 31, 1960.

1961: The National Indian Council is formed.

The unofficial policy of the Canadian government remained the assimilation of the Aboriginal peoples of Canada.

Steps towards significant change came largely from Aboriginal peoples themselves. They created political organizations to make their voices heard, but with so many different groups spread across Canada, there was no single Aboriginal voice. In 1961, the National Indian Council was created to represent three of the four major groups: Treaty and Status Indians (those recognized by the federal government as registered under the *Indian Act*, and entitled to a wide range of programs and services offered by federal agencies, provincial governments, and the private sector); the non-status peoples (persons who considered themselves "Indians" but were not recognized as such by the *Indian Act*, usually because they could not prove their status or had lost their status); and the Métis people. The Inuit were not included. While the National Indian Council hoped to create unity among all Aboriginal peoples, it proved impossible, and in 1968 it broke into two groups—the National Indian Brotherhood, which represented Status and Treaty Aboriginal groups, and the Native Council of Canada, which represented the Métis. Aboriginal groups began to talk about equality, treaty rights, and land ownership.

In 1964, the Hawthorn Commission, which had undertaken a comprehensive investigation into conditions of Aboriginal peoples at the request of the minister of the Department of Citizenship and Immigration, reported that Aboriginal peoples had not been assimilated and recommended that the federal government abandon its racist policy of assimilation. The report did not recommend Aboriginal self-government but preferred what it called "citizens plus." There is no single definition of the concept of Aboriginal self-government, but it was generally assumed to mean that Aboriginal peoples would regain control over the management of affairs that directly affected them and that would allow them to preserve their communities and cultural identities. According to the Hawthorn Commission, Aboriginal Peoples would enjoy all the rights and benefits of Canadian citizenship, but they would remain "Indians" and could expect the federal government to protect their lands and acknowledge their special rights as "charter members of the Canadian community." The Hawthorn report also noted that reserves lacked a sufficient resource base to support the growing Aboriginal population. The Pearson government realized that Aboriginal policy in Canada had to be redefined, but Pearson resigned before he might have reached any accommodation with Aboriginal leaders as he had attempted with Quebec. His replacement, Pierre Trudeau, would counsel no such special status for Aboriginal peoples, even though self-determination, equality, and treaty rights had clearly emerged as part of the Aboriginal discourse.

Inventing Canadian Symbols

Given the divisions that had become apparent in Canada in the 1960s, Pearson hoped that a new definition of Canadian identity would help restore national unity. One of Pearson's most important initiatives in this regard was the adoption of a new Canadian flag. More than 80 percent of Canadians surveyed in 1958 said they wanted a national flag that was not already flown by another country. In 1964, when Pearson first announced that he would introduce a new Canadian flag, he found large numbers of Canadians were either indifferent to his plans or downright hostile. Diefenbaker was opposed to the idea, as was the Royal Canadian Legion. Legionnaires in Winnipeg booed Pearson in May 1964 when he told them that the Red Ensign, a flag of the British merchant marine and used for generations as a Canadian flag, was no longer acceptable for Canadians in the 1960s. He wanted the maple leaf, which had long been seen by many as one of Canada's enduring symbols. Many in French Canada were ambivalent to the debate that ensured, pitting those who favoured a new flag against those that wanted to retain the symbols of Canada's past. A parliamentary committee was tasked with considering various designs for a new flag. They unanimously selected the current maple leaf flag suggested by Liberal MP John Matheson and favoured by Pearson. After passing a closure motion, Parliament voted 163 to 78 to adopt a new flag at 2 A.M. on December 15, 1964. On February 15, 1965, for the first time in the country's 98-year history, Canadians raised an official national flag that eventually became an important Canadian symbol.

1964: Canada adopts the Maple Leaf as the new Canadian flag.

Pearson had no more success, though, with substantive constitutional change than had Diefenbaker. Like so many of Canada's twentieth-century prime ministers, Diefenbaker would have liked to "patriate" the Canadian constitution from the British Parliament so that it could be amended in Canada. Since 1867 each time Parliament had wanted to amend the *British North America Act*, it had had to make a request to the British Parliament. Diefenbaker saw this as a slight to Canadian nationhood. Canada had left its constitution as an act of the British Parliament since 1867 largely because the federal and provincial governments could not agree upon an amending formula. E. Davie Fulton, the minister of justice in Diefenbaker's cabinet, had hoped that the Conservative government could solve the impasse, but it did not.

At a dominion–provincial conference in 1960, Quebec Premier Lesage had raised the matter of constitutional reform. The provinces and the federal government quickly agreed that the consent of all provinces was required before changes were made by the federal Parliament to a variety of items, including the use of the French and English languages, education rights, the assets of a province, the legislative powers of a province, provincial representation in the House of Commons, and the amending formula itself.

There was considerable desire among some of the provinces at the time for a flexible constitution that would allow any province to transfer or delegate a matter of exclusive provincial jurisdiction to the federal government and, at the same time, allow the provinces to assume responsibility for areas within the federal purview. They had also agreed by early December 1961 on an amending formula that allowed the federal Parliament the authority to amend the Constitution if supported by two-thirds of the provinces that together had more than 50 percent of the population of Canada. The Fulton formula, as this constitutional package was called, was rejected by Quebec when it failed to get control over unemployment insurance, which the provinces had surrendered to Ottawa in the early 1940s.

Pearson's Liberal government attempted to bring closure to the Fulton proposal in 1964, when Guy Favreau, then minister of justice, changed the Fulton formula slightly and presented a new proposal for an amending process. His proposal retained the main features of the Fulton formula but added provisions granting Parliament exclusive power to make amendments to the Constitution of Canada concerning the executive government of Canada, the Senate and the House of Commons. At the 1964 conference, all the premiers agreed with the proposed procedure, but Jean Lesage, premier of Quebec, later changed his mind when the deal was opposed in Quebec. He then refused to ratify the agreement. Some in Quebec disagreed with the substance of the agreement, but many were opposed because they disagreed with the process.

1964: Constitutional reform fails.

Women and the Struggle for Equality

The decade was not an easy one for women. In the immediate post-war period, it was clear that domestic duty was the centre of life for most women. Throughout the 1950s, the media and prominent women, such as Dr. Hilda Neatby, one of the pre-eminent historians of her generation, continued to emphasize the centrality of family for Canadian women. Interestingly, though, the role of women outside the home became a frequent topic in women's magazines in both English- and French-speaking Canada. Under the editorship of Doris Anderson after 1957, *Chatelaine/Châtelaine* carried ground-breaking articles on the problems of working mothers, pay equity, abortion, divorce, and family violence. She advocated social change and emerged as one of the leaders of the feminist movement in Canada, committed to bringing about fundamental change for women.

The period saw growth in women's activism, now referred to as the "second wave" of feminism to distinguish it from the earlier women's movement at the beginning of the twentieth century. There was little unity in the women's movement, but most efforts were directed towards the systematic obstacles that helped define women's place in society.

Although only a small number of Canadian women were actually involved with the women's liberation movement, the movement has come to define women's protest during this period. It was most active on university campuses and among middle-class groups and adopted the rhetoric of the liberation movements of colonized people around the world. While some women involved in the liberation of women waged protests against such events as bikini contests in Toronto, other women were working hard to change gender stereotypes about what a woman could and could not accomplish. During the winter of 1968, Nancy Greene earned a place for women in Canadian sport with her gold-medal performance in the giant slalom in the Grenoble Olympics; she worked as a secretary to cover her training costs.

The women's movement responded to some of the major issues of the period, and it included women who were often moved by a particular concern or worry. One issue for many women was the danger posed by the possibility of nuclear war. It was this that prompted Peggy Hope-Simpson, a young mother living in Halifax, to launch the Voice of Women in Nova Scotia. The organization began in 1960, when *Toronto Star* columnist Lotta Dempsey urged women to join together to oppose nuclear war. More than 10 000 women joined, including Maryon Pearson, wife of the federal opposition leader, who became an honorary member. Her husband, Lester B. Pearson, was then leading the fight in Parliament against nuclear weapons in Canada. Voice of Women in Nova Scotia (VOW) organized an international women's conference in 1962 that included women from the Soviet Union and other communist countries; they called on the United Nations to designate an International Year of Peace. The UN declared 1965 as International Cooperation Year. Howard Green later claimed that the VOW contributed to the government's decision in 1962 to delay putting Canadian forces on alert during the Cuban Missile Crisis. A new era had arrived in public participation in the democratic process and it would not belong simply to the nation's youth.

Laura Sabia met the same kind of enthusiasm for her cause. Although she had a privileged upbringing and went to a religious boarding school in Quebec, she never accepted the role that women had in Canadian society. At the convent, she resented the fact that the nuns had to bow to the priests. She went to McGill University with hopes of becoming a lawyer but followed the pattern of so many other female graduates and soon found herself married and raising four children. Somehow, though, she managed to become one of the revolutionaries of her time. In St. Catharines, Ontario, she became active in local politics and the host of a radio phone-in show, and embraced some of the emerging social issues of the day. When she challenged the Catholic Church on abortion, she asked, "What do 100 celibates in Rome know about women's bodies?" When the Royal Bank ran an advertisement of "Mary the Happy Teller," she found it insulting to women and led a campaign to have it withdrawn. Not only was the ad dropped, but her campaign also led to two women being added to the bank's all-male board.[11]

Sabia is best known for pushing the Canadian government to appoint a royal commission to investigate the position of women in Canadian society. She assembled a coalition of 32 women's organizations, including the Fédération des femmes du Québec, to lobby Prime Minister Pearson for the creation of the Royal Commission on the Status of Women. When Pearson refused, Sabia was outraged and told the Toronto *Globe and Mail* that

1967: Royal Commission on the Status of Women is appointed.

Pearson would regret his decision when she led 3 000 000 women to Ottawa. When the newspaper ran Sabia's comments as its lead story, Pearson changed his mind and Sabia got her royal commission. The commission's mandate was to "inquire into and report upon the status of women in Canada, and to recommend what steps might be taken by the Federal Government to ensure for women equal opportunities with men in all aspects of Canadian society." Florence Bird, a CBC journalist, was appointed chair and the commission reported in 1970. The commission was important because, for the first time, it legitimized the concerns women had regarding their status. It also raised women's issues and status to matters of national consciousness.

Between 1960 and 1965, Canadian doctors prescribe the birth-control pill to three-quarters of a million women.

One of the most important developments for women was the development and introduction of the first oral contraceptive, Enovid, known simply as "the Pill" in 1960. Even though doctors agreed that there were adverse side effects to the Pill, it was enormously popular among Canadian women; in its first year on the market, doctors issued more than 10 000 prescriptions for the drug and within five years the number had increased to 750 000. The Pill gave women more control over birth control, and it allowed them greater freedom to choose a career over what had been the only other real option available to many women—motherhood. Nonetheless, Canada still had oppressive laws regarding the display and selling of contraceptive devices. In 1960, Toronto pharmacist Harold Fine was jailed for selling condoms, and it was not until 1968 that the *Criminal Code of Canada* was amended to deal with contraception and abortion.

The federal government had to respond to the changing social mores, and it fell to Pierre Elliot Trudeau, the justice minister in Pearson's government, to change the law to reflect the demands of an increasingly modern and changing society. Although he was a devout Catholic, Trudeau introduced his controversial Omnibus Bill (72 pages in length and containing 109 clauses) in the House of Commons on December 21, 1967, that proposed massive changes to the *Criminal Code of Canada*. It was during debate on the legislation that Trudeau uttered his most famous words: "There's no place for the state in the bedrooms of the nation." The legislation decriminalized some homosexual acts performed in private and between only two people, amended the abortion laws to make it legal for women to get an abortion under certain conditions (although all references to abortion would not be removed from the *Criminal Code* until 1988), legalized lotteries, introduced some restrictions on gun ownership, and permitted police to perform Breathalyzer tests on suspected drunk drivers if they had reasonable and probable cause. It also proposed changes to the laws governing divorce to avoid such charades as those in the "Shady Lady" episode (presented in the opening to this chapter). It also decriminalized the sale of contraceptives. The Bill was passed into law only in 1969 and only after it generated intense and acrimonious debate both inside and outside the House of Commons.

Regardless of the advancements made to improve the lives of Canadian women, for many the major focus was still on the home. Women were largely responsible for the home and it was their role as wives and mothers that concerned many in Canadian society. Although it was far from the reality, the idealized Canadian woman lived in the suburban communities that sprang up around Canada's larger towns and cities. There has been much criticism of the lack of community in the early suburbs and the isolation many women felt there. At the beginning of the 1960s, only one married women in five was in the paid labour force, though by 1970 there had been dramatic gains, as one in three married women worked outside the home. Most women in the paid workforce were still in clerical and retail positions.

Canadian Society

Despite the concern of many Canadians, particularly young university students, about the American influence in Canada, Canada's culture became increasingly American and international at the same time. Like youth throughout the Western world, boys and young men let their hair grow, and young men and women alike wore blue jeans as their attire of choice. This was the baby boom generation that had been born in the post-war period and had become teenagers in the 1960s. They wanted a different life from that of their parents and grandparents, and they would change the music, fashion, and many of the values of an earlier generation. Canada's youth embraced American and British rock groups, and when they found their own stars, such as Gordon Lightfoot, Joni Mitchell, or Neil Young, they were hardly distinguishable from their American and British counterparts. Much of the Canadian protest movement was driven by events in the United States, such as the civil rights movement and protests against the Vietnam War, but the baby boom generation here, as elsewhere, helped shape the new morality of the period. They raised questions about the capacity of governments to control their lives and protect society from the excesses of corporate greed. The public debate that the generation engendered recast old mores and created new social issues. This was particularly true with the degradation of the environment.

Of course, conservation was not new in Canada in the 1960s. John A. Macdonald created the first national park in the 1880s at Sulphur Springs in what is now Banff National Park, but that first environmental movement was aimed at protecting tourist areas for the wealthy, or the efficient management of natural resources. In the 1930s, Ducks Unlimited Canada had been established to protect Canada's wetlands for hunting enthusiasts, and federal and provincial governments attempted to protect forests and manage agricultural land uses. In the late 1950s, Canadians became more concerned about the ecological system and pollution. Some of this was predicated on the fear of nuclear destruction, but pollutants became a huge concern for many Canadians. The concept of ecology was pushed onto the agenda in an influential book by Rachel Carson, an American ecologist who warned about the long-term effects of misusing pesticides in *Silent Spring*, which she published in 1962. For those who dismissed the early environmentalists as alarmists, they finally realized what was happening to the ecosystem in June 1969 when Lake Erie—declared "dead" earlier in the decade—caught fire where the Cuyahoga River empties into the lake at Cleveland, Ohio, because it was so polluted. The Canadian side of the lake was no better, and the Great Lakes became the focus for the fledgling environmental movement in the 1960s.

The first issue was detergents that were being dumped into Lake Ontario from the region of Canada that accounted for much of the nation's manufacturing capacity and its largest post-war growth. Because of the vast industrial and urban activity, a wide range of effluents were discarded into the lake from homes and industries alike. After the Second World War, synthetic detergents had displaced soaps made from biodegradable animal or vegetable fats. A variety of chemicals were added to new detergents to suspend the dirt removed from cotton and other fabrics and not allow it to be redeposited on the wash. However, the foam created by these chemicals was not easily broken down, and it accumulated in the Great Lakes water system. Governments and industry—often reluctantly—worked to solve the problem of the proliferation of foam through the use of more biodegradable materials, but such measures did little to control the massive growth of algae, or cladophora, which fouled local beaches around Toronto.

1969: Pollution Probe is established by students at the University of Toronto.

Algae growth was also linked to the excessive use of phosphorus in detergents, which is added to soften water and suspend dirt. The public outcry against the pollution spawned such organizations as Pollution Probe and helped to create the modern environmental movement in Canada. Pollution Probe began a concerted campaign to force the federal government to amend the *Canada Water Act* to regulate the phosphorus content in detergents.

Pollution was not just a problem in the major industrial centres. In Long Harbour, Newfoundland, a community with a long history in the fishery, experienced environmental and health-related problems after the Electric Reduction Company of Canada Industries Limited (ERCO) was lured to the province with generous subsidies from the provincial government to produce phosphorus. Within months of the plant going into production, fishers began finding dead fish in Placentia Bay, and the minister of fisheries ordered the fishery in the area closed; the plant also closed voluntarily for a brief period on May 2, 1969. Emissions from the plant killed local vegetation; deformed moose and rabbits were found near the plant, and citizens there experienced air pollution for the first time. The plant remained opened until 1989, however.

Expo 67, to celebrate the nation's 100th birthday, was an attempt to mask all problems, including what humankind was doing to the planet. Montreal built an island for the world's fair in the middle of the St. Lawrence River from the soil that had been excavated to build a new subway. The theme for the extravaganza was Man and His World/Terre des Hommes. The 113 pavilions built by participating nations all had a futuristic design, including Germany, which erected a 15-storey-high multi-peak plastic tent. For the millions who visited the site, La Ronde, the amusement park part, and the *Bluenose II*, the a replica of the famed Nova Scotia sailing vessel, were two of the most popular attractions. The fair was proclaimed the greatest ever, and most Canadians celebrated the achievement and were proud that their nation had reached its 100th birthday. The celebration was not just in Montreal. In communities across the country, Canadians celebrated not just with picnics but with the construction of hockey rinks, playgrounds, and arts and cultural centres.

Conclusion

The large birthday party in 1967 did much to mask the troubled and uncertain decade since John Diefenbaker swept into the prime minister's office, but more difficult times lay ahead. Quebec had made it clear that the current situation was unsatisfactory, the regions harboured much discontent towards the centre, women wanted major systemic change, Aboriginal peoples demanded fuller recognition of their treaty rights, multicultural groups wanted equal recognition with citizens of French and English ancestry, and many realized that Canada had too many people who lived in poverty. The nation that the founders had negotiated in 1867 would be shaken to its very core in the years that lay ahead.

Questions to Consider

1. What were the major features of the Quiet Revolution in Quebec?

2. How would you describe federal–provincial relations in the period from 1957 to 1967? Are there differences between how the Conservatives and the Liberals dealt with the provinces?

3. What were the major differences in how Diefenbaker and Pearson attempted to deal with the Americans?

4. What is regional disparity and how successful were governments in dealing with it?

Critical Thinking Questions

1. Why were neither the Liberals nor the Conservatives able to win a majority government throughout most of the 1960s?

2. Was Canada a radical society during the 1960s?

3. Is it inevitable that Canada has strong links with the United States in economic and military affairs?

4. Was Diefenbaker a Canadian nationalist?

Suggested Readings

General

Bothwell, Robert, Ian Drummond, and John English. *Canada since 1945.* 2nd edition. Toronto: University of Toronto Press, 1989.

Granatstein, J.L. *Canada 1957–1967: The Years of Uncertainty and Innovation.* Toronto: McClelland & Stewart, 1986.

Granatstein, J.L. *Yankee Go Home? Canadians and Anti-Americanism.* Toronto: HarperCollins, 1996.

Morton, Desmond. *A Short History of Canada.* 5th edition. Toronto: McClelland & Stewart, 2001.

Palmer, Bryan D. *The Sixties: The Ironies of Identity in a Rebellious Age.* Toronto: University of Toronto Press, 2009.

Prentice, Alison, et al. *Canadian Women: A History.* 2nd edition. Toronto: Harcourt Brace, 1996.

Owram, Doug. *Born at the Right Time: A History of the Baby Boom Generation.* Toronto: University of Toronto Press, 1996.

National Politics

Campbell, Colin, and William Christian, *Parties, Leaders, and Ideologies in Canada.* Toronto: McGraw-Hill Ryerson, 1996.

English, John. *The Worldly Years: The Life of Lester Pearson, Volume II, 1949–1972.* Toronto: Lester & Orpen Dennys, 1992.

Nash, Knowlton. *Kennedy and Diefenbaker: Fear and Loathing Across an Undefended Border.* Toronto: McClelland & Stewart, 1990.

Newman, Peter C. *Renegade in Power: The Diefenbaker Years.* Toronto: McClelland & Stewart, 1989.

Smith, Denis. *Rogue Tory: The Life and Legend of John G. Diefenbaker.* Toronto: Macfarlane Walter and Ross, 1995.

Provincial Politics

Azoulay, Dan. *Keeping the Dream Alive: The Survival of the Ontario CCF/NDP, 1950–63.* Montreal and Kingston: McGill-Queen's University Press, 1997.

Behiels, Michaels. *Prelude to Quebec's Quiet Revolution.* Montreal and Kingston: McGill-Queen's University Press, 1985.

Fournier, Louis. *FLQ: The Anatomy of an Underground Movement.* Toronto: NC Press, 1984.

Gauvreau, Michael. *The Catholic Origins of Quebec's Quiet Revolution, 1930–1970.* Montreal and Kingston: McGill-Queen's University Press, 2006.

Gibbins, Roger. *Prairie Politics and Society: Regionalism in Decline.* Toronto: Butterworths, 1980.

Gibbins, Roger, and Sonia Arrison. *Western Visions: Perspectives on the West in Canada.* Peterborough: Broadview Press, 1995.

Gwyn, Richard. *Smallwood, the Unlikely Revolutionary.* Toronto: McClelland & Stewart, 1972.

Horton, Donald J. *André Laurendeau: French Canadian Nationalist, 1912–1968.* Toronto: Oxford University Press, 1992.

Letourneau, Jocelyn. *Passer à l'avenir.* Montreal: Boréal, 2000.

Linteau, Paul André, René Durocher, François Ricard, and Jean-Claude Robert. *Le Quebéc depuis 1930: Tome II.* Montreal: Boréal, 1989.

Morrison, William R. *True North: The Yukon and Northwest Territories.* Toronto: Oxford University Press, 1989.

Pelletier, Gérard. *Le temps des choix, 1960–1968.* Montréal: Stanké, 1983.

Thomson, Dale C. *Jean Lesage and the Quiet Revolution.* Toronto: Macmillan, 1984.

Economy and Society

Anastakis, Dimitri. *Auto Pact: Creating a Borderless North American Auto Industry, 1960–1971.* Toronto: University of Toronto Press, 2005.

Banting, Keith. "Social Citizenship and the Multicultural State." In Alan C. Cairns, et al., eds., *Citizenship, Diversity, and Pluralism.* Montreal and Kingston: McGill-Queen's University Press, 1999.

Banting, Keith. *The Welfare State and Canadian Federalism.* 2nd edition. Montreal and Kingston: McGill-Queen's University Press, 1987.

Bryden, P.E. *Planners and Politicians. Liberal Politics and Social Policy, 1957–1968.* Montreal and Kingston: McGill-Queen's University Press, 1997.

Campbell, Robert M. *Grand Illusions: The Politics of the Keynesian Experience in Canada, 1945–1975.* Peterborough: Broadview Press, 1987.

Copes, Parzival. *The Resettlement of Fishing Communities in Newfoundland.* Ottawa: Canadian Council on Rural Development, 1972.

Haddow, Rodney S. *Poverty Reform in Canada 1958–1978.* Montreal and Kingston: McGill-Queen's University Press, 1993.

Matthews, Ralph. *The Creation of Regional Dependency.* Toronto: University of Toronto Press, 1983.

Norrie, Kenneth, and Douglas Owram. *A History of the Canadian Economy.* 3rd edition. Toronto: Nelson, 2002.

Struthers, James. *The Limits of Affluence: Welfare in Ontario, 1920–1970.* Toronto: University of Toronto Press, 1994.

Foreign and Defence Policy

Chapnick, Adam. "The Canadian Middle Power Myth." *International Journal* 55 (Spring, 2000): 188–206.

Donaghy, Greg. *Tolerant Allies: Canada and the United States, 1963–1968.* Montreal and Kingston: McGill-Queen's University Press, 2003.

Jockel, Joseph T. *No Boundaries Upstairs: Canada, the United States and the Origins of North American Air Defence, 1945–58.* Vancouver: University of British Columbia Press, 1987.

Labour and Women

Dumont, Micheline, et al. *Quebec Women: A History*. Toronto: Women's Press, 1987.

Korinek, Valarie. *Roughing It in the Suburbs: Reading* Chatelaine *Magazine in the Fifties and Sixties*. Toronto: University of Toronto Press, 2000.

Little, Margaret. *No Car, No Radio, No Liquor Permit: The Moral Regulation of Single Mothers in Ontario, 1920–1997*. Toronto: Oxford University Press, 1998.

Porter, Ann. "Women and Income Security in the Post-War Period: The Case of Unemployment Insurance, 1945–1962." *Labour/Le Travail* 31 (Spring 1993): 111–144.

Prentice, Alison, et al. *Canadian Women: A History*. Toronto: Harcourt Brace, 1966.

Strong-Boag, Veronica. "Home Dreams: Women and the Suburban Experiment in Canada, 1945–1960." *Canadian Historical Review* 72 (1991): 471–504.

Culture

Cameron, David. *More Than an Academic Question: Universities, Government and Public Policy in Canada*. Halifax: Institute for Research on Public Policy, 1991.

Champion, C.P. "A Very British Coup: Canadianism, Quebec, and Ethnicity in the Flag Debate, 1964–1965." *Journal of Canadian Studies* 40, 3 (2006): 68–99.

Grant, George. *Lament for a Nation: The Defeat of Canadian Nationalism*. Toronto: McClelland & Stewart, 1965.

Iguarta, José. *The Other Quiet Revolution: National Identities in English Canada, 1945–1971*. Vancouver: University of British Columbia Press, 2007.

Kendall, Brian. *Our Hearts Went Boom: The Beatles' Invasion of Canada*. Toronto: Penguin Canada, 1997.

MacEachern, Alan. *Natural Selections: National Parks in Atlantic Canada, 1935–1970*. Montreal and Kingston: McGill-Queen's University Press, 2001.

Rutherford, Paul. *When Television was Young: Primetime Canada, 1952–1967*. Toronto: University of Toronto Press, 1990.

First Peoples

Cairns, Alan. *Citizens Plus: Aboriginal Peoples and the Canadian State*. Vancouver: University of British Columbia Press, 2000.

Coates, Ken. *Best Left as Indians: Native-White Relations in the Yukon Territory, 1840–1973*. Montreal and Kingston: McGill-Queen's University Press, 1991.

Dickason, Olive. *Canada's First Nations*. Toronto: McClelland & Stewart, 1997.

Miller, J.R. *Shingwauk's Vision*. Toronto: University of Toronto Press, 1996.

Notes

1. "The Shady Lady Will Help You Get a Divorce," *The CBC Digital Archives Website*, Canadian Broadcasting Corporation, http://archives.cbc.ca/IDC-1-69-760-4654/life_society/divorce/clip1; *Toronto Daily Star*, 5 and 6 July 1960.

2. Canada, Royal Commission on Canada's Economic Prospects, *Final Report* (Ottawa, 1957), 14.

3. Alvin Finkel, *Social Policy and Practice in Canada: A History* (Waterloo: Wilfrid Laurier University Press, 2006), Chapter 8 "The Medicare Debate, 1945–1980."

4. Jamie Glazov, *Canadian Policy Towards Khruschev's Soviet Union* (Montreal and Kingston: McGill-Queen's University Press, 2002), 112–122.

5. Donald Cuccioletta and Martin Lubin, "The Quebec Quiet Revolution: A Noisy Evolution," *Quebec Studies 36* (Fall–Winter 2003): 125.

6. Paul André Linteau, René Durocher, François Ricard, and Jean-Claude Robert, *Le Québec depuis 1930: Tome II* (Montreal: Boréal, 1989); Ronald Rudin, *Making History in Twentieth-Century Quebec* (Toronto: University of Toronto Press, 1997); Michaels Behiels, *Prelude to Quebec's Quiet Revolution* (Montreal and Kingston: McGill-Queen's University Press, 1985); Michael Gauvreau, *The Catholic Origins of Quebec's Quiet Revolution, 1930–1970* (Montreal and Kingston: McGill-Queen's University Press, 2006); Jocelyn Letourneau, *Passer à l'avenir* (Montreal: Boréal, 2000).

7. See Susan Mann Trofimenkoff, *The Dream of Nation: A Social and Intellectual History of Quebec* (Toronto: Gage Publishing, 1983).

8. Ramsay Cook, "Has the Quiet Revolution Finally Ended?" *Queen's Quarterly* 90, 2 (Summer, 1983): 330–342.

9. "Bombs in the Quiet Land," *Time*, 31 May 1963.

10. Kenneth Coates, *Canada's Colonies: A History of the Yukon and Northwest Territories* (Toronto: James Lorimer & Company, 1985); Kerry Abel and Ken S. Coates, *Northern Visions: New Perspectives on the North in Canadian History* (Toronto: University of Toronto Press, 2001).

11. Heather MacIvor, *Women and Politics in Canada* (Peterborough: Broadview Press, 1996), especially pp. 79–81.

Seeking *the*
Just Society:
1968–1984

When 1968 began, Robert Stanfield, the newly elected leader of the Progressive Conservative Party of Canada, was the new kid in Canadian politics. At 53, he was two decades younger than both Prime Minister Lester B. Pearson, who had been in the job for six years, and John Diefenbaker, the previous Conservative leader and former prime minister. Stanfield had been a brilliant student at Harvard University where he edited the prestigious *Harvard Law Journal*. Upon his return to Canada, he chose politics over the family's underwear business and became premier of Nova Scotia in 1956, a position he held easily until he was elected national Tory leader in 1967. Although never a great orator, he appeared honest, sincere, and decent—just what the country needed, it seemed, after years of uncertainty and acrimony in its political life. Public opinion polls had the Conservatives sweeping to victory in the next election, as those lining up to succeed Pearson after he announced his departure late in 1967 seemed old and tired. As Paul Martin, the leading contender for the

top job and the father of a future prime minister, discovered, Canadians might have fallen in love with the Beatles' hit tune "When I'm Sixty-Four," but they clearly did not want a 64-year-old leading the country. When Pierre Elliott Trudeau, the charming, fashionable, bilingual, and wealthy Quebec MP and minister of justice, then 49, won the Liberal leadership, even Stanfield, all of a sudden, seemed much, much older than he was. Canadians, it seemed, wanted someone who appeared youthful and Trudeau did. He even drove one of the few iconic 1960 Mercedes-Benz 300SL roadsters in Canada at that time.

After reading this chapter you will be able to:

1. Understand the events leading to the making of Canada's new Constitution in 1982.
2. Discover some of the regional economic development strategies in the 1970s.
3. Discuss the leadership style of Prime Minister Trudeau.
4. See how Canada changed during the decade.
5. Appreciate the difficulties of trying to reorient Canadian foreign policy away from the United States.

Introduction

The arrival of Pierre Trudeau on the national political stage seemed to signify a new beginning for Canada. He was treated like a rock star and captivated Canadians across the land, arousing such passion, particularly among young voters, that a journalist dubbed the period *Trudeaumania*, stealing a word from the frenzied *Beatlemania* created by the arrival of the British rock group a few years earlier. His election as Liberal leader and prime minister created a manic wave of optimism.

Canadians were impressed with the hard-nosed and determined leader. Many English Canadians were delighted with his resolute stand against those in Quebec who harboured separatist sentiments that threatened to destroy the country. On Saint-Jean-Baptiste Day 1968, one day before a federal election, a group of separatists showered Trudeau and a group of dignitaries with rocks and bottles, some of which contained paint and acid, shouting "*Trudeau au poteau*" (Trudeau to the gallows). An RCMP security detail attempted to usher the prime minister from the grandstand as a riot erupted on the streets of Montreal, but Trudeau refused to leave even as others scurried away. Television cameras captured

Saint-Jean-Baptiste Day Parade Riot: Prime Minister Pierre Elliott Trudeau with Mayor Jean Drapeau seated at the official stand before the riot.

Source: Library and Archives Canada PA-136971.

the prime minister dismissing the Mounties as they attempted to shield him from the hostile crowd. It was clear that he was the one to stand up for Canada and to stand up to Quebec. The following day, his Liberals captured more than 45 percent of the popular vote and 155 seats in the House of Commons, and he won the first majority government in Canada since 1958. Canadians, it seemed, had found their decisive leader for the troubled times that many feared lay ahead. Trudeau was also the flamboyant "non-politician," who many hoped would lead Canada in the apparently liberalizing spirit of the age, chart for it a more independent international role, quell Quebec separatism, build national unity, and forge—as Trudeau famously came to say—a pluralistic "just society" that promised common rights, liberties, and equal opportunity for all.

This chapter will focus on assessing and explaining the results of these goals and aspirations, paying special attention to subjects such as the Third Option, regional economic development, the National Energy Program, the *Official Languages Act*, multiculturalism, passage of the *Constitution Act* and the Charter of Rights, as well as economic management, social welfare initiatives, attempts to redress Aboriginal and regional grievances, and efforts to improve the status of women and sexual minorities. No one could argue that they did not know where Trudeau stood on these or other issues, as his determination and single-mindedness was often resolute. Compromise, long considered an absolute necessity for any successful Canadian prime minister, was not a trait that Trudeau brought to Ottawa. As prime minister, he transformed Canada, but in doing so he alienated large segments of the Canadian population, nearly destroyed the Liberal party, and, many have argued, left the country less unified than he had found it.

Equality and Social Issues

Trudeau dominated Canadian society and politics from the time he was first elected as prime minister on June 25, 1968, until he retired in early 1984. During the 1968 campaign, Trudeau, the charismatic politician, excited Canadians with his promise of a just society. He articulated a vision for Canada that aimed to be more inclusive and fair, whether through enhanced social programs or equalization programs for the regions or language rights for minorities or reform of the *Criminal Code of Canada*. His crusade to remake and modernize Canada when he tackled a number of Canadian taboos that included abortion, divorce, and homosexuality had begun with his revisions of the *Criminal Code* when he was justice minister. Those proposals symbolized the hopes of many Canadians for a new and different Canada, and when as prime minister he pushed those reforms through Parliament, it clearly set him apart from many of his peers. Not surprisingly, those issues had been important in the 1968 election campaign. Although the language used by Trudeau and others in arguing for new laws on a variety of sensitive issues now seems oddly out of place, the changes were clearly meant to create a more liberal Canada. Yet, Trudeau insisted that his government would neither make abortion any easier for Canadian women nor authorize and condone homosexuality. He insisted, however, that it was time to separate "sin" from crime—though those sentiments and the language used in the debate that ensued now seem so backward by the standards of our own time (except, perhaps, among social conservatives). While Trudeau and his minister of justice,

1968: Pierre Elliott Trudeau elected prime minister.

John Turner, often referred to abortion and homosexuality as repugnant and immoral acts, they insisted that what consenting adults did in private should not concern others. In the televised leaders' debate during the federal campaign, Trudeau said "We're not going to send policemen into the nation's bedrooms."

The government's plan to modernize and liberalize Canada came in the Omnibus Bill. It contained 120 clauses, covering a range of social issues, from changing abortion laws to make it legal for women to have an abortion under strict conditions, to legalizing lotteries, to placing restrictions on gun ownership. The law passed in May 1969 after an acrimonious debate in Parliament, and it helped brand Trudeau as progressive and liberal, a crusader for a new Canada.

For many women's groups, however, the new legislation offered a mere veneer of progressive change as it masked the conservative nature of much of the legislation. Their primary target was the new abortion law. Many women continued to be outraged because the reforms did nothing to make abortion more accessible. Section 251 of the Omnibus Bill allowed a woman to obtain an abortion in a hospital but only if it was authorized by the medical profession through a Therapeutic Abortion Committee that had ruled that a woman's health was likely at risk through the pregnancy. Some women's groups saw the legislation as the "medicalization" of abortion and as the continued regulation of women and their reproductive rights. The opposition to the legislation was led by Abortion Caravan, a group organized by the Vancouver Women's Caucus—itself, one of the earliest feminist groups in British Columbia. Abortion Caravan attacked the legislation, claiming that abortion had to be considered from the perspective of women and not as a medical or criminal matter. Abortion was a woman's choice and only when the state recognized that fact could women control their own bodies and be assured a fair measure of equality.

In 1969, although Canada changed its laws governing abortion, many women continued to protest that the changes did not give women control of their bodies.

Source: © The McGraw-Hill Companies, Inc./John Flournoy, photographer.

Some 500 members of Abortion Caravan descended on Ottawa in early May 1970, demanding a meeting with the justice minister. When he refused, they marched to 24 Sussex Drive, the official residence of the prime minister, and placed a coffin on his lawn to represent Canadian women who had died seeking illegal and unsafe abortions. The next day, 30 women from the group chained themselves to chairs in the Parliamentary Gallery, closing the House of Commons for the first time in Canadian history because of a protest in the public galleries. Later in May, members of Abortion Caravan surprised Trudeau at his press conference after a three-week tour of Asia, demanding that he broaden his reforms to immediately change the laws to legalize all abortions in Canada. He refused and in characteristic fashion chided the women to get involved in politics as he had and make the changes themselves.[1]

Even if many Canadians lauded the passage of the Omnibus Bill and saw its adoption as representing significant social and political change in Canada, the outrage from women's groups suggested that many women wanted further changes. One outcome of the opposition to some of the government's reforms was to strengthen the burgeoning women's movement, which became known as "second-wave feminism" to distinguish it from the earlier women's movement at the beginning of the twentieth century. Second-wave feminism developed as part of the general radicalization of the 1960s and 1970s, and the protest against the abortion laws brought together such groups as the National Council of Women, the Canadian Committee on the Status of Women, and a large number of provincial and local women's organizations to fight for equality for women.

One of the landmarks for the women's movement in Canada in the 1970s was the report of the Royal Commission on the Status of Women in Canada that had been appointed in 1967. The long-awaited report confirmed what many women knew already: Women occupied an unequal place in Canadian society and suffered inequality and discriminatory policies in almost all aspects of life. They were clearly underrepresented in political institutions, did not have equal access to either educational opportunities or jobs, were paid only a portion of what men earned, and were treated unfairly under the law, particularly when it came to property. The report offered 167 recommendations on such matters as employment, educational opportunities, and family law, but its greatest contribution came from the fact that women's group now had the irrefutable evidence to argue against discrimination and create in the public consciousness an awareness that the treatment of women had to change.

The report led to the establishment of a large number of women's groups, but none more important than the creation of the National Action Committee on the Status of Women (NAC) as an independent lobby group not only to fight for change but also to keep women's issues on the public agenda. The federal government not only provided NAC with much of its funding, but it also created several bodies within the bureaucracy to deal with women's rights, including a ministry for the status of women, an Office of the Co-ordinator of the Status of Women to monitor the federal government's progress in implementing the Royal Commission's recommendations, an Office of Equal Opportunities in the Public Service Commission to monitor women's progress in the bureaucracy, and an Advisory Council on the Status of Women in 1973. It also removed all instances of discrimination from existing federal legislation.

The new women's movement in Canada was not a unified group, even if most of its members shared similar objectives. At the risk of oversimplification, one element in the women's movement was considered liberal or mainstream feminists. They felt that they could bring about real change, including a change in society's values, through the legislative process and by publicizing their cause through social action and the media. On the other hand, some within the movement believed that the major power relationship in Canadian society was one of the domination and oppression of women and change would only come through radical action. These women were known as radical feminists and they focused on the concept of power; they believed that changing society to bring justice and inequality to women would only happen if women seized power from males and Canadian society was radically reformed. Changing child-rearing practices and the educational system, as well as eliminating stereotypes and sexism in all areas, were some of the matters they focused on.

Unlike the first-wave feminism, which was almost exclusively a middle-class movement, the women who participated in second-wave feminism were as diverse as the causes it targeted. Working-class women, women from the labour movement, Aboriginal women, mothers on welfare, immigrant women, and university students, as well professional and business women, were all involved. Many of the issues they confronted were related to the workplace. Such issues as equal pay legislation, paid maternity leaves, and the removal of the "glass ceiling" all became important, as did the eradication of the sexual exploitation of women and the establishment of rape crisis centres.

By the end of the 1970s, second-wave feminism had become one of the largest and most powerful social movements in Canada. Within a year of its establishment, NAC represented more than 42 associations. In 1969, for instance, British Columbia had two established women's groups but five years later it had more than a hundred. There were at least 39 women's centres across Canada by 1979 and these organizations were forcing change. In 1973, after a spouse in Alberta was denied any claim to the family farm that she and her husband had worked for more than two decades, women's groups mobilized to force government to change family laws to recognize greater equality between spouses. In 1978, the *Canadian Human Rights Act* was passed prohibiting discrimination on the basis of sex for federal employees. In 1982, women's groups forced the government to enshrine gender equality in the Charter of Rights and Freedoms. Change and progress were obvious, but the just society for women still lay some considerable distance into the future.

Equality and Language

Trudeau was also quick to tackle Canada's language laws when he became prime minister. When he worked briefly in the federal civil service in the 1950s, he had been shocked that Ottawa functioned solely in the English language. As a French-speaking citizen, he could not write a memorandum in his native language nor find French-language signs to guide him around Parliament Hill. He introduced in the House of Commons an Official Languages Bill on October 17, 1968, that, he insisted, guaranteed fundamental language rights to all Canadian citizens. The legislation established English and French as the official languages in all branches of the federal civil service, including all federal Crown corporations and all federal courts where either minority group constituted at least 10 percent

Official Languages Bill introduced in 1969.

of the population (called bilingual districts). The legislation built on the program of language training that began in the federal public service in 1964; it also fulfilled Lester B. Pearson's promise in 1966 that the Canadian public service would eventually be bilingual. In introducing the bill, Trudeau insisted that the language legislation reflected the diversity of the country and that the changes were not only a political necessity but also a means of enriching Canada. "We want to live in a country," he said, "in which French Canadians can choose to live among English Canadians and English Canadians can choose to live among French Canadians without abandoning their cultural heritage."[2] A language commissioner was appointed to investigate infractions of the act.

The legislation came under heavy criticism, particularly in Western Canada and from the old guard in the Conservative party. During the 1968 election, the Conservatives had retreated from their *deux nations* in favour of the "One Country, One Canada" slogan. Yet, a group within the party, led by former prime minister John Diefenbaker, saw the legislation as pandering to French Canadians and ignoring the nation's heritage and culture, although Diefenbaker had earlier introduced simultaneous language translation in the House of Commons. When the language bill came to Parliament for a second reading, 17 Conservatives—all but one from Western Canada—were ready to vote against it. Robert Stanfield was able to keep most of them in line. The legislation passed into law in July 1969 but without a recorded vote so as not to emphasize the anti-Quebec sentiment in some quarters of the land.

The new language laws were a further indication of the change that the new government wanted for Canada. It was not compulsory bilingualism but it meant, in principle at least, that both French- and English-speaking Canadians should be able to feel at home in all parts of the country. Trudeau believed that Quebec could be kept in Confederation by ensuring that Francophones could participate significantly at the federal level.

Unity and Regional Economic Disparity

The Trudeau government promoted not only language equality for all Canadians but also social and economic equality, having pledged to eliminate regional income disparities across Canada. Trudeau fully understood that social and economic disparity was as great a threat to national unity as was the issue of language. National unity was Trudeau's central preoccupation, and he declared,

> Economic equality … [is] just as important as equality of language rights … If the underdevelopment of the Atlantic provinces is not corrected, not by charity or subsidy, but by helping them become areas of economic growth, then the unity of the country is almost as surely destroyed as it would be by the French-English confrontation.[3]

Although the federal and provincial governments had been involved in the promotion of economic development since Confederation, not all Canadians had benefited equitably from the governments' economic policies. In fact, there was great economic disparity across Canada. In 1949, when Newfoundland joined the federation after resisting union for more than 80 years, its personal income per capita was only 51 percent of the national average but that was only slightly behind that of the other Atlantic provinces, which was dismal compared with that of Ontario at 120 percent of the national average.

Beginning with Diefenbaker in the late 1950s, Ottawa had demonstrated that it was prepared to intervene directly to promote economic growth in the depressed regions of Canada. Despite a combination of federal initiatives to reduce rural poverty through such programs as the *Agricultural Rehabilitation and Development Act* in 1961 and a host of other regional development policies and interregional transfer payments, the gap between the poorest and the wealthiest provinces narrowed only marginally.

Disadvantaged regions were commonly marked with incomes far below the national average (as Figure 10.1 illustrates) and unemployment rates far above the national average, and little had been agreed upon regarding what should be done about economic inequalities. Canadians who lived in economically challenged regions blamed national economic policies that favoured certain areas of the country for their poor economic performance, while those in economically vibrant regions often criticized the federal government for wasting far too much public money on the inefficient and backward regions of the country. By the time Trudeau became prime minister, only Ontario, Alberta, and British Columbia had per capita incomes that exceeded the national average.

The Trudeau government decided shortly after the 1968 election that it would direct its regional development priorities to the areas east of Quebec City, the most economically depressed region of Canada. As he had done with the language issue by putting Gérard Pelletier in charge, Trudeau turned to his other trusted and loyal friend—Jean Marchand, who had come to Ottawa with Trudeau and Pelletier as the "Three Wise Men" in 1965—to be the first minister of the Department of Regional Economic Expansion (DREE). His mandate was to implement the new regional development strategy and to promote economic growth in the depressed regions of Canada. The federal government adopted a model of economic development known as the *growth pole concept*; it maintains that economic growth does not occur everywhere at once but begins in particular centres and then spreads throughout the larger economic zone. The government hoped to encourage industrial centres that would be successful in attracting manufacturing

1971: Only three provinces with per capita incomes above national average.

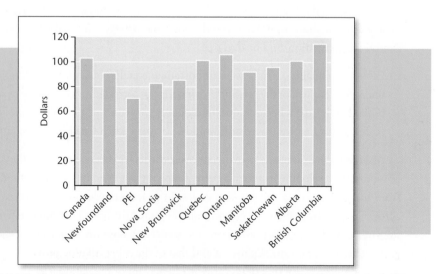

Figure 10.1
Average Weekly Wages and Salaries, 1967

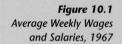

Source: © Statistics Canada, http://www.statcan.ca/english/freepub/11-516-XIE/sectione/E49_59.csv, from Savoie, 108.

and processing industries in the slow-growth regions. By first improving the regional infrastructure in such areas as transportation, water and sewer systems, and educational facilities, the government believed that through generous cash incentives and tax breaks it could encourage new manufacturing industries to set up production in economically challenged regions as a way of fostering industrial growth.

DREE established in 1969.

Marchand soon discovered, however, that all politics in Canada is essentially regional. While the government's strategy was designed to improve the economic situation in the most economically depressed areas of Canada, the wealthier provinces insisted that they, too, had regions with slow economic growth within their borders that would benefit from federal assistance. Ontario, Alberta, and British Columbia—all traditional net contributors to the federal coffers—were subsequently included in the programs to ensure that they, too, received, some of the benefits of the federal monies for economic development. So, too, did some of the major cities.

From 1969 to 1972, nearly 80 percent of DREE's budget was expended in the Atlantic provinces and eastern Quebec, which had been the initial focus of the government's activities in addressing regional disparity. Beginning in 1973, though, the DREE funds were spread more equitably across Canada and to both rural and urban areas to support all types of economic opportunities through General Developments Agreements that had been signed between Ottawa and all the provinces. Twenty-three special areas were subsequently identified throughout the country from Newfoundland's Burin Peninsula to the Renfrew-Pembroke area in Ontario, to the Lesser Slave Lake area of Alberta that would be the targets of the government's growth pole strategy. In those designated areas the federal government provided 50 percent of the cost of most infrastructure projects and provided loans to the provinces for the costs associated with providing water and sewage systems, industrial parks, tourist attractions, educational facilities, and the servicing of industrial lands. Ottawa paid 100 percent of all highway construction in the designated areas and provided grants to firms locating in the designated areas to spur economic development.

The Department of Regional Economic Expansion was not without its political biases and objectives. The Liberal government was particularly anxious to extend funding for regional development to Western Canada, where it had performed poorly in the 1972 election, winning only six of 68 seats. Montreal, which sent a large number of Liberal MPs to Ottawa, lobbied hard from the time DREE was created to have itself included under DREE's mandate. Politicians from Montreal maintained that Quebec's economic strength was dependent on the economic well-being of that city. Montreal was designated as a special case and received economic development assistance. Yet, so as not to create the impression that something special was being done for Quebec, the federal government also added three counties in eastern Ontario to the program. In June 1977, little over a year after the election of the Parti Québécois, DREE allocated a special grant to promote the development of high-tech industries in the Montreal region. Between 1977 and 1978, DREE spent 21 percent of its budget in the Western provinces, 5 percent in Ontario, 31 percent in Quebec, and 39 percent in the Atlantic region. Regional economic development specialist Donald Savoie noted that by 1980, DREE covered "93 per cent of Canada's land mass and over 50 per cent of the population."[4]

The attempt to end regional economic disparity failed to achieve either of the government's objectives. Although Trudeau had initiated his regional development strategy as a way to strengthen national unity, the federal government found itself engaged in bitter quarrels with the provinces even before many of the projects began. The provinces complained that the federal government refused to include them in any meaningful discussion about new economic development strategies undertaken by DREE. Ottawa essentially told the provinces that if they wanted federal funding to deal with economic disparity within their jurisdictions, then they had to accept the new policy as Ottawa had designed it. Most of the provinces did, begrudgingly and with considerable grumbling because the federal government had lots of money to spend. Many provincial politicians and governments were annoyed that federal MPs often used DREE funds to announce new infrastructure projects and job creation programs, and to deliver goodies in their local constituencies.

Despite the steady influx of new monies and countless new announcements across the country, there was no strong evidence that DREE was making any noticeable difference to regional economic disparities across Canada. Several changes had been made in 1973 to foster greater federal–provincial cooperation, including a plan to decentralize DREE operations from Ottawa to each of the ten provincial capitals. In 1982, however, Trudeau disbanded DREE and transferred its policy role and programs to a new Department of Regional Industrial Expansion (DRIE). Trudeau had come to realize that regional economic development could not be achieved by a single department; rather it had to be the responsibility of the whole federal bureaucracy. By that time the government's focus had turned from trying to alleviate regional disparities to preserving the industrial heartland of Canada, particularly that of Ontario where the manufacturing sector was encountering difficult times. Ottawa subsequently signed new Economic and Regional Development Agreements with each of the provinces during its final years in office. This approach served to restore Ottawa's control over regional and economic development and clearly gave Ottawa much more credit for economic development initiatives than had been the case with DREE agreements after 1977. Regional development policies then became an integral part of Trudeau's strategy to strengthen the role of the federal government in Canada.

DREE and DRIE expended more than $7 billion to address regional economic development from 1972 to 1983. Billions more were spent in federal equalization programs. Provincial governments also committed huge financial resources to economic development. While economic disparity was not eliminated in Canada, some progress was made. Incomes per capita narrowed across Canada between the late 1960s and the early 1980s, even if the ranking of those provinces in the have-not category did not change. However, earned income per capita—that is, incomes that do not include government transfer payments, such as unemployment insurance—hardly changed over the period. Regional economic disparity remained as much a factor in Canada at the end of the Trudeau period as it had been at the beginning.

Equality and Social Policy

Just as the Trudeau government hoped to end economic disparity between the various regions in Canada, it had also hoped to create a more equitable social security system for Canadians. Despite the promise of the Pearson era, which saw the introduction of medicare for all

Canadians, improved pensions for the aged with the introduction of a contributory pension plan for workers, and an omnibus Canada Assistance Plan that had Ottawa contributing half of the cost of all social assistance expended by the provinces, many Canadians were shocked when the Economic Council of Canada, a Crown corporation established in 1963 to monitor and study the Canadian economy, reported in its *Fifth Annual Review: The Challenge of Growth and Change* in 1969 that one in five Canadians lived in poverty. Canadians wondered how this could happen when all governments in Canada, combined, spent annually more than $4.4 billion on social welfare. Canada was a prosperous nation: How could so many of its citizens, including many who worked full-time, be poor?

The country was not alone among the nations of the world that rediscovered its poor in the midst of the post-war prosperity; the United States and many European nations did as well. As U.S. President Lyndon Johnson declared war on poverty in the mid-1960s, Trudeau promised his "Just Society" in 1968. Many of the changes in social policy at the federal level were initially motivated by that promise. This was certainly the case with the government's reform of the unemployment insurance (UI) program that had been intro-duced in 1941. The UI program, designed to help people who were temporarily unem-ployed, changed significantly in 1971 when it was broadened to cover virtually all workers in Canada. For the first time, the program added maternity, sickness, and retirement benefits for workers, and increased benefits from 43 percent of earnings to 66.6 percent, to a maximum of $100 per week. With the reforms, some unemployed Canadians could collect benefits for 51 weeks after eight weeks of work.

The notion that Canada was a prosperous nation with a rising standard of living that could afford a social security system that provided a generous array of supports—such as those provided in the revisions to the unemployment insurance program—did not last long. Within 12 months of the changes to UI, the government realized that the cost of the program was more than it could afford. When unemployment rose dramatically in 1972 and the government had to inject $234 million into the UI account and another $800 million a year later, it moved quickly to increase the qualifying period, reduce benefits, and, by 1978, recover through the income tax system some of the benefits that higher-income earners received in unemployment insurance benefits. By the end of the 1970s, the government was motivated more by the needs of fiscal constraint than any notions of a "Just Society."

Family allowances were another important social program that underwent major change. The reforms to the program began as another attempt to achieve Trudeau's Just Society, but by the time the reforms were completed, they were being driven primarily by federal–provincial conflicts and political considerations as regional development programs had been. During the 1968 leadership race, Trudeau had said that the time had come to reconsider the notion of universality in some of Canada's social programs. Universality meant that all citizens received benefits for which they were eligible regardless of their level of income.

Canada's best-known universal social program was family allowances, which paid a monthly allowance to mothers to aid in the raising of their children. By the late 1960s, the federal government was spending about $560 million on the program, or, on average, slightly more than $7.20 monthly for each child under the age of 16 in Canada. Trudeau understood, as did many of the officials in the Department of National Health and

Welfare, which had responsibility for family allowances, that the monthly benefits had to be increased if the program was to help lower-income families move out of poverty. They also knew it would be very expensive to increase family allowance benefits for all children.

The government proposed to eliminate the principle of universality in family allowances, which meant that more affluent families would lose their monthly child benefits. These savings would be then transferred to those families with children considered in greatest need, who would subsequently see a substantial increase in their monthly benefits. When the government announced in 1970 its intention to implement such a strategy to target social spending, public opinion polls found that the majority of Canadians agreed with such an approach. The Liberal government introduced the Family Income Support Program to completely reform the family allowance program, changing it from a universal to a targeted one, and increasing average benefits from about $7 to $20 per month.

Although anti-poverty groups welcomed the proposed reforms, the government's plan failed for three reasons. First, many women's organizations opposed the change because it would have terminated benefits for 1.2 million families, or 39 percent of all recipients. Because the family allowance cheques were paid to mothers, there were loud protests that many middle-class mothers, who did not work outside the home, would lose their only source of income if their family allowance benefits ceased. Second, the Liberals found themselves in a minority government situation after the 1972 election and the New Democratic party, which held the balance of power in Parliament, threatened to withdraw its support if the government changed any of the existing social policy programs. In fact, the government increased social spending to win NDP support. Third, the family allowance program became embroiled in the constitutional quarrel, particularly between Ottawa and Quebec City. When that happened, the issue of who had jurisdiction over family allowances became more important than forging the Just Society.

In 1967, Quebec had demanded that Ottawa transfer control of family allowances and other federal social programs to the provincial governments. After all, it claimed, social policy was a provincial responsibility. Ottawa refused, but when Trudeau launched his initiative to amend the Canadian Constitution, Quebec demanded that Ottawa withdraw from social policy and simply transfer the funds spent on family allowances and other income support programs to the provinces. Because Ottawa refused to meet Quebec's demands, Quebec refused to accept the constitutional reforms that had been worked out at the Victoria Constitutional Conference in 1971.

1971: Victoria Constitutional Conference ends in failure.

Once his constitutional package failed because of an impasse over social policy, the Prime Minister's Office and the Privy Council Office seized control of the file from the Department of National Health and Welfare. Trudeau subsequently named Marc Lalonde, his principal secretary and another of his trusted advisors, the new minister of National Health and Welfare to solve the problem. The government subsequently increased family allowance benefits to $20 per month and allowed the provinces to determine how the benefits were paid in their jurisdiction to allow Quebec a measure of control over the program. Trudeau was determined, however, that the national government retained its right to continue to deliver national programs, and the Government of Canada continued to send family allowance cheques to mothers. Trudeau realized—as had former prime minister Mackenzie King much earlier—that family allowances served as a link between the federal government and individual Canadian citizens in various regions, but especially in Quebec. Ottawa managed to reinforce the nation-building intent of the program even as it made concessions to Quebec, but targeted social spending, which had initially been the primary goal of family allowances reform, would have to wait. In the meantime, the cost of the program continued to increase annually; by 1976 it had reached $1.9 billion.

Throughout the decade, Ottawa and the provinces flirted with introducing a guaranteed income program. Such an initiative would have provided full income support for those not in the workforce and have supplemented the incomes of those who worked but did not earn enough to maintain an adequate standard of living. The costs of the program proved too much for both levels of government and the idea was dropped by the mid-1970s. What governments did discover, however, was that they could use the tax system to deliver social benefits. Ending universal coverage—as the government had attempted earlier—was politically dangerous, but reforming social programs through the income tax system came with much less risk.

Some commentators have called the changes to social policy through the tax system "reform by stealth" because it allowed the federal government to achieve its objectives without incurring the wrath of too many voters. In 1978, the federal government introduced major changes to children's benefits (family allowances) through the tax system when it introduced a Refundable Child Tax Credit Program to funnel more money to lower-income families. It came with virtually no discussion with the provinces and during a serious economic crisis; it also marked a major change in Canadian social policy when it attached income-tested supplements to universal family allowances. Average family allowances benefits were reduced to $20 from $25.68. The money saved was transferred by means of a tax credit to low- and moderate-income families. Families with incomes less than $18 000 received a tax credit of $200 per child under the age of 18; the amount of the tax credit was reduced as incomes rose to $26 000, when it disappeared completely. This was a revolutionary change, and it would be used frequently throughout the 1990s to radically transform Canada's social security system.

Equality and Aboriginal Peoples

If there was a single group in Canada that stood to benefit from Trudeau's promise of a Just Society it was Canada's Aboriginal peoples. The Pearson government had commissioned a study led by Dr. Harry Hawthorn to investigate the situation of Aboriginal peoples with the hope of then preparing a plan to deal with the difficulties that they faced. The *Hawthorn Report* presented a depressing portrait of Aboriginal communities in Canada where earnings per capita, health and education outcomes, mortality rates, and a host of socioeconomic measurements were far below the Canadian average. Hawthorn acknowledged that despite the deplorable state of Canada's Aboriginal peoples, further assimilationist policies were inappropriate and a new policy approach was required. He told the government that it had to accept the fact that there would be a distinct Aboriginal presence in Canada and recommended that the federal government treat Aboriginal peoples as "citizens plus" because of their Aboriginal title and treaty rights.

The Trudeau government began a series of consultations with Aboriginal organizations across Canada as it developed its Aboriginal policy, but in 1969 when it released its *Statement of the Government of Canada on Indian Policy*, better known as the White Paper, it was clear that the government had ignored much of what the Aboriginal communities had told it. The National Indian Council (NIC) had made it clear to Ottawa that Aboriginal peoples wanted to retain their identity as Indians as they improved their position in Canadian society. They also asked for an Indian claims commission to settle the increasing number of land claims that were being launched by groups across Canada, following a similar process that had already begun in the United States. A land claim is a formal request from an Aboriginal community stating that it is legally entitled to land or financial compensation as part of the unfinished treaty-making process, or that the federal government did not fulfill its fiduciary responsibility to look after the interests of Aboriginal peoples who had signed treaties with the Crown.

Aboriginal peoples were terribly disappointed when Indian Affairs Minister Jean Chrétien announced the government's preliminary statement on Aboriginal policy; they saw little of their demands in it. Following on the civil rights movement in the United States and Australia, Trudeau's Aboriginal policy called for the integration of minority and racial groups into mainstream society. Chrétien angered the Aboriginal communities when he said that the disadvantaged position of Aboriginal peoples was attributable not to government policy or racial prejudice but to the fact that they had special status in Canada. Their legal status as "Indians" under the Canadian constitution and the policies that resulted from it, he maintained, had kept them separate and behind other citizens.

Although Trudeau called for fairer treatment of disadvantaged groups and regions across Canada and promised to consult with Aboriginal groups, his strong commitment to liberal values and individualism meant that he was unsympathetic to any special treatment that had been recommended in the *Hawthorn Report*. He found the notion of treaty rights between two groups within the same society clearly at odds with his notions of common citizenship. Moreover, he insisted that no group in Canada required special status. Trudeau resisted all attempts throughout his time in office to redress past injustices. His goal was justice for all citizens in our own time and he believed that as a nation we should not try and undo what had happened in the past.

The White Paper proposed that the special relationship between Aboriginal peoples and the Government of Canada be severed, and all Aboriginal peoples be fully integrated into Canadian life. These legal difference between Aboriginal and non-Aboriginal peoples would be replaced by what the government considered equality, meaning the abolition of Indian status (which entitled Aboriginal peoples to a wide range of programs and services offered by the federal government), the transfer of control of reserve lands to First Nations peoples, and the integration of services for Aboriginal and Métis people into the various federal and provincial departments of government. Aboriginal peoples would then interact with their governments as individuals and not as members of a special group with legal and constitutional rights.

That this was a White Paper (a term given to the government's preliminary position on a particular policy) was not lost on Aboriginal communities. Although there was support among some Aboriginal groups for the government's proposals, most dismissed

Aboriginal peoples reject government's 1969 White Paper.

the White Paper as the ultimate triumph of the government's policy of assimilation to eliminate Canada's Aboriginal peoples. The National Indian Brotherhood (NIB) led the charge; it had been formed after the NIC split into the NIB and the Canadian Métis Society. Historian J.R. Miller has argued that the government's Aboriginal policy "was a response to values within the policymaking arena, not to the basic problems facing Indians."[5] The central agencies in the federal government, such as the Prime Minister's Office, controlled by the prime minister and his political staff, were most concerned with pursuing policies that conformed to Trudeau's philosophy of individualism and equality and the belief that no ethnic and racial group had any special claim in Canada. Not surprisingly, the government dropped the White Paper in the midst of determined Aboriginal opposition. One outcome of the federal debacle, however, was the further politicalization of Aboriginal organizations that felt that they had to defend themselves, their collective identities, and their existence as distinct peoples from the government. Almost immediately, First Nations, Inuit, and Métis people became part of an international network to protect the human rights of Indigenous peoples, and they turned to the courts to build a legal case for their continuity as distinct peoples and separate nations within Canada. The federal government subsequently assisted the Aboriginal organizations by dramatically increasing funding to the NIB and more than 20 other similar organizations across Canada.

Although the socioeconomic condition of Aboriginal peoples improved only slightly during the Trudeau period, they made huge strides in asserting their historical claims, especially through the courts. In 1973, the Supreme Court of Canada ruled against the land claim of the Nisga'a of British Columbia, but for the first time the Court recognized in the *Calder Case* that Aboriginal title existed in Canadian law, prompting Trudeau to quip to a group of First Nations leaders, "Perhaps you had more legal rights than we thought you had when we did the white paper."[6] Ottawa then agreed to deal with Aboriginal claims against lands not under treaty and established the Office of Native Claims. When Quebec began a vast hydroelectric development of the James Bay watershed without addressing the territorial claims of the Cree and Innu who lived there, those groups secured a court injunction to stop the development. In 1975, a deal was worked out in James Bay that gave the Aboriginal groups $150 million in grants and royalties over ten years and control over lands that were not flooded in exchange for surrendering 1 million square kilometres to allow the hydroelectric project to proceed. These were important milestones and, as we will see when we turn to the constitutional renewal, Aboriginal organizations demanded that they, too, participate in that process.

Foreign Policy: Seeking New Directions

If much of Canadian domestic policy during the Trudeau era was to bring a greater measure of equality to Canadians, foreign policy might be characterized as an attempt to bring greater independence for Canada within the community of nations. Trudeau wrote in his *Memoirs* that he was "neither fascinated by the study of foreign policy nor especially attracted by the practice of it," but he knew he did not like how Canada practised foreign policy in the past. He was critical of the style and content of Canadian foreign policy, and he promised a thorough review of both.

Signing ceremony of the James Bay and Northern Quebec Agreement. Included in the photo (right) are Chief Billy Diamond of the Cree Indians, Jean Chrétien, federal treasury board president (second from right), and Robert Bourassa, premier of Quebec (fourth from right).

In his first major foreign policy speech in May 1968, he gave some indication that things needed to change. He promised the diplomatic recognition of the People's Republic of China, a review of Canada's commitment to NATO, and a reassessment of Canada's assistance to Third World countries. After two years of study and consultation, the government outlined its major objectives in a widely discussed document, *Foreign Policy for Canadians.* Economic growth and national unity would replace international security concerns as the major priority. Foreign policy had to be proactive rather than reactive and be based on universal principles. Above all, foreign policy had to be an extension of the domestic policy. The review identified six themes against which foreign policy decisions would be made: sovereignty and independence, peace and security, economic growth, social justice, quality of life, and a harmonious natural environment.

It also promised to promote Canada's Francophone traditions in foreign policy, especially as Canada strove to create better relations with other Francophone states around the world. The review also made it clear that Trudeau and his advisors would control foreign policy; the professional bureaucrats who had played such a strong role in foreign policy since the Second World War would take their direction from the prime minister. Trudeau appointed Ivan Head, his former constitutional advisor, as his principal foreign policy advisor. Throughout the 1970s, Trudeau seemed to personalize Canadian foreign policy as he did with much of Canadian public policy during the period.

Trudeau wanted to reorient Canadian diplomacy away from what he considered Canada's preoccupation with the United States and Europe as a way to exert Canadian independence. He thought this would be achieved through *reapproachement* with the Soviet Union and other communist countries. With his provocative words about the strength of communist Cuba and the need for the West to better understand communist governments around the world, he also took jabs at the Americans. Canada, he believed, was in a unique position to bring these countries into the mainstream of world politics.

One of his first moves in this direction was the recognition of the People's Republic of China with the establishment of official diplomatic relations in 1970. Not only was it an act of independence from American foreign policy, but it was also recognition of the importance of China (with a population of nearly a billion people) as a major and growing market. Good relations with China led to a new era of Sino-Canadian trade. In 1973, Canada and China signed the Canadian-Chinese Trade Agreement, which meant that each country would provide to one another the tariff rate it applied to its most favourable trading partners. That same year, Canada organized a trade fair in Beijing that attracted about 600 Canadian officials and business leaders; Chinese Premier Zhou Enlai even attended. The two countries established a Joint Economic and Trade Committee that sought ways to solve any economic and trade-related concerns between the two nations. By 1973, Canadian exports to China doubled, as had imports from China. With the establishment of "most-favoured nation" status, two-way trade grew further still. By the early 1980s, China had become an important market for Canadian sulphur, wood pulp, newsprint, and metals, such as aluminum and copper, as well as wheat. The Americans were not bothered by what Trudeau was doing, as they themselves had been courting better relations with China since 1969.[7]

1970: Canada recognizes the People's Republic of China.

Canadian attitudes towards NATO were also changing. Even under Pearson, who had helped negotiate the NATO treaty, the government wondered about Canada's future role in an alliance that was increasingly dominated by the United States and one in which European nations seemed unwilling to spend more for their own defence. By the time Trudeau became prime minister, the dangers of communist aggression in Europe seemed much less important than dealing with an array of issues, such as social and economic disparity and national unity, at home and protecting Canada and its culture from American influence. The U.S. war in Vietnam made Canadians more wary of their southern neighbour, but the Soviet-led invasion of Czechoslovakia in 1968 (after it flirted with Western-style democratic reform) suggested to many that the threat from Soviet communism remained real.

Following nearly a decade of détente, or relaxed tensions with Moscow and other Warsaw Pact countries—and without any consultation with its allies—Canada halved its commitments to defending Europe under NATO. Trudeau considered pulling Canada out of NATO, but his Cabinet refused to go along with such a plan. Canada encouraged a reduction in nuclear and conventional arms and reoriented its defence priorities towards protecting Canadian sovereignty. Its allies in NATO complained regularly throughout the 1970s, however, that Canada was not pulling its weight in the alliance.[8]

The Soviet Union was particularly impressed with both Trudeau's rhetoric and his actions as they saw him (as did many Canadians) as simply asserting Canadian independence from the United States. The Soviets invited him to Moscow for a state visit in 1971, the first of any Canadian prime minister to do so. While there, Trudeau emphasized the shared northern experiences of both countries and mused about the dangers of American influence in the cultural, economic, and military life of Canada. Relations went so well during the visit that Trudeau invited Soviet Premier Alexei Kosygin to visit Canada.

Canada–Soviet Union Hockey Summit

It was during these meetings that the two leaders began to discuss the possibility of a hockey competition between the best players in both countries. After all, sport has frequently been used to ease tensions and strengthen bilateral relations between countries; it had been used in 1971 as a way to improve relations between the United States and China when the American National Table Tennis Team travelled to China for a series of games that has become known as "Ping Pong Diplomacy."

In Canada, hockey had long established itself as the national winter pastime, but Canadians had become embarrassed over their poor play in international competition since the early 1950s, when the Soviet Union established itself as the dominant nation in the sport. Even though Canada had won the gold medal in each Olympic Games from 1924 to 1952—except for 1936 when a group of Canadians playing for Great Britain captured gold—and had won the World Championship 19 times between 1920 and 1961, Canada achieved little success in international hockey after that. For Trudeau, hockey, foreign policy, and domestic politics became intertwined. While a hockey tournament might strengthen Canada's relationship with the Soviet Union, it also offered the potential for something greater to Trudeau: If the Canadians emerged victorious, as everyone thought they should, it would also strengthen national unity in Canada.

1972: Canada–Russia Summit Series.

On April 18, 1972, the Canadian government signed a Letter of Agreement on the Canadian–USSR Exchange, providing for an eight-game summit that would allow Canada's professional hockey players with signed contracts with the National Hockey League to represent their country in international competition for the first time. The Soviets had insisted that the negotiations and protocol for the event be handled by each country's foreign affairs office. The Department of External Affairs in Canada established an International Sports Relations desk to handle preparations for the series that began in September 1972. The prime minister and his political staff also played a key role in what was officially considered a cultural exchange between the two countries. Canadian hockey fans were jubilant.

Of course, the Canada–Russia hockey series was no mere cultural event. Both for Leonid Brezhnev, the general secretary of the Soviet Communist party and effectively the political leader of the Soviet Union, and for Trudeau the hockey games were about much more. They both believed that sports played an important role in the development of their nations. For Brezhnev, who took a keen interest in hockey, the series was an opportunity to prove that Russian athletes were the best in the world and to show the West that the communist way of life was working incredibly well. For Trudeau, who often attended major sporting events in Canada and was himself quite athletic, the series would build unity and cohesion at home. For many Canadians, however, the game was a contest between an evil communist empire and a virtuous capitalist liberal democracy.

The Canada–Soviet series became one on the most memorable events in Canadian history and a defining moment for Canadians who watched the games on television. The Soviets surprised the Canadians with their superb and skilful playmaking and their excellent conditioning. They won three of the four games in Canada, prompting Canadian fans in Vancouver—the games were played in four different Canadian cities, itself an act of nation-building—to boo their team for its poor performance. The series moved to Moscow for the final four games.

The games were a virtual war on ice. Bobby Clarke, reportedly with the encouragement of John Ferguson, Team Canada's assistant coach, used his hockey stick like an axe and cracked the ankle of Valeri Kharlamov, the Soviet's star player who missed game seven and was largely ineffective in the final match. Soviet team captain Boris Mikhailov later repeatedly kicked Canadian defenceman Gary Bergman's back leg with his skate; Bergman was cut but not seriously injured in the incident. Both sides cleared their benches after Bergman rammed Mikhailov's head into the chicken wire that was used in the Luzhniki Ice Palace instead of Plexiglas. In the eighth and final game, some of the Canadian players climbed over the boards into the stands to rescue Allan Eagleson, the executive director of the NHL Players' Association and a member of Hockey Canada, who was being ushered out of the arena by police for trying to make his way to the public address announcer after he thought a Canadian goal was disallowed.

The Canadians won the series in dramatic fashion: Paul Henderson scored at 19:26 of the third period after Yvon Cournoyer intercepted a Soviet clearing pass. As Canadians celebrated the victory of their team in Moscow, it was clear that sport had become an aspect of Canada's international relations, a symbol of national unity, and a means for the government to promote its own interest.

Canadian–American Relations: Striving for Cultural and Economic Sovereignty

The Canada–Russia hockey series was only one example of how nationalist sentiment influenced Canadian foreign policy during the Trudeau era. Canadians had historically been wary of the United States but, during the 1960s and early 1970s, with the war in Vietnam and the belief among many Canadians that the American empire had lost its way, that wariness turned to suspicion and hostility. When U.S. President Richard Nixon launched a massive bombing assault purportedly to force North Vietnam to engage in peace talks, Trudeau's minority government, which depended on support from the left-leaning NDP, introduced a motion in the House of Commons condemning American actions.

The United States was furious, and Nixon said that the special relationship with Canada was dead. This was reflected in Nixon's New Economic Program, also launched in 1971, aimed at improving the American economy. It did not recognize a "special relationship" with Canada and considered its northern neighbour as just another trading nation, no different from Western Europeans and the Japanese. Canada considered its options: First, it could attempt to restore its relationship with the United States, or, second, it could try to integrate more closely with the United States. Because there was little appetite for either of these, the government announced that it would pursue what it termed the "Third Option," which was to reorient Canadian trade to Europe and Asia and away from a reliance on the United States. Canada subsequently developed closer ties with both Japan and the European Community, but neither of them proved successful in changing the long-standing trading relations with the United States. It did not help that within government, the Department of Trade and Commerce (the department responsible for international trade) and many in the Canadian business community did not share the government's desire to abandon the American market in favour of others.

These nationalist sentiments were reflected not only in Canada's foreign policy but also in its economic and cultural policies. Under Trudeau, the government ushered in an era of economic nationalism. It introduced the Canada Development Agency in 1971 to foster greater Canadian ownership of businesses by investing heavily in companies operating in Canada. The Foreign Investment Review Agency (FIRA) was created in 1974 to control foreign investment by reviewing all acquisitions of Canadian firms to determine that such transactions were in the national interest. The creation of FIRA resulted in long delays, and angered American entrepreneurs—the real target of the policy—and the Canadian business class alike, but during the period, FIRA turned down very few acquisitions of Canadian firms.

Canada attempted to assert its independence in the energy sector following the Arab–Israeli War in 1973, when the Organization of the Petroleum Exporting Countries (OPEC) imposed an embargo (prohibition) on the shipment of oil to Israel's allies. Because the United States was dependent on foreign supplies of oil and was Israel's strongest ally, it was particularly hard hit and saw Canada as a relatively secure source of oil. However, when Canada adopted an increasingly nationalistic energy policy as it struggled to deal with a rapid increase in world oil prices and its own self-sufficiency, it further angered the Americans. Canada even considered an embargo on oil exports, but settled for a tax increase on exports despite the Americans'—and Alberta's—objections. In response to much of what was going on, Canada created Petro-Canada as a Crown corporation in 1975 to garner a greater share of the oil and gas sector that was largely in American and foreign hands; the National Energy Program was introduced in 1980 to further Canadianize that industry.

Cultural Policy

A similar trend was evident in cultural policy. Since Confederation, Canada had been sensitive about its culture, but many of the disputes with the United States over culture stemmed from a different interpretation of what constituted culture. What Canada saw as culture—television, movies, books, and magazines, for instance—the United States viewed as simply another economic or trade issue and maintained it should not be treated any differently than the movement of potash, for example, when it crossed the Canada–U.S. border. With American cultural exports dominating popular culture in Canada, the government—and Canadians, too—wanted to reverse the trend towards the Americanization of Canada's culture. Through the Canadian Radio-television and Telecommunications Commission (CRTC) established in 1968, the government forced radio stations to include at least 30 percent Canadian content on commercial radio and increase the level of Canadian programming on television to 60 percent. To allow Canadian films and books to compete with American ones, the government increased funding to the Canadian Film Development Corporation and provided subsidies to book publishers. In 1975, the federal government introduced measures to disallow Canadian businesses from claiming advertising costs as a business expense for tax purposes in so-called split-run publications (and on U.S. border television stations) unless those magazines adopted a policy of 75 percent Canadian content. Split-run editions were essentially American magazines reprinted in Canada for the Canadian market with little or no Canadian content. The new measures were aimed primarily at the Canadian editions of *Time* and *Reader's Digest*. *Reader's*

Digest chose to Canadianize, but *Time* did not. *Maclean's*, founded in 1905, emerged as the major news and current affairs magazine in English-speaking Canada in the wake of *Time's* departure from Canada.

One of the greatest ironies of the decade is that Canadians came to realize, just as the Americans had, that cultural industries were an increasingly important economic sector, even if culture was also an expression of a national spirit. As Jonathan Vance points out in his recent history of Canadian culture, culture "employ[ed] thousands of Canadians and generat[ed] billions of dollars in economic activity" during the 1970s. Vance also notes that the decision of governments, both federal and provincial, to promote culture came to "resemble other parts of government: it was over-bureaucratized, filled with agencies whose mandates overlapped or conflicted, consumed excessive amounts of money in administration, dogged by inefficiency, and moved ponderously slowly."[9] Although Saskatchewan had appointed the first provincial arts board in 1948, most of the provinces, including Saskatchewan, did not have ministries or departments of culture until the 1970s, when they all realized that art and culture were industries or commodities that had to be monitored, assisted, and protected.

Despite the fear of the loss of Canadian culture throughout the 1970s, the decade saw a blossoming of Canada's artistic talents. Television programs such as *The Kids of Degrassi Street* and *Second City TV* became successful both in Canada and abroad. The music industry established the Juno Awards in 1970 in honour of Pierre Juneau, the chair of the CRTC when Canadian content regulations were imposed on commercial radio. Anne Murray joined a host of other Canadians to win music fame abroad, and Margaret Atwood, Mordecai Richler, and other writers won international acclaim for their literature. During the debate about preserving and enhancing Canadian culture, CBC television decided that not all culture was important. In 1969, it cancelled the immensely popular weekly Maritime variety show *Don Messier's Jubilee*, which had broadcast nationally a blend of Maritime folk music, jigs and reels, and fiddle music since 1959. For several seasons its rating surpassed that of *Hockey Night in Canada* and it regularly drew larger audiences in Canada than the American import, *The Ed Sullivan Show*. Its cancellation sparked a rally on Parliament Hill. Diefenbaker and other MPs raised the matter in the House of Commons and hundreds of loyal fans complained to newspapers across Canada of CBC's decision to cut the low-budget and inexpensive program. A petition more than nine metres long was presented to the CBC to try and save the show. The CBC, it seemed, was interested in a Canadian culture that appealed to a new, modern, and sophisticated Canada, not the "square"—to use the word of the period, meaning not hip or not cool—image that Don Messier and his toe-tapping music portrayed.

One of the greatest cultural developments in Canada during the Trudeau era was the prime minister's decision to construct new buildings for the national museum and the national art gallery. Both projects came without considerable planning and were part of the government's Special Recovery Capital Works Program, an initiative that was launched in the midst of the economic recession in 1982 to "fast-track" construction projects. The museum, then called the Museum of Man, had to be renamed because of its gender-bias and became the Canadian Museum of Civilization. Like most of the projects that were fast-tracked, the government underestimated the costs of the project: the Museum was originally estimated at $80 million but ended up costing $320 million by the time it opened in 1986. The Museum, designed by Aboriginal architect Douglas Cardinal, is one of the most strikingly beautiful buildings in Canada and regularly attracts nearly 2 million visitors a year. Construction also began in 1982 on a new building for the National Gallery of Canada.

United States: Friend or Foe?

Although Trudeau expressed a deep-seated animosity for any form of nationalism, his policies of economic and cultural nationalism appealed not only to a nationalist sentiment in Canada but also to the sense of anti-Americanism that runs deep in Canadian society. Despite the array of policies aimed at protecting Canada's cultural and economic sovereignty, Canada could not ignore the simple fact that it was a North American state and cooperation was not only inevitable with the United States but also necessary. The 1965 Auto Pact, which provided for an integrated North American automotive free trade zone, was one indication of how economic cooperation might benefit the Canadian economy and, during the tensions of the long Cold War, Canadians realized that their country was at risk if the conflict between the Soviets and American escalated to actual war. Even though Canadians liked to argue that they were not American, the two peoples shared more similarities than differences.

In spite of his bravado and rhetoric during his early years as prime minister, Trudeau came to understand that the United States and Canada were not only military and economic partners, but they were also friends (even if that description has become a cliché), especially after the Cold War heated up with the Soviet invasion of Afghanistan and the American military build-up after Ronald Reagan became president in 1981. In 1983, Trudeau allowed the Americans to test their cruise missiles in Canada. These were essentially guided missiles propelled by a jet engine that flew close to the ground to avoid detection by radar; the Canadian government justified its controversial decision on political and technical terms. The testing demonstrated Canada's commitment to the modernization of NATO as a nuclear deterrent and by testing the missiles in Canada where the terrain was similar to that of the Soviet Union, it allowed the North American Aerospace Defense Command (NORAD) (formerly the North American Air Defense Command until it changed its name in 1981 to reflect its expanded mission to include the monitoring of human-made objects in space, and the detection, validation, and warning of possible attack against North America by aircraft, missiles, or space vehicles) to develop the technology to destroy Soviet cruise missiles heading to North America. And in a complete reversal of Trudeau's early foreign policy, the Canadian government began talks with the Americans in 1983 on the subject of free trade.

It is no wonder that historians J.L. Granatstein and Robert Bothwell titled their book on Trudeau's foreign policy *Pirouette*. They argue that Canadian foreign policy seemed to have come full circle between 1968 and 1984—hence, a foreign policy pirouette. When Trudeau assumed office, he had rejected the Pearsonian mantra that Canada could be a helpful fixer or an "international boy scout" on the world's stage as Canada was sometimes derisively known. Yet, in one of his final acts as prime minister, he embraced Pearson's

Source: CP Images.

Peace activists protest the testing of American Cruise missiles in Canada, 1983.

approach and attempted to play the role of global "helpful fixer" when he undertook a tour of foreign capitals to promote world peace and lessen the growing tensions, especially between the United States and the Soviet Union. As an elder statesman, Trudeau received praise for his peace initiative, but none of the major leaders took him seriously, an indication, perhaps, of how little influence Canada had in international affairs at the end of his years in the prime minister's office. Similarly, Trudeau had earlier dismissed the Commonwealth, but by the 1980s he was one of its strongest proponents and saw it as an important forum to deal with many of the problems in the Third, or Developing, World. His desire to reduce the role of the Department of External Affairs in Canada's foreign policy and centralize power in the Prime Minister's Office seems strange when External Affairs was responsible for many of the major foreign policy accomplishments during his tenure. Most notable was Canada's leadership and success at the United Nations' Third Conference on the Law of the Sea, which met regularly from 1973 to 1982 and negotiated the United Nations Convention on the Law of the Sea (UNCLOS). This agreement provides a virtual constitution for the world's oceans and sets out rules for issues ranging from fisheries, navigation, and mineral resources on the seabed, to marine pollution and scientific research. The Convention effectively recognized Canada's control of its territorial seas to 320 kilometres from the low-tide mark, although it would be 2003 before Canada actually ratified the Convention.

1982: Canada participates in the UN Convention on the Law of the Sea that provides rules governing the world's oceans.

Fiscal Federalism, Public Finances, and Labour

As one way to achieve national unity, the Trudeau government had promised in its 1968 *White Paper on Federalism and International Relations* that it would invite provincial participation in international negotiations when the specific interests of the provinces were affected. During the negotiations leading to the United Nations Convention on the Law of the Sea, for instance, the federal government went to great measures to involve the provinces. Eight provinces sent representatives to the UN-sponsored conferences. Political scientist

Elizabeth Riddell-Dixon has concluded that "the activities of the federal and provincial government in this case were complementary and mutually reinforcing."[10] It was also unusual as the Trudeau era was often marked by tension and unfriendly relations between the federal and provincial governments. When Trudeau resigned as prime minister in 1984, there was little unity across the land and there was not a single provincial government in Canada that was of the same political persuasion as the Liberal government in Ottawa.

Trudeau came to the office of prime minister believing that there should be no special status for anyone. That was evident in the White Paper on Indian policy, but it would also prove true in his dealings with the provinces. Although Trudeau had been Prime Minister Pearson's constitutional advisor in the mid-1960s and later the minister of justice in Pearson's government, he clearly did not share Pearson's commitment to what has been called *cooperative federalism*—the phrase often used to describe Ottawa's attempt to accommodate the provinces, especially Quebec, during Pearson's tenure. This approach has also been referred to as *asymmetrical federalism*, which allows the federal government to work out separate arrangements with the different provinces on a variety of policy matters, meaning that, in essence, one province might have certain powers that the other provinces do not have. To Pearson, allowing Quebec a parallel pension plan with the Canada Pension Plan, for instance, did not matter if all Canadians participated in a similar plan regardless of place of residence. Not so with Trudeau, as he considered the principle of the provinces "opting out" of national shared-cost initiatives with full composition, as Quebec had with health grants, vocational education, old age assistance, and other social programs, a *de facto* special status. He saw it as an erosion of both federal visibility in the provinces and a threat to the nation-state that had to be reversed; otherwise, Trudeau and many others believed, the Canadian state would cease to have a government that could legislate for the nation as a whole.

Trudeau knew that the federal spending power had always been a source of contention with several of the provinces, notably Quebec and Ontario. Since the end of the Second World War, the federal government had the financial resources to create national priorities and programs in areas that some provinces insisted the Constitution had given the provinces the authority to legislate and regulate. For a while, the federal government provided funds to universities, even though education was a provincial responsibility. Later, Ottawa transferred money to the provinces for all sorts of post-secondary education when the federal government decided that the country needed to invest in job training and skills' development, even though the provinces grumbled that education was within their jurisdiction.

The federal government did not simply give money to the provinces; rather, it used its financial resources to encourage—and sometimes coerce—the provinces to embrace federal policy initiatives, as noted earlier with regional development strategies. The provinces usually tolerated Ottawa's intrusion into areas of provincial jurisdiction because they had responsibility for areas that had become incredibly costly, such as education and healthcare. Despite having their own powers of taxation to generate revenue, there was usually a discrepancy between the province's ability to generate revenue and its expenditure responsibilities.

The system of transfer payments or grants from the federal government to the provincial and territorial governments has usually been called *fiscal federalism*. An important instrument in these intergovernmental fiscal relations has been *conditional* and *block grants* going from Ottawa to each of the provinces and territories. These grants have been called conditional because when the federal government transferred money to the provinces it placed significant conditions on how the money was to be spent. This had been true of the federal health grants and universities grants. While the provinces generally needed the money from Ottawa, they came to resist Ottawa's setting of priorities within areas of provincial jurisdiction. As a way to improve federal–provincial relations, the federal government proposed in 1969 to introduce new national programs only if they enjoyed the support of provincial legislatures in at least three of the four regions of Canada. Ottawa promised it would provide financial compensation on a per capita basis to those provinces that chose not to participate in any of the federal programs if they introduced similar programs.

For much of the post-war period, governments had been looked upon to provide economic leadership, and through their Keynesian policies of spending and taxation they attempted to even out the economic ups-and-downs of the business cycle. During the period of prosperity and economic growth, governments continued to improve health, education, income support, and other social benefits for all citizens. By the early 1970s, however, the growth and prosperity that Canada had enjoyed for much of the period since 1945 started to disappear. As the economic growth slowed and government had less money to spend, inflation and unemployment rates rose sharply and the federal deficit ballooned from $1 billion in 1971 to $33 billion in 1984. This not only forced a rethinking of the relationship between the provinces and the federal government but also ushered in a new attitude about economic management and the role of governments.

The economic crisis in the early 1970s was triggered largely by a huge increase in commodity prices around the world, particularly in crude oil after many of the oil-producing countries in the Middle East placed an embargo on oil shipments when the Arab–Israeli War (also known as the Yom Kippur War) broke out in 1973. The Organization of the Petroleum Exporting Countries (OPEC), a cartel of oil-producing nations, refused to sell oil to countries that had supported Israel in the Yom Kippur War in October of that year. Inflation rose to more than 10 percent in 1974 and 1975 and remained high for much of the following decade. Unemployment rose from less than 5 percent in 1973 to 11 percent in 1982.

To deal with rampant inflation, the government introduced a comprehensive system of wage and price controls and appointed the Anti-Inflation Board (AIB) to monitor the situation. The AIB was given the authority to review wage settlements in large companies and reverse increases if it considered them excessive. Similarly, it monitored price increases and profit margins of large companies and had the authority to reverse any increases. These tactics were not particularly effective in helping the economic situation; they not only caused a rift between the federal and provincial governments but also served to mobilize the labour movement.

Labour saw the program as an attempt by both the state and big business to not only limit wage increases for workers but also impose limits on unions to negotiate wages. The labour movement considered wage and price controls as an intrusion into the fundamental right of collective bargaining. On October 15, 1976, the Canadian Labour Congress (CLC) led a day of protest against wage and price control and the Trudeau government. By then, unions had become increasingly militant in protecting the wage gains they had made in the 1960s and early 1970s as both federal and provincial governments sought to limit wage increases. One of the most militant unions was the Canadian Union of Postal Employees, led by Jean-Claude Parrot, who was jailed for refusing to lead his members back to work following back-to-work legislation in 1975. Even as the government removed wage and price controls in 1978, labour realized it had to change its tactics and came to believe it had to become more involved in political and social action. It also embraced new issues, such as the pay and benefit inequities faced by women in the workplace as the female participation rate in the paid labour force reached 50 percent. The times were trying for labour, however, as governments and businesses alike attempted to keep wage rates to a modest increase. In 1982, the federal government imposed wage increases of 6 and 5 percent for two years—a policy later adopted by most provincial governments. Although such policies further angered workers, the situation would get much worse for labour as the economy contracted further in the coming years.

Because of the economic woes, governments faced a significant revenue shortfall as government expenditures began to outstrip revenues beginning in 1974. In its 1975 budget, the federal government made it clear that it had to limit its transfers to the provinces. In Canada, no major social policies were introduced after the 1960s and governments became concerned about how to pay for existing programs. Ottawa was particularly concerned about those cost-shared programs that had been instituted in healthcare, social assistance, and post-secondary education, for instance, where it had promised to reimburse the provinces for 50 percent of their spending. Ottawa realized that this financial arrangement with the provinces left it vulnerable, as it was required to pay for half the costs of many provincial programs.

The federal government wanted greater certainty with the amounts of cash it had to provide to the provinces, and in 1977, it negotiated with them the *Established Programs Financing Act* (EPF). Under this arrangement, Ottawa escaped some of its cost-sharing with the provinces by replacing it with block funding that set limits to the federal contribution. The federal government allowed the provinces greater flexibility in setting their spending priorities and Ottawa provided a cash and tax transfer (a reduced tax rate to allow provinces to raise their tax rates by an equivalent amount) in what amounted to unconditional grants. The advantage for Ottawa during a period of rising deficits was that federal spending became more predictable in those areas as the rate of increase was limited by the growth in per capita gross national product (GNP). It became clear that the move to straight federal transfers and a decline in the number of conditional grants meant that the Canadian federation was becoming even more decentralized, as each province could set its own priorities. One commentator described Canada as the most decentralized federation in the world.

Ottawa and the Provinces: Building a Stronger Nation?

To Trudeau, the movement towards decentralization was disturbing, and his government attempted to create a more centralist and stronger federal government. Not surprisingly, this new orientation heightened tensions between the provinces and the federal government as most of the provinces were in no mood to relinquish any of their constitutional powers to Ottawa. This period of "conflictual federalism" was played out in the West, where Alberta was gaining extraordinary economic wealth with its huge oil reserves, and in Quebec, where the separatist Parti Québécois was elected in 1976 with its goals of sovereignty association with Canada.

Western Canada's discontent with Confederation had a long history. It began shortly after John A. Macdonald introduced the National Policy in 1879, which created a tariff that favoured the manufacturing industries in Quebec and Ontario. The West came to believe that its resources were feeding the wealth of Central Canada and believed its interests were not reflected in the country's political institutions, such as the House of Commons and the Senate. This discontent among the Western provinces has been called "Western Alienation." It has given rise to various forms of populist political parties, such as the Progressives in 1919 and the Co-operative Commonwealth Federation (CCF) in 1932, to voice the discontent or alienation in Western Canada. During the 1970s, Trudeau and the Liberal government not only revived the historical sense of grievance that the West has felt within Confederation, but created new ones with the National Energy Policy that, perhaps more than anything else, have ingrained in the collective consciousness of Western Canada that their interests will always be secondary to the interests of Ontario and Quebec.

In Alberta, the main issue was oil. Oil price increases in 1973–1974 and again in 1979–1980 pitted Western oil-producing provinces against the major consuming provinces in Eastern Canada. These disputes threatened to pull the nation apart. In September 1973, when world prices jumped from around $3 per barrel to more than $12, Ottawa's initial response was to keep the domestic price of oil beneath the world price. It did this by imposing an export tax on oil from Alberta and Saskatchewan shipped to the United States. The federal government then used the extra revenues gained on oil exports to offset the increase that Canadians had to pay in Eastern Canada, which depended on imported foreign oil. The producing provinces responded by increasing the royalty rates charged on Crown lands, but Ottawa refused to allow the oil companies to claim royalty payments as a deduction from the federal corporate taxes that the companies paid. The Western provinces were angry because Ottawa's policies reduced the revenues coming to the provincial treasuries. In the general election following the dispute between the Western provinces and Ottawa, Alberta and Saskatchewan did not elect a single member of the federal Liberal party and British Columbia sent only one Liberal MP to Ottawa. The region's anger against Trudeau helped elect Joe Clark, a Progressive Conservative from Alberta, to a minority government in 1979, but by the time Trudeau returned to office in 1980, the outbreak of the Iran–Iraq War sent Canada into another energy crisis that again saw dramatic increases in the price of oil. Before the new oil crisis renewed the anger in Alberta, Canada had to deal with the threat of Quebec separation.

Quebec: Challenging Canada

Quebec had long argued that it deserved a special place in the Canadian federation, and throughout the 1960s and 1970s Quebec's demands seemed to increase exponentially. Canadians were worried about the bombings of federal buildings and violent deaths in Quebec during the late 1960s. Many feared that the worldwide liberation movement—

marked by race riots and the Black Panther resistance in the United States, the students' confrontation with police in Paris in 1968, and violence in Northern Ireland—would blossom in Quebec. However, when Robert Bourassa led his Liberal party to a decisive victory in April 1970, it seemed that the radical element remained on the margins of Quebec society and it would not pose a serious or immediate threat to the "peaceable" kingdom.

That proved to be an illusion. On October 5, 1970, a few months after the election, Canadians were shocked when the *Front de libération du Québec* (FLQ), a terrorist group promoting the independence of Quebec through revolutionary means, kidnapped British diplomat James Cross from his front lawn. The kidnappers demanded that the FLQ manifesto be read over the radio and that all convicted or detained FLQ members, whom they referred to as political prisoners, be released. The Quebec government agreed to the FLQ demand to read the manifesto, but it refused to release those in custody. On October 10, it offered the kidnappers safe passage out of Canada in exchange for Cross's release; that same day, a second FLQ cell kidnapped Pierre Laporte, the Quebec minister of labour.

The FLQ had been fighting for an independent Quebec since it was created in 1963; it claimed responsibility for setting more than 200 bombings in Quebec between 1963 and 1970, but when it turned to kidnapping, the Quebec government asked Ottawa for assistance. The federal government proclaimed the existence of a state of "apprehended insurrection" and responded with the *War Measures Act*, legislation that had been first used during the First World War. Its invocation effectively suspended the civil rights of all Canadians. The army was sent into Quebec, the FLQ was banned, and more than 465 people were arrested, most of whom were never charged with any crime. Two days after the *War*

Pierre Elliott Trudeau and Robert Bourassa attending the funeral of Pierre Laporte.

Source: Library and Archives Canada PA-151863.

Measures Act was proclaimed, the police found Laporte's body stuffed into the trunk of a car. He had been strangled to death in retaliation for the imposition of the *War Measures Act.* When Cross's kidnappers were discovered by police, he was released in exchange for safe passage of the kidnappers to Cuba. Paul Rose and Francis Simard, two of the terrorists who had kidnapped and participated in the murder of Laporte, were also arrested, convicted for kidnapping and murder, and received life sentences for murder. They were both released in 1982.

The imposition of the *War Measures Act* has remained controversial. At the time, the FLQ claimed it had a membership of 100 000 revolutionary workers who were armed, organized, and ready to achieve independence for Quebec through any violent means possible. Rallies in support of the FLQ were held at the Université de Montréal and the Paul Sauvé Arena; many intellectuals, union leaders, and media personalities appeared sympathetic, and few of them rushed to condemn the FLQ and its tactics. However, more than 88 percent of Canadians (and 85 percent of Quebecers) supported Trudeau's invoking of the *War Measures Act,* but over time many have come to wonder if Trudeau and the federal and provincial governments overreacted to the crisis in Quebec.[11]

Although virtually all of Quebec demonstrated in 1970 that it would not participate in any revolutionary national liberation movement, they were not particularly pleased with Bourassa's leadership. He had won an overwhelming victory in 1973 by stressing the dangers of Quebec's separation from Canada, even though the Parti Québécois (PQ) captured 30 percent of the popular vote. After the election, the PQ, a nationalist social democratic party with strong support from the labour movement, realized it had to broaden its appeal beyond left-wing voters if it hoped to form government. Parti Québécois leader René Lévesque convinced party members and supporters—usually called *péquiste*—to accept sovereignty association with Canada rather than outright independence. Sovereignty association meant that Quebec would be politically independent from Canada but it would continue to have an economic partnership with Canada. The PQ promised that it would hold a referendum on sovereignty association during its first term in office but it would not unilaterally declare independence from Canada.

The party succeeded in changing the rhetoric of independence, making it much more acceptable to Quebec voters. With Bourassa's government mired in scandal, the PQ cruised to an easy victory in 1976, which brought independence and self-determination to the national stage once more. Premier René Lévesque claimed that Confederation was a financial drain on Quebec and the province could only reach its true aspirations—economic as well as social and cultural—if it were free of the burdens of the federal government. Trudeau's promise of a bilingual and bicultural society had done little to satisfy a Quebec that desired greater autonomy and cared little about any attempt to accommodate French-speaking minorities outside of Quebec or Trudeau's promotion of French within the federal civil service.

As the federal government moved to strengthen the French language in Ottawa and throughout the country, Liberal Premier Robert Bourassa had introduced Bill 22, *la Loi sur la langue officielle,* in 1974, making French the official language of Quebec. French became the official language of commerce, and corporations had to acquire a certificate of francization, which was issued only when a company demonstrated it could function

French becomes official language of Quebec.

in French and address its employees in French. What angered many English-speaking Quebecers, or Anglophones as they came to be called, were the restrictions placed on enrolment in English-language schools for the first time. Children had to show they had an understanding of the language before they could be admitted to an English-language school. While many in Quebec's Anglophone community either complained about the legislation or left the province, many nationalists said the legislation did not go far enough to protect the French language. After the PQ defeated the Bourassa Liberals, Lévesque took further steps in 1977 to strengthen the French language through Bill 101, which prohibited the use of English in many instances. In 1978, Sun Life, Canada's largest insurance company, moved its headquarters from Montreal to Toronto, showing the uncertainty of the political and economic situation in Quebec.

Referendum on sovereignty association, 1980.

Quebec Referendum on Sovereignty Association

The Quebec government held its referendum on sovereignty association in 1980. The question put to voters was cumbersome, but its intent was clear:

> The Government of Québec has made public its proposal to negotiate a new agreement with the rest of Canada based on the equality of nations. This agreement would enable Québec to acquire the exclusive power to make its laws, levy its taxes and establish relations abroad—in other words, sovereignty—and at the same time, to maintain with Canada an economic association including a common currency. No change in political status resulting from these negotiations will be effected without approval by the people through another referendum. On these terms, do you agree to give the Government of Québec the mandate to negotiate the proposed agreement between Québec and Canada?

A *oui/yes* vote meant that Quebec would negotiate a new arrangement with Canada that it termed sovereignty association. Under the arrangement Quebec would be politically independent from Canada but maintain its economic ties through a mutual free trade zone that would also share Canada's monetary system. The PQ maintained that goods and people would pass freely across Quebec's borders into Canada and insisted that even with a yes vote, it would be business as usual with the rest of Canada.

The stakes were high and the campaign rhetoric bitter. Many in Quebec had desired their own sovereign state for more than a generation, but others feared a win for the sovereignists would mean the end of Canada. The PQ campaigned not on the basis of the question they posed, but on an impassioned plea for nationhood. Lévesque was clearly the leader of the *oui* side. It was particularly well-organized and fairly effective. In the final days of the campaign, two things happened that perhaps turned the tide against the sovereignists: One was a mistake by a leading PQ minister that the *non* side exploited to great effect, and the other was the intervention of Prime Minister Trudeau, although the decision by Sun Life Assurance to move its headquarters from Montreal to Toronto in 1978, along with other businesses that also left the province, provided useful evidence of the dire economic consequences of separation.

In a speech to Parti Québécois supporters, Lise Payette, the highly respected Québécois feminist and minister of consumer affairs, cooperatives and financial institutions, offhandedly referred to the women supporting the *non* side as "Yvettes" after a submissive young girl that most women in Quebec would have remembered from their days in elementary school (as it was a common basic name in French, akin to Jane in English). Then, she called Madeleine Ryan, the wife of provincial Liberal leader Claude Ryan, an Yvette, inadvertently mobilizing an army of opposition from women and sympathetic media that fuelled the federalist cause in Quebec. More than 14 000 women staged a massive Yvette rally in the Montreal Forum to support the *non* side. Many commentators have suggested that Payette's mistake helped turn the momentum towards the federalist side.

When the PQ announced the referendum, Trudeau had already announced his retirement from politics after losing the June 1979 federal election to the Progressive Conservatives and Joe Clark, who won a minority victory over the Liberals. The PQ saw Clark as less of a threat to their cause than Trudeau, and they were clearly delighted that Trudeau—their long-time nemesis—was no longer prime minister. Clark was only 39, the youngest prime minister in Canada's history, and would serve only seven months before his government was defeated on its first budget. When the Conservative government fell, the Liberals were in the midst of planning a leadership convention. Trudeau was convinced to return, and many Canadians believed that he could lead the federalist forces to victory in the Quebec referendum. In the election held in February 1980, Trudeau seemed to have Quebec in his back pocket. It gave him 74 of 75 of the province's seats, even though it would continue to elect the sovereignist Parti Québécois provincially. Ontario elected 52 Liberals (out of 95 seats), and when combined with Quebec, the two central provinces gave Trudeau nearly 80 percent of his seats in Parliament. He won a majority of the seats in Atlantic Canada, but his party was shutout of seats west of Manitoba. His slim nine-seat majority was hardly a huge endorsement from English-speaking Canada, but Trudeau saw it as a mandate to reform Canada.

Although Claude Ryan, who had replaced Bourassa as the Liberal leader, was the titular head of the referendum's *non* side, Trudeau's entry into the fray proved to be decisive, and it was an eventuality that the PQ had not considered. Trudeau entered the campaign late and gave only three speeches. The last, on May 14, a mere seven days before the vote, was at Montreal's famed Paul Sauvé Arena, a place that had become famous in the province as the site of René Lévesque's 1976 victory speech. Justice Minister Jean Chrétien introduced Trudeau, describing him as "the pride of Québec and the pride of Canada." Trudeau told the gathering he had come as a Quebecer and not as prime minister of Canada. "In one of the great Canadian speeches of the twentieth century, Trudeau brilliantly personified the *appartenance canadienne*, the sense of belonging which most Québeckers shared," L. Ian MacDonald wrote in a review of Canada's greatest prime ministers for the journal *Policy Options*. "I'm telling you in other provinces that we will not agree to your interpreting a *non* vote as an indication that everything is fine and can remain as it was before," Trudeau said.

His promise of constitutional reform helped turn the tide of the campaign, as the Québécois saw a *non* victory as leading to fundamental change to their place in the Canadian Confederation. However, Trudeau never spelled out what his promise meant and it is unlikely—given his views about special status—that he never contemplated greater powers for Quebec. He did not mention anytime during the campaign his hope for a new

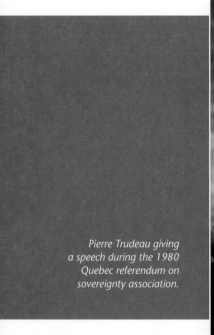

Pierre Trudeau giving
a speech during the 1980
Quebec referendum on
sovereignty association.

Source: Robert Cooper/Library and Archives Canada/PA- (missing) MIKAN No. 358801901.

charter of rights and freedoms that would be the basis of a new Canadian citizenship that would transcend any sense of ethnicity and particularism. Just what Trudeau meant by his promise of change on May 16 and what French Canadians in Quebec thought he meant when he promised to renew the Constitution has been the subject of considerable debate since that time.

Quebec voted 59.5 percent in favour of remaining a part of Canada. More than 85 percent of eligible voters participated in the referendum. The number of *non* votes was 2 187 991, while 1 485 851 voted *yes* in favour of Quebec independence. "We have all lost a little in this referendum," Trudeau remarked. The defeat was emotional, especially for Lévesque, who wept during his concession speech and promised: "*A la prochaine fois.*" Despite the referendum defeat, the Parti Québécois was re-elected in 1981, with René Lévesque as party leader. The premier promised to work with Trudeau to renew Confederation. Quebec politicians were hopeful that they might be able to address some of their particular concerns; after all, Trudeau had insisted that almost everything was negotiable.

Constitutional Odyssey

Twenty-three days following the Quebec referendum, Trudeau met the provincial premiers at 24 Sussex Drive, with the goal of bringing a resolution to the federal–provincial constitutional negotiations. Both Diefenbaker and Pearson had tried to amend the Canadian Constitution and bring it back from London where it had remained since Confederation, but they had both failed to win provincial approval for their proposed changes. Trudeau, too, had attempted to change the Constitution. His first try in 1971 ended in failure when Quebec refused to ratify the Victoria Charter. In 1975, when the premiers met for their annual meetings in St. John's, Trudeau again invited the provincial premiers, or first ministers as they were also called, to consider a constitutional conference to discuss patriation of the Constitution and an amending formula. Frank Moores, the Newfoundland premier and chair of the premiers' conference that year, later told the prime minister that "While all the Premiers agreed that … patriation was a desirable objective, it was generally felt that this issue should be dealt with in the context of a more general review of such aspects as the distribution of powers, control of resources, and related matters."[12]

Between 1975 and 1980, federal–provincial relations were particularly bitter, as we noted earlier. This was perhaps best illustrated by the fact that in those few years, the Supreme Court ruled on 80 constitutional cases dealing with the division of powers between the provinces and Ottawa—two more than it had heard in the previous quarter century. The provinces fought Ottawa on such issues as control over resources, including offshore resource development and greater control over the fisheries, control of telecommunications, and family law.

Although the federalist victory and Trudeau's promise of a new deal for Quebec in the referendum had given an added impetus to the long protracted history of constitutional reform in Canada, there was no indication that success would be imminent. When Trudeau and the first ministers sat down to discuss the Constitution over dinner in September 1980, he dismissed the premiers' list of priorities as just another provincial "shopping list,"[13] and left the formal dinner he was hosting before the dessert arrived. Federal and provincial officials had spent the previous summer negotiating various proposals from the two levels of government, and Trudeau realized that all of the provinces had their pet constitutional projects. A rejuvenated Trudeau, with a new lease on political life—from the Canadian people in the general election and from the Québécois in the referendum—also had his own list and was determined that constitutional renewal would be his legacy and the process would be on his terms. He had broadened his constitutional list to include a Charter of Rights, reform of the Senate and Supreme Court, a commitment to the principles of equalization, and the reduction of regional disparities. Moreover, he wanted to strengthen the Canadian economic union and the ability of Ottawa to manage national economic interests. This added to the bitterness between him and the other first ministers. With the PQ firmly in power in Quebec, constitutional negotiations were bound to be difficult, but a new energy crisis in 1980 not only heightened the tension between the West and the federal government but also gave added impetus to the constitutional negotiations already underway.

Creating a National Economy

Trudeau's attempts to create a strong national government were evident in his economic policy, notably in the introduction of the National Energy Policy (NEP), which still rankles many in Western Canada. After the first oil crisis that occurred in 1973 and 1974, the federal government had negotiated a series of bilateral agreements with the oil-producing provinces, but these agreements expired in mid-1980 during another precipitous rise in oil prices as a result of the Iran–Iraq War, which began on September 22, 1980.

National Energy Policy in 1980 angers Western Canada.

After the federal government failed to negotiate new agreements that satisfied the goals and objectives of the provinces, Trudeau acted unilaterally and announced a new energy policy for Canada in the budget that his minister of finance read on October 28, 1980. The NEP had three objectives: First, it wanted to increase Canadian participation in the oil and gas sector or "Canadianize" it in the view of the media; second, it vowed to make Canada self-sufficient in oil to ensure security of supply for the domestic markets; and third, it implemented fairness in the price of oil by changing the revenue-sharing agreement between the two levels of government to increase the federal share to permit it to keep domestic prices below international values.

Ottawa believed that through the NEP and greater federal control over Canada's energy resources, the Canadian economy could be insulated from the sharp spikes in the cost of oil imports. If the federal government controlled prices and allowed a more gradual increase when world prices spiked precipitously, it would lessen the impact on consumers and the manufacturing sector in Ontario and Quebec. Ottawa decided to subsidize expensive oil imports in Eastern Canada by garnering a greater share of the revenue from the oil produced in the West. The NEP increased Ottawa's share of revenues from 10 to 24 percent and left the remainder to be shared between the provinces and the oil companies. The government also introduced a special tax on the oil and gas sector to finance the purchase by the state-owned Petro-Canada of foreign oil companies operating in Canada.

The oil-producing provinces of Alberta and Saskatchewan were outraged. They claimed that because the export levy was placed only on oil—and excluded other commodities, such as lumber or electricity—it was discriminatory against the oil-producing provinces and was contrary to both the spirit and the intent of Confederation. Alberta Premier Peter Lougheed spoke to Albertans on television and told them what Trudeau had done was akin to "having strangers take over the living room." He immediately reduced oil production by 15 percent, delayed two oil sands projects, and took Ottawa to court. He succeeded in forcing Ottawa to negotiate a new pricing and taxation arrangement for the oil sector. However, the damage was done, and the West never forgave Trudeau for favouring Central Canada. In Alberta, bankruptcies soared, exploration was significantly curtailed, and real estate prices crashed by about 40 percent in Edmonton and Calgary; it has been suggested that the NEP cost Alberta between $50 billion and $100 billion in revenue. Moreover, the Western provinces became more concerned about their power under the Constitution to control their oil and gas reserves when Ottawa introduced the export tax to finance cheaper prices for consumers in Ontario and Quebec at the expense of the Western producers. When the Supreme Court ruled that the province's tax laws aimed at regulating and controlling the oil and gas sector were unconstitutional, Alberta and the other provinces demanded constitutional change. The energy issue developed into a federal–provincial constitutional power struggle. The West insisted the Constitution be reformed to give it a stronger voice in the national policymaking process.

A New Constitution and One Dissenting Province

The constitutional process was not an easy one, and Trudeau pointed his finger at the anger in the West as well as that of the Quebec government as the trends he had to reverse. Trudeau remarked in a year-end television interview in 1981 that "there was a slippage of Canada towards—is it a community of communities or is it ten quasi autonomous states? That slippage has been going on for, perhaps a couple of decades now and I feel that they've been reversed and I think at least the swing of the pendulum has been stopped with the new energy agreements, with the constitutional agreements. There is now, I hope, a line of policy which will keep Canada strong and won't keep it sliding towards this highly decentralized position which it's in and which people don't even know that it's in."[14] Trudeau thought that it was not only the separatist forces in Quebec that were a threat to the country's survival but also excessive decentralization, which was perhaps best illustrated by the growing demands from the provinces for greater control of a variety of policies. This trend had to be countered, Trudeau believed.

At the same time, Trudeau attempted to redefine and strengthen a Canadian national identity. His vision for the country promised to reinvent Canada and, not surprisingly, it encountered stiff opposition. He wanted to reform the Constitution to impose a strong and coherent national state by strengthening the powers of the national or federal government. He also hoped to forge a durable and stable national state as a way to create a renewed political identity through a charter of common and shared rights and freedoms that would transcend the various Canadian identities. In all of this, Trudeau believed his vision and his constitutional reforms would satisfy Quebec as well as build a stronger bond between the national government and all Canadian citizens.

Trudeau wanted to create within Canada a civic nationalism that would replace all forms of ethnic nationalism that was based primarily on a shared language, culture, and heritage—or what Michael Ignatieff has called "blood" in his influential book *Blood and Belonging: Journeys in the New Nationalism*. Civic nationalism was an attempt to replace ethnicity as the defining national characteristic with a new political society based on a philosophical vision around liberal individualism as the organizing principle for the nation-state.

For Trudeau, the ideals of the Canadian nation-state also promoted diversity and the respect for cultural diversity or multiculturalism, which was a reversal of early government policy to assimilate immigrants. Canada introduced a policy of official multiculturalism in 1971, which ensured that all citizens in Canada could keep their identities and take pride in their heritage. This meant that the state would not promote one culture over another as it had attempted to do with promoting the "Britishness" of Canada for generations; rather, culture was an individual matter and all individuals had the right to maintain and celebrate their individual culture. Multiculturalism asked Canadians to accept all cultures and to realize that pluralism and ethnic diversity would strengthen—not threaten—the Canadian identity. The federal government created a Multiculturalism Directorate within the Department of Secretary of State in 1972 to assist with the implementation of its multicultural policies and earmarked about $200 million for its various initiatives. Not surprisingly, not all Canadians supported the government's policy of multiculturalism as they feared it would undermine the British and French heritage; in Quebec, many feared that multiculturalism would weaken Quebec nationalism. Many in the immigrant and multicultural communities appreciated the official recognition of their heritage and culture, but most hoped that official acceptance of multiculturalism would help eliminate the racial prejudice and discrimination that they faced in Canadian society and provide equal access to employment and educational opportunities.

As noted earlier, Trudeau believed that Canadians had the right to communicate with their government in either French or English, but all cultures were equal and none could be given preferential treatment. He also believed that civil and equality rights had to be protected in the Constitution, and it was incumbent upon the state not only to protect the equality of all citizens but also to intervene in society to promote greater equality and social justice as Trudeau had done with regional development plans and reforms to the *Criminal Code of Canada.* As a proponent of civic nationalism, Trudeau considered this the only way to achieve his vision of a Just Society and construct a fair and equitable Canada. There can be no doubt that Trudeau's policies and constitutional reforms embodied a particular ideal for Canada.[15]

Moreover, the act of patriating the Constitution from the British Parliament would be the final act of nationhood. The Mackenzie King government had enacted a *Canadian Citizenship Act* in 1947, Louis St. Laurent had eliminated appeals to the Judicial Committee of the Privy Council in the late 1940s, and L.B. Pearson had replaced the Red Ensign with a new Canadian flag that removed any hint of the British connection. Trudeau himself had attempted to strengthen the Canadian identity when he eliminated the use of the term "Dominion" from Canada to create a "Government of Canada" and began a process to rebrand the nation with bilingual designations, such as for Canada Post and Statistics Canada. Having the ability to amend its own constitution in its own Parliament rather than having to ask the British government to officially change the Canadian Constitution would end years of embarrassment for many Canadians. However, this would not be an easy task, as it had been assumed that sweeping constitutional reform in Canada required the consent of all provinces.

Canadian Constitution is repatriated, 1982.

Less than a month after the September 1980 conference ended in failure, Trudeau took to the national airwaves and told Canadians that given provincial intransigence he would proceed unilaterally with constitutional reform. Trudeau promised an all-Canadian amending formula (eliminating the need to involve the British Parliament), a commitment to the principle of equalization and the reduction of regional disparity, a Charter of Rights and Freedoms, and the use of a referendum to approve future constitutional amendments. By speaking directly to Canadians rather than working through the provincial premiers, Trudeau's proposals were termed the "people's package," clearly an attempt at appealing to the national community of individual citizens that Trudeau believed wanted to create viable national institutions. Nothing in the proposal paid special recognition to Quebec, but there was an expression of equality among Canadians both in the rights provisions of the Constitution and the equality of opportunity principle included in the equalization clause. Trudeau, it seems, had donned a populist mantle.

Only New Brunswick and Ontario supported Trudeau's initiative; the premiers of the other eight provinces were entirely against it. A parliamentary committee on the Constitution subsequently discussed Trudeau's constitutional package in a series of televised hearings and demonstrated it was committed to making the Constitution a people's exercise when the government accepted a series of amendments to its proposal. They included, among others, a constitutional recognition of rights for women, Aboriginal peoples, and people with disabilities, as well as recognition of the multicultural nature of Canada. Trudeau's approach to constitution-making ushered in an era of public and popular

Source: Boris Spremo/GetStock.com.

Women march outside a constitutional conference held by women's group demanding their needs be recognized in the Constitution.

participation in the process and made room for interest-group participation; this change would play a major role in the attempts at constitutional reform during the Mulroney era.

The eight opposing premiers—known as the "Gang of Eight"—were in a dilemma. They found it difficult to argue about the basic tenants of Trudeau's proposal and had to attack the process to get Trudeau to listen to their demands. By flagrantly bypassing the provinces and by proceeding alone, they argued, Trudeau was violating the basic principle of Canadian federalism, and they challenged in the courts his right to proceed unilaterally. The Supreme Court ruled that while Trudeau stood on firm legal grounds, he had clearly violated constitutional convention, or the accepted but unwritten rules of constitutional practice, that held that a substantial provincial consent was required before the federal government requested the British government to amend the *British North America Act*. The Court's decision helped neither side, but Trudeau promised another round of negotiations. The Gang of Eight had a difficult time achieving any consensus given that Premier René Lévesque was not as committed as the other seven premiers to making the country work, even if the Parti Québécois had temporarily put independence on hold and Lévesque had surrendered Quebec's demand for a veto over future amendments.

When Trudeau and the premiers gathered in Ottawa in November 1981, they finally agreed on a constitutional package but how that was achieved has since been the subject of bitter debate. For some, such as Saskatchewan's Allan Blakeney and Manitoba's Sterling Lyon, it was evidence of Canada as a negotiated nation; for others, such as Lévesque, it was a clear indication of how Quebec was really not an integral part of the Canadian polity. On the evening of the third day of the conference, the seven English-speaking premiers broke with Lévesque and agreed to a deal with the federal government. For Quebec it was a betrayal—"the night of the long knives"—that isolated Quebec from the constitutional process as the federal government and the English-speaking provincial politicians hammered out a deal in an Ottawa hotel suite. Despite Trudeau's insistence on a people's constitution, in the end this round in Canada's constitutional odyssey was

1981: Nine English-speaking premiers agreed to a constitutional deal with Ottawa; Quebec did not.

simply another example of elite accommodation. Ottawa later offered two amendments to the package to lure Lévesque into signing the constitutional deal, but he refused. The provincial legislatures did not have to ratify the constitutional package as had been the case with Trudeau's failed Victoria Charter in 1971. Still, the Quebec legislature later voted 70 to 38 to reject the proposals. This prompted Jean Chrétien, the federal minister of justice and a key figure in the late-night negotiations, to describe the Quebec vote as having as much effect as "a decree saying there will be no snow over Québec this winter."[16]

The provinces had been able to force a few amendments to Trudeau's constitutional package, including one on energy. After a heated debate, a new clause (section 92A) was added to section 92 of the *British North America Act*, which granted the provinces legislative authority over natural resources, including the export of those resources, provided that the producing province did not discriminate in prices or supplies available to other provinces. In other words, Alberta could not refuse to sell its oil to other provinces because it wanted to export it at better prices to the United States. Even so, the Constitution also included a clause that states that nothing in section 92A was to derogate "from the authority of Parliament to enact laws in relation to the matters referred to" in that clause, and when the laws of Parliament conflicts with provincial laws, "the law of Parliament prevails to the extent of that conflict." The provinces celebrated that the Constitution recognized their control over natural resources, but some commentators have concluded that the amendments muddled the jurisdictional issue even further. Since Trudeau, no prime minister has attempted to assert Ottawa's control over natural resources and the matter remains a moot point until one does.

When it came to Quebec, Trudeau believed that he and the federal Liberals from Quebec had more legitimacy in speaking for that province than a government committed to destroying Canada. He had repudiated a national polity premised on ethnicity and had erected in its place a civic nationalism as the new ideal for Canada. This was a policy based on a respect for diversity (multiculturalism), equality of individuals, the entrenchment of language rights, social and economic mobility, and the equality of opportunity. Did it fulfill his promise to Quebec made during the referendum campaign? Many in Quebec did not believe it had. In the words of one prominent political scientist, Trudeau's Constitution signified the end of the Canadian dream because it destroyed the duality of Canada. For many federalists in Quebec, their ideal of Canada was that of a compact between two peoples and nations, one Francophone and the other Anglophone, and as long as the each nation respected the rights of the other then there was good reason for the two to cooperate within Confederation. When Trudeau remade Canada with a different national philosophy—one based on liberal individualism and equality under the Charter of Rights and Freedoms—many in Quebec argued that he fundamentally altered the nature of Canada by destroying the duality between French- and English-speaking citizens enshrined in 1867. Others have argued that Trudeau not only remade Canada, but with the Charter he also hoped to undermine the nation-building project that had begun in Quebec with the Quiet Revolution by creating Canada's own nation-building project based on the Charter, with its new notions of political citizenship that left little room for the claims of historic minorities, such as Quebec. Moreover, the Charter gave the courts considerably more power, as it gives them the authority to overrule any law from

New Constitution in 1982 for Canada with Charter of Rights and Freedoms.

Signing of the Constitution.

chapter 10

Source: Library and Archives Canada/Credit: Robert Cooper/Office of the Prime Minister collection/e0028528001.

Parliament that contradicts the rights and freedoms that the Charter guarantees. Before 1982, Parliament was supreme and it could enact any law within its constitutional jurisdiction—even oppressive ones—but the Charter challenges the supremacy of Parliament and puts significantly more power in the hands of citizens to challenge the state.

On April 17, 1982, Queen Elizabeth II came to Ottawa to give royal assent to Trudeau's constitutional package. Much of the *British North America Act* that had been written at the time of Confederation in 1867 was retained, but it was renamed the *Constitution Act, 1867*. The ceremony was a federal affair, as was the constitutional process itself. As he had insisted after his return to power in 1980, Trudeau believed that the national government had to reassert itself and the national interest had to be protected. The 1982 Constitution promoted a pan-Canadian identity based on a new vision of rights.

Conclusion

When Pierre Trudeau announced his resignation in February 1984, after 15 years as prime minister, it was the end of an era in Canadian history. Although Trudeau soon became an elder statesman and was admired by many, Canadians were divided over his impact on their society. The Charter of Rights and Freedoms was his greatest legacy, and his supporters have argued that it transformed Canada, making it the modern secular and tolerant society it has become. Others have seen him as a great disappointment that mismanaged the economy and left Canada more divided than he had found it in 1968; he failed to improve French–English relations even though he tried to make Canada a bilingual and multicultural society where citizenship was based not on ethnicity but on rights. His task of national reconciliation was perhaps doomed to fail, as he did not see Canada as a negotiated nation as the Fathers of Confederation had in 1867.

Trudeau was a Canadian nationalist, even though he was vehemently and ironically opposed to nationalism of all varieties. Throughout his tenure as prime minister, he constantly looked for ways to strengthen the national identity and to strengthen the power of the national government, often through constitutional litigation and constitutional change. He saw the necessity of a strong national state that could create both stability and durability by creating a political identity of pluralism that would transcend the competing identities within Canada and establish a coherent national state that could protect Canadian economic and cultural interests. While many English Canadians embraced Trudeau's vision of Canada, others rebelled. Aboriginal Canadians and Quebec nationalists insisted on their distinctiveness and refused to have their identities manipulated even in a society that promised to be pluralistic and liberal. The West and much of Atlantic Canada saw Trudeau's vision of a national economy as merely serving the interests of Central Canada at their expense. In the decade that followed, Canada continued to struggle with many of the same issues that Trudeau had identified, but no leader would bring the same doggedness and determination to reinvent Canada as he did.

Questions to Consider

1. Why were Canadians so eager to embrace Trudeau in 1968?

2. Was Canadian foreign policy any more independent at the end of the Trudeau period than it was at the beginning?

3. Is national unity possible in Canada?

4. Why did voters in Quebec desert the Liberal party after the 1980 election?

5. What is the Charter or Rights and Freedoms and how has it changed the role of the courts in Canada?

Critical Thinking Questions

1. How effective was Canada's attempts to deal with regional disparity?

2. How successful was Trudeau in promoting Canadian unity?

3. How did Canada change as a nation in the generation from 1968 to 1984?

4. What should the role of the federal government be in addressing regional economic differences in a nation like Canada?

5. Is culture a commodity like wheat?

Suggested Readings
General

Anastakis, Dimitry, ed. *The Sixties: Passion, Politics, and Style.* Montreal and Kingston: McGill-Queen's University Press, 2008.

Axworthy, Thomas S., and Pierre Elliott Trudeau, eds. *Towards a Just Society: The Trudeau Years.* Translations into English by Patricia Claxton. Markham, ON: Viking, 1990.

Bothwell, Robert, Ian Drummond, and John English. *Canada since 1945: Power, Politics and Provincialism.* Toronto: University of Toronto Press, 1989.

Clarkson, Stephen, and Christina McCall. *Trudeau and Our Times*, 2 Vols. Toronto: McClelland & Stewart, 1990–1994.

English, John. *Just Watch Me: The Life of Pierre Elliott Trudeau*, Vol. 2. Toronto: Knopf Canada, 2009.

Fahrni, Magda, and Robert Rutherdale, eds. *Creating Postwar Canada: Community, Diversity, and Dissent, 1945–75.* Vancouver: University of British Columbia Press, 2008.

Finkel, Alvin. *Social Policy and Practice in Canada: A History.* Waterloo, ON: Wilfrid Laurier University Press, 2006.

Ismael, Jacqueline S., ed. *Canadian Social Welfare Policy: Federal and Provincial Dimensions.* Montreal and Kingston: McGill-Queen's University Press, 1985.

Prentice, Alison, et al. *Canadian Women: A History.* 2nd edition. Toronto: Harcourt Brace, 1996.

National Politics, Economics, and Constitutionalism

Cairns, Alan, ed. *Charter versus Federalism: The Dilemmas of Constitutional Reform.* Montreal and Kingston: McGill-Queen's University Press, 1992.

Clippingdale, Richard. *Robert Stanfield's Canada: Perspectives of the Best Prime Minister We Never Had.* Montreal and Kingston: McGill-Queen's University Press, 2008.

French, Richard D. *How Ottawa Decides: Planning and Industrial Policy-Making 1968–1984*, with a new chapter by Richard Van Loon. Toronto: Lorimer, 1984.

Gibbins, Roger, and Guy Laforest, eds. *Beyond the Impasse: Toward Reconciliation.* Montreal: Institute for Research on Public Policy, 1998.

Laforest, Guy. *Trudeau and the End of a Canadian Dream*, translated by Paul Leduc Browne and Michelle Weinroth. Montreal and Kingston: McGill-Queen's University Press, 1995.

McRoberts, Kenneth. *Misconceiving Canada. The Struggle for National Unity.* Toronto: Oxford University Press, 1997.

McWhinney, Edward. *Canada and the Constitution, 1979–1982: Patriation and the Charter of Rights.* Toronto: University of Toronto Press, 1982.

Russell, Peter H. *Constitutional Odyssey.* 3rd edition. Toronto: University of Toronto Press, 2004.

Savoie, Donald. *Regional Economic Development: Canada's Search for Solutions.* Toronto: University of Toronto Press, 1986.

Savoie, Donald J. *The Politics of Public Spending in Canada.* Toronto: University of Toronto Press, 1990.

Whyte, John, Roy Romanow, and Howard Leeson. *Canada … Notwithstanding: The Making of the Constitution, 1976–1982.* Rev. edition. Toronto: Thomson Carswell, 2007.

Provincial Politics

Barmen, Jean. *The West Beyond the West: A History of British Columbia.* Rev. edition. Toronto: University of Toronto Press, 1996.

Bickerton, James. *Nova Scotia, Ottawa and the Politics of Regional Development.* Toronto: University of Toronto Press, 1990.

Bosher, J.F. *The Gaullist Attack on Canada, 1967–1997.* Montreal and Kingston: McGill-Queen's University Press, 1998.

Choyce, Lesley. *Nova Scotia: Shaped by the Sea: A Living History.* Toronto: Viking, 1996.

Cormier, Michel, and Achille Michaud. *Richard Hatfield: Power and Disobedience,* translated by Daphne Ponder. Fredericton: Goose Lane Editions, 1992.

Forbes, E.R., and D.A. Muise, eds. *The Atlantic Provinces in Confederation.* Toronto: University of Toronto Press, 1993.

Friesen, Gerald. *The Canadian Prairies: A History.* Toronto: University of Toronto Press, 1984.

Friesen, Gerald. *The West: Regional Ambitions, National Debates, Global Age.* Toronto: Penguin Books, 1999.

Gauvreau, Michael. *The Catholic Origins of Québec's Quiet Revolution, 1931–1970.* Montreal and Kingston: McGill-Queen's University, 2008.

Gruending, Dennis. *Promises to Keep: A Political Biography of Allan Blakeney.* Saskatoon: Western Producer Prairie Books, 1990.

Gwyn, Richard. *Smallwood: The Unlikely Revolutionary.* Rev. edition. Toronto: McClelland & Stewart, 1999.

Hawkins, John. *Recollections of the Reagan Years: A Political Memoir.* Hantsport, NS: Lancelot Press, 1990.

Hoy, Claire. *Bill Davis. A Biography.* Toronto: Methuen, 1985.

Leeson, Howard, ed. *Saskatchewan Politics: Into the Twenty-First Century.* Regina: Canadian Plains Research Centre, 2001.

MacDonald, L. Ian. *From Bourassa to Bourassa: A Pivotal Decade in Canadian History.* Montreal: Harvest House, 1984.

McAllister, James A. *The Government of Edward Schreyer: Democratic Socialism in Manitoba.* Montreal and Kingston: McGill-Queen's University Press, 1984.

Pratt, Larry, and Garth Stevenson, eds. *Western Separatism: The Myths, Realities & Dangers.* Edmonton: Hurtig, 1981.

Resnick, Phillip. *The Politics of Resentment: British Columbia Regionalism and Canadian Unity.* Vancouver: University of British Columbia Press, 2000.

Tetley, William. *The October Crisis, 1970: An Insider's View.* Montreal and Kingston: McGill-Queen's University Press, 2006.

Tomblin, Stephen G. *Ottawa and the Outer Provinces: The Challenge of Regional Integration in Canada.* Toronto: James Lorimer, 1995.

Tupper, Allan, and Roger Gibbins, eds. *Government and Politics in Alberta.* Edmonton: University of Alberta Press, 1992.

Starr, Richard. *Richard Hatfield: The Seventeen Year Saga.* Halifax: Formac, 1987.

Waiser, Bill. *Saskatchewan: A New History.* Calgary: Fifth House, 2005.

Wiseman, Nelson. *Social Democracy in Manitoba: A History of the CCF-NDP.* Winnipeg: University of Manitoba Press, 1983.

Wonders, William C. *Canada's Changing North.* Rev. edition. Montreal and Kingston: McGill-Queen's University Press, 2003.

Wood, David C. *The Lougheed Legacy.* Toronto: Key Porter, 1985.

Foreign and Defence Policy

Dobell, Peter C. *Canada's Search for New Roles: Foreign Policy in the Trudeau Era.* London: Published for Royal Institute of International Affairs, by Oxford University Press, 1972.

Granatstein, J.L., and Robert Bothwell. *Pirouette: Pierre Trudeau and Canadian Foreign Policy.* Toronto, University of Toronto Press, 1990.

Head, Ivan, and Pierre Trudeau. *Canadian Way: Shaping Canada's Foreign Policy, 1968–1984.* Toronto: McClelland & Stewart, 1995.

Jockel, Joseph T. *Canada in NORAD, 1957–2007: A History.* Montreal and Kingston: McGill-Queen's University Press, 2007.

Kirk, John M., and Peter McKenna. *Canada–Cuba Relations: The Other Good Neighbor Policy.* Gainesville, FL: University Press of Florida, 1997.

Stevenson, Brian J.R. *Canada, Latin America, and the New Internationalism: A Foreign Policy Analysis, 1968-1990.* Montreal and Kingston: McGill-Queen's University Press and the Centre for Security and Foreign Policy Studies/The Teleglobe+Raoul-Dandurand Chair of Strategic and Diplomatic Studies, 2000.

Wright, Robert. *Three Nights in Havana: Pierre Trudeau, Fidel Castro and the Cold War World.* Toronto: HarperCollins, 2007.

Women

Adamson, Nancy, Linda Briskin, and Margaret McPhail. *Feminist Organizing for Change: The Contemporary Women's Movement in Canada.* Toronto: Oxford University Press, 1988.

Cook, Sharon Anne, Lorna R. McLean, and Kate O'Rourke, eds. *Framing Our Past: Canadian Women's History in the Twentieth Century.* Montreal and Kingston: McGill-Queen's University Press, 2001.

McKeen, Wendy. *Money in Their Own Name: The Feminist Voice in Poverty Debate in Canada, 1970–1995.* Toronto: University of Toronto Press, 2004.

Porter, Ann. *Gendered States: Women, Unemployment Insurance, and the Political Economy of the Welfare State in Canada, 1945–1997.* Toronto: University of Toronto Press, 2003.

Rebick, Judy. *Ten Thousand Roses: The Making of a Feminist Revolution.* Toronto: Penguin Canada, 2005.

Report of the Royal Commission on the Status of Women in Canada. Ottawa: Information Canada, 1970.

Strong-Boag, Veronica, and Anita Clair Fellman. *Rethinking Canada: The Promise of Women's History.* Don Mills, ON: Oxford University Press, 1997.

Vickers, Jill, Pauline Rankin, and Christine Appelle. *Politics as If Women Mattered: A Political Analysis of the National Action Committee on the Status of Women.* Toronto: University of Toronto Press, 1993.

Society and Culture

Adams, Ian, William Cameron, Brian Hill, and Peter Penz. *The Real Poverty Report.* Edmonton: Hurtig, 1971.

Banting, Keith. *The Welfare State and Canadian Federalism.* 2nd edition. Montreal and Kingston: McGill-Queen's University Press, 1987.

Behiels, Michael. *Canada's Francophone Minority Communities: Constitutional Renewal and the Winning of School Governance.* Montreal and Kingston: McGill-Queen's University Press, 2004.

Cairns, Alan C., et al., eds. *Citizenship, Diversity, and Pluralism.* Montreal and Kingston: McGill-Queen's University Press, 1999.

Edwardson, Ryan. *Canadian Content: Culture and the Quest for Nationhood.* Toronto: University of Toronto Press, 2008.

Kelley, Ninette, and Michael Trebilcock. *The Making of the Mosaic. A History of Canadian Immigration Policy.* Toronto: University of Toronto Press, 1998.

Pal, Leslie A. *Interests of State: The Politics of Language, Multiculturalism and Feminism in Canada.* Montreal and Kingston: McGill-Queen's University Press, 1993.

Penfold, Steve. *The Donut: A Canadian History.* Toronto: University of Toronto Press, 2008.

Sugunasiri, Suwanda. *Towards Multicultural Growth: A Look at Canada from Classical Racism to Neomulticulturalism.* Toronto: Village Pub. House, 2001.

Trudeau, Margaret. *Beyond Reason.* New York: Paddington Press, 1979.

Warsh, Cheryl Krasnick, ed. *Drink in Canada: Historical Essays.* Montreal and Kingston: McGill-Queen's University Press, 1993.

Young, Scott. *War on Ice: Canada in International Hockey.* Toronto: McClelland & Stewart, 1976.

Aboriginal Peoples

Asch, Michael. *Aboriginal and Treaty Rights in Canada.* Vancouver: University of British Columbia Press, 1988.

Cardinal, Harold. *The Rebirth of Canada's Indians.* Edmonton: Hurtig, 1977.

Hornig, James F., ed. *Social and Environmental Impacts of the James Bay Hydroelectric Project.* Montreal and Kingston: McGill-Queen's University, 1999.

Miller, J.R. *Shingwauk's Vision: A History of Native Residential Schools.* Toronto: University of Toronto Press, 1966.

Weaver, Sally. *Making Canadian Indian Policy: The Hidden Agenda, 1968–70.* Toronto, University of Toronto Press, 1981.

Notes

[1] Christabelle Sethna and Steve Hewitt, "Clandestine Operations: The Vancouver Women's Caucus, the Abortion Caravan, and the RCMP," *Canadian Historical Review* 90 (September 2009): 463–495; CBC, "The Omnibus Bill Doesn't Go Far Enough," CBC Digital Archives Website, http://archives.cbc.ca/politics/rights_freedoms/clips/2702/.

[2] House of Commons Debates, 17 October 1968.

[3] Quoted in Donald J. Savoie, *Regional Economic Development: Canada's Search for Solutions* (Toronto: University of Toronto Press, 1986), 28.

[4] Savoie, *Regional Economic Development*, 73.

[5] J.R. Miller, *Skyscrapers Hide the Heavens: A History of Indian-White Relations in Canada*, 3rd ed. (Toronto: University of Toronto Press, 2000), 334.

[6] Miller, *Skyscrapers Hide the Heavens*, 343.

[7] See, for example, S. Beecroft, "Canadian Policy Towards China, 1949–1957: The Recognition Problem," in P. Evans and M. Frolic, eds., *Reluctant Adversaries: Canada and the People's Republic of China, 1949–1970* (Toronto: University of Toronto Press, 1991); and N. St. Amour, "Sino-Canadian Relations, 1963–1968: The American Factor," in the same publication.

[8] Dean F. Oliver, "Canada and NATO," *Dispatches: Backgrounders in Canadian Military History*, Canadian War Museum, 2009, http://www.warmuseum.ca/cwm/explore/military-history/dispatches.

[9] Jonathan F. Vance, *A History of Canadian Culture: From Petroglyphs, Circuses to the CBC* (Toronto: Oxford University Press, 2009), 398–399. See, Chapter 16, "The Regulatory State" for a fuller discussion of culture during the 1970s.

[10] Elizabeth Riddell-Dixon, *Canada and the International Seabed: Domestic Interests and External Constraints* (Montreal and Kingston: McGill-Queen's University Press, 1989), 104.

[11] Manon Leroux, *Les silences d'octobre: le discours des acteurs de la crise de 1970* (Montreal: VLB Éditeur, 2002); and William Tetley, *The October Crisis: An Insider's View* (Montreal and Kingston: McGill-Queen's University Press, 2006).

[12] Quoted in Peter H. Russell, *Constitutional Odyssey: Can Canadians Become a Sovereign People?* 3rd ed. (Toronto: University of Toronto Press, 2004), 98.

[13] Quoted in Russell, *Constitutional Odyssey*, 110.

[14] Quoted in David Milne, *Tug of War. Ottawa and the Provinces Under Trudeau and Mulroney* (Toronto: James Lorimer & Company, 1986), 15.

[15] These ideas are developed by Andrew Nurse in "Narrating the Nation: An Introduction," in Raymond B. Blake and Andrew Nurse, eds., *Beyond National Dreams* (Toronto: Fitzhenry Whiteside, 2008), 1–8.

[16] *Globe and Mail*, 26 November 1981.

Seeking a
New Consensus:
1984–1993

*O*n June 19, 1985, 63-year-old Solange Denis, who had lived much of her life in Ottawa, joined a protest outside the Centre Block on Parliament Hill. Home to the House of Commons, the Senate, and the Prime Minister's Office, the Centre Block is one of the magnificent Gothic Revival buildings in the nation's capital and one of the most recognizable landmarks in all of Canada. Denis had joined the group to protest the government's decision not to automatically increase Old Age Security unless the consumer price index rose by more than 3 percent annually. The measure had been announced when the new government, led by Prime Minister Brian Mulroney, presented its first budget several weeks earlier. The government had said that the policy was based on fairness and on its desire to target spending on social programs, such as increases to pensions for the elderly, to those in greatest need. Denis and many other senior citizens were outraged. When Mulroney walked out of the Parliament buildings that day, he noticed the group of protesters and—as he was known to do, especially, in his early years as prime minister—he walked over to the crowd to chat and shake a few hands, but he was caught flat-footed by Denis's group. With the television cameras rolling, Denis confronted the prime minister. She would have none of Mr. Mulroney attempts at explaining how de-indexing pensions was a fair policy and scolded him in front of the cameras. "You lied to us," she shouted. "You made promises that you wouldn't touch anything and hello, you lied to us."

chapter 11

Source: Wayne Cuddingham (photographer)—Southam News, Ottawa Citizen, #85-3138R3.

As for voting for him again, "It's goodbye Charlie Brown," she said. Denis emerged as a media star for a few days, and Mulroney's few minutes proved to be a public relations nightmare for the Progressive Conservative Government. Eight days later, it backed down on its proposed cuts to social programs for seniors and, as a group, they escaped many of the reductions that others endured during the years that followed. Some have suggested that Denis was an active Liberal all along, but it really never mattered, as her confrontation with the prime minister shows that Canadians would not easily relinquish the beneficence of the state to which they had become accustomed in the previous generation.

Introduction

When Canadians entered polling stations across the country on September 4, 1984, to vote in the federal election, they gave every indication that they wanted change. Although many Canadians still had a grudging respect for Pierre Trudeau, most were delighted he was no longer at the helm in Ottawa. A summer of never-ending patronage appointments that the former prime minister had orchestrated before the Liberal delegates turned the party and the country over to John Turner at their national convention added to the anger Canadians felt towards the Liberal government, which had held office almost continually since 1963. On voting day, Canadians gave the Progressive Conservatives the largest number of seats ever in any federal election, and Brian Mulroney became the new prime minister. Rarely had so many Canadians turned against their national government.

Mulroney and his Conservatives saw their huge electoral victory of 211 seats in the House of Commons as a mandate for decisive and transformative change—and it was change that the Mulroney government brought during the decade it held office. Canada adopted a new approach to social welfare, established closer relations with the United States, and even negotiated a Canada–U.S. free trade agreement, renewed its commitment to the military, made debt reduction and tax reform a priority, attempted to recognize Quebec as a distinct society, privatized many of the Crown corporations, such as Air Canada and Petro-Canada, moved to entrench self-determination for Aboriginal peoples in the Constitution, tried to create a more decentralized federation through a new relationship between Ottawa and the provinces, and changed the direction and nature of foreign policy. It was an agenda that would transform the nation.

Not surprisingly, this was also a series of public policies that inspired debate and generated controversy. The years from 1984 to 1993 were marked by considerable protest, as many Canadians struggled with the new consensus that seemed to be emerging to deal with the challenges facing their country. It also mobilized citizens like Solange Denis and reinvigorated Canada's social movements, as women's groups, labour, anti-poverty groups, the elderly, and a host of others protested the changes that the state embraced during the period. By 1993, Canadians were once again united in their opposition to their national government. Faced with new regional protest parties, and charges of gutting social services, reneging on the military, and "selling out" Canada to the Americans, Mulroney resigned in early 1993. His Progressive Conservatives suffered even greater losses in the following election in 1993 than the Liberals had after Trudeau's departure, reducing the Conservatives to just two seats in the House of Commons.

As we examine this period of Canadian history, we must ask if it represents an example of failed political management and the sundering of Canadian unity, or if it demonstrates the difficulty of implementing structural change to a nation-state that ushers in a new approach to governing and raises fundamental questions about the role of the state in Canadian society. There are some important questions to consider in this regard: Is the modern Canadian federation really a collection of several regions—each with different and often competing objectives—or is Canada something more? Did the protests generated by various groups against the Conservative government represent a new level of citizen engagement, or did they represent the fact that there were groups that refused to accept a new and different Canada? Can there be a national consensus in Canada, or is the political realignment that we saw emerge during the decade an indication of the realities of a new and even more conflicted Canada than we had seen before?

An Angry Nation Votes for Change

When he swept the country in 1984 with the largest electoral landslide in Canadian history and with more than half of the popular vote, Brian Mulroney capped an extraordinary career in Canadian business and Conservative party politics. Fluently bilingual, he had left Baie-Comeau on Quebec's North Shore to attend St. Thomas College, a private Catholic high school in New Brunswick in 1953. He later studied at St. Francis Xavier University in Antigonish, Nova Scotia, where he first became involved in Conservative politics, before earning a law degree at l'Université Laval in Quebec City. After establishing himself as a successful labour lawyer in Montreal, he moved to the corporate boardroom in 1977 as president of the Iron Ore Company of Canada, a joint subsidiary of three major U.S. steel firms. His first foray into formal politics came in 1976, when he challenged for the leadership of the Progressive Conservative party, but Joe Clark emerged as the winner when fellow-Quebecers Claude Wagner and Mulroney both presented themselves as the best choice to win the province for the Conservatives. Although Canadians elected Clark to a minority government in 1979, Clark never seized the mantle of leadership. He made a number of blunders as prime minister, including the critical one of miscalculating on a vote of confidence that brought down his government and forced an election, which the Liberals won. Soon after, a "Dump Clark" campaign emerged and Mulroney's supporters were among those who worked hard to push Clark out. In 1983, Clark called a leadership convention to silence the persistent critics within his party and Mulroney triumphed in his second bid for the leadership.[1] The Progressive Conservative party then saw him as the best chance to win Quebec and hence move from years of opposition to the government.

Rarely had all Canadians found such common purpose with a national political party than at the end of the Trudeau era. The mood was particularly foul across the land and that certainly helped Mulroney's Conservatives. Western Canada had a profound dislike for Trudeau. He had enacted the National Energy Program and a series of other policies that the West saw as favouring Quebec and Ontario. The West expressed its hostility towards the Liberal government in the 1980 federal election when it sent only two MPs

Brian Mulroney with his wife, Mila, at the announcement of the results of the 1983 PC Leadership Convention.

Source: CP Images.

to Ottawa, and both of them were from Manitoba. Lingering disputes over ownership of the offshore oil reserves had created major rifts between the Atlantic provinces and Ottawa. Quebec continued to smart over the 1982 constitutional process that it claimed had isolated it from the rest of Canada, and every major politician in that province outside the federal Liberal party continued to demand further constitutional reform to accommodate Quebec. Although the Charter of Rights and Freedoms had guaranteed certain rights to Canada's Aboriginal populations, there was a growing frustration and anger within Aboriginal communities over the slow pace of change in their socioeconomic well-being. Many other groups, ranging from women's organizations to Japanese Canadians interned during the Second World War, were disappointed with how slowly the federal government was responding to their demands.

These groups hoped that their grievances would be addressed with a new government. The West, for instance, had long seen the Conservative party as its voice of discontent. Although Mulroney had worked assiduously to undermine Alberta-born Joe Clark, many hoped the system might be different under a leader who talked about national reconciliation as Mulroney had. However, if they had listened closely to him during his leadership campaign and in his first months as the leader of the opposition, they would have known that in some ways he was Trudeau's natural heir when it came to such policies as bilingualism, a policy that many in the West did not support.

"You Had an Option, Sir": The 1984 Canadian Election

Shortly after Mulroney became leader, he made it clear to the Conservatives that he would not tolerate those in the party who opposed official bilingualism. That became evident when Howard Pawley, the NDP Premier of Manitoba, introduced legislation mandating official bilingualism in the provincial legislature and the courts. Pawley's decision to restore section 23 of the *Manitoba Act, 1870* and reinstate the bilingualism that had been abolished in 1890 caused divisions within the federal Conservative party. Many of the Manitoba Tory Members of Parliament sided with provincial Conservative leader Gary Filmon, who opposed the proposed changes to the language laws. Mulroney would have none of it. He emphatically told his party that bilingualism was the law in Canada, and the Conservative party stood squarely behind it. He knew that his policy would not please many in Western Canada, but he was committed to a bilingual Canada.

The Liberals had believed for years that Trudeau understood Quebec and he was essential to their winning that province. Many Conservatives had now come to a similar conclusion about Mulroney: He was essential to their winning Quebec and ending a generation of Liberal domination in federal politics. Yet, in many ways, the Conservative party that Mulroney inherited from Clark was as fractious as the nation itself. The Western Canadian Tories, who were usually "small c" conservative—meaning they were socially and fiscally conservative—and the left-leaning Conservatives under Premier William Davis in Ontario had little in common except that they were usually out of power in Ottawa. Mulroney knew that he could win only if all factions within the party worked together and demonstrated that they could be a party of moderation. He was able to unite the "Red Tories," the name given to the progressive elements within the Conservative party, with the Western Tories and the "Blue Tories," those who were economically and fiscally conservative and primarily from the business elites in Toronto and Montreal. Mulroney attracted to his coalition many of the nationalists from Quebec, as well as many of the disaffected Liberals there who had turned against Trudeau and disliked John Turner more. For a while, the Conservatives established a powerful force in Canadian politics that allowed Mulroney to become prime minister, but it was a coalition that would not stand the test of time.

Most elections in Canada are decided on economic issues; if the economy is doing well and people have secure jobs, it takes something extraordinary for the voters to toss a sitting government out of office. The Conservatives had both the economy and the extraordinary issue working for them in September 1984. The economy had been in turmoil throughout the early 1980s. Five-year residential mortgages averaged about 14 percent in the months before the election. Inflation had been around 10 percent between 1980 and 1982 and had dipped to 5 percent only in 1984, when the economy slipped into recession. Unemployment remained above 10 percent. The National Energy Program in the West, squabbling between Ottawa and the Atlantic provinces (particularly Newfoundland), and the continued constitutional impasse with Quebec all worked against the Liberals.

The Conservatives also had patronage as the extraordinary issue going into the campaign. As is the case for any government so long in power, the Liberals had many friends who wanted their reward as the leadership of the party changed. Reportedly, there was a list of hundreds of full- and part-time appointments circulating within the Prime Minister's Office in Trudeau's final days as Liberal leader. Senior advisors, cabinet members, and party stalwarts were dispatched to the Senate, to Crown corporations, to government agencies, and to Canadian embassies abroad. It was an orgy of patronage, and in a naïve and foolish agreement with the departing Trudeau, those hoping to succeed him had agreed that the appointments should be announced only after the leadership convention. It was the Conservatives, however, who benefited from this decision, even if Mulroney had said

Conservative leader Brian Mulroney (right) won the 1984 leaders' debate when he confronted Liberal leader and prime minister John Turner (left) about Liberal patronage appointments before the election.

Source: CP PHOTO ARCHIVE/ Fred Chartrand.

September 4, 1984: Progressive Conservatives win a record 211 seats in Parliament. Brian Mulroney becomes Canada's 18th prime minister.

during the campaign that his government would only consider appointing Liberals if there was not a single Tory to be found in Canada.

In the televised leadership debate, Mulroney humiliated Turner on the patronage issue. The Liberal leader raised the matter hoping to cast the new Conservative leader as merely wanting power to reward his friends. Mulroney pointed his finger at Turner and chastised him for appointing so many of the Trudeau Liberals to patronage positions. Turner lamely responded that he had no option, giving Mulroney the opportunity to utter the defining phrase of the campaign: "You had an option, sir … You had an option, sir—to say no—and you chose to say yes to the old attitudes and the old stories of the Liberal party. That, sir, if I may say respectfully, that is not good enough for Canadians."[2] From that moment on, Mulroney dominated the campaign and the outcome was never in doubt.

New Ideas and New Approaches: Neoconservatism and Neoliberalism

Mulroney came to office at a time when many nations, notably the United Kingdom and the United States, had already begun to radically reform the role of the government. There was a clear move away from Keynesian economics (pioneered by British economist John Maynard Keynes), which had emerged in the period following the Second World War. Keynesianism was predicated on the notion that governments can play a crucial role in creating economic stability and generating growth. Throughout the post-war decades, this was largely proven to be the case. Canada embraced Keynesianism and enjoyed economic prosperity and continued growth, and its citizens enjoyed a fair measure of social well-being. Throughout the period, there was a huge growth both in the size of government and in the scale of its activities. When Canada and other countries encountered considerable economic difficulties in the late 1970s and early 1980s, many wondered if Keynesianism had been taken too far.

Many wondered, too, if there was a better way to promote economic growth and secure personal liberty. Some people lost faith in government's ability to grow the economy and began to suggest that too much government intervention was inefficient and wasteful. Many came to believe that government was part of the problem. This ideology had started to emerge in the political discourse in the early 1970s and elements of it were evident in Canada as early as the mid-1970s, when Trudeau had become concerned about the rising deficit, slashed government spending, introduced such policies as the income-tested Child Tax Credit in 1978, and began to consider free trade with the United States.

The terms "neoconservatism" and "neoliberalism" have been most generally used to describe the period beginning with the election of the Conservative government in 1984 and lasting until the financial crisis in 2007. Critics of the Mulroney government used "neoconservative" or "neocon" to describe it, but the accuracy of such an ideological label is questionable. Neoconservatism was perhaps best exemplified in the policies and rhetoric of Margaret Thatcher, who was elected prime minster of the United Kingdom in 1979, and Ronald Reagan, who became president of the United States in 1981. The term emerged in the United States to describe the expansion of American military power and the deepening ideological warfare against communist regimes around the world, particularly in Reagan's rejection of détente with the Soviet Union and his support for anti-communist insurgencies worldwide. Neoconservatism also contained an element of social morality; it feared a decline in individualism and the loss of a commitment to civic consciousness that it believed was threatened through such government programs as minority quotas, preferential hiring, and an overly generous welfare state. Numerous neoconservatives attacked feminism, gay activism, the labour movement, and the alleged triumph of "political correctness" in many institutions.

Neoliberalism would be a more appropriate term to describe the new approach to governing in Canada that was embraced, first by the Mulroney Conservatives and later by the Liberal party when it was returned to office in 1993. On the national political scene, Canadian neoconservatives coalesced around the populist Reform Party of Canada that emerged in Western Canada in 1987, notably in Alberta, and tended to support socially conservative policies that emphasized traditional morality and to oppose such policies as same-sex marriages and gun control. It also advocated greater direct democracy and opposed official bilingualism. Provincially, neoconservatives figured prominently in the governments of Alberta and Ontario in the 1990s.

The neoliberal agenda emphasized trade and financial liberalization, privatization of government-run industries, deregulation, openness to foreign direct investment, trade liberalization and freer trade, fiscal responsibility (balanced budgets), and lower taxes, and favoured smaller government. Neoliberals wanted to reform the social-democratic welfare state that emerged in the post-war period by making it more efficient, and they placed considerable hope for greater equality in society by targeting benefits to those in greatest need. As well, they wanted to tie social assistance and unemployment benefits to retraining to encourage participation of all eligible citizens in the labour market. Neoliberalism ushered in an era where the rule of the market place would play a prominent role in all facets of Canadian life. Neoliberals also believed in a new international paradigm where international trade would spawn global growth, and they believed that such organization as the World Trade Organization, the International Monetary Fund, the World Bank, and others would set rules for fair and efficient world trade, believing that global trade would benefit all nations.

Mulroney was not an ideologue in the tradition of British Prime Minister Margaret Thatcher or American President Ronald Reagan. While Mulroney embraced some neoliberal policies, particularly free trade and privatizations, he maintained social spending and was often ambiguous about deficits and taxation. Many of his critics used his policies of close economic relations with the United States as the basis of their accusations of his neoconservative ideology, but the United States had been Canada's strategic ally and primary trading partner for decades. As a labour lawyer, he was skilled in the art of negotiation and compromise. He knew that in Canada compromise, reconciliation, and equity were the principles that had been the trademarks of most successful prime ministers. He understood that Canada was a negotiated nation, one where the state had a role to play. At the beginning of his mandate, however, he was determined to find a different balance between the public and private sectors that had largely prevailed since the 1950s. Mulroney opted for a middle-of-the-road approach, one that followed some of the general tenants of the Thatcher-Reagan revolution to reduce the role of government and increase individual self-reliance but that kept in place much of the welfare state that had been constructed in the post-war period.

New Government, New Direction

The Mulroney government revealed its plans in a White Paper entitled *A New Direction for Canada: An Agenda for Economic Renewal* shortly after it assumed office. In it, Finance Minister Michael Wilson wrote that "refusing change is no longer an option for Canada. If Canadians recoil from the very idea of change ... Canada will be deflected off course in its search for solutions, and for renewal." The government outlined a series of initiatives aimed at strengthening the nation through reconciliation, a decentralized federation, debt and deficit reduction, regional equalization, improvement in Canada–U.S. relations, a greater role for free enterprise and the market, and economic renewal. This approach was about bringing a more entrepreneurial spirit in Canada that the government believed was critical if the country was to maintain, and even improve, its standard of living.

Controlling the burgeoning public debt soon became one of the government's primary focuses and a major preoccupation of opposition parties, think-tanks, the media, and Canadians too. Beginning in the early 1980s and continuing for the next quarter century, the debt (the accumulated annual deficits, which are the difference between government revenue and expenditure) as crisis became an ideology—a problem that had to be solved or the nation faced imminent disaster. Debt was nothing new to Canada: As shown in Figure 11.1, over the generation preceding Mulroney as prime minister, the country had

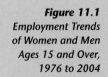

Figure 11.1
Employment Trends of Women and Men Ages 15 and Over, 1976 to 2004

As this figure shows, Canada's federal debt increased substantially beginning in the early 1990s.

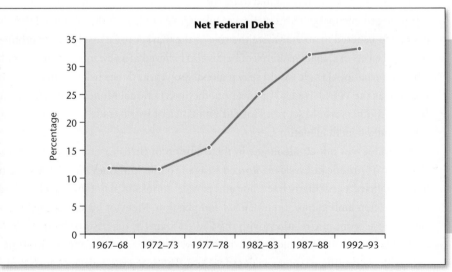

Source: © Department of Finance. Reproduced with the permission of the Minister of Public Works and Government Services, 2010.

incurred a huge debt. In fiscal 1968, the federal debt was $18 billion, or 26 percent of the gross domestic product (GDP); in the year before the Conservatives were elected, the debt was $206 billion, or 46 percent of the GDP. In fiscal 1984—the last year of Trudeau's government—the federal government's expenditures exceeded revenue collected by more than 50 percent. The federal deficit that year was $38.5 billion. Many Canadians were worried that interest payments on the debt consumed nearly one-third of every dollar that Ottawa collected and that amount was growing. The crisis emerged when Canadians and their governments concluded that with the deteriorating fiscal situation, the level of services to which they had grown accustomed might not be sustainable if the level of government spending continued unabated. The federal government had reduced the deficit to $19 billion in fiscal 1988, but it rose to $34 billion again in fiscal 1993. Between 1984 and 1993, the government failed to eliminate the deficit; in fact, during that time, the national debt grew by nearly $300 billion. This amount did not go to new government spending but was used for interest payments on the debt accumulated in the period before 1984. Government spending decreased by $14 billion during the period.

The government's first strategy to deal with the fiscal problem was to reduce the difference between program expenditure and tax collection (the primary deficit). It accomplished this through a combination of tax increases and cuts to government programs that were initially phased in over three years. The government increased revenue by increasing taxes (including the introduction of surtaxes and a minimum federal tax), which disappointed many who had hoped for lower taxes with the Tories; the government eliminated the home ownership savings plan and began partial de-indexing of some social programs. The budget phased out a number of programs, announced the sale of a number of Crown corporations, and substantially reduced grants and subsidies to business. Many of the tax increases were at odds with the Thatcher-Reagan revolution. Privatization reduced employment at the federal level by about 90 000 employees, though the cuts—Canadians were reassured—were supposed to increase economic efficiency and growth.

By 1987, the government had started to back away from its tough deficit reduction measures. However, it introduced a number of budgetary changes that proved both lasting and controversial. First, it reformed a number of universal transfer payments, including family allowances and old age pensions, replaced tax deductions with tax credits, and targeted some of the savings to lower-income Canadians. It also introduced a Goods and Services Tax (GST), a national tax of 7 percent, to replace the existing Manufacturers Sales Tax (MST), that had been levied at the wholesale level on manufactured goods. Both programs were to be revenue-neutral in that they were not designed to increase revenue or to reduce spending.

The sales tax reforms were welcomed by businesses that believed that the MST was a bad tax, as it penalized exporters and producers of goods manufactured in Canada while favouring imported goods, which were not taxed. However, Canadians hated the GST because it was seen as a new and direct tax on most goods and services, and it was one of the reasons Canadians turned so viciously against the Mulroney Conservatives. All ten provinces, the major opposition parties, and lobby groups, such as the Pro-Canada Network, a broad-based coalition of labour and social groups, joined the protest, claiming that the tax would harm lower-income Canadians, as it would add $15 per week to the budget for a family of four.

May 23, 1985: Finance Minister Michael Wilson delivers first budget and announces plan to de-index old age pension.

One poll showed that 80 percent of Canadians objected to the new tax measures. In the three days before the vote on the GST in Parliament, 1.7 million Canadians sent GST protest cards to their MPs. After a noisy and acrimonious debate in the House of Commons, the government passed the bill and the GST came into effect on January 1, 1991. The province of Alberta, which had no provincial sales tax, challenged the constitutionality of the GST, but the Supreme Court of Canada ruled that the measure was permitted under the federal taxing power as defined in section 91(3) of the *Constitution Act, 1867*. By the end of the 1990s, the GST accounted for slightly more than 15 percent of all federal tax revenues, and it became a major weapon after 1993 in the Liberal arsenal to eliminate the deficit.

The fiscal relationship between Ottawa and the provinces also changed as a part of the government's deficit reduction strategy. Ottawa had transferred funds to the provincial governments in support of health and post-secondary education for a generation. Since 1977, the Established Program Financing (EPF) provided block funding independent of provincial expenditures through a complicated system of cash transfers and tax points whereby the federal government reduced its tax rates and the provinces increased theirs. The transfers were initially designed to mirror increases in the rate of growth of GDP. In the economically challenging early 1980s, the Trudeau government had limited Ottawa's increase to its 5 and 6 percent austerity program, effectively reducing the size of the federal cash transfer. Mulroney continued this policy of reducing the rate of growth of the total transfer and effectively transferred some of the cost of fighting the deficit to the provinces. The period brought a new approach to intergovernmental relations that was confrontational and contested that had Ottawa unilaterally off-loading programs to the provinces and withdrawing federal monies from a variety of health and social services. Some social scientists have labelled this approach as social policy based on "stealth."

Social Policy in a Period of Retrenchment

Since the Second World War, Canadians had placed great faith in the state to try to solve most of the social ills that the country faced. There was widespread support for the development of social programs to help families with raising their children, to provide a measure of protection against unemployment, and to fund a series of programs offering a measure of protection against ill health and old age. By the 1980s, Canadians were worried about the state's ability to provide for their well-being. Even though the Conservatives maintained that Canada's social safety net was a "sacred trust," during the decade that they held office, there was a noticeable change in Canada's welfare state. It moved from a system based on universal access and financial entitlements for all Canadians to one that was decidedly neoliberal and emphasized the payment of social programs based on need. Yet, the government did not simply dismantle the welfare state.

This was a period of shifting social policy regimes around the globe, and the Canadian government believed that a number of the existing programs were simply ineffective and had to be reformed. It should be understood that Canada was not immune to international trends. Just as Canada adopted a new approach to social welfare after the Second World War in step with the United Kingdom and a host of other countries, Canada's reforms were also a part of the reorientation of social policy internationally. In the United Kingdom, the government introduced legislation limiting the rights of workers and brought labour unions to heel. Similarly, the U.S. government cut social programs in the name of market liberalism. In Canada, where social welfare played an important role in the national psyche, the government moved to reassure Canadians that the welfare state would not be dismantled. As Figure 11.2 illustrates, federal social spending did not decline during the Mulroney period. In constant 1992 dollars, spending on social programs increased from 1984 to 1993; it also increased as a percentage of total government expenditure and as a percentage of GDP. The Mulroney government wanted to be compassionate and caring, but it also vowed to manage more effectively the existing programs as it dealt with the burgeoning debt and fostered a program of economic growth. To do this, the government pursued a "strategy of containment rather than neo-conservative dismantlement," in the view of Michael J. Prince and J. Rice, who have written widely on this period.

Canada did this by changing the rates at which benefits were paid or the rates at which people were taxed. Many of these incremental changes came through the Department of Finance, such as through the *clawback* (paying benefits and then taxing all or a portion back) of family allowance and Old Age Security benefits. The federal government doubled the Child Care Expense Deduction (CCED) from $2000 to $4000 per year for children under six or with a disability and to $2000 for older children; in 1992, the CCED increased to a maximum of $5000 per child. The government also introduced legislation to create an additional 200 000 new child-care spaces that would create an expansion of child-care facilities for both the non-profit and the commercial sectors, as well as the use of the tax system that gave parents some choice over how they wanted their children cared for. Many child-care activists and women's organization opposed the plan, arguing that allowing such choice in the system would make the universal publicly funded system that many had advocated impossible. The bill died on the order paper when the 1988 election was called and was not revived in the government's second mandate.

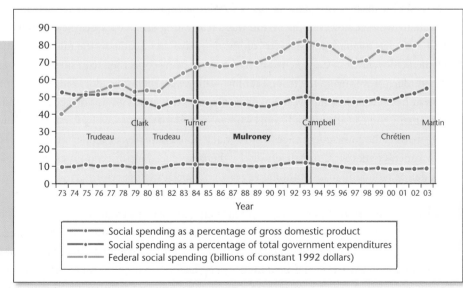

Figure 11.2
Federal Social Spending

Contrary to popular belief, federal social spending increased during the period Mulroney was prime minister.

Source: *Transforming a Nation*. McGill-Queen's Press.

There were also significant changes made to the unemployment insurance (UI) program. While benefits were improved for maternity, sickness, and parental leave, and coverage began for workers over 65 to comply with the Canadian Charter of Rights and Freedoms, some of the reforms brought fundamental change to the program that had been first introduced in 1940. The government wanted to remove disincentives to work and foster greater attachment to the labour force; they stopped contributing to the UI Account for regions that faced particularly difficult employment prospects. Ottawa ended the five-decade practice of funding unemployment insurance in Canada and placed the total burden on employees and employers. Not surprisingly, premiums paid by workers and employers increased substantially from 1990 to 1992 to offset the $2.9 billion that the federal government withdrew from the program. The federal government also increased the penalty for those who quit their job voluntarily, causing an outcry particularly from women's groups that such a policy would penalize those who were fleeing sexual harassment in the workplace.

There was a shift from universality to selectivity in social programs, as the government believed that a well-managed program provided assistance to those most in need. Because of this, the government moved to end universal family allowance benefits that had been paid to mothers for their children since 1945 in favour of increased benefits for lower-income Canadians. The government also abolished universality of the Old Age Security program in 1991. Directing funds to those most in need might explain why both poverty and income inequality declined during the Mulroney years. The period represented a shift in the approach to social welfare that continued with abandon after the Liberals returned to power in 1993.

Feminists on the Defensive

Women's groups were hopeful going into the 1984 election campaign. More than 200 women stepped forward as candidates and all three party leaders agreed to participate in a debate on women's issues. Twenty-seven candidates won election, including 19 Conservatives, the most ever for any party in Canadian history. Mulroney appointed six women to his cabinet. For many women, however, the period was a frustrating one. As political scientist Sylvia Bashevkin has noted, feminists were "on the defensive" in Canada. By the mid-1980s, the women's movement in Canada had moved beyond being concerned with such matters as the number of women in the federal cabinet—they were intent on addressing systematic discrimination and substantive inequalities. Organized women's groups moved away from what many had considered traditional women's issues to become involved in many of the core items in the government's agenda that many would have seen as gender-neutral issues.

Women's issues were overshadowed by the large questions of economics, trade policy, deficit reduction, constitutional reform, and social welfare reform. At a time when governments were intent on reducing the role of the state, it was not surprising that many women's groups were disappointed with their accomplishments. There was no greater disappointment than with the issue of violence against women. The magnitude of the problem had been made amply clear in 1989 when a young man, embittered by his hatred of feminists, murdered 14 female engineering students at the École Polytechnique in Montreal. The Montreal Massacre, as it became known, moved recognition of

December 6, 1989: Fourteen women are murdered in Montreal Massacre at École Polytechnique.

violence against women into mainstream society. In a response to a petition from women's groups across the country, the government promised in 1991 a blue-ribbon panel to undertake an enquiry into violence against women. Women's groups demanded a royal commission, however. As the Conservative tenure was coming to an end in 1993, the Canadian Panel on Violence Against Women issued its report, *Changing the Landscape: Ending Violence—Achieving Equality.* While the report provided a comprehensive documentation of violence against women and concluded that violence could only be eliminated when women were finally equal to men, many women's groups were disappointed with the report because it did not provide either a timetable or a strategy for implementing its 400 recommendations, and the government was not bound by the report's findings.

Each year, students like Simon Lacombe place flowers to mark the anniversary of the Montreal Massacre.

Source: CP Images

Nevertheless, the period saw continued advances for women's equality and women's rights that had become one of the hallmarks of the era. The dramatic growth in the share of women in the paid workforce continued to increase, as shown in Figure 11.3. In 1984, 47.7 percent of women 15 and over were employed in the workforce; that number grew to 51.6 percent by 1993. Similarly, women continued to make gains as a percentage of the workforce, moving from 42 percent when Mulroney was elected to 45 percent when his government was defeated. Women also saw a marked increase in their numbers in management and professional roles: In 1987, women occupied 28 percent of managerial positions but by 1993 held down 35 percent, although that number also reflected the difficulty women had moving into traditional male roles. In the professions, women increased their share from 49.8 to 52 percent, though women also continued to overwhelmingly occupy clerical and administrative roles. Increasing numbers of women with children

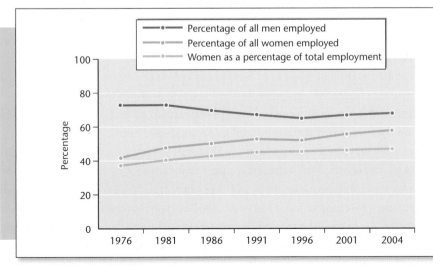

Figure 11.3
Employment Trends of Women Ages 15 and Over, 1976 to 2004

Women's increased participation in the paid labour force has been one of the most significant social trends in recent Canadian history. This graph shows the sharp rise in the employment of women after the 1970s.

Source: © Statistics Canada 2010.

continued to work outside the home: In 1983, 49.9 percent of all women with children under age 16 were in the labour force, but the number jumped to 62.8 percent in 1993. Not all women enjoyed the same gains, though. The number of lone female parents in the labour force remained static at about 50 percent, while the number of women with partners jumped from 51 percent to 65 percent. The numbers of women between the ages of 15 and 24 equalled that of men in paid labour, but those women between 55 and 64 had participation rates way behind those of men of similar age.[3]

The equality provisions of the Charter of Rights and Freedoms enacted in 1982 came into force in 1985, offering additional protection for women in Canadian society. The Royal Commission on Equality in Employment, headed by Judge Rosalie Abella, issued its report shortly after the Conservatives were elected. The report called for a massive policy intervention to solve the problem of women's inequality. The federal government responded with a new *Employment Equity Act* in 1986 to address inequalities of four target groups: women, people with disabilities, Aboriginal peoples, and visible minorities. The legislation covered the federal civil service as well as federally regulated employers with more than 100 employees doing business with the government through the Federal Contractors Program. The Act required employers to produce an annual report showing how the target groups fared in terms of participation rates, occupational distribution, and salary comparisons, as well as plan for the greater representation of the four groups in the organization.

Women also made important gains through the courts. The Supreme Court of Canada struck down certain restrictions with respect to abortion found in section 251 of the *Criminal Code*, which it claimed violated women's rights to "life, liberty and security of the person" because of the lack of access and delays in the operation of the abortion system in Canada. The Court also offered a new interpretation of "maternity" benefits when it ruled that the 15-week benefit period at the birth of a child could not be denied to the father. The government subsequently introduced a 10-week parental benefit leave, available to either parent, in addition to the 15 weeks available to the mother.

One of the most important changes came for Aboriginal women in 1985 when the Mulroney government removed the discriminatory provisions of the *Indian Act* that had stripped women of their legal status when they married outside their race. Although the Supreme Court had upheld the law in a divided decision in 1973, the ruling proved to be very controversial and certainly did not settle the issue. Sandra Lovelace, a Maliseet woman from the Tobique Reserve in New Brunswick, was instrumental in forcing the government to change the legislation. She had married an American soldier and moved to the United States in 1970, but when the marriage ended a few years later she returned home and discovered that she and her children were denied housing, education, healthcare, and other services provided to those with status under Canada's *Indian Act*. Under the 1869 legislation, the legal status of women was determined by the male head of the household. What this meant, in effect, was that women, such as Lovelace, who married non-status men lost their status at marriage. Two Aboriginal women's organizations, the Indian Rights for Indian Women and National Native Women's Association, were determined to change the law. With the support of National Action Committee on the Status of Women (NAC) and the Voice of Women, they waged a vigorous campaign but with little success, until 1977 when Lovelace joined the group. She took the matter to the Human Rights Committee of the United Nations, which ruled in 1981 that Canada was violating the International Covenant on Civil and Political Rights by insisting on the legislation. In 1985, the Mulroney government unilaterally passed Bill C-31, an *Act to Amend the Indian Act*—despite opposition from some bands: First Nations women who married non-status men no longer lost their status, nor did their children.

However, the organized women's movement found itself in conflict with the federal government at nearly every turn. This was in part an expected outcome of a more left-wing feminism that found itself in conflict with a government that believed the state had been poor managers and placed considerable faith in the marketplace. Most feminist groups saw the state as being a positive force in society that could regulate the workplace, provide social and health benefits, and help ensure a greater measure of equality for women. The Conservatives, on the other hand, were concerned not only with the fiscal realities but also with the efficiency and limits of social programs and other types of state support. It was a classic clash of ideologies. The conflict between the National Action Committee on the Status of Women, the major women's organization in Canada, and the Mulroney government over free trade indicates how difficult the relationship was between the state and women's groups. NAC had passed a resolution opposing free trade at its annual convention in 1984 after it became apparent that the Royal Commission on Canada's Economic Prospects (the *Macdonald Report*) would recommend a free trade agreement with the United States. NAC was also a founding member of the Council of Canadians, one of the groups in the social movement that sprang up to oppose free trade. In fact, the first anti–free trade coalition held its inaugural meeting at NAC offices in Toronto, and free trade became one of the first mainstream economic issues in which women's groups played a leading role. Women's groups opposed free trade because they feared that the sectors of the economy, such as clothing and textiles, where women predominated would be most affected by the removal of tariffs, and because they feared that trade harmonization with the United States would adversely impact social programs. Women's groups were also at the forefront of bringing public attention to the implications of increased globalization and international agreements, such as the North American Free Trade Agreement, on Canadian society, which was being considered as Mulroney left office.

The relationship between women's groups and the government worsened in the Conservatives' second term as it moved to deal more aggressively with the deteriorating economic situation and the growing debt. When Finance Minister Michael Wilson announced major budgetary cuts in the early 1990s, few sectors escaped unscathed; funding for women's centres, feminist organizations, and women's magazines were all cut. NAC had relied on the federal government for nearly two-thirds of its funding, but that was reduced to about half after the cuts. But Ottawa supported other women's organizations, including REAL Women of Canada (Realistic, Equal, Active, for Life), that promised a different perspective from the established feminist organizations, such as NAC. For REAL women, the family was the most important social unit in society, and they believed that the role of motherhood should not be discouraged but rather supported through taxation and government policies. The government had come to consider NAC as just another lobby group—this was evident in the reduction in state funding and shift of support away from feminist groups to those more committed to traditional family values. In its effort to save more than $7 billion in spending, the government announced it would not proceed with retroactive pay settlements for pay equity primarily for women in the civil service. Retrenchment within the civil service also had a profound impact on women, as the civil service had provided in the preceding decade an important model in advancing gender and wage equality. In the social reform package there was a definite shift away from framing policy in terms of women and towards children, child development, and attachment to the labour force.

Leap of Faith: Free Trade with the Americans

A large group of academics and journalists assembled by the public policy magazine *Policy Options Politiques*[4] in 2003 rated Mulroney as the second most effective prime minister of the last 50 years, just behind Lester B. Pearson. The prime ministers were rated on unity and management of the federation, the economy and fiscal framework, foreign affairs and Canada's place in the world, and social policy and concern for Canadians. As Pearson had created a new "social" Canada, Mulroney ushered in a new "economic" Canada. Mulroney committed future governments to a fundamentally different Canada because of the Canada–U.S. Free Trade Agreement. At the time, many argued that Mulroney had no legitimacy to negotiate free trade with the Americans; after all, he had not campaigned on the issue in 1984. Moreover, he had opposed free trade during the Conservative leadership campaign. Once in power, though, he believed that free trade was one way to improve the Canadian economy and ensure prosperity.

By the mid-1970s, freer trade with the United States, at least as part of a larger system of multilateral trade, was finding its way back onto the Canadian agenda. One of the first groups to float the idea was the Economic Council of Canada (ECC) in its 1975 report *Looking Outward: A New Trade Strategy for Canada*. Like earlier proponents of free trade, the ECC linked free trade with increased productivity and economic prosperity. "Canadians are, in general," the report observed, "relatively complacent about the future of the country's economy, [believing that] Canada's economic outlook is that of a bountiful land growing ever more prosperous."[5] Given Canada's low productivity, its small internal market, an inadequate industrial plant size, and high tariffs, the ECC warned that the key factors contributing to sustainable economic growth and improving the material living standards of Canadians were missing. Free trade, it concluded, would help improve Canadian productivity in manufacturing through improved economies of scale when producing for a larger market. It would also encourage greater specialization and more innovation in Canada's industrial sector, which more than anything else would improve the economic and social well-being of Canadians.

There were several factors pushing Canada towards a renewed interest in some sort of trade agreement with the Americans. First, exports of natural resources, particularly to the United States, were finding new competition from developing nations and Canada felt it needed a secure market. Second, the Canadian economy was becoming more diversified and dependent on the U.S. market and could not afford to lose it. Third, investment and growth in the non-resource sectors of the economy meant that Canadian firms had to be more competitive to compete outside the protected domestic market that it had enjoyed for decades. Fourth, the American market was becoming increasingly protective and Canada needed certainty in at least one export market. Of course, the United States wanted guaranteed access to the vast oil reserves in Western Canada as its own oil and gas reserves declined rapidly. Canada was also becoming concerned about the creation of trading blocs, such as the European Union, and considered it advantageous to have one in North America.

When Mulroney became prime minister, senior officials in the government warned him that Canada's economic circumstances were bleak and that relations with the United States were in serious trouble. The government was greatly influenced by Derek Burney, assistant undersecretary for trade and economic policy in the Department of External Affairs and the author of "Trade Policy Review" in 1981–1982, which offered an assessment for the government of Canada–U.S. economic relations. The Liberal government of Pierre Trudeau was considering various options for Canada's trade with the United States. By 1983, it was clear that Trudeau's nationalist policies, which had resulted in the creation of the Canada Development Corporation (1971), the Foreign Investment Review Agency (1973), and the National Energy Program (1980), as well as his much-vaunted "Third Option" to reduce Canada's dependence on trade with the United States in favour of enhanced economic links with Asia Pacific and the European Community, had largely failed. The Liberal government had begun to discuss the prospects of sectoral free trade with the Americans as the NEP and rising protectionism in the United States jeopardized Canada's trading relations with its southern neighbour. When International Trade Minister Gerald Regan released his department's review of Canada's trade policy on August 31, 1983, "he proclaimed the death of the third option and the dawning of a new era in trade relations with the United States."[6] A major royal commission appointed by the Liberals and headed by Donald Macdonald, a former Liberal finance minister, recommended a bilateral Canada–U.S. free trade agreement. The Canadian Manufacturers' Association, long the major voice of central Canadian protectionism and long opposed to free trade, changed its position. Canadians also seemed supportive, as public opinion polls showed that a majority favoured a free trade deal with the United States, even though some surveys warned that many Canadians saw potential problems in such an economic arrangement and continued to worry that Canadian sovereignty might be adversely affected.

After months of internal study and debate, public consultations, and media scrutiny of free trade, the government announced on September 26, 1985, that Canada would seek a bilateral trade agreement with the United States, in part, to protect Canadian exporters from growing protectionism in the United States. It would be nearly three years before an agreement was negotiated between Canada and the United States. There was very little symmetry between the two nations, as Canada needed American markets more than the United States needed the Canadian one, except for oil and other sources of energy. As a result, Canada was disadvantaged throughout the entire round of negotiations. President Ronald Reagan had adopted a policy of "managed trade" to solve the trade imbalance between the United States and Japan, and he and Mulroney were both committed to the bilateral trade deal. The Conservatives introduced the legislation for the trade deal in the House of Commons in June 1988.

Reaction to the Canada–U.S. Free Trade Agreement

The regional cleavages were immediately evident on the free trade issue. The West and Atlantic Canada generally supported free trade. Both regions had long resented the economic dominance of Central Canada, which had benefited enormously under the protection provided by the National Policy, and they had long demanded freer trade with the United States. The West, especially the province of Alberta, was also philosophically and ideologically predisposed to closer economic relations with the United States. Although Ontario had benefited immensely from the Auto Pact, it remained worried that free trade would have a detrimental impact on many of the manufacturing firms in the province. In Quebec, where much of the Canada's textile, footwear, and clothing was established, there was also considerable fear of the impact of free trade in those quarters, but it did not share Ontario's level of opposition. In fact, there was considerable support for free trade in the province. Many of those who saw free trade as leading to the destruction of Canadian culture were in Ontario.

The opposition to free trade was determined and fierce. It was not based primarily on economics and the fate of Canada's manufacturers, but on what the opponents of the Canada–U.S. deal feared would be the increasing Americanization of Canada and the further weakening of Canadian values, culture, and sovereignty. As political scientist Michael Hart has pointed out, the debate on free trade pitted a market-oriented internationalist view against a government-centred nationalist one. The opponents were able to invoke nationalism in their fight against free trade.

The opposition can be divided into two groups. First, there emerged a social movement combined of a multitude of groups who shared a common ideology and participated in a sustained campaign to defeat the Mulroney Conservatives and prevent the ratification of the Canada–U.S. free trade deal. Second, the two opposition parties—the Liberals and the New Democratic party—fought against the deal in Parliament and in an election campaign. The social movement included a coalition of what might be called populist groups concerned with a variety of issues—culture, healthcare, environmental protection, gender equality, and other largely non-economic concerns—that many believed would be threatened by greater continental integration. Most of these Canadian nationalists regarded the state as the primary defender against the continental forces led by the United States. Women, for example, led by the National Action Committee on the Status of Women believed that their equality would be best promoted by the state and any limitation placed on the state by the free trade agreement would jeopardize the progress they had made in recent years. They were worried that free trade would limit the ability of the federal government to improve and expand the welfare state. The social movement that fought free trade in 1988 was traditional in the sense that they were on the left of the political spectrum and wedded to the political system that called for the political mobilization of its members to defeat the government. A new social movement would emerge out of the free trade debate that would challenge the globalization movement of the 1990s and called for direct action of a new civil society.[7]

The Liberals (historically proponents of free trade) and the New Democrats also attacked free trade. Liberal leader John Turner warned that free trade "will finish Canada as we know it and replace it with a Canada that will become nothing more than a colony of the United States." It took 120 years to build the Confederation, he told the House of Commons, but Mulroney was going to destroy it in the time it took to sign his name.[8] Later, as the debate intensified, Turner warned that

> the price [for free trade] is our sovereignty, our freedom to make our own choices, to decide what is right for us, to go on building the kind of country we want. That freedom, that sovereignty, is our most valuable asset. When you strip away all the technical jargon of this deal, that is what the Government wants to give away, our freedom to be different, our freedom to be ourselves, to do things our own way, not the American way ... we do not want to become Americans."[9]

In August 1988, Turner announced that he had instructed the Liberal-dominated Senate not to ratify the implementation legislation for free trade until the Canadian people had had the opportunity to consider the matter in a general election. Mulroney had little choice but to ask the governor-general to dissolve Parliament and call an election to settle the debate. The election was essentially a referendum on free trade with the United States.

All three of the major political parties waged nationalist campaigns based largely on fear. For the Progressive Conservatives, the issue was nation-building and, in their continentalist approach one can argue that they were adopting a view that had long been envisioned by the Liberal party. As Mulroney told the press in front of Rideau Hall after the election writ was issued, "Our view of Canada is confident and outward looking. We see a country and world changing before us and we are determined to respond positively and aggressively to that change." Mulroney believed that free trade with the United States was an important step in nation-building, and throughout the campaign, he argued repeatedly that the deal would permit Canada to end some of the lingering problems with regional disparity, become a prosperous nation, and guarantee Canada's entry into the American market, which was becoming increasingly protective. He argued with equal fervour and passion that all the progressive legislation in social welfare, culture, foreign policy, and a host of other areas that Canada had introduced in the post-war era would be threatened without free trade. During the election campaign, several prominent artists, including Mary Pratt, Christopher Pratt, Alex Colville, and Morley Callaghan, among others, signed a national advertisement that appeared as "Artists and Writers for Free Trade—We Are Not Fragile." The pro–free trade Canadian Alliance for Trade and Job Opportunities noted in a full-page advertisement in the nation's newspapers that Canadian culture would not only survive but would thrive under free trade. Many of the country's largest businesses also supported free trade.

The Liberals and New Democrats attacked free trade, arguing that the agreement with the Americans would destroy everything Canadians had worked to achieve in their country, if not the country itself. Both parties told voters that free trade with the United States would undermine Canada's social security system, destroy pensions and healthcare, and reduce Canada to little more than a ward of the United States. Similarly, John Turner built his campaign on the Canadian government "selling out" Canada to the United States, and repeatedly warned Canadians that free trade would lead to the end of Canada as an independent, sovereign nation. At times it all got a little silly as Mulroney presented himself as "Brian the Builder" and took to describing Turner as "John the Ripper" after Turner threatened to tear up the free trade agreement.[10]

The Conservatives won a second consecutive majority government on the issue, and with their 1988 win became the first party in nearly three decades to win back-to-back majorities. Most of the headlines in newspapers and in radio and television news across the country saw the election outcome as support for free trade. The Conservatives captured 169 seats, compared with 82 for the Liberals and 44 for the New Democrats;[11] Atlantic Canada, Metropolitan Toronto, parts of Manitoba, and Saskatchewan voted against the Conservatives. In all, the Conservatives won only 43 percent of the popular vote, but the Liberal-dominated Senate had little choice but to pass the legislation implementing free trade. The agreement between Canada and the United States came into effect on January 1, 1989.

A New Dependence

The impact of the free trade deal has been staggering for the Canadian economy. In 1980, two-way bilateral trade in goods and services with the United States represented about 40 percent of Canadian GDP. By 2000, that figure had reached nearly 75 percent, and Canada–U.S. trade was valued at $700 billion annually or $2 billion dollars each day. About 30 000 trucks carrying a variety of goods crossed the border daily in 2000. The products that flowed across the border changed to include a much higher level of value-added and finished products. Two-way flows of foreign direct investment reached new highs of about $10 billion annually. All this activity meant that Canadians had become dependent on the U.S. market, which took about 85 percent of all of Canada's export of goods and services in 2000. Some economists have argued that Canada did not need a formal free trade agreement because a booming U.S. economy and the broader impact of globalization would have produced similar results. Others have argued that the free trade agreement helped to reorient Canadian producers from an east–west to a north–south axis. What it had done was integrate the Canadian economy with the American one. It also helped Canadian investors to direct more of their savings towards foreign opportunities, and in 1997 Canada became a net exporter of capital for the first time. Some economists have argued that this development was a sign of the emergence of a more mature and confident economy.

The Canada–U.S. Free Trade Agreement did not eliminate trade disputes between Canada and the United States. Because Canada did not get an exemption from the U.S. countervailing duties (additional import duties imposed by an importing country to offset subsidies granted by an exporting country to its export manufacturers) or anti-dumping duties (penalties imposed on abnormally low-priced imports), the agreement did not eliminate trade disagreements between the two countries. This remained for some time one of the most controversial aspects of the agreement for Canadians. What the agreement did provide, however, was a means of resolving conflict through Chapter 19 of the agreement dealing with anti-dumping and countervailing duties. Even with this clause, it was agreed that the new dispute settlement panels would apply the U.S. law and standard of review in the same manner as U.S. courts, even though in Canada the free trade agreement effectively takes precedence over other Canadian laws. With the exception of softwood lumber and durum wheat, the dispute settlement mechanism has worked fairly effectively, even though Canada has learned that protectionism in the United States makes poor economics but good politics, especially in election years. A recent review concluded that Chapter 19 dispute panels have produced outcomes more favourable to Canadian exporters than have U.S. courts.[12]

Ambiguity about Culture

Canadians wrestled with the issue of culture in their search for consensus, especially during debate over free trade between 1987 and 1988. Those who were opposed to free trade, including many in Canada's cultural and artistic community, argued that free trade would destroy Canadian culture. Yet some of the nation's best-known artists and writers, as noted earlier, were not at all worried. Novelist Mordecai Richler represented the views of those supporting free trade with an incendiary quip that "Nationalists are lobbying for the imposition of Canadian content quotas in our bookshops and theatres ... In a word, largely second-rate writers are demanding from Ottawa what talent had denied them, an audience."[13] Culture had become a major concern of governments by this time, however, and it was expected that the federal and provincial governments would have a strategy for dealing with it, especially as cultural activities became increasingly seen as an engine of economic growth.

Despite a promise that culture mattered, the Mulroney government never had a clear cultural policy. For instance, in 1985 it cut $75 million from the approximately $1.7 billion arts and culture budget, but it restored the money a year later. It then provided Telefilm Canada with $33 million to promote feature films and movies. As the Canadian television industry had flourished under the Canadian Broadcast Program Development Fund that had been introduced in 1984 and had spawned such television series as *Street Legal*, the film industry had lobbied hard for a similar fund for the film industry. Telefilm Canada received $85 million from 1986 to 1991 for the Feature Film Fund and an additional $102 million in 1992–1993.

The fund resulted in a number of new productions, but as the Liberal government had done earlier with the Broadcast Fund for television, the funding was intended to encourage the private sector to increase both the quantity and the quality of Canadian programming. Federal funding for film encouraged a laissez-faire approach to developing a national film industry. As a result of the new funding, Canadian filmmakers began to enter co-production agreements with the American industry and, as had happened in television, there was an enormous increase in production. Although the Canadian film industry became increasingly reliant on government subsidies and U.S. investment, it produced a number of remarkable and award-winning films, including *I've Heard the Mermaids Sing* (Patricia Rozema), *Jésus of Montréal* (Denys Arcand), and *The Adjuster* (Atom Egoyan). In 1988, the government created the Feature Film Distribution Fund, which made credit available to Canadian distributors to ensure the widest possible distribution of Canadian films. Despite a new *Broadcast Act* in 1991 promising that Canadian programming should be predominately and distinctively Canada and should contribute to shared national consciousness and identity, the government then reduced funding for the CBC by $276 million and closed a number of regional bureaus across the country. Funding was also reduced for the Department of Canadian Heritage that was responsible for promoting Canadian culture. Even so, from 1986 to 1990, the viewing of Canadian programs on English-language television during peak hours increased from 19.6 to 25.4 percent, and the viewing of drama nearly doubled from 2.4 to 4.0 percent. Canadian programs on French-language television had a significantly larger presence.

There were also many accomplishments in the cultural sector throughout the period. In February 1994, *Billboard* magazine wrote a story entitled "Oh Canada! One Nation Under a Groove" that highlighted the growing prominence of Canadian musicians, such as Celine Dion, Bryan Adams, Crash Test Dummies, Barenaked Ladies, and a host of others on the international music charts. These successes came in part because the federal government had imposed Canadian content in 1971 as a condition for licensing radio stations. A decade later, a number of private radio stations were concerned about the shortage of popular Canadian music and created the Fund to Assist Canadian Talent on Radio (FACTOR). In 1986, the federal government contributed to the sound-recording industry following a similar model as FACTOR. This was the type of public–private collaboration that the Mulroney government favoured.

There were other notable events and accomplishments in Canadian culture and sports. In 1984, Guy Laliberté and Daniel Gauthier created Cirque du Soleil, which combined street entertainment and circus arts, and grew into one of the most successful entertainment companies in Canadian history. Sprinter Ben Johnson, who had come to Canada as a child from Jamaica, set a world record for the 100-metre dash in 1987, and Canadians were excited about his winning gold at the Seoul Olympic Games in 1988. When he won the gold medal, Canadians were jubilant as Johnson came to represent the new multicultural spirit of Canada. However, when Johnson tested positive for anabolic steroids, he was stripped of the medal. A few days later, the *Toronto Globe and Mail* ran a cartoon with three sequential headlines: "Canadian Sprinter Wins Gold in 100 Metres"; "Jamaican-Canadian Athlete Tests Positive for Steroids"; "Jamaican Athlete Stripped of Gold Medal." The Canadian government appointed a Commission of Inquiry into the Use of Drugs and Banned Practices to Increase Athletic Performance (the Dubin Inquiry) to investigate the use of drugs in sports. It concluded that performance-enhancing drugs were common in all sports, and over the decade that followed it became clear that drug use was pervasive among high-performance and professional athletes. Still, Canadians celebrated the Winter Olympics in Calgary in 1988 and became wrapped up in baseball as the Toronto Blue Jays (which had became Canada's second major league professional team in 1977) became the first Canadian team to win the World Series, a feat it accomplished in 1992 and 1993.

Diplomatic Departures: Canadian Foreign Policy

If there was considerable ambiguity over culture during this period, the same could not be said about foreign policy. The decade saw major changes in foreign policy—it was here that the government proved itself both surprising and influential. There was little evidence before September 1984 that Canada could expect a major reorientation in its foreign policy under the Conservatives, but the following decade would see one of the most activist governments ever in Canadian foreign policy. Canada broke with a number of traditions in Canadian statecraft and took the country in a different policy direction from that of either the Pearson or the Trudeau Liberals. Most Canadians expected a different approach to Canada–U.S. relations, as Mulroney had promised to "refurbish" Canada's relationship with the United States. He promised to be a better friend to the Americans and give the United States the benefit of the doubt as friends are wont to do. For Mulroney, it was important that Canadians knew where he stood on particular foreign policy matters. When a Soviet fighter aircraft shot down Korean Airlines Flight 007, a passenger plane en route to Seoul, South Korea, from New York in September 1983, Mulroney called the incident that claimed 269 lives an act of cold-blooded murder; Trudeau, on the other hand, had simply called it "a tragic accident, an accident of war."[14] Mulroney promised to make Canada "a first-class nation" in the world. He appointed Joe Clark, the former prime minister, as the secretary of state for external affairs, or foreign minister, as the post was then called.

Mulroney believed that a close personal relationship between the prime minister and the U.S. president was essential to maintaining good relations between Canada and the United States. He established close friendships with both Ronald Reagan and George H.W. Bush, although many Canadians were uncomfortable with their cosiness. They did not take kindly to Mulroney, Reagan, and their wives joining hands on stage to sing "When Irish Eyes are Smiling" at the first summit meeting between the two leaders—known as the "Shamrock Summit"—held in Quebec City in March 1985, even if Mulroney enjoyed a level of access and influence in the White House rarely seen among Canadian prime ministers.

March 17, 1985: Mulroney hosts U.S. President Ronald Reagan in "Shamrock Summit" in Quebec City.

Still, this close relationship did not mean that Canadian–American relations were free from conflict. The reality was far from it. There were disputes over extraterritoriality on Cuba, American unilateralism towards international institutions, U.S. policy in Central America, intrusions on Canadian sovereignty in the Arctic, defence policy, and American contribution to acid rain falling in Canada. Throughout all these issues there was a sense that Canadian–American relations had to be *managed* somehow, however. This was evident, for instance, in the Strategic Defense Initiative (SDI), or "Star Wars" as it was dubbed by its critics. This was an American plan to develop a space-based defence shield against ballistic missile attack. While Mulroney appeared to personally favour the initiative, his government rejected the SDI after a parliamentary committee reviewing Canadian foreign policy recommended that Canada not participate. Even though the Canadian government rejected with what has been termed a "polite no" to minimize conflict between Ottawa and Washington, it allowed Canadian industries to participate in the project. When the United States refused to recognize Canada's territorial sovereignty claims over the Northwest Passage through the Arctic, Mulroney intervened with President Reagan and was able to negotiate the Arctic Cooperation Agreement in January 1988. Although the United States continued to press that the passage through the region was an international waterway, it agreed that it would seek Canadian consent before sending U.S. icebreakers through the region. But Mulroney declared the U.S. denial of Canada's claim to the Arctic "an unfriendly act," the two countries managed to find accommodation on many of the issues that divided them. Mulroney was also successful in convincing Reagan that the United States was a major contributor to the acid rain that was killing Canadian forests and streams. The two sides negotiated the Acid Rain Accord in 1991 that significantly reduced emissions from U.S. factories. This level of cooperation was a significant change after the frosty relationship Canada had with the United States during the Trudeau era.

Canada also joined the Organization of American States (OAS) in 1989, which was an indication of its commitment to fuller participation in the Americas; it hoped to bring greater multilateralism to the region. An observer at OAS since 1972, Canada had refused full membership because the organization was at the time quite polarized between the United States and many of the Latin American nations. Rather than having to take sides and alienate either the United States or the other members, Canada decided to stay outside the organization. Mulroney maintained that Canada could no longer maintain such a position as OAS members became more democratic and began to focus more on economic issues and trade. After joining the OAS, Canada found—as earlier governments had feared—that it would have to side either with the United States or with the Latin American members. When the United States invaded Panama and overthrew the dictator Manuel Noriega (whom the Americans had assisted for years) after the U.S. Drug and Enforcement Administration indicted him on drug charges, Canada was the only OAS member besides El Salvador to support the American invasion. However, Canada did not follow U.S. policy towards Cuba.

Another indication of the major new directions in Canadian foreign policy came when news broke of the famine in Ethiopia in October 1984, a few weeks after the Mulroney government took office. The situation in Ethiopia had been a long time in the making. Earlier, in 1983, the Trudeau government had rejected a proposal of emergency relief because it did not consider the situation sufficiently grave. When the CBC broadcast images from war-ravaged Ethiopia, the Canadian government responded in a way that represented a major shift in foreign policy. Instead of working through the Department of External Affairs or the Canadian International Development Agency, the government appointed a Canadian Emergency Co-ordinator for African Famine to organize the government's efforts. It also created a Special Fund for Africa and promised to match financial contributions from ordinary Canadians and brought non-governmental organizations into the process of making program allocation decisions—a first for a Canadian government. The government held a series of community meetings across Canada and involved ordinary members of Parliament when the Standing Committee on External Affairs and National Defence held hearings on famine relief in early 1985. The response to the crisis in Ethiopia demonstrated the government's willingness to open up the policy process to a broader public.

During this time, Canada also made important changes in its position on human rights. On the issue of apartheid in South Africa, the government wanted to end diplomatic relations with the regime in South Africa. This put the prime minister in direct opposition with Margaret Thatcher and Ronald Reagan, who both opposed sanctions against South Africa. Mulroney was the only G-7 leader favouring a tough stand on the country. Similarly, Canada angrily denounced the Tiananmen Square massacre of June 1989 in what was among the harshest statements ever by a Canadian government on an internal matter in a foreign country. The world watched the events unfold in Beijing, but Canadians who read the *Globe and Mail* were offered a unique perspective into the events from Jan Wong, a third-generation Chinese Canadian and the newspaper's correspondent in China. She watched the Chinese crackdown from her hotel room overlooking Tiananmen Square. Canada subsequently imposed sanctions against China that prevented all trade in arms. In the fall of 1991, Canada announced that human rights and good governance would be a "cornerstone of Canada's foreign policy," and that Canadian foreign aid would be conditional on the satisfactory performance of all recipients of aid of both human rights and good governance. Mulroney was particularly interested in children's issues and as co-chair of the World Summit for Children in 1990, he promised to put children's issues at the top of the international agenda.

There was also a rethinking in the Canadian government of the notion of national sovereignty, as the period saw a decline in wars between nations but a rise in bloody internal conflicts. One of the most vicious internal conflicts occurred in the Balkans in the early 1990s. Barbara McDougall, who had replaced Joe Clark as secretary of state for external affairs, said, "National sovereignty should offer no comfort to repressors, and no protection of those guilty of breaches of the common moral codes enshrined in the Universal Declaration of Human Rights." In 1991, Mulroney was the first Western leader to call for United Nations intervention in the growing civil war in Yugoslavia to impose a peace on the region; he also promised Canadian participation in such a mission. Mulroney also changed Canada's position on state sovereignty when his government openly supported the move for Ukrainian independence from Russia. Largely because of the threat of Quebec separatism, Canadian governments had traditionally avoided the issue of the possible disintegration of any state. Canada was so wary of such issues that during the Nigerian–Biafran War (1967–1970), Trudeau quipped, "Where's Biafra?" when a reporter asked him about Canada's policy towards the breakaway region. Canadian foreign policy had certainly changed. Also noteworthy was Canada's support of the U.S.-led war to evict Iraqi troops from Kuwait in January and February 1991, marking it the first time since the Korean War of 1950–1953 that a Canadian government had sent its military to war.

In defence policy, the Canadian government was concerned primarily with Canada's sovereignty and credibility. The government issued a discussion paper on defence, the first since 1971 that promised change through the maintenance of strategic deterrence, credible conventional defence, and the protection of Canadian sovereignty. Canadians have since forgotten that the world was a dangerous place in the 1980s before the fall of communism. It was not uncommon during the period for Soviet fishing trawlers, called "tattletales," which fished off Canada's east coast, to interfere with Canadian army exercises at Canadian Forces Base Gagetown, New Brunswick, by intercepting, jamming, and manipulating communications. The government never promoted Canada as a pseudo-neutral in the Cold War, and even participated in several covert activities internationally during the 1980s. Canadian forces often lent support to groups fighting communism in the Developing World and were known to airlift seriously injured Afghan mujahedeen fighting the pro-Soviet Afghan government to Canada for specialized medical treatment. However, the government's need to cut spending to deal with the massive debt, combined with the collapse of the Soviet communist system, meant that many of the plans for spending on defence were not followed through, and the planned purchases for the Canadian Navy and the land forces, for instance, were either scaled back or cancelled. The fiscal crisis and the peace dividend of 1990 meant that there were few new priorities in defence policy. The Canadian forces were, in fact, reduced in size from 86 000 to 76 000 between 1986 and 1993, even though military expenditure as a percentage of GDP remained unchanged at 2.1 percent.

A new form of peacekeeping that was more akin to peacemaking emerged during this period. Canada despatched a mechanized infantry battalion to Croatia in 1991 and subsequently moved it to Bosnia to secure the airhead at Sarajevo International Airport. Canada also deployed the Canadian Airborne Regiment to Somalia, but the brutal 1993 beating death of a Somali teenager, Shidane Arone, by two Canadian soldiers shocked Canadians and raised serious questions about the elite forces in Canada's military and the nature of peacekeeping. Those military operations had changed and, as Somalia demonstrated, the Canadian Forces had much to learn about planning, command and control, joint operations, and training in the post–Cold War world. In part because of Somalia and the hope for new world order that would see the international community join in the pursuit of justice and the quest for peace and prosperity after the end of hostilities with the Soviet Union, Canada hoped that large conventional forces would be less important, but it might require its elite military units for deployment in troubled areas around the world.

Consequently, Canada created the Joint Task Force 2 (JTF2) in the spring of 1993. It consisted of volunteers from the three branches of the Canadian Armed Forces and took over the counter-terrorist duties from the Royal Canadian Mounted Police. JTF2 was modelled on Britain's Special Air Service (SAS) and the super-elite American Delta Force. It could be deployed to troubled spots instantly and operate with stealth and deadly force. (The unit would come to prominence after September 11, 2001, and the emergence of the Al Qaeda network.) In 1985, Canada had its first encounter with "non-state actors" that would rise to international prominence in the 1990s, when terrorists placed a bomb on Air India Flight 182 departing from Vancouver on June 22, 1985, killing 329 people, making it Canada's worst case of mass murder. The army was also deployed as an Aid of the Civil Power to deal with what the media called the "Mohawk civil war" at Akwasasne, near Cornwall, Ontario, and at Khanesatake, south of Montreal, where a land dispute between the municipal authorities and the Khanesatake Mohawk nation escalated into a violent confrontation in 1991.

Constitutional Reconciliation: Triumph and Failure

During Mulroney's nine-year term as prime minister, the debate over the Constitution might have replaced hockey as the national pastime. When the Conservatives rolled into Ottawa, they promised national reconciliation and, for the government, an important part of this was bringing Quebec into the Constitution and finishing the business not completed in 1982. One can argue that with the defeat of the Parti Québécois in 1985 by a rejuvenated Robert Bourassa and his Liberal party, constitutional matters were pushed from centre stage where they had been for much of Trudeau's term as prime minister. Some have seen Mulroney's attempt to have Quebec sign the Constitution as an egotistical desire on the part of the prime minister to best Pierre Trudeau. This view ignores Bourassa's promise to the electorate of Quebec to make constitutional reform one of the most important policies in his party's platform. Bourassa had laid out five minimum conditions for Quebec's acceptance of the *Constitution Act* of 1982: explicit recognition of Quebec as a distinct society; increased powers over immigration; limitation of federal spending power; recognition of Quebec's traditional veto rights; and participation in the appointment of Supreme Court judges.

Moreover, the Quebec government warned the rest of Canada that "Quebec nationalism is not dead.... It is thriving more than ever but in a different form. It is no longer synonymous with isolation or xenophobia, but rather with excellence."[15] The other premiers supported Quebec's position and wanted to bring some measure of closure to the constitutional discussions of the previous two decades. Of course, Mulroney believed that it was incumbent upon the national government to bring a measure of harmony to Canadian federalism that had been lacking for much of the previous decade.

What Canada's political leaders had forgotten when they began their discussion of the Constitution in the late 1980s was that the political culture of Canada had changed in the short time since the patriation of the Constitution in 1982. The constitutional process that had been ongoing intermittently since Confederation in 1867 and had reached its zenith in Trudeau's final term as prime minister exposed two important tenets of Canadian democracy and our conception of federalism. First, the adoption of the Canadian Charter of Rights and Freedom created among Canadians, especially among the equality groups identified in section 15 (multicultural, linguistic-minority, Aboriginal, and women), the sense that all Canadians had fundamental rights that could not be tampered with. Fundamental to this, was the notion of equality of all citizens and no special rights for anyone. Second, the Constitution had committed Canada to the notion of equality of the provinces and no single province—not even Quebec—had a veto over proposed constitutional changes. Since the 1960s, Quebec had demanded that it be empowered with jurisdictional powers that the other provinces did not have—special status, in other words—to preserve its distinctiveness. Most of English-speaking Canada was not prepared to accept Quebec's demands. The *Constitution Act, 1982* did not recognize the distinctiveness of Quebec or provide Quebec with the right of veto over further constitutional change. Moreover, the model of elite accommodation of intergovernmental relations and constitutional change that had been in place since Confederation was obsolete by the time Mulroney came to office. After more than two decades of trying to meet Quebec's aspirations, many English-speaking Canadians were less than enthusiastic about restarting conversations regarding the Constitution, with the aim of having their governments accommodate Quebec's wishes.

When in April 1987 Mulroney and the premiers began the process of trying to secure Quebec's acceptance of the 1982 Constitution, they reverted to the traditional method of intergovernmental negotiations: 11 men in suits negotiating behind closed doors. On June 3, 1987, however, they successfully negotiated a new constitutional package that became known as the Meech Lake Accord. If ratified, it would have Quebec accepting the constitutional amendments negotiated in 1982. That this arrangement of "11 men in suits" was unacceptable became the default position of many of those that came forward to oppose the Meech Lake Accord, but it had succeeded in getting Quebec to agree to sign on to the Constitution. The price for agreement was a radical decentralization of the Canadian federation and a strengthening of the role of the provinces. That, too, had its critics.

The Meech Lake Accord has two essential parts. The first recognized Quebec as a distinct society, even as it emphasized the principle of equality of all the provinces. It also recognized the duality of Canada by acknowledging that the English-speaking minority in Quebec and the French-speaking minority in the rest of Canada contributed to a fundamental characteristic of Canada. The second section increased the relative powers of the provinces against those of the federal government. The Accord gave the provinces a role in the nomination of Supreme Court judges and appointments to the Senate, limited the power of the federal government to spend on national programs, and agreed to provide financial compensation to those provinces that did not participate in a national program initiated by the federal government. It also called for an annual constitutional conference to discuss such issues as Senate reform (particularly important to Alberta) and the roles and responsibilities in the fisheries (particularly important to Newfoundland) and gave the provinces much greater power over immigration. All premiers and the prime minister agreed to the constitutional amendment, but the sticky part was that all provincial legislatures had to ratify the Accord.

Aside from the process, many of the opponents argued that the "distinct society" clause that was to become section 2 of the Constitution was an assault on the equality principle that Canadians had come to see as basic to their liberal democracy. This clause stated that "The Constitution of Canada shall be interpreted in a manner consistent with ... (b) the recognition that Quebec constitutes within Canada a distinct society.... The role of the legislature and Government of Quebec to preserve and promote the distinct identity of Quebec ... is affirmed." This was the clause that generated the fiercest criticism. The contradictory messages coming from the leaders also worried many Canadians. The Quebec premier said that the amendment was an important gain for the province, but in English-speaking Canada, Canadians were told that the clause brought non-substantive change to the Constitution.

Difficulties aside, Canadians had welcomed the Meech Lake Accord when it was first announced. Polls indicated that the public was in favour. Both the Liberals and the NDP in the House of Commons supported the deal. The early criticism came largely from academics, but when Pierre Trudeau returned to oppose the Accord, the opposition to it mushroomed. Many women's groups in English-speaking Canada opposed the Accord for fear that special status for Quebec would jeopardize the equality rights for Quebec women, though, ironically, women in Quebec did not share those concerns.

What the framers of Meech did not anticipate was that some of the architects would be gone before the Accord could be ratified. The Progressive Conservative government of New Brunswick was the first to fall when Liberal newcomer Frank McKenna swept every seat in the province on October 13, 1987. Then, Howard Pawley lost in Manitoba to be replaced by Conservative Gary Filmon. In that election, Liberal leader Sharon Carstairs won 20 seats in the minority legislature. Perhaps, most important, Clyde Wells defeated the Conservative government in Newfoundland. This brought three premiers to office that had not participated in negotiating the Meech Lake Accord, and all three were worried about the decentralizing intent of the Accord, as well as the much-debated distinct society clause.

The fate of Meech was placed in further jeopardy when the Government of Quebec used the Constitution's "notwithstanding clause" to override the Supreme Court of Canada's decision against Quebec's repressive language legislation. The Court had ruled on December 15, 1988, that the 1977 Quebec legislation prohibiting the use of any language other than French on commercial signs in the province was unconstitutional. The notwithstanding clause has been one of the most controversial sections of the Canadian Charter of Rights and Freedoms. When it has been invoked, commentators have charged that it

June 3, 1987: Meech Lake Accord is finalized. If ratified, Quebec will sign 1982 Constitution Act.

is unconstitutional, but it is very much a part of the Constitution. The clause is found in section 33(1) of the Charter, and it allows a provincial or federal legislature to pass legislation that overrides section 2 of the Charter (which contains such fundamental rights as freedom of expression, freedom of conscience, freedom of association, and freedom of assembly) and sections 7–15 (containing the right to life, liberty, and security of the person, freedom from unreasonable search and seizure, freedom from arbitrary arrest or detention, a number of other legal rights, and the right to equality). While Bourassa considered his options, the Supreme Court ruling invigorated the independence movement in Quebec. More than 18 000 nationalists gathered at the Paul Sauvé Arena, warning Bourassa not to tamper with the language laws guaranteed in Bill 101. While Bourassa allowed for languages other than French inside stores and shops in Quebec, his use of the notwithstanding clause to override the Court's decision on language rights confirmed for many throughout Canada the illiberal nature of Quebec nationalism, which Meech Lake seemed to strengthen.

December 15, 1988: Supreme Court of Canada rules that Quebec's controversial French-only sign law is unconstitutional. Quebec uses the notwithstanding clause to override the decision three days later.

Premier Filmon, who had earlier introduced a motion in the Manitoba Legislature to ratify the Meech Lake Accord, withdrew it on December 19, the day following Quebec's use of the notwithstanding clause. Premier Wells of Newfoundland quickly became a national hero for his insistence on the equality of all Canadians, and he had the Newfoundland legislature vote on April 6, 1990, to rescind its earlier approval of the Accord. He said that he would do so four days after Trudeau publicly denounced the Accord as a "bad deal" in October 1990. Bourassa called Wells an "extremist" and federal cabinet minister Lucien Bouchard said Canadians would have to choose between Quebec and Newfoundland. To further aggravate the situation, Aboriginal leaders and the territorial governments complained about their exclusion from both the process and the substance of the Meech Lake Accord. The West was particularly annoyed with the absence of Senate reform from the Accord. This issue gave the fledgling Reform party the ammunition it needed to launch a major offensive against both the deal and the Mulroney government in Western Canada.

These were some of the most tumultuous and divisive times in Canada's history. Bouchard resigned from the federal government and the Conservative party, arguing that Meech Lake had been a bare minimum for Quebec and any changes or side deals to bring the opposing premiers on side was totally unacceptable. A few other Quebec Conservatives also resigned, as did a few disgruntled Liberals, prompting Bourassa to warn that the country could fall apart if the Accord was not ratified.

In the final days leading to the deadline for ratification of Meech Lake, a series of intergovernmental bargaining almost saved the Accord. Prime Minister Mulroney convened a make-it-or-break-it constitutional conference in Ottawa that lasted for a week. New Brunswick subsequently ratified the Accord and Newfoundland's Clyde Wells promised a free vote in the province's legislature. However, on June 12, 1990, Elijah Harper, an Oji-Cree from Red Sucker Lake and the first treaty Indian to be elected as a provincial politician when he served in the Manitoba legislature from 1981 to 1992, refused to give his consent to discuss a motion that would provide for the initiation of hearings on the Accord. Although Harper won the admiration of many who opposed the Accord, some Aboriginal peoples, including the Métis National Council, had supported it, but Harper wanted to protest the exclusion of First Nations and Aboriginal peoples from the constitutional

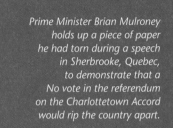

Prime Minister Brian Mulroney holds up a piece of paper he had torn during a speech in Sherbrooke, Quebec, to demonstrate that a No vote in the referendum on the Charlottetown Accord would rip the country apart.

Source: CP/Fred Chartrand.

process. Holding a single eagle feather, Harper refused to grant unanimity to waive the usual two-day period to debate a new motion that would have enabled a vote on Meech Lake. Although Filmon introduced a motion on June 20 to ratify the Meech Lake Accord, the procedural rules of the legislature meant that Manitoba could not ratify the Accord until after the June 23 deadline. When Manitoba did not vote on the Accord, Wells decided it was futile to have another vote in the Newfoundland legislature. The Meech Lake Accord had failed in the ratification process.

The reaction to the defeat of the Meech Lake Accord was severe. In Quebec, the failure was seen as another example of the humiliation of the Québécois nation by English Canada. A month after the defeat of the Accord, Lucien Bouchard and six other MPs created the Bloc Québécois as a separatist party in the House of Commons to protect Quebec's interests in Ottawa. On August 13, 1990, Gilles Duceppe become the first Bloc member elected to the House of Commons, and support for independence in Quebec reached an all-time high of 64 percent in November 1990. Robert Bourassa raised the prospect of radical reform of the federation or outright sovereignty for Quebec, and he introduced a Referendum Bill in Quebec's National Assembly. He said that he would not negotiate with the rest of Canada and would await offers from the Government of Canada. Bourassa imposed a deadline of October 26, 1992, for an acceptable offer; otherwise, he would hold a referendum either on renewed federalism if an offer was forthcoming or sovereignty. The mood across the country was sombre. It was clear that Bourassa no longer saw Quebec as one of ten provinces but as a nation equal to Canada: There would only be bilateral discussion between Quebec and Ottawa. In the words of many, Bourassa had "put a knife to the throat of English Canada."

His strategy worked. Many Canadians told pollsters that they feared that their nation would not survive to the millennium. Governments and citizens alike wanted the matter resolved. Several provinces asked their citizens to participate with commissions or task forces on the future of Canada. The federal government also created its own process to engage Canadians. When Keith Spicer went across Canada as chair of the Citizens' Forum on Canada's Future, some 400 000 Canadians came forward either to vent their anger or offer solutions; some did both. Canadians told the Commission that they had little regard for their prime minister, their provincial premiers, and their opposition leaders. The *Forum Report* concluded that "The concept of equality applies both to individuals and to their provinces, territories and regions.... Participants strongly disapprove of government policies which seem to promote the rights of groups over individuals, especially in comparison with citizens in other Canadian jurisdictions. Similarly, ... the Canadians who spoke to the Forum will not countenance apparent inequality among provinces or 'special privileges' for one or more provinces."

Canada's political leaders were listening. If the Meech Lake Accord had been negotiated in private, the following round of constitution-making became a virtual open house where everything was on the program and the guest list was broadened. As Ottawa began the process of putting together an acceptable offer to Quebec before the provincially imposed deadline in what became known as the Charlottetown Accord, it promised to include institutional parliamentary reform, the division of powers, amendments to the Charter of Rights, interprovincial trade and commerce, Aboriginal issues, territorial issues, and intergovernmental relations. When the federal and provincial governments started to put together a package for Quebec, Ontario premier Bob Rae insisted that representatives of Canada's Aboriginal peoples join with federal, provincial, and territorial leaders. The leaders eventually hammered out a deal that was changed slightly in the negotiations with Quebec to give Bourassa what he thought he needed to win a referendum on keeping Quebec in Canada. The Charlottetown Accord was put to Canadians in a fall national referendum in 1992. Before the vote was taken, Trudeau entered the fray once more, calling the Accord "a big mess."

In the end, the Charlottetown Accord was defeated by vote of 54 percent to 46 percent, with only four provinces and one of the territories voting for it. More than 56 percent of those voting in Quebec (which held its own referendum) voted against the Accord. So, after several years of constitutional negotiations between Ottawa and the provinces from 1987 to 1992, the Quebec National Assembly had still not ratified the *Constitution Act, 1982*, and the country was more divided than it had been in 1983.

October 26, 1992: Charlottetown Accord is defeated in a national referendum. Six provinces, including Quebec, vote against the Accord.

Aboriginal Peoples: Seeking a New Voice

The failure to address Aboriginal concerns during the Meech Lake and Charlottetown constitutional negotiations was just one of the major issues for Aboriginal peoples during the 1980s and early 1990s. Others included the armed confrontation at the Mohawk reserve of Kanesatake near Oka, a new status for some Aboriginal women, and a new role for First Nations governments in managing their own affairs. As one commentator who watched the Aboriginal file closely has noted, the Mulroney government inherited "a legacy of frustration" among Aboriginal peoples, even though they had been guaranteed certain rights by the Charter of Rights and Freedoms.[16] There had been little real substantive change for Aboriginal peoples in either their well-being or in Aboriginal–state relations after Trudeau introduced the White Paper and, despite several accomplishments during the Mulroney era, the legacy of frustration continued throughout the period.

Aboriginal leaders held great hope for the future as the Mulroney government took office. At the First Ministers' Conference on the Rights of Aboriginal Peoples in 1985—one of four constitutionally mandated conferences under section 37 of the 1982 Constitution to deal with Aboriginal issues—the government promised to make space for Aboriginal governments. That these meetings had to be guaranteed in such a manner suggests that there was a high level of mistrust between the state and Aboriginal groups. At the end of the four meetings, no decisions had been reached on such critical issues as self-government and land claims. It was just a few months after the final meeting in 1987 that the premiers met, without Aboriginal leaders, with the purpose of securing Quebec's signature on the Constitution. This was the Quebec Round, Aboriginal leaders were told, but they were disappointed nonetheless that the Meech Lake Accord did not address their concerns, notably the inherent right of self-government.

The closed-door constitutional process that had led to Meech represented for Aboriginal peoples a reversal of what Mulroney had promised. Yet, as part of the last-ditched effort to save Meech Lake in June 1990, Mulroney and the premiers offered a six-point plan for Aboriginal peoples that included a federal–provincial process to set the agenda for the First Ministers Conference on Aboriginal matters, a commitment by the government of Canada to fully recognize Aboriginal peoples as a fundamental characteristic of Canada, the participation of representatives of Aboriginal peoples at any future first ministers conferences held to discuss the "recognition clause," an invitation to participate in all first ministers conferences where matters being discussed directly affected Aboriginal peoples, the joint definition of treaty rights, and the establishment of a Royal Commission on Aboriginal Affairs.

Aboriginal–state relations reached a low point shortly after the collapse of Meech Lake, when Mohawks from the Kanesatake reserve erected a blockade near Oka, Quebec, to protest the construction of a golf course on sacred land. Mohawks from the nearby Kahawake reserve blockaded the Mercier Bridge, a major access route to Montreal from the surrounding suburbs, in support of the initial protest. The Mohawk Warrior Society, an armed militant group committed to defending Aboriginal rights and allegedly involved in the smuggling of cigarettes and liquor across the Canada–U.S. border, joined the blockades. An armed standoff ensued, and the Sûreté du Québec (the provincial police force) moved in to remove the barricade at Oka. After a police officer was killed in the melee, Quebec Premier Robert Bourassa asked that the Canadian Army be dispatched to the area in aid of the civil power. Under the terms of the *National Defence Act*, once a provincial government requests aid, the federal government has to comply. For 78 days, Canadians focused their attention on the Oka Crisis, which saw both sides ready for a shoot-out. The crisis was finally resolved by the end of September 1990, when the Warriors Society gave up the struggle. Some of the Warriors were arrested and relations between the two sides remained tense long after. Plans for the golf course were subsequently dropped.

After the crisis was resolved, the government announced a new federal Aboriginal agenda. It promised to establish a new working relationship between the Canadian state

Marchers mark the anniversary of the start of the Oka Crisis.

Source: CP Images.

and Aboriginal peoples; expedite land claims settlements; improve the social and eco-nomic well-being of Aboriginal peoples; renew and reform Aboriginal relations and processes with the government; and deal with accommodating self-government within the constitutional framework.[17] The Royal Commission on Aboriginal Peoples (RCAP) was appointed in August 1991 as part of that new arrangement with Aboriginal peoples, though its primary purpose was to offer recommendations to solve the problems that had long-plagued Aboriginal–state relations in Canada. It was the most comprehensive and inclusive attempt to study the complex world of Aboriginal policy in Canada, but like so many such commissions, it had considerable cost overruns and did not report on schedule. A report was delivered in November 1996.

As part of the democratization of the constitutional process that saw the government promise citizens a voice through public consultation forums and a national referendum, Aboriginal groups also became more important constitutional actors. The process that led to the Charlottetown Accord in 1992 seemed to mark a new beginning in Canada as Aboriginal leaders participated for the first time in constitutional negotiations. If the Accord had been successful, it would have represented major constitutional gains for Aboriginal peoples by entrenching Aboriginal government as one of the three orders of government in Canada, by recognizing the inherent right of self-government, and creating Aboriginal seats in the Senate. The Accord was rejected by Canadians, including many First Nations reserve residents and the Native Women's Association of Canada. Many Aboriginal women feared that the Accord undermined women's rights under Aboriginal self-government, and many objected to the fact that they were excluded from the Aboriginal national representa-tion. Without a doubt, there was as wide a gulf between Aboriginal leadership and their people as there was between the Canadian leadership and the non-Aboriginal population.

Another important aspect of Aboriginal policy in the period was the restructuring of the funding arrangement between the federal government and First Nations. Aboriginal policies, like so many others at the time, were threatened by Ottawa's neoliberal agenda to control federal spending. In its review of government spending when they assumed office, the Conservatives seemed to favour deep cuts to Indian and Northern Affairs Canada, the federal department responsible for Aboriginal peoples. Internally, the plan was referred to as "The Buffalo Jump of the 1980s" and elicited a rapid response from First Nations who remembered only too well the 1969 assimilationist White Paper on Indian policy. To control the damage that had been done, Mulroney and David Crombie, the minister of Indian and Northern Affairs Canada, promised that the current levels of funding for programs and services for First Nations would be maintained. It was, in fact, the only department during the period of retrenchment that escaped the cutbacks.

The government moved to increase First Nations control of and decision making over managing federally run programs that were in place after 1986. Some have argued that this was simply an attempt by the government to offload federal responsibility to other jurisdictions, while others have seen such changes as a means of allowing Aboriginal peoples to assume greater responsibility and control over their own affairs. By 1991, more than 77 percent of program spending was managed by First Nations. However, the socioeconomic evidence suggests that the level of Indian and Inuit well-being was far below the national averages.

Some important gains were made on the issue of land claims. Land claims policy had been influenced by decisions of the Supreme Court and the *Constitution Act, 1982*. When the Court ruled in the *Calder Case* in 1973 that Aboriginal title was recognized in common law, it forced the federal government to negotiate with Aboriginal peoples to resolve some outstanding land claims and move to settle breaches of treaty obligations. Section 35 of the *Constitution Act, 1982* explicitly recognized and affirmed the existing Aboriginal and treaty rights of Aboriginal peoples, including those that resulted from comprehensive land claims. The process for resolving this complex issue is still far from complete, but the Mulroney government established the clear connection between resolving land and self-government issues together. The government created a task force to review the policy on comprehensive lands claims. Its report recommended that the resolution of land claims disputes would affirm Aboriginal rights rather than extinguish them. Research into Aboriginal lands claims became a virtual cottage industry during the period, but there were some significant accomplishments as well. This was most notable in 1993, when the Inuit people of the Eastern Arctic reached an agreement with the federal government to create Nunavut as a third territory in Canada's North. The relevant legislation for this agreement was passed in Parliament just as Mulroney was leaving Ottawa. It effectively allowed the Inuit control of their collective future but with a small population and huge costs and impending global warming, the North continued to face considerable challenges in the decades that followed.

Two other developments were also important. In 1985, the *Indian Act* was amended in Bill C-31 (as noted earlier) to give Registered Indian Status to women who had been removed from the Indian Register because they had married non-status Indians. Their children were also permitted to register under the Act, and new rules were enacted giving entitlement to all children born to a Registered Indian parent on or after April 17, 1985. Individual First Nations were also given the authority to establish their own rules governing membership. Across Canada, the impact was enormous, as the government estimated that the incremental growth associated with Bill C-31 totalled about 174 500 individuals. This included 106 781 Bill C-31 registrants, 59 798 children who would not have qualified under the old Act, and 5986 women and 1937 children gained through Bill C-31 changes regarding marriages.[18] For the first time, the federal government recognized people who had been referred to as "non-status" Indians. This included Métis, urban Aboriginals, and other Aboriginal peoples who were not recognized in federal legislation and not included in the *Indian Act*. The government created the office of a federal interlocutor for Métis and Non-Status Indians, with a cabinet minister responsible for relations between the federal government and the representatives of these groups. In all, important progress was made, but the standard of living for many Aboriginal peoples remained far below the national standard.

The West: Frustration and Change

Many of the provincial governments shared some of the frustration felt by Aboriginal and First Nations communities. Achieving intergovernmental harmony is no easy task in Canada, but the early years with Mulroney as prime minister seemed to suggest that it was possible. The first meetings between the premiers and the prime minister were positive affairs without the acrimony so evident during the Trudeau years. Moreover, long-standing grievances with the provinces were solved quickly. Newfoundland, a province that had struggled economically since joining Canada in 1949, finally secured revenue rights to the vast offshore oil reserves in the Canada–Newfoundland Atlantic Accord, which was signed in February 1985. A month later, Ottawa eliminated a series of federal taxes in the oil and gas sector with the Western Accord, an agreement between the governments of Canada, Saskatchewan, Alberta, and British Columbia on oil and gas pricing and taxation, ending the feud with the Western provinces that had marked much of the previous decade.

The new style of cooperation did not last long, however, as the fundamentally different interests among the provinces emerged that had always made intergovernmental harmony difficult. On the issue of free trade, for example, Alberta Premier Peter Lougheed and Premier Bourassa of Quebec were in favour because of their provinces' reliance on the export of raw and semi-processed materials. David Peterson, the premier of Ontario, on the other hand, was opposed. He feared for his province's vast manufacturing sector. Some reports suggested that Ontario might lose nearly 300 000 manufacturing jobs if the borders were open to American producers. At a first ministers meeting to discuss how to proceed on free trade, Mulroney agreed to the principle of provincial participation in the trade talks. The premiers, especially Peterson, believed this to mean that the first ministers would have a voice in the negotiations. However, Ottawa had no intention of making the premiers partners in the process; they would be kept informed during the negotiations, but there was little of the intergovernmental collaboration that many had anticipated. It was clear during this period that Ottawa would act unilaterally when it felt necessary. In the case of the Atlantic and Western Accords, for example, there had been little consultation with the provinces, as both agreements resulted from unilateral federal action even if the spirit and letter of the accords met with provincial approval.

The same was true of intergovernmental negotiations over Canada's equalization program, a program established in 1957 to redistribute tax dollars from the wealthier provinces ("haves") to the poorer ones ("have-nots"). The program is renegotiated every five years. When negotiations began in 1986, Finance Minister Michael Wilson offered the provinces an additional $175 million in equalization payments. The provinces rejected the offer, hoping to win more from Ottawa. Wilson eventually offered substantially less when he discovered that the nation's financial crisis was worsening. Again, Ottawa demonstrated that it would have the final say.

As a way of addressing the deficit, the federal government unilaterally decided to limit its contribution to the Canada Assistance Plan, a cost-shared program between the federal and provincial governments to provide comprehensive social services across Canada. While Ottawa's decision allowed it to address its deficit problem, it increased the disagreements between the two orders of government. In fact, the federal government came to realize that intergovernmental relations was one of the most difficult files to manage, as the various intergovernmental files could not be kept separate. For instance, the country was dealing with free trade and the Constitution at the same time that Ontario and British Columbia were quarrelling with Ottawa over how best to deal with American duties on Canada's export of softwood lumber. Mulroney learned that free trade affected constitutional negotiations and the equalization program had an impact on all others. With so many contentious issues, none of them could be dealt with in an entirely independent manner. Intergovernmental relations are complex in Canada, made doubly so by the extent of regional diversity in Canada. This lesson was perhaps most apparent in Western Canada.

In 1986, the government awarded the billion-dollar maintenance contract for the CF-18 aircraft fighter jet used by the Canadian Forces to Montreal-based Canadair instead of Winnipeg-based Bristol Aerospace—even though the Western firm had a cheaper and technically superior bid. This decision sealed Mulroney's fate in the West. It had the same effect emotionally as Trudeau's National Energy Program and led in part to the creation of a new Western political party. In 1987, Preston Manning, son of former Alberta premier Ernest Manning, created the Reform Party of Canada as an expression of Western discontent. The party was formed by Conservatives in the West who were disappointed with Mulroney, and one of its primary objectives was to achieve what it termed a Triple-E Senate—elected, equal, and effective.

The Reform party immediately became a threat to the Conservative base in Western Canada. In 1988, Deborah Grey, singing the Reform's "the West wants in" message, won a by-election in east-central Alberta to become the first Reform member in the House of Commons. The Mulroney coalition of the West and Quebec held in the 1988 election, but it was beginning to show signs of strain. As Mackenzie King discovered much earlier, Mulroney had to choose between the two sections of Canada. In 1988, the government introduced Bill C-72 "to fulfill the bilingualization of Canada in general and the Canadian government in particular." The West saw this as another sign of appeasing Quebec. When Manitoba Tory Dan McKenzie refused to vote for the bill, he was fired as parliamentary secretary to the minister responsible for Veteran's Affairs. He was replaced by a Quebec MP, Charles Hamelin, who threatened to quit the party and join the Parti Québécois if Tory backbenchers blocked the legislation. At the same time, a poll found that 71 percent of those in the Prairies and British Columbia felt that the Mulroney government had done too much for Quebec. Only 60 percent of all English-speaking Canada felt that way.

In the 1988 election, the Reform party failed to win a single seat but it captured 15 percent of the vote in Alberta. After the election, Mulroney continued to lose support in the West as the region, and particularly Alberta, felt increasingly alienated from the party. In fact, in April 1991, the Alberta Progressive Conservative party severed all ties with the national party. Much of the alienation came from a perception in the West that Mulroney was even more obsessed with Quebec than was the region's earlier nemesis, Pierre Trudeau. A public opinion poll gave the Conservatives 15 percent of support and the Reform party 43 percent. This came at a time when the West had 10 of the 30 seats in the federal cabinet, but the Conservative party had lost touch with the West, which had shifted to the ideological right and had become even more "small c" conservative.

Like so many politicians, Mulroney was held captive to his own region and his own vision of a bilingual and bicultural Canada, and that vision of Canada demonstrated to the West that the Conservatives were no different from the Liberals. As Don Braid and Sydney Sharpe have noted, "Western mistrust of Ottawa is built into Canadian history and the national system ... [and] westerners believe the country isn't fair."[19] By the end of the Mulroney period, the Reform party had replaced the Conservatives as the dominant political force in Western Canada.

A Conservative Is a Conservative

On February 25, 1993, with the economy mired in a stubborn recession, unemployment rates at a 20-year high, the country deeply divided, and his own approval rate the lowest of any sitting prime minister, Mulroney resigned. The coalition he had forged among Quebec nationalists and Western conservatives to lead the Progressive Conservatives to two consecutives majorities had come unravelled. The Reform party stood poised to win Western Canada, the Bloc Québécois had wrestled control of Quebec from the Tories, and Ontario was smarting over the prolonged economic downturn. The prospects for Mulroney and the Conservatives were bleak.

During Mulroney's term, Canada had successfully negotiated a Canada–U.S. free trade arrangement and had prepared a more extensive agreement with the United States to include Mexico. Mulroney's Conservatives had ushered in considerable economic change—some of which was very unpopular—such as the Goods and Services Tax and other tax reforms, and curbed government spending on programs and reduced the current account deficit. It had deregulated important sectors of the economy, including energy and transportation. There were clear failures, as well, principally two unsuccessful attempts at constitutional reform to meet the needs of Quebec and First Nations peoples. Many English-speaking Canadians had a visceral dislike of Mulroney and were delighted when he left the Prime Minister's Office. The *Toronto Star*, which had been hostile to Mulroney for much of his two terms, reflected that he made us "less Canadian and less secure."[20] He had much greater support in Quebec, however. At the end of his mandate, he took to the media in his own defence: "I always tried to do what I thought would be right for Canada in the long term, not what would be politically popular in the short term."[21] It did little to change people's minds about him.

Kim Campbell succeeded Mulroney to become leader of the Progressive Conservatives and Canada's first woman prime minister on June 13, 1993. She had come to Ottawa in 1988 and made her presence felt immediately. Appointed the justice minister and attorney general in 1990—the first woman to hold the positions—she successfully pushed for stricter gun control after the Montreal Massacre, despite strong opposition within her own party. In 1993, she became the first woman to serve as minister of National Defence and Veterans Affairs.

Her term as prime minister was brief. In October 1993, Campbell led the Conservatives to one of the most disastrous defeats in Canadian political history. The Tories saw their popularity drop from 43 percent and 169 seats in 1988 to 16 percent and just two seats in 1993. Campbell even lost her own seat in British Columbia.

Brian Mulroney did not disappear from Canadian politics after he resigned as prime minister. During his years in office, he was dogged with allegations of corruption and wrongdoing within his government and by those around him. The rumours persisted after he left office and the RCMP even launched an investigation into his dealings with businessman Karlheinz Schreiber over the purchase of

1993: Kim Campbell becomes the first woman to be prime minister of Canada.

Kim Campbell was Canada's 19th prime minister.

Source: Jeff Goode/GetStock.com.

new airplanes from Airbus Industrie for Air Canada. When word of the investigation was leaked to the media, Mulroney successfully sued the Canadian government and in 1997 it issued him an apology for the investigation, which uncovered no evidence of wrong-doing, and paid his legal fees. Later, it came to light that Mulroney had accepted $300 000 in cash from Schreiber but did not report the amount to the Canada Revenue Agency for tax purposes until 1999. In early January 2008, Parliament's Ethics Committee launched an investigation into Mulroney's dealings with Schreiber, who was later extradited to Germany and convicted on charges of corruption and tax evasion. Prime Minister Stephen Harper appointed a Commission of Inquiry into Certain Allegations Respecting Business Dealings Between Karlheinz Schreiber and the Right Honourable Brian Mulroney with Mr. Justice Jeffrey J. Oliphant, associate chief justice, Court of Queen's Bench for Manitoba, as sole commissioner. Justice Oliphant said in a stern report released in May 2010 that the financial dealings between Mulroney and Schreiber were "inappropriate." Mulroney had failed to live up to the ethics code he had introduced in 1985 as prime minister, the report concluded.

Conclusion

Many of Mulroney's policies—from the GST to free trade to peacekeeping to at least a stated commitment to debt reduction—did not disappear when Canadians voted the Conservatives from office in 1993. Many of these policies were continued, and even embraced, by the Liberal government that followed. Did the Mulroney government succeed in building a new consensus among Canadians from 1983 to 1993? The answer is clear: It did not.

At the end of the period, there had emerged in Canada three sectional parties representing the various regions of Canada: the Reform party in the West, the Bloc Québécois in Quebec, and the Liberals in Ontario and Atlantic Canada. The old Conservative party of John A. Macdonald that had negotiated the founding of Canada and had assumed power by building an effective coalition was in danger of disappearing. Canadians themselves were angry and, unlike 1984 when they turned to an alternative national party to govern the nation, in 1993 they turned to regional parties that they thought would best represent their interests. The results demonstrated that the national reconciliation that the Conservatives had promised a decade earlier had not happened.

It would perhaps be easy to explain this period as simply an example of failed political management at the federal level and blame Mulroney and the Conservatives for the state the nation was in by 1993. Some of the cleavages within Canada had manifested themselves much earlier, and the West, Quebec, the First Nations, and some women's groups, for instance, hoped in 1984 that a new national government would address their concerns. All came with expectations—some of which were in conflict—and when their particular concerns were not met, once again, the result was a level of anger and disappointment that has been seen only rarely in Canada's history.

Compromise and negotiation, which had been the hallmarks of national politics for much of the period since Confederation, no longer seemed to work; the tensions long evident in the national polity, it seemed, finally reached a breaking point. The 1993 election demonstrated that Quebec and the West, both with longstanding grievances with the centre, turned their backs on the traditional parties, opting instead to create new regionally based parties to represent their interests in Parliament. That meant that the party that won Ontario controlled the national government, which was a new phenomenon in Canada. Regardless, the decade was a momentous one in Canadian history, one that brought profound change that breathed new life into Canada's social movement and destroyed one of the founding political parties created at Confederation. But more than anything, the period demonstrated that Canada had become a nation with deep-rooted conflicts that would not easily be resolved.

Questions to Consider

1. Did women and women's issues make much progress during the Mulroney era?

2. Why did Canadians reject the attempts at constitutional change in this period?

3. Why did Prime Minister Mulroney become so unpopular?

4. Would the period you just studied be considered a positive or negative experience for First Nations and other Aboriginal peoples?

5. How did the economic conditions of the period force new approaches to state–societal relations?

6. What was the relationship between Canada's adoption of free trade and the emergence of a new social movement?

Critical Thinking Questions

1. Do prime ministers make a difference?

2. Even though government spending on social policy remained constant from 1984 to 1993, do you think the welfare state was dismantled or at least significantly altered? Explain.

3. How can governments effectively manage change?

4. On an issue such as free trade with the United States, should a government have a clear majority of the popular vote before it can enact such legislation?

Suggested Readings
General

Blake, Raymond B., ed. *Transforming the Nation: Canada and Brian Mulroney.* Montreal and Kingston: McGill-Queen's University Press, 2007.

Gollner, Andrew, and Daniel Salée, eds. *Canada Under Mulroney: An End-of-Term Report.* Montreal: Véhicule Press, 1988.

Mulroney, Brian. *Memoirs, 1939–93.* Toronto: McClelland & Stewart, 2007.

Newman, Peter C. *The Canadian Revolution: From Deference to Defiance.* Toronto: Penguin Books of Canada, 1996.

Sawatsky, John. *Mulroney: The Politics of Ambition.* Toronto: Macfarlane Walter & Ross, 1991.

The North

Coates, Kenneth, and William R. Morrison, eds. *Interpreting Canada's North: Selected Readings.* Toronto: Copp Clark Pitman, 1989.

Dacks, Gurston. *Devolution and Constitutional Development in the Canadian North.* Ottawa: Carleton University Press, 1990.

Dickerson, Mark O. *Whose North? Political Change, Political Development, and Self-Government in the Northwest Territories.* Vancouver: University of British Columbia Press, 1992.

White, Graham, and Kirk Cameron. *Northern Governments in Transition.* Montreal: Institute for Research on Public Policy, 1995.

Constitutional Negotiations

Cohen, Andrew. *A Deal Undone: The Making and Breaking of the Meech Lake Accord.* Vancouver and Toronto: Douglas & McIntyre, 1990.

Fournier, Pierre. *Meech Lake Post-Mortem: Is Quebec Sovereignty Inevitable?* Montreal and Kingston: McGill-Queen's University Press, 1991.

Johnston, Richard, André Blais, Elisabeth Gidengil, and Neil Nevitte, "The People and the Charlottetown Accord." In Ronald L. Watts and Douglas M. Brown, eds., *Canada: The State of the Federation 1993.* Kingston: Institute of Intergovernmental Relations, 1993.

McRoberts, Kenneth. *Misconceiving Canada: The Struggle for National Unity.* Toronto: Oxford University Press, 1997.

Monahan, Patrick. J. *Meech Lake: The Inside Story.* Toronto: University of Toronto Press, 1991.

Politics

Ayres, Jeffrey M. *Defying Conventional Wisdom: Political Movements and Popular Contention against North American Free Trade.* Toronto: University of Toronto Press, 1998.

Bercuson, David, J.L. Granatstein, and W.R. Young. *Sacred Trust: Brian Mulroney and the Conservative Party in Power.* Toronto: Doubleday, 1986.

Braid, Don, and Sydney Sharpe. *Breakup: Why the West Feels Left Out of Canada.* Toronto: Key Porter Books, 1990.

Harrison, Trevor. *Of Passionate Intensity: Right-Wing Populism and the Reform Party of Canada.* Toronto: University of Toronto Press, 1995.

Ornstein, Michael, and H. Michael Stevenson. *Politics and Ideology in Canada: Elite and Public Opinion in the Transformation of a Welfare State.* Montreal and Kingston: McGill-Queen's University Press, 2003.

Aboriginal Issues

Graham, Katherine. "Indian Policy and the Tories: Cleaning Up After the Buffalo Jump." In M. Prince, ed., *How Ottawa Spends 1987–99: Restraining the State.* Toronto: Methuen, 1988.

Hawkes, David C. *Negotiating Aboriginal Self-Government: Developments Surrounding the 1985 First Ministers' Conference*, Background Paper 7. Kingston: Institute of Intergovernmental Relations, 1985.

White, Graham, with Jack Hicks. "Nunavut: Inuit Self-determination Through a Land Claim and Public Government?" In Keith Brownsey and Michael Howlett, eds., *The Provincial State in Canada: Politics in the Provinces and Territories.* Peterborough: Broadview Press, 2001.

York, Geoffrey, and Loreen Pindera. *People of the Pines: The Warriors and the Legacy of Oka.* Toronto: Little, Brown & Company, 1991.

Women

Baskevkin, Sylvia. "Losing Common Ground: Feminists, Conservatives and Public Policy in Canada during the Mulroney Years." *Canadian Journal of Political Science / Revue canadienne de science politique* 29, 2 (June 1996): 211–242.

Bashevkin, Sylvia. *Women on the Defensive: Living through Conservative Times.* Toronto: University of Toronto Press, 1998.

Dobrowolsky, Alexandra. *The Politics of Pragmatism: Women, Representation, and Constitutionalism in Canada.* Don Mills, ON: Oxford University Press, 2000.

Timpson, Annis May. *Driven Apart: Women's Employment Equality and Child Care in Canadian Public Policy.* Vancouver: University of British Columbia Press, 2001.

Vickers, Jill, Pauline Rankin, and Christine Appelle. *Politics as if Women Mattered: A Political Analysis of the National Action Committee on the Status of Women.* Toronto: University of Toronto Press, 1993.

Social Welfare

Battle, Ken. "The Politics of Stealth: Child Benefits under the Tories." In Susan D. Phillips, ed., *How Ottawa Spends: A More Democratic Canada…?* Ottawa: Carleton University Press, 1993.

Blake, Raymond B. *From Rights to Needs: A History of Family Allowances in Canada, 1929–1992.* Vancouver: University of British Columbia Press, 2009.

Jenson, Jane, and Mariette Sineau, ed. *Who Cares? Women's Work, Childcare, and Welfare State Redesign.* Toronto: University of Toronto Press, 2001.

Porter, Ann. *Gendered States: Women, Unemployment Insurance and the Political Economy of the Welfare State in Canada, 1945–1997.* Toronto: University of Toronto Press, 2003.

Rice, James R., and Michael J. Prince. *Changing Politics of Canadian Social Policy.* Toronto: University of Toronto Press, 2000.

Economy

Doern, G. Bruce, and Brian W. Tomlin, *Faith and Fear: The Free Trade Story*. Toronto: Stoddart, 1991.

Hart, Michael. *A Trading Nation: Canadian Trade Policy from Colonialism to Globalization*. Vancouver: University of British Columbia Press, 2002.

Hart, Michael, with Bill Dymond and Colin Robertson. *Decision at Midnight: Inside the Canada–US Free Trade Negotiations*. Vancouver: University of British Columbia Press, 1994.

McQuaig, Linda. *The Quick and the Dead: Brian Mulroney, Big Business and the Seduction of Canada*. Toronto: Penguin Books, 1991.

Savoie, Donald J. *Thatcher, Reagan, Mulroney: In Search of a New Bureaucracy*. Pittsburgh: University of Pittsburgh Press, 1994.

Tomlin, Brian, and Max Cameron. *Negotiating NAFTA: How the Deal Was Done*. Ithaca, NY: Cornell University Press, 2000.

Intergovernmental Relations

Bakvis, Herman. *Regional Ministers—Power and Influence in the Canadian Cabinet*. Toronto: University of Toronto Press 1991.

Savoie, Donald J. *Governing from the Centre: The Concentration of Power in Canadian Politics*. Toronto: University of Toronto Press, 1999.

Defence and Foreign Policy

Andrew, Arthur. *The Rise and Fall of a Middle Power: Canadian Diplomacy from King to Mulroney*. Toronto: James Lorimer, 1993.

Freeman, Linda. *The Ambiguous Champion: Canada and South Africa in the Trudeau and Mulroney Years*. Toronto: University of Toronto Press, 1997.

Frost, Mike, and Michel Gratton. *Spyworld: Inside the Canadian and American Intelligence Establishments*. Toronto: Doubleday Canada, 1994.

Maloney, Sean M. *War Without Battles: Canada's NATO Brigade in Germany 1951–1993*. St. Catharines, ON: McGraw-Hill Ryerson, 1997.

Martin, Lawrence. *Pledge of Allegiance: The Americanization of Canada in the Mulroney Years*. Toronto: McClelland & Stewart, 1993.

Michaud, Nelson, and Kim Richard Nossal. *Diplomatic Departures: The Conservative Era in Canadian Foreign Policy, 1984–1993*. Vancouver: University of British Columbia Press, 2001.

Morrison, David R. *Aid and Ebb Tide: A History of CIDA and Canadian Development Assistance*. Waterloo: Wilfrid Laurier University Press, 1998.

Nossal, Kim Richard. *The Politics of Canadian Foreign Policy*. 3rd edition. Scarborough: Prentice Hall Canada, 1997.

Thompson, John Herd, and Stephen J. Randall, *Canada and the United States: Ambivalent Allies*. Montreal and Kingston: McGill-Queen's University Press, 1994.

Notes

[1] See CBC News, *The Fifth Estate*, "The Dump-Clark Movement," 31 October 2007, http://www.cbc.ca/fifth/unauthorizedchapter/clark.html.

[2] CBC News, CBC Digital Archives, Mulroney vs. Turner, 25 July 1984, http://archives.cbc.ca/politics/federal_politics/clips/6516/.

[3] Statistics Canada, *Women in Canada: Work Chapter Updates*, August 2001, Catalogue No. 89F0133XIE.

[4] Institute for Research on Public Policy, *G8/G10 Policy Options*, http://www.irpp.org/po/index.htm.

[5] Economic Council of Canada, *Looking Outward: A New Trade Strategy for Canada* (Ottawa: Economic Council of Canada, 1975).

[6] Quoted in Bill Dymond and Colin Robertson, *Decision at Midnight: Inside the Canada–US Free-Trade Negotiations* (Vancouver: University of British Columbia, 1994), 18.

[7] Rod Bantjes, *Social Movements in a Global Perspectives: Canadian Perspectives* (Toronto: Canadian Scholars' Press, 2007), Chapter 11, "Coalition Politics."

[8] House of Commons *Debates*, 29 June 1988.

[9] House of Commons *Debates*, 30 August 1988.

[10] *Winnipeg Free Press*, 19 November 1988.

[11] Eighty-two percent of the electorate saw free trade as the "most important election issue," although only about half of voters claimed to have made up their mind on how to vote mainly on the basis of free trade. See Alan Frizzell, Jon H. Pammett, and Anthony Westell, eds., *The Canadian General Election of 1988* (Ottawa: Carleton University Press, 1989), 122–125.

[12] Juscelino F. Colares, "Alternative Methods of Appellate Review in Trade Remedy Cases: Examining Results of U.S. Judicial and NAFTA Binational Review of U.S. Agency Decisions from 1989 to 2005," *Journal of Empirical Legal Studies* 5, 1 (March 2008): 171–196.

[13] Cited in Michael Hart, with Bill Dymond and Colin Robertson, *Decision at Midnight: Inside the Canada–US Free-Trade Negotiations* (Vancouver: UBC Press, 1994), 264.

[14] House of Commons *Debates*, 4 October 1983.

[15] Gil Rémillard, "Unofficial English Language Text of the Speech to the 5 May, 1986 Mont-Gabriel Conference, 'Rebuilding the Relationship; Quebec and its Confederation Partners,'" in Peter M. Leslie, ed., *Canada: The State of the Federation 1986* (Kingston: Institute of Intergovernmental Relations, Queen's University, 1986), 97–105.

[16] Katherine Graham, "Indian Policy and the Tories: Cleaning Up After the Buffalo Jump," in M. Prince, ed., *How Ottawa Spends 1987–99: Restraining the State* (Toronto: Methuen, 1988): 237.

[17] Brian Mulroney, *CARC—North Perspectives* 21, 3 (Fall 1993). See also, Augie Fleras and Jean Leonard Elliott, *The Nations Within: Aboriginal-State Relations in Canada, the United States, and New Zealand* (Toronto: Oxford University Press, 1992), 97.

[18] Stewart Clatworthy, *Re-assessing the Population Impacts of Bill C-31*. Report prepared for Indian and Northern Affairs Canada, 2001.

[19] Don Braid and Sydney Sharpe, *Breakup: Why the West Feels Left Out of Canada* (Toronto: Key Porter Books, 1990), 14.

[20] *Toronto Star*, Editorial, 25 February 1993.

[21] *Montreal Gazette*, 25 February 1993.

12

Canada's New Century

On March 6, 2006, Canada was in the midst of its annual "Roll Up the Rim to Win" contest at Tim Hortons, and Marilou, a 10-year-old student from St. Jerome, Quebec, and her parents found themselves locked in a battle with a 12-year-old girl and her parents from her school. Marilou had found a Tim Hortons paper coffee cup in the trash on her school playground and, after struggling to see what lay hidden under the rim, she asked her schoolmate for help, only to discover that they held a winning cup for a new Toyota SUV. A teacher called the parents, and the two dads headed to Tims—as the popular Tim Hortons donut chain is affectionately known. However, there was only one form to complete and one prize to claim; Marilou's parents said the prize was theirs, but the mother of the other girl demanded a half-share of the vehicle, which was valued at almost $33 000. Then, the janitor at the school said he was hiring a lawyer, claiming the cup was his, and threatened a DNA test to prove his case. The story, not surprisingly, became national news—Tim Hortons is not just a donut shop.

Tim Hortons and the humble donut have assumed a curiously important place in Canadian society and culture. Donuts seem to have become the official food of Canada, and Tim Hortons has come to symbolize the mythical essence of the country—humble, hard-working, honest, and not at all pretentious. To give a glimpse into the "real" Canada at the start of the new millennium, a book by award-winning *Globe and Mail* reporter John Stackhouse was titled *Timbit Nation: A Hitchhiker's View of Canada*. Historian Steve Penfold's Ph.D. dissertation on the donut in Canada also won a major prize before it became a successful book, *The Social Life of Donuts:*

chapter 12

Source: THE CANADIAN PRESS/Richard Buchan.

Commodity and Community in Postwar Canada. As Penfold reminds us, there are many donut stores in Canada, but Canadians seem to have made Tim Hortons theirs.

Tim Hortons began in Hamilton in 1964 when Tim Horton, a hockey star with the Toronto Maple Leafs, opened a donut shop. It started out as Tim Horton's Donuts with an apostrophe. When the language laws in Quebec in the late 1980s required signs to be in French unless it was a personal name, the company opted for "Tim Hortons" rather than "Les donuts de Tim Horton." The company struggled for years and only emerged as a major player in the fast-food industry when Ron Joyce, a kid from Tatamagouche, Nova Scotia, moved to Ontario, became a police officer, and later bought out Horton's partner and subsequently developed a successful and clever marketing strategy. Horton died tragically in a car crash in 1974, and Joyce eventually bought Horton's half of the company from his widow, Lori, for $1 million dollars and a new Cadillac. She later sued Joyce, demanding half of the business be returned to her, along with $10 million in compensation. She claimed Joyce had swindled her out of millions. The court dismissed Lori Horton's claim. In 1995, Joyce sold Tim Hortons to Wendy's, the American hamburger chain, for $400 million, an executive position in Wendy's, and a bundle of stock options. In September 2009, Tim Hortons executives announced the company would be reorganized as a Canadian corporation and moved back to Canada.

Canada has more donut shops per capita than any other country on the planet. Canadians love Tim Hortons, the most popular donut chain, with more than 3000 stores in 2009; an outlet even opened in Kandahar to service Canadian troops in Afghanistan. Not even the American donut giant Krispy Kreme could make any headway in Canada against Tim Hortons, and words such as "Timbits" and "double-double" have become fixtures of the Canadian lexicon and can be found in the *Canadian Oxford Dictionary*, and the "Roll Up the Rim to Win" contest is more welcomed than spring itself. As Penfold notes, Tim Hortons is to many communities the town hall where the local political matters are discussed and debated. And one shouldn't belittle Tim Hortons, either. Columnist Leah McLaren of the *Globe and Mail* discovered that when she wrote in one of her 2001 columns that Tim Hortons did not belong in her upscale Toronto neighbourhood. How Toronto, the rest of Canada complained, when most towns and villages across the country would give almost anything to have a Tim Hortons nearby! Even Tims could not bridge the urban–rural divide.

Tim Hortons, for a time an American-owned donut chain, has emerged as a truly Canadian symbol. When something happens at Tims, it rapidly becomes national news, as it did when the two young girls had a spat over a used coffee cup. The two girls and the janitor must have already known that if your name "ain't on it" in elementary school, its finders keepers: Marilou got the Toyota RAV4.

After reading this chapter you will be able to:

1. Appreciate how the fiscal situation in Canada throughout the 1990s changed the role and policies of governments.
2. Understand the importance of the issue of violence against women in women's struggle for equality.
3. Assess the campaign of the two sides in the 1995 Quebec Referendum.
4. Explain Canada's reasons for the Turbot War.
5. Consider the issue of multiculturalism in the age of global terrorism.

Introduction

When the Dominion Institute, an organization committed to promoting Canadian history, and the Department of Citizenship and Immigration Canada issued the results of a 2008 Canada Day survey on what defines Canada, Tim Hortons was on the list; none of Canada's major art and cultural icons, such as Margaret Atwood, the Group of Seven, or Neil Young, were. Hockey legends Wayne Gretzky and Don Cherry both made the list of the top 101 things that best describe Canada. The Maple Leaf, Vimy Ridge, the beaver, the Canadian Flag, and hockey were the top five. Most university and college students might agree that the list defines their Canada, but they would probably add multiculturalism, the Charter of Rights and Freedoms, and a few other things.

Canadians have long struggled with what defines their country; they have a strong sense of what their nation is, but this does not mean that all Canadians sees their nation in the same way. The issues that have resonated in the period since 1993, such as Canada's economic situation, Quebec's place in Canada, Western alienation, the viability of east coast fisheries, Aboriginal self-government, relations with the United States, a new approach to the social safety net, government scandals, environmental challenges, women, the impact of globalization, and the role of Canada's military, have been about the very nature of Canada and the type of nation Canadians want. As we consider Canada's contemporary history, it is important to see that many of the same issues that animated Canadians for decades continue to be important, including the role of the state, the nature of Canada's social programs, the relationships between the state and Aboriginal peoples, gender equality, federal–provincial relations, the military, and multiculturalism. On most issues, Canadians continue to hold different views, but the history of Canada has been about negotiating those differences and finding enough common ground to make the country work.

The Triumph of Regionalism and the Fracturing of Canada's Political System

Canadians were in a foul mood again when they were called to vote in the 35th general election since Confederation on October 25, 1993. The country was in the midst of a stubborn economic downturn. The unemployment rate hovered around 11 percent and personal and business bankruptcies continued to set new records each month. Economic forecasters warned that a fiscal crisis loomed that would make it nearly impossible for governments to continue the level and quality of services to which Canadians had become accustomed. On the east coast, more than 42 000 workers were thrown out of work as the fishery collapsed from overfishing. Ontario continued to grumble about the economic costs of free trade, and the West complained that it was being ignored as usual. Political commentators and some economists were warning that the only solution was deep cuts to government spending and a rethinking of the role of governments. Others suggested that the focus on spending cuts in social programs was a political choice and only confirmed for them an entrenched neoliberal agenda among the nation's political and economic elites.

It was not just the economy that angered Canadians; many other things were not right either. Two of Canada's famed peacekeepers from the Canadian Airborne Regiment in Somalia were charged with second-degree murder and torture following the death of Somali teenager Shidane Arone. The federal government had ordered a public inquiry into the safety of Canada's blood supply after more than 1200 patients were infected with the deadly HIV virus through blood transfusions. The United Nations Committee on Economic, Social and Cultural Rights criticized Canada for its high level of poverty and homelessness, especially among Aboriginal peoples, despite the fact that it was one of the world's richest countries. Quebec, it seemed, couldn't wait for another chance to vote on sovereignty or independence. With all of these issues, it is little wonder that many Canadians feared their country would break apart before they reached the year 2000.

The one bright spot, for a brief moment at least, seemed to be Kim Campbell—she was intelligent, enthusiastic, and rising in the public opinion polls. She became Canada's first female prime minister on June 25, 1993, after easily winning the leadership of the Progressive Conservative party. During the leadership campaign, though, her inexperience showed, especially in her impromptu comments. Like most politicians of that era, she made annual deficits and the accumulated debt her major priority, but she described those who were not concerned with such matters as "enemies of Canada." She labelled those who took no interest in politics and voting "apathetic s.o.b.s," and she had to defend her handling of the defence department, as she had been minister when Arone was beaten to death. On Canada Day, when she jetted across the country, taking in the sunrise ceremonies on Signal Hill in St. John's, the noon-time celebrations in Ottawa, and the evening festivities in Vancouver, her critics dismissed such extravagance as a subsidized pre-election gimmick. Three days later, Ontario NDP Premier Bob Rae, bruised and battered from his own struggles, refused to meet with Campbell and the other premiers because he saw the meetings as another pre-election photo opportunity. Everyone was cranky.

When Campbell called the election, the Liberals and Conservatives were tied in the polls. Campbell had tried to distance herself from the Mulroney government but, she warned, as Mulroney had, that deficit reduction, controlled spending, and curtailing inflation were all priorities. She pledged to reduce pensions for federal politicians and get tough on crime—two of the major issues of the Reform party, the new party of Western protest.

During the campaign, the Conservatives made a number of fatal mistakes. Campbell admitted that unemployment would remain high and not improve until after 2000—scant comfort for an angry electorate that had become disillusioned with its leaders and many of its political institutions. When asked about transforming Canada's social programs, she remarked that an election campaign was too short to "get involved in a debate on very, very serious matters." The party's greatest blunder, however, was to run an election ad that mocked the facial features of Jean Chrétien, the new Liberal leader. Chrétien had been afflicted in his youth with an illness that left the muscles in his face partially paralyzed. The ads were pulled, but the personal attacks served to demonstrate that Campbell and the Conservatives were desperate. Mulroney's unpopularity was another problem for Campbell. The coalition that Mulroney had built in 1984 collapsed and spawned two new parties—the Bloc Québécois and the Reform party—which cut into Campbell's support.

Only 69.6 percent of those eligible bothered to vote in the 1993 election, the lowest turnout since 1925, when Mackenzie King was re-elected to a minority government. Although the Conservatives captured 16 percent of the popular vote, the party was decimated, winning only two seats. The Liberals won a majority government with 177 seats, and Chrétien became prime minister. Although Chrétien's Liberals won seats in every province, the regional cleavages within the nation were clear. They captured all but one of the 99 seats in Ontario and 30 in Atlantic Canada, but were swamped by the Bloc Québécois in Quebec and the Reform party in the West. Led by the popular and charismatic Lucien Bouchard, a former Mulroney cabinet minister, the Bloc had the support of nearly 50 percent of Quebecers (13.5 percent nationally) and won 54 of 75 seats there, enough to make the Quebec separatist party the official opposition in the House of Commons, an outcome that angered many in English-speaking Canada.

Reform, a new political party that had become the voice of Western discontent, was two seats behind the Bloc and had 18.7 percent of the popular vote. Under Preston Manning, Reform captured 52 of 86 ridings west of the Ontario–Manitoba border. Manning had emerged on the national political scene during the referendum on the Charlottetown Accord in 1992, which he always described as Mulroney's deal to great effect. The Reform party fielded 207 candidates but avoided Quebec and Atlantic Canada. Stephen Harper, then just 35, was elected for Reform in Calgary. Its campaign focused on controlling the deficit by promising to cut federal spending by $18 billion and reduce the size of government. The rapid rise of Reform in the West also destroyed much of the support for the New Democrats, which dropped from 43 seats to 9, and 6 percent of the vote; more than half of its MPs came from Saskatchewan, where NDP support ran deep. Like the Conservatives, the NDP lost official party status in the House of Commons. The old political system, characterized by two major parties and one or two significant minor ones that had endured for much of the twentieth century, was replaced by a new multiparty system in which the various parties held their allegiances to particular regions of the country. Politically, Canada was a fragmented nation.

New Government, Old Issues

Although 1993 marked a changing of political parties at the national level, the issues confronting the country remained much the same as they had for more than a decade: the fiscal situation, federal–provincial relations (especially the place of Quebec in Canada), immigration, social policy, the rights of minorities, Aboriginal Canadians, and Canada's place in the world. With a few minor and perhaps symbolic changes, the Chrétien government soon made it clear that it had no intention of reversing the changes that the Mulroney Conservatives had introduced. In many instances, Chrétien pursued those policies with a greater determination than had his predecessor and, during the course of three majority governments, he demonstrated that most of Mulroney's policies did eventually pay dividends.

The Mulroney government had talked a lot about putting the nation's fiscal house in order. While it had managed to keep spending in line with the revenues that the government collected, it continued to borrow to pay the interest charges on the national debt. The 1993 deficit of $34 billion was used to pay interest on the national debt of $423 billion. However,

Controlling the deficit and dealing with the national debt become a major public policy issue.

Mulroney had helped convince many Canadians that as a nation we were living beyond our means, and they regularly told pollsters that the fiscal situation was the major issue facing the nation. Managing it better had become the chief priority of all the major political parties by 1993; they differed only on how much and how quickly the deficit and debt had to be reduced.

Chrétien and Finance Minister Paul Martin took control of the government, convinced that action had to be taken to reduce public spending. With most Canadians on side, the Liberals could be ruthless in cutting government expenditures and transfers to the provinces. Their greatest legacy would be improving Canada's fiscal position and returning the government to annual surpluses. Unlike previous Liberal governments, such as those led by Lester B. Pearson and Pierre Trudeau, who had believed activist governments could solve any national problem, Chrétien instead followed the Conservative neoliberal agenda.

The task of confronting the nation's fiscal situation fell largely to Martin. When he delivered his first budget in 1994, he followed pretty much the same course as the Conservatives had. He reduced spending on the military by closing bases and reducing personnel, including cancelling a contract that the previous government had signed for new helicopters; cut benefits for unemployment insurance and increased the qualifying period for unemployed workers; froze transfers to the provinces for education and welfare; and promised to reduce the deficit. However, a rise in interest rates, precipitated by inflationary pressure in the United States and fears about another referendum in Quebec, severely limited any gains Martin had made in bringing the deficit under control with modest reductions in government spending.

A tour of the world's financial markets and a visit to the International Monetary Fund headquarters in Washington following his first budget demonstrated to Martin that he had to be more aggressive in dealing with the fiscal situation. He was told that Canada had been talking about eliminating its deficit for more than 25 years, but it had not made any real progress. He was warned that Canada was "going down the tubes," and he realized that the new economy that he had hoped to create through increased spending on infrastructure and training was not possible without first getting Canada's deficits under control.[1] The influential *Wall Street Journal* described Canada as an honorary member of the Third World and warned that, like Mexico, Canada was about to hit the "debt wall" and drop into the financial abyss if the government failed to manage its debt problem more effectively. Also in 1994, Moody's Investors Services downgraded Canada's sovereign bonding rate, making it more expensive for the government to borrow money. Rising expectations would have to be tempered, and polls told Martin that most Canadians were ready for the bitter medicine.

By 1994, the federal deficit was nearly $40 billion; the national debt exceeded $500 billion and was growing by $85 000 a minute. This information is shown in Figure 12.1, which also shows how the deficit and the debt (the accumulated deficits) had increased dramatically from the early 1960s to the mid-1990s. More than 30 cents of every dollar the government collected in taxes in 1995 went to service the debt. In Martin's view, the $6 billion needed for interest payments was money that was not available for new government spending. He reportedly told his officials that wrestling the deficit to the ground was not about ideology but arithmetic. To appear credible, Martin believed he had to be harsh, and harsh he was: His second budget was perhaps the most severe in the history of Canada. In his 1995 Budget Speech he said, "There are times in the progress of a people

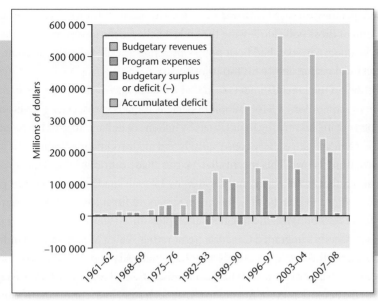

Figure 12.1
An Overview of Canada's Fiscal Situation from 1961 to 2008

Source: © Department of Finance, Reproduced with the permission of the Minister of Public Works and Government Services, 2010.

when fundamental challenges must be faced, fundamental choices made—a new course charted. For Canada, this is one of those times."[2]

Martin outlined budget cuts of $80 billion between 1994–1995 and 1998–1999. This brought government spending as a percentage of gross domestic product (GDP), as shown in Figure 12.2, to levels not seen since 1961,[3] and it continued to transform Canada with the neoliberal agenda first introduced under Mulroney. Martin reduced expectations and abandoned the interventionist policies of earlier Liberal governments. He reduced the civil service by 45 000 jobs or 14 percent. Every department in the federal government—with the exception of Indian and Northern Affairs Canada—suffered major cuts, subsidies to businesses were either eliminated or reduced, and many government services were told to operate on a commercial model; that is, they could not lose money. The government continued to privatize many of its Crown corporations, including Canadian National (the nation's railway system) and Petro-Canada (the state-run oil company). Air traffic control that provided navigation for the country's airline industry was privatized, and the Crow Rate, the subsidy that assisted Western farmers in moving their grains to market, was eliminated. Canada reduced its expenditure on foreign aid, and substantially increased the fee for immigrants. The Liberal plan for a national child-care program, at about $360 million, was scrapped—to the disappointment of many women's groups—and the federal government

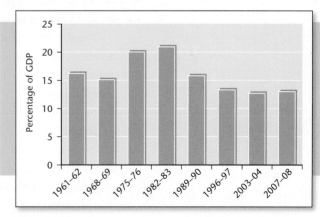

Figure 12.2
Federal Government Spending as a Percentage of GDP
Note the decline in spending after 1982–1983.

Source: © Department of Finance, Reproduced with the permission of the Minister of Public Works and Government Services, 2010.

New transfer agreement between Ottawa and the provinces.

stopped spending on social (low-income) housing. Even with such aggressive cuts, nearly 70 percent of those polled following the budget believed the government was doing what had to be done; Chrétien had been politically astute as well as fiscally prudent, it seems, to make fiscal responsibility his top priority.

Martin and the Liberals understood that it was best to overstate the problem in their fiscal forecasting. With a $160 billion budget, as Canada's was, even a slight mistake of 1 or 2 percent meant missing their targets by billions of dollars. To avoid that, the Liberals built their annual budgets very conservatively and made room for economic circumstances and forecasting errors. This meant that Martin made cautious budgetary forecasts, but his final numbers were always impressive; the Liberals made a trademark of painting a terrible picture and then beating their own targets. In fiscal 1997–1998, Martin reported a surplus of $2.9 billion—the first federal surplus since 1969—and after several years of surpluses, Moody's upgraded Canada's credit rating, which Martin saw as vindication of his handling of the fiscal crisis. In his view, his neoliberal policy agenda was a success, and when Martin delivered more than he had promised, Canadians came quickly to regard him as one of the best ministers of finance in Canadian history and a prime minister in waiting.

Changing the Federal–Provincial Relationship

The new Liberal government changed the relationship between Ottawa and the provinces. The federal government had, for more than a generation, transferred to the provinces funds to support health, social welfare, and post-secondary education under two separate programs: the Canada Assistance Plan (CAP) and the Established Programs Financing (EPF), although Ottawa had been cutting the amount of the transfers to the provinces since 1991. Both CAP and EPF enabled the federal government to set national standards for social programs in the provinces and to impose some consistency in social citizenship across Canada. These types of grants were known as conditional transfers because the provinces had to adhere to national standards, or conditions, to receive funds from the federal government.

These funding arrangements were replaced in fiscal 1996 by the Canada Health and Social Transfer (CHST). When Martin made the changes, he further reduced transfers to the provinces by more than $14 billion from fiscal 1995 to fiscal 1998. Planned cuts of more than $6 billion for fiscal 1998 were restored as an election promise in the 1997 general election, but the cuts resumed again in 2000 as Table 12.1 illustrates. The cuts announced after 1994 represented about 3 percent of all provincial revenues, and the provinces complained that Ottawa was saving money— and eliminating the federal deficit—by cutting transfers to the them and "off-loading" responsibility for health, education, and social welfare to the provincial governments. The provinces were right: The CHST no longer earmarked funding for social assistance, for instance, but allowed the provinces to spend the money as they wished. The Liberal government insisted that conditional transfers had been a source of irritation in federal–provincial relations, and that Ottawa was simply allowing the provinces to spend the transferred funds as they chose—even if the amounts were

Table 12.1

Federal Transfers to Provinces and Territories as a Percentage of GDP, 1992–1993 to 2007–2008

Year	Federal Cash Transfers
1992–93	4.2
1993–94	3.9
1994–95	3.8
1995–96	3.7
1996–97	2.9
1997–98	2.7
1998–99	2.9
1999–00	2.8
2000–01	2.8
2001–02	3.0
2002–03	3.0
2003–04	3.1
2004–05	3.3
2005–06	3.4
2006–07	3.4
2007–08	3.6

Source: Provincial/territorial Public Accounts and 2008 Budgets and *National Income and Expenditure Accounts* (13-001).

significantly reduced. The problem, however, was that most of the provinces were nearly broke and were forced to implement their own austerity programs.

In the area of health, the federal government continued to enforce the *Canada Health Act* and the provinces were required, as they were under the rules of the CAP, to provide social assistance without any minimum residency requirements. Under the old arrangement, the provinces received federal funding to offset the costs of social spending in the provinces, but with the new CHST the provinces had to fund new program spending out of their own funds. Many simply reduced social spending to fit within the funds transferred under the CHST. Michael Prince, a social policy professor at the University of Victoria, described the CHST as "a child of federal deficit reduction and a cousin of provincial demands for greater autonomy in social policy."[4] The introduction of the CHST was an attempt by the federal government to reduce the deficit rather than to foster a new role for itself. In some cases, the cuts meant the end of national standards, which was ironic given that Chrétien had campaigned against the Meech and Charlottetown Accords, claiming that the proposed constitutional changes would lead to a more decentralized federation; several years later, he was doing precisely that to prevent financial exigency.

One result of Ottawa's financial plan was to download responsibility for much of the social spending to the provinces. Reduced federal transfers exacerbated the plight of the provinces that had to deal with their own deficit and debt problems. All provinces, it seemed, were amalgamating and restructuring school boards, hospitals, and municipalities to save money. In Saskatchewan, where the province had a brush with bankruptcy, NDP Premier Roy Romanow focused on the government deficit reduction through spending cuts and privatization and even introduced balanced budget legislation—showing how far-reaching the fiscal crisis had become. It was the same across the country. In Ontario, for instance, NDP Premier Bob Rae cut spending in virtually every sector, including municipalities, universities, schools, hospitals, and social welfare. This was particularly difficult for a socialist government, and Rae attempted to negotiate a social contract with the public sector that he thought would ameliorate the difficulties in the province. The social contract was an attempt to negotiate with labour on how best to achieve the province's fiscal objectives rather than arbitrarily announcing a series of cuts as the federal government had.

Labour disputes were common in the early 1990s. Here, a student protests a strike that shut down the ferry to the Toronto Islands, preventing him from getting to his summer job.

Source: Richard Lautens/GetStock.com.

Rae's policies were a failure and his attempts to balance the budget through wage freezes and rollbacks, early retirement, and unpaid days off (called "Rae days" by workers) earned Rae and the NDP nothing but contempt from his supporters and detractors alike. Although Rae had pursued a progressive social agenda, including a ban on nuclear plants in the province, the inherent right of Aboriginal peoples to self-government, an affirmative action program for visible minorities and women in the public service, and a bill to provide benefits to same-sex couples (which was defeated when his own party refused to support it), he was badly beaten in the 1995 provincial election that saw his party go from 74 seats to 17. Rae and the NDP were replaced with Progressive Conservative Mike Harris, who promised a *Common Sense Revolution*, which was predicated on restoring fiscal responsibility to government through tax and spending cuts. During his seven years as premier, Harris embraced a policy of restraint adopted in most provinces, which saw a diminished role for the state and huge cuts in public spending aimed, in many cases, at reducing the size of the civil service. Harris was more zealous than other premiers in his spending reductions on welfare, social programs, and what became known as the MUSH (municipalities, universities, schools, and hospitals) sector.

An economic neoconservative, Harris generated considerable opposition among labour and social groups, but he had little interest in such issues as same-sex marriage and abortion, which animated so many neoconservatives. Alberta's Ralph Klein, premier from 1992 to 2006, was Canada's other neoconservative and he launched what became known as the *Klein Revolution*, though it soon became apparent that Klein was more interested in simply reducing spending than revolutionizing Alberta politics. Although he privatized Alberta's liquor stores, those on the right wing of his party were disappointed that he did not pursue the more radical ideas within the Conservative party to embrace private health clinics and eliminate funding for abortion clinics. As Jason Kenny, then president of the Canadian Taxpayers' Federation, complained, "This isn't a revolution … we have just traded a Rolls-Royce for a Cadillac."[5]

Cutting Back on Equality

The Canadian women's movement saw the concern over fiscal matters as an attack on women and their struggle for equality. Throughout the period, women's organizations saw their influence reduced and funding for a variety of them were cut. This might have been anticipated, as Chrétien had refused during the 1993 campaign to participate in an election debate on women's issue; he even mused that the government should get out of funding lobby or special interest groups, which many in government believed included the various women's groups. In 1995, for instance, the federal government closed the Canadian Advisory Council on the Status of Women, which Trudeau had established in 1973 to provide research and advice on women's issues inside the federal government.

Women's groups believed that when the government enacted the huge cutbacks, especially in social policy, it ignored the gendered dimension of such policies. They believed that women were substantially more affected by reductions in social spending than males. This was evident, they claimed, in cuts to the unemployment insurance program in 1996. As the program was revamped to become employment insurance, the new rules regarding coverage, benefit periods, and ineligibility made it difficult for part-time workers to qualify, many of whom were women. Yet, the new hourly based approach to qualifying for benefits meant more women were covered when the changes took affect.

It has been argued by some scholars that the Chrétien government's attitude to gender equality can be demonstrated by examining its policy on violence towards women. By the time the Liberals won power in 1994, the Canadian government had made violence against women an important issue. Not only that, S. Laurel Weldon, a specialist on policies on violence against women at Purdue University, argues, Canadian policy had incorporated language and analyses developed by radical feminists. Canada was a leader in addressing the issue of violence against women and recognized the problem in gender-specific terms as wife battering, rape, and other forms of violent acts directed specifically against women. Violence against women was recognized as a symptom of sexual inequality between women and men, but during the Liberal regime, the government ceased seeing violence against women as an issue of gender inequality and started using gender-neutral language to describe the problem. Violence against women became, for instance, linked to a "law and order" agenda that emphasized the need to protect citizens against criminals and increasingly saw crime as a wider social problem. Such a reorientation removed violence against women from a discussion about traditional gender roles to the broader issue of social inequality than had been the case in the previous decade.

Government support for the women's movement declined dramatically and can be seen in the withdrawal of funding for shelters for victims of violence. In 1994, the federal government shut down its Family Violence Initiative, and only restored funding in 1997 (an election year), and in 1995 it shifted funding responsibility for shelters for victims of violence to the provinces. The number of new shelters had increased by 400 percent between 1979 and 1989, but the rate of growth slowed considerably after that, with only a 25 percent increase between 1995 and 1998, and 5 percent between 1998 and 2000, even as their use grew by more than 20 percent during the same period. Moreover, government funding for women's groups working with victims of violence was cut substantially during the period.[6] In the 12-month period from April 1, 2007, to March 31, 2008, more than 62 000 women and their 38 000 children sought refuge in one of Canada's nearly 600 known shelters that provide residential services to abused women and their children. In 2008, women were the victims of 83 percent of all incidents of spousal violence reported to police.

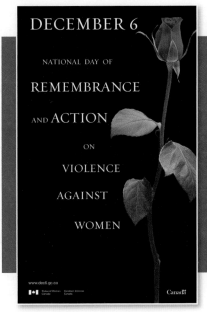

December 6 is the National Day of Remembrance and Action on Violence Against Women in Canada. It was established in 1991 by the Parliament of Canada to mark the anniversary of the murders in 1989 of 14 young women at l'École Polytechnique de Montréal, who were killed because they were women.

Source: www.swc-cfc.gc.ca/dates/vaw-vff/poster-affiche-eng.pdf. Reproduced with the permission of the Minister of Public Works and Government Services, 2010.

Reinvesting in Canada

Following several years of dramatic spending cuts, the federal government believed it had the fiscal situation under control. It then altered its approach, signalling that it could begin to reinvest in the country. By 1998—after declaring a budgetary surplus in 1997—Ottawa introduced a series of new programs that, it claimed, was to enhance social solidarity in Canada by "preserving and modernizing the social union so that the Canadian commitment to a caring and sharing society remained truly Canada-wide in scope."[7] The federal government attempted to reassert its position with the provinces in the areas of child policy, post-secondary education, and health, but it was not a return to the system of cost-sharing with the provinces that had existed from the 1960s to the 1980s. This time, Ottawa hoped to achieve its policy goals through three mechanisms: (1) direct transfers to individuals and families; (2) changes to the CHST; and (3) the creation of foundations.

One priority was children in low-income families. Under the system existing prior to 1997, child benefits were often reduced when parents left social assistance (welfare) to enter the workforce. Parents also lost other valuable benefits, such as health, dental, and prescription drug benefits for their children. It was often financially better for those parents to remain on welfare than take a low-paying job. While a variety of government programs provided various forms of support to families with children, they had inadvertently created a "welfare wall" that made it difficult for parents to move from welfare to work. The existing system created significant financial disincentives for parents to leave social assistance. Ottawa and the provinces wanted a system that would make parents better off financially if they were working as opposed to remaining on social assistance.

1998: Canada introduces the new National Child Benefit.

The federal government introduced a National Child Benefit (NCB)—the first major national social program in more than three decades. The goals were to reduce child poverty, to help parents participate in the labour market without losing their child benefits, and to reduce overlap and duplication of government programs. The program involved the federal, provincial, and territorial governments and First Nations and began in July 1998. Quebec did not participate in the National Child Benefit program, but it received the NCB supplements from Ottawa and used the money saved from reducing its social assistance payments to finance other family programs. It subsequently developed one of the most progressive programs for early childhood care and education, including a $5-a-day child-care program in regulated centres, a full-day kindergarten for all five-year-olds, and a half-day program for younger children from low-income families whom the government considered at risk of encountering learning problems once they entered the school system.

There are two components to the National Child Benefit, as shown in Figure 12.3. The first was a monthly payment from the Government of Canada to families with children. The direct federal benefit, known as the Canada Child Tax Benefit (CCTB), was designed to help low- and middle-income families with the costs of raising their children, though the level of benefits decreased as family income increased and was fully phased out when family incomes reached $99 128 (in 2007). In 2007, 3.5 million families and 6 million children received the CCTB. In addition, some 2.8 million children and 1.6 million families with income less than $36 387 received additional benefits through the NCB Supplement. The new program, totalling $6 billion, provided considerable support to all low-income families across Canada and was billed as "an important national project." Pierre S. Pettigrew, the minister of Human Resources Development, admitted that the National Child Benefit Supplement would not eliminate child poverty, but he believed that "it would improve the living standards of thousands of Canadian children."[8] The *National Child Benefit Progress Report: 2006* shows that the percentage of families with children living in low income had declined from 17.6 percent in 1996 to 11.6 percent in 2005.

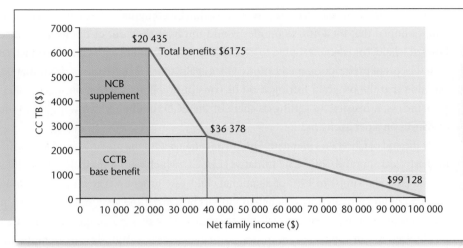

Source: *The National Child Benefit Progress Report: 2006*. Reproduced with the permission of the Minister of Public Works and Government Services Canada, 2010.

Figure 12.3

This graph represents the maximum Canada Child Tax Benefit (CCTB) base benefits and the NCB supplement for the benefit year July 2006 to June 2007, for a family with two children.

The second component of the NCB included a variety of benefits and services designed and delivered by the provinces, territories, and First Nations to improve the lives of low-income families with children. When the federal government introduced the NCB Supplement, the other orders of government were allowed under the NCB initiative to reduce their payments for social assistance recipients with children. However, these savings could not be removed from the social assistance programs; in fact, when the National Child Benefit initiative was first established, the provinces agreed that all social assistance savings would be reinvested to benefit low-income families with children. The provincial funds saved because of increases to federal programs had to be redirected towards improved income support and children's services for low-income working families. The provinces, territories, and First Nations agreed to a national reinvestment framework that would provide new or enhanced supports for low-income families with children, including, child-care/daycare initiatives, child benefits and earned income supplements, special services for early childhood development and children-at-risk, and supplementary health benefits for children. By 2005–2006, more than $870 million had been reinvested by the provinces. While the National Child Benefit was not a traditional federal–provincial conditional transfer because the federal funds were paid to individuals rather than the provinces, the NCB did allow the provinces to redirect funds to related areas that the federal government set as priorities.

A second initiative under what the government called its National Child Agenda was the Early Childhood Development (ECD). It was a more traditional "conditional" grant, and designed to increase and expand provincial programs for children and their families by adding $2.2 billion to the Canadian Health and Social Transfer between 2001–2002 and 2005–2006. The provinces had to spend the funds in four general areas: promoting healthy pregnancy, birth, and infancy; improving parenting and family supports; strengthening early childhood development, learning, and care; and strengthening community supports. The provinces were permitted to establish their own programs and services within these general areas and did not have to satisfy any federal conditions or performance measures, but they had to publish an annual progress report aimed at their residents.

The expectation here was that the provinces had to be accountable to their citizens, and Ottawa hoped that by doing so monies would not be moved out of the sector. Prince Edward Island, for example, opted to assist low-income families with children under 18 with the cost of prescription medications. Once again, Quebec opted out of this initiative, claiming that the program infringed on its constitutional jurisdiction on social policy. Nonetheless, it insisted on getting its share of the ECD funding, which was paid to the provinces on a per capita basis.

At the end of Chrétien's mandate, Ottawa negotiated with the provinces and territories the Early Learning and Child Care Initiative (ELCCI), which went some distance to fulfilling the Liberal promise in 1993 of a national child-care program. The initiative, costing nearly $1 billion initially, was designed to support provincial and territorial investment in early learning and child care, especially for low-income families. A side agreement focused on children in Aboriginal communities. As prime minister, Paul Martin attempted to build on these child-care provisions initiated by Chrétien and signed separate agreements with all ten provinces for more child-care spaces, but his national daycare program was replaced in 2006 by the Conservatives, who made a $1200 cash payment to parents of children under six for help with child-care costs.

The Rising Cost of Health

Another priority for the reinvesting in Canada initiative was healthcare. Canada had introduced a publicly funded national health insurance program (though administered by the ten provinces and three territories) in the late 1960s. The federal contribution to medicare—as the program was commonly called—was reduced significantly as Ottawa attempted to deal with its budgetary deficits. Total healthcare spending as a percentage of GDP fell each year between 1993 and 1997, to reach 8.9 percent in 1997. These reductions came even as costs soared for the health sector, as Table 12.2 shows. Much of the increase was driven by new technology, the demand from citizens to reduce the waiting list for various medical procedures (such as hip replacement and cataract surgery), and increased labour costs. Because of the huge public concern over the state of healthcare, it became the subject of several major studies, including one by former Saskatchewan premier Roy Romanow, amid worries that Canada's medicare system was on the verge of collapse.

The crisis in healthcare prompted a heated debate that often pivoted on the issue of whether or not healthcare was a public good that had to be delivered only through a publicly administered system or through private clinics, or a combination of both. This is an issue that will not go away; in 2008, the Canadian Medical Association elected a president that favoured a mixed private and public healthcare system, but there is little indication that governments will move away from a system of predominately public service delivery anytime soon. Support appears to be strong for the federal health insurance legislation, known as the *Canada Health Act*, which outlines the national principles that govern the medicare system: public administration, comprehensiveness, universality, portability, and accessibility, principles that the all major political parties insist symbolize the underlying Canadian values of equity and solidarity.

Table 12.2
Total Health Expenditure, Canada, 1975 to 2009

Year	Total ($000 000)
1975	12 199.4
1980	22 298.4
1985	39 841.7
1990	61 022.6
1995	74 089.2
2000	98 427.5
2005	141 061.1
2009	183 120.9

Source: http://www.cihi.ca/cihiweb/en/media_20091119_tab1_e.html.

Healthcare costs account for nearly 40 percent of all provincial spending, making it the largest and fastest-growing segment of provincial expenditures. How much of its revenue each province spends on healthcare can vary greatly: Total health expenditure as a percentage of provincial GDP ranged from 6.9 percent in Alberta and 8.8 percent in Newfoundland and Labrador to 14.6 percent in Nova Scotia and 15.3 percent in Prince Edward Island in 2008. In 1975, the total costs for healthcare throughout Canada consumed 7.5 percent of GDP; that number had risen to nearly 11 percent by 2008, or $172 billion.

In 1999, the federal government responded to the growing crisis in healthcare and promised to add $11.5 billion in new funding for health in the CHST over the coming five years. A year later, another $2.5 billion was added, but it did little to solve the problem. In September 2000, a first ministers conference on health resulted in the creation of two new provincial health funds, one of $1 billion for equipment, and another of $800 million for a health transition fund to test and evaluate innovative ways to deliver healthcare services. The only condition placed on the provinces was to publish reports on how the money was spent. The Canadian Medical Association was alarmed when it later completed a study of the funds and found that nearly half of the new monies went to replace provincial expenditures on health, which meant that those funds did little to address problems in the system. Some of the monies for health equipment were spent on lawn mowers, printers, and cooking utensils—not exactly what Canadians had expected.

In February 2003, the provinces and the federal government reached a health accord mainly to improve access to healthcare. This agreement separated the CHST into a Canada Health Transfer and a Canada Social Transfer, with health taking more than 60 percent of the total. The federal government committed $34.8 billion in new funding over the five-year period from 2003–2004 to 2007–2008 and added an additional $2 billion in 2004. The fund was aimed at primary healthcare, home care, particularly for people with mental illnesses and end-of-life care, and catastrophic drug care, but it was not enough. A year later, a new ten-year plan was negotiated, with the federal government committing to an additional $18 billion to the provinces and territories over the next six years to sustain the public healthcare system, and the federal government guaranteed to increase federal health transfers by 6 percent annually until 2015. According to the federal government, this amounted to an additional $41 billion in new funding over ten years, above the $36.8 billion agreed to in the 2003 Health Accord. A separate deal was worked out with Quebec. Although the early period of the Chrétien era was marked by considerable acrimony over federal cuts to healthcare, much of the funding had been restored by 2005. Since then, healthcare has not received as much attention as other issues. Under the Conservative government of Stephen Harper, the government has tried to show that it does not want to have greater private involvement in the healthcare system. After all, the government is keenly aware—as was demonstrated in separate surveys by Nanos Research and a Harris/Decima polling in 2009—that Canadians overwhelmingly support their public health system.

New Ways of Funding Education

The third area of federal reinvestment was in post-secondary education. The federal government has played an important role in financing post-secondary education since the 1950s, but in the 1990s it opted for two approaches that moved it away from the federal–provincial transfers that had become the norm. In the 2000 budget, Ottawa created the Canada Research Chairs Program at a cost of $900 million to fund salaries and research costs of university chairs across Canada. This was part of the government's innovation agenda, and its goal was to attract top researchers, both foreign and Canadian-born, who had left the country to do research elsewhere; for the government, innovation through research was a necessary condition for economic prosperity.

The other funding approach for post-secondary education was the creation of foundations. Since 1996, the federal government has transferred more than $10 billion to nine foundations. The Canada Foundation for Innovation (CFI) is one of the most important. It was created to make strategic infrastructure investments in the areas of science, engineering, health, and the environment. Another, the Canada Millennium Scholarship Foundation (CMSF), provides funds for students with financial need through the provincial student aid programs and has undertaken a wide array of research projects on post-secondary education in Canada. The Harper government announced in its 2008 budget that it would not renew the mandate of the CMSF when it expired in 2010 and that it will be replaced with a national system of grants aimed at students from low- and middle-income families, part-time students, students with dependants, and students with permanent disabilities. The foundations, although creations of the federal government, operated at arm's length, but they were very much tied to the government's "competitiveness" agenda that placed an important role on research and development, especially in those sectors that made up what was called the new economy. These initiatives also demonstrated the government's belief that research at Canada's universities would promote innovation and increase productivity and economic development across the country.

Unity and a Second Referendum

National unity is always a major issue in Canada. Some governments, such as Mackenzie King's, used brokerage politics and delay to keep the nation united. More recently, others, such as Pierre Trudeau, believed that they could construct a liberal society built on individual rights that would bridge the differences that existed in Canada. When Canada faced one of its greatest threats to national unity in the 1990s, many Canadians feared that it had a leader with neither the vision nor the political smarts to handle the problem. Although Prime Minister Chrétien claimed that national unity was his primary goal during a lifetime in politics, the rhetoric did not support his claim. Chrétien was minister of Indian Affairs when the government angered Aboriginal peoples with the White Paper in 1969; he was justice minister and played a pivotal role in patriating the Constitution in 1982, which alienated many in Quebec who insisted that the process was not only a failure but also unfinished; and he was minister of energy during the early 1980s when the West rose in protest over Ottawa's energy policy and ignited a new round of Western alienation. Two years after he became prime minister, vowing not to have any discussion on the Constitution to please Quebec, he had to face a second referendum and nearly lost the country.

When the Meech Lake Accord, a constitutional agreement that recognized Quebec as a distinct society, failed in 1990, it signalled the inevitability of a second referendum on Quebec independence. The Parti Québécois was returned to office in 1994, promising to hold such a vote within a year. The referendum had all the excitement of a good Hollywood drama, and most Canadians would have enjoyed watching it unfold if the stakes had not been so huge. Jacques Parizeau, the new Quebec premier, aristocratic and distant, was never suited for the lead in such a dramatic event—that fell to Lucien Bouchard, who emerged as one of the most charismatic and effective politicians in Canadian history in the months before the referendum. Although Bouchard had been a committed Québécois nationalist who supported the "Yes" side in the 1980 referendum, he had served for a time in the Mulroney cabinet before he quit over proposed changes to the Meech Lake Accord to create the Bloc Québécois.

Not only was he passionate, brilliant, and determined, Bouchard was also handsome and accompanied everywhere by his wife, Audrey Best, a beautiful Californian 20 years his junior. The comparison with Trudeau was obvious. But tragedy struck him just before Christmas in 1994. Bouchard was rushed to a Montreal hospital suffering from necrotizing fasciitis, the one-in-a-million flesh-eating disease. His life was in grave danger and the national media gave hourly updates. Doctors were forced to amputate his leg in hopes of saving his life. At first it appeared that the amputation had failed, and there were rumours that he had died and that Parizeau's office was planning a state funeral. During his ordeal he had scribbled a note to his doctors—"*Que l'on continue, merci*"—which many in Quebec saw as a political message that the battle for independence had to continue, even if Bouchard died. Miraculously, he survived, his popularity soared, and he was about to emerge as saviour of the separatist cause.

Parizeau was consumed with sovereignty; he saw no need for any negotiation or partnership with Canada as René Lévesque had proposed in 1980. With 40 percent support according to the polls, he was leading the "Yes" side to certain defeat. Bouchard understood that many in Quebec wanted to keep some link with Canada or, at least, it was the necessary condition to winning the referendum. In early March 1995, he challenged Parizeau to offer Canada a partnership and promise Quebec another referendum before declaring sovereignty. The Quebec premier had no choice but to relent. He invited Bouchard to become co-chair of the "Yes" side, as the sovereignist campaign showed signs of collapsing.

Bouchard united the sovereignist forces. He brought Mario Dumont, the young dynamic leader of the fledgling Action Démocratique, into the sovereignist camp. They negotiated with Parizeau a Tripartite Agreement on Sovereignty to coordinate their efforts in the referendum. There would be no outright declaration of sovereignty. The sovereignists once again sought a mandate to launch formal negotiations for a new economic and political association with Canada in the event of a "Yes" majority. If the negotiations failed to produce a deal after a year, the government would then have the power to declare Quebec sovereign. While the federalist forces—those that wanted Quebec to remain in Canada—dismissed the agreement as the last gasp of desperation, Marie Huhtala, the U.S.

1995: Second Quebec referendum on independence.

consul-general in Quebec, told the U.S. State Department that "Canadians and Quebeckers would be well advised to fasten their seat belts. The sovereignty train has left the station and is picking up speed. We are lucky we can stay on the sidelines; it is likely to be a rough ride."[9] The referendum was set for October 30, 1995.

Federalists denounced the question as confusing and misleading largely because it made no reference to Quebec as an independent country; they were confident that the polls were correct and that Quebeckers would vote as they had in 1980. They focused primarily on telling Quebecers that a "Yes" vote meant Quebec's separation from Canada, attacking the sovereignists' economic arguments, and warning that the costs of separation were immense. Prime Minister Chrétien dismissed those who warned that the low-key approach might backfire. There is no need to worry, he told the CBC: "I'm selling the best product on the market: Canada." Because of the antipathy of many voters in Quebec towards him, Chrétien was largely kept out of the province, as his presence could jeopardize the federalist lead.

Aboriginal peoples in Northern Quebec, who had quarrelled with the Quebec government over hydroelectric development projects, announced that if Canada was divisible, then so was Quebec. They refused to participate in the PQ referendum and held their own; the Cree voted "No" to Quebec sovereignty by 96.3 percent and the Inuit by 95 percent in a referendum held a week before the main event.

The Quebec referendum outcome seemed sealed, but in the eleventh hour Parizeau yielded centre stage to Bouchard, who was appointed chief negotiator for Quebec in the event of a "Yes" victory. This essentially meant that Bouchard became the leader of the sovereignist forces in Quebec. Bouchard turned the campaign around immediately. Some observers adopted the term "Bouchardmania" to describe the excitement he created. His title as chief negotiator brought credibility to the idea of a partnership with Canada and his passionate speeches throughout the province ignited those "soft-nationalists" who never related to Parizeau. The "Yes" side finally had momentum, and the "No" campaign faltered badly. The federalists, it seemed, were no match for Bouchard. With less than two weeks to go, a new poll put the "Yes" side ahead at 50.6 to 49.4 percent.

Many of Quebec's business leaders, who supported the federalist side, were worried and blamed the federalist politicians for mishandling the situation. English-speaking Canadians, too, were in a state of shock. Their political leaders had assured them that the federalist cause would triumph; then, suddenly, their country was on the verge of breaking apart. Many started to point a finger at the prime minister, questioning his abilities and judgment. Chrétien had earlier thanked Westerners in Calgary for their silence and for not provoking Quebecers during the campaign. English Canadians, who had kept out of the campaign, realized that they could no longer keep quiet.

It was not just ordinary citizens who were worried—so were many in Chrétien's cabinet who only now realized that Quebec might leave the federation. What was equally troubling for them was that there were no contingency plans in case the unthinkable happened. With little more than a week before the referendum and the polls indicating a "Yes" victory, they realized that they had no idea what Chrétien might do in the event of a sovereignist victory. They wondered if he had the moral authority to remain as prime minister if Quebec voted to leave. Moreover, Chrétien was on a three-day trip to New York from October 22 to 24 to participate in the United Nations' 50th anniversary celebrations, and his cabinet ministers had not received any instructions from him on how to prepare for the possible breakup of the country. In the week before the referendum, several fighter jets stationed at CFB Bagotville, in Quebec, were moved to U.S. bases in Virginia and South America, and the army had made plans to secure major defence installations in Quebec and at key federal institutions like the CBC/Radio-Canada building in Montreal if Quebec voted for sovereignty.

On October 25—five days before the vote—a shaken and worried Chrétien addressed the nation for the first time since he became prime minister. This was a clear indication of the gravity of the crisis. He warned Quebecers that a "Yes" vote would destroy Canada and asked if their lives and their families' lives would be better with Canada in tatters. Chrétien also changed his tactics: Perhaps its was time to recognize Quebec as a distinct society, to move towards greater decentralization, and to grant a constitutional veto to Quebec on matters that affected the powers of the provincial government, he told Canadians—all of the changes he had railed against earlier. Bouchard had been given equal airtime. He began by holding up a 1981 newspaper showing Chrétien and Trudeau smiling for the cameras after they patriated the Canadian constitution without the support of Quebec Premier René Lévesque. Bouchard's message was powerful: Chrétien was not to be trusted.

Love for Quebec!

Days before the Quebec vote, Brian Tobin, the federal minister of fisheries, helped organize a federal rally dubbed "The Crusade for Canada" at Montreal's Place du Canada to allow Canadians from across the country to express their love for Quebec. On Friday, October 27—a mere three days before the vote—Canadians from all parts of the country converged on Montreal, aided by huge discounts offered by the major airlines and Via Rail. More than a 100 000 attended the rally and listened to speeches from the prime minister and other "No" campaign leaders. They were showing their commitment to Quebec and while the "No" side welcomed the support, Bouchard dismissed the rally as an act of desperation on the part of the federalists. He also charged that the rally violated Quebec electoral laws, which set strict limits on campaign spending.

As Canadians outside Quebec tuned in to watch the results on October 30, many realized how closely divided Quebecers were on the issue. The vote was extremely close for hours, with the "Yes" side leading for much of the evening. At one point, the two sides were separated by a mere 29 votes. More than 93 percent of eligible voters turned out to cast a ballot, and it was late in the evening before it became clear that the country would remain united. When all votes were counted, 50.58 percent had voted against sovereignty. A mere 54 288 votes separated the two sides or, as one television commentator put it, less than the capacity crowd for a CFL game at Montreal's Olympic Stadium.

The drama continued when Premier Parizeau took the stage to concede defeat. It was the second loss for the sovereignist movement, and Parizeau was anything but gracious. He lashed out at those who did not vote for sovereignty. Six out of ten Francophones had voted for independence, but in Parizeau's mind their dream had been denied by "money and the ethnic vote" within the province. Bouchard, who would soon replace Parizeau as premier, promised that there would be another chance, but he and the other sovereignist leaders knew that it would not be anytime soon.

Plan A … and B

Chrétien promised to reach out to the Parti Québécois, but many Canadians were convinced that he had bungled the referendum and almost lost the country. Many English Canadians had had enough of the secessionists in Quebec, and they were in no mood for their national government to make further constitutional concessions to a province that seemed intent on destroying their country. Quebec, too, had had enough of the issue, and support for sovereignty dropped to traditional levels of about 40 percent.

Nonetheless, Chrétien attempted to restore Canada's credibility in Quebec. Because there was little support among the other provinces for recognizing Quebec as a distinct society through a constitutional amendment, Chrétien passed a resolution to that effect in the House of Commons, but it had no real impact. He also introduced legislation that limited Ottawa's right to propose a constitutional amendment without the consent of regional majorities, and he attempted to negotiate with Quebec and the other provinces to transfer jurisdiction over such areas as employment training and immigration, and promised to limit federal spending in social policy without provincial consent. Quebec was not interested, but in 1999 Ottawa negotiated these things and a set of principles governing social policy in the Social Union Framework Agreement (SUFA) with all the other provinces. Quebec refused Ottawa's constitutional authority in the area and would not participate, but it more or less endorsed the principles included in the Agreement:

- Ottawa's decision not to introduce new national programs in a variety of social programs including post-secondary education, health, and social assistance without provincial agreement;
- federal recognition of the provinces' role in defining national priorities and objectives; and
- provincial authority to design social programs.

These measures, referred to as Plan A, were designed to meet Quebec's aspirations and to show that federalism could be flexible. Social policy advocates criticized the SUFA, claiming it limited the federal authority to introduce new national social programs and created too much decentralization in the federation.

The second strategy, Plan B, was to play hardball with the sovereignists and discredit the movement to take Quebec out of Canada. Some have termed this tactic "combative federalism" and it took several forms. First, Chrétien launched an advertising campaign run largely out of his office to increase the federal presence and encourage a positive perception of Canada in Quebec. The program, which lasted from 1997 to 2003 and cost $250 million, provided financial support to nearly 2000 sports and cultural events in exchange for using the Canada word mark and displaying other symbols, such as the Canadian flag, at their events and on their promotional materials. The expenditure of such huge sums of money for advertising, often with lax (or no) accounting rules that often passed through Liberal-friendly advertising agencies in Quebec, was uncovered and became known as the Sponsorship Scandal. It contributed to the defeat of the Liberal government in 2006.[10]

Second, Ottawa decided to set the rules for any future referenda in Quebec. It began by submitting in September 1996 a reference to the Supreme Court on the rules for the secession of Quebec from Canada. The Court ruled that Quebec does not have the constitutional right to secede unilaterally from Canada; however, the rest of Canada has an obligation to negotiate Quebec's separation if a clear majority of Quebecers vote in favour of separation on a clear referendum question. Following the Court's ruling, Ottawa passed the *Clarity Act*, which attempted to establish rules under which the Government of Canada would negotiate the secession of any province. Incidentally, Chrétien had refused an opposition proposal in 1994 and 1996 to assert federal authority over a referendum process in any province to ensure a clear and unequivocal question. When he did act in 2000, he declared that, first, any referendum on independence would have to be clear about the issue of independence, and, second, the result would have to have the support of a clear majority in that province—50 percent plus one would not be acceptable. The federal Parliament will decide if a referendum question and results meet these conditions. While Chrétien often claimed the *Clarity Act* as his greatest achievement, many commentators, including historian Michael Behiels, have pointed out that states rarely follow constitutional protocol on the road to independence. Ottawa has not said how it would respond if Quebec unilaterally declared independence after the federal Parliament declared a question or vote unclear. Would Canada, for instance, enforce its legislation through the use of force?

2000: The federal Parliament passes the Clarity Act on succession.

While support for independence declined after the 1995 referendum—perhaps because many in Quebec finally realized that the strategy of playing the separatist card to strengthen the province's negotiating position with Ottawa could be taken too far—there is no evidence to suggest that sovereignist support dropped because of the *Clarity Act*. In fact, sovereignists liked the legislation, as it now forces Canada to negotiate with Quebec after a referendum victory. The Parti Québécois was re-elected to a second term in 1998, but it stopped talking about sovereignty. When the Liberal party under Jean Charest defeated the PQ in 2003, the issue of Quebec secession disappeared. In February 2010, former premier and Bloc Québécois leader Lucien Bouchard said that Quebec sovereignty was nothing more than a dream that would not be achieved anytime soon.

Aboriginal Struggles

Aboriginal issues have not disappeared from the policy agenda; indeed, few have been resolved to the satisfaction of Aboriginal leaders. Although Aboriginal self-government had been promised in the 1992 Charlottetown Accord, the Liberal government claimed that it wanted to negotiate "practical and workable" self-government agreements at the provincial, treaty, or regional levels rather than through constitutional means. The government subsequently announced four foundational principles that would govern this process: (1) Aboriginal peoples had the right to negotiate agreements in such specific areas as healthcare, education, child welfare, housing, and economic development that affected their communities; (2) each agreement on self-government would reflect the differences within Aboriginal communities; (3) the costs of self-government would be shared among federal, provincial, territorial, and Aboriginal governments; and (4) it was the responsibility of Aboriginal peoples to initiate negotiations on self-government.

The federal government saw comprehensive claims settlement and the land claims settlement as important parts of the self-government process. Comprehensive claims are negotiated between First Nations and the federal government for areas that are not covered under existing treaties and that Aboriginal peoples claim they have a legal right over; specific land claims are negotiations between Aboriginal groups and the government over the administration of lands covered by a treaty, where grievances over the fulfillment of the treaties abound. The term "land claims" refers generally to both types of Aboriginal claims.

More than a thousand outstanding land claims have been registered with Indian and Northern Affairs Canada (277 claims have been filed in Ontario and 522 have been filed in British Columbia alone). Between 1973 and 2005, governments in Canada were able to settle only a fraction of the claims. Since 1975, the federal Crown has entered into 21 modern treaties with Aboriginal peoples across Canada. One of the most important was negotiated among Ottawa, British Columbia, and the Nisga'a, and it was finalized in 2000.

Nisga'a Treaty is signed in 2000.

The Nisga'a Treaty is the first modern-day treaty in British Columbia; it gives the Nisga'a government the authority to make laws in many areas and authority over the administration of its own government, management of its lands and assets, and its citizenship, language, and culture. However, there are limits on its government. For example, the Nisga'a cannot enact laws about Nisga'a citizenship that deal with immigration or Canadian citizenship, and their laws must be consistent with the Canadian Constitution. As the agreement demonstrated, modern treaties can be expensive. When the agreement was completed, the Nisga'a received $487 million from Ottawa in capital transfers for lost revenue from the forestry sector and to implement the agreement. An additional $462 million was promised to allow Nisga'a to provide a variety of social services and economic development over the first five years of the treaty. More support was to be negotiated later.

Many Aboriginal leaders had placed great faith in the Royal Commission on Aboriginal Peoples (RCAP) that had been appointed in 1991 to investigate Aboriginal–state relations in Canada. Its five-volume report, released in 1996 and plagued by huge cost over-runs and delays, called for major changes to the relationship between Aboriginal peoples, non-Aboriginal people, and governments in Canada. The report argued that the economic marginalization and social problems facing Aboriginal communities could be reversed only by establishing a new relationship between the Canadian state and Aboriginal peoples, one that recognized them as self-governing nations: The colonial relationship between the state and Aboriginal peoples had to be replaced with one based on the principles of equality, mutual respect and consent, and strict adherence to historic treaties. By the time the report was released, more than half of Canada's Aboriginal peoples lived not on reserves but in urban centres.

Most Aboriginal groups supported the Royal Commission's recommendations. The government did not respond until April 1997, when it released *Gathering Strength: Canada's Aboriginal Action Plan*. The first step in the federal response was an apology delivered by Jane Stewart, the minister of Indian and Northern Affairs Canada, to Aboriginal peoples for decades of mistreatment and abuse suffered at the hands of the Canadian government. Many Aboriginal leaders considered the apology, referred to as a "Statement of Reconciliation," less than sincere, as it was delivered in a conference room and not in Parliament and not by the prime minister, who was noticeably absent from the ceremony. Stewart

Twenty-month-old Janice Papatie stands in front of her home in the Algonquin Anicinape community of Kitcisakikin Northern Quebec. Many of the homes do not have electricity or running water.

Source: The Canadian Press Images/Francis Vachon.

acknowledged the damage done to Aboriginal communities since the arrival of Europeans in the fifteenth century, noting particularly the physical and mental abuse at government-run residential schools. With the apology, the government created a $350 million "healing fund" to address the legacy of abuse in the residential school system. The other initiatives—including policies to strengthen Aboriginal governance, to build a new fiscal relationship with Aboriginal governments that emphasized financial stability, self-reliance, and accountability, and to work with Aboriginal peoples to improve their social conditions and build strong communities—showed Ottawa's intent to create a new relationship with Aboriginal peoples and cease the assimilative policies that existed as late as the 1960s.

Phil Fontaine, grand chief of the Assembly of First Nations, described the apology and the government's initial response to the RCAP report as an important first step in forging a new relationship. Other Aboriginal groups did not share his enthusiasm, including those representing Inuit, Aboriginal women, and Métis. They said that the apology was too weak and the measures the government promised insufficient to solve the tremendous difficulties confronting Aboriginal peoples.

Both national and international human rights organizations were soon agreeing with the critics of the government's proposals. In its 1999 annual report, the Canadian Human Rights Commission criticized the government for its tardiness on responding to the pressing needs of Aboriginal communities. In 1998, the United Nations Committee on Economic, Social and Cultural Rights had also criticized the Canadian government for ignoring the urgency of addressing Aboriginal issues. A year later, the United Nations Human Rights Committee expressed concern that Canada had failed to implement the recommendations of the RCAP report. This criticism was particularly distressing for Chrétien, who liked to point out that while he was prime minister the United Nations had consistently ranked Canada among the top countries on its social indicators.

In a speech in Parliament in 2001, Chrétien said that he was concerned that "we may be spending too much time, too much energy, and too much money on the past, and not nearly enough on what is necessary to ensure a bright future for the children of today and tomorrow.… Our approach will be to focus on the future."[11] In other words, the government did not really see the redress of historical grievances as part of the process of moving forward. The government subsequently ceased negotiating approximately 30 land claims and self-government negotiations that had stalled, claiming that the "Aboriginal industry" lawyers and consultants were more interested in continuing the negotiations than reaching an agreement. Critics blamed the government for the lack of progress because it had insisted on dominating the process and on extinguishing Aboriginal rights in any negotiated settlement.

Chrétien's approach was perhaps best demonstrated by the introduction of Bill C-7, known as the *First Nations Governance Act*. The Act was an attempt to strengthen governance in Canada's 600 First Nations communities and Indian Bands. It established governance codes and procedures in matters of leadership selection, the administration of government, and financial accountability. Mostly, it was an attempt to modernize Aboriginal governance and foster economic independence and autonomous decision-making powers, as the federal government reduced its involvement with Aboriginal government. This legislation was seen by some critics as another attempt to change the *Indian Act* without the consent of First Nations. The major criticism from Aboriginal organizations was that the legislation had been introduced following consultation with Aboriginal communities but not negotiations with them. They claimed that such a process reinforced paternalism in Aboriginal–state relations rather than negotiations as equals that the Liberals had promised. Moreover, the emphasis on governance ignored the long-standing and urgent social and economic issues in First Nations communities. When Paul Martin replaced Chrétien as prime minister, he scrapped the legislation, which meant the attempt to reform the *Indian Act* had failed once again.

While the social and economic conditions for Aboriginal peoples improved only marginally, great strides were made on clarifying Aboriginal treaty rights in the courts. One of the most important came in December 1997, when the Supreme Court of Canada provided its first interpretation on Aboriginal title in Canada. The decision in *Delgamuukw* v. *British Columbia* also provided some clarification of Aboriginal title as included in subsection 35(1) of the *Constitution Act, 1982*, which affirmed existing Aboriginal and treaty rights. In *Calder* v. *The Attorney General of British Columbia* (1973), the Supreme Court acknowledged the Aboriginal legal rights to use the land other than those provided for by treaty or statute since the British Conquest in 1763. In 1984, the Gitxsan and 13 Wet'suwet'en peoples of British Columbia took the province to court to secure title to 58 000 square kilometres of land in northern British Columbia. By 1996, the matter was before the Supreme Court. The Court did not rule on the merits of the Gitxsan and Wet'suwet'en Aboriginal title claim and, in fact, ordered a new trial, but Chief Justice Lamer clarified what Aboriginal title means. His ruling was seen as a turning point in treaty negotiations. The decision confirmed Aboriginal title to the land and not just the right to hunt, fish, or gather on the land. Aboriginal title bestows a property right and is much more extensive than the right to use the land, which was not limited to traditional usage. The Court— which accepted oral history as evidence for the first time in any proceeding—recognized Aboriginal title as communal right (not an individual right) and ruled that the lands could be sold only to the government. The Court also recommended against further litigation and urged the parties to negotiate a solution to the thorny land claims issue. That process continues.

The Peculiar Ways of Foreign Policy

Foreign aid, the military, and the nation's diplomatic corps—many of the items usually associated with foreign policy—were all victims of government cuts in the 1990s. Foreign policy was never an important issue for the Chrétien government, and when the prime minister turned his attention to such matters, it was usually driven more by domestic political concerns than a concern for Canada's role in the international community. As Ken Nossal notes, "Chrétien … came to power … actively seeking to avoid the kind of activist foreign policy that had been pursued by the Mulroney government."[12] Still, during this period, the government broke with two traditions in Canadian foreign policy. First, it took military action against one of its North Atlantic Treaty Organization (NATO) allies; and second, it refused to participate with its two major allies, the United States and Britain, in military action against Iraq. Many Canadians cheered both developments.

One trend was undisputable, however: Canada was becoming more inextricably part of a North American economy. The Canada–U.S. Free Trade Agreement was signed in 1988, and although Chrétien had vowed during the 1993 campaign to cancel the treaty, he did not. Chrétien rejected the close personal relationship that Mulroney had with U.S. presidents Ronald Reagan and George H.W. Bush and came to office determined to distance Canada from this type of relationship. Still, he ratified the North American Free Trade Agreement (NAFTA) that had been negotiated by the out-going Conservative government, creating a larger free trade zone in North America. As a skilled politician, Chrétien knew that anti-Americanism played well in domestic politics, but he had come to realize that Canada needed access to all of the North American and Mexican market.

Those trade agreements further reinforced Canada's economy away from an east–west axis to a north–south one. All of the provinces with the exception of Manitoba now trade more with the United States than with the rest of Canada. This has been particularly noteworthy in Quebec: In 1989, exports to the rest of Canada accounted for 21.2 percent of Quebec's GDP and those to the United States 16 percent; by 2001, exports to the United States contributed 33.6 percent of its GDP and those to the rest of Canada had dropped to 19.4 percent.[13] More than 80 percent of Canada's exports went to the United States in 2006. Canadians seemed quite comfortable with all of this. Public opinion polls showed that 70 percent of Canadians supported NAFTA by 2003, and 69 percent of Canadians told pollsters that closer relations between the Canadian and American economies were a good thing; that number jumped to 80 percent for those under the age of 35. Even the anti-globalization forces protesting Canada's new trade relationships fizzled after major confrontations with police at the 2001 Free Trade Area of the Americas Summit in Quebec City and the Group of Seven meeting in Kananaskis, Alberta, in 2002.

The percentage of Canada's exports going to the United States surpasses 80 percent in 2006.

By the time the Liberals took power in Ottawa, Canada's relationship with the United States was not an issue of great public concern. For a time, Canadians gauged the strength of their nation by how often politicians appeared to be standing up to the Americans, but by the time Chrétien became prime minister in 1993, Canadians did not seem overly concerned about the United States, although they did want some indication that their country had not become a nation of weaklings among the nations of the world. Canadians found their cause—for a few brief moments —when their leaders fired upon Spain, a NATO ally.

There was no denying the reality of an environmental and economic catastrophe on Canada's coasts by the early 1990s. With a dramatic decline in fish stocks off the east coast, the federal government had closed much of the fishery in 1992; the British Columbia fishery was in a similar state of collapse. A year later, the ban, or moratorium on ground fish on the east coast, was expanded, effectively shutting down the entire industry in Atlantic Canada. The closure displaced 36 000 workers, the vast majority in Newfoundland, and created havoc in one of Canada's most economically challenged regions. The government told fishers and others employed in the industry that it would take at least a decade for the fish population to recover; some even warned that the resource was so overfished that nothing short of a miracle could save the industry. It was a catastrophe of enormous proportions.

"No Longer a Wimp": The Turbot War

In 1995, fisheries and foreign policy became intertwined—as they had been in the nineteenth century—and led to the Turbot War, named after a slimy, spineless flatfish of which the vast majority of Canadians had never heard. In fact, the fish had become important only after the collapse of the traditional species, and Canada was determined to get as much of it for its fishers as possible and protect it from being fished to extinction. However, much of the stock was outside Canada's 320-kilometre exclusive economic zone, and Canada had no authority on the high seas outside that boundary line. Many in Canada had been demanding for more than three decades that the government take decisive action against foreign fleets fishing in or just outside Canadian waters. In the late winter of 1995, after a tough federal budget was delivered on February 27, a federal report acknowledging the rapid depletion of west coast salmon stocks, an impending showdown with sovereignist forces in Quebec, and with a growing environmental lobby, it was an opportune time for Canada to assert itself on the international stage, even if it was against fishing vessels from its allies, Spain and Portugal.

The North Atlantic Fishery Organization (NAFO) is responsible for setting quotas, or catch limits, for the fishing nations, including Canada, in international waters. It is a murky process, as members states can disregard the allotments handed out by NAFO and simply set their own quotas. That is what happened in early 1995, when NAFO set the total allowable catch at 24 500 metric tons (27 000 tonnes) and slashed the share for the European Union (all of which went to Spain and Portugal) from 80 percent of the quota in 1993 and 1994 to just 12 percent for 1995; NAFO awarded Canada 60 percent of the quota. This decision was disastrous for Spain and Portugal, which were facing declining stocks in their waters and faced huge social and economic problems if their fisheries were shut down. They ignored the international quotas and sent their vessels to the fishing grounds on the Grand Banks to catch 18 100 metric tons (20 000 tonnes) of turbot.

Brian Tobin, the minister of fisheries, made it clear that Canada could not permit what he considered such illegal fishing by the Europeans. In Canada, he had tremendous support from the labour movement, the provinces, and even the Reform party; from Europe came a warning that if Canada interfered with fishing in international waters, there would be serious repercussions. Chrétien proposed to European Union president

Jacques Santer a 60-day moratorium to allow the two sides to negotiate. When Santer refused, Canada announced it would arrest any European trawler fishing illegally in the area. Spain countered that it was sending a naval vessel to protect its fishing fleet.

On the morning of March 9, Chrétien put Canada on a war footing, and authorized the deployment of submarines and warships to enforce Canada's ban on foreign fishing. A few minutes later, the prime minister personally gave Canadian fisheries officers and the RCMP in the fisheries patrol vessels the authority to seize any Spanish vessel violating conservation practices and to discharge their weapons if it became necessary.

Later that day, Canada targeted the *Estai*, a Spanish fishing vessel. Three Canadian patrol vessels chased the vessel for suspected illegal fishing and having undersized fish stashed in a concealed hold. The *Estai* had eluded the Canadians several times, had foiled two boarding attempts, and had even cut its nets and disappeared in the fog. Finally, and well into international waters, the *Cape Roger* closed in on the fleeing Spanish trawler. It warded off five other Spanish trawlers with water cannons, and fired four volleys from a large ship-mounted machine gun across the bow of the *Estai*. The Canadians gave Captain Enrique Davila Gonzalea five minutes to stop. If he refused, the next round would be at his ship. Gonzalea surrendered. Armed Canadian fisheries officers, backed by an RCMP emergency response team, scurried over the side and seized the Spanish ship. It was only the second time Canada had fired upon another nation in peacetime; the first, in 1968, was also at a fishing boat, but in 1995 Canada had planned its aggressive action well in advance of the discharge of its guns.

Spain dispatched a second naval patrol vessel, the *Vigia*, armed with a 76-mm gun and two machine guns, to the Grand Banks. Spanish Prime Minister Felipe Gonzalez warned that the Spanish warships had been authorized to fire on any Canadian assault team attempting to board any of the Spanish fishing trawlers. Ironically, Canadian officials were

Spain and Canada confront each other in 1995 over fishing outside Canada's 320-kilometre limit.

Source: CP PHOTO/Fred Chartrand.

The Spanish fishing vessel Estai in St. John's harbour after being seized by Canadian officials on March 12, 1995.

worried that the *Vigia*, not designed for the ice-filled waters of the Northwest Atlantic, would sink, as it became top-heavy from the ice that formed on its guns. A Canadian patrol plane constantly monitored the two Spanish vessels for fear they might sink, even though the prime minister had authorized in the Canadian Rules of Engagement to sink any Spanish vessel that uncovered its guns. Even with six armed fisheries patrol vessels and a Canadian submarine already in the area, Chrétien ordered the deployment of a Canadian frigate and a destroyer for additional support. The prime minister informed the European Union on March 10 that Canada would seize other Spanish vessels if they continued to fish. The following day, Canada's national newspaper the *Globe and Mail* ran a story comparing the strength of the navies of Spain and Canada.[14] No other vessels were stopped, and a compromise was reached on the quotas a few days later. For all of the talk about conservation, Canada arrested only one Spanish fishing trawler. Even in that single case, the charges were dropped, the cargo of fish was returned to the owners of the vessel at Canada's expense, and within days, more than 20 European vessels, mostly from Spain, were back fishing in the disputed seas.

During the incident, Canadians showed that they, too, are flag-waving patriots who want the national interest defended. Even though most Canadians could not identify a turbot at their local supermarket, they praised Chrétien's actions and that of his determined minister of fisheries and oceans. More than 90 percent of Canadians supported the government's action. The Halifax *Daily News* noted that "few events have brought such a sense of common cause across the sprawling, argumentative width of Canada as the clash with Spanish trawlers."[15] John Wright, senior vice-president of the Angus Reid polling firm, said Canadians saw this as "Green Ramboism. Canadians are feeling feisty enough," he concluded, "that they would want Brian Tobin to go over there and dump a bag of fish on the desk of the European Union diplomats."[16] The *Toronto Sun* reflected the Canadian jingoism when it declared, "Most Canadians are happy we fired the first shots. In fact, we would have aimed lower after the *Estai* didn't stop at the first two machine-gun bursts." Later, one of its columnists noted that "Canada is no longer a wimp. We made a show of force and stand proud, unrepentant and ready to strike again."[17] In a rare moment of solidarity, every Canadian MP rose and cheered when Tobin returned to the House of Commons following the arrest of the *Estai*.[18]

Unilateralism and the flouting of international law were not the preferred options in foreign policy when the Government of Canada completed its foreign policy review in 1995. Instead, it said foreign policy would be based on three related aims or pillars: the protection of Canada's security within a stable global framework, the promotion of prosperity and employment, and the promotion of the values and culture that Canadians cherish. As several foreign policy experts, notably Denis Stairs, have pointed out, "it is difficult not to be impressed by the speed, and the ease, with which Canada's values—or the things, at least, that Canadians collectively claim as their values—are abandoned whenever a competing self-interest comes down the pike." Stairs also notes that Canada ditched another important value—the rule of law, especially international law—when such recourse has not coincided with Canadian interest. He suggests that in foreign policy, despite its insistence on multilateralism, the rule of law, and the promotion of Canadian values, Canada's response to the overfishing of turbot in the international waters outside the 320-kilometre exclusive economic zone on the Grand Banks "had nothing to do with what Canadians like to think of as their 'values' and everything to do with the desire to enhance their prosperity."[19]

Canadian foreign policy enjoyed considerable success on two other fronts. The first was what Foreign Minister Lloyd Axworthy touted as evidence of Canada's commitment to international multilateralism. This was reflected in the successful campaign for a human security agenda, including a landmine treaty, an international criminal court, and a campaign against child soldiers. These policies reflected what Chrétien called Canadian values. The Axworthy initiatives were an attempt to create a sense of a more independent role for Canada in foreign policy. The second was the use of foreign policy through the Team Canada Missions to drum up business for Canadian enterprises. All prime ministers are salespeople for their nation's businesses and exporters, but Chrétien raised this role to a new level. Trade promotion and liberalization were the mainstays of Chrétien's foreign policy.

9/11

The confrontation with Spain paled in comparison to the devastating terrorist attack on the Twin Towers of the World Trade Center in New York City and the Pentagon in Washington, D.C., which killed almost 3000 people and downed four commercial airliners on September 11, 2001. It made Al Qaeda, the War on Terror, and "security" household words across Canada. While it was not the target of the terrorists, Canada had been identified in tapes released by Osama bin Laden, the apparent mastermind behind 9/11, and it made Al Qaeda's list of enemies several times because of its support of American policy in the Middle East.

After 9/11, the Canadian government moved quickly to contribute to the security of North America. First, Prime Minister Chrétien reorganized his cabinet to create the Cabinet Committee on Public Security and Anti-terrorism (a counterpart to the U.S. Homeland Security Office) that was responsible for protecting Canada and spending $8 billion over five years to do so. Second, Canada contributed a military contingent to Afghanistan. Third, the government made border improvements with the United States one of its top priorities, as well as airport security across the country. Given the volume of goods that cross the Canada–U.S. border daily, Canada had to ensure that border security did not disrupt the Canadian economy. By September 2002, Canada and the United States had put in place a series of electronic programs dubbed the Smart Border Declaration to facilitate the movement of frequent travellers across the border. Still, the United States requires that all Canadians entering into the country have a valid passport or another approved form of identification. Fourth, Canada enacted new and controversial legislation in the *Anti-Terrorism Act* days after the 9/11 attack.

This legislation was Canada's first anti-terrorist legislation. It gave Canada's security forces new powers to monitor and investigate suspected terrorists and terrorist organizations and allowed for the investigation, prosecution, and prevention of terrorist activities both within Canada and abroad. Even as it was being debated in Parliament, concerns were being raised that the legislation trampled civil liberties because it gave police sweeping new powers, including the ability to arrest people and hold them without charge for up to 72 hours if they were suspected of planning a terrorist act. The legislation defined a terrorist act as one committed "for a political, religious or ideological purpose, objective or cause." The legislation passed quickly and without any amendments.

As governments moved to "secure" Canada, Canadians were also trying to understand the societies and countries that had produced the 9/11 terrorists. Perhaps the best-known recent presentation of Muslim culture in Canada is in the CBC series *Little Mosque on the Prairie*. It first aired in 2007 and explores through satire the widely held prejudices about Islam. Nelofer Pazira, who fled Afghanistan in 1989 and immigrated to Canada after a year in Pakistan, has tried to help Canadians understand Afghanistan. She is now a journalist, filmmaker, and human rights activist, and in 2001, she starred in the film *Kandahar*, a quasi-documentary about her return to Taliban-run Afghanistan in search of her sister. Two years later she co-directed and produced the documentary *Return to Kandahar*, which won a 2003 Gemini award. In 2006, she won the Drainie-Taylor Biography Prize for her *A Bed of Red Flowers: In Search of My Afghanistan*. Yet, many Canadians might be more influenced by Kiefer Sutherland's Jack Bauer, an American counter-intelligence agent in the hit TV series *24* who often relied on violent and savage interrogation methods to keep the United States safe from terrorists.

The 9/11 attack also contributed to the American–British decision to invade Iraq in March 2003. By mid-2008, the war, widely accepted as misguided and wrong, had resulted in the death of more than 4000 U.S. and British soldiers and more than 40 000 civilians. Unlike American President George W. Bush, Chrétien insisted that Canada did not support military action to bring about regime change in Iraq nor anywhere around the world. While he admitted that there where many governments that Canada did not like, he added that "If we change every government we don't like in the world where do we start? Who is next?" Canada also believed that the diplomatic progress of disarming Iraq was working and given more time would have proven successful. And, Chrétien insisted, given Canada's long-standing commitment to multilateralism in foreign policy, it could not consider participating in a war against Iraq without a resolution sanctioning the action from the United Nations Security Council. However, Chrétien had committed Canadian troops to U.S.-led missions in Kosovo and Afghanistan, even though the United Nations had sanctioned neither.

Chrétien's critics, who had earlier heaped scorn on him for not following through on his pledge to renegotiate NAFTA, hailed him as a great Canadian nationalist for not participating in the "coalition of the willing," as those nations that supported the Iraq War were called. In 1998, though, Chrétien had told the House of Commons that Canada was ready to join with then-U.S. President Bill Clinton to wage a military strike against Iraq without a UN mandate to enforce Security Council Resolution 6878 that required Iraq to destroy all chemical, nuclear, and biological weapons, as well as all ballistic missiles with a range greater than 150 kilometres. Consistency was not a strong point in Canada's foreign policy during the Chrétien era, but the prime minister was able to gauge public opinion fairly accurately. Seventy-one percent supported his decision not to go to war in Iraq.

Although most Canadians cheered the decision to stay clear of the Iraq War, Canada did not seem to have a clear sense of the role it wanted to play in the world. After noting how Canada's influence in the world had declined, *Time* magazine asked in a May 2003 cover story "Would anyone notice if Canada disappeared?" The *Toronto Star* considered such a question a "slur" on Canada, and its editorial on May 22 included a number of e-mail comments from American readers who criticized their nation's invasion of Iraq. Yet, for many commentators, Canada's foreign policy was not simply about participation in Iraq, but about the general lack of direction of Canada's role in world affairs. In a 2003 bestseller, *While Canada Slept: How We Lost Our Place in the World*, Andrew Cohen asked, "We are not mediocre at home. So why be mediocre abroad?" Norman Hillmer, a historian of foreign policy at Carleton University, has argued that Canada is really the Walter Mitty of foreign policy: Canada dreams of much more than it can deliver. Hillmer has argued that Canada is like most other nations and it followed "its interests directly, ruthlessly, relentlessly."[20] He also argued that Canada constructs masks and convinces itself that it acts either multilaterally or independently. While this might be good politics for a while, it surely wasn't the reality of Canadian foreign policy. Michael Ignatieff, a noted Canadian scholar and later leader of the Liberal party, noted that "we are living off a Pearsonian reputation that we no longer deserve."[21]

By staying out of Iraq, Canada opted for Afghanistan, and by 2009 that initiative had also become a quagmire. Canadians remain divided over the participation in Afghanistan. One of the major problems for both the Liberal and Conservative governments has been explaining why Canada was there in the first place. The Taliban, a fundamentalist Islamist organization, ruled Afghanistan, and they attracted international condemnation for their repressive human rights regime. It was not the Taliban's treatment of women, nor its repressive regime that precipitated a U.S.-led military force to drive the Taliban government from power in October 2001; it was the Taliban's support for Al Qaeda militants led by Osama bin Laden. Canada had a limited role in the initial forays into Afghanistan, and it supported the American-led invasion. It secretly sent Joint Task Force Two (JTF2) elite troops to Afghanistan in late 2001 and formally deployed troops with other NATO forces in February 2002. A second deployment followed in 2003, demonstrating support for the Americans' War on Terror without committing to Iraq. The Taliban troops retreated to the mountains in southern Afghanistan, but by 2005 they had adopted the improvised explosive device (IEDs), better known as roadside bombs, as their primary means of attacking coalition forces, including Canadian troops.

Canada's participation in the war in Afghanistan starting in late-2001 becomes longest military conflict in Canadian history.

Sending troops to Afghanistan was one of the ways that Canada could participate in the War on Terror. Some have argued that Canada is in Afghanistan because of the mistake that the Americans made in invading Iraq and if the United States had not made such a mess of that, Canadian soldiers would not be in Afghanistan. Others contend that Canada's involvement in Afghanistan runs counter to its traditional peacekeeping role and the government should pull the troops out. What Canadian soldiers were fighting in Afghanistan has been described as a multinational religious-political movement in the Taliban, a proponent of radical Islam. Because of its long history with outside powers, including the Soviet Union in the 1970s, the Afghan population is particularly wary of foreign soldiers in their country.

By 2006, Canada was one of the major forces operating in the dangerous southern regions of Afghanistan for the NATO-led International Security Assistance Force (ISAF). Prime Minister Stephen Harper appointed an independent commission to study Canada's role and recommended a course of action. Former Liberal cabinet minister John Manley

The body of Sergeant John Faught heads back to Canada. He was killed by an IED while on foot patrol in Afghanistan on January 16, 2010.

Source: AR2010-0010-17.JPG www.forces.gc.ca. National Defence. Reproduced with the permission of the Minister of Public Works and Government Services, 2010.

headed the investigation and recommended against an immediate withdrawal of troops, but he did call for a greater emphasis on diplomacy and reconstruction. The Conservatives and Liberals agreed that Canada would support the Afghan military mission until 2011 and provide annually $100 million in development assistance. By July 2010, 151 Canadian soldiers had died in the mission, and the task of reconstruction and building a legitimate governance system or a viable state in Afghanistan is proving elusive.

Social and Cultural Canada

While fiscal policy, healthcare, national unity, and foreign policy have largely defined the public agenda since 1993, there has also been considerable discussion about a crisis in the Canadian community. In many ways the discussions over fiscal and health policy, for instance, have also been about the type of community Canada is and should be, but we have come to identify other issues as defining the Canadian community. The dividing lines have never been clear, and most Canadians watched from the sidelines as a variety of issues moved in and out of the public agenda over the past decade. On one side were the Canadians, usually referred to as social conservatives, who have railed against the gun registry, the right to abortion, same-sex marriages, and certain aspects of Canada's immigration policy, notably the admission of large numbers of refugees; on the other side were Canadians, usually referred to as liberals, who have argued for a more inclusive society based on the Charter of Rights and Freedoms. In many ways, the Charter has sharpened the debate about the nature of Canada rather than having defined it.

What is clear is that Canada as essentially a "British" nation with a French-speaking minority has been replaced by Canada as a nation-state that shares a national philosophy based on liberal individualism. It is the individual rather than the collective that has become important, even though many point out that this was following an American model based primarily on individual rights. This change also meant that the courts now play an important role in determining public policy—an issue that also concerns many Canadians. Governments are more likely to follow in the promotion of social justice rather than lead it.

The response from the courts and governments on a variety of social issues has often been presented as either an indication of progress or the lack of it depending on where one stands on many hot-button issues. What remains to be seen are the long-term implications of the ascendency of individualism in Canada. In the view of Peter C. Newman, who described the changes in his bestselling book *The Canadian Revolution: From Deference to Defiance*, the national trait of deference and respect for authority and a sense of collective well-being has been replaced by a belief in individualism and a culture of self-interest. A new Canada emerged that had as a national philosophy a liberal individualist ideal.[22] This was the liberalism of Pierre Trudeau that has emerged in the post-Charter period; some have called this a rights revolution and it has redefined Canada's national identity. The rights revolution has empowered some groups, while others feel that their country is changing beyond recognition. It has often meant that the courts had to be called upon to protect diversity and individualism from the harmful policies of elected majorities that might sit in the provincial and federal legislatures. This liberalism has been manifested in various ways, such as the decriminalization of the possession of small amounts of marijuana and the legalization of same-sex marriages.

In 2006, more than 90 percent of Canadians lived in urban areas.

The 2006 census also revealed that a new Canada had emerged. More than 90 percent of Canada's population of 31.6 million lived in large metropolitan areas, compared with less than 20 percent at the time of Confederation in 1867. Ontario and Quebec still had the largest share of the population, but Alberta had the largest increase since the 2001 census—a 10.6 percent increase, compared with a 5.4 percent increase for the country, while Newfoundland and Labrador and Saskatchewan registered declines. The Census Metropolitan Areas of Toronto, Vancouver, and Montreal remained the largest cities and together with Ottawa-Gatineau, Calgary, and Edmonton were home to 68 percent of all Canadians.

The rural–urban cleavage in Canada is being played out in a number of ways. It is not unusual to hear complaints that several cities have larger populations than any of the provinces in Atlantic Canada, and questions have been raised about why a province such as Prince Edward Island with 140 000 residents (0.4 percent of the national population) should have equality with Ontario and its 12 million people (40 percent of national population) in constitutional matters, for instance. The urban–rural divide emerged as an issue after the 2006 federal election. Although the Conservative party was largely shunned by urban voters and did not win a single seat in the three largest cities, it formed the government. Could a government, it was asked, be legitimate if it had no representation from the largest urban areas? Historically, rural constituencies have been larger in size than urban ones and had fewer voters, but some commentators began to talk for

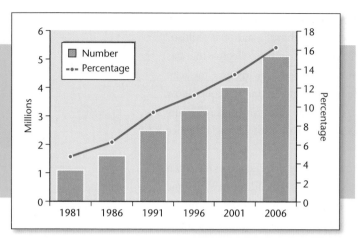

Figure 12.4
Number and Share of Visible Minority Persons in Canada, 1981–2006

Source: Statistics Canada. *Canada's Ethnocultural Mosaic, 2006 Census* (Ottawa: Ministry of Industry). Catalogue no. 97-562-X.

the first time about the diminishing value of an urban vote. In November 2009, a controversial private member's bill in the House of Commons to end the gun registry passed only because rural MPs in the Liberal and New Democratic parties supported the measure. More and more issues, it seems, are exposing the growing rural–urban divide in Canada.

The face of Canada has changed, too. Those with Aboriginal identity—that is, those who identified themselves as North American Indian, Métis, or Inuit and/or those who reported they were members of an Indian Band or First Nation— surpassed the 1 million mark, or 3.8 percent of the population. These numbers represented a 44.9 percent increase over the previous census, making Aboriginal peoples the fastest-growing group within Canada. Visible minorities numbered 5 million, or 16.2 percent of the population, compared with 11.2 percent in 1996, as Figure 12.4 shows. There were more than 200 ethnic groups identified in the census, and South Asians (from the Indian subcontinent) surpassed Chinese as the largest visible minority group in 2006. The vast majority of visible minorities (95.9 percent) lived in a large metropolitan area, and reflecting the changing face of Canada's population, 41.4 percent reported more than one ethnic origin, giving rise to the concept of multiple identities in Canada. As a way of comparison, 32.3 percent of the total population reported Canadian as their only ethnic origin.

Although it was not unusual to hear criticisms of Canada's immigration policies and charges that it was racist, Canada continued to have one of the most liberal immigration policies of any country in the world. At the time of Confederation, Canada had a white-only immigration policy, but by the 1960s colour had been removed as a criteria. In 1967, the point system was introduced for all immigrants, making education and skills the main criteria, and reducing—if not eliminating—many of the discriminatory features of Canada's immigration and refugee policies. There is, however, considerable criticism of the point system: In 2007, Canada had a backlog of 800 000 applicants and a four-year waiting period. Labour market analysts have said that the emphasis on education has created overcapacity in some professions and shortages in skilled blue-collar and trade sectors. In 1986, Canada became the only country ever to receive the Nansen Refugee Award from the United Nations High Commission on Refugees for its policies in support of refugees, and in 1993 Canada became the first country to formally recognize people that faced gender prosecution as refugees. The Chrétien government placed considerable emphasis on attracting immigrants who were self-sufficient and especially those who brought investment dollars with them. After September 11, 2001, security became an additional issue for those wanting to come to Canada.

The events of 9/11 also raised a number of questions about multiculturalism, a policy that Canada had officially adopted in 1971. The policy of multiculturalism did not simply recognize the reality of pluralism in Canada but also made it clear that the long-held policies of assimilation would stop. For nearly two decades, multiculturalism held a place of pride in Canada, and it was celebrated as a multi-ethnic and multinational state that did not simply accommodate but embraced ethnic diversity. The equality provisions in the Charter of Rights and Freedoms have served to strengthen these views.

In the new century, however, there has been considerable discussion about how far should Canada go to accommodate its immigrant communities. This has given rise to the term "reasonable accommodation." For many, the issue is apparent: Canada must provide its ethnic and religious groups with the collective rights necessary to maintain their culture and identity; for others, society must remain secular and everyone must be treated the same as newcomers are integrated into Canada.

The matter made national headlines in 2007 when a small Quebec town, Hérouxville, passed a bylaw that outlined a code of conduct for immigrants that outlawed stoning and female circumcision. There has been considerable discussion over the years about such matters—from RCMP officers wearing turbans and the use of hijabs, kirpans, and various religious symbols in school and the workplace. The Supreme Court has usually allowed such items, but all of them have been a source of resentment in some quarters. When such matters make the evening news, such as the request from Hasidic leaders in Montreal requesting a local YMCA cover its windows to prevent young Hasids from seeing women in aerobic wear or the demands from Muslim university students that they should not have to sketch a nude model in their introductory drawing course, the question of reasonable accommodation comes to the surface.

Immigration, multiculturalism, and identity became an issue in the 2007 Quebec provincial election, and Premier Jean Charest appointed a commission to investigate the cultural and social accommodation of religious and ethnic minorities. Gérard Bouchard and Charles Taylor, two well-respected university professors, were appointed to chair the Consultation Commission on Accommodation Practices Related to Cultural Differences. Similarly, in a recent Ontario election, the Conservative leader, John Tory, unleashed a wave of protest when he proposed funding religious-based schools and was forced to change his mind throughout the campaign. *Maclean's* magazine asked in an October 2007 cover story "Are we becoming a nation of bigots?" Polling data has suggested that more than 53 percent of Canadians believe immigrants should fully adapt to Canadian culture, while 18 percent favoured accommodation of immigrants.[23]

When Taylor and Bouchard reported, they said that Quebec was no longer a French-Canadian society but an increasingly pluralistic one that they described as embodying the concept of interculturalism (rather than multiculturalism). The government, they recommended, must work to create a secular society in Quebec and as a first step recommended that the legislature vote to remove the crucifix from the Assemblée nationale du Québec to show the government's secular nature and function. The legislature's reaction? It voted unanimously to keep the crucifix hanging over the Speaker's chair. This issue is not limited to Quebec, and it is certain—as it has been since before Confederation—that debates on Canadian identity, citizenship, and nationalism will continue. It will be interesting to see the impact of the explosion of social media networks, such as Facebook and Twitter, on such debates.

From Cheers to Dithers

Jean Chrétien's leadership of the Liberal party was never easy, largely because of Paul Martin's presence. Even when Chrétien won the Liberal leadership in 1990, many considered it only a matter of time before Martin, who became his minister of finance in 1993, would replace him as prime minister. The relationship between the two was always tense and the "feud" was well known. Although Chrétien won three consecutive majority governments from 1993 to 2003—according to many of the pundits because of the dominance of regionally based opposition parties from 1993 to 2005, who had no hopes of forming the government—Martin was a prime-minister-in-waiting and his supporters began the process of scheming to replace Chrétien before the end of Chrétien's first term in Ottawa. In his autobiography published in 2007, Chrétien wrote: "I was hurt by (Martin's) betrayal [and] I was damned if I was going to let myself be shoved out the door by a gang of self-serving goons" who were only interested in power. Chrétien fired Martin in 2002 but in late 2003 resigned himself and allowed Martin to become prime minister.

By the time he resigned, Chrétien was dogged by persistent rumours of scandal and financial mismanagement in his government. It had begun when an internal audit of the Department of Human Resource Development found that the Liberal government had failed to account for employment program grants worth more than $1 billion, creating what the media called "the billion-dollar boondoggle." The RCMP launched 12 different investigations and traced several grants to the prime minister's riding of Saint Maurice in Quebec. By 2006, 26 individuals had been charged for fraud or attempting to commit fraud. Another scandal was dubbed "Shawinigate," which raised questions about two properties Chrétien owned in his riding. Chrétien had sold both the Grand-Mère resort and the Grand-Mère golf course in 1993 but he was not paid for the golf course shares until 1999. On two separate occasions, though, the prime minister intervened with the federal Business Development Bank of Canada for a $2 million loan that the new owners had requested while he still owned the premises. Although the ethics counsellor—appointed by the prime minister—cleared him of any wrongdoing, the media and opposition parties continued to see the matter differently.

These scandals were minor compared with what became known as the Sponsorship Scandal, which played a major role in the Liberal defeat in 2006. The scandal had its beginning in the aftermath of the 1995 Quebec referendum. Auditor General Sheila Fraser investigated the program and concluded in her 2004 report that the entire project amounted to a "breakdown in the proper conduct of public business."[24] She famously claimed that the Department of Public Works "broke just about every rule in the book" when it came to paying $100 million to communication agencies in the form of fees and commissions under the sponsorship program. Support for the Liberal party dropped nine points in the week following Fraser's comments.

In 2004, Auditor General Sheila Fraser tabled a scathing report on the Sponsorship Scandal that contributed to the Liberal's defeat in the next election.

Source: THE CANADIAN PRESS/ *Whitehorse Star*—Vince Federoff.

On December 12, 2003, his first day as prime minister, Martin cancelled the sponsorship program. He also fired several of Chrétien's high-profile ministers who had been given patronage appointments, including former minister Alphonso Gagliano, who had been appointed as Canada's ambassador to Denmark when the scandal first surfaced; Jean Pelletier, Chrétien's chief of staff who had been appointed head of Via Rail; and André Ouellet, another minister, who had been appointed to run Canada Post. Martin appointed Mr. Justice John Gomery to head a Commission of Inquiry to investigate the program, an attempt to distance himself from Chrétien. Still, as minister of finance and a senior Quebec minister, many Canadians assumed that Martin had to have known what was going on in the government and if he didn't, he should have. Either way, he was in trouble, even though Gomery later exonerated him from any wrongdoing while he was minister of finance.

Gomery Commission reports on Liberal Sponsorship Scandal, 2005.

The scandal had a tremendous impact on Liberal fortunes, especially in Quebec. Not only were Quebec voters—like many across Canada—upset over the misuse of taxpayers' money, but the whole program was also an insult to the province. Did Chrétien really think he could strengthen the federal presence in Quebec simply by advertising Canada and flying the Maple Leaf at events throughout the province? If so, what did that say about the intelligence of Quebecers? Such attitudes contributed to the drastic loss of support for the party and rejuvenated a struggling Bloc Québécois. In 1993, the Liberals had 33 percent of the popular vote in Quebec, and although it had jumped to 44.2 percent in 2000, it dropped precipitously to 33 percent in 2004 and 20 percent in 2006. In Quebec, support for sovereignty rose above 50 percent, showing how quickly the sovereignty movement can be mobilized in the province.

The Gomery Commission sealed Martin's fate, even though the sponsorship program had run amok under Chrétien's watch. Across the country, Canadians watched the Gomery hearings with eagerness and shock, and they took their vengeance out on Martin. When it issued its first report in November 2005, the Commission revealed how federal funds had gone to "Liberal-friendly" firms; some of it had found its way back to the Liberal party. While Gomery did not directly implicate Chrétien in his final report, he did suggest that the former prime minister and his chief of staff, Jean Pelletier, had to shoulder much of the responsibility for the scandal, but he did not consider either of them guilty of corruption. The RCMP conducted a criminal investigation and several advertising executives and one official who formerly worked in the Department of Public Works were convicted of fraud and fraud-related charges.

When he moved to 24 Sussex Drive, the official home of Canada's prime minister, Martin had every reason to think he would be living there for a decade at least. Opinion polls showed that more than half of the country planned on voting Liberal in the next election, and he was even more popular than his party. To help matters, the opposition was still in serious trouble. Preston Manning had led the right-wing populist Reform party to Ottawa in the 1993 election, and even though it had succeeded in forming the official opposition in 1997, Reform was unable to challenge for control of the government. Manning had attempted to unite the Western-based Reform with the Progressive Conservative party (which was then led by former Prime Minister Joe Clark) into a new Canadian Reform Conservative Alliance (known as the Canadian Alliance), but that did not boost their electoral fortunes. Even replacing Manning with former Alberta Treasurer Stockwell Day, who was regarded as more photogenic and flamboyant than Manning, made little difference. Day resigned in 2002 and Stephen Harper became leader. A year later, the Canadian Alliance and the Progressive Conservative party merged to become the Conservative Party of Canada. For the first time in more than a decade, the Conservatives in Canada were united within a single party.

It was not the popularity of the Conservatives, however, that dealt Martin's government such a crushing blow, first with a minority in 2004 and then defeat in 2006. Martin had been regarded as an excellent minister of finance, but he failed to distinguish himself as prime minister. His team of advisors and supporters had been determined to make him prime minister—some detractors noted that they had not managed that particularly well since it took them nearly a decade to dethrone Chrétien—but when they came to the seat of power, they did not know what to do. Pundits noted that Martin set for himself 39 top priorities; after years of planning for the top job, he obviously lacked vision. The influential magazine *The Economist*, which had once praised Martin as finance minister, dismissed him as "Mr. Dithers" for being so indecisive. Martin simply was not up to the challenge.

It was the results of the Gomery Commission into the alleged Liberal mismanagement and corruption that spelled the end for the Liberals and for Martin. Martin managed to hang on to a minority in 2004 by stressing to Canadians that a government under Stephen Harper and his right-wing supporters threatened the things that Canadians valued, such as medicare, individual freedoms and liberties, and social justice. In 2006, this tactic failed to work a second time when the January federal election was in many ways—as CBC news described it—a referendum on the Liberal party itself. The Conservatives under Stephen Harper ran a superb campaign that tightly controlled their message and won a minority government, ending a 13-year stretch of Liberal control.

Harper—A New Mackenzie King?

Harper was an unlikely prime minister. He had become involved in politics first with the Progressive Conservatives and then left the party to become a founding member of the Reform party and a senior advisor to Preston Manning. He quit active politics to become president of the National Citizen's Coalition, a right-wing think-tank committed to tax cuts, reduced government spending, and privatization of healthcare. However, he ran successfully for the leadership of the Canadian Alliance and then worked to create a new Conservative party by merging Reform with the old Progressive Conservative party. He presented a moderate set of proposals as party leader and, despite his lack of charisma, started to appear prime ministerial. He spent much of the 2006 campaign in Ontario and Quebec and was able to convince enough Canadians that he was the better choice to lead Canada. He secured a minority government and, less than 24 months later in October 2008, he won a second minority government, 11 seats shy of a majority (see Map 12.1 for the election results).

It is too early to know what type of Canada Prime Minister Harper will create, but it is becoming clear that—like former Prime Minister Brian Mulroney—he wants to replace the Liberals as the natural governing party. Despite the Liberals' warning about social

Harper wins minority government in 2006 and 2008.

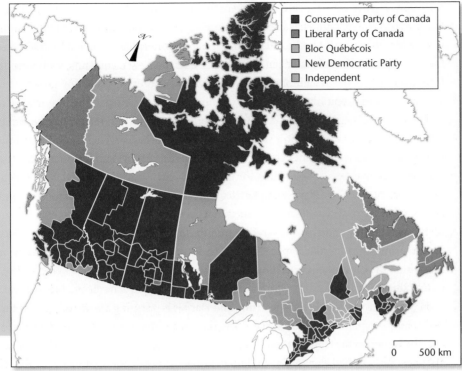

Map 12.1
The 40th Federal Election Results, 2008

This map of the 2008 elections shows the political cleavages that have emerged in Canada.

Source: The Atlas of Canada. Natural Resources Canada.

conservatism under Harper, it has not been born out. As he promised in the 2006 election, he allowed a free-vote on same-sex marriages in Parliament, but it was defeated, as Harper knew it would be. He has prevented his backbenchers from putting any limits on abortion rights and has apologized to several groups in Canada, including Aboriginal peoples and Ukrainians, for past injustices inflicted by the Government of Canada. In his apology to First Nations and Aboriginal peoples in 2008—unlike the earlier apology from the Liberal government—he invited five Aboriginal leaders and six residential school survivors to the floor of the House of Commons and he gave the apology: "Today, we recognize that this policy of assimilation was wrong, has caused great harm and has no place in our country," Harper said. "The Government of Canada sincerely apologizes and asks the forgiveness of the Aboriginal Peoples of this country for failing them so profoundly. We are sorry."[25]

Harper renewed Canada's commitment to a continued military presence in Afghanistan and promises to spend $490 billion over the coming 20 years to improve the capacity of the Canadian military. He was able to get the opposition Liberals to agree with his decision to extend Canada's mission, but when Canadians began to wonder if it was a wise policy, Harper announced that Canada would end its military commitment in 2011. Canadians, it seems, take pride in a more active military, but they are not sure what they want their armed forces to do; they know, however, that they would prefer them not to be engaged in such wars as that in Afghanistan. At the top of his government's defence priorities is the protection of Canadian sovereignty in the Arctic, another issue on which most Canadians agree.

Despite Harper's ideological commitment to smaller government and less public spending, government spending has increased in each of the Conservative budgets. When the worldwide financial crisis hit Canada in 2008, Harper's government at first underestimated the severity of the problem. When the Liberals and the New Democrats, with support from the Bloc Québécois, announced that they had agreed upon a coalition government and intended to defeat him in a vote of confidence, Harper learned the importance of compromise and negotiations. After consultations with the opposition parties, he immediately announced a $29 billion economic stimulus package. Deficit spending would have been inconceivable under Harper a few months earlier, but some estimates have the federal deficit in excess of $40 billion for fiscal 2009–2010 and additional deficits for the foreseeable future. While Harper emphasizes that he will not permit a return to "structural deficit"—the term used to describe a deficit that persists over the long term even when the economy is healthy and growing—recent months have shown him to be as pragmatic as former prime minister Mackenzie King and to do what is necessary to retain power and to position the Conservatives as the natural governing party.

Harper returns to deficit to deal with recession in 2009–2010.

Canadian prime ministers who have been able to do that have been able to govern from the centre of the political spectrum, and Harper is pursuing a series of policies that are broadly acceptable to the majority of voters to stake out the middle ground. He introduced a motion in the House of Commons that acknowledged that "the Québécois form a nation within a united Canada," even though he had earlier denounced the appeasement of ethnic nationalism. The Liberals, the Bloc Québécois, and the NDP had either planned or adopted such a policy towards Quebec. This was an attempt by Harper to bring Quebec nationalists into his coalition, which already included neoliberals and social conservatives.

He has promised a more open and flexible federalism, and all the provinces seem to welcome the change. The Harper government believes that greater autonomy must be given to the provinces and they cannot all be treated the same. Although it is not certain what this means, Harper sees a more decentralized federation as necessary not only to avoid the continual bickering with most of the provinces, but as a way to deal with the cleavages within the country. At the time of Confederation, it was generally recognized that there were two solitudes in Canada: one French-speaking and the other English-speaking. By the early 1990s, there were many more—the West, Atlantic Canada, Ontario, Quebec, and First Nations and other Aboriginal peoples—and more than any other political party, the Harper Conservatives seem to have recognized the cleavages and embraced a form of brokerage politics to build a new coalition through negotiation and compromise to make the country work.

Conclusion

Many of the tensions that have marked Canada in its infancy in the years following Confederation in 1867 remain; only the specifics have altered. The federal and provincial governments continued, in the period from 1993 to the present, to fight over fiscal policy and jurisdiction, but the sources of such quarrels recently have been healthcare, post-secondary education, and social programs rather than liquor licensing or timber rights as it was in the late-nineteenth century. Canada's relationship with the United States and Britain remains as an important issue as it was in the early years of Confederation. While the demographics have changed considerably since 1867, Canadians continue to struggle to find ways to live together in an ever-changing environment. Yet, for all of the uncertainties of the recent past, Canadians have developed a nation that others around the world look on with envy. Canadians have created a nation that is, in many ways, one of the best in the world, even as they continue to search for what best defines them as a people and a nation.

Questions to Consider

1. What strategies did the federal and provincial governments follow to deal with the fiscal situation? Were they effective and what were their long-term impacts?

2. What were the major social issues facing Canada from 1993 to 2008?

3. How would you describe Canada's foreign policy during this period?

4. How would you characterize Canada's reaction to the 9/11 attacks?

Critical Thinking Questions

1. In an era of post-colonial political negotiations, what are the best ways for the federal and Aboriginal governments to approach such issues as Aboriginal resource claims and self-government?

2. Was the Turbot War necessary? Explain.

3. Do governments lose their legitimacy when they start to reduce spending and transfers to individuals, or are governments about more than providing services?

4. How many referenda on sovereignty of independence should the province of Quebec be allowed to hold?

Selected Readings
General

Bogart, W.A. *Good Government? Good Citizens? Courts, Politics, and Markets in a Changing Canada.* Vancouver: University of British Columbia Press, 2005.

Harder, Lois, and Steve Patten, eds. *The Chrétien Legacy: Politics and Public Policy in Canada.* Montreal and Kingston: McGill-Queen's University Press, 2006.

Hillmer, Norman, and Adam Chapnick, eds. *Canadas of the Mind: The Making and Unmaking of Canadian Nationalisms in the Twentieth Century.* Montreal and Kingston: McGill-Queen's University Press, 2007.

Hubbard, Ruth, and Gilles Paquet. *Gomery's Blinders and Canadian Federalism.* Ottawa: University of Ottawa Press, 2007.

Smith, Miriam. *A Civil Society? Collective Actors in Canadian Political Life.* Peterborough: Broadview Press, 2005.

Wells, Paul. *Right Side Up: The Fall of Paul Martin and the Rise of Stephen Harper's New Conservatism.* Toronto: McClelland & Steward, 2006.

National Politics, Economics, and Constitutionalism

Chrétien, Jean. *My Years as Prime Minister.* Toronto: A.A. Knopf Canada, 2007.

Flanagan, Tom. *Harper's Team: Behind the Scenes in the Conservative Rise to Power.* Montreal and Kingston: McGill-Queen's University Press, 2007.

Gray, John. *Paul Martin: The Power of Ambition.* Toronto: Key Porter Books 2003.

Ibbitson, John. *The Polite Revolution: Perfecting the Canadian Dream.* Toronto: McClelland & Stewart, 2005.

Martin, Lawrence. *Chrétien: The Years in Power.* Toronto: Penguin Books Canada 2003.

Martin, Paul. *Hell or High Water: My Life in and out of Politics.* Toronto: McClelland & Stewart, 2008.

Plamondon, Bob. *Full Circle: Death and Resurrection in Canadian Conservative Politics.* Toronto: Key Porter Books, 2006.

Provincial Politics

Dunn, Christopher, ed. *The Provinces: Canadian Provincial Politics.* 2nd edition. Peterborough, ON: Broadview Press, 2006.

Harrison, Kathryn, ed. *Racing to the Bottom? Provincial Interdependence in the Canadian Federation.* Vancouver: University of British Columbia Press, 2006.

Henderson, Ailsa. *Nunavut: Rethinking Political Culture.* Vancouver: University of British Columbia Press, 2008.

Jackson, Robert J., and Doreen Jackson. *Politics in Canada: Culture, Institutions, Behaviour and Public Policy.* Toronto: Pearson Prentice Hall, 2009.

Laplante, Benoit. "The Rise of Cohabitation in Quebec: Power of Religion and Power over Religion." *Canadian Journal of Sociology* 31, 1 (2006): 1–24.

Leeson, Howard, ed. *Saskatchewan Politics: Into the Twenty-First Century.* Regina: Canadian Plains Research Centre, 2009.

Mau, Tim. "Referendum Rhetoric and National Mobilization: A Comparison of the 1980 and 1995 Referenda." *British Journal of Canadian Studies* 18, 1 (2005): 93–119.

Pickup, Mark. "Globalization, Politics, and Provincial Government Spending in Canada." *Canadian Journal of Political Science* 39, 4 (2006): 883–917.

Smith, Doug. *"As Many Liars": The Story of the 1995 Vote-Splitting Scandal.* Winnipeg: Arbeiter Ring Publishing, 2003.

Foreign and Defence Policy

Barry, Donald. "Chretien, Bush, and the War in Iraq," *The American Review of Canadian Studies* 35, 2 (2005): 215–245.

Jockel, Joseph T. *Canada in NORAD, 1957–2007.* Montreal and Kingston: McGill-Queen's University Press, 2007.

Maginley, Charles D. *The Canadian Coast Guard, 1962–2002: Auxilio Semper.* St. Catharines, ON: Vanwell Publishing 2003.

Nossal, Kim Richard. "Defense Policy and the Atmosphere of Canada–US Relations: The Case of the Harper Conservatives." *American Review of Canadian Studies* 37, 1 (2007): 23–34.

Women

Beach, Charles M., et al. "Earnings Variability and Earnings Instability of Women and Men in Canada: How Do the 1990s Compare to the 1980s?" *Canadian Public Policy* 29 (supplement) (2003): 41–63.

Brooks, Bradley, et al. "Occupational Gender Segregation in Canada, 1981–1996: Overall, Vertical, and Horizontal Segregation." *Canadian Review of Sociology and Anthropology/ Revue canadienne de sociologie et d'anthropologie* 40, 2 (2003): 197–214.

Myles, John, et al. "Why did Employment and Earnings Rise Among Lone Mothers in Canada during the 1980s and 1990s?" *Canadian Public Policy* 33, 2 (2007): 53–63.

Newman, Jacquetta, and Linda A. White. *Women, Politics, and Public Policy: The Political Struggles of Canadian Women.* Toronto: Oxford University Press, 2006.

Rebick, Judy. *Ten Thousand Roses: The Making of a Feminist Revolution.* Toronto: Penguin Group, 2005.

Society and Culture

Edwardson, Ryan. "'Kicking Uncle Sam Out of the Peaceable Kingdom': English-Canadian 'New Nationalism' and Americanization." *Journal of Canadian Studies/Revue d'études canadiennes* 37, 4 (2002–2003): 131–150.

Gildiner, Alina. "Measuring Shrinkage in the Welfare State: Forms of Privatization in a Canadian Health-Care Sector." *Canadian Journal of Political Science* 39, 1 (2006): 53–75.

Lippert, Randy. "Rethinking Sanctuary: The Canadian Context, 1983–2003." *International Migration Review* 39, 2 (2005): 381–406.

Razavy, Maryam. "Sikh Militant Movements in Canada." *Terrorism and Political Violence* 18, 1 (2006): 79–93.

Aboriginal Peoples

Depasquale, Paul, ed. *Natives and Settlers Now and Then: Historical Issues and Current Perspectives on Treaties and Land Claims in Canada.* Edmonton: University of Alberta Press, 2006.

Phillips, Ruth B. "Disrupting Past Paradigms: The National Museum of the American Indian and the First Peoples Hall at the Canadian Museum of Civilization." *Public Historian* 28, 2 (2006): 75–80.

Ray, Arthur J. "Aboriginal Title and Treaty Rights Research: A Comparative Look at Australia, Canada, New Zealand, and the United States." *New Zealand Journal of History* 37, 1 (2003): 5–21.

Notes

1   Quoted in John Gray, *Paul Martin: In the Balance* (Toronto, Key Porter Books, 2003), 114.

2   Quoted in Canada, Department of Finance, *Budget Speech*, 27 February 1995.

3   *Maclean's*, 18 March 1996.

4   Michael Prince, "La Petite Vision, Les Grands Decisions: Chrétien's Paradoxical Record in Social Policy," in Lois Harder and Steve Patten, eds., *The Chrétien Legacy: Politics and Public Policy in Canada* (Montreal and Kingston: McGill-Queen's University Press, 2006): 215.

5   Quoted in David Leyton-Brown, ed., *Canadian Annual Review of Politics and Public Affairs: 1995* (Toronto: University of Toronto Press, 2000), 211.

6   S. Weldon, "Citizen, Victims, Deviants, Restructuring Government Response to Violence Against Women in Canada," Paper presented at the annual meeting of the American Political Science Association, Hilton Chicago and the Palmer House Hilton, Chicago, IL, 2 Sept. 2004, http://www.allacademic.com/meta/p61822_index.html.

7   Privy Council Office, *Renewing the Canadian Federation: A Progress Report* (Ottawa, 1996), 2.

8   Department of Finance, *Working Together Towards a Child Benefit System* (Ottawa, 1997), 1–2.

9   http://www.cbc.ca/breakingpoint/chapter3_3.shtml.

10 Office of the Auditor General of Canada, *2003 November Report of the Auditor General of Canada*, Chapter 3, "The Sponsorship Program," http://www.oag-bvg.gc.ca/internet/English/parl_oag_200311_03_e_12925.html.

11 Quoted in Michael Murphy, "Looking Forward Without Looking Back: Jean Chrétien's Legacy for Aboriginal-State Relations," in Lois Harder and Steve Patten, eds., *The Chrétien Legacy: Politics and Public Policy in Canada* (Montreal and Kingston: McGill-Queen's University Press, 2006): 169.

12 Kim Richard Nossal, "Mission Diplomacy and the 'Cult of the Initiative' in Canadian Foreign Policy," in Andrew Cooper and Geoffrey Hayes, eds., *Worthwhile Initiatives: Canadian Mission-Oriented Diplomacy* (Toronto: Irwin Publishing, 2000): 1–12.

13 Tom Courchene, *The Changing Nature of Canada-Quebec Relations: From the 1980 Referendum to the Summit of the Canadas* (Montreal: Institute for Research on Public Policy, 2004), 15.

14 *Globe and Mail*, 29 March 1995.

15 Halifax *Daily News*, 3 April 1995.

16 Halifax *Daily News*, 16 March 1995.

17 *Toronto Sun*, 19 March 1995.

18 *Maclean's*, 10 April 1995.

19 See Denis Smith, "Moral, Mythic and Reality in Canadian Foreign Policy," *International Journal* 58, 2 (Spring 2003).

20 Norman Hillmer, "The Secret Life of Canadian Foreign Policy," *Policy Options* (February 2005): 32.

21 Michael Ignatieff, "Canada in an Age of Terror—Multilateralism Meets a Moment of Truth," *Policy Options* 24, 2 (2003): 14–19.

22 This idea comes from Andrew Nurse, director of the Centre for Canada Studies at Mount Allison University in Sackville, New Brunswick.

23 Institute for Research of Public Policy. News Release, "Canadians Overwhelming Support Limits to Accommodation," 25 September 2007, http://www.irpp.org/newsroom/archive/2007/092507e.pdf.

24 Quoted in "Something Rotten," *Time Magazine*, 23 February 2004.

25 "The Long-awaited Apology," CBC News, 11 June 2008, http://archives.cbc.ca/society/native_issues/clips/15394/.

Appendix

Canada's Prime Ministers

Prime Minister	Party	Term(s)
John Alexander Macdonald	Cons.	July 1, 1867 – Nov. 5, 1873
Alexander Mackenzie	Liberal	Nov. 7, 1873 – Oct. 8, 1878
John Alexander Macdonald	Cons.	Oct. 17, 1878 – June 6, 1891
John Joseph Caldwell Abbott	Cons.	June 16, 1891 – Nov. 24, 1892
John Sparrow David Thompson	Cons.	Dec. 5, 1892 – Dec. 12, 1894
Mackenzie Bowell	Cons.	Dec. 12, 1894 – Apr. 27, 1896
Charles Tupper	Cons.	May 1, 1896 – July 8, 1896
Wilfrid Laurier	Liberal	July 11, 1896 – Oct. 6, 1911
Robert Laird Borden	Cons.	Oct. 10, 1911 – Oct. 12, 1917
Robert Laird Borden	Unionist	Oct. 12, 1917 – July 10, 1920
Arthur Meighen	Unionist	July 10, 1920 – Dec. 29, 1921
William Lyon Mackenzie King	Liberal	Dec. 29, 1921 – June 28, 1926
Arthur Meighen	Cons.	June 29, 1926 – Sept. 25, 1926
William Lyon Mackenzie King	Liberal	Sept. 25, 1926 – Aug. 7, 1930
Richard Bedford Bennett	Cons.	Aug. 7, 1930 – Oct. 23, 1935
William Lyon Mackenzie King	Liberal	Oct. 23, 1935 – Nov. 15, 1948
Louis Stephen St. Laurent	Liberal	Nov. 15, 1948 – June 21, 1957
John George Diefenbaker	P.C.	June 21, 1957 – Apr. 22, 1963
Lester Bowles Pearson	Liberal	Apr. 22, 1963 – Apr. 20, 1968
Pierre Elliott Trudeau	Liberal	Apr. 20, 1968 – June 3, 1979
Charles Joseph Clark	P.C.	June 4, 1979 – Mar. 2, 1980
Pierre Elliott Trudeau	Liberal	Mar. 3, 1980 – June 30, 1984
John Napier Turner	Liberal	June 30, 1984 – Sept. 17, 1984
Martin Brian Mulroney	P.C.	Sept. 17, 1984 – June 25, 1993
A. Kim Campbell	P.C.	June 25, 1993 – Nov. 4, 1993
Joseph Jacques Jean Chrétien	Liberal	Nov. 4, 1993 – Dec. 12, 2003
Paul Edgar Philippe Martin, Jr.	Liberal	Dec. 12, 2003 – Feb. 6, 2006
Stephen Joseph Harper	Cons.	Feb. 6, 2006 – present

Cons. = Liberal Conservative   P.C. = Progressive Conservative

Source: Library and Archives Canada.

Index